Also by Stephen E. Ambrose

Upton and the Army

Halleck: Lincoln's Chief of Staff

Ike's Spies: Eisenhower and the Espionage Establishment

Rise to Globalism: American Foreign Policy, 1938–1970

Crazy Horse and Custer: The Parallel Lives of Two American
Warriors

Eisenhower and Berlin, 1945

Duty, Honor, Country: A History of West Point

The Supreme Commander: The War Years of General Dwight D.
Eisenhower

Eisenhower: Soldier, General of the Army, President-Elect, 1890–1952

Eisenhower: The President

Pegasus Bridge: June 6, 1944

Nixon: The Education of a Politician, 1913–1962

Nixon: The Triumph of a Politician, 1962–1972

Band of Brothers: E Company, 506th Regiment, 101st Airborne
from Normandy to Hitler's Eagle's Nest

D-Day, June 6, 1944: The Climactic Battle of World War II

Undaunted Courage: Meriwether Lewis, Thomas Jefferson,
and the Opening of the American West

Citizen Soldiers: The U.S. Army from the Normandy Beaches
to the Bulge to the Surrender of Germany, June 7, 1944–May 7, 1945

The Victors: Eisenhower and His Boys: The Men of World War II

Comrades: Brothers, Fathers, Heroes, Sons, Pals

Nothing Like It in the World: The Men Who Built the
Transcontinental Railroad, 1863–1869

The Wild Blue: The Men and Boys Who Flew the B-24s Over
Germany

To America: Personal Reflections of an Historian

EISENHOWER

Soldier and President

STEPHEN E. AMBROSE

SIMON & SCHUSTER PAPERBACKS
New York London Toronto Sydney

SIMON & SCHUSTER PAPERBACKS
Rockefeller Center
1230 Avenue of the Americas
New York, NY 10020

First Simon & Schuster paperback edition 2003
SIMON & SCHUSTER PAPERBACKS and colophon are
registered trademarks of
Simon & Schuster, Inc.

For information regarding special discounts for bulk purchases,
please contact Simon & Schuster Special Sales at 1-800-456-6798
or business@simonandschuster.com.

Designed by Edith Fowler
Manufactured in the United States of America

21 23 25 27 29 30 28 26 24 22

The Library of Congress has cataloged the hardcover edition as follows:
Ambrose, Stephen E.
Eisenhower: soldier and president/
Stephen E. Ambrose.—[Rev. ed.]
p. cm.
Condensed version of a two volume work
originally published as : Eisenhower. © 1983–© 1984.
Includes bibliographical references and index.
1. Eisenhower, Dwight D. (Dwight David), 1890–1969.
2. Presidents—United States—Biography. 3. Generals
—United States—Biography. 4. United States Army—
Biography. I. Ambrose, Stephen E. Eisenhower.
II. Title.
E836.A828   1990
973.921'092—dc20
(B)   90-9701

ISBN-13: 978-0-671-70107-9
ISBN-10:   0-671-70107-X
ISBN-13: 978-0-671-74758-9 (Pbk.)
ISBN-10:   0-671-74758-4 (Pbk.)

This is a condensed version of two works originally published as
Eisenhower: Soldier, General of the Army, President-Elect
1890–1952 *and* Eisenhower: The President.

TO THE MEN OF D-DAY

CONTENTS

10 | CONTENTS

FOREWORD

DWIGHT DAVID EISENHOWER was a great and good man. This is an assertion I hope to prove; let me begin by defining the terms.

In 1954, Dwight Eisenhower wrote his childhood friend Swede Hazlett on the subject of greatness. Ike thought greatness depended either on achieving preeminence in "some broad field of human thought or endeavor," or on assuming "some position of great responsibility" and then so discharging the duties "as to have left a marked and favorable imprint upon the future."[1]

The qualities of a great man, he said, were "vision, integrity, courage, understanding, the power of articulation, and profundity of character." To that list, I'd add two others: decisiveness (the ability to take command, decide, and act) and luck.

The qualities of goodness in a man, I believe, include a broad sympathy for the human condition, that is, an awareness of human weaknesses and shortcomings and a willingness to be forgiving of them, a sense of responsibility toward others, a genuine modesty combined with a justified self-confidence, a sense of humor, and most of all a love of life and of people.

Eisenhower was one of the outstanding leaders of the Western world of this century. As a soldier he was professionally competent, well versed in the history of war along with modern strategy, tactics, and weaponry, decisive, disciplined, courageous, dedicated, popular with his men, his superiors, and his subordinates.

As President, he was a leader who made peace in Korea and kept the peace thereafter, a statesman who safely guided the free world through one of the most dangerous decades of the Cold War, and a politician who captured and kept the confidence of the American people. He was the only President of the twentieth century who managed to preside over eight years of peace and prosperity.

As a man, he was good-looking, considerate of and concerned about others, loyal to his friends and family, ambitious, thin-skinned and sensitive to criticism, modest (but never falsely so), almost embarrassingly unsophisticated in his musical, artistic, and literary tastes, intensely curious about people and places, often refreshingly naive, fun-loving—in short, a wonderful man to know or be around. Nearly everyone who knew him liked him immensely, many—including some of the most powerful men in the world—to the point of adulation.

The aim of this work is to explain and describe this man, to record his accomplishments and failures, his triumphs and shortcomings, his personal life and his personality. In the process, I hope that I convey some sense of what a truly extraordinary person he was, and of how much all of us who live in freedom today owe to him.

This book is basically a condensation of my two-volume biography of Eisenhower. There are some revisions and several new sections. My aim has been to provide a readable one-volume life, free of scholarly paraphernalia and excessive detail on plans, organization of military and government offices, bureaus, Cabinets, and the like.

As I made the condensation, the passage of time and the perspective of the end of the decade let me read the two volumes with fresh eyes. I've been struck by how right Ike was about so many things —and how wrong he was on others. Most particularly, I am impressed with his determination to do all that he could to foster the United States of Europe. I did the work of condensing in the evenings in Caen, Normandy. I spent the days walking the battlefield and swimming off the invasion beaches. Visitors from all over Europe come to the American, British, and German cemeteries in ever-increasing numbers. Many of them are students, and they get along with each other so well that I came away convinced that Ike's dream is on the verge of becoming a reality.

That impression was strongly reinforced by the political activity in Europe in the summer of 1989. Elections were being held for the European Parliament. The campaign was active and positive, and voter turnout was high. Discussion about the future of a united Europe was spirited and imaginative. In 1992, at the least the Europeans will form an economic union, dropping trade barriers, customs duties, and internal passport controls. At a maximum, they will create a common currency and form an all-European army. As readers of this book will see, President Eisenhower made an all-European army one of his top priorities; it all but broke his heart when the French turned it down. Now the idea has been revived and may soon become a reality.

Just before going to Normandy, I taught a course at the University of New Orleans on the Vietnam War, so it was very much on my mind. Reading about Ike's insistence in early 1944 on the necessity of bombing France to prepare for the invasion, and about his threat to resign if he was not given complete control of the Allied air forces to use as he saw fit, I could not help but note the contrast between him and the American high command in Vietnam. No commander in Vietnam ever threatened to resign if not allowed to fight the war as he thought necessary.

I was also impressed more than ever by Ike's refusal to send American troops to Vietnam in 1954, and by his warning that the jungles of Southeast Asia would just swallow up our divisions.

As a prophet, he missed badly on the Reagan Revolution. In the mid-fifties, Ike told one of his brothers that if he ever expected to see the elimination of the graduated income tax he certainly planned to live a long time. The brother didn't quite make it, but he didn't miss by much.

Ike was also badly wrong in his frequently expressed fears about the effect of *Brown* v. *Topeka*. He thought it would lead the South to abandon its public school system altogether. That has not happened —although admittedly in some places, such as my own city of New Orleans, we have come perilously close.

Most of all I was struck by how much Ike has to say to us today. On such fundamental issues as national defense, the relationship between the economy and arms expenditures, the importance of a balanced budget, the need to speak out for freedom everywhere for all men, the wisdom of waiting for the Communist system to collapse because of its inherent internal contradictions, and many others, his words, his thoughts and actions provide leadership for us today just as they did for the generation of World War II and the first decade of the Cold War.

STEPHEN E. AMBROSE
Caen
July 22, 1989

CHAPTER ONE

Abilene, West Point, World War I

HE WAS BORN on October 14, 1890, in a small rented frame house, not much more than a shack, beside the railroad tracks in Denison, Texas. He was the third son of David and Ida Stover Eisenhower. They were members of the Mennonites, fundamentalists in their religion, and pacifists. David was a common laborer—he had once owned a general store in Hope, Kansas, purchased with an inheritance from his father, but it had failed. In 1891 he moved to Abilene, Kansas, where a relative had found him a job as a mechanic at the Belle Springs Creamery. When the Eisenhowers stepped onto the train platform in Abilene, David had in his pocket the sum total of his capital, $10.

In a small two-story white frame house at 201 South East Fourth Street, set on a three-acre plot, David and Ida raised six strong, healthy boys—Arthur (born 1886), Edgar (1889), Dwight, Roy (1892), Earl (1898), and Milton (1899). The Eisenhowers were respected around town, but the family was in no way prominent. David held no elective office, provided no community leadership. Still the Eisenhowers were content. The parents were frugal out of necessity, but they were proud and ambitious, if not for themselves, then for their sons.

"I have found out in later years we were very poor," Dwight said on June 4, 1952, on the occasion of laying the cornerstone of the Eisenhower Museum in Abilene, across the street from his boyhood home, "but the glory of America is that we didn't know it then. All that we knew was that our parents—of great courage—could say to us, 'Opportunity is all about you. Reach out and take it.' "[1]

By most standards, David and Ida never reached out to take that opportunity themselves. Instead they invested in their sons the hopes they once had for themselves. They taught the simple virtues of honesty, self-reliance, integrity, fear of God, and ambition. They wanted their sons to succeed in a wider setting than Abilene, or even Kansas. They gave the boys the feeling, as one of them later put it, that "if you stay home you will always be looked upon as a boy."[2]

Eisenhower's home life revolved around worship. Every day, morning and night, the family members got down on their knees to pray. David read from the Bible before meals, then asked for a blessing. After the meals the boys washed the dishes, then gathered around David for Bible reading. "Finally there was bedtime," Earl recalled, "when Dad got up and wound the clock on the wall. You could hear the ticking no matter where you were. When Dad started winding, you might as well get ready for bed, for that was the bedtime signal."[3]

During the day, the boys saw little of their father, who worked in the creamery from 6:00 A.M. to 6:00 P.M. "Mother was by far the greatest personal influence in our lives," Dwight remembered.[4] She supervised their chores, made their meals, selected and mended their clothes, soothed their hurts, praised their accomplishments, and lightened the atmosphere. Milton, the youngest, said that "Father and Mother complemented one another. Mother had the personality. She had the joy. She had a song in her heart. Dad had the authority."[5]

In a family of six boys, competition was the natural order of things. Who could do the best job at this or that task? Who could run the fastest? Jump the highest? Lift the heaviest weight? Read the Bible aloud most accurately? Daily, in countless ways, the boys tested themselves against one another. David and Ida encouraged this competition, encouraged them to be ambitious to do the best. Most of all, each of the boys wanted to be the toughest, and they fought among themselves to find out who was the best scrapper.

One day Ida was baking in the kitchen. Dwight and Edgar began a fight on the kitchen floor. Soon the older and heavier Edgar was sitting astride the prostrate Dwight, giving him a pounding. "Give up?" Edgar shouted. "No!" Dwight gasped. Edgar grabbed Dwight's hair and began to thump his head against the floor. Earl rushed in to help Dwight. Ida, without turning away from the stove, said sharply to Earl, "Let them alone."[6]

David encouraged his sons to stand up for themselves, with one another and in their relations with boys outside the family. Dwight recalled that his father never wanted to see his sons beaten by their playmates in anything, least of all in a fight. One evening David returned from work to see Dwight being chased by a boy about his own size. "Why do you let that boy run you around like that?" he demanded.

"Because if I fight him," Dwight replied, "you'll give me a whipping, whether I win or lose!" Instantly, David replied, "Chase that boy out of here." Dwight did.[7]

The chief characteristic of Abilene in the 1890s was that it was typical of small-town midwestern America, which meant, for young Dwight, that it reinforced everything he learned from his parents. There was, first of all, the emphasis on self-sufficiency. Contact with the outside world was minimal. There were few taxes to pay to, and almost no services provided by, the government, save on the local level. The city paid for and ran the school system. Families took care of their own sick, insane, crippled, elderly, or just down-on-their-luck members. There was no police force because in a town small enough (less than four thousand population) for everyone to know, and trust, everyone else, there was no need for one.

There was a strong emphasis on hard work, on getting things done. Little or no time was wasted on reflection or introspection. Everyone in Abilene worked, most of them at hard physical labor. Unemployment was virtually unknown, even among children. The youngest worked around the house; eight- to twelve-year-olds held odd jobs; teen-agers found regular employment.

Abilene was cautious and conservative in its social outlook, religion, and politics. Everyone was Christian, of European descent, and nearly all voted Republican. There was a strong sense of community, a feeling that the world was divided into "us" (the residents of Abilene, Dickinson County, and to some extent the state of Kansas) and "them" (the rest of the world). Abilene was like a large extended family, giving to its residents a feeling of security. Threats to that security came not from within but from without, primarily in the form of adverse weather or falling commodity prices.

A man was judged by how hard he worked and whether he paid his bills on time, a woman by how well she ran her household. It was assumed that a man's success depended solely upon his output and that the unsuccessful had no one to blame but themselves. "The isolation was political and economic," Milton recalled, "as well as just a prevailing state of mind. Self-sufficiency was the watchword; personal initiative and responsibility were prized; radicalism was unheard of."[8]

To the Eisenhower boys, Abilene seemed an ideal place. It provided more than sufficient scope for a growing boy to discover himself and develop his physical capacity in an atmosphere of security, friendliness, and tolerance of boyish pranks. In 1947, Dwight Eisenhower spoke from his heart about the town that he loved. He said that Abilene "provided both a healthy outdoor existence and a need to work. These same conditions were responsible for the existence of a society which, more nearly than any other I have encountered, eliminated prejudices based upon wealth, race or creed, and maintained a standard of values that placed a premium upon integrity, decency, and consideration for others. Any youngster who has the opportunity to spend his early youth in an enlightened rural area has been favored by fortune."[9]

Just as Dwight loved Abilene, so did Abilene love him. He was a popular boy, well known for his curiosity, his fun-loving ways, his big smile, and his energy. He had a catchy nickname, "Little Ike" (his older brother Edgar was called "Big Ike").

But Little Ike had a terrible temper. Anger would possess him, take complete control, make him oblivious to anything else. The adrenalin rushed through his body, raising the hair on the back of his neck, turning his face a bright beet-red. On Halloween night, 1900, his parents gave Arthur and Edgar permission to go "trick or treating." Little Ike begged, pleaded, and argued to be allowed to go along, but his parents insisted that he was too young. Anger overwhelmed him. He rushed outside and began pounding the trunk of an apple tree with his bare fists. He sobbed and pounded until his fists were a raw bleeding mass of torn flesh. Finally his father grabbed him by the shoulders and shook him until he gained some control over himself.

Dwight went to his bed and cried into his pillow for an hour, out of resentment and rage. His mother came into the room and sat beside him. She took up his hands, putting salve on them and then bandages. After what seemed to him to be a long time, she said, "He that conquereth his own soul is greater than he who taketh a city." She went on to tell him how futile and self-destructive anger was, and how he, of all her boys, had much the worst temper and the farthest to go in conquering it. When he was seventy-six years old, Eisenhower wrote, "I have always looked back on that conversation as one of the most valuable moments of my life." [10]

Getting control of his temper, however, did not come easily or quickly. Two years after the apple-tree incident, when Dwight was twelve and Arthur sixteen, Arthur incurred his little brother's wrath over some trifling matter. Raging, but frustrated because Arthur was much too big for him to attack with his fists, Dwight looked around. Seeing a brick at his feet, he grabbed it and flung it with all his might at Arthur's head. Arthur just managed to duck out of the way— Dwight had fully intended to hit him.

Dwight attended Lincoln elementary school, directly across the street from his home. The curriculum emphasized rote learning. "The darkness of the classrooms on a winter day and the monotonous hum of recitations," Eisenhower wrote in his memoirs, " . . . are my sole surviving memories. I was either a lackluster student or involved in a lackluster program." [11] He came to life for the spelling bee and arithmetic. Spelling contests aroused in him his competitive drive and his hatred of careless mistakes—he became a self-confessed martinet on the subject of orthography. Arithmetic appealed to him because it was logical and straightforward—an answer was either right or wrong.

The subject that really excited him, however, was one that he pursued on his own, military history. He became so engrossed in it, in fact, that he neglected his chores and his schoolwork. His first hero was Hannibal. Then he became a student of the American Revolution, and George Washington excited his admiration. He talked history to his classmates so frequently that his senior yearbook predicted that he would become a professor of history at Yale (it also predicted that Edgar would become a two-term President of the United States).

During Dwight's high school years his interests were, in order of importance, sports, work, studies, and girls. He was shy around the girls and in any case wanted to impress his male classmates as a regular fellow, just one of the gang. Paying too much attention to the girls was considered somewhat sissy. He was careless of his dress, his hair was usually uncombed, and he was a terrible dancer on the few occasions he tried the dance floor.

Studies came easily to him and he made good to excellent grades without extending himself. He got all Bs in his freshman year, when the subjects were English, physical geography, algebra, and German.

He did a bit better the next year, and as a junior and senior he was an A or A-plus student in English, history, and geometry. His sole B was in Latin.

Sports, especially football and baseball, were the center of his life. He expended far more energy on sports than he put into his studies. He was a good, but not outstanding, athlete. He was well coordinated, but slow of foot. He weighed only 150 pounds. His chief asset was his will to win. He loved the challenge of the games themselves, enjoyed the competition with older and bigger boys, bubbled over with pleasure at hitting a single to drive in the winning run or at throwing the other team's star halfback for a loss.

It was in sports that he first discovered his talents as a leader and an organizer. As a boy, he provided the energy and leadership that led to a Saturday-afternoon game of football or baseball. Later, he was the one who organized the Abilene High School Athletic Association, which operated independently of the school system. Little Ike wrote to schools in the area to make up a schedule, and solved the problem of transportation by hustling his team onto freight trains for a free ride from Abilene to the site of the contest.

He also organized camping and hunting trips. He got the boys together, collected the money, hired the livery rig to take them to the camping site, bought the food, and did the cooking.

The central importance of sports, hunting, and fishing to Little Ike cannot be overemphasized. He literally could not imagine life without them, as was shown by the most dramatic incident of his childhood.

During his freshman year in high school, he fell and scraped his knee. This was a common enough experience, and his only thought was for his ruined brand-new pants, which he had bought with his own earnings. Since there was no bleeding, he went to school the next day. Infection set in, however, and that evening he fell into a delirium on the sofa in the front room. His parents called in Dr. Conklin, but despite his treatment, the infection began spreading. For the next two weeks, Dwight slipped into and out of a coma. Conklin called two or three times a day; Ida stayed at his bedside; they painted a belt of carbolic acid around his leg; still the poison spread and crept up his leg toward his abdomen. Conklin called in a specialist from Topeka. The two doctors agreed that only amputation would save his life.

During one of his conscious moments, Dwight heard his parents discussing amputation. They distrusted surgery, but the doctors insisted on it. Fourteen-year-old Dwight listened, then said, quietly but firmly, "You are never going to cut that leg off." When his parents told Conklin of his decision, the doctor warned, "If the poisoning ever hits his stomach he will die."

By this time the infection had reached his groin and his periods of consciousness were few and short. He called in Edgar and said, "Look, Ed, they are talking about taking my leg off. I want you to see that they do not do it, because I would rather die than to lose my leg." Edgar understood. He made the promise, and from then on stayed at his brother's bedside to make certain that no amputation took place. Conklin grew angry, began mumbling about "murder," but he could not persuade Edgar, or David and Ida, to allow him to amputate. Edgar even slept at night on the floor across the threshold of the door, so that Conklin could not get into the room while Edgar was sleeping.[12]

At the end of the second week, the poison began to recede, the fever left Dwight's body, consciousness returned. After a two-month convalescence, which caused him to have to repeat his freshman year, Dwight recovered completely. It was miraculous enough, but became much embellished decades later. Sunday School tracts and inspirational literature ·described the whole family as down on its knees, night and day, praying for recovery.

The Eisenhower boys hated such talk, with its implication that their parents believed in faith healing. They insisted that they prayed no more, and no less, than at other times. "We always prayed," Edgar recalled. "It was just as natural for us to pray, to call upon God for help as it was for us to get up and eat breakfast." And Dwight dismissed the night-and-day-praying stories as "ridiculous."[13]

During the summer of 1910, Dwight got to know Everett "Swede" Hazlett, son of one of the town's physicians. He had known Swede only casually before, because Swede had gone to a military school in Wisconsin. Swede had obtained an appointment to the Naval Academy at Annapolis, but in June 1910 had failed the mathematics section of the entrance examination. He had come home to study for a year, in order to repeat the examination the following June. He struck up a friendship with Dwight that became intimate and lasted for the remainder of their lives.

Ike's intentions at this time were to work, save his money, and go to the University of Michigan in the fall of 1911. He wanted a college education and an opportunity to play college football and baseball.

Michigan had one of the best football teams in the country. Swede pointed out to him that the Naval Academy played football too, that it had at least as much prestige as Michigan, that it guaranteed an interesting useful career to its graduates, and best of all it was free. He wanted Ike to seek an appointment and become his classmate. Ike agreed to try.

In September 1910, Ike read in the local paper an announcement of a competitive examination for applicants for the service academies. He took the exam and scored second among the eight candidates, which was good enough for the appointment to West Point, but not the Naval Academy. Swede was disappointed, but Ike was delighted. Ida did not want her boy to become a soldier, but she held back her tears until he boarded the train headed east. David, typically, showed no emotion whatsoever.

As he swung onto the train, Ike made a striking picture. He had filled out in the past two years, putting on twenty pounds, none of which was fat. At nearly six feet tall, now weighing 170 pounds, with strong broad shoulders and rock-hard muscles, he was the embodiment of an athlete. He was rawboned, with big hands. He walked on the balls of his feet and carried himself gracefully, as good athletes do.

Most people thought him extremely good-looking. He had light-brown hair, large eyes that were clear blue and quite fetching to the girls, and an oversized nose and mouth that fit nicely with his large head. His face was full, round, and symmetrical. His blue eyes sparkled, danced, and looked intently at whatever he saw. He grinned as easily as he breathed, a big lopsided grin that most people found irresistible. He laughed easily, too. He had a marvelously expressive face that still turned beet-red when he was angry, scowled furiously when he was disapproving, lit up when he was pleased.

He had an active, curious mind. He wanted to know about history, about sports, about mathematics, about opportunities, about how things worked and what people had done. His curiosity, however, was neither creative nor original. He had no interest in music, or painting, or any of the fine arts, or literature, or political theory. He directed his great energy and powers of concentration on making things work better, not differently. Internally his goal was self-improvement, whether in sports or studies, not self-change.

Most of all he knew himself and his capabilities, and as he swung himself up on the train and headed east, away from Abilene, his family, and his friends, he broke into one of his biggest grins. He had no doubts about himself. There was not, for him, the self-searching or identity crisis so often associated with young men. Ike Eisenhower knew who he was and where he was going.

The train ride took Eisenhower across the Mississippi River for the first time, and on to the East Coast. At West Point, he found an institution that regarded its own past with veneration and concentrated on instilling that concept in the plebes, or freshmen, filling them with the feeling that the past was a living thing, all around them. Here was Grant's room, there Lee's, there Sherman's. Over there Winfield Scott lived. Here Custer learned to ride. Eisenhower, with a strong sense of military history, responded enthusiastically. In his free time, of which there was precious little, he liked to wander about the Plain, climb the cliffs, look down on the Hudson, reflect on the Point's crucial role in the American Revolution, wonder at what might have happened had Benedict Arnold's attempt to betray the post to the British been successful. Years later he told his son he never tired of such speculation.

Hazing, the uglier side of West Point, had little appeal to him, obviously not as a recipient, but not as a Yearling either. Only once, at the beginning of his own third-class year, did he yield to the temptation to haze. A plebe, dashing down the street to carry out an order, ran into him and tumbled to the ground. Reacting with a "bellow of astonishment and mock indignation," Eisenhower scornfully demanded, "Mr. Dumgard, what is your P.C.S. [Previous Condition of Servitude]?"—adding sarcastically, "You look like a barber."

The plebe pulled himself together and replied softly, "I was a barber, sir."

Eisenhower turned red with embarrassment. Without a word, he returned to his room, where he told his roommate, P. A. Hodgson, "I'm never going to crawl [haze] another plebe as long as I live. As a matter of fact, they'll have to run over and knock me out of the company street before I'll make any attempt again. I've just done something that was stupid and unforgivable. I managed to make a man ashamed of the work he did to earn a living."[14] Eisenhower's reaction to the incident typified his four years at the Academy. He took from West Point what was positive and rejected that which was negative.

West Point was even more cut off and isolated from the rest of the world than Abilene had been. Like Abilene, its self-satisfaction was complete; like Abilene, it had a revealed truth and felt no need to examine it. And that truth reinforced much of what Eisenhower had absorbed in his upbringing.

Eisenhower's studies were overwhelmingly narrow and technical, with the emphasis on civil and military engineering. His teachers were, to a man, recent graduates of the USMA. The method of teaching had not changed since the War of 1812. Every day, in every class, every cadet was expected to recite, to give an approved answer to a standard question, and to receive a carefully recorded grade on each response.

Often the instructors knew little more than their students. In integral calculus one day, the teacher ordered Eisenhower to do a long, complicated problem on the blackboard. The instructor had previously explained the problem and supplied the answer, but since it had been obvious to Eisenhower that the instructor was doing it entirely by rote he had paid no attention. Thus, when called upon, he had "not the foggiest notion of how to begin." After struggling for almost a full hour, he finally tried a solution that, to his amazement, worked. He was asked to explain his solution; it was shorter and simpler than the rote answer. But the instructor interrupted him to charge that he had merely memorized the answer and then put down a lot of figures and steps that had no meaning.

Eisenhower could not abide being called a cheat. He began to protest so vehemently that he was soon in imminent danger of being expelled on a charge of insubordination. Just then, a senior officer from the Mathematics Department walked in. He inquired about the trouble, had Eisenhower go through the solution again, then pronounced it superior to the one being used in the department and ordered it incorporated into the Mathematics Department's teaching.[15]

Eisenhower was saved, but just barely, for a flexible and sympathetic response from the authorities was unusual at West Point. In most cases, there was no room for discussion or exploration of new answers to old problems. English was composition, never literature; history was fact, never inquiry. It was all rote learning, and Eisenhower was good enough at it that he could stay comfortably in the top half of his class without undue exertion. He was especially good in English; while others struggled for days over a theme, he could produce a high-scoring essay a half hour before class. The chief requirement of a good essay at West Point was a logical presentation of fact. At the end of his plebe year, when his class had shrunk from 265 to 212, he stood tenth in English.

In other subjects, Eisenhower was content to stay in the middle. He preferred enjoying his classmates to competing with them. These classmates were, generally, like him—white, rural or small town in origin, middle class, intelligent, and athletic. Eisenhower's own class later became the most famous in West Point's history, "the class the stars fell on." In 1915, 164 of them graduated. Of the 164, 59 rose to the rank of brigadier general or higher, three to the rank of full general, and two to the rank of general of the army. Members included Vernon Prichard, George Stratemeyer, Charles Ryder, Stafford Irwin, Joseph McNarney, James Van Fleet, Hubert Harmon, and Omar Bradley. Eisenhower knew and liked them all, especially Bradley, who became a close friend, and of whom he wrote, in the 1915 yearbook, the *Howitzer,* "Brad's most important characteristic is 'getting there,' and if he keeps up the clip he's started some of us will someday be bragging that, 'Sure, General Bradley was a classmate of mine.' "[16]

The West Point system is designed to find and break the nonconformist, and is usually successful—Edgar Allan Poe, a cadet in 1830, hated the "God-forsaken place" and, after less than a year, simply walked away. Others, less extreme than Poe, enjoyed testing or bending the regulations, finding out what they could get away with, more or less cheerfully paying the price when they got caught. Eisenhower was one of these. His cadet pranks, which he told with great relish in his old age, as if they were originals, were in fact part of a traditional pattern followed by generations of cadets who managed to adjust to West Point without losing their individuality.

Cigarette smoking was strictly forbidden. "So," Eisenhower recorded laconically, "I started smoking cigarettes." He smoked roll-your-own Bull Durhams. His roommate did not approve; other plebes were worried; Eisenhower smoked anyway. When caught by an officer, he walked punishment tours or served room confinement for a number of hours. He continued to smoke.[17]

This was only one of his small acts of rebellion. He could not or would not keep his room as neat as the regulations required, was frequently late for formation or guard mounting, often failed in his attempts to dress according to the regulations. For all these, and other, sins, he paid a price in demerits, which counted against him in his final class standing. Of the 164 men in his class who graduated, he stood 125th in discipline. It hardly bothered him; he later admitted that he "looked with distaste on classmates whose days and nights were haunted by fear of demerits and low grades." During World

War II, he expressed astonishment at the news that one of his classmates had made general office rank; "Christ," he said, "he's always been afraid to break a regulation."[18]

His own favorite story about a cadet prank centered on the sometimes absurd literalness of the regulations and orders. Eisenhower and another plebe, named Atkins, were guilty of an infraction. The cadet corporal who caught them, named Alder, ordered them to report to his room after tattoo in "full-dress coats," meaning a complete dress uniform. The two plebes decided to do exactly as ordered, and that night reported to Adler wearing their coats and not another stitch of clothing.

Adler roared in anger. He ordered them to return after tattoo "in complete uniform including rifles and crossbelts and if you miss a single item I'll have you down here every night for a week." They did as ordered and suffered through a long session of bracing and lecturing, but the laughs they and their fellow plebes got from Adler's discomfort made it worthwhile.[19]

Eisenhower's major escape from the grind was not in petty pranks, but in athletics. Sports remained the center of his life. He said later that he had "a lack of motivation in almost everything other than athletics, except for the simple and stark resolve to get a college education."[20] In his plebe year, he played football for the Cullum Hall team, or junior varsity. Over the winter, to build up his weight, he ate until he thought he would burst. In the spring, he played baseball—Omar Bradley was a teammate. By the fall of 1912, he was faster, stronger, and bigger—at 174 pounds—than he had ever been. He was determined to make the varsity. In the first practice game, he did well. He was, in his words, "as high as a kite."[21]

With his improved speed, Eisenhower shifted from the line to the backfield. He got his chance when Army's star ballcarrier, first-classman Geoffrey Keyes, was injured before the first game. Eisenhower led Army to a victory in that game, against Stevens Institute, and was again the star the next week in a win over Rutgers. *The New York Times* described him as "one of the most promising backs in Eastern football" and carried a two-column photograph of him punting a football. In a victory over Colgate, the West Point yearbook reported that "Eisenhower in the fourth quarter could not be stopped."[22]

The following week against Tufts, Eisenhower twisted his knee. There was some swelling and he spent a few days in the hospital, hoping that he would recuperate in time to play in the final game of the season against Navy. But that week, while participating in the "monkey drill" in the riding hall—leaping off and back onto a galloping horse—his knee crumbled when he hit the ground. The cartilages and tendons were badly torn. The doctors put his leg in a plaster cast; the pain was so intense that for days he could hardly sleep. His spirits sank even lower when Navy won the game. "Seems like I'm never cheerful anymore," he wrote a friend. "The fellows that used to call me 'Sunny Jim' call me 'Gloomy Face' now. The chief cause is this game pin of mine—I sure hate to be so hopeless and worthless. Anyway, I'm getting to be such a confirmed grouch you'd hardly know me." [23]

He hit bottom when the doctors took off the cast and informed him that he would never play football again. So great was his depression that several times his roommate had to talk him out of resigning from the Academy. "Life seemed to have little meaning," he later recalled. "A need to excel was almost gone." [24]

His studies suffered. As a plebe, he had stood fifty-seventh in a class of 212; in his Yearling year, when he hurt his knee, he slipped to eighty-first in a class of 177. But although his playing days were ended, his interest in football was not. He became a cheerleader, which gave him his first experience as a public speaker—he would address the entire Corps of Cadets the night before a big game, exhorting the members to make an all-out effort as fans the next afternoon.

His enthusiasm was matched by his intense study of the intricacies of the game, to the point that the football coach suggested that he coach the junior varsity. He did so eagerly, and with success, sending a number of players on to the varsity and winning most of his games.

His experiences as a coach—and there were to be many more—strengthened his love for the game. Like many other fans, he made football into something more than just an athletic contest. The act of coaching brought out his best traits—his organizational ability, his energy and competitiveness, his enthusiasm and optimism, his willingness to work hard at a task that intrigued him, his powers of concentration, his talent for working with the material he had instead of hoping for what he did not have, and his gift for drawing the best out of his players.

During World War II, a number of associates compared his techniques as a general with those of a good football coach, pacing up and down the line, urging his team forward. In his private talks with his corps and division commanders, and in his Orders of the Day, Supreme Commander Eisenhower used football slang extensively, urging his men to "pull an end run" and "hit the line" and "break through" and "get that ball across the goal line."

Most of all, as a general and as President, he urged teamwork. At the end of his life, he wrote, "I believe that football, perhaps more than any other sport, tends to instill in men the feeling that victory comes through hard—almost slavish—work, team play, self-confidence, and an enthusiasm that amounts to dedication."[25] Millions of Americans would agree that the act of playing or coaching football built successful men who could go out and get a job done.

Eisenhower graduated from West Point in June 1915. He had drifted into the Academy and, as a student, drifted through it. He had obtained a free education and the Academy had sharpened his sense of duty.

Following graduation, and before going on active duty, Second Lieutenant Eisenhower spent the summer in Abilene. His constant companion was Gladys Harding, the blond daughter of the man who owned the freight business in town. They had dated when in high school, but at that time they were not "serious." Ike also dated Ruby Norman and other local girls. In July 1915, however, he fell madly in love. Evidently Gladys' father warned her that the "soldier boy" was not for her, but when Ike reached his first duty post in San Antonio, in August, he wrote her: "More than ever now I want to hear you say the three words more than I ever have. . . . For, girl, I do love you and want you to *know* it. To be as certain of it as I am. To believe in me and trust in me as you do your dad."

A week later, he wrote her that "your love is my whole world. Nothing else counts at all." On reading her letter to him, "my eyes filled with tears and I simply had to stop and whisper over and over I love you Gladys, I love you Gladys. And now my beautiful lady, I'm going to read your letter once more, then I'll meet you in dreamland, if you will meet me there. And there, as sometime in reality, you shall be my dearest and closest friend, my own sweetheart and true blue *wife*."

It was not to be. Whether because of her father's opposition, or because she wanted to pursue a career as a serious piano player, Gladys put him off. On the rebound, he found another. Feeling rebuffed, so did she. Each married, and lived their separate lives, she in Abilene, he around the world. In his letters to friends back in Abilene during the war, Ike included Gladys in a list of four or five people he wanted to say hello to; when her husband, Cecil Brooks, died in 1944, he wrote Gladys a short letter of condolence. When Ike became President, Gladys bound up his love letters, along with a faded rose, and gave them to her son with a note: "Letters from Dwight Eisenhower when we were young and happy, 1914 and 1915. Not to be opened or published in any way whatsoever until after his death and Mamie's and also after my death." They remained under seal until more than three-quarters of a century after they were written.

As he set off for his first assignment, at Fort Sam Houston, Texas, he was determined so long as he was an officer in the United States Army, he would do his best to be a good one. It was a resolve rather than an ambition, and sprang from a sense of obligation and responsibility rather than from a competitive drive, for he felt that with the end of his sports career, his competitive days were over.

His duties in the peace-time Army were light, and hardly took up all of his time. When on his own, he played poker with the other junior officers, winning consistently, went drinking and hunting with them, and generally got on fine with his contemporaries. He made some lifelong friendships, including Walton Walker, Leonard Gerow, and Wade Haislip (each of these lieutenants became a four-star general).

And he fell in love. The romance began on a Sunday afternoon in October 1915, one of those perfect autumn days in South Texas. Ike was Officer of the Day. Putting on his newly cleaned and pressed uniform, his boots, brightly polished by his orderly, and his service revolver, he walked out of the Bachelor Officers' Quarters to make an inspection of the guard posts. Across the street, on the lawn of the Officers' Club, sitting on canvas chairs enjoying the sunshine, a small group of women was gathered.

Ike walked across the street to say a polite hello to the ladies. "The one who attracted my eye instantly," he later recalled, "was a vivacious and attractive girl, smaller than average, saucy in the look about her face and in her whole attitude."[26] She was wearing a starched white linen dress and big, floppy black hat. She had just arrived in Texas for the season—she lived in Denver during the hot months—and she was renewing her many friendships at Fort Sam.

She was eighteen years old. Her name was Mary Geneva Doud, but she was known as Mamie.

Mamie's first thought on seeing Ike walk out of the BOQ resplendent in his brass buttons, determined in his stride, big in his shoulders, had been, "He's a bruiser." As he came closer, her next thought was, "He's just about the handsomest male I have ever seen." When he asked her to accompany him as he walked his rounds, she accepted.[27]

The following day, when Mamie returned home from a fishing expedition, her maid informed her that a "Mr. I-something" had been calling every fifteen minutes all afternoon. The phone rang. It was "Mr. I-something."

Very formally, Ike asked "Miss Doud" to go dancing that night. She said she had a date. The next night? Another date. And so on until finally he made a date for a dance four weeks away. Having established her popularity, before hanging up Mamie also established her feelings—"I'm usually home about five," she said. "You might call some afternoon." Ike said he would be there the next day.[28]

Ike persuaded her to cancel her dates; they went out together every evening. His $141.67-per-month pay, even though supplemented by poker winnings, limited them to dollar-per-couple meals at a Mexican restaurant and a once-a-week show at the vaudeville house. To save money, he gave up store-bought cigarettes and returned to rolling his own.

On Valentine's Day, 1916, he proposed and she accepted. They sealed the engagement with his West Point ring. When he formally asked Mr. Doud for his daughter's hand in marriage, Doud consented, but only if he would agree to wait until November, when Mamie would be twenty years old.

Doud told Eisenhower that the couple would be on their own financially, and warned him that Mamie might not be able to adjust from her carefree life to that of an Army wife. She was accustomed to having her own maid and a generous allowance. He made a similar speech to his daughter, in addition pointing out to her that she was agreeing to a life in which she would be constantly on the move, frequently separated from her husband, and often worried about him. She said that she understood and looked forward to the challenge.

That spring of 1916, Ike and Mamie decided to push forward the date of their wedding. The Douds agreed. Ike got ten days' leave, and on July 1, 1916, in the Douds' spacious home in Denver, they were married. Ike wore his tropical dress uniform, stiffly starched and dazzling white, the crease so sharp he would not sit down; Mamie wore a white Chantilly lace dress, her hair in bangs over her forehead. Doud's chauffeur drove them to Eldorado Springs, Colorado, for a two-day honeymoon. Then they took the train for Abilene, so that Mamie could meet the Eisenhower family.

They arrived at 4 A.M. David and Ida were up, waiting for them. They liked Mamie at once, and she them, especially after they told her they were so glad to finally have a daughter (Dwight was the first of their sons to marry). When Earl and Milton came downstairs, Mamie charmed them by saying, "At last I have some brothers." Ida served a fried chicken breakfast.[29]

Back at Fort Sam, they settled into Ike's three-room quarters in the BOQ. He concentrated on his work; she concentrated on him. Ike had a firm expectation about his wife's role, which was to center her life around his. That suited Mamie. She was six years his junior; she had been trained for such a role in her Denver finishing school; she had watched her mother devote herself to pleasing her father.

As an Army wife, she was ideal. She loved to entertain, as did he, and in a society in which everyone knew exactly how much everyone else earned, there was no need for pretense. Beans, rice, and beer more than satisfied the junior officers and their wives who were their guests. They sang popular songs at the top of their lungs, Mamie playing a rented piano. Eisenhower's favorite was "Abdul the Bulbul Amir," to which he knew some fifty verses. Their apartment came to be known as "Club Eisenhower." Mamie taught her man some of the social graces. "She takes full credit for smoothing the edges off the rough-and-ready Kansan," her son John told an interviewer, "and for teaching him some of the polish that later put him in good stead."[30]

She did not share his love of the out-of-doors, nor of athletics or physical exercise of any kind. But they both enjoyed talking, to each other and to other people, and playing cards together, and music and entertaining. Best of all she never complained, although she had much she might have complained about. In the first thirty-five years of their marriage, they moved thirty-five times. Not until 1953 did they have a home they could call their own. Until World War II, with one exception, in 1918, he was never the CO, so she always had to defer to someone else's wife. His progress in the Army, after World War I, was excruciatingly slow. She had to manage the money to the penny, and watched as he turned down numerous offers for civilian employment at substantially higher salaries. But she never nagged him to leave the Army, never told him that the time had come for him to make something of himself.

In April 1917, the United States entered World War I. Eisenhower stayed at San Antonio, training the 57th Infantry. He did well at it, using the same skills he had developed as a football coach, and earned the high praise his superiors gave him in his 201 file, the official record of an officer's career. He was promoted to captain. But he was impatient to get to France. Training troops was like coaching football all week without ever being able to play a game on Saturdays. He had more than the normal American male's mystique about combat; he had been trained, at considerable expense, to fight; his place was on the fighting line, not on the sidelines. He was dismayed, therefore, when in mid-September his orders finally came, and he learned that the War Department was sending him to Fort Oglethorpe, Georgia, to train officer candidates.

In Georgia, he helped construct a miniature World War I battlefield, complete with trenches and dugouts, in which he and the trainees lived while they practiced assaults across no-man's-land. Oglethorpe had none of the advantages of active service, but many of the disadvantages, the chief being that Mamie could not be with him and was thus in San Antonio, when, on September 24, 1917, their first son was born. She named him Doud Dwight and called him "Icky."

As a trainer of troops, Eisenhower managed to impress his superiors and his trainees. One of the latter wrote, "Our new Captain, Eisenhower by name, is, I believe, one of the most efficient and best Army officers in the country . . . He has given us wonderful bayonet drills. He gets the fellows' imaginations worked up and hollers and yells and makes us shout and stomp until we go tearing into the air as if we meant business."[31]

In February 1918, he received orders to report to Camp Meade, Maryland, to join the 65th Engineers, the parent group of the 301st Tank Battalion, which was slated to go to the battlefield in the spring. Elated, he threw himself into the job. The men were all volunteers, morale was high, expectations even higher. Although none of the men had actually seen a tank, they were convinced that with the new weapon they would break through the German lines and drive straight to Berlin.

Insofar as he could do so from newspaper accounts, Eisenhower studied the Battle of Cambrai (November 1917), where the British for the first time used tanks to achieve a breakthrough. They had not gathered together enough tanks to exploit the victory, but they had shown what could be done. In mid-March, he was informed that the 301st would soon be embarking for France from New York, and that he was to be its commander. Exuberant, he rushed to New York to make certain that the port authorities were prepared for the 301st. "Too much depended on our walking up that gangplank," he wrote, "for me to take a chance on a slip anywhere." [32]

Back at Meade, elation gave way to more despair. The War Department had changed his orders. His superior's praise of his "organizational ability" had been so lavish that the authorities had decided to send him to Camp Colt, in Gettysburg, Pennsylvania. It was an old, abandoned camp, on the site of the great Civil War battle. The War Department had decided to reorganize its armored units, take them away from the 65th Engineers and give them an organization of their own, the Tank Corps. The tankers were to be trained at Camp Colt, with Eisenhower in command.

It was, on the face of it, a choice assignment. At twenty-seven years of age, Eisenhower was to be in command of thousands of men, all of them volunteers. He would be working with the weapon of the future (although he was given no actual tanks, nor training manuals, nor experienced armored officers to work with). He could expect a promotion. He was able to rent a house in town, so his wife and son could live with him. Nevertheless, he later confessed, "my mood was black." [33] He completed the preparations for the 301st to embark, then watched the unit sail with a sinking heart.

Eisenhower was certain that the War Department had made a terrible mistake, but in fact, in its wisdom, it had made an excellent selection for the commander at Camp Colt. Working with whatever materials he could find, he transformed the historic ground of Pickett's charge from an open wheat field into a first-class Army camp. He obtained tents, food, and fuel for his men. He taught them to drill, got them into shape, kept up their morale by establishing a telegraph school, then a motor school. By mid-July, he had ten thousand men and six hundred officers under his command, but still no tanks.

He went to Washington, badgered the War Department into giving him some old Navy cannons, and drilled his men in their use until they were proficient. He managed to obtain some machine guns; soon his men could take them apart and put them back together again while blindfolded. He mounted the machine guns on flatbed trucks and taught the men to fire the weapons from a moving platform. He used Big Round Top as a backstop and soon the firing there was heavier than it had been during the battle fifty-five years earlier.

He was always trying to improve the training and lift the morale. To that end, he wanted suggestions and ideas from his subordinates, not praise. One of his young lieutenants, anxious to please, nevertheless praised every aspect of his administration. "For God's sake," Eisenhower cut him off one day, "get out and find something wrong with the camp! It can't be as good as you say it is. Either you're not being frank, or you're as big a fool as I am." [34]

The men responded to his leadership. "Eisenhower was a strict disciplinarian," his sergeant major, Claude J. Harris, declared, "an inborn soldier, but most human, considerate, and his decisions affecting the welfare of his officers and men were always well tempered . . . This principle built for him high admiration and loyalty from his officers perhaps unequaled by few commanding officers." [35]

On October 14, 1918, his twenty-eighth birthday, Eisenhower was promoted to lieutenant colonel (temporary). Even more welcome were his orders—he was to embark for France on November 18, there to take command of an armored unit. He put Mamie and Icky on a train for Denver and went to New York to make certain that the port authorities were ready for his men and that nothing would go wrong with the embarkation. Then, on November 11, the Germans signed the Armistice.

Captain Norman Randolph was sitting in Eisenhower's office when the news arrived. "I suppose we'll spend the rest of our lives explaining why we didn't get into this war," Eisenhower moaned. "By God," he added, "from now on I am cutting myself a swath and will make up for this." [36] But whatever his determination, glittering combat possibilities had turned into demobilization realities. Eisenhower supervised the discharge of thousands of men, the tearing down of Camp Colt, the movement of the remnants of the Tank Corps to Fort Benning, Georgia.

Eisenhower was deflated and depressed. He could hardly believe it had happened to him—he was a professional soldier who had missed action in the greatest war in history. He had never heard a shot fired in anger and now did not expect to in his lifetime. He worried about what he would tell Icky when his son asked him what he did during the war. He envisioned having to sit silent at class reunions when his fellow officers talked about their experiences and exploits in combat. When he met a young officer at Benning who had been in France and who complained that there had been no promotions over there, he snapped back, "Well, you got overseas—that should be promotion enough!" [37]

In 1919, Colonel Ira C. Welborn recommended him for the Distinguished Service Medal. The award finally came through in 1922. It praised Eisenhower for his "unusual zeal, foresight, and marked administrative ability." [38] To Eisenhower, it was more a bitter reminder than a welcome award.

CHAPTER TWO

Between the Wars

EISENHOWER WAS twenty-eight years old when the war ended. His ambitions had been thwarted: now he was a member of an organization that was being practically dismantled. By January 1, 1920, the Army had only 130,000 men on active duty. Through the 1920s and 1930s it continued to shrink. By 1935, the Army did not have a single combat-ready unit of any size. It ranked sixteenth among the world's armies. It was more a school than an army.

But, for Eisenhower, the schooling was excellent, and almost continuous. The first problem he studied was the role of the tank in the next war; his fellow student was George S. Patton, Jr. Eisenhower first met Patton in the fall of 1919, at Camp Meade, Maryland. It was an ideal assignment for Eisenhower, as he had Mamie and Icky with him and he was working with tanks. Best of all, he had some real tanks to work with, British heavies, French Renaults, German Marks, and even some American-built tanks.

Eisenhower and Patton immediately became and remained fast friends, despite their much different personalities and backgrounds. Patton came from a wealthy, aristocratic family. He was an avid polo player, well able to afford his own string of ponies. He was extreme in his mannerisms, his dress, and his talk. Eisenhower could swear as eloquently as most sergeants, but he went easy on the curse words in mixed company; Patton, who could outswear a mule skinner, swore at all times as if he were in a stag poker game. Eisenhower's voice was deep and resonant, Patton's high-pitched and squeaky. Eisenhower enjoyed being one of the gang, wanted to be well liked and popular. Patton was more of a loner, did not much care what his associates thought of him. Where Eisenhower tended to qualify all his observations and statements, Patton was dogmatic. Where Eisenhower had no particularly strong views on race and politics, Patton was viciously anti-Semitic and loudly right wing. Where Eisenhower was patient and let things happen to him, Patton was impatient and took charge of his own career. Patton had been in combat, with tanks, and Eisenhower had not. And to hear Patton tell it, as he loved to do, he had ridden into battle on one of his tanks as if it were a polo pony and then single-handedly (well, almost) breached the Hindenburg Line.[1]

But Eisenhower and Patton had enough in common to overcome these differences. Both were West Pointers (Patton graduated in 1909). Both had been athletes—Patton played football as well as polo for the Army—and remained interested in athletics. Both were married, and their wives got along well together. Both had a deep interest in military history, both were serious students of war. Most of all, both were enthusiastic about tanks, sharing a belief that the weapon would dominate the next war.

It was thanks to Patton that Eisenhower first met General Fox Conner, a man who was destined to play a critical role in his life, one that cannot be exaggerated.

In 1964, in his retirement, after a career that had put him in intimate working contact with scores of brilliant and talented men, including most of the great statesmen and military leaders of World War II and the Cold War, Eisenhower could still say, "Fox Conner was the ablest man I ever knew."[2]

He met Conner at a Sunday-afternoon dinner in the fall of 1920 in Patton's quarters at Camp Meade. Patton had known Conner in France; Eisenhower knew him by reputation as one of the smartest men in the Army. A wealthy Mississippian who had graduated from West Point in 1898, Conner had served as Pershing's operations officer in France, where he was generally acknowledged to have been the brains of the AEF. He was currently Pershing's chief of staff in Washington. Both the general and Mrs. Conner—herself an heiress —were charming, soft-spoken southerners, formal and polite in their manners, but genuinely interested in younger officers and their wives. Eisenhower and Mamie felt drawn to them at once. The Patton dinner was a great success, highlighted by wide-ranging conversations.

After dinner, Conner asked Patton and Eisenhower to show him their tanks and explain to him their ideas about the future of the weapon. This was the first—and was to be the only—encouragement they had from a superior officer, and they spent a long afternoon with him, showing him around Camp Meade, explaining to him their ideas. When the time came for him to return to Washington, Conner praised them for their work and encouraged them to keep at it.

Eisenhower's family life was a warm, happy one. He and Mamie thoroughly enjoyed each other and the Army social scene, but most of all they delighted in their son. Icky, three years old in the fall of 1920, was an active, energetic boy, his father's delight and his mother's joy. The soldiers adopted him as a mascot. They bought him a tank uniform, complete with overcoat and overseas cap, and took him along on field maneuvers. He was enthralled by his tank rides. His father took him in the afternoon to football practice, where he would stand on the sidelines, cheering madly at every play in the scrimmage. He would put on his uniform and stand at stiff attention as the band played and the colors passed during parades.

The Eisenhowers made plans for a glorious Christmas. Mamie went to Washington to buy presents; Eisenhower put up a tree in their quarters and bought a toy wagon for Icky. But, a week or so before Christmas, Icky contracted scarlet fever. He evidently got it from the maid, a young local girl who had, unknown to the Eisenhowers, just recovered from an attack of the disease. Eisenhower called in a specialist from Johns Hopkins; the doctor could only advise prayer. Icky had to go into quarantine; Eisenhower was not allowed to enter his room. He could only sit outside it and wave to his son through the window. Mamie was also ill and confined to bed. Eisenhower spent every free minute at the hospital, desperate with worry, remembering his younger brother Milton's own struggle with the dreaded scourge of scarlet fever seventeen years earlier, hoping that Icky, like Milton, would somehow pull through.

He did not. On January 2, Icky died. "This was the greatest disappointment and disaster in my life," Eisenhower wrote in his old age, "the one I have never been able to forget completely."[3] For the next half century, every year on Icky's birthday he sent flowers to Mamie. The Eisenhowers arranged to have Icky's remains laid beside them in their own burial plot.

Inevitably, they blamed themselves. If only they had not hired that maid, if only they had checked on her more carefully, if only . . .

These feelings had to be suppressed if the marriage was to survive the disaster, but suppression did not eliminate the unwanted thoughts, only made them harder to live with. Both the inner-directed guilt and the projected feelings of blame placed a strain on their marriage. So did the equally inevitable sense of loss, the grief that could not be comforted, the feeling that all the joy had gone out of life. "For a long time, it was as if a shining light had gone out in Ike's life," Mamie said later. "Throughout all the years that followed, the memory of those bleak days was a deep inner pain that never seemed to diminish much."[4]

At the end of 1921, General Conner took command of the 20th Infantry Brigade in the Panama Canal Zone. He requested Eisenhower for his executive officer. Chief of Staff John J. Pershing granted the request.

The Eisenhowers arrived in January 1922. The accommodations were miserable. Mamie described their house as "a double-decked shanty, only twice as disreputable." Built on stilts, it had been abandoned for a decade and stank of mildew. She had household help, which cost practically nothing in Panama and was worth about as much; she had to do the shopping herself and provide minute supervision of the cooking and housework.[5]

The Conners lived next door; Mamie and Mrs. Conner became close friends. Mamie called on her daily—Virginia Conner became her confidante and adviser. When Mamie complained about some of her difficulties with her husband, Mrs. Conner was forthright in her advice. She told Mamie to cut her hair, change her clothes, brighten herself up. "You mean I should vamp him?" Mamie asked. "That's just what I mean," Mrs. Conner replied. "Vamp him!"[6]

Eisenhower and General Conner, meanwhile, developed a teacher-student relationship. They both enjoyed riding horseback through the jungle, spreading their bedrolls on the ground at night, chatting around a campfire. On weekends, they went on fishing expeditions together.

Conner pulled Eisenhower out of the lethargy that had threatened to engulf him after Icky's death. He insisted that Eisenhower read serious military literature and forced the younger man to think about what he was reading by asking probing questions. Eisenhower read memoirs of Civil War generals, then discussed with Conner the decisions Grant and Sherman and the others had made. What would have happened had they done this or that differently? Conner would ask. What were the alternatives? Eisenhower was anxious to please, so anxious that he read Clausewitz' *On War* three times through—a difficult enough task to complete even once, made more difficult by Conner's insistent questioning about the implications of Clausewitz' ideas.

They also discussed the future. Conner insisted that there would be another war in twenty years or less, that it would be a world war, that America would fight with allies, and that Eisenhower had better prepare himself for it. He advised Eisenhower to try for an assignment under Colonel George C. Marshall, who had been with Conner on Pershing's staff. Marshall, Conner insisted, "knows more about the techniques of arranging allied commands than any man I know. He is nothing short of a genius." Indeed, Conner's highest praise was "Eisenhower, you handled that just the way Marshall would have done." Conner had witnessed at first hand the price the Allies had paid for divided leadership in war, knew the cost of not giving Marshal Foch sufficient powers to go with his grand title. He told Eisenhower that in the next war, "We must insist on individual and single responsibility—leaders will have to learn how to overcome nationalistic considerations in the conduct of campaigns . . . "[7] Prophetic words for Foch's successor.

Eisenhower almost worshiped Conner. His three years in Panama, he later said, were "a sort of graduate school in military affairs . . . In a lifetime of association with great and good men, he is the one figure to whom I owe an incalculable debt." Virginia Conner noted, "I never saw two men more congenial than Ike Eisenhower and my husband." Conner, in his 1924 efficiency report on Eisenhower, wrote that he was "one of the most capable, efficient, and loyal officers I have ever met."[8]

Adding to Eisenhower's happiness in Panama was the birth of a second son. In the early summer of 1922, Mamie went to Denver to escape the heat and have her child in a modern hospital. In July, Eisenhower took a leave and was present on August 3 when John Sheldon Doud Eisenhower was born. John's presence was a great help in getting over Icky's death; as parents the Eisenhowers tended to be protective of him. Mamie, John later remarked, "was exceedingly affectionate, almost smothering me with concern," and Mamie told an interviewer, "It took me years, many years, to get over my 'smother love'—it wasn't until Johnnie had children of his own that I finally stopped all worry." His father, while stern ("Dad . . . was a terrifying figure") and rigid in his discipline, was afraid enough of his own temper that he never laid a hand on his son.[9] Instead, he gave John sharp verbal dressing downs for transgressions, which, given Eisenhower's standards, were frequent. But overall they got on fine, and as soon as John was old enough, Eisenhower included his son in as many of his activities as possible, a practice that grew as the years went by and continued to the father's death.

In 1925, Conner used his influence with the War Department to get Major Eisenhower assigned to the Command and General Staff School at Leavenworth, Kansas. In the year that followed, Eisenhower worked as he never had before. He was in direct competition with 275 of the best officers in the Army. The work load, like the competition, was nearly overwhelming. The students looked on an assignment to C&GS as a reward as well as a challenge, but the Army regarded it as a test. The school was designed to discover not only who had brains, but who could take the strain.

The method was war gaming by case studies. Students were given problems. A hostile force of such-and-such strength was either attacking or defending a position. Students commanding the Blue Force had to decide what actions should be taken. After the student had handed in his answer, he was given the approved solution. He then had to work out the movements of the combat units and the supply services to support that solution—in short, the basic staff work that would be required in time of war.

C&GS was notorious for its pressure. Students would stay up half the night studying. The tension was such that nervous breakdowns were fairly common, and there was an occasional suicide. Eisenhower found this atmosphere "exhilarating."[10] He decided that a fresh mind was more important than one crammed full of details, so he limited himself to two and one-half hours of study per night, always going to bed at nine-thirty. He got together with one old friend from Fort Sam, Leonard Gerow. They set up a command post on the third floor of Eisenhower's quarters, covered the walls with maps, filled the shelves with reference works. No sound reached them there; it was off limits to his family.

One of John Eisenhower's earliest memories was of the night he invaded this sanctuary. He saw his father and "Gee" bending over a large table, eyeshades protecting them from the glare of the lamp. "I was too small to see what was on the table but stared in wonderment at the huge maps tacked on the wall. The two young officers were going over the next day's tactical problem. Dad and Gee welcomed me with a laugh and shoved me out the door in the course of perhaps half a minute."[11]

The course brought out the best in Eisenhower, his ability to master detail without getting bogged down in it, his talent for translating ideas into action, his positive (almost eager) reaction to pressure, his mastery of his profession, and his sense of being a team player (the emphasis of the course was on the smooth functioning of the machine). When the final rankings were posted, he stood first in his class. Gerow was second, two-tenths of a point behind.

Eisenhower, elated, informed all his friends. Messages of congratulations poured in. Fox Conner was delighted with his protégé. Mrs. Doud wired, "Oh boy what a thrill hurrah I am broadcasting the news love and kisses Mother."[12] Patton wrote Eisenhower a letter of congratulations. "That certainly is fine. It shows that leavenworth is a good school if a HE man can come out one." He added that Eisenhower's record proved that "if a man thinks war long enough it is bound to effect [sic] him in a good way."

Then Patton put in a cautionary note. "Good as leavenworth is," he said, "it is still only a means not an end." Since his own graduation two years earlier he had continued to work through all the C&GS problems, but he warned Eisenhower, "I don't try for approved solutions any more but rather to do what I will do in war." Warming to his subject, Patton added, "You know that we talk a hell of a lot about tactics and such and we never get to brass tacks. Namely what is it that makes the Poor S.O.B. who constitutes the casualty lists fight and in what formation is he going to fight. The answer to the first Leadership that to the second—I don't know." But he did know that any doctrine based on "super trained heroes is bull. The solitary son of a bitch alone with God is going to skulk as he always has and our advancing waves will not advance unless we have such superior artillery that all they have to do is to walk."

Patton told Eisenhower that now that he had graduated from C&GS, he should stop thinking about drafting orders and moving supplies and start thinking about "some means of making the infantry move under fire." He prophesied that "victory in the next war will depend on EXECUTION not PLANS."[13]

Eisenhower's next assignment was to the War Department, where General Pershing put him to work on preparing a history of the American Army in France. Fortunately, Eisenhower had his youngest brother, Milton, to help him. Milton was the number-two man in the Department of Agriculture, well known around Washington as a rising star. His special talent was journalism, and he helped his brother put the history together. The brothers, although nine years apart in age, were similar in many ways. Both loved a good game of bridge, as did their wives, and they frequently played together. They looked alike, with the same big grin and hearty laugh, although Dwight was leaner in the face, tougher in the body. Their voices were so similar that, practical jokers both, they would call the other man's wife on the telephone and carry on a conversation, pretending to be each other. The wives never caught on.

Milton, who had married a wealthy girl, could afford to entertain frequently. Cabinet members, other bureaucrats, Washington lawyers, and the Washington press club were his usual guests. Dwight and Mamie joined in the fun; to Milton's secret delight, Dwight became known in Washington as "Milton's brother." At one party, as a reporter was leaving, Milton stopped him and said, "Please don't go until you've met my brother; he's a major in the Army and I know he's going places." Shaking hands with thirty-seven-year-old Major Eisenhower, the reporter thought, "If he's going far he had better start soon." But the firm handshake, the lopsided grin, and the complete concentration of Eisenhower's blue eyes on his all impressed the reporter. He decided Milton might be right.[14]

Pershing thought so too. He was delighted when Eisenhower handed in the work, on time, and sent a lavish letter of commendation: Eisenhower, he said, "has shown superior ability not only in visualizing his work as a whole but in executing its many details in an efficient and timely manner. What he has done was accomplished only by the exercise of unusual intelligence and constant devotion to duty."[15]

Pershing was so pleased, in fact, that he sent Eisenhower to the Army War College for a year, then to Paris to study the ground and expand the history. Mamie found a furnished apartment at 68 Quai d'Auteuil, near Pont Mirabeau, on the Left Bank of the Seine, and a school for John. Eisenhower himself spent much of his time on the road, examining on the spot the American battlefields east of Paris. That was excellent preparation, in the event there would ever be another war and if he got involved and if it was fought in France.

In November 1929, Eisenhower returned to Washington, where he went to work as an aide to the new Chief of Staff, General Douglas MacArthur. He was destined to spend a decade under MacArthur, who became, after Fox Conner, one of the two most important men in Eisenhower's life. The other was George C. Marshall. It was Eisenhower's luck to know and work for these outstanding generals, each one a powerful personality and a historic figure. They were vastly different in their leadership techniques.

MacArthur was bombastic, flamboyant in dress, egotistical, outrageous in his flattery, intensely partisan, keen to enter the political fray. Marshall was soft-spoken, reserved in dress, modest, slow to praise, staunchly nonpartisan, reluctant to enter the political fray. Both served Franklin Roosevelt as Chief of Staff, but their conceptions of the relationship of the head of the Army to the President were sharply different. MacArthur's was one of antagonism, Marshall's of complete support. They also differed on a fundamental strategic question, the relative importance of Europe and Asia to America. One result was to divide the U.S. Army and its General Staff into two groups, the "MacArthur clique" and the "Marshall clique," or the "Asia-firsters" and the "Europe-firsters."

Eisenhower spent fourteen of his thirty-seven years in the Army working directly under these two men, ten with MacArthur, four with Marshall. Each general liked and respected Eisenhower. They had good reason to do so. Eisenhower did his work brilliantly. It was always done on time. He loyally supported his chief's decisions. He adjusted himself to his chief's time schedule and to other whims. He was able to think from the point of view of his chief, a quality that both MacArthur and Marshall often singled out for praise. He had an instinctive sense of when to make a decision himself, when to pass it up to the boss.

MacArthur said of Eisenhower in a fitness report in the early 1930s, "This is the best officer in the Army. When the next war comes, he should go right to the top."[16] In 1942, Marshall showed that he agreed with that assessment by implementing the recommendation.

Because of his frequent disagreements with MacArthur, a conviction developed that Eisenhower hated working for MacArthur and tried desperately to obtain a transfer. Reportedly, too, MacArthur was bitter toward Eisenhower and deliberately held him back, which supposedly explains why Eisenhower was still lieutenant colonel in 1940, on his fiftieth birthday. But an account of the Eisenhower-MacArthur relationship that concentrates on bitterness, hatred, and jealousy, with the emphasis on their fights, is much too simple.

Their relationship was rich and complex, with many nuances, and was highly profitable to each man. Eisenhower later said that he had always been "deeply grateful for the administrative experience he had gained under General MacArthur," without which he confessed he would not "have been ready for the great responsibilities of the war period." Eisenhower also pointed out the obvious: "Hostility between us has been exaggerated. After all, there must be a strong tie for two men to work so closely for so many years." [17]

In his memoirs, Eisenhower described MacArthur as "decisive, personable, amazingly comprehensive in his knowledge . . . possessed of a phenomenal memory." MacArthur was a "peculiar fellow," Eisenhower said, who had a habit of referring to himself in the third person. Of MacArthur's well-known egotism, Eisenhower commented, "[He] could never see another sun . . . in the heavens." But MacArthur's idiosyncrasies, little and great, were not matters of substance. Eisenhower said of MacArthur "he did have a hell of an intellect! My God, but he was smart. He had a *brain*." [18] So did Marshall, of course, and Eisenhower too for that matter, although of the three, only MacArthur could read through a speech or a paper once, then repeat it verbatim.

Eisenhower was much closer to MacArthur personally than he ever was to Marshall. Eisenhower and MacArthur frequently exchanged jokes; Eisenhower and Marshall seldom did. Marshall, a graduate of the Virginia Military Institute, did not much care who won the Army-Navy game, while Eisenhower and MacArthur were fanatic followers of West Point's football fortunes. Each fall they engaged in lively discussions about prospects for and the results of the Army-Navy game. Eisenhower and Mamie had almost no social contact with the Marshalls, while they frequently attended parties and dinners with MacArthur and his wife, Jean.

Eisenhower learned a great deal from MacArthur, far more than simply administrative skills. When he took a position on an issue, MacArthur was very stubborn in maintaining it, especially when the Army was concerned. He mastered the details of an issue and spoke with authority on them. He matched the persistence of his argument with a logical presentation of the facts. Whether consciously or not, during the war and as President, Eisenhower copied MacArthur in debate.

Nevertheless, many of the lessons Eisenhower learned from MacArthur were negative ones, a reflection of the markedly different styles of the two men. MacArthur did not attempt to teach or instruct, to make Eisenhower a protégé as Marshall tended to do; instead, Eisenhower learned from MacArthur by observing him in action.

MacArthur was certainly a fascinating man to observe. Reporters accompanied him wherever he went, and his pronouncements or activities often made headlines. He was deliberately outspoken on some of the most volatile emotional issues of the day. He lambasted the Communists, the New Dealers, the pacifists, the Socialists, any and all groups that did not meet his definition of 100 percent Americans. He never refused a challenge; he loved to charge into the battle.

MacArthur made no secret of his political ambitions; everyone knew that unlike Pershing he would welcome a presidential nomination. During the Roosevelt years and on into Truman's Fair Deal, right-wing Republicans tried again and again to organize a MacArthur-for-President boom, even in 1944. Such activities always excited the general but never got far. One reason for the failure was obviously MacArthur's extremism, but another was his inability to understand the American people. Eisenhower had a much better intuitive understanding of his fellow citizens' political preferences.

During the 1936 presidential campaign, for example, when Eisenhower and MacArthur were in Manila, MacArthur convinced himself that Republican nominee Alf Landon was sure to win, probably by a landslide. Eisenhower protested that he was wrong. MacArthur insisted that he was correct, and cited a *Literary Digest* poll to prove it. He even bet several thousand pesos on Landon's election and advised the Philippine government to prepare for a change in administrations in Washington. Eisenhower predicted that Landon could not even carry his home state, Kansas. MacArthur indulged himself in an "almost hysterical condemnation" of Eisenhower's "stupidity." When another of MacArthur's aides, T. J. Davis, supported Eisenhower's position, MacArthur loudly denounced them both as "fearful and small-minded people who are afraid to express judgments that are obvious from the evidence at hand." Eisenhower's comment in a diary that he was beginning to keep on a sporadic basis was "Oh hell."

After the election, in which Landon carried only two states, MacArthur accused the *Literary Digest* of "crookedness," but Eisenhower noted, "he's never expressed to TJ or to me any regret for his awful bawling out . . ."[19]

In his first years of working for MacArthur, Eisenhower was often astonished at the way in which the Chief of Staff brushed aside the usual "clean-cut lines between the military and the political. If General MacArthur ever recognized the existence of that line, he usually chose to ignore it." To Eisenhower's dismay he found that "my duties were beginning to verge on the political, even to the edge of partisan politics."[20]

The tradition in the Army was to deny that it was ever involved in any way in politics. The Army refused to see itself as a vast bureaucracy, even while it lobbied among congressmen for appropriations (a task on which Major Eisenhower spent much of his time). The Army and Army officers were supposed to be above politics. But, as Eisenhower confessed to Merriman Smith in a 1962 off-the-record interview, when Smith said it was his impression that Eisenhower did not like the role of politician, "What the hell are you talking about? I have been in politics, the most active sort of politics, most of my adult life. There's no more active political organization in the world than the armed services of the U.S. As a matter of fact, I think I am a better politician than most so called politicians."

When Smith asked why, Eisenhower explained, "Because I don't get emotionally involved. I can accept a fact for what it is, and I can also accept the fact that when you're hopelessly outgunned and outmanned, you don't go out and pick a fight."[21]

MacArthur embraced controversial issues; Eisenhower avoided them. When Eisenhower became President, the nation paid a price for his avoidance of controversy, as in the desegregation crisis or in dealing with Senator Joseph R. McCarthy. But the avoidance clearly helped Eisenhower's career, as he well knew. MacArthur was famous, but he was never popular enough to win a nomination, much less an election. Watching MacArthur in the thirties, and observing the results of his political activity, reinforced Eisenhower's determination to keep himself above politics. That attitude was crucial to his success as a general and a politician.

MacArthur operated differently, and MacArthur never became President, although he wanted the job much more than Eisenhower ever did. There is an irony here. MacArthur, the most political of generals, never succeeded in politics, while three of the most apolitical generals in American history, Washington, Grant, and Eisenhower, did. They were the true American Caesars, the only American soldiers to hold both supreme military and political power.

As a young officer, Eisenhower wanted to get some service with troops, as a line officer, away from Washington and the staff, but MacArthur would not let him go. In 1935, MacArthur's tour as Chief of Staff came to an end (Roosevelt had extended it by one year already), and Eisenhower looked forward to a field assignment. But then MacArthur "lowered the boom on me." Congress had voted "commonwealth" status for the Philippines, with complete independence to come in 1946. The new Philippine Commonwealth government, led by Manuel Quezon and the Nacionalista party, would need an army. Quezon asked MacArthur to come to Manila as his military adviser, to take charge of creating one. MacArthur accepted and insisted that Eisenhower accompany him as his assistant.[22]

In late September 1935, Eisenhower joined MacArthur on a train headed west for San Francisco, where they would board a ship for Manila. Eisenhower had been in Washington for six years. He had precious little to show for it. No promotions had come to him; neither he nor any other Army officer had been able to persuade the government to begin rebuilding the nation's defenses; he had had no service with troops and seemed fated to be forever a staff officer.

He could, however, take pride in MacArthur's assessment of his service and abilities. On September 30, 1935, the Chief of Staff wrote him a letter, praising him for his "success in performing difficult tasks whose accomplishment required a comprehensive grasp of the military profession in all its principal phases, as well as analytical thought and forceful expression." MacArthur thanked Eisenhower for his "cheerful and efficient devotion . . . to confining, difficult, and often strenuous duties, in spite of the fact that your own personal desires involved a return to troops command and other physically active phases of Army life, for which your characteristics so well qualify you." He assured Eisenhower that his experiences would be valuable to him as a commander in the future, "since all problems presented to you were necessarily solved from the viewpoint of the High Command."

All that praise, so typical of MacArthur (and so well deserved), was welcome, but MacArthur's concluding paragraph must have seemed to Eisenhower just a bit painful. MacArthur wrote, "The numbers of personal requests for your services brought to me by heads of many of the Army's principal activities during the past few years furnish convincing proof of the reputation you have established as an outstanding soldier. I can say no more than that this reputation coincides exactly with my own judgment."[23] Eisenhower wished that MacArthur would meet one of those requests and let him go. But the chief did not, and now Eisenhower was off for Manila.

In January 1939, shortly after his forty-eighth birthday, Eisenhower wrote his personal definition of happiness. His brother Milton had asked his advice about a job offer. Eisenhower wrote that "only a man that is happy in his work can be happy in his home and with his friends." He continued, "Happiness in work means that its performer must know it to be worthwhile, suited to his temperament, and, finally, suited to his age, experience and capacity for performance of a high order."[24]

Eisenhower served in the Philippines from late 1935 to the end of 1939. Nothing that he did there met any of the criteria he himself had set down for a happy life. His work was neither rewarding nor suited to his age or abilities. It was also terribly frustrating and, when the test came, proved to be worthless, as the Japanese in 1941 easily conquered the Philippine Army he had labored to help create. His close and warm relationship with MacArthur became distant and cold. His best friend died in an accident. Mamie was ill and bedridden much of the time. John was the only member of the family who enjoyed the Philippines and prospered there. The best that can be said for Eisenhower's years with the Philippine Army was that he gained some experience in juggling and cutting national budgets.

That came about because MacArthur's style was to leave all details to his subordinates, which in practice meant that Eisenhower met daily with Quezon on the problems of preparing and paying for the new army. He all but begged MacArthur to see Quezon at least once a week, but MacArthur refused. "He apparently thinks it would not be in keeping with his rank and position for him to do so."[25]

As a result, Quezon gave Eisenhower a private office in the Malacañan Palace, next to the president's office. Eisenhower spent two or three hours a day there, the rest of his time in his regular office, next to MacArthur's, in the Manila Hotel. One day in 1936 MacArthur strode in, beaming. He said Quezon was going to make him a field marshal in the Philippine Army. At the same time, Quezon wanted to make Eisenhower and his assistant Major James B. Ord general officers. Eisenhower turned pale. He said he could never accept such an appointment. Ord agreed with Eisenhower, "though in somewhat less positive fashion." Eisenhower explained in his diary that he felt that because "so many American officers [stationed in the Philippines] believe that the attempt to create a Philippine army is somewhat ridiculous, the acceptance by us of high rank in an army which is not yet formed would serve to belittle our effort."[26]

To MacArthur directly, Eisenhower said, "General, you have been a four-star general [in the U.S. Army]. This is a *proud* thing. There's only been a few who had it. Why in the *hell* do you want a *banana* country giving you a field-marshalship? This . . . this looks like you're trying for some kind of . . ." MacArthur stopped him. "Oh, Jesus!" Eisenhower later remembered. "He just gave me hell!" [27]

MacArthur, obviously, did not share Eisenhower's sensibilities. He believed, and often said, that Asians were peculiarly impressed by rank and title. Since that suited his own tastes, he accepted the field-marshal rank, explaining to Eisenhower that "he could not decline it without offense to the president." Eisenhower noted that MacArthur "is tickled pink." [28]

MacArthur designed his own uniform for the ceremony, which took place on August 24, 1936, at Malacañan Palace. Resplendent in a sharkskin uniform consisting of black trousers and a white coat covered with braid, stars, and unique lapel designs, MacArthur graciously accepted his gold baton from Mrs. Quezon. MacArthur gave a typically grandiloquent speech, which one of his officers, Captain Bonner Fellers, later a close associate, told him was "a Sermon on the Mount clothed in grim, present-day reality. I shall never forget it."

To Eisenhower, however, the whole affair was "rather fantastic." Five years later, in 1941, it became even more fantastic to him when Quezon told him "that he had not initiated the idea at all; rather, Quezon said that MacArthur himself came up with the high-sounding title." [29]

In early January 1938, MacArthur conceived the idea, according to Eisenhower, that "the morale of the whole population would be enhanced if the people could see something of their emerging army in the capital city, Manila." He ordered his assistants to arrange to bring units from all over the islands to a field near Manila, where they could camp for three or four days, winding up the whole affair with a big parade through the city. Eisenhower and Ord did a quick cost estimate, then protested to MacArthur "that it was impossible to do the thing within our budget." MacArthur waved aside their objections and told them to do as ordered.

They did. Soon Quezon learned about the preparations. He called Eisenhower into his office to ask what was going on. Eisenhower was astonished—he had assumed that MacArthur had discussed the project with the President. When he learned that such was not the case, he told Quezon that they should discuss the matter no further until he had had a chance to confer with MacArthur. But when Eisenhower returned to his office in the Manila Hotel, he found a furious MacArthur. Quezon had called him on the telephone, said he was horrified at the thought of what the parade would cost, and wanted it canceled immediately.

MacArthur then told his staff that "he had never meant for us to proceed with preparations for the parade. He had only wanted us to investigate it quietly." Eisenhower, "flabbergasted, didn't know what to say. And finally I said to him, I said, 'General, all you're saying is that I'm a liar, and I am *not* a liar, and so I'd like to go back to the United States right away.' Well, he came back . . . and he said, 'Ike, it's just fun to see that damn Dutch temper'—he put his arm right over my shoulder—he said, 'It's fun to see that Dutch temper take you over,' and he was just sweetness and light. He said, 'it's just a misunderstanding, and let's let it go at that.' " [30]

But Eisenhower could never let it go at that; thirty years later he still grew incensed when describing the scene. He commented, "Probably no one has had more, tougher fights with a senior than I had with MacArthur. I told him time and again, 'Why in *hell* don't you *fire* me?' I said, 'Goddammit, you do things I don't agree with and you know damn well I don't.' " [31]

MacArthur did not fire Eisenhower for the best of reasons—he needed him. Eisenhower was his liaison with Quezon, his "eyes and ears" for reports on developments in the various camps, the manager of his office, the man who drafted his speeches, letters, and reports. MacArthur knew that Eisenhower was close to indispensable, and as often as he shouted at his assistant, he found cause to praise him lavishly. In a typical handwritten note, praising Eisenhower for a policy paper, MacArthur said, "Ike—This is excellent in every respect. I do not see how it could be improved upon. It accomplishes the purpose in language so simple and direct as to preclude confusion and is flexible enough for complete administration." Quezon too was grateful to Eisenhower for his efforts. When Eisenhower drafted a speech for Quezon, the president wrote him a note saying, "It is excellent. You have completely absorbed my thought and expressed it better than I ever could do it." [32]

So, despite his own intense desire for service with American troops, despite his unhappy wife, despite his fights with his boss, Eisenhower had no chance of getting out of the Philippines. MacArthur would never consider his requests for a transfer, in fact would not even allow him to make such a request on a formal basis or enter it on his record.

There were compensations. The extra pay was welcome, the new apartment was luxurious, John was in a good school, and in July 1936 Eisenhower was finally promoted, along with the rest of his class, to lieutenant colonel.

●　●

In September 1939, World War II began. To Eisenhower, although war would mean advancement in his own career and although he had dedicated his life to preparing for the challenge, the coming of the conflict was a disaster. On the day war was declared, he wrote Milton, "After months and months of feverish effort to appease and placate the mad man that is governing Germany, the British and French seem to be driven into a corner out of which they can work their way only by fighting. It's a sad day for Europe and for the whole civilized world—though for a long time it has seemed ridiculous to refer to the world as civilized. If the war . . . is . . . long-drawn-out and . . . bloody . . . then I believe that the remnants of nations emerging from it will be scarcely recognizable as the ones that entered it."

He feared that Communism, anarchy, crime and disorder, loss of personal liberties, and abject poverty "will curse the areas that witness any amount of fighting." He said it scarcely seemed possible "that people that proudly refer to themselves as intelligent could let the situation come about." He blamed Hitler, "a power-drunk ego-centric . . . one of the criminally insane . . . the absolute ruler of eighty-nine million people." And he made a prophecy: "Unless [Hitler] is successful in overcoming the whole world by brute force, the final result will be that Germany will have to be dismembered."[33]

Eisenhower's attitude contrasted sharply with that of his friend Patton, who signed off a 1940 letter to Eisenhower, "Again thanking you and hoping we are together in a long and BLOODY war."[34]

After the Germans overran Poland, stagnation set in as the Wehrmacht and the Western Allies stared at each other across the Maginot Line. In October 1939, Eisenhower confessed to Leonard Gerow that "the war has me completely bewildered . . . It seems obvious that neither side desires to undertake attacks against heavily fortified lines. If fortification, with modern weapons, has given to the defensive form of combat such a terrific advantage over the offensive, we've swung back to the late middle ages, when any army in a fortified camp was perfectly safe from molestation. What," Eisenhower wondered, "is the answer?"[35]

By this time, Eisenhower had a fixed date for his return to the States—December 13, 1939. MacArthur had tried to talk him into staying, as had Quezon, who offered him a blank contract for his services and said, "We'll tear up the old contract. I've already signed this one and it is filled in—except what you want as your emoluments for remaining. You will write that in." Eisenhower thanked him but declined, explaining "no amount of money can make me change my mind. My entire life has been given to this one thing, my country . . . my profession. I want to be there if what I fear is going to come about actually happens." [36]

The liner pulled out of its dock at noon. By Christmas, 1939, the Eisenhowers were in Hawaii; they celebrated New Year's Eve in San Francisco. The ordeal of their four years in the Philippines was over.

During the voyage, and after they arrived in California, John talked to his father about his future. Then seventeen years old, he was considering going to West Point. Eisenhower had tried not to push him in that direction (although it was clear to John that his father would be delighted if he became a cadet), and before John committed himself, his father wanted to make certain that the young man was fully aware of what he was getting into.

In terms of a career, Eisenhower pointed out that if John became a lawyer, doctor, or businessman, "he could probably go just as far as his character, abilities, and honorable ambitions could carry him." In a grand understatement, he added that "in the Army . . . things are ordered somewhat differently." No matter how good an officer was, no matter how well he did his duty, his promotion was governed strictly by the rules of seniority.

Using himself as an example, Eisenhower pointed out that he had been in the Army since 1911. During the past twenty-nine years, he had consistently been praised by his superiors and classed in the top category for his age and rank. He had attended the Army's leading postgraduate schools and graduated first at C&GS. But nothing that he had done had had the slightest influence in pushing him ahead. Seniority govered all promotions until a man became a colonel, when he was eligible for selection to a one-star rank, regardless of seniority. But Eisenhower's class would not reach the grade of colonel until 1950, at which time he would be sixty years old, and the War Department would not promote colonels to general office grade when they had only a short time remaining before compulsory retirement. Thus, Eisenhower told his son, his own chances of ever obtaining a star in the Army "were nil."

At this point in the discussion, Eisenhower wrote later, "John must have wondered why I stayed in the Army at all." Indeed he must have. Eisenhower explained that he had found his life in the Army "wonderfully interesting . . . it had brought me into contact with men of ability, honor, and a sense of high dedication to their country." He claimed that he had refused to bother himself about promotion. "I said the real satisfaction was for a man who did the best he could. My ambition in the Army was to make everybody I worked for regretful when I was ordered to other duty."[37]

In 1940 Eisenhower had the best year of his career to that date. He was regimental executive to the 15th Infantry Regiment of the 3d Division, and commander of the 1st Battalion of the 15th. He did not just enjoy being with troops, he relished it, reveled in it, filled his letters with enthusiasm. To Omar Bradley, for example, he wrote on July 1, 1940, "I'm having the time of my life. Like everyone else in the army, we're up to our necks in work and in problems, big and little. But this work is fun! . . . I could not conceive of a better job."[38] The relatively leisurely life he had led in Manila gave way to one of constant physical activity, which suited him perfectly. After field maneuvers in Washington State in August—through country that he said "would have made a good stage setting for a play in Hades—Stumps, slashings, fallen logs, tangled brush, holes, and hills!"—he commented to Gerow: "I froze at night, never had, in any one stretch, more than 1¾ hours sleep, and at times was really fagged out—but I had a swell time." His experience strengthened his conviction that "I belonged with troops; with them I was always happy."[39]

At age fifty, he was in excellent physical condition. When he returned from the Philippines, a friend told him that he appeared to be thin and worn-out. Eisenhower insisted that he felt fine, that Mamie was the one who had been sick in the tropics, that although the heat had worn him down a bit, he expected to gain some weight and bounce back quickly.

He did. By the fall of 1940, he was robust again. Most people thought he looked ten years younger than his actual age. The outdoor life and service with troops restored him to his full strength. Broad of chest and shoulder, he still had the physical grace of the natural athlete. His whole body was animated. He walked with a bounce to his step, swinging his arms, eyes darting, missing nothing.

His voice was deep and resonant. When he talked, his hands flashed through the air as he enumerated his points on his fingers. His powers of concentration were greater than ever. He would fix his blue eyes on a listener, compelling attention and respect.

He was almost completely bald by now, with only a few strands of light-brown hair on the back and sides of his head, but the exposed pate somehow added to his good looks, perhaps because it balanced his broad, mobile mouth. He retained his infectious grin and hearty laugh.

He was mentally alert, ideas coming into his head so rapidly that his words tumbled out. Most of all, he exuded self-confidence. He was good at his job, he knew it, and he knew that his superiors realized it. He expected to be called to challenging posts, and to make a major contribution to the Army and to the nation.

He was at his post up to eighteen hours a day, seven days a week; he set up training schedules, made inspections, lectured his newly commissioned junior officers, supervised field exercises, studied the war in Europe and applied the lessons to his own unit. He was concerned with morale, did all he could to build it up and keep it high. He was convinced that "Americans either will not or cannot fight at maximum efficiency unless they understand the why and wherefore of their orders," so wherever he went he talked, asked questions, listened, observed. He was patient, clear, and logical in his explanations to his officers and men about why things had to be done this way or that. He mingled with the men on an informal basis, got to know them, listened to their gripes, and, when appropriate, did something about them.

He believed that "morale is at one and the same time the strongest, and the most delicate of growths. It withstands shocks, even disasters of the battlefield, but can be destroyed utterly by favoritism, neglect, or injustice." Eisenhower would not abide favoritism or neglect, and tried to be just in his dealings with his men. But he also knew that "the Army should not be coddled or babied, for that does not produce morale, it merely condones and encourages inefficiency."[40] Consequently, he drove his men hard, all day, every day, without letup, just as he did himself.

Eisenhower hated any sign of lassitude, most especially when a Regular Army officer displayed it. He would grow furious when he saw one of his Regulars scanning the training programs "carefully and fearfully to see whether they demand more hours; whether their execution is going to cause us some inconvenience!" He told his old friend Everett Hughes, "I was never more serious in my life than I am about the need for each of us, particularly in the Regular Army, to do his whole chore intelligently and energetically. If ever we are to prove that we're worth the salaries the government has been paying us all these years—now is the time!"[41]

Eisenhower was delighted in September 1940 when Colonel Patton, commanding the 2d Armored Brigade in Fort Benning, wrote to say that two armored divisions would soon be formed, the first in the Army's history and the fulfillment of their hopes as young officers back at Fort Meade in 1920. Patton said he expected to command one of the armored divisions. He wondered if Eisenhower would want to serve under him.

"That would be great," Eisenhower responded immediately. "I suppose it's too much to hope that I could have a regiment in your division, because I'm still almost three years away from my colonelcy, but I *think* I could do a damn good job of commanding a regiment." Patton wrote back, "I shall ask for you either as Chief of Staff which I should prefer or as a regimental commander you can tell me which you want for no matter how we get together we will go PLACES."[42]

Through the winter of 1940–1941, as the Army expanded, so did Fort Lewis. As at every other Army post, construction crews were everywhere, while recruits came in by the thousands. Eisenhower did his usual efficient job, and his responsibilities grew as a result. In March 1941, General Kenyon Joyce, commanding the IX Army Corps, which covered the entire Northwest, asked for Eisenhower as his chief of staff. That same month, on the eleventh, he was promoted to the rank of full colonel (temporary).

No promotion he ever received delighted him more. Being made a colonel fulfilled his highest ambitions. Mamie and John arranged a celebration. His fellow officers, congratulating him, said it would not be long before he had a star on each shoulder. "Damn it," he complained to John, "as soon as you get a promotion they start talking about another one. Why can't they let a guy be happy with what he has? They take all the joy out of it."[43]

Three months later, he joined General Walter Krueger as chief of staff for the Third Army. In late June 1941, the Eisenhowers set off for Fort Sam Houston. They arrived on July 1, their twenty-fifth wedding anniversary. Mamie was pleased to be back at such a familiar place, with all its happy memories, especially since her husband was now a colonel, which entitled them to one of Fort Sam's fine old brick houses, with shady verandas all around and a large lawn.

A colonel rated a striker and an executive officer. Mamie put up a notice on the bulletin board for a striker. A few days later, Pfc. Michael J. McKeogh volunteered. "Mickey," whose parents had immigrated to the United States from Ireland, had been a bellhop at the Plaza Hotel in New York before he was drafted. He liked Eisenhower "straight off," he later said, because the colonel was "absolutely straight" and "you always knew exactly where you stood with him."

He thought Mamie "a very gracious lady." Mickey soon became Eisenhower's most fervent admirer and remained with him for the next five years.[44]

As his executive, Eisenhower selected Lieutenant Ernest R. Lee (everyone called him "Tex"), a native of San Antonio, who had been an insurance and a car salesman. Bright, breezy, cheerful, anxious to please, Lee had all the qualities of a good salesman. Eisenhower enjoyed his company, came to rely on him to handle office details. Lee, like Mickey, stayed with Eisenhower to the end of the war. Together, they formed the nucleus of what would become Eisenhower's "family," a close-knit group of enlisted men and women and junior officers who were devoted to Eisenhower and who served him well.

The greatest experience of Eisenhower's tour as chief of staff to the Third Army was the Louisiana maneuvers, held in August and September 1941. These were the largest maneuvers held by the U.S. Army before America entered the war. They pitted Krueger's Third Army against General Ben Lear's Second Army. Krueger, with 240,000 men, was "invading" Louisiana, while Lear, with 180,000 men, was "defending" the United States. Marshall had insisted on such a large-scale war game because he wanted to uncover deficiencies in training and equipment, and because he needed to uncover hidden talent in the officer corps.

Eisenhower got his first publicity almost immediately. Krueger's Third Army, operating under plans Eisenhower had helped draw up, outflanked Lear's Second Army, forcing it to retreat. "Had it been a real war," young reporter Hanson Baldwin wrote for *The New York Times,* "Lear's force would have been annihilated."[45] In their syndicated column, "Washington Merry-Go-Round," Drew Pearson and Robert S. Allen reported that it was "Colonel Eisenhower . . . who conceived and directed the strategy that routed the Second Army." They said that Eisenhower "has a steel-trap mind plus unusual physical vigor [and] to him the military profession is a science . . ."[46]

Eisenhower professed to be unaware of why he received the credit, which he said should have gone to General Krueger. His modesty was genuine and typical. It was also one of his most endearing traits, an essential part of his popularity with the press and the public. His "Aw shucks, who me?" look, his embarrassment at being singled out, his insistence that others, not he, really deserved the praise, became one of his best-known characteristics, something millions of people found irresistibly appealing. In late September, on Krueger's recommendation, he was promoted to brigadier general (temporary).

Congratulations came pouring in. Eisenhower responded by writing, "When they get clear down to my place on the list, they are passing out stars with considerable abandon."[47]

Thanks to the promotion, Eisenhower's photograph, stern-faced and saluting the flag, went out over the wire services. The American people—and press corps—began to discover something Mamie had always known, that Eisenhower was one of the most photogenic men in the country, even in the world.

A Denver friend, Aksel Nielsen, whom he had met through the Douds, wrote Eisenhower to ask for an autographed print of the photograph. Eisenhower replied, "I'm so tremendously flattered by the thought of anyone asking for my photo that I'm hurrying it off at once—it would be tragic to have you change your mind. Wouldn't you like three or four???"[48]

On Sunday morning, December 7, 1941, Eisenhower went to his office—over Mamie's protests—to catch up on his paper work. About noon, he told Tex Lee that he was "dead tired" and said he "guessed he'd go home and take a nap." He told Mamie he did not want to be "bothered by anyone wanting to play bridge" and went to sleep. An hour or so later, Lee called him with the news from Pearl Harbor.[49]

Five hectic days later he was at his desk with more of the inevitable paperwork when he got a call from the War Department. "Is that you, Ike?" Colonel Walter Bedell Smith, secretary of the General Staff, asked. "Yes," Eisenhower replied. "The Chief says for you to hop a plane and get up here right away," Smith ordered. "Tell your boss that formal orders will come through later."[50]

Eisenhower assumed that Marshall wanted to talk to him about the state of the defenses in the Philippines, and that he would not be gone long. He told Mickey to pack only one bag for him, assured Mamie that he would be back soon, and got an afternoon plane leaving San Antonio for Washington.

Bad weather forced the aircraft down in Dallas. Eisenhower switched to a train. After the train passed Kansas City and headed east, Eisenhower was riding over the same tracks he had traveled on thirty years earlier, on his trip from Abilene to West Point. As he rode along, he tried to prepare himself for the conference with Marshall. He knew it was not only a great responsibility but also a great opportunity.

Perhaps his thoughts strayed, once or twice, to his parents' injunction, which had been in his mind in 1911: "Opportunity is all about you. Reach out and take it."

By most standards, he had failed to take the advice. Instead of taking opportunity, he had given his life and his talents to the Army. He was fifty-one years old; only the coming of war had saved him from a forced retirement and a life with no savings and but a small pension to live on. Although he had impressed every superior for whom he had worked, he had no accomplishments to his credit that he could point to with pride for his grandchildren. Had he died in 1941, at an age when most great men have their monumental achievements behind them, he would be completely unknown today.

As his train sped across the Midwest toward Washington, he may have dared to hope that the war would give him an opportunity to use his talents and skills, which were considerable, for the good of his country and perhaps even for the good of his own career.

CHAPTER THREE

Preparing
the First Offensive

ON SUNDAY MORNING, December 15, 1941, Eisenhower arrived at Union Station in Washington. He went immediately to the War Department offices in the Munitions Building on Constitution Avenue (the Pentagon was then under construction) for his initial conference with the Chief of Staff. After a brief, formal greeting, Marshall quickly outlined the situation in the Pacific—the ships lost at Pearl Harbor, the planes lost at Clark Field outside Manila, the size and strength of Japanese attacks elsewhere, troop strength in the Philippines, reinforcement possibilities, intelligence estimates, the capabilities of America's Dutch and British allies in Asia, and other details. Then Marshall leaned forward across his desk, fixed his eyes on Eisenhower's, and demanded, "What should be our general line of action?"

Eisenhower was startled. He had just arrived, knew little more than what he had read in the newspapers and what Marshall had just told him, was not up to date on the war plans for the Pacific, and had no staff to help him prepare an answer. After a second or two of hesitation, Eisenhower requested, "Give me a few hours."

"All right," Marshall replied. He had dozens of problems to deal with that afternoon, hundreds in the days to follow. He needed help and he needed to know immediately which of his officers could give it to him. He had heard great things about Eisenhower, from men whose judgment he trusted, but he needed to see for himself how

Eisenhower operated under the pressures of war. His question was the first test.

Eisenhower went to a desk that had been assigned to him in the War Plans Division of the General Staff. Sticking a sheet of yellow tissue paper into his typewriter, he tapped out with one finger, "Steps to Be Taken," then sat back and started thinking. He knew that the Philippines could not be saved, that the better part of military wisdom would be to retreat to Australia, there to build a base for a counter-offensive. But the honor of the Army was at stake, and the prestige of the United States in the Far East, and these political factors outweighed the purely military considerations. An effort had to be made. Eisenhower's first recommendation was to build a base in Australia from which attempts could be made to reinforce the Philippines. "Speed is essential," he noted. He urged that shipment of planes, pilots, ammunition, and other equipment be started from the West Coast and Hawaii to Australia immediately.

It was already dusk when Eisenhower returned to Marshall's office. As he handed over his written recommendation, he said he realized that it would be impossible to get reinforcements to the Philippines in time to save the islands from the Japanese. Still, he added, the United States had to do everything it could to bolster MacArthur's forces, because "the people of China, of the Philippines, of the Dutch East Indies will be watching us. They may excuse failure but they will not excuse abandonment." He urged the advantages of Australia as a base of operations—English-speaking, a strong ally, modern port facilities, beyond the range of the Japanese offensive—and advised Marshall to begin a program of expanding the facilities there and to secure the line of communications from the West Coast to Hawaii and then on to New Zealand and Australia. "In this," Eisenhower said, ". . . we dare not fail. We must take great risks and spend any amount of money required."

Marshall studied Eisenhower for a minute, then said softly, "I agree with you. Do your best to save them." He thereupon placed Eisenhower in charge of the Philippines and Far Eastern Section of the War Plans Division (WPD). Then Marshall leaned forward—Eisenhower recalled years later that he had "an eye that seemed to me awfully cold"—and declared, "Eisenhower, the Department is filled with able men who analyze their problems well but feel compelled always to bring them to me for final solution. I must have assistants who will solve their own problems and tell me later what they have done."[1]

Over the next two months Eisenhower labored to save the Philippines. His efforts were worse than fruitless, as MacArthur came to lump Eisenhower together with Marshall and Roosevelt as the men responsible for the debacle on the islands. But throughout that period, and in the months that followed, Eisenhower impressed Marshall deeply, so deeply that Marshall came to agree with MacArthur's earlier judgment that Eisenhower was the best officer in the Army.

Marshall was not an easy man to impress. He was a cold, aloof person—"remote and austere," Eisenhower called him—a man who forced everyone to keep his distance. Franklin Roosevelt had tried at their first meeting to slap him on the back and call him "George," but Marshall drew back and let the President know that the name was "General Marshall," and "General Marshall" it remained. He had few intimate friends. When he relaxed he did it alone, watching movies or puttering in his garden. He kept a tight grip on his emotions and seldom displayed any sign of a sense of humor. His sense of duty was highly developed. He made small allowance for failings in others, but to those who could do the work, Marshall was intensely loyal. He also felt deep affection toward them, though he seldom showed it.

Hardly anyone, for example, could resist Eisenhower's infectious grin and he was known throughout the Army by his catchy nickname, but Marshall did resist. In all their years together, Marshall almost always called him "Eisenhower" (except after November 4, 1952, when he called him "Mr. President").

Marshall slipped only once, at the victory parade in New York City in 1945, and called him "Ike." "To make up for it," Eisenhower recalled with a smile, "he used the word 'Eisenhower' five times in the next sentence."[2]

For his part, Eisenhower always called Marshall "General." After the years with MacArthur, he found Marshall to be the ideal boss, both as a man to work for and as a teacher. In October 1942, he told an assistant, "I wouldn't trade one Marshall for fifty MacArthurs." He thought a second, then blurted out, "My God! That would be a lousy deal. What would I do with fifty MacArthurs?" As he later wrote more formally, Eisenhower conceived "unlimited admiration and respect" for Marshall, and came to have feelings of "affection" for him.[3] Marshall came to have the dominant role not only in Eisenhower's career, but also in his thinking and in his leadership techniques. He was the model that Eisenhower tried to emulate; he set the standards Eisenhower tried to meet.

The two men, although ten years apart in age, had much in

common. Marshall had the build and grace of an athlete, was about Eisenhower's height (six feet), and was equally well proportioned. He had been a football player in college. He was a great fan of Fox Conner and a student of military history. Like Eisenhower, he loved exploring the Civil War battlefields and habitually illustrated his points or strengthened his arguments by drawing on examples from past battles and campaigns. The way he exercised leadership coincided nicely with Eisenhower's temperament. He never yelled or shouted, almost never lost his temper. He built an atmosphere of friendly cooperation and teamwork around him, without losing the distinction between the commander and his staff—there was never any doubt as to who was the boss.

Marshall headed a stupendous organization. To do so effectively he needed assistants he could trust. In picking them, he took professional competence for granted and concentrated on personality traits. Certain types were, in his view, unsuited for high command. Foremost among these were those who were self-seeking in the matter of promotion. Next came those who always tried to "pass the buck." Officers who tried to do everything themselves and consequently got bogged down in detail were equally unsatisfactory. Men who shouted or pounded on the desk were as unacceptable to Marshall as men who had too great a love of the limelight. Nor could he abide the pessimist. He surrounded himself with men who were offensive-minded and who concentrated on the possibilities rather than the difficulties.

In every respect, Eisenhower was exactly the sort of officer Marshall was looking for. Eisenhower himself, as Supreme Commander and later as President, used Marshall's criteria in picking his subordinates.

The first three months of 1942 were terribly trying on Eisenhower. Until February 7, he lived with Milton and Helen in Falls Church, Virginia, but he never saw the house in daylight. His driver would pick him up before dawn to take him to his office on Constitution Avenue, and bring him back at 10:30 P.M. or later. He wolfed down his meals, often no more than a hot dog and coffee, at his desk. When he got to Falls Church, Helen would have a snack for him, and he would wake up his nephew and niece for a chat before going to bed himself. Always thoughtful, he arranged to send flowers to Helen for a big dinner party he could not attend, and had an aide purchase Christmas presents for the children.

But he missed Mamie and was delighted when she came up to Washington in February and found a small apartment at the Wardman Park Hotel. Mickey, who drove the family Chrysler east from Texas, was shocked when he first saw Eisenhower: "He was more tired-looking than I'd ever seen him; all of his face was tired. His voice was tired, like his face."[4] Small wonder; on February 22 Eisenhower noted that he had gone to a Sunday dinner in honor of two visiting Chinese and that this was the "longest I've been out of the office in daytime since coming here ten weeks ago today."[5]

Part of the strain was due to the nature of his job. He wanted to be in the field, with troops, not behind a desk. "My God, how I hate to work by any method that forces me to depend on someone else," he complained. Considering the whole Washington-in-wartime scene, he remarked, "There's a lot of big talk and desk hammering around this place, but very few doers. They announce results in advance in a flashy way and make big impressions, but the results often don't materialize, and then the workers get the grief."[6]

On March 10, David Eisenhower died. His son could barely take the time to record the fact in his diary. The following day, Eisenhower wrote that "war is not soft, it has no time to indulge even the deepest and most sacred emotions." That night he quit work at 7:30 P.M., noting, "I haven't the heart to go on tonight." On March 12, the day of the funeral in Abilene, he closed his office door for a half hour, to think about his father and to compose a eulogy. He praised his father for his "sterling honesty, his pride in his independence, his exemplary habits" and for his "undemonstrative, quiet, modest" manner. "I'm proud he was my father," Eisenhower wrote, and then expressed his only regret—"It was always so difficult to let him know the great depth of my affection for him."[7]

Worn-out, angry at his country for not having prepared for the war, angry at MacArthur and the Navy for the way they were fighting it, angry at being stuck in Washington, one day Eisenhower almost lost his temper completely with Marshall. It happened on March 20, in Marshall's office. Marshall and Eisenhower had settled a detail about an officer's promotion. Marshall then leaned forward to say that in the last war, staff officers had gotten the promotions, not the field officers who did the fighting, and that he intended to reverse the process in this war. "Take your case," he added. "I know that you were recommended by one general for division command and by another for corps command. That's all very well. I'm glad that they have that opinion of you, but you are going to stay right here and fill your position, and that's that!" Preparing to turn to other business, Marshall muttered, "While this may seem a sacrifice to you, that's the way it must be."

Eisenhower, red-faced and resentful, shot back, "General, I'm interested in what you say, but I want you to know that I don't give a damn about your promotion plans as far as I'm concerned. I came into this office from the field and I am trying to do my duty. I expect to do so as long as you want me here. If that locks me to a desk for the rest of the war, so be it!"

He pushed back his chair and strode toward the door, nearly ten paces away. By the time he got there he decided to take the edge off the outburst, turned, and grinned. He thought he could see a tiny smile at the corners of Marshall's mouth.[8]

Whether Marshall smiled or not, Eisenhower's anger returned full force after he left the office. He went to his desk and filled his diary with his feelings. The thought of spending the war in Washington, missing combat again, was maddening. It seemed so unfair. Marshall's cold, impersonal attitude just added to the anger. He cursed Marshall for toying with him; he cursed the war and his own bad luck.

The next morning, Eisenhower read what he had written, shook his head, and tore the page out of his diary, destroying it. Then he wrote a new entry. "Anger cannot win, it cannot even think clearly. In this respect," he continued, "Marshall puzzles me a bit." Marshall got angrier at stupidity than anyone Eisenhower had ever seen, "yet the outburst is so fleeting, he returns so quickly to complete 'normalcy,' that I'm certain he does it for effect." Eisenhower envied Marshall that trait and confessed, "I blaze for an hour! So, for many years I've made it a religion never to indulge myself, but yesterday I failed."[9]

A week later Marshall recommended Eisenhower for promotion to major general (temporary). In his recommendation to the President, Marshall explained that Eisenhower was not really a staff officer, but was his operations officer, a sort of subordinate commander. Surprised and delighted, Eisenhower's first reaction was "This should assure that when I finally get back to the troops, I'll get a division." Decades later, in his memoirs, he wrote that he "often wondered" if his outburst and the way in which he had been able to control his emotions and end the session with one of his big lopsided grins had led Marshall to take a greater interest in him.[10]

Perhaps, but unlikely. Marshall had already been pushing Eisenhower ahead, increasing his responsibilities at a rapid pace. In January, he had taken Eisenhower along as his chief assistant to the first wartime conference with the British, and had given Eisenhower the task of preparing the basic American position on organization and strategy for global war. In mid-February he made Eisenhower the head of WPD, and thus his principal plans and operations officer. On March 9, as a part of a general reorganization of the War Department, WPD was renamed the Operations Division (OPD), and given expanded functions, with Eisenhower as its commanding officer. This steady progress surely indicated that Marshall, with or without that display of what MacArthur called "Ike's damn Dutch temper," thought Eisenhower's potential unlimited.

By the beginning of April, Eisenhower had 107 officers working directly under him in OPD. As its responsibilities included both plans and operations, OPD was in effect Marshall's command post, and it was concerned with all Army activities around the world, which gave Eisenhower a breadth of vision he could not have obtained in any other post.

Working in daily contact with the units in the field, as well as preparing plans on grand strategy, gave Eisenhower a realistic sense of the scope of modern war. In late February, he had been complaining in his diary about both MacArthur and Admiral Ernest J. King, Chief of Naval Operations. He called King "an arbitrary, stubborn type, with not too much brains and a tendency toward bullying his juniors." The outburst led him to write a sentence that described the essence of Eisenhower's leadership style, both as a general and as President. "In a war such as this, when high command invariably involves a president, a prime minister, six chiefs of staff, and a horde of lesser 'planners,' there has got to be a lot of patience—no one person can be a Napoleon or a Caesar." [11]

Eleven years later he made the same point more vividly, when as President-elect he wrote in his diary, "Winston [Churchill] is trying to relive the days of World War II. In those days he had the enjoyable feeling that he and our president were sitting on some . . . Olympian platform . . . and directing world affairs from that point of vantage. But . . . many of us who, in various corners of the world, had to work out the solutions for . . . problems knew better." [12]

Of all the generals, Eisenhower himself came closest to a Napoleonic role, but he would never make such a comparison. Having been a staff officer for so long himself, he was acutely aware of the importance of his staff to him; he was just as acutely aware of the indispensability of the subordinates in the field commands who carried out his orders. He had no false modesty, was conscious of the crucial nature of the role he played, but he never thought of himself as a Napoleon. Always, his emphasis was on the team. The only difference in his Presidency was that he applied the principle on an even wider scale. He was not self-effacing, but realistic, aware that there were definite limits on his powers, and keeping his self-image in perspective.

Throughout the winter and early spring of 1942, Eisenhower continued to move up in Marshall's esteem. Among other things, Marshall had been impressed by the smooth relations Eisenhower had established with the British at the Arcadia conference, held in Washington from late December to mid-January.

The main concern of Arcadia was to agree on a plan for an offensive in the European Theater in 1942. That Europe would be the main theater was taken for granted, despite MacArthur's plea that Asia generally and the Philippines particularly should come first. Sitting behind Marshall at the conference, listening daily to discussions of global strategy, Eisenhower's own views broadened.

At first, he had protested against sending American troops to Northern Ireland, and by implication against the concentration of resources against the European enemy. He managed to stop part of one convoy destined for Ireland and sent it to Australia instead, but that did not satisfy him. "Damn 'em, I tried," he scribbled in his diary, "but I don't wear 45s. We're going to regret every damn boat we sent to Ireland." [13] On January 17, he had wanted to "drop everything else" and go all out in the Far East. [14]

By January 22, however, a dramatic switch had occurred. "We've got to go to Europe and fight," he wrote, "and we've got to quit wasting resources all over the world, and still worse, wasting time." Arcadia, Marshall's persuasive abilities, hard military facts, and broadened responsibilities had caused him to change his mind. He criticized the British, the American General Staff (and himself), when he wrote, "Everybody is too much engaged with small things of his own" adding, five days later, "We can't win by giving our stuff in driblets all over the world." Piecemeal reinforcement should give way to concentrated counterattacks. Eisenhower now advocated a program of keeping Russia in the war, holding a defensive line in the Far East, and then "slugging with air at West Europe, to be followed by a land attack as soon as possible." [15]

By late March, Eisenhower and his staff had a specific plan ready. The code name was Roundup. It called for a force of 5,800 combat airplanes and an eventual total of 48 infantry and armored divisions, half of them British, assaulting the French coast between Le Havre and Boulogne, northeast of the mouth of the Seine River, with a target date of April 1, 1943. Meanwhile raids and forays along the coast should be mounted to harass the Germans. If necessary, Sledgehammer, a suicide operation designed to take the pressure off the Russians in the event a Russian surrender appeared imminent, could be mounted in September 1942. The emphasis, however, was on Roundup, the 1943 cross-Channel assault.

Marshall took Eisenhower's plan to Roosevelt, who approved and told Marshall to fly to London to obtain British agreement. Marshall left on April 7 for six days of conferences. The British finally agreed to Roundup, although as Marshall told Eisenhower when he returned, many British officers "hold reservations." Eisenhower noted in his diary, "I hope that, at long last, and after months of struggle by this division, we are all definitely committed to one concept of fighting. If we can agree on major purposes and objectives, our efforts will begin to fall in line and we won't be just thrashing around in the dark." [16]

Marshall returned to Washington worried about the depth of the British commitment to Roundup and about the American commander in London, General James Chaney, who seemed not to understand the urgency of the situation. He decided to send Eisenhower to Britain to see what could be done.

On May 23, Eisenhower flew to Montreal, then on to Goose Bay, Labrador. Bad weather forced him to spend a night and a day at Gander, Newfoundland, where he shot skeet while taking his first day off in half a year.

On May 25 he made it to Prestwick, Scotland, where a British driver, Mrs. Kay Summersby (a divorcée), a young and attractive Irishwoman with sparkling eyes and a pert smile, extremely chatty but a bit awed by being in the presence of a general, met him. She drove him to an exercise involving landing craft, and they visited the birthplace of Robert Burns and scenes associated with Robert Bruce.

That evening Eisenhower took the train to London, arriving the next morning and spending the day in conference with Chaney and his staff. He was appalled by what he saw. Chaney and his assistants "were completely at a loss," stuck in a "back eddy," still wearing civilian clothes, working an eight-hour day, and taking weekends off.

They knew none of the British high command and had no contacts with the British government.[17]

On May 27 Eisenhower observed a field exercise in Kent, under the direction of Lieutenant General Bernard Law Montgomery. Later Eisenhower attended a lecture at which Montgomery explained the exercise. Montgomery wore a field greatcoat which emphasized his own small physical stature and tiny steps. He had a permanent scowl that gave him a crabbed look. He was, by nature, condescending, especially toward Americans, most of whom regarded him with extreme distaste. While he lectured, Eisenhower calmly lit a cigarette. He had taken about two puffs when Montgomery broke off in midsentence, sniffed the air with his nose held high, and demanded, "Who's smoking?"

"I am," Eisenhower replied.

"I don't permit smoking in my office," Montgomery said sternly.

Eisenhower did not let the bad start color his view of Montgomery. When he got back to the States, he reported that Montgomery was "a decisive type who appears to be extremely energetic and professionally able."[18]

During his ten days in Britain, Eisenhower met two other officers with whom he was destined to spend a great deal of time. One was General Alan Brooke, the Chief of the Imperial General Staff. Brooke, a fiery Irishman with impressive credentials, carried throughout the war the handicap of a deep-seated prejudice against the Americans. After his first meeting with Marshall, Brooke had commented that Marshall was "rather overfilled with his own importance," a unique judgment. Brooke admitted that Marshall was "a pleasant and easy man to get on with [a conclusion he would later change]. But I should not put him down as a great man."[19]

Brooke's comments on Eisenhower, from beginning to end, were similar but more scathing. He put Eisenhower down as an affable type with no strategic sense or command ability. Eisenhower's own practice was to either say something nice about an associate or not mention him at all, and he seldom mentioned Brooke.

With Vice-Admiral Lord Louis Mountbatten, however, Eisenhower struck up an immediate and lifelong friendship. Mountbatten, young, titled, handsome, wealthy, already had a distinguished record in the Royal Navy, but unlike Montgomery and Brooke, he rather enjoyed Americans and responded with special warmth to Eisenhower. The two men got on famously from their first meeting. What drew them together aside from personality was that both were offensive-minded, committed to the earliest possible attack against the French coast, and thus keenly interested in the development of landing craft. They agreed that the bigger those craft, the better, and they wanted as many as possible. Eisenhower was also much impressed by the way Mountbatten had created a joint staff of British Army, Navy, and Air officers at Combined Operations, an organization that was planning amphibious assault techniques.

On June 3, Eisenhower returned to Washington. He was dissatisfied with what he had seen in London. Except for Mountbatten it was clear that none of the British high command really believed in Roundup, much less Sledgehammer. It was equally clear that Chaney would have to be replaced.

Marshall in fact already had Eisenhower in mind for the job. Churchill had reported to Marshall that the British high command liked Eisenhower personally and were impressed by his dedication to the Alliance. The day before Eisenhower returned from England, Mountbatten had arrived in Washington for a conference; to both Roosevelt and Marshall, Mountbatten praised Eisenhower and said the British were quite ready to work with him as the senior American officer in Britain. Army Air Force Chief of Staff Henry Arnold, who had accompanied Eisenhower to Britain, and Mark Clark, who had also been on the trip, had agreed among themselves that Chaney's successor "should be Ike." Arnold had passed this recommendation on to Marshall.[20]

Not that Marshall needed any urging. For six months he had been in daily, often hourly, contact with Eisenhower. He had given Eisenhower broad responsibilities and a wide scope. Not once had Eisenhower let him down. Eisenhower had become his protégé, showing a remarkable ability to think like Marshall, to anticipate his chief's wishes, to accept his views and translate them into action. Marshall appreciated the manner in which Eisenhower accepted responsibility and, even more, Eisenhower's offensive-mindedness, his calm confidence that if the Allies made an all-out effort, they could successfully invade France in 1943. Marshall also felt that Eisenhower could get along with the British better than any other officer in the U.S. Army.

On June 8, Eisenhower took to Marshall a draft directive for the commander of the European Theater of Operations (ETO), a name Eisenhower himself had given the London command. Eisenhower urged "that absolute unity of command should be exercised by the Theater Commander," who should organize, train, and command the American ground, naval, and air forces assigned to the theater. As Eisenhower handed the draft to Marshall, he asked the Chief to study it carefully because it could be an important document in the further waging of the war. Marshall replied, "I certainly do want to read it. You may be the man who executes it. If that's the case, when can you leave?" Three days later Marshall appointed Eisenhower to the command of ETO.[21]

With her husband leaving Washington, Mamie had to move out of their just acquired quarters at Fort Myer. Luckily, she found a small apartment at the Wardman; to save money, she asked Ruth Butcher to share the apartment and the expenses. Harry Butcher, a friend of Milton's and Ike's, who had joined the Navy and been commissioned as a lieutenant commander, was going along to London with Eisenhower as the "naval aide"—King had made special arrangements at Eisenhower's request after Eisenhower explained that he wanted one old, close friend with him.

The weekend before Eisenhower left, John got a leave and took the train from West Point to spend two days with his parents. Father and son discussed life at the Academy, some of the conversations taking place in Eisenhower's bedroom, as he was flat on his back as a result of taking his typhus, tetanus, smallpox, and typhoid injections all on the same day. When John had to leave, on Sunday afternoon, he hugged his mother, shook hands with his father, and marched down the gravel path to a waiting taxi. At the door he stopped, did an about-face, and—wearing his full cadet uniform—snapped his hand up to his visor in a formal salute. It was more than Mamie could bear; she burst into tears. It was the last family get-together until after the war.

On June 19, just before leaving, Eisenhower wrote a friend, Brigadier General Spencer Akin, who was on MacArthur's staff, a summary of his six months' experience in WPD-OPD. It had been a "tough, intensive grind," Eisenhower said, "but now I'm getting a swell command." It meant the world to him that he had gained Marshall's confidence, because he felt "the Chief is a great soldier." Eisenhower described Marshall as "quick, tough, tireless, decisive and a real leader. He accepts responsibility automatically and never goes back on a subordinate."[22] The last point was particularly important; Eisenhower felt that his greatest asset in London would be the knowledge that as long as he did his job, Marshall would stand behind him.

Marshall had almost as high an opinion of Eisenhower, but all of

Eisenhower's achievements, to date, had been as a staff officer serving under strong-willed superiors. All his superiors, including MacArthur, thought he would be a success as an independent commander, but that was only prediction. No one really knew how he would react when commanding on his own, away from the daily influence of a decisive superior. But Eisenhower himself was confident.

On June 24, Eisenhower arrived in England. There were no bands to greet him, no speeches at the airport, no ceremonies. It was almost the last time in his life he would have such a quiet arrival anywhere. On June 24, he was still unknown to the general public, in America as well as in Britain. But the day following his arrival in London, he held a press conference. An announcement was passed out identifying him as the commander of the American forces in Britain.

From that moment forth, his life was dramatically and unalterably changed. He suddenly became a world figure—in the jargon of World War II, a Very Important Person, or VIP. It hardly mattered that his role was more that of an administrator than a commander, or that the numbers of men under him were relatively small (55,390 officers and men). Precisely because there were so few American forces in Britain, in fact, and because they were not involved in combat, Eisenhower received more coverage. His appointment was a front-page story. Every reporter in London, whether British or American, who could do so attended Eisenhower's first-ever press conference.

Eisenhower proved to be outstanding at public relations. There was, first and foremost, the man himself. He *looked* like a soldier. He stood erect, with his square, broad shoulders held back, his head high. His face and hands were always active, his face reddening with anger when he spoke of the Nazis, lighting up as he spoke of the immense forces gathering around the world to crush them. To cameramen, he was pure gold—for them a good photo of Eisenhower, whether tight-lipped and grim or laughing heartily, was usually worth at least two columns on the front page. His relaxed, casual manner was appealing, as was the nickname "Ike," which seemed to fit so perfectly. His good humor and good looks attracted people. Most reporters found it impossible to be in Eisenhower's presence and not like him.

His mannerisms complemented his good looks. Recording before a newsreel camera for the movie-theater audience back in the States, he spoke with great earnestness directly into the camera, his eyes riveted on the invisible audience. It was a perfect expression of a devotion to duty that he felt deeply, and it electrified viewers. So too did his manner of speaking bluntly about the difficulties ahead, the problems that had to be met and overcome, all followed by that big grin and a verbal expression of Eisenhower's bouncy enthusiasm.

He habitually used expressions that immediately identified him as just plain folks. He would speak of someone who "knows the score," someone else as a "big operator," or he would say, "I told him to go peddle his papers somewhere else." He called his superiors the "Big Shots." He made innumerable references to "my old home town, Abilene," and described himself as a "simple country boy," sighing and responding sadly to a question, "That's just too complicated for a dumb bunny like me."[23]

Eisenhower, in short, was an extremely likable person who came to the public's attention at exactly the right moment in the war. Nothing was happening in the European Theater to write about, but London was overrun with reporters looking for copy.

Throughout the war, Eisenhower manipulated the press, for his own purposes and for the good of the Allied cause. He was more aware of the importance of the press, and better at using it, than any other public figure of his day. This recognition was a result of his instincts and his common sense. In addition, he enjoyed meeting with the press, liked reporters as individuals, knew some of them himself from his long years in Washington, called them by their first names, posed for their photographs, flattered them not only by the attention he paid to them but by telling them that they had a crucial role to play in the war. Eisenhower believed that a democracy could not wage war without popular, widespread support for and understanding of the war effort, which only the press could create. At his first press conference, he told the reporters that he considered them "quasi members of my staff," part of the "team," a thought that delighted the reporters no end, and he promised to be open and honest with them always.[24] Only the most cynical of reporters could fail to respond to such blandishments.

Eisenhower's sense of public relations extended far beyond himself. He used the press to sell the idea of Allied unity. He believed that Anglo-American friendship was a *sine qua non* of final victory, and did all he could to make that friendship genuine and lasting. In the summer of 1942, his major effort was to smooth relations between the British public and the American soldiers, airmen, and sailors who were coming to British Isles in ever-increasing numbers—eventually, more than two million came to the United Kingdom.

Eisenhower, the man at the top, was the most important individual in molding the British attitude toward the U.S. Army. He was aware of it, accepted the responsibility, and met it magnificently. London took him to her heart. He was so big, so generous, so optimistic, so intelligent, so outspoken, so energetic—so American.

Besides being good copy personally, he represented the American military machine that was coming to win the war, so inevitably he was a center of attention. His relations with the London press were as good as with the American. The British appreciated reports that he took them as they were, neither trying to ape their mannerisms nor make fun of their ways. They laughed at an item that related Eisenhower's practice of levying on the spot a fine of twopence on any American who used a British expression such as "cheerio."

Another favorite London story concerned Eisenhower's heavy smoking—he consumed four packs of Camels a day. The American ambassador, deeply embarrassed, had told Eisenhower after a dinner party that it was the custom in England not to smoke at the dinner table before the toast to the King had been drunk. Eisenhower's response was that he would attend no more formal dinners.

When Mountbatten nevertheless invited him to a dinner, Eisenhower said no. When Mountbatten pressed the point and assured Eisenhower he would not have to curtail his smoking, Eisenhower reluctantly agreed to go. After the sherry, the party sat down to soup. As soon as it was consumed, Mountbatten jumped to his feet and snapped, "Gentlemen, the King!" After the toast, he turned to Eisenhower and said, "Now, General, smoke all you want." [25]

With such stories making the rounds, and with his picture in the papers frequently, Eisenhower became a great favorite in London. Taxi drivers would wave; people on the street would wish him good luck.

Beyond the rapport he established with the British public, he got on well with British leaders, best of all with Churchill himself. He soon became a regular weekend visitor at Churchill's country home, Chequers. Eisenhower's informality appealed to Churchill, and the Prime Minister responded to him in kind. On the evening of July 5, for example, Eisenhower recorded in his diary, "We spent the early part of the evening on the lawn in front of the house, and . . . took a walk . . . into the neighboring woods, discussing matters of general interest in connection with the war." After dinner, they saw a movie, then talked until 2:30 A.M. Eisenhower slept that night in a bed Cromwell had slept in.[26]

Mountbatten frequently accompanied Eisenhower on field exercises; when they went south of London they stayed overnight at Mountbatten's spacious country estate, Broadlands; when they went north, to Scotland, they stayed on his yacht.

Admiral Sir Andrew B. Cunningham was another member of the British elite who, although he had little in common with the self-described "simple Kansas farmboy," became one of Eisenhower's close friends. Cunningham was the embodiment of the Royal Navy, a man of dignity and grace, striking in appearance, cool, competent, and aggressive in action. Cunningham, in a postwar tribute, described how he—and most Britons—reacted to Eisenhower: "I liked him at once. He struck me as being completely sincere, straightforward and very modest. In those early days I rather had the impression that he was not very sure of himself; but who could wonder at that? He was in supreme command of one of the greatest amphibious operations of all time, and was working in a strange country . . . But . . . it was not long before one recognized him as the really great man he is—forceful, able, direct and far-seeing, with great charm of manner, and always with a rather naive wonder at attaining the high position in which he found himself."[27]

Throughout the war, Eisenhower's good relations with the British leadership would be one of his great strengths. The friendships included the leading politicians, the RAF generals, the admirals, and the various British staff officers who worked at his headquarters. The only exceptions were the British Army generals, especially their two leaders, Montgomery and Brooke. Otherwise, Eisenhower's relations with the British could not have been better, or done more good for the cause of Anglo-American unity.

While Eisenhower was trying to sell the idea of Anglo-American unity in July 1942, on the strategic front little unity in fact existed. The British wanted to invade North Africa in the fall of 1942, while Eisenhower—promoted to lieutenant general that month—wanted to prepare for Roundup, the invasion of France, in April 1943. He was also ready to launch Sledgehammer, a late 1942 invasion of Normandy, if it appeared essential to draw German strength from the Eastern Front.

He recognized that Sledgehammer would almost certainly be a

suicide operation, but, he wrote, *"we should not forget that the prize we seek is to keep 8,000,000 Russians in the war."* To fail to make an effort to help the Red Army if it appeared on the verge of collapse would be "one of the grossest military blunders of all history."[28]

But the British would have no part of Sledgehammer. Roosevelt, meanwhile, wanted an offensive somewhere, and the American Army was not strong enough to launch one on its own. Churchill said it was North Africa or nothing in 1942. Roosevelt decided on North Africa.

Eisenhower was deeply depressed by the decision. He thought that the day it was made, July 22, 1942, could well go down as the "blackest day in history."[29] He felt so strongly because he believed the decision for North Africa (code name Torch) represented passive and defensive thinking.

For Eisenhower personally, the decision was a great break, as Marshall decided to make him the commander of Torch. Putting aside his doubts, Eisenhower went to work with a will. He was determined that the first Anglo-American offensive of the war would be a success and that in the process British and American officers would learn to work together. To that end, he established an integrated staff at Allied Force Headquarters (AFHQ).

Eisenhower's commitment to the Alliance became legendary. Many stories circulated to illustrate it; one concerned the time General Hastings Ismay, Churchill's chief staff officer, reported to Eisenhower that he had heard of an American officer who, when drinking at Claridge's, boasted that the Americans would show the British how to fight. Eisenhower "went white with rage." He summoned an aide and told him to arrange for the officer to report the next morning. As the aide left the office, Eisenhower hissed to Ismay, "I'll make the son of a bitch swim back to America."[30] The officer was sent home— by boat.

A week later, Eisenhower heard of a fracas between an American and a British officer on the AFHQ staff. He investigated, decided that the American was at fault, ordered him reduced in rank, and sent back to the States. The British officer involved called on Eisenhower to protest. "He only called me the son of a bitch, sir, and all of us have now learnt that this is a colloquial expression which is sometimes used almost as a term of endearment." To which Eisenhower replied, "I am informed that he called you a *British* son of a bitch. That is quite different. My ruling stands."[31]

AFHQ was located at Norfolk House on St. James's Square. Eisenhower's deputy was Mark Clark. The naval commander was Admiral Cunningham, an appointment that delighted Eisenhower. The British ground troops, organized as the British First Army, would be commanded by Lieutenant General Sir Kenneth Anderson. One part of the American contingent would combat-load in Norfolk, Virginia, and sail across the Atlantic directly to its assault beaches. Eisenhower told Marshall he wanted Patton to command that force, and Marshall complied. The American troops coming out of Britain, organized as II Corps, would be led by Major General Lloyd Fredendall. Marshall had made the selection—Eisenhower hardly knew Fredendall—but the Chief assured Eisenhower that Fredendall was one of the best.

On the basis of his own experience, Eisenhower believed that the most crucial appointment was his chief of staff. He knew the man he wanted, Brigadier General Walter Bedell Smith, currently serving in the War Department as the secretary of the General Staff. Eisenhower sent numerous requests for Smith to Marshall, but Marshall would not let Smith go. The tug-of-war lasted until the end of August, when Marshall finally relented and allowed Smith to go to London.

Smith remained with Eisenhower to the end of the war. He was indispensable. His square jaw and Prussian appearance dominated Eisenhower's headquarters. He decided who would see the boss and who could not, handled most of the administrative duties, was the "No" man in the office, and frequently represented Eisenhower at meetings, always confident that he was speaking for his boss and represented his thinking. Eisenhower trusted Smith completely and regarded him as a "godsend—a master of detail with clear comprehension of the main issues." Years later Eisenhower said Smith was like a crutch to a one-legged man, "the perfect chief of staff."[32]

Smith was also, as Eisenhower politely put it, "strong in character and abrupt by instinct." Or, as Eisenhower explained to a British officer, "Remember Beetle [Smith's nickname] is a Prussian and one must make allowances for it."[33]

Smith suffered from an ulcer, and looked it, his face pinched together in constant pain, while his nervous energy kept him in constant motion. Although he could be suave and conciliatory when on a diplomatic mission, he was a terror in his own office, reducing his subordinates to a bundle of shaking nerves. He yelled, bellowed, threatened, and insulted them.

Once when he was holding a conference in his own office his secretary, Ruth Briggs, a gracious lady who later ran for governor of

Rhode Island, stuck her head in the door. Smith shouted, "Get the hell out of here." Without pausing for breath, and before the startled Miss Briggs could withdraw, Smith turned to the officers around the table and declared, "You'll have to excuse her, gentlemen. She's an idiot."[34] (After the war, Smith served for a time as the U.S. ambassador to Russia. Eisenhower said he did not approve of professional soldiers serving as diplomats, but then, thinking about the men in the Kremlin having to put up with Smith and his ulcer, he grinned and remarked, "It served those bastards right.")[35]

Smith's most important duty was to be the channel through which the various assistant chiefs of staff at AFHQ communicated with Eisenhower. This duty he handled without strain or fuss. Smith "takes charge of things in a big way," Eisenhower told a friend shortly after Smith arrived. "I wish I had a dozen like him. If I did, I would simply buy a fishing rod and write home every week about my wonderful accomplishments in winning the war."[36] Smith had two deputies, General Alfred Gruenther, an old friend of Eisenhower's and one of his favorite bridge partners, and the British Brigadier John F. M. Whiteley; both Gruenther and Whiteley stayed with Eisenhower through the war.

Ike's life was an unending series of conferences, meetings, debates, trips, and inspections. He was constantly surrounded by people. Yet he complained to Mamie, "This is a lonely existence," precisely because "I live in a gold fish bowl."[37] He had "no home to go to . . . no exercise, either." When he was in his hotel room, he found himself constantly wondering, "Why isn't Mamie here?" He told her he missed her, because "You're good for me—even for my official efficiency. And please be good to yourself."[38]

Like millions of other Americans in World War II, Ike had to face the problem of communicating with his wife for the period of an indefinite separation, with no phone calls allowed for security reasons, when he could not discuss his work and had long since run out of new ways to say, "I love you." Or, as Ike himself put it, "I take my pen in hand with a feeling of 'what can I say except to tell her I'm well and just as much in love with her as ever?' "[39]

Ike wrote 319 letters to Mamie during the course of the war (he hated writing by hand, and did so only to Mamie; during one extremely busy period, he dictated a letter, but Mamie's objections were such that he never did it again). They are love letters of a high quality, not in any literary sense, but in the sense that they provided the reassurance so necessary in a wartime husband-to-wife letter.

"It's impossible for me to tell you how tremendously I miss you," he would write, and then assure her that he had her photograph on his office desk, "right in front of my eyes." He said he thought of her always and wished he could write more often so that she would know "you're the only person I'm in love with." On her forty-sixth birthday, he told her, "I've loved you for 26 years," and, "Your love and our son have been my greatest gifts from life." He worried about her health, and said again and again that he wished she could be with him.

He fantasized about a three-day leave in Miami for the two of them—"I can get all excited just thinking about it"—and about their future. He looked forward to retiring to a rural setting, where "with a few pigs and chickens we can be as happy as a pair of Georgia crackers with a good still! . . . I know that no matter how I fumble the pen . . . you'll read between the lines that I'm thinking of you, and wishing again that we could have, together, a life in a home of our own."

Many of his themes were common to men at war. He worried that Mamie was buying too many clothes, and expressed concern about having enough money to pay the income tax. He told her to get the oil changed in the car and to make sure to run it every other day.

He noted the passing of time—"Tomorrow, Sept. 24, Icky would have been 25 years old. Seems rather unbelievable doesn't it? We could well have been grandparents by this time. I'm sorry we're not! Lord knows that at times I feel old enough to tack a 'great, great' on to it."

John and his progress at West Point were standard features of the letters. "I'm so tied up in him it hurts," Ike wrote on August 9. Like every parent, he wondered why John could not write more often. "After all," Ike wrote, speaking for all fathers, "suppose he'd have had to start at 13 or 14 getting up at 4 or 5 in the morning working through a hot summer day to 9:00 at night—day after day —or doing his winter work with cold chapped hands and not even gloves—maybe he'd think writing a letter wasn't so terribly difficult!"[40]

The doings of mutual friends helped fill many a paragraph. Ike usually managed to get in a story about Mickey, or Butch, or Tex Lee. In a typical middle-aged man's inept way, he had enthusiastically described Kay Summersby to Mamie when he returned from his trip to London in May.

Mamie responded to the news that this good-looking, lively

younger woman was suddenly a part of her husband's life with a predictable coldness. In his next letter, Ike reassured her: "This time they have assigned me an old time Britisher as a chauffeur. He is safe and sane, and seems to know every nook and cranny of the country." He never mentioned Kay or her new duties as one of his secretaries.

Ike's special problem was that his every move was reported on, so Mamie nevertheless knew all about Kay, who was one of the featured members of the "Eisenhower family." Gossip about the general and his former chauffeur was inevitable. In the summer of 1942, it was also baseless; Kay was engaged to be married, and Ike and Kay never had a moment alone together. But to those who knew them both, it was obvious that they enjoyed each other's company—telling stories and sharing observations and a laugh—enough so to start the rumors. The gossip may have been on Eisenhower's mind when he wrote to Mamie on October 27, "I've liked some—been somewhat intrigued by others—but haven't been in love with anyone else and don't want any other wife."

Although he could not discuss his work, Ike was able to use his letters to Mamie as an outlet for the kind of complaints only she would understand. He was not getting enough sleep; he was smoking too much; British food was awful; he never got a chance to see a movie. And she was the person to whom he could describe the complexities and demands of his job without seeming to brag: "In a place like this the C.G. . . . must be a bit of a diplomat—lawyer—promoter —salesman—social hound—*liar* (at least to get out of social affairs) —mountebank—actor—Simon Legree—humanitarian—orator— and incidentally . . . a soldier!" Becoming a bit wistful, he wrote, "Soldiering is no longer a simple thing of shouting 'Turn boys turn!'" To Mamie, he could confess that he was delighted to have *"no conferences"* on his schedule that day. "I'm getting to hate the sound of that word."

Most of all, Ike used his wartime letters to Mamie to clear his mind and spend a half hour thinking only of her, and John, and their life together, and not about the war. "When I see the unhappiness here," he wrote, "I thank the Lord that somewhere, some people, can have their minds relatively free . . . I want you to be happy as you can—and how I wish you were living here! You cannot imagine how much you added to my efficiency in the hard months at Washington. Even I didn't realize it then; at least not fully—but I do now, and I'm grateful to you."[41]

Eisenhower planned to go to Gibraltar on November 2, to take command of the Rock, the best communications center in the area, and direct the invasion from there. Bad weather prevented the flight on November 2 and again on the third; on the fourth, Eisenhower ordered his reluctant pilot, Major Paul Tibbets (by reputation the best flier in the Army Air Forces; he later flew the *Enola Gay* on the first atomic-bomb mission), to ignore the weather and take off. Six B-17 Flying Fortresses, carrying Eisenhower and most of his staff, got through safely, but only after engine trouble, weather problems, and an attack by a German fighter airplane had been overcome.

After a bumpy landing, Eisenhower went to his headquarters, which were in the subterranean passages. Offices were caves where the cold, damp air stagnated and stank. Despite the inconveniences, Eisenhower got a great kick out of being in actual command of the Rock of Gibraltar, one of the symbols of the British Empire. "I simply must have a grandchild," he scribbled in his diary, "or I'll never have the fun of telling this when I'm fishing, gray-bearded, on the banks of a quiet bayou in the deep South."[42]

He had little time to gloat or enjoy. British and American troops under his command were about to invade a neutral territory, without a declaration of war, without provocation, and with only a hope, not a promise, that the French colonial army would greet them as liberators rather than aggressors. He hoped he could find a high-ranking French officer who would cooperate, but was frustrated. Disgusted, he exploded, "All of these Frogs have a single thought—'ME.' "[43]

Patton was leading an invading force that had loaded, combat-ready, in Norfolk, Virginia, thousands of miles away from its destination at Casablanca, where to add to the worries the surf was one of the highest in the world. The British contingent had to sail past Gibraltar, where the Spanish might turn on them. What the French would do, no one knew.

In short, Eisenhower, in his first experience in combat or in command, faced problems that were serious in the extreme, and as much political as military. His staff was at least as tense as he was, and looked to him for leadership. It was a subject he had studied for decades. It was not an art in his view, but a skill to be learned. "The one quality that can be developed by studious reflection and practice is the leadership of men," he wrote John at West Point.[44] Here was his chance to show that he had developed it.

In the event, he not only exercised it, but learned new lessons. It was "during those anxious hours" in Gibraltar, he later wrote in a draft introduction to his memoirs that he finally decided to discard, "that I first realized how inexorably and inescapably strain and tension wear away at the leader's endurance, his judgment and his confidence. The pressure becomes more acute because of the duty of a staff constantly to present to the commander the worst side of an eventuality." In this situation, Eisenhower realized, the commander had to "preserve optimism in himself and in his command. Without confidence, enthusiasm and optimism in the command, victory is scarcely obtainable."

Eisenhower also realized that "optimism and pessimism are infectious and they spread more rapidly from the head downward than in any other direction." He saw two additional advantages to a cheerful and hopeful attitude by the commander: First, the "habit tends to minimize potentialities within the individual himself to become demoralized." Second, it "has a most extraordinary effect upon all with whom he comes in contact. With this clear realization, I firmly determined that my mannerisms and speech in public would always reflect the cheerful certainty of victory—that any pessimism and discouragement I might ever feel would be reserved for my pillow. I adopted a policy of circulating through the whole force to the full limit imposed by physical considerations. I did my best to meet everyone from general to private with a smile, a pat on the back and a definite interest in his problems."[45]

He did his best, from that moment to the end of his life, to conceal with a big grin the ache in his bones and the exhaustion in his mind.

There was a great deal more that went into Eisenhower's success as a leader of men, of course. As he put it on another occasion, the art of leadership is making the right decisions, then getting men to *want* to carry them out. But the words he wrote about his learning experience on the Rock, words that he was too modest to put into the published version of his memoirs, are a classic expression of one of the most critical aspects of leadership, perfectly said by a man who knew more about the subject than almost anyone else.

CHAPTER FOUR

North Africa, Sicily, and Italy

THE FRENCH did resist, to Eisenhower's fury. He hated wasting bullets on Frenchmen that had been made to kill Germans. He therefore approved when Clark, in Algiers, entered into a tentative deal with the French commander-in-chief, Admiral Jean Darlan. Although Darlan was a double-crosser who had an odious record as a collaborator with Hitler, he promised to have the French Army lay down its arms if Eisenhower would make him governor general of French North Africa. Eisenhower, anxious to move east toward the Germans in Tunisia and in need of a secure rear area to do so, agreed.

On November 13, Eisenhower flew from the Rock to Algiers to meet with Darlan and seal the deal. The tiny, fidgety French admiral was more than happy to shake and sign an agreement, promising to respect it "scrupulously" and to turn the "full fury" of the French colonial army and the fleet against the Germans.[1] It was a momentous agreement that was to have far-reaching repercussions.

The irony was that by following the seemingly more cautious path of completing arrangements with Darlan to secure his rear area, Eisenhower took a much greater political risk, one that almost cost him his job.

When the Darlan Deal was announced, there was a tremendous storm of criticism. In their initial offensive of the war, the first thing the Allies had done was to make a deal with one of Europe's leading fascists. Press and radio commentators were uniformly hostile, some

83

passionately so. The intense reaction took Eisenhower by surprise; his usual good sense of public relations had deserted him. He was hurt by it, not so much at the criticism of the deal itself, which in some measure he had anticipated, but by the intensity of the criticism and, even more, at the charge that he was a simpleminded general who had gotten himself into political waters well over his depth. He grew to be defensive about the Darlan Deal, and refused to admit that he had been surprised by the reaction.

Despite the charges of the critics, Eisenhower was no fascist. To his son, John, he wrote, "I have been called a Fascist and almost a Hitlerite," when the fact was that he had "one earnest conviction" about the war: "It is that no other war in history has so definitely lined up the forces of arbitrary oppression and dictatorship against those of human rights and individual liberty." His single goal was to do his full duty in helping "to smash the disciples of Hitler."[2]

Indeed, Eisenhower thought of himself as an idealist; "I can't understand why these long-haired, starry-eyed guys keep gunning for me," he declared. "I'm no reactionary. Christ on the Mountain! I'm as idealistic as Hell."[3]

He could be eloquent in describing and defending democracy. He said that the Allied cause was an inspiring one, because it was "completely bound up with the rights and welfare of the common man." He ordered his commanders to make sure that every GI was made to realize that "the privileged life he has led . . . His right . . . to engage in any profession of his own choosing, to belong to any religious denomination, to live in any locality where he can support himself and his family, and to be sure of fair treatment when he might be accused of any crime—all of these would disappear" if the Germans won the war.[4]

But his passion for democracy was essentially conservative, a defense of the basic principles of Anglo-American liberties. It was not offensive, a vigorous attempt to spread either democracy or its meaning. He had not come to North Africa to improve the condition of the Arabs, or relieve the persecution of the Jews. As he wrote Mamie, "Arabs are a very uncertain quantity, explosive and full of prejudices. Many things done here that look queer are just to keep the Arabs from blazing up into revolt. We sit on a boiling kettle!!"[5]

Deeply fearful of a revolt, Eisenhower never went beyond mildly urging Darlan to make some small reforms in the anti-Semitic legislation. Darlan asked for time, arguing that if "sensational steps to improve the lot of the Jews" were taken, there would be a violent Muslim reaction which the French could not control.[6]

Eisenhower agreed that governing the tribes was a "tricky business" that had best be left to the French. There were no changes in the anti-Jewish laws. Eisenhower had seen, in the Philippines, how to deal with natives—work through the local elite, don't ask questions about local conditions, don't interfere. Given Eisenhower's beliefs and experiences, it never occurred to him not to deal with Darlan. It was because he could see no alternative that he was so surprised at the criticism.

Still in London, Smith was the first to inform him of the intensely hostile British response. Churchill claimed to be thunderstruck by the deal, and the British Foreign Office said that Darlan's record was so odious that he could not be considered for the permanent head of North Africa. "There is above all our own moral position," the British declared. "We are fighting for international decency and Darlan is the antithesis of this."[7]

Roosevelt too was indicating that he was anxious to repudiate the deal and in the process, perhaps, repudiate the general who had made it. Eisenhower's military campaign, to date, had been marked by hesitation and lost opportunities. Torch was already a strategic failure, and Eisenhower's political activities had unleashed a barrage of criticism. He was vulnerable.

Realizing this, he reacted quickly and decisively. On the morning of November 14 he sent a long cable to the CCS, written to defend his actions. "Can well understand some bewilderment in London and Washington with the turn that negotiations with French North Africans have taken," he began. In explanation, he said that "the actual state of existing sentiment here does not repeat not agree even remotely with some of prior calculations."

The first fact about life in North Africa was that "the name of Marshal Pétain is something to conjure with." All French officers tried to create the impression that they lived and acted "under the shadow of the Marshal's figure." Frenchmen agreed that only one man had a right "to assume the Marshal's mantle," and "That man is Darlan." They would follow Darlan, "but they are absolutely not repeat not willing to follow someone else."

Eisenhower realized that "there may be a feeling at home that we have been sold a bill of goods," but he insisted that without Darlan, he would have to undertake a complete military occupation of North Africa. The cost in time and resources "would be tremendous."[8]

The message made a strong impression on Roosevelt. So did Secretary of War Henry L. Stimson, who barged into the President's office and insisted that Roosevelt absolutely had to support Eisenhower. Marshall told him the same thing. In addition, Marshall held a press conference, where he lambasted American reporters. He said that planning estimates had declared American losses might go as high as 18,000 in the Torch landings; since they were in fact only 1,800, the Darlan Deal had saved 16,200 American casualties.

Press reports from Morocco and Algeria had continued to emphasize that under Darlan the natives had no political rights, that the Jews were still persecuted, that Communists, Jews, Spanish Republicans, and anti-Vichy Frenchmen filled the prisons, while fascist organizations continued to bully the population and Vichy officials were still in office.

Marshall denied none of this, but told the reporters their criticism of Eisenhower and the Darlan Deal was "incredibly stupid." It would play into the hands of the British, who would demand Eisenhower's replacement by a Britisher. So, Marshall concluded, the press was criticizing American leadership, which, if successful, would put the United States into a position of world prestige beyond anything the country had previously experienced. One of Marshall's aides said, "I have never seen him so concerned as he was on this occasion." As a result of his press conference, a number of American newspapers refused to print critical stories about the North African situation.[9]

For Eisenhower, the main result was that he had survived the crisis. He would have survived much more easily if he had had any progress on the battlefront to show as a result of the deal, but he did not. That was partly Darlan's fault, partly Eisenhower's. As early as the fourth day of Torch, Eisenhower was showing that as a field commander he would not take chances. He had a floating reserve, part of the British 78th Division; because it was at sea it had outstanding mobility. He could have sent it into Bizerte, but on November 11 he decided that Bizerte was too risky and instead put the men ashore in Bougie, only one hundred miles east of Algiers. Meanwhile, the Germans, taking much larger risks, continued to build their strength in Tunis.

The CCS had hoped for more from the employment of the floating reserve. The Chiefs proposed that Eisenhower broaden his operations in the Mediterranean by invading Sardinia. It would have to be a shoestring operation, the Chiefs recognized, but Sardinia was garrisoned by poorly equipped, dispirited Italian troops who would not put up much resistance. The Chiefs said that Eisenhower could divert the Torch follow-up troops from Algiers to Sardinia. The potential gain, for such a small investment, was great—possession of Sardinia would give the Allies airfields from which to attack Tunis, Sicily, and Italy, and it would threaten the southern French coast. Best of all, the entire Italian peninsula would be outflanked.

But to Eisenhower's orderly, staff-oriented mind, now burdened in addition by the responsibility of command, it was a shocking proposal. He had no maps, no plans, no intelligence, no preparations, and was by no means satisfied with the situation in North Africa. "I am unalterably opposed to any suggestion at this time for reducing contemplated Torch strength," he told the Chiefs. Like them, he said, he wanted to take advantage of any opportunity, but he insisted on moving ahead in an orderly fashion. "For God's sake," he said, "let's get one job done at a time." The first requirement was to create a stable rear area. "I am not crying wolf nor am I growing fearful of shadows," he declared defensively, but as he told Smith later in the day, "Don't let anybody get any screwy ideas that we've got the job done already." [10]

In retrospect, it was one of the great missed opportunities of the war. Had the Allies captured Sardinia by a *coup de main* in November 1942, the entire campaign in the Mediterranean would have been drastically changed. But it involved a degree of risk that Eisenhower was unwilling to accept.

Eisenhower might have done better in his first command had he left behind him the emphasis on an orderly, systematic advance that he had imbibed at C&GS, and instead adopted the attitude Patton had expressed back in 1926, when he told Eisenhower always to remember that "victory in the next war will depend on EXECUTION not PLANS." [11] But Eisenhower had been a staff officer for twenty years and could not shake the patterns of thought that had become second nature to him. He concentrated on administrative matters and politics, and insisted on an orderly, rather than a bold and risky, advance, even when his superiors urged him to take more chances.

In mid-December, after Eisenhower had decided that the Allies were not strong enough to attack yet and ordered another delay in mounting the offensive toward Tunis, the CCS reminded him that "large initial losses in a determined assault were much preferable to the wastage inherent in a war of attrition." [12] That was tantamount to accusing him of being too cautious, a charge that in Eisenhower's view was completely unfounded. Yet shortly thereafter, when General Lloyd Fredendall, commanding the American troops on the right flank of the British First Army, proposed to attack in the direction of Sfax or Gabès, Eisenhower strongly disapproved. To make sure there would be "no misunderstanding," he met personally with Fredendall and instructed him to concentrate on securing his position. "Only when . . . the whole region was safe from attack" could Fredendall contemplate any offensive action, and even then he was to make certain that no lead elements got cut off and isolated.[13]

In his diary, Eisenhower wrote that he had learned in his first month of combat that "rich organizational experience and an orderly logical mind are absolutely essential to success," and that "the flashy, publicity-seeking type of adventurer can grab the headlines and be a hero in the eyes of the public, but he simply can't deliver the goods . . ."[14]

Then and later, Eisenhower insisted that he had no choice but to wait for more men and supplies, and he may well have been right. One cannot help but wonder, however, what a bolder commander— Patton, for example, or Rommel—might have accomplished.

Eisenhower was "like a caged tiger," Butcher recorded, "snarling and clawing to get things done."[15] He was snapping at his subordinates, irritated by his superiors. Political problems continued to plague him. He resented the way his staff officers thrust their burdens on to him. He complained that they never seemed to realize that "when they receive orders to do something, they themselves have been relieved of a great load of moral responsibility." To Mamie, he admitted that he had never worked so hard nor been so tired— "London was a picnic compared to this"—and added, "I hope I get home before I'm decrepit with age but since I sometimes think that I live ten years per week, I'm not so sure I'll be any young, gay, darling blade!" He began one letter with the hope that it "won't sound as irritated and mean as I feel this evening."[16]

In public, Eisenhower had a remarkable ability to shed his weariness, self-pity, and pessimism. He held weekly press conferences and was consistently cheerful in his assessment of the situation. As he explained to Mamie, when "pressure mounts and strain increases everyone begins to show the weaknesses in his makeup. It is up to the Commander to conceal his; above all to conceal doubt, fear and distrust."[17] How well he was able to do so was indicated by a member of his staff, who wrote at this time, "[Eisenhower] was a living dynamo of energy, good humor, amazing memory for details, and amazing courage for the future."[18]

On December 22, Eisenhower started for the front, where he

wanted to see conditions for himself and, he hoped, get an attack started. On Christmas Eve, he visited the units in the field. Steady rain had turned the entire countryside into a quagmire. It was impossible to maneuver any type of vehicle off the roads, and hard enough on them. Eisenhower decided to call off any attack, to wait for better weather and more reinforcements. He told the CCS that "the abandonment for the time being of our plan for a full-out effort has been the severest disappointment I have suffered to date," and called it a "bitter decision." [19] The race to Tunis had been lost. A protracted campaign loomed ahead.

In his first command experience, Eisenhower had shown both strengths and weaknesses. His greatest success had been in welding an Allied team together, especially at AFHQ. His ability to get along with others and to see to it that British and American officers got along with each other was much appreciated. But at the point of attack, he had shown a lack of that ruthless, driving force that would lead him to take control of a tactical situation and, through the power of his personality, extract that extra measure of energy that might have carried the Allies into Tunis or Sardinia. He had not forced himself or his subordinates to the supreme effort; there had been an element of drift in the operations he directed.

Between January 14 and 24, Churchill, Roosevelt, and their staffs met in Casablanca to agree on a strategy for 1943, to make the appropriate command arrangements, and to discuss world politics. Eisenhower went to Casablanca for a day, January 15, to report on the situation in his theater. Initially, he made a poor impression on Roosevelt, who remarked to his adviser Harry Hopkins, "Ike seems jittery." Hopkins explained that it was the result of a harrowing plane ride (over the Atlas Mountains, Eisenhower's B-17 had lost two engines, and he had almost had to bail out), a case of the flu, and his disappointment over losing the race to Tunis.[20] He might have added that concern about his future was upsetting Eisenhower.

Eisenhower need not have worried. His report was satisfactory and upbeat; Churchill and Roosevelt agreed to keep him in command. The CCS then made General Harold Alexander the deputy commander in chief of land operations, Admiral Cunningham the deputy in command of the naval forces, while Air Marshal Arthur Tedder took charge of the air forces, with Eisenhower as overall commander.

This solution to the command problem pleased Marshall, as it kept Eisenhower on top; it also pleased Brooke, who took the lead in arranging it, because it put control of day-to-day operations in the hands of Eisenhower's British deputies. Brooke had been impressed by the way Eisenhower built an Allied staff at AFHQ, but distinctly unimpressed by Eisenhower's handling of the campaign. "He had neither the tactical nor strategical experience required for such a task," Brooke said of Eisenhower.

Just as bluntly, Brooke admitted his motive in elevating Eisenhower to the supreme command of the combined forces: "We were pushing Eisenhower up into the stratosphere and rarefied atmosphere of a Supreme Commander, where he would be free to devote his time to the political and inter-allied problems, whilst we inserted under him . . . our own commanders to deal with the military situations and to restore the necessary drive and co-ordination which had been so seriously lacking."[21]

All three of the deputies outranked Eisenhower, whose permanent rank was still lieutenant colonel; he wore the three stars of a lieutenant general on a temporary basis, while his deputies all wore four stars. But Eisenhower was never awestruck by rank or title. He intended to work with his deputies, not by imposing his will on them, but through persuasion and cooperation, to draw on their talents by establishing a close personal relationship with them.

He already knew, admired, and got on perfectly with Cunningham. At Casablanca, he had a long talk with Alexander and was impressed. What Churchill called Alexander's "easy smiling grace and contagious confidence" charmed Eisenhower, as it did everyone else.

With Tedder, he quickly hit it off. When they were introduced, Eisenhower gave his big grin and thrust out his hand. "Well, another Yank," Tedder thought to himself. Once Eisenhower started to talk, however, Tedder decided "he made a good deal of sense."[22] Suave and handsome, Tedder had strong prejudices and concepts which he did not hesitate to express. He usually had a pipe stuck in his mouth and the amount of smoke it gave forth was a good indication of the amount of emotion he was feeling. Like Eisenhower, he preferred to work informally and hated conferences. He was to stay with Eisenhower through to the end of the war and become the British officer who had the greatest influence on Eisenhower's thought and action.

Brooke's hopes that the three deputies would get Eisenhower out of the way were soon dashed, primarily by Eisenhower himself, who resisted all attempts to impose the British system of command by committee on Mediterranean operations. When on January 20 the CCS issued a directive that indicated that actual control of operations would be in the hands of the deputies, Eisenhower—who described himself as "burning inside"—dictated a "hot message challenging such intrusion" into his command setup and insisted on maintaining the principle of unity of command.[23] Smith pleaded with him to moderate the message, but Eisenhower would only allow Smith to tone it down, not change its meaning. As long as he was supposed to be the commander, he was determined to exercise that authority. "Manifestly, responsibility . . . falls directly on me," he told Marshall.[24]

Marshall was equally determined to maintain unity of command. To help Eisenhower, he told him privately that he was recommending him for the rank of full general. The promotion came through on February 10. The four-star rank was the highest in the U.S. Army at that time (and was fairly recent; even Grant had worn only three stars) and had been reserved for the Chief of Staff. In 1943, only Marshall and MacArthur were full generals.

Two years earlier, Eisenhower had been a temporary colonel, and had told John that he expected to be retired at that rank. With his staff he downplayed the importance of the new rank, while with his wife he was appropriately modest. "Loneliness is the inescapable lot of a man holding such a job." Subordinates could advise, urge, help, and pray, but only he could decide, "Do we or don't we?" Furthermore, at his level, "the stakes are always highest, and the penalties are expressed in terms of loss of life or major or minor disasters to the nation." In summary, he told Mamie that "I feel damned humble" as a result of the promotion, "but I do not feel that I've 'arrived'—or that my major job is finished. I've just begun." He promised "always to do my duty to the extreme limit of my ability."[25]

In Tunisia, American troops occupied the southern end of the line. They had seen little action and tended to be complacent, poorly disciplined, and unprepared to face Erwin Rommel's Afrika Korps, which was arriving on their front after its long retreat from the Egyptian border. Eisenhower tried to tighten their discipline and improve their battle readiness, but without much success. Part of the fault was his, part of it Fredendall's.

The II Corps (consisting of the 1st Infantry Division, the 34th Infantry, and the 1st Armored) was badly stretched out. Further, the 1st Armored was divided into two parts, Combat Command A and B

(CCA and CCB). Worst of all, Fredendall was excessively concerned with his own command post, which he had located miles to the rear and far up a canyon, where he had two hundred engineers blast underground shelters for security. "Most American officers who saw this command post for the first time," an observer later wrote, "were somewhat embarrassed, and their comments were usually caustic."

Eisenhower's method was to lead through persuasion and hints, rather than direct action. Although he worried about Fredendall's burying himself in his tunnels, all he did about it was to tell Fredendall that "one of the things that gives me the most concern is the habit of some of our generals in staying too close to their command posts," and asking him to "please watch this very, very carefully among all your subordinates." Eisenhower reminded Fredendall of the advantage of personally knowing the ground and that "generals are expendable just as is any other item in any army."[26] Fredendall ignored the hints and stayed at his command post.

On February 11 the AFHQ head of intelligence, or G-2, reported that the German commander in northern Tunisia, General von Arnim, was receiving reinforcements from Rommel's Afrika Korps and would shortly be launching a major attack at Fondouk, the northern limit of the II Corps line. The information came from radio intercepts.

Eisenhower decided to go to the front personally to prepare for Arnim's attack. On the afternoon of February 13, he arrived at Fredendall's headquarters for a conference, followed by an all-night tour of the front lines. He was disturbed by what he saw. The American troops remained complacent. Eisenhower drove down to CCA headquarters, where he went for a stroll in the moonlit desert. Looking eastward, he could just make out the gap in the black mountain mass that was the Faid Pass. Beyond the pass, Rommel and his Afrika Korps were assembling, but in the pass itself, nothing moved.

At about 3:30 A.M. Eisenhower drove on to Fredendall's headquarters, where he arrived two hours later to learn that thirty minutes after he had been at Faid Pass, the Germans had launched an attack through it against CCA. Still assuming that the main attack would be in the north, Eisenhower thought it was probably a feint and decided to drive on to his own advance headquarters at Constantine, where he could keep an eye on the whole front.

When he reached Constantine, about midafternoon of February 14, he learned that the attack out of Faid was a major one. Rommel's panzers had destroyed an American tank battalion, overrun a battalion of artillery, and isolated the remaining American troops. Eisenhower spent the day trying to get reinforcements to the Faid area, but the distances involved and the poor road network made it virtually impossible to help the beleaguered CCA. Rommel continued his attack on February 15, in the process knocking out ninety-eight American tanks, fifty-seven half-tracks, and twenty-nine artillery pieces. For practical purposes, CCA had been destroyed.

On February 16, the Afrika Korps drove toward the next range of mountains and through the pass, named Kasserine. Beyond lay open ground and the major supply base at Le Kef. The situation was intolerable. Eisenhower could try to patch things up by relieving Fredendall, or by relieving all his subordinates. The second alternative was hardly feasible, and Eisenhower did not want to relieve Fredendall in the middle of a battle. He did relieve his G-2 because he was "too wedded to one type of information"—the radio intercepts.[27] (The intercepts had been accurate enough, but Rommel had simply disobeyed his orders and launched the attack on his own.) He refused to relieve Fredendall, as the situation demanded.

He rushed reinforcements to the battle. He got the 9th Division artillery started on a 735-mile march for the front, stripped the 2d Armored and 3d Infantry of equipment to send to Fredendall, and cannibalized other units in Algeria and Morocco in order to get trucks, tanks, artillery, and ammunition to the front.

Despite the embarrassing and costly losses, Eisenhower was not disheartened. He realized that all his lectures on the need to eliminate complacency and instill battlefield discipline among the American troops had had little effect, but he also realized that the shock of encountering the Wehrmacht on the offensive was accomplishing his objectives for him.

"Our soldiers are learning rapidly," he told Marshall at the height of the battle, "and while I still believe that many of the lessons we are forced to learn at the cost of lives could be learned at home, I assure you that the troops that come out of this campaign are going to be battle wise and tactically efficient."[28] The best news of all was that American soldiers, who had previously shown a marked disinclination to advance under enemy fire, were recovering rapidly from the initial shock of Rommel's attack. The troops did not like being kicked around and were beginning to dig in and fight.

Nevertheless, on February 21, Rommel got through Kasserine Pass. Eisenhower regarded this development as less a threat, more an opportunity, because by then his efforts had produced a preponderance of American firepower at the point of attack, especially in artillery. Rommel had a long, single supply line that ran through a narrow pass, which made him vulnerable.

"We have enough to stop him," Eisenhower assured Marshall, but he expected to do more than that.[29] He urged Fredendall to launch an immediate counterattack on Rommel's flanks, seize the pass, cut off the Afrika Korps, and destroy it. But Fredendall disagreed with Eisenhower's conclusion that Rommel had gone as far as he could; he expected him to make one more attack and insisted on staying on the defensive to meet it. Rommel, accepting the inevitable, began his retreat that night. It was successful, and a fleeting opportunity was lost.

In a tactical sense, Rommel had won a victory. At small cost to himself, he had inflicted more than five thousand American casualties, destroyed hundreds of tanks and other equipment. But he had made no strategic gain, and in fact had done Eisenhower a favor. In his pronouncements before Kasserine, Eisenhower had consistently harped on what a tough business war is and on the overwhelming need to impress that fact on the troops.

But the man most responsible for American shortcomings was Eisenhower himself, precisely because he was not tough enough. He had allowed Fredendall to retain command, despite his serious and well-founded doubts. He had allowed a confused command situation to continue. He had accepted intelligence reports based on insufficient sources. And at the crucial moment, when Rommel was at his most vulnerable, he had failed to galvanize his commanders, which allowed Rommel to get away.

Kasserine was Eisenhower's first real battle; taking it all in all, his performance was miserable. Only American firepower, and German shortages, had saved him from a humiliating defeat.

But Eisenhower and the American troops profited from the experience. The men, he reported to Marshall, "are now mad and ready to fight." So was he. "All our people," he added, "from the very highest to the very lowest have learned that this is not a child's game and are ready and eager to get down to . . . business." He promised Marshall that thereafter no unit under his command "will ever stop training," including units in the front line.[30] And he fired Fredendall, replacing him with Patton.

When Patton arrived, Eisenhower gave him advice that might better have been self-directed. "You must not retain for one instant," Eisenhower warned Patton, "any man in a responsible position where you have become doubtful of his ability to do the job. . . . This matter frequently calls for more courage than any other thing you will have to do, but I expect you to be perfectly cold-blooded about it."[31]

To his old friend Gerow, then training an infantry division in Scotland, Eisenhower expanded on the theme. "Officers that fail," he said, "must be ruthlessly weeded out. Considerations of friendship, family, kindliness and nice personality have nothing whatsoever to do with the problem . . . You must be tough." He said it was necessary to get rid of the "lazy, the slothful, the indifferent or the complacent."[32] Whether Eisenhower could steel himself sufficiently in this regard remained to be seen.

Patton tightened discipline to a martinet standard while his whirlwind tours in his open command car, horns blaring and outriders roaring ahead and behind him, impressed his presence on everyone in the Corps. His flamboyant language and barely concealed contempt for the British created pride in everything American. When British officers made slighting remarks about American fighting qualities, Patton thundered, "We'll show 'em," and then demanded to know where in hell the Brits had been during the crisis of Kasserine. But Alexander told Patton to avoid pitched battles and stay out of trouble.

Not being allowed to attack, forced to stand to one side while Montgomery delivered the final blow to the Afrika Korps, was galling to Patton. He asked Eisenhower to send him back to Morocco, where he could continue his planning for the invasion of Sicily. Eisenhower did so, replacing Patton with the recently arrived General Omar Bradley, his old West Point classmate. Then Eisenhower told Alexander that it was essential that the Americans have their own sector in the final phase of the Tunisian campaign. Alexander replied that the Americans had failed at Kasserine and thus their place was at the rear.

Eisenhower held his temper, but his words were firm. He told Alexander that the United States had given much of its best equipment to the British. If the American people came to feel that their troops would not play a substantial role in the European Theater, they would be more inclined to insist on an Asia-first strategy. But most of all, Eisenhower insisted, Alexander had to realize that in the ultimate conquest of the Nazis, the Americans would necessarily provide the bulk of the fighting men and carry most of the load. It was therefore imperative that American soldiers gain confidence in their ability to fight the Germans, and they could not do so while in the rear. Alexander tried to debate the point, but Eisenhower insisted, and eventually Alexander agreed to place II Corps in the line, on the north coast.

Having persuaded the reluctant Alexander, Eisenhower turned his attention to Bradley. He told Bradley that he realized the sector assigned to II Corps was poorly suited to offensive action, but insisted that Bradley had to overcome the difficulties and prove that the U.S. Army "can perform in a way that will at least do full credit to the material we have." He instructed Bradley to plan every operation "carefully and meticulously, concentrate maximum fire power in support of each attack, keep up a constant pressure and convince everyone that we are doing our full part . . . " He concluded by warning Bradley to be tough. Eisenhower said he had just heard of a battalion of infantry that had suffered a loss of ten men killed and then asked permission to withdraw and reorganize. That sort of thing had to cease. "We have reached the point where troops *must* secure objectives assigned," Eisenhower said, "and we must direct leaders to get out and *lead and to secure the necessary results.*"[33]

Eisenhower spent the last week of April touring the front lines, and was pleased by what he saw. Bradley was "doing a great job," he concluded, and he was delighted to hear a British veteran say that the U.S. 1st Infantry Division was "one of the finest tactical organizations that he had ever seen."[34]

By the first week in May, Arnim's bridgehead was reduced to the area immediately around the cities of Bizerte and Tunis. On May 7, British troops moved into Tunis itself; that same day, Bradley sent Eisenhower a two-word message—"Mission accomplished." The II Corps had captured Bizerte. Only mopping-up operations remained to clear the Axis completely out of Tunisia.

Eisenhower spent the last week of the campaign at the front, and it made a deep impression on him. In February, he had told Mamie that whenever he was tempted to feel sorry for himself, he would think of "the boys that are living in the cold and rain and muck, high up in the cold hills of Tunisia," and be cured.[35]

In May, he heard about a story in the American press on his mother; the story stressed Ida's pacifism and the irony of her son being a general. Ike wrote his brother Arthur that their mother's "happiness in her religion means more to me than any damn wisecrack that a newspaperman can get publicized," then said of the pacifists generally, "I doubt whether any of these people, with their academic or dogmatic hatred of war, detest it as much as I do."

He said that the pacifists "probably have not seen bodies rotting on the ground and smelled the stench of decaying human flesh. They have not visited a field hospital crowded with the desperately wounded." Ike said that what separated him from the pacifists was that he hated the Nazis more than he did war. There was something else. "My hatred of war will never equal my conviction that it is the duty of every one of us . . . to carry out the orders of our government when a war emergency arises." Or, as he put it to his son,"The only unforgivable sin in war is not doing your duty." [36]

On May 13, the last Axis forces in Tunisia surrendered. Eisenhower's forces captured 275,000 enemy troops, more than half of them German, a total bag of prisoners even larger than the Russians had gotten at Stalingrad three and a half months earlier. Congratulations poured in on Eisenhower from all sides. He told Marshall he wished he had a disposition that would allow him to relax and enjoy a feeling of self-satisfaction, but he did not. "I always anticipate and discount, in my own mind, accomplishment, and am, therefore, mentally racing ahead into the next campaign. The consequence is that all the shouting about the Tunisian campaign leaves me utterly cold." [37]

Eisenhower knew that the North African campaign had taken too long—six months—and cost too much—his forces had lost 10,820 men killed, 39,575 wounded, and 21,415 missing or captured, a total of 71,810 casualties. But it was over, and his men had won. His own great contribution had been not so much directing the Anglo-American victory, but insisting that they won as Allies. Thanks in large part to Eisenhower, the Alliance had survived its first test and was stronger than ever.

Following a victory parade in Tunis, Eisenhower joined his British political adviser, Harold Macmillan, for the flight back to Algiers. As their Flying Fortress passed over Bizerte, they looked down to see a huge Allied convoy proceeding unmolested toward Egypt. Macmillan touched Eisenhower's arm. "There, General," he said, "are the fruits of your victory." Eisenhower turned to Macmillan, smiling with tears in his eyes. "Ours, you mean, ours." [38]

As the Tunisian campaign was drawing to an end, Eisenhower looked ahead to Sicily and beyond. He told Marshall that after Sicily was taken, he wanted to invade Sardinia and Corsica, then use them as springboards to invade western Italy. He realized that such an extension of the Mediterranean offensive ran directly counter to

Marshall's views. "I personally have never wavered in my belief that the Roundup conception is the correct one,"[39] Eisenhower assured Marshall, but meanwhile—and here he sounded exactly like Churchill in July 1942—wasn't it a pity that nothing could be done in the summer of 1943? Especially when it could be done so cheaply. The Mediterranean was a major theater already, Eisenhower pointed out, and the troops had to be maintained anyway, so with a relatively minor additional expenditure the Allies could keep the pressure on Germany and satisfy the public that something was being done.

In Marshall's view that was precisely the problem: it was doing something for the sake of doing something. There was no strategic objective. Knocking Italy out of the war would be more of a burden than a help, as Allied shipping would have to be used to support the population. Marshall told Eisenhower, "The decisive effort must be made against the Continent from the United Kingdom sooner or later," and it would come sooner if there were no more offensives after Sicily in the Mediterranean.[40]

In May, the CCS met in Washington to decide the issue. They argued for two weeks. The Chiefs finally agreed to a commitment to a cross-Channel attack in 1944, but made no decision on what to do in the Mediterranean after Sicily. They left that decision up to Eisenhower, directing him "to plan such operations in exploitation of Husky [code name for Sicily] as are best calculated to eliminate Italy from the war and to contain the maximum number of German forces." Eisenhower could decide for himself how to accomplish those goals. He could use the forces he already had in the theater, minus seven divisions that would be transferred to the United Kingdom on November 1.[41]

No one was satisfied with the result. Since Eisenhower would decide, Churchill flew to Algiers to persuade the general to go for Italy. Brooke and other staff officers accompanied him, as did Marshall—Churchill had insisted that he come along, completing the spectacle of the superiors come to woo the subordinate.

They stayed a week, Churchill talking constantly. He did not want Eisenhower to invade Sardinia, but Italy; Sardinia would be a "mere convenience," he said, while Italy would be "a glorious campaign." The glory would come from the capture of Rome, which "would be a very great achievement" and a fitting climax to the Eighth Army's odyssey.

"The PM recited his story three different times in three different ways last night," Eisenhower complained on May 30. That night,

Churchill called after dinner to ask if he could come over. It was nearly 11 P.M. and Eisenhower wanted to sleep. He said he was tired of going over the same ground again and again. Churchill insisted. Eisenhower said all right. Churchill arrived fifteen minutes later, then talked steadily for two hours. Butcher finally more or less had to push him out the door. Brooke saw the "very sleepy Eisenhower" the next day and admitted, "I smiled at his distress, having suffered from this type of treatment [from Churchill] repeatedly."[42]

Marshall did not want either Sardinia or Italy. He urged Eisenhower to begin drawing down in the Mediterranean as soon as Sicily was over. He was suspicious of the British, doubted their resolve for the cross-Channel attack. On this point he was right. Brooke came privately to Eisenhower to have his say, which was that the Allies ought to apply their naval and air strength toward blockading Germany and leave the ground fighting to the Russians. He said that in northwest Europe, the Allies would be fighting at "a great disadvantage and would suffer tremendous and useless losses." They should therefore limit themselves to fighting in Italy.[43]

Eisenhower heard them all out and kept his own counsel. Much would depend on how hard the Germans fought for Sicily, and whether or not they moved additional divisions into Italy. Eisenhower was left with the power to decide, based on enemy reactions, what to do after Sicily.

In addition to all his official responsibilities, only just outlined here, Ike had some worries about Mamie. By May of 1943 the couple had been separated for almost a full year. Ike had his never-ending work to occupy him, and in addition was surrounded by old and new friends. But except for Ruth Butcher, Mamie was alone, and Ruth was not much help, as she was a heavy drinker and her marriage was in trouble (when the war ended, the Butchers were divorced). Ike, robust as usual, could drive himself right through an occasional cold or touch of diarrhea; Mamie, delicate as always, was ill and bedridden much of the time. She had little interest in food and her weight had slipped to 112 pounds. In her own words, she "lived after sorts, read mystery thrillers through the nights—and waited."[44] She was being plagued to make public appearances, which she detested, and was receiving voluminous mail, which helped her pass the time, as she answered by hand every letter.

Writing letters to her husband was much more satisfying, to her and to him (the first thing he looked for in every incoming mail

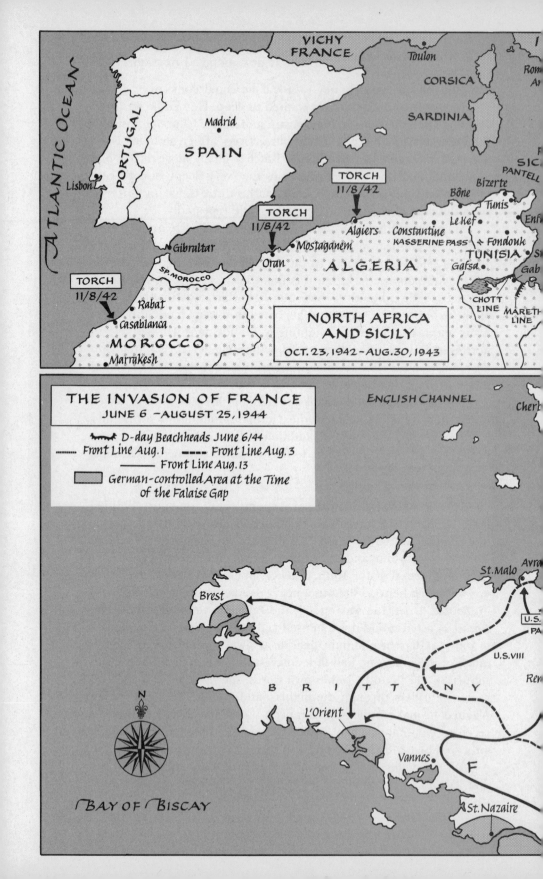

NORTH AFRICA AND SICILY
OCT. 23, 1942 – AUG. 30, 1943

VICHY FRANCE

ATLANTIC OCEAN

PORTUGAL

Madrid
SPAIN

Lisbon

Gibraltar
SP. MOROCCO

TORCH
11/8/42

Rabat

Casablanca

MOROCCO

Marrakesh

TORCH
11/8/42

Oran

Mostaganem

TORCH
11/8/42

Algiers   Constantine
KASSERINE PASS

ALGERIA

Toulon

CORSICA

SARDINIA

Rom
At

SIC
PANTELL

Bizerte

Bône

Tunis

Le Kef   Enf

Fondouk

TUNISIA   Sw

Gafsa   Gab

CHOTT
LINE   MARETH
LINE

THE INVASION OF FRANCE
JUNE 6 – AUGUST 25, 1944

〰️ D-day Beachheads June 6/44
.... Front Line Aug. 1   - - - - Front Line Aug. 3
———— Front Line Aug. 13
▨ German-controlled Area at the Time
    of the Falaise Gap

ENGLISH CHANNEL

Cher

St. Malo   Avra

Brest

U.S.
PA

U.S. VIII

B R I T T A N Y

L'Orient

Vannes

Rer

F

N

BAY OF BISCAY

St. Nazaire

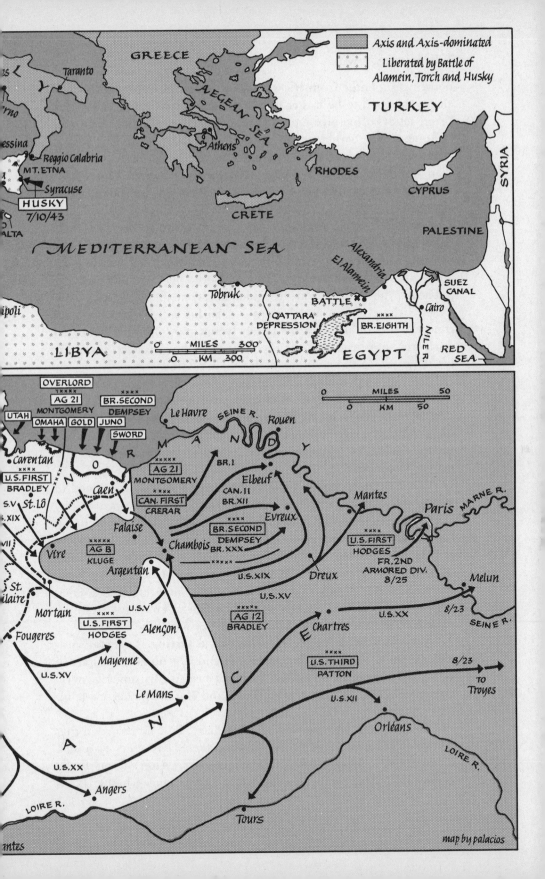

Map 1 (top):

GREECE

Taranto

AEGEAN SEA

TURKEY

Reggio Calabria
MT. ETNA
Syracuse

HUSKY
7/10/43

Athens

RHODES

CYPRUS

SYRIA

CRETE

PALESTINE

MEDITERRANEAN SEA

Alexandria
El Alamein

SUEZ
CANAL

Tobruk

BATTLE

Cairo

QATTARA
DEPRESSION

BR. EIGHTH

LIBYA

0   MILES   300
0   KM   300

EGYPT

NILE R.

RED
SEA

Axis and Axis-dominated

Liberated by Battle of
Alamein, Torch and Husky

Map 2 (bottom):

OVERLORD
AG 21
MONTGOMERY

BR. SECOND
DEMPSEY

0   MILES   50
0   KM   50

UTAH

OMAHA GOLD JUNO

Le Havre

SEINE R.

Rouen

SWORD

N   O   R   M   A   N   D   Y

Carentan

U.S. FIRST
BRADLEY

Caen

St. Lô

AG 21
MONTGOMERY

BR. 1

Elbeuf

Mantes

MARNE R.

Paris

S.V.

CAN. FIRST
CRERAR

CAN. 11
BR. XII

Evreux

S. XIX

Falaise

AG B
KLUGE

Chambois

BR. SECOND
DEMPSEY
BR. XXX

Dreux

U.S. FIRST
HODGES

Vire

Argentan

FR. 2ND
ARMORED DIV.
8/25

VII

U.S.XIX

Melun

St.
Hilaire

Mortain

U.S.V

U.S.XV

SEINE R.

8/23

Fougeres

U.S. FIRST
HODGES

Alençon

AG 12
BRADLEY

Chartres

U.S.XX

8/23

Mayenne

E

U.S. THIRD
PATTON

8/23
TO
Troyes

U.S.XV

Le Mans

N

U.S.XII

Orléans

LOIRE R.

A

U.S.XX

Angers

LOIRE R.

Tours

map by palacios

ntes

pouch was a letter from his wife), but no matter how cheerful and chatty she tried to be in her notes, he could read between the lines. "Your letters often give me some hint of your loneliness," Ike wrote in June, "your bewilderment and your worries in carrying on . . . when you're lonely, try to remember that I'd rather be by your side than anywhere else in the world." He was also concerned by reports from Washington that people were "darn near placing you on a royalty basis."

Mamie's biggest problem—aside from living without her husband—was her realization that the price she had to pay for the thrill of being married to a world-famous man was that that man was no longer her "personal property." Ike reassured her: "In spite of all the publicity," he wrote, "you are quite mistaken in saying that I no longer belong to you and Johnny. . . . So far as I, as a person, am concerned—I'm just ⅓ of the family (yours and Johns and mine). So don't fret your head about that phase of the thing. At least no crackbrain has yet started running me for political office."[45]

He indulged himself in fantasies about their getting together. "Last night I dreamed you had come over here," he wrote in July. "We were having a lot of fun fixing things up the way you wanted them—particularly my house at my main headquarters. Then you found out that I was leaving at once for quite a trip; and did you give me hail Columbia!"[46]

What she was really giving him hell for was Kay. It seemed to Mamie that Kay was with her husband constantly. She appeared frequently in photographs, standing beside or just behind the general. And indeed Ike could hardly deny that he liked Kay, enjoyed being with her, responded to her warmth, charm, good looks, and flirtatious manner, even if he was twenty years her senior. In his highpowered world of generals, admirals, prime ministers, and French politicians, he needed a soft touch, a light laugh, an escape from the constant pressure of war and death, and Kay met those needs.

She was driving for Ike again, as well as serving as a secretary at AFHQ. She often joined Ike and his friends for dinner, and served as his partner in an occasional game of bridge. Brigadier General Everett Hughes, an old friend of Ike's, and Harry Butcher made up the opposition.

Hughes kept an extensive, gossipy diary; in it he recorded that his own driver was worried "over Kay and Ike. She foresees a scandal. . . . I tell her . . . Kay will help Ike win the war." After one party, he sat around with Ike and "discussed Kay. I don't know whether Ike is alibiing or not. Says he wants to hold her hand, accompanies her to house, doesn't sleep with her."[47] Ike's obvious enjoyment of her company, and the fact that she was around so much of the time, fueled the gossip, in Algiers and in Washington, about the general and his driver. Mamie grew heartily sick of reading about and being asked about Kay.

In Ike's mind, his relationship with Kay was perfectly innocent and lots of fun. He deeply resented but would not comment upon the gossip, just as having Kay's presence singled out left him furious but helpless. Once he told Patton, "The other day Kay and I were out riding and a soldier yahooed at us."[48] Ike said he could do nothing more than glare at the man and ride on.

At first glance, Ike seems particularly inept in carrying on a middle-aged flirtation with a woman young enough to be his daughter, and equally insensitive to his wife's reaction to seeing Kay standing next to him whenever his picture was in the newspapers. But the truth was that if he wanted to see and be with Kay at all—and he certainly did—it had to be in public, as they never had time alone together.

Until June of 1943, there was a limit to how far the gossip could go, because of Kay's impending marriage. But then her fiancé was killed by a land mine. Kay, naturally, took it hard; Ike, naturally, tried to console her. Mamie continued to ask about Kay in her letters; Eisenhower responded, "She is a very popular person in the whole headquarters and everyone is trying to be kind. But I suspect she cannot long continue to drive—she is too sunk!"[49] He thought Kay should go back to London, but she insisted on continuing her work at AFHQ, and he cheerfully agreed. Mamie's anxieties increased, needlessly in Ike's view, inevitably in everyone else's.

Sicily was next. "Everybody is tremendously keyed up," Eisenhower told Marshall on July 1.[50] It was natural enough, considering the complexity of the operation and the size of the force involved. Sicily was the largest amphibious assault ever attempted. At dawn on July 10 seven divisions, preceded by airborne operations involving parts of two parachute divisions, would go ashore simultaneously along a front of one hundred miles.

On July 7 Eisenhower flew to Malta, Cunningham's command post, to direct the invasion. Eisenhower said he felt "as if my stomach were a clenched fist."[51] On D-Day minus one—July 9—the weather turned bad. The wind came up from the west and increased in force, piling up whitecaps in the Mediterranean, tossing about the landing craft in which Patton's men were crossing from Tunisia to Sicily. Staff officers suggested to Eisenhower that he postpone the invasion before it was too late. But Cunningham's meteorological experts said that the wind would drop around sundown. Marshall sent a wire asking if the invasion was on or off. As Eisenhower later put it, "My reaction was that I wish I knew!"[52] But as the wind did indeed slacken, he decided to go ahead. After giving the orders, accompanied by Cunningham he climbed to the highest point in Malta to watch the transports of the British 1st Airborne Division fly through the rain toward Sicily. He silently prayed for the safety and success of all the troops under his command.

He returned to his office to wait. He wrote a letter to Mamie. "In circumstances such as these men do almost anything to keep them from going slightly mad," he said. "Walk, talk, try to work, smoke (all the time)—anything to push the minutes along to find out a result that one's own actions can no longer affect in the slightest degree. I stand it better than most, but there is no use denying that I feel the strain."[53]

In the morning, waiting for reports, Eisenhower went for a walk on the beach with Butcher. He had no immediate decisions to make, it was a rare free time, and he took the opportunity to do some reflecting. He said he had 150,000 men going ashore against a mostly undefended coast, with a follow-up force of 350,000, supported by the largest armada assembled to that date, and a correspondingly large air force. It suddenly seemed an awfully big force to be throwing against such a small target, a tremendous expenditure of effort for so slight a return on the investment. Eisenhower thought that the Germans would breathe a sigh of relief when they realized the Allies were only going after Sicily, not something bigger. He anticipated that they would throw up a defensive cordon around Messina and Mount Etna, fight a delaying action, tie up the Allied armies for some weeks, then withdraw to the mainland.[54]

He was exactly right. His troops got ashore without serious opposition, and the Italians surrendered in droves, but the two German divisions fought skillfully and fiercely, so that the campaign that ensued in Sicily followed his prediction and in consequence has been condemned by nearly all military historians.

Montgomery did not drive for Messina; he hardly even crawled. He and Patton fought among themselves until Patton, furious at the passive role he had been assigned, struck out on his own, toward

Palermo, in western Sicily, away from the Germans but toward the headlines.

Then he turned right, to race Monty to Messina. On August 17, Patton's men won. That, and the excellent showing of the GIs in the rough mountain fighting, was the only bright spot in an otherwise dismal conclusion. The Germans had gotten away, after holding back a half million Allied troops for thirty-eight days and inflicting twenty thousand casualties, at a cost of twelve thousand. They were delighted with the results; Eisenhower and his commanders were correspondingly deflated.

On the day Patton reached Messina, Eisenhower's surgeon general handed him a report from one of his doctors. It said that Patton, a week earlier, had lost his temper while visiting a field hospital when he saw a young GI who had nothing visibly wrong with him. Patton wanted to know why he was a patient.

The soldier replied, "It's my nerves. I can't stand the shelling any more," and began sobbing. Patton, cursing and screaming, slapped the man, twice, accused him of cowardice, and ordered the doctors not to admit him.

Eisenhower read the report. He was feeling friendly toward Patton that day, for he was secretly pleased that the Americans had beaten Montgomery to Messina, so his initial reaction was mild. "I guess I'll have to give General Patton a jacking up," he said, then praised Patton for the "swell job" he had done in Sicily. He told the surgeon general to go to Sicily and conduct a full investigation, but to keep it quiet. "If this thing ever gets out," he feared, "they'll be howling for Patton's scalp, and that will be the end of Georgie's service in this war. I simply cannot let that happen. Patton is *indispensable* to the war effort—one of the guarantors of our victory." [55]

Eisenhower then wrote, by hand, a long personal letter to Patton. "I clearly understand that firm and drastic measures are at times necessary in order to secure desired objectives," he began, "but this does not excuse brutality, abuse of the sick, nor exhibition of uncontrollable temper in front of subordinates." Eisenhower warned that if the reports were true, he would have to "seriously question your good judgment and your self-discipline." This would raise "serious doubts . . . as to your future usefulness." But exasperating as Patton was, Eisenhower would go to almost any length to keep him, and he assured Patton that "there is no record of the attached report or of my letter to you, except in my own secret files." He also promised there would be no official investigation. He did, however, order Patton to make a private report of his own, and to apologize to the soldier he had struck and to the nurses and doctors in the hospital.[56]

Eisenhower found writing the letter painful in the extreme. Since the days at Fort Meade, almost a quarter of a century ago, Eisenhower and Patton had dreamed of fighting together. Now they were actually doing it, side by side in history's greatest war. Patton's temper had jeopardized everything. Eisenhower confessed, "No letter that I have been called upon to write in my military career has caused me the mental anguish of this one, not only because of my long and deep personal friendship for you but because of my admiration for your military qualities." But he concluded, sternly, "I assure you that conduct such as described in the accompanying report will not be tolerated in this theater no matter who the offender may be."[57]

Eisenhower hoped that with that the incident would die, but when a general slaps a private the story gets around. The press corps in Sicily got hold of it. On August 19, Demaree Bess of *The Saturday Evening Post,* Merrill Mueller of NBC, and Quentin Reynolds of *Collier's* came to see Smith, to tell him that they had the facts but did not want to embarrass General Eisenhower. They offered a deal—if Patton were removed from command, they would hold the story.

When Smith took that offer into Eisenhower's office, Eisenhower commented sadly, "I might have to send Georgie Patton home in disgrace after all." He called Bess, Mueller, and Reynolds into his office, where he nearly begged the reporters to let him keep Patton. Eisenhower told them that Patton's "emotional tenseness and his impulsiveness are the very qualities that make him, in open situations, such a remarkable leader of an army. The more he drives his men the more he will save their lives." Eisenhower made it seem that victory over Germany depended on George Patton; under the circumstances, the reporters felt they could do nothing other than agree to hold the story of the slapping.[58]

Patton, meanwhile, had made the apologies Eisenhower had required, then wrote his boss, "I am at a loss to find words with which to express my chagrin and grief at having given you, a man to whom I owe everything and for whom I would gladly lay down my life, cause for displeasure with me."[59]

The incident was closed, or so Eisenhower hoped. He was so anxious to keep it a secret that he did not inform Marshall, even after Marshall asked him for a candid assessment of the generals under his command. In reply, Eisenhower said that Patton's chief characteristics were energy, determination, and unflagging aggressiveness. He kept the troops going when anyone else would have let them stop and rest. Eisenhower did hint at the slapping by adding: "Patton continues to exhibit some of those unfortunate personal traits of which you and I have always known and which during this campaign caused me some uncomfortable days." His explanation was vague; he said Patton's "habit of . . . bawling out subordinates" had extended to "personal abuse of individuals." Eisenhower said he had taken "the most drastic steps; and if he is not cured now, there is no hope for him." He believed Patton was cured, partly because of his "personal loyalty to you and to me," but mainly because "he is so avid for recognition as a great military commander that he will ruthlessly suppress any habit of his own that will tend to jeopardize it."[60]

On August 10, Eisenhower submitted to a physical exam (a routine requirement before he could be promoted to full colonel). The doctors thought he was hypertensive and found his blood pressure too high. They ordered a week's rest, in bed. Five days later, Eisenhower actually did take two days off, staying in his bedroom, but not in his bed. Butcher found him pacing the room nervously, worrying about his responsibilities, but nevertheless in a reflective mood. With Butcher for an audience, he did a critique of his own generalship.

He thought he had made two serious errors, both the result of overestimating the enemy and therefore advancing too cautiously. He felt he should have gone farther east with the Torch landings, all the way to Tunis. He also wished that he had invaded Sicily at its northeastern tip, landing on both sides of Messina, thus cutting off the Germans and forcing them to attack Allied defensive lines.[61]

It was an accurate, if painful, self-criticism, and a mark of the man that he was forthright in engaging in it. There were many campaigns to go, and he did not want to repeat his mistakes. He was determined to seize whatever opportunities opened up to him, to avoid the small solutions and the resulting long-drawn-out, wasteful battles of attrition that had characterized Tunisia and Sicily.

One opportunity was an Italian double-cross of the Germans. The government, headed by Marshal Pietro Badoglio, was eager to quit. Eisenhower, despite the criticism he had been subjected to because of the Darlan Deal, was eager to accept an Italian surrender and willing to make concessions to Badoglio despite the marshal's fascist politics. Churchill and Roosevelt were unhappy with this development, and put up various roadblocks that slowed the secret surrender negotiations.

Badoglio wanted to be saved from the Germans. To that end, he demanded that Eisenhower send the 82nd Airborne Division to Rome before he announced the surrender. Eisenhower agreed, but on September 8, as the division was taking off from airfields in Sicily, the Germans moved into Rome in force, and at the last minute he called the transports back. Meanwhile, the landing craft began moving toward Salerno, south of Rome, for the invasion of Italy.

Now Eisenhower entered the waiting period before an invasion, that maddening time when he could only pray. He wrote two letters to Mamie. "Here I am once more," he said, "waiting. This thing is making an old man of me!" He made up pipe dreams about things they would do together after the war—the "predominant note is laziness, soft climate, and utter contentment."[62]

Clark's men were on their way to the beaches. The Germans were taking control of Rome. They had a division in Salerno and could quickly get more there. "I am frank to state," Eisenhower told Marshall, "that there is more than a faint possibility that we may have some hard going."[63]

When Eisenhower awoke on September 9, he learned that Clark's Fifth Army was getting ashore successfully, but that the Germans had taken control of Rome, where the Italian government had panicked. At 5 A.M. the King, Badoglio, and the most important military leaders had fled the capital, headed for the south and safety under Allied protection.

No one bothered to send any orders to the Italian ground forces (numbering some 1.7 million men); the Germans disarmed most of them, while the rest threw away their uniforms and merged into the civilian population. Almost overnight, the Italian Army ceased to exist and Italy was an occupied country.

Eisenhower cabled Badoglio, who had made it to Brindisi, urging him to take action. "The whole future and honor of Italy depends upon the part which [Italy's] armed forces are now prepared to play," Eisenhower said. He asked Badoglio to issue a clarion call to all patriotic Italians to "seize every German by the throat."[64]

It did little good. The Italian fleet did sail from its ports, eventually to join the Allies, which left the ports of Bari, Brindisi, and Taranto open to Cunningham's ships, who took possession and allowed the British 1st Airborne Division to occupy the heel of Italy. But as for the ground forces, asking the Italians to act was like beating a dead horse. Aside from the fleet, all the Allies had gotten out of the armistice was a symbol of leadership in the persons of the King and Badoglio, and those two had fled their capital.

At Salerno by midmorning the initial success was giving way to disturbing developments. There was a twenty-five-mile gap between the British and the American beaches, and efforts to link up were meeting increasingly heavy resistance. Clark wanted Eisenhower to rush the 82nd Airborne into the gap; Eisenhower was trying to find the landing craft with which to do the job. "I feel that Salerno will be a matter of touch and go for the next few days," he told the CCS at noon on September 9. If he had sufficient landing craft to put the 82d ashore immediately, "the matter would be almost a foregone conclusion," but as it was, "we are in for some very tough fighting."[65]

They were indeed. On September 10, the Germans began a series of counterattacks against the beachhead, concentrating on the gap between the British and the American forces. By the eleventh, the Germans had five divisions in the area and seemed on the verge of destroying Clark's Fifth Army. Eisenhower had no landing craft available to reinforce Clark. He did have the 82d Airborne drop by parachute onto the beachhead. He urged Montgomery to speed up his movement north, from the Italian toe, in order to threaten the German left flank (the British Eighth Army had advanced only forty-five miles during its first seven days on the mainland, against negligible resistance). Eisenhower rushed fighter aircraft to the small airfield on the constricted beachhead, and prepared another infantry division to go to Salerno as soon as the landing craft were available. He begged the CCS for more B-24s, saying "I would give my next year's pay for two or three extra heavy groups right this minute."[66]

It was a most dangerous moment. An army of four divisions was on the verge of annihilation. Eisenhower received a message from Clark that indicated Clark was making plans to put his headquarters on board ship in order to control both sectors and to continue the battle in whichever one offered the greater chance for success.

The message made Eisenhower almost frantic. He told Butcher and Smith that the headquarters should leave last, that Clark ought to show the spirit of a naval captain and if necessary go down with his ship. He thundered: "By God!, the Fifth Army ought to emulate the Russians at Stalingrad and stand and fight."[67] He wondered aloud if it had not been a mistake to give Clark the command—he wished he had selected Patton.

But neither then nor later, after Clark continued to disappoint him, did he seriously consider removing Clark from command. For one reason, he liked and respected Clark; for another, he blamed the CCS for the situation, not Clark.

If his bosses had listened to reason and given him the bombers and landing craft he had asked for, there would be no problem at Salerno. As it was, "we have such a painfully slow buildup and the enemy can constantly bring so much strength against us" that the situation was critical.[68]

Eisenhower admitted, in a diary entry of September 14, that his deputies had warned him there was insufficient landing craft and air cover for the invasion, which they had wanted to call off, and that the decision to go ahead, "was solely my own, and if things go wrong there is no one to blame except myself."[69] In a note to Marshall, he said that he thought Clark could hold on, but if he did not, "I would . . . merely announce that one of our landings had been repulsed— due to my error in misjudging the strength of the enemy at that place." But he had "great faith that even in spite of currently grim reports, we'll pull out all right."[70]

All that day, September 14, the Germans attacked. At the critical point, American artillerymen stood to their guns and prevented a German breakthrough. Eisenhower sent words of encouragement to Clark, told Tedder to put "every plane that could fly" over Salerno, including all the bombers, and told Cunningham to bring up close to shore every ship that could fire so that they could pound the Germans.[71] The air forces dropped 3,020 tons of bombs that day, while the naval forces—mostly Royal Navy—delivered more than 11,000 tons of shells in direct support of the ground forces on the beachhead. By nightfall, the crisis was over. The next day, lead elements of the Eighth Army made contact with a Fifth Army patrol. On September 18, the Germans began a deliberate disengagement and withdrawal.

Within two weeks, Eisenhower's forces had a continuous line across Italy, as Montgomery's right wing met with the left of the British 1st Airborne coming from the heel. Losses had been high but unevenly distributed—Fifth Army had suffered fourteen thousand casualties to Eighth Army's six hundred. The drive for Naples and the airfields at Foggia, on the east coast, then began.

At this point, Marshall sent Eisenhower some criticism of his generalship and a suggestion on how to improve. Marshall said he had been disappointed at Eisenhower's failure to seize Rome with the 82nd Airborne, and disappointed too by the landings in the Italian toe, which struck him as unduly conservative. He said he feared that if Eisenhower took time to secure his position around Naples, the Germans would have time to prepare their defenses and thus make the road to Rome long and difficult. He wondered if Eisenhower had considered the possibility of halting Fifth and Eighth Army efforts toward Naples once the city was "under the guns" and making a dash for Rome, perhaps by amphibious means.[72]

Eisenhower replied with some heat that he too wanted to be bold —"I would give my last shirt to be able to push a strong division landing into the Gulf of Gaeta" (north of Naples)—but he simply did not have the landing craft. As Eisenhower dictated his defense of himself, his face set in a deep scowl of concentration. His usual practice while dictating was to pace the room, talking rapidly, or else to shift from chair to chair. This time he became so engrossed that he walked right out the open door into the hallway and kept on dictating. His secretary scurried after him, taking shorthand all the while.

Eisenhower reminded Marshall that he did not have sufficient landing craft, and that the Germans had a panzer division in the Gulf of Gaeta, another in Rome, and a reserve division that could reinforce either one. Eisenhower felt that if he landed a small force it would be quickly eliminated, while a force large enough to sustain itself could not be mounted or maintained.

Eisenhower felt unfairly accused, by a man who should have known better and yet one whom he respected more than anyone else in the world. "As a final word," he concluded, "I want to say that we are looking every minute for a chance to utilize our air and naval power to turn the enemy positions . . . I do not see how any individual could possibly be devoting more thought and energy to speeding up operations or to attacking boldly and with admitted risk than I do."

As Eisenhower was dictating, a message came in from Churchill. The Prime Minister congratulated Eisenhower on the Salerno landings and commented, "As the Duke of Wellington said of the Battle of Waterloo, 'It was a damned close-run thing.'" Churchill said he was proud of Eisenhower for his policy of "running risks." Eisenhower triumphantly passed the message along to Marshall and commented, "I feel certain that [Churchill] looks upon me as a gambler."[73]

Gambler or not, by September 26 Eisenhower was committed to the slow, direct, expensive overland approach to Rome. He still expected to take the city before the end of October, but he was badly mistaken. Problems with weather, terrain, and enemy resistance slowed the offensive to a crawl. The Allied air forces could not operate because of the torrential rains, tanks could not maneuver off the roads, artillery got bogged down in the mud, and there were no landing craft to take advantage of control of the sea, so all of Eisenhower's assets were relatively useless, while the Germans used their more than two-to-one manpower advantage (Eisenhower's eleven divisions were engaging twenty-five German divisions) to make every step forward bloody and costly. All through October and November, the Fifth and Eighth Armies tried to attack, but with minimal success. The Germans had imposed a stalemate in Italy.

Eisenhower's new office was in the Caserta Palace north of Naples. He had a room large enough to serve as a railroad station. He protested at the excess space, in vain. His staff had a conqueror's complex, as did his generals. On a cruise around the Isle of Capri, Eisenhower spotted a large villa.

"Whose is that?" he asked. "Yours, sir," someone replied—Butcher had arranged it. Nodding at another, even larger villa, Eisenhower asked, "And that?" "That one belongs to General Spaatz."

Eisenhower exploded. "Damn it, that's *not* my villa! And that's not General Spaatz' villa! None of those will belong to any general as long as I'm Boss around here. This is supposed to be a rest center—for combat men—not a playground for the Brass!" He meant it. When he returned to shore, he wired Spaatz, "This is directly contrary to my policies and must cease at once."[74]

Such concern with the men under his command was typical of Eisenhower. It enhanced his popularity. The Capri story, and others similar to it, quickly got out to the troops and delighted them. Nothing pleased the footslogger struggling in the mud of Italy more than hearing that Eisenhower had put Spaatz or some other general in his place. The fact that Eisenhower swore like a sergeant was much appreciated by the men. So were his frequent visits to the front lines, especially because he listened to the troops' complaints and, when he could, did something about them.

For his part, Eisenhower enjoyed escaping from the VIPs, who were coming into his theater in large numbers, by going to the front. Chatting with troops restored his energy. "Our soldiers are wonderful," he told Mamie. "It always seems to me that the closer to the front the better the morale and the less the grumbling. No one knows how I like to roam around among them—I'm always cheered up by a day with the actual fighters."[75]

Also cheering was news from Washington that Mamie was doing well; indeed, that was the best part about the constant stream of VIP visitors. Many of them had seen Mamie recently and "all report you [Mamie] in tip-top shape [and] fine fettle—and a person of whom the whole army is proud—because of your tact, good sense and modesty." Ike reported that his sister-in-law had written him, asking him to "order" Mamie to San Antonio for the winter; his comment to Mamie was "I give lots of orders, but I'd play——trying to give you one!"[76]

The President came to the Mediterranean, on his way to Cairo for a meeting of the CCS. Eisenhower flew to Oran to meet Roosevelt, then accompanied him to Tunis, where they went on a motor trip to inspect battlefield sites, both recent and ancient, and had a long talk. Roosevelt shifted quickly from subject to subject and Eisenhower found him a fascinating conversationalist.

At one point the President touched on Overlord, the new code name for the cross-Channel attack. He said he dreaded the thought of losing Marshall in Washington, but added, "You and I, Ike, know the name of the Chief of Staff in the Civil War, but few Americans outside the professional services do."[77] He thought it only fair that Marshall have an opportunity to make his mark on history as commander of a field army. Later that day Admiral King, who had accompanied Roosevelt, told Eisenhower that he had urgently and persistently advised the President to keep Marshall in Washington, but had lost. "I hate to lose General Marshall as Chief of Staff," King told Eisenhower, "but my loss is consoled by the knowledge that I will have you to work in his job." Eisenhower took King's statement as "almost official notice that I would soon be giving up field command to return to Washington."[78]

Roosevelt, Churchill, and the CCS meanwhile went on to Teheran, Iran, for a meeting with Stalin. Stalin's concern continued to be the Second Front. When Roosevelt assured him that the invasion was definitely on for the spring of 1944, Stalin demanded to know who was in command. Roosevelt replied that the appointment had not yet been made. Stalin said in that case he did not believe the Western Allies were serious about the operation. Roosevelt promised to make the selection in three or four days.

Despite his promise, Roosevelt shrank from the distasteful task of making the decision. His preferred solution—Marshall for Overlord, Eisenhower as his replacement in the War Department—had little to recommend it. It would make Eisenhower Marshall's boss, an absurd situation, and—worse—put Eisenhower in a position of giving orders to MacArthur, which MacArthur was certain to resent. Nevertheless, Roosevelt desperately wanted to give Marshall his opportunity. When they got back to Cairo in early December, he asked Marshall to express his personal preference, and thus, he hoped, make the decision for him. But Marshall replied that while he would gladly serve wherever the President told him to, he would not be the judge in his own case.

Roosevelt made his decision. As the last meeting at Cairo was breaking up, Roosevelt asked Marshall to write a message to Stalin for him. As Roosevelt dictated, Marshall wrote, "From the President to Marshal Stalin," it began. "The immediate appointment of General Eisenhower to command of Overlord operation has been decided upon." Roosevelt then signed it.[79]

It was the most coveted command in the history of warfare. It gave Eisenhower his great, unique opportunity. Without it, he would have been only one among a number of famous Allied generals rather than the Great Captain of World War II and, as a consequence, President of the United States.

He got the appointment, it seemed, by default. In explaining his reasoning afterward, Roosevelt said that he just could not sleep at night with Marshall out of the country. Eisenhower was the logical choice because Marshall was too important to be spared, even for Overlord. Since the commander had to be an American, a process of elimination brought it down to Eisenhower.

There were, nevertheless, manifold positive reasons for Eisenhower's selection. Overlord, like Torch, was going to be a joint operation, and Eisenhower had proved that he could create and run an integrated staff and successfully command combined British-American operations. No other general had done so. Admiral Cunningham, now a member of the CCS (he had assumed the duties of First Sea Lord in mid-October), had said it well when he left the Mediterranean. He told Eisenhower it had been a great experience for him to see the forces of two nations, made up of men with different upbringings, conflicting ideas on staff work, and basic, "apparently irreconcilable ideas," brought together and knitted into a team. "I do not believe," Cunningham said, "that any other man than yourself could have done it."[80]

The key word was "team." Eisenhower's emphasis on teamwork, his never-flagging insistence on working together, was the single most important reason for his selection, much more important than his generalship, which in truth had been cautious and hesitant. Eisenhower's dedication to teamwork was, of course, a theme that had characterized his whole life, stretching back to the Abilene High School baseball and football games.

Gathering the disparate forces for Overlord, welding them into a genuine team, making the plans for the actual engagement, and directing the action once the conflict began were challenges rather like coaching a football team, albeit on an immensely larger scale. The job required an ability to spot and exploit each player's strength, and to force each player—many of them "stars," egotistical and self-centered—to merge his talents with the others in order to fight together in a common cause. Marshall, for all his awesome abilities, did not have the patience required to work smoothly and efficiently with prima donnas, especially British prima donnas. Nor did Marshall have Eisenhower's experience in commanding amphibious operations. Brooke, a man who was consistently and scathingly critical of Eisenhower's professional competence, recognized this truth. "The selection of Eisenhower instead of Marshall," he wrote, "was a good one."[81]

Another, related factor in Roosevelt's choice was Eisenhower's popularity. Everyone liked him, responded positively to his outgoing personality, even when they disagreed with his decisions. His hearty laugh, infectious grin, relaxed manner, and consistent optimism were irresistible.

Equally important, he was physically strong enough to withstand the rigors and pressures of a long and arduous campaign. Fifty-three years old, he was tough enough to get along on four or five hours sleep a night, to shake off a cold or the flu, to rouse himself from near-total exhaustion and present a cheerful face to his subordinates. It was not that he did not pay a price for all his activity, but that he did not let it show. In September 1943, a friend told him that he was pleased to see from some snapshots taken in Sicily that Eisenhower looked so healthy. In reply, Eisenhower said, "I must admit that sometimes I feel a thousand years old when I struggle to my bed at night."[82] Nevertheless, the overriding impression he gave was one of vitality. Dwight Eisenhower was an intensely alive human being who enjoyed his job immensely.

That quality showed in his speech, his mannerisms, his physical movements, most of all in his eyes. They were astonishingly expressive. As he listened to his deputies discuss future operations, his eyes moved quickly and inquisitively from face to face. His concentration was intense, almost a physical embrace. The eyes always showed his mood—they were icy blue when he was angry, warmly blue when he was pleased, sharp and demanding when he was concerned, glazed when he was bored.

Most of all, they bespoke his supreme self-confidence, a certainty of belief in himself and his abilities. It was neither a blind nor an egotistical confidence. As has been seen, he was a sharp and insightful critic of his own decisions. Like the successful football coach studying the movies of the preceding week's game, his self-criticism was searching and positive, designed to eliminate errors and improve performance.

He had made, and would have to make, countless decisions, decisions that involved the lives of tens of thousands of men, not to speak of the fate of great nations. He did so with the certainty that he had taken everything into account, gathered all relevant information, and considered all possible consequences. Then he acted. This is the essence of command.

His self-confidence inspired confidence in him. When associates described Eisenhower, be they superiors or subordinates, there was one word that almost all of them used. It was trust. People trusted Eisenhower for the most obvious reason—he was trustworthy. Disagree as they might (and often did) with his decisions, they never doubted his motives. Montgomery did not think much of Eisenhower as a soldier, but he did appreciate other qualities. While he thought Eisenhower intelligent, "his real strength lies in his human qualities . . . He has the power of drawing the hearts of men towards him as a magnet attracts the bit of metal. He merely has to smile at you, and you trust him at once."[83]

With his staff and with his troops, with his superiors and with his subordinates, as with foreign governments, Eisenhower did what he said he was going to do. His reward was the trust they placed in him. Because of that trust, and because of the qualities he possessed that brought it about, he was a brilliant choice as Supreme Commander, Allied Expeditionary Force, quite possibly the best appointment Roosevelt ever made.

On December 7, Eisenhower met Roosevelt in Tunis, where the President was stopping on his way back to Washington. Roosevelt was taken off his plane and put in Eisenhower's car. As the automobile began to drive off, the President turned to the general and said, almost casually, "Well, Ike, you are going to command Overlord."[84]

The news electrified Eisenhower and his AFHQ associates. Their morale had declined as they prepared for Eisenhower's imminent departure for Washington. "We now feel," Harry Butcher wrote, "that we have a definite and concrete mission. This adds zest to living and interest in pursuing the objective. It has already made a remarkable difference in Ike. Now he is back to his old system of incessant planning and thinking out loud of qualifications of this or that man for certain jobs." [85]

Personnel selection was crucial, and Eisenhower threw himself into the task. Bradley had already been selected to command the U.S. First Army, which delighted Eisenhower. For his British ground commander, he wanted Alexander, but accepted Montgomery when Churchill insisted on keeping Alexander in Italy. He kept Smith as chief of staff. He also insisted on bringing his "family" to London with him—Butcher, Tex Lee, Mickey, Kay, two stenographers (WAACs), two drivers (also WAACs), his cook, and the two black enlisted men who served as his houseboys.

The American general he most wanted, next to Bradley, was Patton (although unwilling to relieve Clark in Italy, he never considered taking Clark to England for an Overlord command). He wanted Patton badly. It cost him something to get Patton, because just as he was making his selections, radio commentator Drew Pearson broke the news of the Patton slapping incident in a garbled and exaggerated broadcast.

Eisenhower, the War Department, and the White House all received hundreds of letters, most demanding that any general who would strike a private in a hospital be summarily dismissed from the service. Marshall asked for an explanation. Eisenhower's reply ran to four single-spaced pages. He assured Marshall that despite reports that Patton had received no official reprimand (which was true), he had taken "corrective action" that was "adequate and suitable." Eisenhower thought the best thing to do was "to keep still and take the brunt of the affair myself." [86] He refused to make a public defense of his actions, or lack of them, and advised Patton to keep quiet, since "it is my judgment that this storm will blow over." [87] Eventually, it did, and Eisenhower took Patton to England with him, along with almost everyone else he wanted from the Mediterranean.

Marshall began urging Eisenhower to come to the States and take a furlough. That suited Eisenhower's repeatedly expressed desire to spend a few days with Mamie, but ran counter to his sense of duty and anxiety to plunge into his new job. He begged off, telling Marshall that there was too much work to be done. Marshall finally made it a direct order. "You will be under terrific strain from now on," Marshall pointed out. "I am not interested in the usual rejoinder that you can take it. It is of vast importance that you be fresh mentally and you certainly will not be if you go straight from one great problem to another. Now come on home and see your wife and trust somebody else for 20 minutes in England."[88]

Eisenhower capitulated. He decided to fly to the United States and take two weeks off. He left at noon on the last day of 1943. Just before departing the Mediterranean, he wrote a friend, "I have put in a hard year here and I guess it is time to go."[89]

It had been a year marked by great gains on the map. The forces under Eisenhower's command had conquered Morocco, Algeria, Tunisia, Sicily, and southern Italy. The strategic gains, however, had been small at best. Germany had not lost any territory that was critical to its defense. It had not been forced to reduce its divisions in France or in Russia. Taken as a whole, Eisenhower's campaigns from November 1942 to December 1943 must be judged a strategic failure.

By no means was it altogether his fault. In the summer of 1942 he had warned his political bosses about what was going to happen if they turned down Roundup for Torch. But some of the blame was his. The excessive caution with which he opened the campaign, his refusal to run risks to get to Tunis before the Germans, his refusal to take a chance and rush troops into Sardinia, his refusal to relieve Fredendall, his refusal to take a grip on the battle in Sicily, his refusal to seize the opportunity to take Rome with the 82nd Airborne, all contributed to the unhappy situation he left behind in Italy. The Allied armies were well south of Rome as winter set in, with little hope of any rapid advance. The Allies had expended great resources for small gains.

On the political side, the legacy of the campaign was one of profound mistrust of the Americans and the British by the French and the Russians, each of whom wanted a second front in northwest France, and each of whom was deeply suspicious of the Darlan Deal, and of Eisenhower's negotiations with Badoglio. The campaign brought minimal military rewards at the cost of diplomatic disaster.

But there was one clear gain from 1943 for the Allies—it gave the high command in general, and Eisenhower particularly, badly needed experience. The troops, too, learned what a tough business war is. Further, Eisenhower learned which of his subordinates could stand up to the strain of battle, and which could not. Had it not been for Torch, had Roundup been launched in 1943 instead of Overlord in 1944, the Allies would have gone ashore with an insecure Eisenhower in command of inexperienced troops led by Lloyd Fredendall. The idea of Fredendall in charge at Omaha Beach during the crisis is by itself enough to justify the Mediterranean campaign.

In his first combat experience, Eisenhower had been unsure of himself, hesitant, often depressed, irritable, liable to make snap judgments on insufficient information, defensive in both his mood and his tactics. But he had learned how critical it was for him to be always cheery and optimistic in the presence of his subordinates, how costly caution can often be in combat, and who he could rely upon in critical moments.

In the Mediterranean campaign, Eisenhower and his team had improved dramatically. As they now prepared for the climax of the war, the invasion of France, they were vastly superior to the team that had invaded North Africa in November 1942. In that respect, the payoff for Torch was worth the price.

CHAPTER FIVE

D-Day and the
Liberation of France

IKE ARRIVED in Washington at 1:30 A.M. on Sunday, January 2. Mamie had learned only a few hours earlier that he was coming; she was still awake when her husband rushed to the Wardman Park Hotel to greet her. The Eisenhowers talked through the night, the words tumbling out—about the doings of old friends, taxes, the car, Ike's assignment, John's progress, and a dozen other subjects.

Mamie noticed changes in her husband. He was heavier, noticeably older, more self-assured than he had been eighteen months ago. She thought he was more serious, his voice a shade more decisive than it had been. She was worried about his excessive smoking, pleased by his infectious confidence in himself and in Overlord.

After breakfast, he announced that he was off to the War Department to see Marshall, and just that quick he was gone. Time was precious to him now, in a way that it had never been before. In the two weeks that followed, Mamie learned that it had become habitual for him to terminate a conversation or interview abruptly, not because he had grown rude, but simply because he was accustomed to it and expected everyone around him to understand that he had to get on to the next problem.

On January 6, the Eisenhowers got into Marshall's private railroad car to go to White Sulphur Springs, where the Chief of Staff had arranged for them to stay at a small, private cottage, for two days of complete privacy. It was not an altogether restful and relaxing vacation, because twice Ike slipped and called Mamie "Kay," which made Mamie furious. Ike blushed, explained that Kay really meant nothing to him; it was just that she was practically the only woman he had seen in a year and a half and her name just naturally popped out. Mamie found it a less than satisfactory explanation.[1]

Back in Washington, Eisenhower attended a series of conferences. He met with Marshall and General Henry Arnold, who commanded the Army Air Forces. Eisenhower was concerned about the organization and command structure of the air forces in Britain. The CCS had assigned the tactical air forces, the fighters, to Overlord. Their activities would be controlled by Marshal of the Royal Air Force Trafford Leigh-Mallory, who was directly responsible to Eisenhower (Tedder, although Eisenhower's deputy supreme commander, was without portfolio). The bombers were not a part of the Overlord structure. General Arthur Harris headed the RAF Bomber Command, while General Carl Spaatz had the U.S. Eighth Air Force. Both Harris and Spaatz had their own strategy, Harris to bring about a German capitulation through terror bombing of German cities, Spaatz to force a German surrender through the selective destruction of certain key industries, especially oil production facilities. Neither man believed Overlord was necessary. Spaatz' subordinates had been heard to say that they wanted only twenty or thirty clear operational days and they would finish the war on their own.

To Eisenhower, this was dangerous nonsense. He believed that Germany would have to be defeated on the ground before it would ever quit. Overlord was therefore the great operation of the war. In the initial stages, the Allies would be outnumbered on the ground ten to one in France; only air superiority made Overlord feasible. Eisenhower wanted to take the bombers away from the campaign inside Germany and use them for purposes that would be immediately helpful to Overlord. To that end, he had to have personal command of RAF Bomber Command and the Eighth Air Force. The issue remained unsettled.

On January 12, Eisenhower went to the White House for a private conference with Roosevelt. He found the President in bed, ill with the flu. They talked for two hours, mainly about French and German affairs. Eisenhower was upset at the attitude toward Free French leader Charles de Gaulle that he found in Washington. Just before leaving Algiers, Eisenhower had met with de Gaulle, in what Butcher described as a "love fest." "I must have your help," Eisenhower had told de Gaulle, "and I have come to ask you for it." De

Gaulle had replied, "Splendid! You are a man! For you know how to say, 'I was wrong.' " [2] What Eisenhower had in mind was the French Resistance. He counted on it for sabotage operations on D-Day, and for information on German dispositions and movements, and he knew that the Resistance would respond only to de Gaulle. Smith and de Gaulle had worked out an agreement whereby the Resistance would obey Eisenhower, in return for which Eisenhower promised that French forces would participate in the liberation of Paris and the Free French would take control of civil affairs in the liberated areas of France.

But in Washington, to his distress, Eisenhower discovered that no one wanted to deal with de Gaulle. Roosevelt insisted that the French people would not submit to the authority of the Free French and that any attempt to impose de Gaulle on France could lead to civil war. Eisenhower thought the President's position unrealistic, and politely told the President so, but Roosevelt was adamant. The difficulties that ensued from the Allied attempt to ignore de Gaulle, Eisenhower later said, caused him some of the "most acutely annoying problems" he had to face before D-Day. [3]

Eisenhower then turned to the problem of the occupation of Germany. He told the President that the plan to divide Germany into three zones, one for the Americans, one for the British, and one for the Russians, was a mistake. Germany, he declared, should not be divided into zones; the military government ought to be conducted by a coalition of the Allied forces, under a single commander. This would make administration simpler and make it easier to control the Red Army's behavior in the areas it occupied. Roosevelt, unconvinced, said he could deal with the Russians.

The following day, Eisenhower's furlough ended. Mamie was unhappy at her husband's single-minded concentration on Overlord, his obvious anxiety to get back to London, and the little time he had spent with her. Watching him pack for yet another lengthy separation, her heart nearly broke. "Don't come back again till it's over, Ike," she said. "I can't stand losing you again." [4]

A week later, he wrote her: "I find myself very glad I came home —even though things did seem to be a bit upsetting! I guess it was just because we'd been separated so long, and before we could get really acquainted again, I was on my way." Four days after that, he thanked Mamie for "the third letter I'd received since coming here and all of them have been wonderful—quite the nicest you've written since I left home in June '42." His conclusion was that, although everything had not gone as well as he had hoped, "My trip home has paid dividends!"[5]

Back in London, Eisenhower set up his headquarters on familiar grounds, at 20 Grosvenor Square. "Right now we are busy getting settled and going through the business of ramming our feet in the stirrups," he wrote a friend shortly after his arrival.[6] The process was much easier than it had been in June 1942. The SHAEF staff came primarily from AFHQ; the commanders of the field forces, with the exception of Leigh-Mallory, had had combat experience in the Mediterranean; Eisenhower now had three amphibious operations behind him; taken together, Eisenhower's team was battle-tested, committed to Allied unity, full of faith in Eisenhower, and eager to get to work. Compared to the team that had started on Torch, it was far superior; as Eisenhower put it, "Order had replaced disorder and certainty and confidence had replaced fear and doubt."[7]

There was also a single-mindedness not present in Torch. As Eisenhower said, at SHAEF there was "a very deep conviction, in all circles, that we are approaching a tremendous crisis with stakes incalculable." Everyone was "working like dogs," he was pleased to note. As always, his emphasis was on the positive. "Our problems are seemingly intricate and difficult beyond belief," he said, but he refused to allow anyone even to hint that they would not be overcome.

Privately, he was more worried than anyone else, but he never let his subordinates know it. "As the big day approaches," he wrote in early April, "tension grows and everybody gets more and more on edge. This time, because of the stakes involved, the atmosphere is more electric than ever before." Under the circumstances, "a sense of humor and a great faith . . . are essential to sanity."[8]

Another great difference between the pre-Torch and the pre-Overlord periods was that in 1944 Eisenhower did not have to prove himself to the British. His relations with Churchill were such that he could disagree violently with the Prime Minister over issues without affecting their friendship or mutual respect in any way. Except for Brooke, he got on well with the British Chiefs of Staff. His relations with Montgomery were formal and correct, rather than warm; with Tedder, by way of contrast, he had struck up a close friendship. With Cunningham, Eisenhower had established a mutual admiration society.

Closer personal relations with the British were possible in 1944, in contrast to 1942, partly because this time the place, time, and date of the assault were all fixed, rather than subjects for dispute. The place would be Normandy, west of the mouth of the Orne River, the time would be shortly after dawn, the date May 1.

A complex set of factors had gone into these selections. The state of German defenses was the overriding consideration; they were strongest around the French ports and especially in the Pas de Calais, which otherwise would have been the obvious target as it was on the shortest line between England and Germany. Dawn was the time because it would allow the fleet to cross the Channel under the cover of darkness and give the troops a full day to establish a beachhead. May 1 was the date because of moon and tidal conditions; the AEF had to come ashore shortly after dead low tide to avoid the German underwater obstacles, and the bombers and paratroopers needed at least a half-moon the night before. The assault had to come late enough in the year to allow for final training of troops in the British Isles, but soon enough to give the Allies at least four months of good campaigning weather in France. These conditions were met only three times in the spring of 1944—during the first days of May and the first and third weeks of June.

The issue that was not settled, and thus the one that would cause Eisenhower a great deal of anguish, was the scope of the commitment in landing craft and air power to Overlord. To Eisenhower, convinced that Overlord was *the* great operation of the war, it was almost inconceivable that there should be any question about a total commitment. "Every obstacle must be overcome," he declared in his initial report to the CCS, "every inconvenience suffered and every risk run to ensure that our blow is decisive. We cannot afford to fail."[9]

That meant, above all else, that he had to have sufficient landing craft to mount a five-division assault, with enough additional craft for two follow-up divisions to go ashore on D-Day. "Nothing less will give us an adequate margin to ensure success," he warned, and to get it he was willing to make sacrifices elsewhere. He had to have 271 landing craft beyond those already assigned to Overlord, and to have them he had decided, within a week of his arrival in London, to put D-Day back a month, from May 1 to early June, in order to have available an extra month's production of landing craft (amounting to almost 100 vessels).[10]

The worldwide shortage of landing craft colored the entire situation and made all events related. At one point Churchill growled that "the destinies of two great empires . . . seem to be tied up in some Goddamned things called LSTs."[11]

• •

Living in London caused constant interruptions, because Churchill, the American ambassador, and other VIPs felt free to call him at any hour, and the staff found the temptations of London night life too much to pass up. In February, Eisenhower moved his headquarters outside the city, to Bushey Park. Tents went up, camouflage covered them, and the SHAEF staff, grumbling, moved in.

For himself, Eisenhower selected living quarters in a small house on the edge of the park, called Telegraph Cottage. The Supreme Commander thus had the least pretentious home of any general officer in England, but Eisenhower was happy, for at Telegraph he could work, think, relax, play a hole or two of golf, and read Westerns without being interrupted. He could even enjoy an occasional moment alone with Kay.

In public, Kay was very much in evidence. She accompanied Eisenhower to meetings with Churchill, King George VI, and others. Although she was a British subject, Eisenhower was arranging to have her commissioned as a WAAC lieutenant. Decades later, in a book published after her death, Kay claimed that they had fallen in love, and that both had realized it when he returned from Washington. "His kisses absolutely unraveled me," she wrote.

According to her account, it was a passionate but unconsummated romance, partly because—save for an odd moment or two at Telegraph Cottage—they were seldom alone together, mainly because, on the one evening they did try to make love, Eisenhower was flaccid. This may have been because, as one aide put it in a grand understatement, "Ike had a lot on his mind," or because his stern sense of morality overrode his passion. Or it may be that the incident never happened, that it was merely an old woman's fantasy. No one will ever know. What is important to note is that not even Kay ever claimed that they had a genuine love affair.[12]

Other generals did have affairs, as men at war have done since time out of mind, but no other general was so completely exposed to public scrutiny, or so busy, as Eisenhower. When Mamie wrote to him about the "tales . . . I've heard" about the "night clubs, gayety and loose morals" of the American officers in London, he quickly responded, "So far as I can see 99% of officers and men are too busy to have any time for anything else [but work] . . . the pictures painted by gossips are grossly exaggerated. So far as the group around me is concerned, I know that the principal concern is work—and that their habits are above reproach."[13]

• •

Overlord was a direct frontal assault against a prepared enemy position. The German line, or Atlantic Wall, was continuous, so there was no possibility of outflanking it. The Germans had a manpower advantage and the benefit of land lines of communication, so Eisenhower's forces could not hope to overwhelm them. Eisenhower's advantages were control of the air and of the sea, which meant that Allied bombers and ships could pound the enemy emplacements and trenches on a scale even larger than the World War I artillery barrages. In addition, he was on the offensive, which meant that he knew where and when the battle would be fought. Even better, he had no defensive lines to maintain, so he could concentrate all his resources on a relatively narrow front in Normandy, while the Germans had to spread their resources along the coast.

Harris' and Spaatz' bombers would play a key role. There was no dispute about this point; all agreed that on the eve of D-Day every bomber that could fly would participate in the attack on the Normandy coastal defenses. There was, however, intense debate over the role of the bombers in the two months preceding the invasion. Eisenhower persisted in his demand that the bombers come under SHAEF control, and that they then be used to implement the so-called Transportation Plan, designed to destroy the French railway system and thus hamper German mobility.

On March 6, Patton came to visit Eisenhower at Bushey Park. He was shown into Eisenhower's office while Eisenhower was on the telephone with Tedder.

"Now, listen, Arthur," Eisenhower was saying, "I am tired of dealing with a lot of prima donnas. By God, you tell that bunch that if they can't get together and stop quarreling like children, I will tell the Prime Minister to get someone else to run this damn war. I'll quit." Patton took careful note of the tone of command in his voice; Eisenhower was obviously taking charge, and Patton could not help but be impressed.[14]

Marshall supported Eisenhower in the dispute; Churchill supported Harris and Spaatz. Eisenhower then told Churchill that if his bosses refused to make anything less than a full commitment to Overlord by holding back the bombers, he would "simply have to go home."[15]

This extreme threat (as with Eisenhower's relations with the press, what a contrast with the American Army leaders in Vietnam!) brought Churchill around. Tedder then prepared a list of more than seventy railroad targets in France and Belgium. The bombers went to work on the French railway system. By D-Day the Allies had dropped seventy-six thousand tons of bombs on rail centers, bridges, and open lines. The Seine River bridges west of Paris were virtually destroyed. Based on an index of 100 for January and February 1944, railway traffic dropped from 69 in mid-May to 38 by D-Day.

Eisenhower had dozens of major and hundreds of minor disagreements with Churchill and the CCS during the war, but the only occasion on which he threatened to resign was over the issue of command of the strategic air forces. He was certain at the time that he was right, and he never saw any reason to question that belief. In 1968, in one of his last interviews, he told this author that he felt the greatest single contribution he personally made to the success of Overlord was his insistence on the Transportation Plan.

There were many aspects to Overlord in which Eisenhower's role was more supervisory than direct, including such items as the artificial harbors, the specially designed tanks, assault techniques, the deception plan, the logistical problems involved in getting the men and equipment to the southern English ports, transporting them across the Channel, and supplying them in Normandy.

Overlord was the greatest amphibious assault in history, with the largest air and sea armadas ever assembled. It required, and got, painstakingly detailed planning, with thousands of men involved. SHAEF alone had a total strength of 16,312, of whom 2,829 were officers (1,600 Americans, 1,229 British). There were in addition the staffs of the U.S. and British armies, corps, and divisions, all devoting their entire energy to Overlord.

These vast bureaucracies did very well what they were created to do, but their limitations were obvious. They could suggest, plan, advise, investigate, but they could not act. Nor could any single member of the bureaucracies see the problem whole. Every individual involved had a specific given role to play and could concentrate on one set of problems; each staff officer was an expert struggling with his specialty. The officers could study and analyze a problem and make recommendations, but they could not decide and order.

Someone had to give the bureaucracies direction; someone had to be able to take all the information they gathered, make sense out of it, and impose order on it; someone had to make certain that each part meshed into the whole; someone had to decide; someone had to take the responsibility and act.

It all came down to Eisenhower. He was the funnel through which everything passed. Only his worries were infinite, only he carried the awesome burden of command. This position put enormous pressure on him, pressure that increased geometrically with each day that passed.

"Ike looks worn and tired," Butcher noted on May 12. "The strain is telling on him. He looks older now than at any time since I have been with him." It would get worse as D-Day got closer and innumerable problems came up each day, many unsolved and some unsolvable. Still, Butcher felt that all would turn out all right, that Eisenhower could take it. "Fortunately he has the happy faculty of bouncing back after a night of good sleep."[16]

Unfortunately, such nights were rare. Eisenhower's tension and tiredness began to show in his face, especially when he was inspecting training exercises, watching the boys he would be sending against Hitler's Atlantic Wall. The anxieties also showed in his letters to Mamie. Almost without exception, every letter he wrote her in the pre-Overlord period had a fantasy about his retirement plans when the war was over. The emphasis was on loafing in a warm climate.

Writing to Mamie was practically the only time he was free to think about issues that went beyond Overlord. He took the opportunity to express some of his deepest feelings. He loathed war and hated having to send boys to their death. "How I wish this cruel business of war could be completed quickly," he told Mamie. He was the man who had to total up all the casualties, bad enough in the air war, with worse to come when Overlord began. Counting the human costs was "a terribly sad business." It made him heartsick to think about "how many youngsters are gone forever," and although he had developed "a veneer of callousness," he could "never escape a recognition of the fact that back home the news brings anguish and suffering to families all over the country. Mothers, fathers, brothers, sisters, wives and friends must have a difficult time preserving any comforting philosophy and retaining any belief in the eternal rightness of things. War demands real toughness of fiber—not only in the soldiers that must endure, but in the homes that must sacrifice their best."

"I think that all these trials and tribulations must come upon the world because of some great wickedness," he said in another letter, "yet one would feel that man's mere intelligence to say nothing of his spiritual perceptions would find some way of eliminating war. But man has been trying to do so for many hundreds of years, and his failure just adds more reason for pessimism when a man gets really low!"[17]

The contrast between Eisenhower and those generals who gloried in war could not have been greater. Small wonder that millions of Americans in the 1940s felt that if their loved one had to join the fight, Eisenhower was the general they wanted for his commander. Patton, MacArthur, Bradley, Marshall, and the others all had their special qualities, but only Eisenhower had such a keen sense of family, of the way in which each casualty meant a grieving family back home.

Eisenhower's concern was of such depth and so genuine that it never left him. In 1964, when he was filming with Walter Cronkite a television special entitled "D-Day Plus 20," Cronkite asked him what he thought about when he returned to Normandy. In reply, he spoke not of the tanks, the guns, the planes, the ships, the personalities of his commanders and their opponents, or the victory. Instead, he spoke of the families of the men buried in the American cemetery in Normandy. He said he could never come to this spot without thinking of how blessed he and Mamie were to have grandchildren, and how much it saddened him to think of all the couples in America who had never had that blessing, because their only son was buried in France.

One reason, more rational than emotional, that Eisenhower was concerned about his troops was his realization that while he, SHAEF, the generals, and the admirals could plan, prepare the ground, provide covering support, ensure adequate supplies, deceive the Germans, and in countless other ways try to ensure victory, in the end success rested with the footslogger carrying a rifle over the beaches of Normandy. If he was willing to drive forward in the face of German fire, Overlord would succeed. If he cowered behind the beached landing craft, it would fail. The operation all came down to that.

For that reason, Eisenhower spent much of his pre D-Day time visiting troops in the field. He wanted to let as many men as possible see him. He made certain that every soldier who was to go ashore on D-Day had the opportunity to at least look at the man who was sending him into battle; he managed to talk to hundreds personally. In the four months from February 1 to June 1 he visited twenty-six divisions, twenty-four airfields, five ships of war, and countless depots, shops, hospitals, and other installations. He would have the men break ranks, gather around him while he made a short speech, then go around shaking hands.

He always managed to talk to the enlisted men as individuals. Other generals did so too, of course, but none had Eisenhower's touch. Bradley, Patton, Montgomery, and the rest would ask a man about his military specialty, his training, his unit, his weapons.

Eisenhower's first question invariably was "Where are you from?" He wanted to know about their families, what they did in civilian life back in the States, what their postwar plans were. He enjoyed discussing cattle ranching in Texas with them, or dairy farming in Wisconsin, or logging in Montana. To Eisenhower's associates, the men were soldiers; to Eisenhower, they were citizens temporarily caught up in a war none of them wanted, but which they realized was necessary. His face would light up whenever he met a boy from Kansas; he kept hoping to find one from Abilene, but never did. The British and Canadians responded as enthusiastically to Eisenhower's friendliness, informality, curiosity about them as individuals and sincerity as did the Americans.

To the graduating class at Sandhurst, in the spring of 1944, Eisenhower delivered an impromptu, ad-lib address that ranks as one of his best. He spoke of the great issues involved, and made each individual aware that his own chances for a happy, decent life were directly tied up in the success of Overlord. He reminded them of the great traditions of Sandhurst. He told the newly commissioned officers that they must be like fathers to their men, even when the men were twice their age, that they must keep the enlisted men out of trouble, and stand up for them when they committed a transgression. Their companies, he said, returning to his favorite theme, must be like a big family, and they must be the head of the family, ensuring that the unit was cohesive, tough, well trained, well equipped, ready to go. The response of the Sandhurst graduates, according to Thor Smith, a public-relations officer at SHAEF, was "electric. They just loved him." [18]

The commander of the U.S. First Army, Bradley, had already been selected by Marshall, on the basis of Eisenhower's enthusiastic recommendation. Eisenhower had selected Patton to lead the follow-up army, the Third. Until the Third Army was activated, Patton's role was to command a fictitious army group at Dover as part of the deception plan. This kept him out of the active preparations and made him even more nervous and irritable than usual. To increase his visibility to the Germans, he attended numerous public functions. On April 25, at the opening of a club sponsored by British women for American servicemen, he spoke on Anglo-American unity. He told the audience it was an important subject, "since it is the evident destiny of the British and Americans to rule the world, [and] the better we know each other the better job we will do." A reporter covering the event put the statement out over the wire services; it was widely circulated. A storm of criticism at Patton's indiscretion broke, and Eisenhower had another problem to deal with. Marshall, much upset, wired Eisenhower. The Chief said he had just sent a list of "permanent makes," that is, permanent Regular Army promotions, to the Senate, and Patton's name was on the list. Marshall sadly noted, "This I fear has killed them all." He asked Eisenhower to investigate and report.[19]

"Apparently he is unable to use reasonably good sense," Eisenhower said of Patton. "I have grown so weary of the trouble he constantly causes you and the War Department to say nothing of myself, that I am seriously contemplating the most drastic action." Marshall responded the same day. "You carry the burden of responsibility as to the success of Overlord." If Eisenhower thought the operation could succeed without Patton and wanted to relieve him, "all well and good." If Eisenhower felt that he had to have Patton, "then between us we can bear the burden . . . of keeping him."[20]

Eisenhower sent a stinging letter to Patton. He said that he was not so upset at the press reaction as at "the implication that you simply will not guard your tongue. . . . I have warned you time and again against your impulsiveness in action and speech . . ." The incident forced Eisenhower to doubt Patton's "all-around judgment, so essential in high military position." He concluded by saying he had not decided on what action to take, but if in the meantime Patton did anything that in any way embarrassed the War Department or SHAEF, "I will relieve you instantly."[21]

At 11 A.M. on May 1, Patton was ushered into Eisenhower's office. An old hand at getting out of a fix, Patton let out all the stops. He was plunged into despair, said he felt like death, but he would fight if "they" would let him. He dramatically offered to resign his commission to save his dearest friend from embarrassment. Although wearing his helmet (he was the only officer who ever wore a helmet for an interview with Eisenhower at Bushey Park), he was the picture of remorse, looking like a small boy who had inadvertently committed a big sin and who was deeply ashamed of himself.

Eisenhower could not bring himself to send "Georgie" home. He said he had decided to keep him on. Tears streamed down Patton's face. He assured Eisenhower of his gratitude and loyalty. As Eisenhower later described it, "in a gesture of almost little-boy contriteness, he put his head on my shoulder." That caused his helmet to fall off and tumble across the floor. The whole scene struck Eisenhower as "ridiculous," and he terminated the interview.[22]

Patton, now smiling and jaunty, returned to Dover, where he noted in his diary that he had pulled a fast one on Ike. He claimed his retention in command "is not the result of an accident," but rather was "the work of God."

Butcher was never as taken in by Patton as Eisenhower was. He noted that Patton "is a master of flattery and succeeds in turning any difference of views with Ike into a deferential acquiescence to the views of the Supreme Commander." But if Butcher saw something that Eisenhower missed, there was a reverse side to the coin. Patton bragged that he was tolerated as an eccentric genius because he was considered indispensable, and he was right. The very qualities that made him a great actor also made him a great commander, and Eisenhower knew it. "You owe us some victories," Eisenhower told Patton when the incident was closed. "Pay off and the world will deem me a wise man."[23]

On May 15, Eisenhower's commanders met at the ancient St. Paul's School, in West Kensington, for a final review. St. Paul's was Montgomery's 21st Army Group Headquarters (it had also been his boyhood school) and the show was primarily his. It was a distinguished, rather than a large, gathering. SHAEF sent out formal, engraved invitations. The King was there, the Prime Minister, and other notables. Eisenhower made a brief speech of welcome, then turned the stage over to Montgomery. He had a huge relief map of Normandy the width of a city street on the floor and—as Bradley recalled—"with rare skill, Monty traced his 21st Group plan of maneuver as he trampled about like a giant through Lilliputian France."[24]

In deference to Eisenhower and Churchill, Montgomery even broke his long-standing rule and allowed smoking in his presence. He began by reminding the audience of the problem—the Germans had sixty divisions in France, ten of them armored, commanded by the redoubtable Rommel. Montgomery called his opponent "an energetic and determined commander; he had made a world of difference since he took over [in January]. He is best at the spoiling attack; his forte is disruption; he is too impulsive for the set-piece battle. He will do his level best . . . to prevent our tanks landing, by using his own tanks well forward."

German morale was high. The enemy believed that, through a combination of the underwater obstacles, the fixed coastal defenses, and the extensive, well-manned trench system, the Allies could be stopped at the beaches. Then Rommel would call up his reinforcements, and his ability to do so, according to Allied intelligence, was impressive. Montgomery said Rommel might have nine divisions in the battle for Normandy by the second day, and thirteen by the third. By D-Day plus six, Rommel might counterattack with all ten panzer divisions. The SHAEF buildup, by contrast, would be exceedingly slow; the Germans thus expected to drive the Overlord forces back into the sea.

In spite of the gloomy predictions, when Montgomery turned to the Allied picture, he exuded optimism. As he talked and explained, he grew expansive. Storming the beaches was the least of his problems. He wanted to get well inland on D-Day itself and "crack about and force the battle to swing our way." It was possible, he said, that he would get to Falaise, thirty-two miles inland, the first day. He intended to send armored columns quickly toward Caen, for "this will upset the enemy's plans and tend to hold him off while we build up strength. We must gain space rapidly and peg claims well inland." He said he intended to take Caen the first day, break through the German lines on that (left, or eastern) flank, then drive along the coast toward the Seine River.

After Montgomery spoke, the King made a brief address. Then Churchill "let go with a slow-starting but fast-ending stemwinder. He preached bravery, ingenuity and persistence as human qualities of greater value than equipment." The King had to leave early; before he left, Eisenhower thanked him for his attendance and told him not to worry. There would be seven thousand planes overhead on D-Day, he said. The navies had "marshalled the greatest armada . . . the world had ever seen." All the ground troops had to do was to land and capture some villas for the VIPs, "particularly one to accommodate the King who would be . . . welcome in France."

Spaatz, Harris, Bradley, and the naval commander, Admiral Bertram Ramsay, then spoke on the role of the forces under their command in the great undertaking. Brooke, who was in a sour mood, was unimpressed. Spaatz bored him. In his diary, Brooke complained that "Harris told us how well he might have won the war if it had not been for the handicap imposed by the existence of the two other

Services." Brooke was especially worried about Eisenhower. "The main impression I gathered was that Eisenhower was no real director of thought, plans, energy or direction." He feared that the Supreme Commander was "just a co-ordinator, a good mixer, a champion of inter-Allied co-operation." He wondered if those abilities were sufficient for the task at hand and doubted it. As the meeting broke up (thus ending, the minutes noted, "the greatest assembly of military leadership the world had ever known"), Brooke was still shaking his head.[25]

But the meeting did help dispel Churchill's long-standing doubts. At the beginning of 1944 the Prime Minister had still wondered about the wisdom of a cross-Channel attack, saying to Eisenhower on one occasion, "When I think of the beaches of Normandy choked with the flower of American and British youth . . . I have my doubts . . . I have my doubts." Early in May, Eisenhower had lunched alone with Churchill. As they were parting, the Prime Minister grew emotional. With tears in his eyes he said, "I am in this thing with you to the end, and if it fails we will go down together." But after the St. Paul's briefing, Churchill told Eisenhower, "I am hardening toward this enterprise."[26]

Eisenhower, for his part, had never doubted that it could be done, not since that day in January 1942 when he had scribbled in his diary, "We've got to go to Europe and fight." Now his confidence was higher than ever. As he put it, "The smell of victory was in the air."[27]

He could not escape last-minute problems and worries. On May 29 Leigh-Mallory wrote him to say that he was disturbed over intelligence information acquired during the past week that indicated the Germans were reinforcing the area where the American paratroopers were going to drop. Leigh-Mallory said that it was probable that "at the most 30 percent of the glider loads will become effective for use against the enemy." He concluded that the airborne operation was likely "to yield results so far short of what [you] expect and require that if the success of the seaborne assault . . . depends on the airborne, it will be seriously prejudiced." He wanted the airborne assault canceled. Thinking the matter over, Leigh-Mallory then decided that his letter alone was not sufficient, and on May 30 he called on Eisenhower to present his case personally. He spoke of the "futile slaughter" of two fine divisions (the 82d and 101st Airborne), warning that losses might run as high as 70 percent.[28]

As Eisenhower later put it, "It would be difficult to conceive of a more soul-racking problem." He knew that Bradley counted on the paratroopers. He went to his tent, alone, and thought about the alternatives. He decided that the greater risk was in cancellation, went to the telephone, and told Leigh-Mallory that the operation would go ahead as scheduled.

He followed up the call with a latter, telling Leigh-Mallory that there "is nothing for it" but for the commanders to "work out to the last detail every single thing that may diminish the hazards." Eisenhower also ordered him to see to it that the troops involved were not needlessly depressed. "Like all the rest of the soldiers, they must understand that they have a tough job to do but be fired with determination to get it done." [29]

On June 2, Eisenhower drove from London to Southwick House, just north of Portsmouth, a lovely country estate with broad vistas, site of Admiral Ramsay's headquarters, which Eisenhower now took over for SHAEF, making it his advance command post.

There, he wrote an Order of the Day: "Soldiers, Sailors and Airmen of the Allied Expeditionary Force: You are about to embark upon the Great Crusade, toward which we have striven these many months. The eyes of the world are upon you. The hopes and prayers of liberty-loving people everywhere march with you. In company with our brave Allies and brothers-in-arms on other Fronts you will bring about the destruction of the German war machine, the elimination of Nazi tyranny over oppressed peoples of Europe, and security for ourselves in a free world. I have full confidence in your courage, devotion to duty and skill in battle. We will accept nothing less than full victory! Good luck! And let us all beseech the blessing of Almighty God upon this great and noble undertaking."

At Southwick House, on June 3, Eisenhower also wrote a memorandum for his diary. It gave him a chance to occupy his time and allowed him to put his worries into perspective. At the top of his list was de Gaulle, and he dictated three paragraphs on the difficulties of dealing with the French. Next came weather. "The weather in this country is practically unpredictable," he complained. If it turned bad, he knew he would be advised by at least some of his associates to call off the invasion. That might mean a delay of some weeks. "Probably no one that does not have to bear the specific and direct responsibility of making the final decision as to what to do," he declared, "can understand the intensity of these burdens." Only the Supreme Commander could sort out conflicting weather reports and decide on which one to act. Only he could make the kind of judgment involved if, for example, the weather were suitable for all other plans, but unsuitable for the airborne operation. In that case should he risk the airborne movement anyway, or defer the whole operation in hopes of getting better weather?

Outside Eisenhower's tent the wind was coming up and the sky darkening. He would soon have to make the final decision. "My tentative thought," he recorded before going to meet with the weathermen again, "is that the desirability for getting started on the next favorable tide is so great and the uncertainty of the weather is such that we could never anticipate really perfect weather coincident with proper tidal conditions, that we must go unless there is a real and very serious deterioration in the weather." [30]

Then he found time to think of John. His son was about to graduate from West Point, a great day in John's life, and for his father too. Ike wrote Mamie, who was going to the Academy for the ceremonies, "There's nothing I would not have given to have been with you and John on June 6, but c'est la guerre!" [31]

The AEF was set to go, living on the edge of fearful anticipation. "The mighty host," in Eisenhower's words, "was tense as a coiled spring," ready for "the moment when its energy should be released and it would vault the English Channel." [32]

SHAEF had prepared for everything except the weather. It now became an obsession. It was the one thing for which no one could plan, and the one thing that no one could control. In the end, the most completely planned military operation in history was dependent on the caprice of winds and waves. Tides and moon conditions were predictable, but storms were not. From the beginning, everyone had counted on at least acceptable weather for D-Day. There had been no contingency planning. Eisenhower's inclination, as he noted in his diary, was to go, whatever the weather, but if he held to a rigid timetable and conditions became really bad, the invasion might fail. Wind-tossed landing craft could founder before reaching the shore, or the waves might throw the troops up on the beaches, seasick and unable to fight effectively. The Allies would not be able to use their air superiority to cover the beaches. If Overlord failed, it would take months to plan and mount another operation, too late for 1944.

The evening of June 3, Eisenhower met in the mess room at Southwick House with his commanders and RAF Group Captain J. M. Stagg, his chief weatherman. Stagg had bad news. A high-pressure system was moving out, and a low was coming in. The weather on June 5 would be overcast and stormy, with a cloud base of five hundred feet to zero and Force 5 winds. Worse, the situation was deteriorating so rapidly that forecasting more than twenty-four hours in advance was highly undependable. It was too early to make a final decision, but word had to go out to the American Navy carrying Bradley's troops to Omaha and Utah beaches, since they had the farthest to travel. Eisenhower decided to let them start the voyage, subject to a possible last-minute cancellation. He would make the final decision at the regular weather conference the next morning.

At 4:30 A.M. on Sunday, June 4, Eisenhower met with his subordinates at Southwick House. Stagg said sea conditions would be slightly better than anticipated, but the overcast would not permit the use of the air forces. Montgomery said he wanted to go ahead anyway. Tedder and Leigh-Mallory wanted postponement. Ramsay said the Navy could do its part but remained neutral when asked whether or not the whole operation should go.

Eisenhower remarked that Overlord was being launched with ground forces that were not overwhelmingly powerful. The operation was feasible only because of Allied air superiority. If he could not have that advantage, the landings were too risky. He asked if anyone present disagreed, and when no one did he declared for a twenty-four-hour postponement. The word went out to the American fleet by prearranged signal. Displaying superb seamanship, the fleet drove through the incoming storm, regained its ports, refueled, and prepared to sail again the next day.

That evening, June 4, Eisenhower ate at Southwick House. After dinner he moved into the mess room. Montgomery, Tedder, Smith, Ramsay, Leigh-Mallory, Strong, and various high-ranking staff officers were already there. The wind and the rain rattled the window frames in the French doors in staccato sounds. The mess room was large, with a heavy table at one end and easy chairs at the other. Two sides of the room were lined with bookcases, most of which were empty and forlorn. A third side consisted of the French doors; the fourth wall was covered with a huge map of southern England and Normandy, filled with pins, arrows, and other symbols of Allied and German units. The officers lounged in easy chairs. Coffee was served and there was desultory conversation. Stagg came in about nine-thirty with the latest weather report. Eisenhower called his associates to order and they all sat up to listen intently.

Stagg reported a break. Kenneth Strong, the SHAEF G-2, recalled that at Stagg's prediction, "a cheer went up. You never heard middle-aged men cheer like that!" The rain that was then pouring down, Stagg continued, would stop in two or three hours, to be followed by thirty-six hours of more or less clear weather. Winds would moderate. The bombers and fighters ought to be able to operate on Monday night, June 5–6, although they would be hampered by clouds.

Leigh-Mallory remarked that it seemed to be only a moderately good night for air power. Tedder, his pipe clenched between his teeth and forcibly blowing out smoke, agreed that the operations of heavy bombers were going to be "chancy." Eisenhower countered by pointing out that the Allies could call on their large force of fighter-bombers.

The temptation to postpone again and meet the following morning for another conference was strong and growing, but Ramsay put a stop to that idea by pointing out that Admiral Alan G. Kirk, commanding the American task force, "must be told in the next half hour if Overlord is to take place on Tuesday [June 6]. If he is told it is on, and his forces sail and are then recalled, they will not be ready again for Wednesday morning. Therefore, a further postponement would be forty-eight hours." A two-day delay would put everything back to June 8, and by that time the tidal conditions would not be right, so in fact postponement now meant postponement until June 19.

Whatever Eisenhower decided would be risky. He began pacing the room, head down, chin on his chest, hands clasped behind his back.

Suddenly he shot his chin out at Smith. "It's a helluva gamble but it's the best possible gamble," Smith said. Eisenhower nodded, tucked his chin away, paced some more, then shot it out at Montgomery, huddled in his greatcoat, his face almost hidden.

"Do you see any reason for not going Tuesday?" Montgomery straightened up, looked Eisenhower in the eye, and replied, "I would say—Go!"

Eisenhower nodded, tucked away his chin, paced, looked abruptly at Tedder. Tedder again indicated he thought it chancy. Finally Eisenhower halted, looked around at his commanders, and said, "The question is just how long can you hang this operation on the end of a limb and let it hang there?"

If there was going to be an invasion before June 19, Eisenhower had to decide now. Smith was struck by the "loneliness and isolation of a commander at a time when such a momentous decision was to be taken by him, with full knowledge that failure or success rests on his individual decision." Looking out at the wind-driven rain, it hardly seemed possible that the operation could go ahead. Eisenhower calmly weighed the alternatives, and at 9:45 P.M. said, "I am quite positive that the order must be given."

Ramsay rushed out and gave the order to the fleets. More than five thousand ships began moving toward France. Eisenhower drove back to his trailer and slept fitfully. He awoke at 3:30 A.M. A wind of almost hurricane proportions was shaking his trailer. The rain seemed to be traveling in horizontal streaks. He dressed and gloomily drove through a mile of mud to Southwick House for the last meeting. It was still not too late to call off the operation.

In the now familiar mess room, steaming hot coffee helped shake the gray mood and unsteady feeling. Stagg said that the break he had been looking for was on its way and that the weather would be clearing within a matter of hours. The long-range prediction was not good, to be sure, but even as he talked the rain began to stop and the sky started to clear.

A short discussion followed, Eisenhower again pacing, shooting out his chin, asking opinions. Montgomery still wanted to go, as did Smith. Ramsay was concerned about proper spotting for naval gunfire but thought the risk worth taking. Tedder was ready. Leigh-Mallory still thought air conditions were below the acceptable minimum.

Everyone stated his opinion. Stagg withdrew to let the generals and admirals make the decision. No new weather reports would be available for hours. The ships were sailing into the Channel. If they were to be called back, it had to be done now. The Supreme Commander was the only man who could do it. Eisenhower thought for a moment, then said quietly but clearly, "O.K., let's go." And again, cheers rang through Southwick House.[33]

Then the commanders rushed from their chairs and dashed outside to get to their command posts. Within thirty seconds the mess room was empty, except for Eisenhower. The outflow of the others and his sudden isolation were symbolic. A minute earlier he had been the most powerful man in the world. Upon his word the fate of thousands of men depended, and the future of great nations. The moment he uttered the word, however, he was powerless. For the next two or three days there was almost nothing he could do that would in any way change anything. The invasion could not be stopped, not by him, not by anyone. A captain leading his company onto Omaha, or a platoon sergeant at Utah, would for the immediate future play a greater role than Eisenhower. He could now only sit and wait.

Eisenhower was improving at killing time. He visited South Parade Pier in Portsmouth to see some British soldiers climb aboard their landing craft, then returned to his trailer. He played a game of checkers on a cracker box with Butcher, who was winning, two kings to one, when Eisenhower jumped one of his kings and got a draw. At lunch they exchanged political yarns. After eating, Eisenhower went into a tent with representatives of the press and announced that the invasion was on. Smith called with more news about de Gaulle. After hanging up, Eisenhower looked out the tent flap, saw a quick flash of sunshine, and grinned.

When the reporters left, Eisenhower sat at his portable table and scrawled a press release on a pad of paper, to be used if necessary. "Our landings . . . have failed . . . and I have withdrawn the troops," he began. "My decision to attack at this time and place was based upon the best information available. The troops, the air and the Navy did all that bravery and devotion to duty could do. If any blame or fault attaches to the attempt it is mine alone."[34]

Putting the note in his wallet, Eisenhower went to dinner. Then at 6 P.M. he and a group of aides drove to Newbury, where the 101st Airborne was loading up for the flight to Normandy. The 101st was one of the units Leigh-Mallory feared would suffer 70 percent casualties. Eisenhower wandered around among the men, whose blackened faces gave them a grotesque look, stepping over packs, guns, and other equipment.

A group recognized him and gathered around. He chatted with them easily. He told them not to worry, that they had the best equipment and leaders. A sergeant said, "Hell, we ain't worried, General. It's the Krauts that ought to be worrying now." When he met a trooper from Dodge City, Eisenhower gave him a thumbs up and said, "Go get 'em, Kansas!" And a private piped up, "Look out, Hitler, here we come." A Texan promised Eisenhower a job after the war on his cattle ranch. Eisenhower stayed until all the big C-47s were off the runway.[35]

As the last plane roared into the sky Eisenhower turned to Kay, who was his driver that night, with a visible sagging in his shoulders. She saw tears in his eyes. He began to walk slowly toward his car. "Well," he said quietly, "it's on." It took nearly two hours to get back to camp on the narrow British country roads. Eisenhower arrived at his trailer at 1:15 A.M., June 6. He sat around and chatted with Butcher for a while, then finally went to bed.[36]

Shortly before 7 A.M. Ramsay called to tell him everything was going according to plan. Then Butcher came over to his trailer with good news fom Leigh-Mallory—the air drop had been a success and casualties were light. Butcher found the Supreme Commander sitting up in bed, smoking a cigarette and reading a Western novel.

Through the morning, news from the beachhead was spotty and sometimes contradictory. Eisenhower sent a brief message to Marshall, informing him that everything seemed to be going well and adding that the British and American troops he had seen the previous day were enthusiastic, tough, and fit. "The light of battle was in their eyes."[37]

At noon, a messenger brought a note from Leigh-Mallory; he said that it was sometimes difficult to admit that one was wrong, but he had never had a greater pleasure in doing so than on this occasion. He congratulated Eisenhower on the wisdom of his command decision in sending the airborne troops in and apologized for having added to the Supreme Commander's worries.

For the remainder of the day Eisenhower paced, his mood alternating between joy and worry as he received news of the situation on the British and Canadian beaches, where the opposition was remarkably light; from Utah, where the Americans were well established; and from Omaha, where the troops were pinned down by surprisingly heavy German fire. After eating, Eisenhower retired to get a good night's sleep.

At a cost of only 2,500 casualties, mainly at Omaha, his men had gained a striking victory. More than 23,000 airborne troops had dropped into Normandy the night of June 5–6 and 57,500 Americans and 75,215 British and Canadian troops had come ashore during the day. More than 156,000 Allied soldiers had breached Hitler's much-vaunted Atlantic Wall.

The figures give an indication of the scope of Overlord. It was as if a city the size of Madison, Wisconsin, or Baton Rouge, Louisiana, or most of the state capitals in the United States, had been picked up —vehicles, buildings, people, everything—and moved sixty to one hundred miles in one night, against determined opposition. Nothing like it had ever been seen before, or would again.

The next few days were spent in consolidating gains. Nowhere along the front had initial objectives been fully achieved on D-Day or even D plus one and two, but the Allies held the initiative by putting the pressure on the Germans everywhere. By the end of the first week of the invasion Eisenhower's forces had consolidated a bridgehead eight to twelve miles deep and sixty miles wide. Eisenhower kept busy, holding press conferences, answering messages of congratulations, dealing with de Gaulle, talking to Churchill, gathering incoming information, and urging all his subordinates to redouble their efforts. He removed a division commander who had failed the test of combat.

On June 10, Marshall, Arnold, and King arrived in London, ostensibly for a meeting of the CCS, in reality because they wanted to see the great invasion for themselves. On June 12 Eisenhower, Marshall, King, Arnold, and members of their staffs crossed the Channel in a destroyer and went ashore on Juno Beach. They lunched on C rations and discussed recent operations with some of the corps and division commanders. Marshall praised Eisenhower, although characteristically not to his face. "Eisenhower and his staff are cool and confident," the Chief reported to Roosevelt, "carrying out an affair of incredible magnitude and complication with superlative efficiency."[38]

The trip to Juno symbolized the success of Overlord. If that much brass could safely go ashore in France, the beachhead was clearly secure. More than ten divisions were now engaged on the Allied side, with more coming in every day. There were still problems, but the great invasion had worked.

Eisenhower's gamble on the weather had paid off. What Churchill rightly called "the most difficult and complicated operation that has ever taken place" had put the Allies back on the Continent.

Ike, typically, was as excited by family news as by the great event. On June 9, he had sent a teletype to Mamie and John, at West Point, saying that "Due to previous plans it was impossible for me to be with you and John [for the graduation exercises] . . . but I thought of you and hope you and he had a nice time . . ." Then Marshall told him that he had made special arrangements for Second Lieutenant Eisenhower to spend his two-week graduation leave with his father. Ike beamed. "How I look forward to seeing Johnny. It will be odd to see him as an *officer of the Army!* I'll burst with pride!" On June 13, expecting his son to arrive in a couple of hours, he told Mamie, "I'm really as excited as a bride."[39]

When John arrived, late in the afternoon of June 13, he walked into his father's office, threw his arms around him, and kissed him on the cheek. "Ike was just one big grin," Kay reported.[40] She drove them to Telegraph Cottage, where they talked through most of the night. John had not seen his father since 1942, and he was both surprised and a bit amazed at the number of people who surrounded Ike and devoted their energies to translating his wishes into reality. Drivers, cooks, aides, houseboys—John had not sufficiently appreciated his father's importance until he saw them scurrying around whenever Ike indicated that he wanted this or that done. In the days that followed, John was further impressed by his father's easy familiarity with some of the most famous and powerful men in the world, and by the way in which the press reported on his every move.

Ike enjoyed impressing his son, but he did not like the notoriety. He wrote a friend, "When this war is over I am going to find the deepest hole there is in the United States, crawl in and pull it in after me."[41] John had brought with him a letter from Mamie that dealt with publicity—a Hollywood firm had offered Eisenhower a large financial inducement for the right to do a film biography. Mamie wrote that she felt he ought to accept the money.

Ike replied, "I can understand your feelings . . . but my own convictions as to the quality of a man that will make money out of a public position of trust are very strong! I couldn't touch it—and would never allow such a thing to occur. We don't need it anyway—it's fun to be poor!"[42]

During the two weeks that followed, John was constantly at his father's side. Ike assured Mamie that "I love to be with him," that "he and I have talked, every night, well past midnight," and—on the eve of John's departure—"I hate to see him go!" But he also admitted that "it is difficult to tell when he is pleased."[43]

In truth, there was a certain awkwardness in their relationship. Ike's position and the never-ending demands on his concentration added to the normal difficulties inherent in a father-son relationship when the son has emerged into manhood. John was a bit stiff and shy to begin with, and very much the recent West Point graduate, shouting out his "Yes, sir!" and "No, sir!" responses, bracing to full attention and snapping out his salutes.

When Second Lieutenant Eisenhower offered textbook advice on military problems to Supreme Commander Eisenhower, the general would snort and exclaim, "Oh, for God's sake!" Concerned about military protocol, one day John asked his father, "If we should meet an officer who ranks above me but below you, how do we handle this?

Should I salute first . . .?" Annoyed, Ike snapped, "John, there isn't an officer in this theater who doesn't rank above you and below me."

John got to know Kay and, as did almost everyone else, had liked her immediately. He noted her popularity and how relaxed his father was in her presence. In the evenings, he and Butcher took on Kay and Ike in a few rubbers of bridge. Ike was highly critical—almost embarrassingly so—of John's play.

John wanted to see the battle zone. On June 15 his father took him along on a flight to the British sector. Together with Tedder, they drove to Bayeux, headquarters of the British Second Army and home of William the Conqueror, the only other man—save Eisenhower and Caesar—to have successfully commanded a cross-Channel attack.

Driving around the beachhead area, John was startled to see vehicles moving bumper to bumper, in complete violation of textbook doctrine. "You'd never get away with this if you didn't have air supremacy," he told his father. Ike snorted, "If I didn't have air supremacy, I wouldn't be here." [44]

The Normandy battle was not going well. The Americans, on the right, or western, flank, found themselves fighting in a country of small fields separated by hedges, banks, and sunken roads. Tanks could not operate, while the infantry had to advance from hedgerow to hedgerow, a painfully slow and expensive process against the skillful and determined German resistance. On the left, Montgomery had promised to take Caen on the first day, but had not done so even by the end of June. Less than two weeks after the exultation over the success of D-Day came the letdown, and with it a severe strain on Anglo-American relations in general, and the relations between Eisenhower and Montgomery specifically.

That the two men would have difficulty in dealing with each other was almost inevitable, given the contrasts between them. Eisenhower was gregarious, while Montgomery lived in isolation. Eisenhower mixed easily with his staff and discussed all decisions with his subordinates; Montgomery set himself up in a lonely camp, where he slept and ate in a wood-paneled trailer he had captured from Rommel in the desert. Montgomery wrote his directives by hand and handed them down from on high, while Eisenhower waited for general agreement among his staff and usually had his operations officer write the final directive. Montgomery had shunned the company of women after his wife's death and did not smoke or drink. Eisenhower was modest, Montgomery conceited. "I became completely dedicated to my profession," Montgomery once said of himself.[45]

He had indeed made an intensive study of how to command. What he had not studied was how to get his ideas across. He always seemed to be talking down to people, and his condescension became more marked the more intensely he felt about a subject. Montgomery's arrogance offended even British officers, while most Americans found him insufferable. What one American called "his sharp beagle-like nose, the small grey eyes that dart about quickly like rabbits in a Thurber cartoon," his self-satisfaction, all irritated.[46]

The personality differences were significant factors in the always strained Eisenhower-Montgomery relationship, but what mattered more was fundamental disagreement over strategy and tactics, and their different structural positions. Eisenhower's military theory was straightforward and aggressive. Like Grant in the Virginia Wilderness in 1864, he favored constant attack, all along the line. He was an advocate of the direct approach and put his faith in the sheer smashing power of great armies. He was once accused of having a mass-production mentality, which was true but beside the point. He came from a mass-production society, and like any good general he wanted to use his nation's strengths on the battlefield.

To Montgomery, "it was always very clear . . . that Ike and I were poles apart when it came to the conduct of the war." Montgomery believed in "unbalancing the enemy while keeping well-balanced myself." He wanted to attack on a narrow front, cut through the German lines, and dash on to his objective.[47]

Further, Eisenhower was responsible to the CCS, and beyond that body to the two governments. Montgomery was in theory responsible to Eisenhower, but in reality he looked to Brooke, not Eisenhower, for guidance. Montgomery was the senior British officer on the Continent, and as such saw himself as responsible for his nation's interests. The British had neither the manpower nor the material resources to overwhelm the Germans, and they had learned, from 1914 to 1918, that it was near suicidal for them to attempt to do so. The British strength was brains, not brawn. Montgomery proposed to defeat the Germans in France by outthinking and outmaneuvering them; Eisenhower wanted to outfight them.

The initial difficulty centered around the taking of Caen. Montgomery had promised it, did not have it, would not attack it. By mid-June, he was claiming that he had never intended to break out of the beachhead at Caen, on the direct road to Paris; rather, his strategy was to hold on the left while Bradley broke out on the right. His critics charge that he changed his plan because of his failure at Caen; Montgomery himself insisted that he had all along planned to pin the German panzers down in front of Caen while Bradley outflanked them. There is a fierce, continuing, and unresolvable controversy among military experts on this point.

On July 1, Eisenhower went to Normandy to see what he could do to galvanize his commanders. He told Bradley he was bringing "nothing but a bedroll, one aide and an orderly" and wanted "nothing but a trench with a piece of canvas over it."[48] He stayed five days, visiting with troops, inspecting the battlefield, talking with Bradley and the American corps and division commanders. None of them liked having Eisenhower around, because their various headquarters were all subject to sporadic German artillery fire. Eisenhower's old friend Wade Haislip, commanding the XV Corps, told him flatly to get out. "Don't think I'm worrying about your possible demise," he added. "I just don't want it said that I allowed the Supreme Commander to get killed in my corps area. Now if you want to get killed, go into some other area."[49]

At one point Eisenhower commandeered a jeep and, accompanied by his British aide, James Gault, and an orderly, with no other escort, personally drove around the countryside, and even managed to wander behind the German lines. No startling events occurred, and he did not know he had been in danger until he reached 90th Division headquarters and was told where he had been. The GIs were delighted to see Eisenhower driving the jeep and shouted and whistled as he drove past.

On July 4, Eisenhower went to a fighter airfield; while there, he learned that a mission was about to be flown. Eisenhower said he wanted to go along in order to see the hedgerow country from the air. Bradley, who was with him, demurred, but Eisenhower insisted. His last words, as he climbed into a Mustang, were "All right, Brad, I am not going to fly to Berlin."[50]

When he got back to Bushey Park, disappointed at the lack of progress in the hedgerows, despairing of ever breaking out in that awful country, Tedder and Smith both told him that it was all Montgomery's fault. They insisted that Eisenhower had to force him to act. Tedder complained that Montgomery was unjustly blaming the air forces for his own failure and said that "the Army did not seem prepared to fight its own battles."[51]

Eisenhower wrote a letter to Montgomery, but it was too weak—more a statement of desired objectives than a firm order—to impel action. On July 12, Patton commented in his diary, "Ike is bound hand and foot by the British and does not know it. Poor fool. We actually have no Supreme Commander—no one who can take hold and say that this shall be done and that shall not be done."[52] There was a general uneasy feeling around SHAEF that Eisenhower would never take hold of Montgomery. Gossips at SHAEF were speculating on "who would succeed Monty if sacked." This simple solution was, to Eisenhower, out of the question, because of Montgomery's popularity with the British troops, Brooke, and the British public. Further, Eisenhower had no right to remove the senior British commander. The Supreme Commander seems to have been the only man at SHAEF to recognize these obvious truths, and they provide the answer to the nagging question, Why did Eisenhower put up with Montgomery? He had no choice. He had to cooperate with the difficult and exasperating British general, for Montgomery's place in the command structure was secure.

The real threat to Montgomery's position was Tedder's recommendation that Eisenhower move his headquarters to Normandy and take personal control of the land battle. Montgomery knew that he needed to buy time, not so much to protect his position as to keep Eisenhower in England so that he could run the land battle.

On July 18 Montgomery finally launched an attack, code name Goodwood. In its initial stages, assisted by the tremendous air bombardment, it went well. But after Montgomery lost 401 tanks and suffered 2,600 casualties, he called it off. The British Second Army had taken Caen, gained a few square miles, and inflicted heavy casualties on the Germans, but there had been nothing like a breakthrough. Montgomery announced that he was satisfied with the results.

Eisenhower was angry. He thundered that it had taken more than seven thousand tons of bombs to gain seven miles and that the Allies could hardly hope to go through France paying a price of a thousand tons of bombs per mile. Tedder blamed Montgomery for "the Army's failure," and SHAEF officers wondered aloud whether Montgomery should be made a peer and sent to the House of Lords or given the governorship of Malta.[53]

This was all wild and irresponsible talk. After the war, Eisenhower said he felt the powers of a supreme commander should be greater, that he should have the right to dismiss any subordinate, whatever his nationality. But even had Eisenhower had that power in 1944, he would not have exercised it. Sensitive to the morale factor and keenly aware of Montgomery's great popularity, he would not consider asking for Montgomery's removal.

At Smith's and Tedder's urging, Eisenhower sent a letter to Montgomery. *"Time is vital,"* he said, and he urged Montgomery to resume the attack. Many American officers thought that Montgomery hesitated because of the critical British manpower situation. The United Kingdom could no longer make good the losses in the Second Army, so it could not afford the cost in casualties of an all-out attack. Eisenhower argued that an attack now would save lives in the long run.[54]

Everyone was depressed, irritable. After seven weeks of fighting, the deepest Allied penetrations were some twenty-five to thirty miles inland, on a front of only eighty miles, hardly enough room to maneuver or to bring in the American forces waiting in England for deployment. The Americans were still struggling in the hedgerow country, measuring their advance in yards rather than miles. Goodwood had failed and Montgomery refused to mount another attack. The newspapers were full of the ugly word "stalemate."

There were two bright spots. Ultra radio intercepts revealed that the Germans were stretched to the limit, and Bradley was working on a plan, code name Cobra, to break out on the right. As Eisenhower noted in his letter to Montgomery, "Now we are pinning our hopes on Bradley."

By July 23, the Americans had landed a total of 770,000 troops in Normandy. First Army had suffered 73,000 casualties. The British and Canadians had landed 591,000 troops and suffered 49,000 casualties. There was a large, immediately available reserve of American divisions in England waiting to enter the battle. The Germans in Normandy, meanwhile, had twenty-six divisions in place, six of them armored, to face the AEF's thirty-four divisions. As the Allies were on the offensive, their superiority on the ground was only marginal; in addition, the German Fifteenth Army was still intact in the Pas de Calais, which meant that the German ability to reinforce was greater than that of the Allies.

Eisenhower's great advantage continued to be control of the air. Bradley planned to use it in Operation Cobra to break through the German lines; once he was through, Eisenhower intended to rush divisions over from England, activate Patton's Third Army, and send it racing for Brittany to open the ports there.

The problem with air power was weather; it was a weapon that could be used only under suitable conditions. Cobra was scheduled to begin on July 21. That day Eisenhower flew over to Normandy to witness the beginning. The sky was overcast and his B-25 was the only plane in the air. By the time he arrived it was raining hard. Bradley told him the attack had been called off and dressed him down for flying in such weather. Eisenhower tossed away his soggy cigarette, smiled, and said his only pleasure in being Supreme Commander was that nobody could ground him.

"When I die," he added, looking at the steady rain, "they ought to hold my body for a rainy day and then bury me out in the middle of a storm. This damned weather is going to be the death of me yet."[55]

The next day, as the rains continued, he flew back to London; on the twenty-fourth, still waiting for a clear day, he wired Bradley, urging him to an all-out effort when the weather permitted. "A break through at this juncture will minimize the total cost," he said, and added that he wanted First Army to "pursue every advantage with an ardor verging on recklessness." If it broke through, "the results will be incalculable."[56]

Bradley hardly needed urging, but Montgomery did. Eisenhower wanted Second Army to attack when Cobra began—indeed had promised Bradley he would see to it—so after sending his message to Bradley, Eisenhower flew to Montgomery's headquarters. What he wanted, as Smith noted, was "an all-out co-ordinated attack by the entire Allied line, which would at last put our forces in decisive motion. He was up and down the line like a football coach, exhorting everyone to aggressive action."[57]

All this was highly irritating to Montgomery and Brooke. "It is quite clear that Ike considers that [General Miles] Dempsey [commanding Second Army] should be doing more than he does," Brooke wrote to Montgomery. "It is equally clear that Ike has the very vaguest conception of war." The British officers agreed that Eisenhower had no notion of balance. If everybody was to attack, Montgomery argued, nobody would have the strength to make a decisive breakthrough or to exploit it. Eisenhower "evidently . . . has some conception of attacking on the whole front," Brooke complained, "which must be an American doctrine."[58]

Tedder too was unhappy with Eisenhower, but as usual he disagreed with Montgomery and Brooke. Cobra got started on the morning of July 25; that day, Tedder called Eisenhower on the telephone, demanding to know why Montgomery was not doing more and what Eisenhower was doing about it. Eisenhower said he had talked with Churchill and that they were satisfied that this time Montgomery's attack would be in earnest. Tedder "rather uh-huhed, being not at all satisfied, and implying the PM must have sold Ike a bill of goods." Eisenhower told Butcher of the conversation and said he thought he could work things out satisfactorily, for "there's nothing so wrong a good victory won't cure."[59]

He was right. On the second day of Cobra, U.S. First Army broke through. Eisenhower activated Patton's Third Army. General Courtney Hodges took command of First Army as Bradley moved up to command of 12th Army Group, consisting of First and Third Armies.

On August 1, Patton was unleashed and began his race through Brittany. The nightmare of a static front was over. "This is great news," Eisenhower exulted. Just before lunch on August 2, Butcher met Eisenhower in the hall at Bushey Park. The Supreme Commander was all smiles. "If the intercepts are right," he said, "we are to hell and gone in Brittany and slicing 'em up in Normandy."[60]

On August 7, Eisenhower set up an advance command post in Normandy, a tented headquarters in an apple orchard near Granville, which was less than twenty-five miles from Mortain and almost directly in the path of an expected German counterattack. He met with Bradley, and they immediately agreed to hold Mortain with minimal forces while rushing every available division south. They bolstered the flanks of the salient with American artillery and called in the fighter-bombers. Eisenhower told Bradley that "if the Germans should temporarily break through from Mortain to Avranches and thus cut off the southward thrust, we would give the advance forces two thousand tons of supply per day by air." The following morning, Eisenhower told Marshall, "The enemy's . . . counter attacks . . . make it appear that we have a good chance to encircle and destroy a lot of his forces."[61]

The gamble at Mortain paid off; in a classic defensive action, the 30th Division held, while the artillery and air forces virtually destroyed the German tanks. On August 9, the Germans broke off the counterattack. The Canadians and Patton were posing a threat to encircle them. The Allied offensive was in full swing, all forces meshing, aiming for the destruction of the German Seventh and Fifth Panzer Armies, which were in a huge salient, with the tip at Mortain and the base on the Falaise-Argentan line. "Ike keeps continually after both Montgomery and Bradley," Butcher noted, "to destroy the enemy now rather than to be content with mere gains of territory."[62]

The Canadian attack, however, went slowly. Patton, facing slimmer resistance, made a steady advance. By August 10, the Germans were nearly trapped; Patton's units had cut off all but one of the supply roads for the German armies. On August 12, Patton's lead corps reached Argentan. The Canadians were still short of Falaise.

Patton, impatient, wanted to cross the army boundary line and close the gap. He called Bradley on the telephone and pleaded, "Let me go on to Falaise and we'll drive the British back into the sea for another Dunkirk." Bradley refused. He did not believe Patton was strong enough to hold the gap once the Germans started the rush to escape. Besides, he thought the Canadians could complete the encirclement.[63]

By August 14 the Allies were on the verge of closing the trap. Eisenhower, Butcher reported, was "sunny, if not almost jubilant." He called for an all-out effort. On the fourteenth, he issued a rare Order of the Day (he sent out only ten in the course of the war), exhorting the Allied soldiers, sailors, and airmen. "The opportunity may be grasped only through the utmost in zeal, determination and speedy action," Eisenhower declared. If everyone did his job, "we can make this week a momentous one in the history of this war—a brilliant and fruitful week for us, a fateful one for the ambitions of the Nazi tyrants."[64] The Order of the Day was broadcast over BBC and the Allied radio network, and distributed to the troops in mimeographed form.

There was the greatest excitement at SHAEF, and indeed through the Allied world. Churchill, Roosevelt, Marshall, and Brooke all felt it. In New York, the stock market tumbled in anticipation of peace. Newspaper correspondents who had been overly pessimistic during the Normandy stalemate now asked Eisenhower, at an August 15 press conference, how many weeks it would take to end the war. In the days that followed, he would hear that question again and again. People thought of November 1918, when the German Army cracked, and expected a repetition in August or September of 1944. The thought persisted, indeed grew stronger and plagued Eisenhower until October.

The expectation of a German collapse was based on a misreading of the lesson of November 1918, an inaccurate assessment of the situation in August 1944, and a failure to understand the German character. In 1918 the Germans had been pushed behind their last defensive line, while in 1944 they still had the West Wall to fall back to. In 1918 the Germans had fallen behind in the technological race (it was the Allies who had the tanks), while in 1944 the Nazis could legitimately ask the Wehrmacht to hold on just a little longer, because Germany's secret weapons might well win the war for them; many of those weapons, such as the V-1s and V-2s, jet aircraft, and diesel submarines, were already realities. In 1918, it was the dim-witted, indecisive Kaiser and the shattered Ludendorff who had agreed to an armistice; Eisenhower knew that Hitler was made of sterner stuff.

Most of all, Eisenhower knew that the Germans would not quit until they were incapable of resistance. He knew it, in part, because of his own German heritage. He expected the Germans to fight until it was impossible for them to continue. He knew that they could retreat to the West Wall, and in the process fall back on their supply base, while the AEF supply lines grew longer. He also realized that because of the Transportation Plan, because his ground commanders had called on the heavy bombers so often in Normandy, and because of the bombing effort against the V-1 and V-2 sites, Germany itself was still relatively untouched. He knew that the Germans were producing more tanks, artillery, and other weapons in 1944 than in any previous year; he knew that the AEF was, therefore, in for a tremendous fight.

The theme appears again and again in his letters to his wife. On August 11, he told her, "Don't be misled by the papers. Every victory . . . is sweet—but the end of the war will come only with complete destruction of the Hun forces." In September, when expectations of a German collapse were even higher, he said, "I wonder how the people at home can be so complacent about finishing off the job we have here. There is still a lot of suffering to go through. God, I hate the Germans!"[65]

So, when reporters asked him on August 15 how many weeks to the end, he was furious. Butcher recorded, "Ike vehemently castigated those who think they can measure the end of the war 'in a matter of weeks.' He went on to say 'such people are crazy.' " Eisenhower reminded the press that Hitler knew he would hang when the war ended so he had nothing to lose in continuing it. In 1918, the Kaiser had had reason to hope for a soft peace on the basis of Wilson's Fourteen Points; in 1944, Hitler had only Roosevelt's unconditional surrender demand to contemplate.

Eisenhower told the reporters that he expected that Hitler would end up hanging himself, but before he did he would "fight to the bitter end," and most of his troops would fight with him.[66] It was a leap into the mind of the enemy, the highest form of the military art, and he was exactly right.

• •

Just how right Eisenhower was, the Germans demonstrated in the Falaise pocket. They rejected the easy way out—surrender—and fought to hold open their escape route. Despite Eisenhower's plea in his Order of the Day, it was the Germans, not the Allies, who made the supreme effort at Falaise. The rigidity with which the field commanders held to the boundary lines at Argentan and Falaise helped the Germans, to be sure, but the main factors were German fighting ability and determination. The gap was not closed until August 19; some forty thousand Wehrmacht troops escaped.

Eisenhower was disappointed but not downcast. "Due to the extraordinary defensive measures taken by the enemy," he explained to Marshall, "it is possible that our total bag of prisoners will not be so great as I first anticipated."[67] Falaise left a taste of bitterness and led to recrimination between the British and the Americans as to whose fault it was that any Germans escaped, much less forty thousand.

Still, the disappointment should not obscure the fact that Falaise *was* a victory. Some fifty thousand Germans were captured, another ten thousand were killed. Those who escaped left their equipment behind. Later in August, Eisenhower toured the battlefield with Kay, Jimmy Gault, and press representatives. Gault wrote, "We were certainly not disappointed in the results, because the scene was one of masses of destroyed tanks, guns, transports and equipment of all sorts lying around, including many dead Germans and horses. The smell was tremendous."[68]

Eisenhower said that the scene "could be described only by Dante. It was literally possible to walk for hundreds of yards at a time, stepping on nothing but dead and decaying flesh."[69] Falaise, in fact, ended the Battle of France. The Germans, those who were left, were retreating pell-mell toward the border. They could not defend the line of the Seine, nor any other in France; their only safety lay in the West Wall. But, as Eisenhower knew, although everyone around him seemed at one time or another to forget, victory in France did not mean the end of the war, and as he told Mamie in early August, "In war there is no substitute for victory."[70]

Following Falaise, the AEF overran France. Montgomery's 21st Army Group drove along the coast toward Belgium, while the First and Third Armies headed east, toward Paris and beyond to the German border. On August 23, the SHAEF G-2 summary declared, "The August battles have done it and the enemy in the West has had it.

Two and a half months of bitter fighting have brought the end of the war in Europe within sight, almost within reach." Patton said that he could cross the German border in ten days, then drive on almost at will to Berlin. And Montgomery told Eisenhower, "I consider we have now reached a stage where one really full-blooded thrust toward Berlin is likely to get there and thus end the German war."[71]

It was inevitable that the high command should feel so optimistic. The last two weeks of August and first week of September 1944 were among the most dramatic of the war, with great successes following one another in rapid succession. In France, First Army liberated Paris and 21st Army Group swept forward, covering in hours distances that had taken months and cost tens of thousands of lives to cross in World War I. In the last week of August alone, 21st Army Group covered two hundred miles. Rumania surrendered to the Soviets, then declared war on Germany. Finland signed a truce with the Russians. Bulgaria tried to surrender. The Germans pulled out of Greece. The Allies landed in the south of France and drove to Lyons and beyond, and 6th Army Group joined the AEF.

American troops continued to come from England to France, enough for the creation of yet another army, the Ninth, under Lieutenant General William Simpson. It was assigned to 12th Army Group. British and American paratroopers in England were organized into the First Allied Airborne Army and constituted a highly mobile reserve, ready to strike wherever Eisenhower directed. Alexander was attacking in Italy. The Russians' summer offensive carried the Red Army to Yugoslavia, destroying twelve German divisions and inflicting 700,000 casualties. The end of the war did indeed seem at hand.

But not to Eisenhower, who was more realistic than Marshall and the others. One of his major functions was the allocation of supplies to the field armies, which made him acutely aware that every step Montgomery's forces took to the northeast, and that Patton's army took toward the east, carried them farther away from the Normandy ports, adding to an already serious supply problem. On August 20 Eisenhower told reporters that his forces had advanced so rapidly and supply lines were so strained that "further movement in large parts of the front even against very weak opposition is almost impossible."[72]

The supply situation, which soon turned critical, raised the questions of priority and the nature of the advance into Germany. There are two natural invasion routes—north of the Ardennes, through

Belgium and Holland into northern Germany, and south of the Ardennes, straight east from Paris past Verdun and Metz to cross the Rhine at Mainz.

On August 19, Eisenhower told Montgomery and Bradley that it was his intention to take personal control of the land battle as soon as SHAEF could set up in France a forward command post with adequate communication facilities. He also outlined a plan of campaign that would send 21st Army Group northeast, toward Antwerp and the Ruhr, with 12th Army Group heading straight east from Paris toward Metz.

Now it was Montgomery's turn for anger. On August 22 he sent his chief of staff, Freddie de Guingand, to see Eisenhower and protest against both decisions. Montgomery argued that the quickest way to end the war was to hold Patton in Paris, give control of U.S. First Army and all incoming supplies to 21st Army Group, and send it to Antwerp and beyond to the Ruhr.

This force had to operate as a single unit under single control, which was "a WHOLE TIME job for one man." Montgomery warned that "to change the system of command now, after having won a great victory, would be to prolong the war." De Guingand pressed these points in a two-hour meeting with Eisenhower, but Eisenhower refused to change his mind. Montgomery then invited Eisenhower to come to his tactical headquarters at Condé for lunch the next day, August 23, to discuss future operations.[73]

Eisenhower drove to Condé for the meeting. Smith was with him, but when they arrived Montgomery abruptly announced that he wanted to see Eisenhower alone and thus Smith would have to stay outside. Eisenhower meekly accepted Montgomery's really quite insulting demand that Smith be locked out, even though de Guingand was with Montgomery.

Once inside the trailer, Montgomery tried his best to be tactful, but his idea of tact was to deliver a patronizing lecture on elementary strategy that a Sandhurst or West Point cadet would have found insulting. Standing before the map, his feet spread, hands behind his back, head up, eyes darting about, Montgomery outlined the situation, said the immediate need was for a firm plan, discussed logistics, told Eisenhower what the plans should be (a single thrust to the Ruhr by 21st Army Group, with First Army in support), declared that if Eisenhower's plan were followed the result would be failure, and told Eisenhower that he "should not descend into the land battle and become a ground C-in-C." He said that the Supreme Commander "must sit on a very lofty perch in order to be able to take a detached view of the whole intricate problem" and that someone must run the land battle for him. Eisenhower replied that he would not change his mind and intended to take control on September 1.

Unable to move Eisenhower on the question of command, Montgomery shifted to the real issue, the nature of the advance into Germany. He wanted Patton stopped where he was; he wanted the Airborne Army and First Army assigned to him; he wanted all available supplies; he wanted a directive that would send him through the Pas de Calais, on to Antwerp and Brussels, and beyond to the Ruhr.

Eisenhower, after an hour's argument, made some concessions, of which the most important were to give Montgomery control of the Airborne Army and the "authority to effect the necessary operational coordination" between the right flank of 21st Army Group and Bradley's left (i.e., First Army). In addition, 21st Army Group would have "priority" in supplies. Still, Eisenhower insisted, to Montgomery's dissatisfaction, "on building up . . . the necessary strength to advance eastward from Paris toward Metz." After the meeting, Montgomery reported to Brooke that "it has been a very exhausting day," but overall he was pleased, as he felt he had won the main points, "operational control" over the Airborne and the First Armies, plus priority in supplies.[74]

Eisenhower's attempt to appease Montgomery made both Bradley and Patton furious. The two American generals met; Patton recorded in his diary that Bradley "feels that Ike won't go against Monty . . . Bradley was madder than I have ever seen him and wondered aloud 'what the Supreme Commander amounted to.' " Patton felt that the southern advance offered much better tank terrain than the water-logged country to the north, but noted in disgust that Montgomery "has some way of talking Ike into his own way of thinking." He suggested to Bradley that they threaten to resign. "I feel that in such a showdown we would win, as Ike would not dare to relieve us."[75]

Bradley would not go so far, but he did spend two days with Eisenhower, arguing against giving First Army to Montgomery. Tedder agreed with Bradley, as did Eisenhower's operations officer (G-3), Major General Harold Bull, and his G-2, General Strong. Eisenhower yielded to their pressure. When he issued his directive, on August 29, he did not give operational control of First Army to Montgomery; instead, Montgomery was only "authorized to effect"— through Bradley—"any necessary coordination between his own forces" and First Army.[76] That decision, and its sequel, strengthened

Montgomery's and Brooke's—and Bradley's and Patton's—conviction that Eisenhower always agreed with the last man he talked to.

It was a most serious charge, but a bit off the mark. Montgomery tended to hear what he wanted to hear, read what he wanted to read; Eisenhower tended to seek out words or phrases that would appease. There was, consequently, a consistent misunderstanding between the two men. Nevertheless, Eisenhower never yielded on the two main points, command and single thrust, not in August and September 1944, nor again when they were raised in January and March 1945. He took—and kept—control of the land battle, just as he said he would. And he never wavered, from the moment he first saw the SHAEF plans for a two-front advance into Germany to the last month of the war, on the question of the so-called "broad front."

He did waver, sometimes badly, on some important issues, primarily the relative importance of Arnhem and Antwerp, and the meaning of the word "priority." But he never told Montgomery anything that a reasonable man could have construed as a promise that Patton would be stopped in Paris and 21st Army Group be sent on to Berlin. Nor did he ever encourage Patton to believe that he would be sent to Berlin alone. He always insisted on invading Germany from both north and south of the Ardennes.

His reasons were manifold. His analysis of German morale and geography played a large role. Even after the Allies got through the West Wall, there was still a major barrier between them and the German heartland, the Rhine River. A single thrust, especially beyond the Rhine, would be subject to counterattacks on the flanks. Eisenhower believed that the counterattacks might be powerful enough to sever the supply lines and then destroy the leading armies. Currently, with the Allies' limited port capacity, the Allies could not bring forward adequate supplies to sustain an army beyond the Rhine. Every mile that the advancing troops moved away from the Normandy ports added to the problems. For example, forward airfields had to be constructed to provide fighter support for the troops. But to construct them it was necessary to move engineers and building materials forward, at the expense of weapons and gasoline. One senior engineer involved pointed out that if Patton had gone across the Rhine in September, he would have done so without any logistical or air support at all. "A good task force of Panzerfaust, manned by Hitler Youth, could have finished them off before they reached Kassel." [77]

As for 21st Army Group, de Guingand pointed out that when

(and if) it reached the Rhine, bridging material would have to be brought forward, at the expense of other supplies. Like Eisenhower, de Guingand doubted that there would be a collapse of German morale; he expected the enemy to fight to the bitter end.

As, of course, the Germans did; it took the combined efforts of 160 Russian divisions *and* the entire AEF *and* Alexander's Italian offensive *and* eight additional months of devastating air attack to force a German capitulation. After the war, de Guingand remarked, a bit dryly, that he had to doubt that Montgomery could have brought about the same result with 21st Army Group alone. "My conclusion, is, therefore," de Guingand wrote, "that Eisenhower was right."[78]

The personality and political factors in Eisenhower's decision are obvious. Patton pulling one way, Montgomery the other; each man insistent; each certain of his own military genius; each accustomed to having his own way. Behind them, there were the adulating publics, who had made Patton and Montgomery into symbols of their nation's military prowess. In Eisenhower's view, to give one or the other the glory would have serious repercussions, not just the howls of agony from the press and public of the nation left behind, but in the very fabric of the Alliance itself. Eisenhower feared it could not survive the resulting uproar. It was too big a chance to take, especially on such a risky operation. Eisenhower never considered taking it.

Montgomery and Patton showed no appreciation of the pressures on Eisenhower when they argued so persistently for their plans, but then Eisenhower's worries were not their responsibility. Montgomery wanted a quick end to the war, he wanted the British to bring it about, and he wanted to lead the charge into Berlin personally. Patton would have given anything to beat him to it. Had Eisenhower been in their positions, he almost surely would have felt as they did, and he wanted his subordinates to be aggressive and to believe in themselves and their troops.

Eisenhower's great weakness in this situation was not that he wavered on the broad-front question, but rather his eagerness to be well liked, coupled with his desire to keep everyone happy. Because of these characteristics, he would not end a meeting until at least verbal agreement had been found. Thus he appeared to be always shifting, "inclining first one way, then the other," according to the views and wishes of the last man with whom he had talked. Eisenhower, as Brooke put it, seemed to be "an arbiter balancing the requirements of competing allies and subordinates rather than a master of the field making a decisive choice."[79] Everyone who talked to him left the meeting feeling that Eisenhower had agreed with him, only to find out later that he had not. Thus Montgomery, Bradley, and Patton filled their diaries and letters and conversations with denunciations of Eisenhower (Bradley less so than the others).

The real price that had to be paid for Eisenhower's desire to be well liked was not, however, animosity toward him from Montgomery and Patton. It was, rather, on the battlefield. In his attempts to appease Montgomery and Patton, Eisenhower gave them great tactical leeway, to the point of allowing them to choose their own objectives. The result was one of the great mistakes of the war, the failure to take and open Antwerp promptly, which represented the only real chance the Allies had to end the war in 1944. The man both immediately and ultimately responsible for that failure was Eisenhower.

CHAPTER SIX

The West Wall
and the
Battle of the Bulge

THE GROUND COMMAND issue that Montgomery persisted in raising was essentially phony. It hardly mattered, except for publicity purposes, if Bradley reported to Eisenhower directly or through Montgomery. As Eisenhower emphasized to Montgomery, nothing happened without his approval, whether or not he had direct control of the land battle. What did matter was logistics, the flow of supplies. Eisenhower allocated supplies, and that was his real power. The way in which Eisenhower distributed the available supplies would determine the direction and the nature of the offensive, no matter who had the title of land commander.

So, where Eisenhower could afford to be generous with Montgomery, he was, while retaining the reality of power. Words of praise cost nothing and gained much, and Eisenhower was free with them. On August 31, Eisenhower called a press conference in London. "Now," he told the reporters, "the time has come when we have broken out of that initial beachhead and General Bradley is taking over his part of the job, reporting directly to SHAEF headquarters, and anyone that interprets this as a demotion for General Montgomery simply won't look facts in the face. He is not only my very close and warm friend, but a man with whom I have worked for two years, and for whom I have a tremendous admiration, one of the great soldiers of this or any other war."

He gave Montgomery credit for the victories in France. As to the

American criticism that Montgomery had been too cautious before Caen, Eisenhower said he would not hear of it. "Every foot of ground he [the enemy] lost at Caen was like losing ten miles anywhere else. Every piece of dust there was more than a diamond to him." [1]

Churchill, as aware as Eisenhower of the blow to Montgomery's ego from the command changes, also helped soften the blow. On September 1, Churchill announced that Montgomery had been promoted to field marshal (which created a situation in which Montgomery outranked Eisenhower, five stars to four). The field marshal's baton, however, led Montgomery to increase, not slacken, his demand that his plan be implemented. Nor did it impress Patton sufficiently to persuade him to give in to Montgomery.

At the beginning of September, Eisenhower declared that Montgomery's 21st Army Group should have priority in supplies. But he also wanted 12th Army Group under Bradley to "build up" east of Paris and to "*prepare* to strike rapidly eastwards." Exactly as Montgomery had feared, Bradley allowed Patton to advance to Reims and beyond. On August 30, Patton crossed the Meuse River, which put him more than a hundred miles east of Paris and not much more than that distance from the Rhine. He was, however, out of gas; that day, he received only 32,000 gallons of the 400,000 gallons of gasoline he needed. Still, he wanted to push on. When one of his corps commanders reported that he had stopped because if he went any farther his tanks would be without fuel, Patton told him "to continue until the tanks stop and then get out and walk." Patton realized that when his tanks ran dry Eisenhower would have to give him more gasoline, even at the expense of the 21st Army Group. [2]

On September 2, Eisenhower went to Versailles to see Bradley, Hodges, and Patton to discuss future operations. Before the meeting, Kay noted in the SHAEF office diary that "E. says that he is going to give Patton hell because he is stretching his line too far and therefore making supply difficulties." But Patton seized the offensive; he gleefully told Eisenhower that he had patrols on the Moselle and—stretching the truth—in Metz. "If you let me retain my regular allotment of tonnage, Ike, we could push on to the German frontier and rupture that Goddamn Siegfried Line [the West Wall]. I'm willing to stake my reputation on that."

"Careful, George," Eisenhower responded, thinking of Patton's recent difficulties, "that reputation of yours hasn't been worth very much." Patton, thinking of this recent dash through France, rejoined, "That reputation is pretty good now." [3] Patton then convinced Eisenhower that the opportunities on his front were too good to pass up, and got Eisenhower to agree to allocate additional gasoline to Third Army. Eisenhower also gave Patton permission to attack toward Mannheim and Frankfurt, and agreed to Bradley's demand that First Army stay on Patton's left, south of the Ardennes.

When Montgomery learned that Patton was getting more gasoline and that Hodges had been detached from his right flank, he exploded. There were not enough supplies for two offensives, Montgomery thundered, and Eisenhower had to choose one or the other. The one selected "must have all maintenance resources it needs without qualifications." Time was vital. "If we attempt a compromise solution and split our maintenance resources so that neither thrust is full-blooded we will prolong the war," he warned. Eisenhower replied that he still gave priority to 21st Army Group and was allocating supplies on that basis.[4]

Two days later, September 7, Montgomery protested that he was *not* getting priority in supplies. After reciting the facts and figures of his shortages, Montgomery added, "It is very difficult to explain things in a message like this." He wondered if it would be possible for Eisenhower to come to see him.[5]

It was typical of Montgomery that he should make such a request. It never seems to have occurred to him that he, not Eisenhower, was the supplicant. Only once during the entire campaign did he visit Eisenhower at SHAEF, even though he was regularly invited to attend conferences. He always insisted that Eisenhower come to him.

Montgomery's request of September 7 was particularly untactful, because Eisenhower had hurt his knee and every movement was painful for him. The accident happened on September 2, when Eisenhower was returning to Granville from his meeting with Bradley and Patton at Versailles. Eisenhower's B-25 broke a muffler and he switched to a small L-5, a one-passenger plane with a limited range, designed for liaison work. A storm came up; the pilot lost his way and could not find the airstrip. The L-5 was about to run out of gasoline, and they made an emergency landing on a beach. Eisenhower hopped out to help the pilot push the plane above the tideline and, in the wet sand, slipped and twisted his knee. The pilot helped him limp across the salt marshes to the road, where a GI passing in a jeep picked them up and drove them to Granville.

Wet, exhausted, bedraggled, Eisenhower had two aides carry him up to his bedroom. The knee swelled; the pain was bad; Eisenhower was immobile. A doctor flew over from London and ordered him to stay in bed for a week; a few days later, as the swelling went down, the doctor put Eisenhower's knee in a plaster cast.

From his bed, Eisenhower had a grand view of Mont St. Michel, but it did little to raise his spirits. He had a ringing in his ears, caused —he supposed—by high blood pressure (he would not allow the doctors to check for fear they might send him home); the pain in his knee drained his energy; he was irritated with all his subordinates, American as well as British. Most of all, he hated having to use crutches or a cane just to get around in his bedroom.

The pain persisted; two weeks later he told Mamie he was taking daily treatments, one and a half hours of baking and rubbing, but it hardly helped. A bit later, he told Mamie that "my leg is improving, but not as rapidly as if I were 30 instead of almost 54. It is OK except for soreness, and I have to be so d----- careful! Annoying."[6] Until the end of the war, the knee continued to bother him, occasionally forcing him to spend a day or two in bed, often requiring the aid of a cane or crutches (but never in public).

Montgomery knew about the injury, but still decided it would be better for Eisenhower to come to Brussels than for him to fly to Granville, despite Eisenhower's request that he do so. On the afternoon of September 10, Eisenhower therefore flew to Brussels. Getting aboard the plane was painful, getting off out of the question. So Montgomery came aboard. Pulling Eisenhower's latest directive from his pocket, waving his arms, Montgomery damned the plan in extreme language, accused the Supreme Commander of double-crossing him, implied that Patton, not Eisenhower, was running the war, demanded that control of the land battle be returned to him, and asserted that the double thrust would result in certain failure.

As the tirade gathered in fury Eisenhower sat silent. At the first pause for breath, however, he leaned forward, put his hand on Montgomery's knee, and said, "Steady, Monty! You can't speak to me like that. I'm your boss."[7]

Montgomery mumbled an apology. He then proposed that 21st Army Group make a single thrust through Arnhem to Berlin. Eisenhower, according to Tedder, who was present, thought "it was fantastic to talk of marching to Berlin with an army which was still drawing the great bulk of its supplies over beaches." Montgomery insisted that it could be done if he got all the supplies, but Eisenhower refused even to consider the possibility. As Eisenhower put it in his office diary later, "Monty's suggestion is simple, give him everything, which is crazy."[8]

Sitting in Eisenhower's B-25 on the Brussels airfield, the Supreme Commander and the field marshal argued for another hour. Eisenhower finally agreed to a plan, code name Market-Garden, that Montgomery said promised great results. It called for a crossing of the Lower Rhine in Arnhem, in Holland, with the Airborne Army and British Second Army.

Eisenhower agreed to the plan because, like Montgomery, he wanted to get a bridgehead across the Rhine before the momentum of the offensive was lost. He also liked the idea of using the Airborne Army for a major operation. But Market-Garden had some obvious disadvantages. By moving northward from the Belgian-Dutch border, rather than east, Second Army would open a gap between its right flank and First Army's left. Hodges would have to slide his divisions to his left to cover the gap, which meant an even broader front than before, with more stretching by everyone. The direction of the attack would carry 21st Army Group away from the Ruhr and give it another river to cross. Worst of all, it would delay the opening of Antwerp.

Antwerp had always been emphasized in SHAEF's pre-Overlord plan. It was Europe's biggest port, and the one closest to the German heartland. SHAEF had reckoned that no major operations could be conducted in Germany without Antwerp. Yet Eisenhower allowed Montgomery to ignore Antwerp in favor of a reckless operation, at Arnhem, that promised no great results even if successful. Similarly, Eisenhower had said, "There is no point in getting there [to the West Wall] until we are in a position to do something about it."[9] But, because he allowed Patton to advance willy-nilly, and because he failed to insist on Antwerp, that is exactly what happened. It was his worst error of the war.

Montgomery, with his eyes on Arnhem, diverted supplies from the Canadians to Second Army. Thus although the Canadians took the city of Antwerp in early September, the Germans still held the Scheldt Estuary, making it impossible for the Allies to use the port, and the Canadians were not strong enough to drive them out. On September 11 Eisenhower wrote in his office diary, "Monty seems unimpressed by necessity for taking Antwerp approaches," but Eisenhower himself was just as guilty.[10] By agreeing to Market-Garden, the Supreme Commander had in practice agreed to take supplies from Patton and to ignore Antwerp in order to achieve a tactical, not a strategic, gain. All the AEF was involved in half measures, or less. It would have been impossible to say at this point which the Supreme Commander wanted most, Antwerp, or Arnhem, or a penetration of the West Wall south of the Ardennes.

In his own defense, Eisenhower wrote, long after the war, "I not only approved Market-Garden, I insisted upon it. What we needed was a *bridgehead* over the Rhine. If that could be accomplished, I was quite willing to wait on all other operations. What this action proved was that the idea of 'one full-blooded thrust' to Berlin was silly."[11] But of all the factors that influenced Eisenhower's decisions—to reinforce success, to leap the Rhine, to bring the highly trained but underutilized paratroopers into action—the one that stands out is his desire to appease Montgomery. At no other point in the war did Eisenhower's tendency toward compromise and his desire to keep his subordinates happy exact a higher price.

On September 17, Market-Garden began. The first day went badly for Second Army, but well for the paratroopers. By September 21, due to a variety of factors, of which bad weather, German counterattacks, and Montgomery's strange passivity in prodding Second Army were the most important, Market-Garden was on the verge of failure.

On September 20, Eisenhower moved SHAEF headquarters to the Hotel Trianon at Versailles. Eisenhower's office was too large for his tastes, so he had it partitioned, giving the other half of the room to Kay and the other secretaries. The secretaries lived together in a flat above what had once been the stables of Louis XV, while Eisenhower lived in a handsome mansion that had recently been occupied by Field Marshal Gerd von Rundstedt.

His knee continued to hobble him; the ringing in his ears was still there; he had a cold; a cyst on his back added to his discomfort.

But what bothered him most was the German resistance. He told Mamie that people kept asking him what he was going to do when the war was over. "The question makes me angry, because you can be certain this war is not 'won' for the man that is shivering, suffering and dying up on the Siegfried Line." When he had a rare idle moment, his mind went backward rather than forward. "Yesterday I thought so frequently of Icky," he wrote on September 25. "He would have been 27 years old!"

That thought, plus a letter from Mamie saying that she feared he had changed so much that she would not know him, led to a bit of reflection. "Of course we've changed," he wrote her. "How could two people go through what we have . . . without seeing each other except once in more than two years, and still believe they could be exactly as they were. The rule of nature is constant change. But it seems to me that the thing to do is to retain our sense of humor, and try to make an interesting game of getting acquainted again. After all, there is no 'problem' separating us—it is merely distance, and that can some day be eliminated." [12]

On the battlefield in northwest Europe, everything had turned out badly. The great offensive of August in France had not led to victory in Europe. Market-Garden had failed and Antwerp was not opened in time to do any good in 1944. The ultimate blame for this situation rested with the man who had the ultimate responsibility, the Supreme Commander himself.

On October 9, Eisenhower finally began to give Montgomery a shaking. The immediate provocation was a report from Admiral Ramsay's office that the Canadians would be unable to accomplish anything until November 1 because of ammunition shortages. A furious Eisenhower wired Montgomery, "Unless we have Antwerp producing by the middle of November our entire operations will come to a standstill. I must emphasize that, of all our operations on our entire front from Switzerland to the Channel, I consider Antwerp of first importance, and I believe that the operations designed to clear up the entrance require your personal attention." He took all the sting out of the message, however, by adding, "You know best where the emphasis lies within your Army Group." [13]

Montgomery fired back a cable the same day. "Request you will ask Ramsay from me by what authority he makes wild statements to you concerning my operations about which he can know nothing rpt nothing." The Canadians, Montgomery said, were already attacking. He reminded Eisenhower that there "is *no* rpt *no* shortage of ammunition." He hotly claimed that at the Versailles conference the Supreme Commander had made the attack in Holland the "main effort"; as for Antwerp, he insisted that "the operations [there] are receiving my personal attention." [14]

Eisenhower replied that "the possession of the approaches to Antwerp remains . . . an objective of vital importance." He added, "Let me assure you that nothing I may ever say or write with respect to future plans . . . is meant to indicate any lessening of the need for Antwerp." [15]

Shortly thereafter Smith called Montgomery on the telephone and demanded to know when SHAEF could expect some action around Antwerp. Heated words followed. Finally Smith, "purple with rage," turned to his deputy, General Morgan, and thrust the telephone into his hand. "Here," Smith said, "you tell your countryman what to do." Morgan, expecting that Montgomery would be head of the British Army after the war, thought to himself, "Well, that's the end of my career." [16] He then told Montgomery that unless Antwerp was opened soon his supplies would be cut off.

Morgan was right about his career. Neither he, nor any other British officer who served at SHAEF, nor for that matter de Guingand, prospered in the postwar Montgomery-run British Army. As Eisenhower once said of Montgomery, "He's just a little man, he's just as little inside as he is outside." [17]

Montgomery, incensed by this threat, put down the phone and wrote to Smith. He blamed the failure of Market-Garden on a lack of coordination between his forces and Bradley's and once again demanded that he be given sole control of the land battle. This was too much. Eisenhower's patience with the field marshal was almost limitless, but not quite. "The Antwerp operation does not involve the question of command in any slightest degree," Eisenhower told Montgomery. In any event, as far as command went, he would not, ever, turn 12th Army Group over to Montgomery.

Then Eisenhower used his ultimate threat; he said that if Montgomery, after reading the SHAEF plan of campaign, still characterized that plan as "unsatisfactory, then indeed we have an issue that must be settled soon in the interest of future efficiency." Eisenhower said he was well aware of his own powers and limitations, "and if you, as the senior Commander in this Theater of one of the great Allies, feel that my conceptions and directives are such as to endanger the success of my operations, it is our duty to refer the matter to higher authority for any action they may choose to take, however drastic." [18]

Montgomery knew full well that if Eisenhower told the CCS it was "him or me," Eisenhower would win. "I have given you my views and you have given your answer," Montgomery hastened to reply. "I and all of us will weigh in one hundred percent to do what you want and we will pull it through without a doubt." He said he had given Antwerp top priority and would terminate the discussion on command arrangements. "You will hear no more on the subject of command from me," he promised, and signed off, "Your very devoted and loyal subordinate, Monty." [19]

Montgomery could be as abject as Patton when it had to be done, but like Patton, he still insisted on going his own way. Despite this exchange, he continued to emphasize Second Army's attack, at the expense of the Canadians. It was October 16 before Montgomery gave up on operations in Holland. Then, the taking of the approaches to Antwerp proved to be a difficult and time-consuming tactical problem; the Allies did not drive the Germans out of the Scheldt Estuary until November 8. After that, the mines had to be cleared; not until November 28 did the first Allied convoy reach Antwerp's docks.

By then, bad weather had long since set in, and any chance of ending the war in 1944 was gone. As Brooke declared, "I feel that Monty's strategy for once is at fault. Instead of carrying out the advance on Arnhem he ought to have made certain of Antwerp in the first place. Ike nobly took all the blame on himself as he had approved Monty's suggestion to operate on Arnhem."[20]

The Germans had pulled off "the miracle of the West." They had established a firm defensive line from the North Sea to the Swiss border, a defensive line that was based on the West Wall, which was proving to be much more formidable than Allied intelligence had anticipated. The Germans had rebuilt their once-shattered divisions, brought new ones into the fight, and were superior in numbers (although not in tanks or artillery) to the AEF. Worst of all, they were fighting in defense of their homeland just as hard as Eisenhower had feared they would. The rosy Allied expectations of August and September were gone.

Fall was never Eisenhower's best season. In 1942 he had been stuck in the mud of Tunisia, in 1943 bogged down on the Italian peninsula, and in 1944 the rains came again to turn the fields of northwest Europe into quagmires. As Eisenhower told Marshall, "I am getting exceedingly tired of weather."[21] His airplanes could not fly, his tanks were unable to maneuver, and his soldiers marched only with difficulty. He was still short on supplies and was beginning to have replacement problems. Under these circumstances, the fall battles resulted in little beyond heavy casualties on both sides.

Throughout the fall, Eisenhower traveled incessantly. "Weather is so miserable that all my travel is by auto," he told Mamie, "which takes lots of time." He usually traveled with only his driver, Sergeant Dry, and Jimmy Gault (who read the maps), while he sat alone in the back seat. "I have hours to think," he wrote Mamie, "and since the staff is not there to plague me, I think of you a lot. Some of the roads I travel are the ones we rode over 15 years ago, and I always wish you were along to see them, with me, again."[22]

It was a discouraging period all around. "Well sweet, I'd like to think that this mess would be over soon, so I could come home," Ike wrote his wife on November 22. "But the fighting and the dying go on—and the end is not yet. 'Civilization' is not pretty when it resorts to war. Anyway, some day victory will be ours, and I'll come a running!"

"It's all so terrible, so awful," he said in another letter, "that I constantly wonder how 'civilization' can stand war at all." The strain of the long separation on his marriage was getting worse, Mamie's complaints about her loneliness and his indifference harder to bear. "It's true we've now been apart for 2½ years," he wrote in November, and he recognized how "painful" this was for her. "Because you don't have a specific war job that absorbs your time and thoughts I understand also that this distress is harder for you to bear. But you should not forget that I do miss you and do love you, and that the load of responsibility I carry would be intolerable unless I could have the belief that there is someone who wants me to come home—for good." In a heartfelt plea for understanding, he added, "Don't forget that I take a beating, every day."

In mid-December, he told her he prayed that this would be their last Christmas apart, and promised her endless hours of talking when the war was over. "We'll have to take a three month vacation on some lonely beach—and oh lordy, lordy, let it be *sunny!!*"[23]

Almost as vexing to Eisenhower as his problems with the British field marshals were his problems with Second Lieutenant John Eisenhower, or, more precisely, with John's mother. John had been assigned to the 71st Division, which was scheduled to leave Fort Benning for France in the near future. Mamie found out about this development before Ike did and complained, "You didn't tell me what you had cooked up."

Ike protested, "I've cooked up nothing, and I don't know where he is or what he is going to do. I did make sure that *if he wanted* to go to a division coming to this theater, the W.D. would not object merely because I was in command here." Five days later he learned of John's assignment to the 71st, and commented, "I will have a hard time keeping from 'interfering.' I'm so wrapped up in that boy—but I keep reminding myself that he is a man, with a man's job to do and his own career to make. How I wish I dared go and stay with him."[24]

To John, Ike offered an old infantryman's advice on how to train his platoon. "Go around and see every man, see that he gets into warm, dry clothing . . . that he gets a good hot meal and that his weapons are in tiptop shape. Shoes, socks and feet are of tremendous importance, and you should try to wear exactly the same kind of materials as your men do when in field training or in combat. By pursuing these methods you will not only have a splendidly trained platoon, but one that will follow you anywhere."

When the moment for John's departure came, Mamie felt hurt, angry, deserted. Despite her husband's disclaimers, she was sure he had arranged the assignment. "I fully understand your distress . . . ," Ike reassured her, "but it always depresses me when you talk about 'dirty tricks' I've played and what a beating you've taken, apparently because of me. You've always put your own interpretation on every act, look or word of mine, and when you've made yourself unhappy, that has, in turn, made me the same. . . .

"So far as John is concerned," he continued, "we can do nothing but pray. If I interfered even slightly or indirectly he would be so resentful for the remainder of his life that neither I (nor you, if he thought you had anything to do with it) could be comfortable with him. . . . But, God, how I do hope and pray that all will be well with him." Eisenhower assured Mamie, "I'm not 'fussing' at you. But please try to see me in something besides a despicable light and at least let me be *certain* of my welcome home when this mess is finished.

"I truly love you and I do know that when you blow off steam you don't really think of me as such a black hearted creature as your language implies. I'd rather you didn't mention any of this again." [25]

Through the fall, the great offensive continued. The only place the Allies were not on the attack was in the Ardennes itself, which was thinly held by Troy Middleton's corps. On his way to Maastricht on December 7 Eisenhower had noted how spread out the troops in the Ardennes were, and he questioned Bradley about the vulnerability of this sector of the front. Bradley said he could not strengthen the Ardennes area without weakening Patton's and Hodges' offensives, and that if the Germans counterattacked in the Ardennes they could be hit on either flank and stopped long before they reached the Meuse River. Although he did not expect a German counterattack, he said he had taken the precaution of not placing any major supply installations in the Ardennes. Eisenhower was satisfied by Bradley's explanation.

December 16 was a day of celebration at SHAEF Main in Versailles, featuring a wedding, a promotion, and a medal. In the morning, Mickey McKeogh married one of the WAC sergeants. Eisenhower hosted a champagne reception in his house in Saint-Germain. He had something else to celebrate; the Senate had just announced his promotion to the newly created rank of General of the Army, which made him equal in rank to Marshall, MacArthur,— and Montgomery.

Late in the afternoon, Bradley arrived, to complain about the replacement situation. The United States now had all but one of its divisions committed, the flow of replacements was not keeping pace with the casualty rate, and because of the general offensive that Eisenhower insisted on conducting, SHAEF had few men in reserve.

While they talked in Eisenhower's office, British General Kenneth Strong interrupted to inform them that a German attack had been launched that morning in the Ardennes. Bradley's initial reaction was to dismiss it as a mere spoiling attack, designed to draw Patton's forces out of the Saar offensive. But Eisenhower immediately sensed something bigger. "That's no spoiling attack," he said, explaining that since the Ardennes itself offered no worthwhile objective, the Germans must be after some strategic gain. "I think you had better send Middleton some help," he told Bradley. Studying the operations map with Strong, Eisenhower noticed that the 7th Armored Division was out of the line, in First Army sector, and that the 10th Armored Division, a part of Third Army, was currently uncommitted. He told Bradley to send the two divisions to Middleton, in the Ardennes. Bradley hesitated; he knew that both Hodges and Patton would be upset at losing the divisions, Patton especially, as the 10th Armored was one of his favorites. With a touch of impatience, Eisenhower overruled Bradley.

Having made these arrangements, Eisenhower and Bradley, joined by Everett Hughes, settled down to enjoy what was left of the champagne, open a bottle of Highland Piper Scotch that Hughes had brought, and play five rubbers of bridge. They would make another assessment of the situation in the morning, when Strong would have more information for them.[26]

The news Strong brought, based on identification of German divisions in the Ardennes and on captured documents, was about as bad as it could have been. Eisenhower's rapid and intuitive judgment had been right—the Germans were engaged in a counteroffensive, not just a counterattack. Two German panzer armies of twenty-four divisions had struck Middleton's corps of three divisions. The Germans had managed to achieve both complete surprise and overwhelming local superiority, an eight-to-one advantage in infantrymen and a four-to-one advantage in tanks.

Eisenhower accepted the blame for the surprise, and he was right to do so, as he had failed to read correctly the mind of the enemy. Eisenhower failed to see that Hitler would take desperate chances, and Eisenhower was the man responsible for the weakness of Middleton's line in the Ardennes, because he was the one who had insisted on maintaining a general offensive.

But despite his mistakes, Eisenhower was the first to grasp the full import of the offensive, the first to be able to readjust his thinking, the first to realize that, although the surprise and the initial Allied losses were painful, in fact Hitler had given the Allies a great opportunity. On the morning of December 17, Eisenhower showed that he saw the opportunity immediately, when he wrote the War Department that "if things go well we should not only stop the thrust but should be able to profit from it."[27]

After dictating that letter, Eisenhower held a conference with Smith, Whiteley, and Strong. SHAEF now had only two divisions in reserve, the 82d and 101st Airborne, which were refitting from the battles around Arnhem. The SHAEF generals anticipated that the Germans would attempt to cross the Meuse River, thus splitting 21st and 12th Army Groups, and take the huge Allied supply dumps at Liège. The dumps were crucial to the Germans, as they contained the fuel Hitler counted on to sustain a drive to Antwerp.

Whiteley put his finger on the small Belgian town of Bastogne and declared that the crossroads there was the key to the battle. Bastogne was surrounded by rolling countryside, unusually gentle in the rough Ardennes country, and had an excellent road network. Without it the Germans would not be able to cross the Ardennes to the Meuse. Eisenhower decided to concentrate his reserves at Bastogne. He ordered a combat command of the 10th Airborne to proceed immediately to the town, and told the 101st to get there as soon as possible. He also sent the 82d Airborne to the northern edge of the penetration, where it could lead a counterattack against the German right flank. Finally the Supreme Commander ordered the cessation of all offensives by the AEF "and the gathering up of every possible reserve to strike the penetration in both flanks."[28]

The following morning, December 18, Ike called Smith, Bradley, and Patton to a conference. The generals met in a cold, damp squad room in a Verdun barracks, on the site of the greatest battle ever fought. There was only one lone potbellied stove to ease the bitter cold. Eisenhower's subordinates entered the room glum, depressed, embarrassed. Noting this, he opened by saying, "The present situation is to be regarded as one of opportunity for us and not of disaster.

There will be only cheerful faces at this conference table." Patton quickly picked up on the theme. "Hell, let's have the guts to let the _____ _____ _____ go all the way to Paris," he said. "Then we'll really cut 'em off and chew 'em up."[29]

Eisenhower said he was not *that* optimistic: the line of the Meuse had to be held. But he was not thinking defensively. He informed his commanders that he was not going to let the Germans get away with emerging from the West Wall without punishing them. He asked Patton how long it would take him to change the direction of his offensive, from east to north, to counterattack the Germans' left, or southern, flank.

Patton replied, "Two days." The others chuckled at this typical Patton bravado; Eisenhower advised him to take an extra day and make the attack stronger. He told Patton to cancel his offensive in the Saar, change directions, and organize a major counterblow toward Bastogne by December 23. He was going to have Montgomery organize an attack in the north, against the German right flank.[30] In short, by December 18, on the third day of the Bulge, well before the issue was settled at Bastogne or on the Meuse, Eisenhower had already put in motion a counterattack designed to destroy the German panzer armies in the Ardennes.

The Germans would soon have a wedge driven between Bradley's forces, making it difficult for Bradley to communicate with First Army. Strong thought that under the circumstances, Eisenhower should give Montgomery command of all forces north of the Ardennes. This would mean that Bradley would keep Third Army, while Montgomery got First and Ninth Armies. Such a command arrangement was what Montgomery had all along been proposing and Eisenhower refusing, and a transfer of command at this point would look as if the Americans had to turn to the British to rescue them from the crisis. But the communications problem was so serious that the step had to be taken.

Smith called Bradley on the telephone. Bradley insisted that it was not necessary, but Smith told Bradley, "It seems the logical thing to do. Monty can take care of everything north of the Bulge and you'll have everything south." Bradley protested that such a shift would discredit the American command. "Bedell," he added, "it's hard for me to object. Certainly if Monty's were an American command, I would agree with you entirely."[31]

Then Eisenhower telephoned Bradley. By now, Bradley was set

against any such change. Strong could hear him shouting at Eisenhower: "By God, Ike, I cannot be responsible to the American people if you do this. I resign." Eisenhower, flushed with shock and anger, drew a deep breath, then said, "Brad, I—not you—am responsible to the American people. Your resignation therefore means absolutely nothing." There was a pause, then another protest from Bradley, but this time without any threats. Eisenhower declared, "Well, Brad, those are my orders." He then turned the conversation to Patton's counterattack, which he declared he wanted mounted in the greatest possible strength.[32]

After hanging up, Eisenhower placed a call to Montgomery to inform him of the command switch. The telephone connection was unfortunately indistinct. Montgomery heard what he wanted to hear and attached his own meaning to the garbled conversation. He told Brooke that Eisenhower had called. "He was very excited," Montgomery said, "and it was difficult to understand what he was talking about; he roared into the telephone, speaking very fast." The only thing Montgomery understood was that Eisenhower was giving him command of First and Ninth Armies. "This was all I wanted to know. He then went on talking wildly about other things."[33]

Within two hours of his conversation with Eisenhower, Montgomery had visited with Hodges and General William Simpson, commander of the Ninth Army. A British officer who accompanied him said he strode into Hodges' headquarters "like Christ come to cleanse the temple." Montgomery reported to Brooke that Simpson and Hodges "seemed delighted to have someone to give them firm orders."[34]

In his efforts to find infantry replacements, Eisenhower ordered the entire Services of Supply combed out for men who could fight. He also ordered service units organized for the defense of the Meuse bridges, stressing "the vital importance of insuring that no repeat no Meuse bridges fall into enemy hands intact."[35] To Bradley, the order seemed to indicate that Eisenhower was getting "an acute case of the shakes," while Bradley's chief of staff, after reading the message, asked, "What the devil do they think we're doing, starting back for the beaches?"[36]

Adding to the impression of panic at SHAEF were the elaborate security precautions instituted at Versailles. SHAEF intelligence had learned that the Germans had organized a special group of English-speaking German soldiers, dressed them in American uniforms, given them captured American jeeps to drive, and spread them behind the American lines. Their mission was to issue false orders, spread defeatism, and capture bridges and road junctions. Rumor quickly spread, however, that their main intention was to assassinate the Supreme Commander. Thus everyone at SHAEF became super security-conscious. Eisenhower was sealed into the Trianon Palace. Guards with machine guns were placed all around the palace, and when Eisenhower went to Verdun or elsewhere for a meeting, he was led and followed by armed guards in jeeps.

Despite the security flap, Eisenhower and SHAEF were quietly confident, and eagerly anticipating the AEF counterattack. On December 22, while waiting for the skies to clear, so that the air forces could get into action, and for Patton to shift directions, so that he could attack toward Bastogne, Eisenhower issued an Order of the Day. "We cannot be content with his mere repulse," he said of the enemy. "By rushing out from his fixed defenses the enemy may give us the chance to turn his great gamble into his worst defeat. . . . Let everyone hold before him a single thought—to destroy the enemy on the ground, in the air, everywhere—destroy him!"[37]

Inside the Bulge, at Bastogne, the encircled 101st Airborne was doing just that. At noon on December 22, the Germans paused in their attacks to demand a surrender; Brigadier General Anthony McAuliffe made his famous "Nuts" reply. The Germans attacked again; again the 101st beat them back with heavy losses.

The best news came on December 23, when day broke clear and cold, with virtually unlimited visibility. From the first, Hitler had counted on a sustained period of bad weather to neutralize the Allied air forces. With the sunrise on the twenty-third, every Allied plane that could fly got into the air. Lumbering C-47s dropped tons of supplies to the 101st inside Bastogne; fighter planes strafed the Germans in the Bastogne ring; P-47s hit them with fragmentation bombs, napalm, and machine-gun fire. Patton began his thrust, which by the day after Christmas had carried him into Bastogne and lifted the siege.

For Eisenhower, victory in the defensive phase of the battle brought with it more problems from his two chief subordinates. Montgomery made no effort to conceal his pleasure and delight at the Americans' discomfort, nor any attempt to soothe Bradley's injured pride. At a Christmas Day meeting, he told Bradley that the Americans deserved the German counteroffensive, saying that if there had been a single thrust none of this would have happened. "Now we are in a proper muddle."

Montgomery reported that Bradley "looked thin, and worn and ill at ease" and claimed that the American general agreed with everything he said. Montgomery noted of Bradley: "Poor chap; he is such a decent fellow and the whole thing is a bitter pill for him."[38] Then the field marshal expressed his view that Patton's attack would not be strong enough to "do what is needed [and] I will have to deal unaided with both Fifth and Sixth Panzer Armies." He therefore demanded that Eisenhower give him more American troops. Bradley, meanwhile, came away from his meeting with Montgomery in a furious state of mind. He demanded that Eisenhower return First and Ninth Armies to his command.[39]

Eisenhower resisted the pushing and pulling on him from both sides and rejected both Montgomery's and Bradley's demands. He did agree that troops should be taken from the southern end of his line, but not that they should then be assigned to 21st Army Group. Instead he started to build a strategic reserve. Nor would he restore First and Ninth Armies to Bradley, not yet anyway, because he felt it was still logical for Montgomery to control the forces on the northern flank of the Bulge.

On December 26, Eisenhower met with his staff in the Trianon. Standing before a huge operations map, he told his G-3, General Harold "Pinky" Bull, " 'Pink,' you'd better go and see [General Jacob] Devers [commanding the 6th Army Group on the southern flank] today. I think the best line is this." Eisenhower outlined a withdrawal in the Strasbourg area. "I'll tell you, boys," he continued, "what should be done. See Devers and give this line. It will be a disappointment giving up ground, but this area is not where I told Devers to put his weight."[40]

Eisenhower's confidence in himself had grown tremendously during the crisis. His initial intuitive judgment had been proved right; his decision to rush the 7th and 10th Armored, and the 82d and the 101st Airborne, into the battle had been proved right; he still felt that his handing over the northern flank to Montgomery was right; his decision to have Patton attack toward Bastogne was right. Now he was laying down the line, telling the boys how it should be done. Whatever Brooke and Montgomery might say about his lack of experience, he had taken control of this battle and made it his.

But Eisenhower still had the supreme test to face. Giving firm orders to Bradley, Patton, and Devers was one thing, giving them to Field Marshal Montgomery quite another.

Eisenhower was beginning to worry that, as at Kasserine, the

Allies would be too late in their counterattack. Montgomery, it appeared, was going to insist that every condition was optimum before he moved forward. Two days after Christmas, at the regular SHAEF 8 A.M. meeting, the discussion centered upon the need to begin soon. Tedder emphasized that the good weather would not last much longer and that it was important to hit the Germans while the airplanes could still fly. At this point word arrived that Montgomery had a new plan for attack, one that involved two corps. "Praise God from whom all blessings flow," Eisenhower remarked.[41]

The tension that had characterized the Eisenhower-Montgomery relationship since mid-June 1944 now reached its height. As before Caen, it centered around differing perceptions of the Germans' intentions and the timing and strength of the Allied attack. Eisenhower believed the German divisions in the Bulge were understrength and badly battered, with their supply lines in poor shape. He wanted to hit them, hard and quickly.

Montgomery hesitated. He told Eisenhower, at a December 28 meeting at his headquarters, that the Germans would make one last big attack on the northern shoulder of the Bulge. He thought the best thing to do would be to receive that attack, then launch his counterattack with First Army after the Germans had been stopped. To add to Eisenhower's dismay, Montgomery wanted to strike against the tip of the Bulge, driving the Germans back to the West Wall, rather than attacking on the flank in an attempt to cut them off.

Eisenhower told him that if he waited, Rundstedt would either withdraw from the Bulge or put infantry divisions into the line, pulling out his tanks and putting them in reserve. The latter, Eisenhower said, "we must not allow to happen," and he again urged Montgomery to attack quickly. Montgomery repeated that first he had to receive and stop the expected German attack. Eisenhower grumbled that there would be no attack, and finally got Montgomery to agree that if one did not come that day or the next, First Army would counterattack against the German flank on January 1. Or at least Eisenhower thought Montgomery agreed.[42]

On December 30, however, de Guingand came to SHAEF with the bad news that Montgomery would not attack until January 3 or later. The blow to their hopes was more than any of the SHAEF officers could take. "What makes me so Goddam mad," Smith exploded, "is that Monty won't talk in the presence of anyone else." Speaking for Montgomery, de Guingand claimed that Eisenhower had misunderstood—there had been no agreement on a January 1 attack. "Damn it, there was!" Eisenhower responded. He felt that he had been lied to, that Montgomery was trying to lead him by the nose, that a great opportunity was about to be lost, and that therefore the time had come to make a break with Montgomery.

Eisenhower dictated a blistering letter to Montgomery, demanding that Montgomery live up to his promises. If he did not, Eisenhower continued, he would be sacked. De Guingand, shown a copy of the letter, begged Eisenhower to hold it. He said he would talk to Montgomery and straighten things out. Eisenhower liked de Guingand, as did everyone at SHAEF; his affable personality, common sense, and reasonableness stood in sharp contrast to his boss and made him the perfect broker between Montgomery and SHAEF. Eisenhower agreed to hold the letter until de Guingand could consult with Montgomery.[43]

On New Year's Eve de Guingand conferred with Montgomery, then flew back to Versailles, where he reported that Montgomery held firm to his view that the proper strategy was to let the Germans exhaust themselves with one last attack before taking up the offensive. Eisenhower, angry, said that Montgomery had definitely promised him an attack on January 1. De Guingand repeated that Eisenhower must have misunderstood.

Bradley, meanwhile, was already attacking, believing that Montgomery would begin his offensive on January 1. But Montgomery did not, and the Germans switched panzer divisions from the north to the south to stop Bradley.

Eisenhower thought Montgomery's sense of timing in military operations was seriously deficient. That point may be open to question, but there can be none about Montgomery's total lack of a sense of timing in personal relations, or his complete inability to see things from someone else's point of view. At the height of the debate over what Montgomery had or had not promised, Montgomery sent a letter to Eisenhower, damning the Supreme Commander's policies and demanding that he, Montgomery, be given full control of the land battle. And, of course, there must be a single thrust, in the north, with Patton held where he was. Montgomery even wrote out a directive to those ends for Eisenhower's signature.

Instead of doing as told, Eisenhower issued his own directive, which ran counter to Montgomery's draft on every point. He returned First Army to Bradley's control and insisted on a double thrust into Germany. "The one thing that must now be prevented," he emphasized, "is the stabilization of the enemy salient with infantry, permitting him opportunity to use his Panzers at will on any part of the front. We must regain the initiative, and speed and energy are essential."[44]

In a covering note to Montgomery accompanying the directive, Eisenhower was simple, direct, and forceful. "I do not agree," Eisenhower said, referring to Montgomery's contention that there should be a single ground commander. He said he had done all he could for Montgomery and did not want to hear again about placing Bradley under Montgomery's command. "I assure you that in this matter I can go no further." He added, "I have planned an advance" to the Rhine on a broad front, and ordered Montgomery to read his directive carefully. All the vagueness of earlier letters and directives to Montgomery was now gone.

In conclusion, Eisenhower told Montgomery that he would no longer tolerate any debate on these subjects. "I would deplore the development of such an unbridgeable gulf of convictions between us that we would have to present our differences to the CCS," he said, but if Montgomery went any further that was exactly what he would do. "The confusion and debate that would follow would certainly damage the good will and devotion to a common cause that have made this Allied Force unique in history," Eisenhower admitted, but he could do nothing else if Montgomery persisted.[45]

De Guingand, meanwhile, was working on Montgomery. He told his boss that the depth of feeling against him at SHAEF was very great. Smith "was more worried than I had ever seen him." The general sentiment was that Montgomery had to go. Montgomery scoffed at this. "Who would replace me?" he demanded.

"That's already been worked out," de Guingand replied. "They want Alex."

Montgomery paled. He had forgotten about Alexander. He began pacing his trailer, finally turning to de Guingand to ask, "What shall I do, Freddie? What shall I do?"

De Guingand pulled out the draft of a message he had already prepared for Montgomery's signature. "Sign this," he said. Montgomery read it, and did.[46] The cable said that Montgomery knew there were many factors Eisenhower had to consider "beyond anything I realize." It asked Eisenhower to tear up the letter demanding sole command of the ground forces.[47]

Montgomery followed up the cable with a handwritten letter. "Dear Ike," he began, "you can rely on me and all under my command to go all out one hundred percent to implement your plan." [48] On January 3 he began his attack. It was not all that Eisenhower wanted, but much better than Montgomery had originally proposed. For the next month the Allies battered away at the Bulge. The Germans, schooled in winter warfare from the Russian front, waged a fighting retreat, and not until February 7 had the original line been restored. Eisenhower had hoped for better results, but these were satisfactory, for most of the German armor was destroyed in the process. The enemy had practically no mobility left, and once Eisenhower's forces broke through the West Wall they would be able to dash through Germany almost at will. In that dash, in fact as well as in name, their commanding general would be Eisenhower.

Meanwhile, Montgomery held a press conference to explain how he had won the Battle of the Bulge. It was a quite incredible manifestation of Montgomery's insensitivity. He told the press that on the very first day, "as soon as I saw what was happening I took certain steps myself to ensure that if the Germans got to the Meuse they would certainly not get over the river. And I carried out certain movements so as to provide balanced dispositions to meet the threatened danger . . . i.e., I was thinking ahead." Soon Eisenhower put him in command of the northern flank, and he then brought the British into the fight, and thus saved the Americans. "You have thus the picture of British troops fighting on both sides of American forces who have suffered a hard blow. This is a fine Allied picture." It had been an "interesting" battle, he said, rather like El Alamein; indeed, "I think possibly one of the most interesting and tricky battles I have ever handled." What came next nearly destroyed Allied unity. Montgomery said the GIs made great fighting men, when given proper leadership. [49]

Bradley, Patton, and nearly every American officer in Europe were furious. As they saw the battle, they had stopped the Germans before Montgomery came onto the scene. Almost no British forces were even engaged in the Bulge. Far from directing the victory, Montgomery had gotten in everyone's way and botched the counterattack.

But what was especially galling about Montgomery's version of the Battle of the Bulge was his immense satisfaction with the outcome. Patton ranted and raved to every reporter who would listen, telling them publicly what he had already written privately in his diary—that had it not been for Montgomery, "we [could have bagged] the whole German army. I wish Ike were more of a gambler, but he is certainly a lion compared to Montgomery, and Bradley is better than Ike as far as nerve is concerned. . . . Monty is a tired little fart. War requires the taking of risks and he won't take them."[50]

CHAPTER SEVEN

The Last Offensive

In mid-January 1945, Eisenhower envisioned a campaign in which all his armies would fight their way forward to the Rhine, in the process inflicting great damage on the Wehrmacht. Montgomery would make a major crossing north of the Ruhr, with Hodges and Patton making secondary crossings to the south. Eisenhower could then use his reserve to support whatever opportunities presented themselves. Eisenhower expected that with Montgomery coming down from the north, and Bradley coming up from the south, the two army groups could encircle the Ruhr, Germany's industrial heart. In preparing this plan, Eisenhower went back to his childhood reading and his first hero, Hannibal. He and Smith discussed in some detail Hannibal's encirclement of the Romans at Cannae.

Once the Ruhr was encircled, Eisenhower intended to fan out and overrun Germany. Again Montgomery and Brooke disagreed with his plan; they thought 21st Army Group ought to get all the supplies for a thrust to Berlin. But Eisenhower already had in mind using Bradley for the main campaign east of the Rhine. This was based in part on his faith in Bradley, and in part on his lack of confidence in Montgomery. As Whiteley put it after the war, "the feeling [at SHAEF] was that if anything was to be done quickly, don't give it to Monty. . . . Monty was the last person Ike would have chosen for a drive on Berlin—Monty would have needed at least six months to prepare."[1] Or, to slip into the football jargon Eisenhower was so fond of using, when the Allies got down near the goal line, the back Eisenhower relied upon was Bradley and he wanted Bradley to carry the ball.

That was the plan. Marshall agreed with it, but Brooke and Eisenhower's field subordinates had objections. Patton wanted a larger role; Bradley thought there was too much emphasis on Montgomery's crossing; Montgomery thought there was not enough. But Eisenhower held firm and saw to it that it was his plan that was implemented. Smith, in an April press conference, when the operation had been successfully completed, said, "Of all the campaigns I have known this one has followed most exactly the pattern of the commander who planned it. With but one small exception, it proceeded exactly as General Eisenhower originally worked it out."[2]

John Eisenhower, who visited his father around this time, noted, "Probably at no time in his life did I ever see the Old Man enjoying such peace of mind . . . He was . . . exercising the professional skills and knowledge that he had been developing for thirty years. And he was doing so at the highest levels." It was this period Eisenhower had in mind some years later, when he told a reporter that war brought on an "exhilaration that you can feel everywhere you go." It came from the "matching of wits . . . in the intellectual and spiritual contest." But he was no war lover; he immediately went on to quote Robert E. Lee that it was well that war was so terrible, or else "we would grow too fond of it."[3]

John's assignment to the European Theater was, naturally, a major concern for Ike. It was unthinkable that John should be sent into the front lines, because of the possibility that he might become a POW (not to speak of Mamie's reaction). Bradley solved the problem by detaching John from the 71st Division and assigning him to a special communications unit. On January 30, a week before John arrived, Ike confessed to Mamie, "I'm so anxious to see him that I feel like a June bride ten days before her wedding." In another letter, he reassured her about John's job and commented, "It will be one to broaden and instruct him, and at the same time will be one where I can see him reasonably often."

When John got to Europe, Bradley gave him four days off to spend with his father at Versailles. "John and I sat up until very late last evening," Ike reported to Mamie. They discussed John's girlfriends, his new job, his training, and his career prospects. Ike gave his son a fur-lined coat, a new combat jacket, and gloves, but when John left to take up his duties, he forgot them. "He has a habit of vagueness," Ike told Mamie, "out of which I hope he will grow. . . . He's lots of fun and we have a thoroughly good time when he is here. But I can't quite figure him out when he gets just sort of roaming about in his mind."[4]

During John's visit, Ike's knee was bothering him again, and he was submitting to daily rubdowns. He had a cold he could not shake; the cyst on his back was getting worse. He kept this information from Mamie, telling her only that he had had a medical checkup and "except for a stinging lecture [the doctor] gave me on the number of cigarettes I smoke, he seemed pleased with my condition. BP was 138/82. Then, of course, I'm eight pounds overweight." But John noted his physical discomfort immediately, and Kay commented that "Ike complained that there was not one part of his body that did not pain him." When he was in public, "he pulled himself together by sheer willpower and looked healthy and vigorous and exuded his usual charm. But the moment he got back to the office . . . he slumped."[5]

Simpson got across the Roer on February 23; by March 2 he had reached the Rhine, in the process achieving one of Eisenhower's basic purposes in the Rhineland campaign—Ninth Army killed six thousand Germans and took thirty thousand prisoners. Farther north, the British Second and Canadian First Armies closed to the Rhine and Montgomery began his preparations for crossing the river. To the south, Hodges reached the Rhine on March 5 at Cologne; Patton got to the river three days later.

Just as Eisenhower had expected, the Germans had insisted on fighting west of the Rhine. At the conclusion of the campaign, Eisenhower held a press conference. A reporter asked him if he thought it was Hitler or the German General Staff that made the decision. Eisenhower replied, "I think it was Hitler. I am guessing because I must confess that many times in this war I have been wrong in trying to evaluate that German mind, if it is a mind. When it looks logical for him to do something he does something else. . . . When we once demonstrated . . . that we could break through the defense west of the Rhine, any sensible soldier would have gone back to the Rhine . . . and stood there and said, 'Now try to come across.' . . . If they had gotten out the bulk of their force they would have been better off."[6]

As a result of Hitler's decision, the Germans had taken a fearful beating. In the Rhineland campaign they lost 250,000 prisoners and untold killed and wounded. More than twenty divisions had been effectively destroyed. The Germans had only thirty or so divisions to defend the Rhine. Spaatz' oil campaign, now going full blast, had virtually eliminated the German fuel reserves. The Allied air forces took full advantage of the lengthening days and better weather, blasting every German who moved during daylight hours, flying as many as eleven thousand sorties in one day.

Eisenhower's plan had worked. Late in March he met Brooke on the banks of the Rhine. Brooke had come to observe Montgomery's crossing. "He was gracious enough," Eisenhower reported to Marshall, "to say that I was right." Eisenhower added that he did not want to sound boastful, "but I must admit to a great satisfaction that the things that . . . I have believed in from the beginning and have carried out in face of some opposition from within and without, have matured so splendidly."[7] Best of all, however, was the creation of a large and powerful reserve, which was now available to Eisenhower to exploit any opportunity that might arise.

On March 7, Eisenhower returned to Reims from a week of travel along the front. That evening he planned to relax and asked a few of his corps commanders to dinner. They had just sat down to eat when the telephone rang. It was Bradley, who said that one of Hodges' divisions had taken intact the Ludendorff railroad bridge at Remagen.

"Brad, that's wonderful," Eisenhower boomed. Bradley said he wanted to push all the force he had in the vicinity over to the east bank. "Sure," Eisenhower responded, "get right on across with everything you've got. It's the best break we've had." Eisenhower's G-3, Pinky Bull, was with Bradley, and Bradley said that Bull objected to establishing a bridgehead at Remagen, because the terrain on the east bank was unsuitable to offensive exploitation and in any case a crossing at Remagen was not part of the SHAEF plan.

Eisenhower dismissed Bull's objections out of hand. "To hell with the planners," Eisenhower said. "Sure, go on, Brad, and I'll give you everything we got to hold that bridgehead. We'll make good use of it even if the terrain isn't too good."[8]

The next morning, Eisenhower informed the CCS that he was rushing troops to Remagen "with the idea that this will constitute greatest possible threat" to the Germans.[9] Because he had insisted on closing to the Rhine, SHAEF had sufficient divisions in reserve for Eisenhower to exercise flexibility and exploit the opportunity. Over the following two weeks, he sent troops to Hodges, who used them to extend the bridgehead. The Germans made determined efforts to wreck the bridge, using air attacks, constant artillery fire, V-2 missiles, floating mines, and frogmen, but Hodges' defenses thwarted their efforts. By the time the big railroad bridge finally collapsed, the bridgehead was twenty miles long and eight miles deep, with six pontoon bridges across the river. It constituted a threat to the entire German defense of the Rhine. To the north, meanwhile, Montgomery was preparing his crossing, as was Patton to the south. Ike told Mamie, "Our attacks have been going well . . . The enemy becomes more and more stretched . . ." Unfortunately, "he shows no signs of quitting. He is fighting hard. . . . I never count my Germans until they're in our cages, or are buried!" [10]

Eisenhower spent the evening of March 16 with Patton and his staff. Patton was in a fine mood and set out to kid and flatter Eisenhower. He said that some of the Third Army units were disappointed because they had not had an opportunity to see the Supreme Commander. "Hell, George," Eisenhower replied, "I didn't think the American GI would give a damn even if the Lord Himself came to inspect them."

Patton smiled. "Well," he said, "I hesitate to say which of you would rank, sir!" The banter went on through the evening. Patton noted in his diary, "General E stated that not only was I a good general but also a lucky general, and Napoleon preferred luck to greatness. I told him this was the first time he had ever complimented me in 2½ years we had served together." [11]

General Arnold paid a visit to Eisenhower's headquarters at Reims. Eisenhower confided that he was feeling the pressure. The war, Arnold noted, "had taken a whole lot out of him but he forced himself to go on and would until [the] whole mess was cleaned up." [12] His physical condition worried those closest to him. He had a touch of the flu. The cyst on his back had been cut out, leaving a deep and painful wound that required a number of stitches. His knee was swollen. Smith told him frankly that he was pushing himself too hard and that he would have a breakdown if he did not take some time off. Eisenhower started to get angry; Smith cut him off by saying, "Look at you. You've got bags under your eyes. Your blood pressure is higher than it's ever been, and you can hardly walk across the room." A wealthy American had offered Eisenhower and his staff the use of his luxurious villa on the French Riviera, Sous le Vent, in Cannes. Smith insisted that Eisenhower accept and take a leave. Eisenhower finally said he would do so if Bradley came along.

On March 19 Eisenhower, accompanied by Bradley, Smith, Tex Lee, and four WACs, including Kay, took the train to Cannes. They stayed four days. Eisenhower was so run-down that he spent the first two days sleeping. He would wake for lunch, have two or three glasses of wine, and shuffle back to bed. One afternoon Kay suggested a game of bridge. Eisenhower shook his head. "I can't keep my mind on cards," he said. "All I want to do is sit here and not think."[13]

Other generals came to Cannes, among them Everett Hughes. Hughes had a talk with Tex Lee about the Eisenhower-Summersby relationship. Lee shared an office with Kay and told Hughes that in his opinion they were not sleeping together. Hughes was not convinced, but remarked, "There is nothing we can do about it." By this stage of the war there was, in fact, a noticeable cooling in Eisenhower's relationship with Kay. He still thought she was great fun to be with, still the only woman he saw on a regular basis, still someone he could talk to privately and frankly. But the intimacy that had prevailed in North Africa and in England was gone. Partly this was due to Eisenhower's almost constant travels, partly to the imminent end of the war. Eisenhower's early 1945 letters to Mamie were filled more than ever with references to their getting together as quickly as the war ended. When that time came Eisenhower knew there would be no place for Kay in his life.

Shortly after returning to Reims from Cannes, Ike wrote Mamie that he had been thinking about "the problem of devising a 'policy' once the Germans stop fighting, under which I could get you over here quickly. It is difficult, of course, to do anything like that arbitrarily. I must not give others the chance to say 'The Boss doesn't care how long he stays here, he has his family, while we . . . we are still separated from ours.' About such things it is impossible to 'reason'—we have to be most careful. But when the shooting stops I'm going to figure out something—you can bet on that! We've been far too long apart."

They needed to get together for many reasons, not the least of which was John. "Mamie gives me hell," Ike told Hughes. Rumors about the supposedly loose morals and high living of the American Army in Europe had reached her, and she told Ike she was worried about exposing John to such influences. Ike was aghast at such charges. "It's amazing to read what you have to say about the 'pitfalls' of last summer," he wrote Mamie. "[John] scarcely left my side, going, I think to only one party—and that attended by a large number of people. So where he could have been in jeopardy is beyond me."

His own worries about John, in fact, were the opposite of Mamie's. "I must say I find him conservative and rather sedate," Ike wrote. "I wish he'd have a bit more fun, or get more laughs out of life." One major complaint was that "he's the champion non-letter writer!" Ike kept reminding himself that "[John] is a man now with his own problems—daily life, etc. It is exceedingly hard for him to realize how important he is to us. But it is difficult to be philosophical."

Mainly, however, Ike's letters to his wife during the last months of the war were filled with the hope that they would soon be together. "Just when this mess is to be over," he wrote her in early April, " . . . I cannot even guess. But, thereafter, if I have to stay here indefinitely, you must come as soon as I can get a permanent abode." [14]

Even at Cannes, Eisenhower could not enjoy the luxury of not thinking. After catching up on his sleep, he spent hours discussing the options in the final campaign with Bradley. The result of their talks was a SHAEF directive that instructed Bradley to send Third Army over the Rhine in the Mainz-Frankfurt area, then make "an advance in strength" toward Kassel. Hodges should meanwhile push east from Remagen. This would lead to a linkup between First and Third Army, to be followed by an encirclement of the Ruhr. It would also make 12th Army Group's offensive greater in size and scope than that of 21st Army Group. Since January, and especially after Remagen, Eisenhower's inclination had been to keep increasing the strength of the attack on Bradley's front. At first it had been intended as a diversion, then as a secondary effort to help Montgomery, then as an alternative major thrust if Montgomery had difficulties. By the third week in March, Bradley's operations had become, in Eisenhower's mind, the main thrust.

On March 22, the day after he received the SHAEF directive, Patton made a surprise crossing of the Rhine. The following day Eisenhower flew from Cannes to Wesel, on the lower Rhine, where he watched Simpson's Ninth Army (attached to 21st Army Group) make its practically unopposed crossing of the Rhine. To the north, meanwhile, Second Army made an assault crossing. Simultaneously, Hodges and Patton extended their bridgeheads. The final offensive was rolling.

On March 25 Eisenhower went to Montgomery's headquarters for a quick visit. Churchill and Brooke were already there. The Prime Minister showed Eisenhower a note he had received from Soviet

Foreign Minister Molotov. Molotov accused the West of dealing "behind the backs of the Soviet Union, which is bearing the brunt of the war against Germany," by conducting surrender negotiations with the German military command in Italy. Eisenhower, Churchill later recorded, "was much upset, and seemed deeply stirred with anger at what he considered most unjust and unfounded charges about our good faith." Eisenhower told Churchill he would accept surrenders in the field whenever offered; if political matters arose he would consult the heads of governments. Churchill responded that he thought the AEF ought to make a definite effort to beat the Russians to Berlin and hold as much of eastern Germany as possible "until my doubts about Russia's intention have been cleared away."[15]

Thus was raised what would be the last great controversy of World War II. Once the AEF was over the Rhine, and given the Red Army position on the Oder-Neisse line, the fate of Germany was sealed. For almost three and one-half years, the Wehrmacht had been at the center of Eisenhower's thoughts. Now Churchill wanted him to think rather less about the Germans, more about the Russians. Eisenhower resisted such a switch. There were political reasons for his resistance, which will be discussed later, but there were also some immediate military factors, of which the most important was the simplest—Eisenhower would not believe the Wehrmacht was finished until it had surrendered unconditionally.

Aside from his general analysis of the German character, Eisenhower had a specific fear—that the Nazis intended to set up a mountain retreat in the Austrian Alps, from which Hitler would direct guerrilla warfare. Eisenhower wanted a quick, sharp, definitive end to the war; to get it, he believed, the AEF had to occupy the Alps. They were, to him, a more important objective than Berlin. He thus rejected Churchill's argument that he should race the Russians to the German capital.

That decision represented a change in plan and was a bitter blow to British pride. It has been much criticized since, and not just by the British. Eisenhower's detractors, on both sides of the Atlantic, regard it as his worst mistake of the war.

The capture of Berlin was the obvious culmination of the offensive that began in 1942 in North Africa. The Western press, and the British and American people, assumed that SHAEF was directing its armies toward Berlin. The SHAEF planning staff had in fact planned for it. In September 1944, when it seemed that the AEF would soon

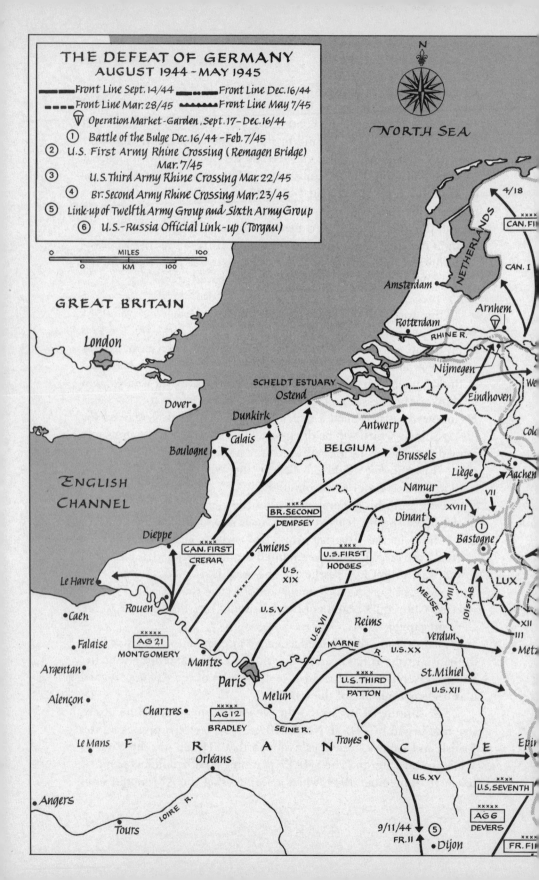

THE DEFEAT OF GERMANY
AUGUST 1944 - MAY 1945

━━━━ Front Line Sept. 14/44   ▄▄▄▄ Front Line Dec. 16/44
▬ ▬ ▬ Front Line Mar. 28/45   ◆◆◆◆ Front Line May 7/45
▽ Operation Market-Garden, Sept. 17 – Dec. 16/44
① Battle of the Bulge Dec. 16/44 – Feb. 7/45
② U.S. First Army Rhine Crossing (Remagen Bridge)
     Mar. 7/45
③ U.S. Third Army Rhine Crossing Mar. 22/45
④ Br. Second Army Rhine Crossing Mar. 23/45
⑤ Link-up of Twelfth Army Group and Sixth Army Group
⑥ U.S.-Russia Official Link-up (Torgau)

MILES
0 ——————— 100
0 ——————— 100
KM

N

NORTH SEA

GREAT BRITAIN

London

Dover

ENGLISH
CHANNEL

NETHERLANDS

Amsterdam

Rotterdam

Arnhem

RHINE R.

Nijmegen

Eindhoven

We

4/18

CAN. FI

CAN. I

SCHELDT ESTUARY

Ostend

Dunkirk

Calais

Boulogne

Antwerp

BELGIUM

Brussels

Liège

Namur

Aachen

Col

Dieppe

CAN. FIRST
CRERAR

Amiens

U.S.
XIX

BR. SECOND
DEMPSEY

Dinant

U.S. FIRST
HODGES

VII

XVIII

① Bastogne

LUX.

Le Havre

Caen

Rouen

U.S. V

U.S. VII

MEUSE R.

IOIST AB

VIII

XII

III

Falaise

AG 21
MONTGOMERY

Reims

Verdun

Met

Argentan

Mantes

MARNE R.

U.S. XX

St. Mihiel

Alençon

Paris

Melun

U.S. THIRD
PATTON

U.S. XII

Chartres

AG 12
BRADLEY

SEINE R.

Le Mans   F   R   A   N

Orléans

Troyes

C

E

Épin

U.S. XV

U.S. SEVENTH

Angers

LOIRE R.

AG 6
DEVERS

Tours

9/11/44 ▽ ⑤
FR. II

Dijon

FR. FI

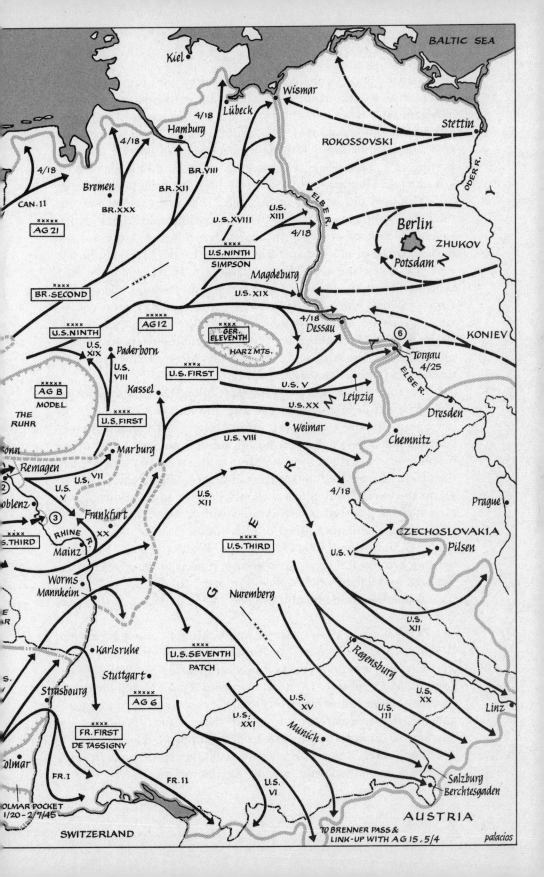

be advancing into Germany, the planners drew up a proposal for the final offensive. "Our main object must be the early capture of Berlin," it began, "the most important objective in Germany." The way to accomplish this was to make the major advance north of the Ruhr with 21st Army Group; 12th Army Group would operate in a supporting role. Eisenhower accepted this plan; on a number of occasions he told Montgomery, "Clearly Berlin is the main prize." [16]

Why then did he change his mind? The main reason was that the military situation in March 1945 was far different from that prevailing in September 1944. In September, the Red Army was still outside Warsaw, more than three hundred miles from Berlin; the AEF was about the same distance away. In March 1945, the AEF remained more than two hundred miles from Berlin, while the Red Army was only thirty-five miles away. At a March 27 press conference, a reporter asked Eisenhower, "Who do you think will be into Berlin first, the Russians or us?" "Well," Eisenhower replied, "I think mileage alone ought to make them do it. After all they are thirty-three miles [away]. They have a shorter race to run." [17]

A second factor in Eisenhower's decision was Bradley's advice. His influence on Eisenhower's thinking was always great, and in the last months of the war it grew even stronger. At Cannes, the two generals had a long talk about Berlin. Bradley pointed out that even if Montgomery reached the Elbe River before the Red Army reached the Oder, fifty miles of lowlands separated the Elbe from Berlin. To get to the capital, Montgomery would have to advance through an area studded with lakes, crisscrossed with streams, and interlaced with canals. Eisenhower asked Bradley for an estimate on the cost of taking Berlin. About 100,000 casualties, Bradley replied. "A pretty stiff price to pay for a prestige objective, especially when we've got to fall back and let the other fellow take over" (Berlin was well within the occupation zone already assigned to the Russians at the Yalta Conference.) [18]

Personality, as always, played a role. "Monty wanted to ride into Berlin on a white charger," as Whiteley put it. By this stage of the war, however, Eisenhower was barely on speaking terms with Montgomery. As Eisenhower later told Cornelius Ryan, "Montgomery had become so personal in his efforts to make sure that the Americans—and me, in particular—got no credit, that, in fact, we hardly had anything to do with the war, that I finally stopped talking to him." [19]

Eisenhower wanted Bradley to lead the last campaign. Had Bradley been on the northern flank, Eisenhower might well have sent him to Berlin. But 12th Army Group was in the center, so Eisenhower decided to make the main thrust there, with Dresden as the objective. This line offered the shortest route to the Red Army and would divide the remaining German forces roughly in half. To provide Bradley with sufficient force, Eisenhower took Ninth Army away from 21st Army Group and gave it to Bradley. To insure cooperation with the Russians, he wired Stalin to inform him of his intentions, to suggest that the Red Army meet the AEF around Dresden, and to ask for information as to Russian intentions.

Eisenhower's cable to Stalin, dated March 28, set off a flurry of activity in the capitals of the Big Three. The Russians acted first. Stalin agreed that Dresden was the best area for a meeting between the AEF and the Red Army, and added that Berlin had lost its former strategic significance. Stalin said that the Red Army planned to allot only secondary forces to the capture of the German capital. In fact, however, the Red Army had already begun a major redeployment, carried out "in almost frantic haste," designed to make Berlin its primary objective, assigning to that objective 1.25 million soldiers, supported by twenty-two thousand pieces of artillery.

The British agreed with the Russians about the importance of Berlin; consequently they were decidedly unhappy with Eisenhower's plan to aim toward Dresden instead, and unhappy too with Eisenhower for opening direct communications with Stalin. They feared that Stalin would make a dupe of Eisenhower. "I consider we are about to make a terrible mistake," Montgomery wired Brooke. The British Chiefs sent their own strong protest directly to Marshall.[20]

In the United States, where Roosevelt was sick and Marshall had taken charge of the conduct of the war, the Americans in their turn were upset by the British protests. They resented the way their British allies called into question the strategy of the most successful field commander of the war. After Eisenhower's success in the Rhineland campaign, Marshall thought that for the British to display such a lack of trust in Eisenhower was incredible, and he told them so.

Unaware of Marshall's response to the British, Eisenhower sent a justification of his own to the Chief of Staff. He denied that he had made any changes in plans—which was simply not true—and then turned British criticism of his strategy on its head. "Merely following the principle that Field Marshal Brooke had always shouted to me," he said, "I am determined to concentrate on one major thrust and all that my plan does is to place the Ninth U.S. Army back under Bradley" for that thrust. He showed some of his long-suppressed irritation with the British in his concluding paragraph: "The Prime Minister and his Chiefs of Staff opposed my idea that the Germans should be destroyed west of the Rhine. Now they apparently want me to turn aside on operations in which would be involved many thousands of troops before the German forces are fully defeated. I submit that these things are studied daily and hourly by me and my advisors and that we are animated by one single thought which is the early winning of this war." [21]

The next day, March 31, Churchill tried again. He wired Eisenhower, "Why should we not cross the Elbe and advance as far eastward as possible? This has an important political bearing, as the Russian Army of the south seems certain to enter Vienna . . . If we deliberately leave Berlin to them, even if it should be in our grasp, the double event may strengthen their conviction, already apparent, that they have done everything." He wanted the British to get to Berlin first, and he wanted Ninth Army given to 21st Army Group to make it possible. Such a solution, Churchill said, "avoids the relegation of His Majesty's Forces to an unexpected restricted sphere." [22]

Churchill's plea, according to the SHAEF office diary, "upset E quite a bit." He immediately dictated a reply. He repeated that he had not changed his plan. He said he still intended to send Montgomery over the Elbe River, but toward Lübeck, not Berlin. By going to Lübeck, 21st Army Group would seal off the Danish Peninsula and keep the Russians out of Denmark. This was an important objective, Eisenhower insisted, and he confessed that "I am disturbed, if not hurt, that you should suggest any thought on my part to 'relegate His Majesty's Forces to an unexpected restricted sphere.' Nothing is further from my mind and I think my record over two and a half years of commanding Allied forces should eliminate any such idea." [23]

The British, realizing that nothing they could say or do would change Eisenhower's mind, made the best of it. The storm began to subside, as neither side wanted a split. The British agreed in practice to the relegation of Montgomery to a secondary role. Churchill, keenly aware of the need for Anglo-American solidarity in the postwar world, took the lead in calming the waters. In a message to Roosevelt he said, "I wish to place on record the complete confidence felt by His Majesty's Government in General Eisenhower, our pleasure that our armies are serving under his command and our admiration of his great and shining quality, character and personality." Churchill sent a copy to Eisenhower, saying in addition that it would "be a grief to me" if anything he had said "pains you." The Prime Minister could not resist the opportunity, however, to add that he still felt the AEF should take Berlin. "I deem it highly important that we should shake hands with the Russians as far to the east as possible." [24]

Thus, although the British had accepted the transfer of Ninth Army from Montgomery to Bradley, and resigned themselves to seeing the major thrust in central Germany, they still wanted the question of Berlin left open. Montgomery pushed that position on April 6, when he told Eisenhower that although he realized Eisenhower did not feel Berlin had much value, "I personally would not agree with this; I consider that Berlin has definite value as an objective and I have no doubt whatever that the Russians think the same; but they may well pretend that this is not the case!!" [25]

Meanwhile, however, Marshall was telling the British Chiefs, "Only Eisenhower is in a position to know how to fight his battle, and to exploit to the full the changing situation." As to Berlin, the JCS felt that such "psychological and political advantages as would result from the possible capture of Berlin ahead of the Russians should not override the imperative military consideration, which in our opinion is the destruction and dismemberment of the German armed forces." [26]

The next day, Eisenhower set the controversy in perspective while making his own position in the structure of the high command clear. He said he was making his decisions on military grounds and that he would require a new directive from his superiors on the CCS if the CCS wished him to operate on political grounds. He said a drive to Berlin was militarily unsound, then added, "I am the first to admit that a war is waged in pursuance of political aims, and if the Combined Chiefs of Staff should decide that the Allied effort to take Berlin outweighs purely military considerations in this theater, I would cheerfully readjust my plans and my thinking so as to carry out such an operation." [27] The British, knowing that they could not change Marshall's mind, did not even try. The CCS made no change in Eisenhower's directive. He therefore continued to operate under orders that required him to aim at the destruction of the German armed forces.

Through the first weeks of April the AEF rolled forward. Superiority in quality of troops, mobility, air power, material, and morale was enormous. Regiments, companies, squads, sometimes even three men in a jeep dashed on ahead, leaving their supply bases far behind, ignoring wide gaps on the flanks and enemy units in their rear, roaming far and wide with only sketchy knowledge of the enemy's positions, all the time certain that there was little or nothing the Germans could do about it. The German high command was, for all practical purposes, nonexistent; most German units were immobilized because of lack of fuel. There was no coherent defense.

On April 11, the leading units of Simpson's Ninth Army reached the Elbe River at Magdeburg. Simpson got two bridgeheads over the river, one north of Magdeburg on April 12, another to the south on April 13. The one to the north was driven back by a German counterattack on April 14, but the one to the south held.

Suddenly it seemed that the Americans had an opportunity to take Berlin. The Russian drive for the capital had not yet begun and Simpson was within fifty miles of the city. He felt he could get to Berlin before the Red Army got there and asked Bradley's permission to try. Bradley checked with Eisenhower. Eisenhower said no. Simpson was stopped where he was.

Patton was appalled. His romanticism, his strong sense of the dramatic, and his deep knowledge of military history all led him to believe that Eisenhower was passing up an a historic opportunity. "Ike, I don't see how you figure that one," Patton told his boss. "We had better take Berlin and quick." [28]

Eisenhower disagreed. He felt that taking Lübeck in the north and occupying the Alpine redoubt area to the south were tasks "vastly more important than the capture of Berlin." He also thought that Simpson could not get to the capital before the Russians and so it was foolish to try. "We'd get all coiled up for something that in all probability would never come off." While it was true that Simpson had a bridgehead over the Elbe, "it must be remembered that only our spearheads are up to that river; our center of gravity is well back of there." [29]

The British nevertheless urged Eisenhower to send Simpson to Berlin. On April 17, Eisenhower flew to London to confer with Churchill on the subject. He convinced the Prime Minister of the soundness of his views; Churchill admitted that the immense strength of the Red Army on the eastern edges of Berlin, in comparison with Simpson's force (Simpson had fewer than fifty thousand men over the Elbe, and had gone beyond the range of fighter support), inevitably meant that it would be the Russians who first battered their way into the ruins.

• •

By 1952 Eisenhower was embarrassed by his failure to take Berlin. In various ways he tried to rewrite the historical record, asserting in his memoirs references to this or that warning he gave to this or that politician about the Russians. In *At Ease,* written in 1967, he claimed that he told FDR in January 1944 that he anticipated trouble with the Russians, but that Roosevelt would not listen. He further claimed that he warned Brooke, in 1943, that if the Allies did not get to Europe soon, the Red Army would overrun it, and that the Russians would then be impossible to deal with. He may well have uttered such warnings, but he did not mention them in *Crusade in Europe,* written almost two decades before *At Ease,* nor did he ever write anything during the war to indicate that he was fearful of Russian intentions. When he claimed to have done so, it was noticeable that in both cases he said he made his point in private, and in both cases the man he made it to was dead.

Eisenhower also became highly defensive about the Berlin decision, especially after the 1948 Russian blockade of the city, and explained again and again—mainly to Republicans who feared that Stalin had made a fool of him—that he made the decision solely on military grounds, that he really was already aware of the Russian threat, and that he was warning others about the Soviets. The truth was that he may have wished by 1952 that he had taken a hard line with the Russians in 1945, but he had not. Instead, he was scrupulously fair in upholding their interests in the surrender negotiations and in the movements of his armies in the last weeks of the war.

In the spring of 1945 the Germans were eager to join the Americans in an anti-Soviet alliance. Hitler's suicide, on April 30, seemed to the remaining German leaders to eliminate the major obstacle to such an alliance. They felt that with Hitler gone, the West would be more inclined to see Germany as a bulwark against Communism in Europe.

Specifically, the way Admiral Karl Doenitz, Hitler's successor, tried to speed up the East-West split and salvage something for Germany was through piecemeal surrender to the Western Allies only. President Truman replied that the only term acceptable was unconditional surrender of all German armies to the Big Three. Churchill supported Truman. Eisenhower too was in complete agreement with Truman's policy. "In every move we make these days," Eisenhower assured Marshall, "we are trying to be meticulously careful in this regard."[30]

Meticulous care was essential, as by both word and act the Germans continued their effort to split the Alliance. Their soldiers on the Eastern Front, rightfully fearing above all else capture by the Red Army, fought desperately. On the Western Front, they surrendered at the first sight of an AEF unit. German civilians tried to flee to the West so that they would be inside the Anglo-American lines when the end came. And on May 1, Doenitz, in a radio address to the nation, said the Wehrmacht would "continue the struggle against Bolshevism until the fighting troops and the hundreds of thousands of families in Eastern Germany have been preserved from destruction."[31] But by May 2 or 3, Doenitz realized that Eisenhower would not accept a general surrender in the West only; he therefore tried to achieve the same end by surrendering armies and army groups to SHAEF while fighting on in the East.

Eisenhower rebuffed him and continued to insist on a general, unconditional surrender. Nevertheless, Doenitz kept hoping. On May 4, he sent Admiral Hans von Friedeburg to SHAEF with instructions to arrange for the surrender of the remaining German forces in the West. Eisenhower insisted that a general surrender had to take place on the Eastern and Western Fronts simultaneously. Smith and Strong (Strong had been military attaché in Berlin before the war and spoke perfect German) carried on the discussion with Friedeburg, for Eisenhower refused to see any German officers until the document of unconditional surrender had been signed. Smith told Friedeburg that there would be no bargaining and ordered him to sign the surrender document; Friedeburg replied that he had no power to sign. Smith insisted. He showed Friedeburg some SHAEF operational maps, which were quite convincing of the overpowering might of the AEF and the hopelessness of the German position. Friedeburg cabled Doenitz, asking for permission to sign an unconditional surrender.

Late on the evening of May 5, Strong informed Eisenhower of these developments. Eisenhower grunted, then lay down on the cot in his office. The next morning he wrote Mamie, "Last night I really expected some definite developments and went to bed early in anticipation of being waked up at 1, 2, 3, or 4 A.M. Nothing happened and as a result I was wide awake, very early—with nothing decent to read. The Wild Wests I have just now are terrible—I could write better ones, left-handed."[32]

Doenitz did not give Friedeburg permission to sign. Instead, he made one last effort to split the Alliance, sending Generaloberst Alfred Jodl, the German Chief of Staff, to Reims to arrange for a surrender in the West only. Jodl arrived on Sunday evening, May 6.

He conferred with Smith and Strong, emphasizing that the Germans were willing, indeed anxious, to surrender to the West, but not to the Red Army. Doenitz, he said, would order all German troops remaining on the Western Front to cease firing no matter what SHAEF did about the offer to surrender. Smith replied that the surrender had to be a general one to all the Allies. Jodl then asked for forty-eight hours "in order to get the necessary instructions to all their outlying units." Smith said that was impossible. After the talks dragged on for over an hour, Smith put the problem to Eisenhower.

Eisenhower felt that Jodl was trying to gain time so that more German soldiers and civilians could get across the Elbe and escape the Russians. He told Smith to inform Jodl that "he would break off all negotiations and seal the western front preventing by force any further westward movement of German soldiers and civilians" unless Jodl signed the surrender document. But he also decided to grant the forty-eight-hour delay before announcing the surrender, as Jodl requested.

Smith took Eisenhower's reply to Jodl, who thereupon sent a cable to Doenitz, explaining the situation and asking permission to sign. Doenitz was enraged; he characterized Eisenhower's demands as "sheer extortion." He nevertheless felt impelled to accept them, and was consoled somewhat by the thought that the Germans could still save many troops from the Russians during the forty-eight-hour delay. Just past midnight, therefore, he cabled Jodl: "Full power to sign in accordance with conditions as given has been granted by Grand Admiral Doenitz."[33]

At 2 A.M on May 7, Generals Smith, Morgan, Bull, Spaatz, Tedder, a French representative, and General Susloparoff, the Russian liaison officer at SHAEF, gathered in the second-floor recreation room of the École Professionelle et Technique de Garçons, Reims. Strong was there to serve as translator. The war room was L-shaped, with only one small window; otherwise, the walls were covered with maps. Pins, arrows, and other symbols showed how completely Germany had been overrun. It was a relatively small room; the Allied officers had to squeeze past one another to get to their assigned chairs, gathered around a heavy oak table. When they had all sat down, Jodl, accompanied by Friedeburg and an aide, was led into the room. Tall, perfectly erect, immaculately dressed, his monocle in place, Jodl looked the personification of Prussian militarism. He bowed stiffly. Strong found himself, to his own surprise, feeling a bit sorry for him.

While the somewhat elaborate procedures for the signing went on, Eisenhower waited in his adjacent office, pacing and smoking. The signing took a half hour. In the war room, Jodl was delivering the German nation into the hands of the Allies and officially acknowledging that Nazi Germany was dead; outside, spring was bursting forth, promising new life.

Eisenhower knew that he should feel elated, triumphant, joyful, but all he really felt was dead beat. He had hardly slept in three days; it was the middle of the night; he just wanted to get it over with. At 2:41 A.M., Strong led Jodl into Eisenhower's office. Eisenhower sat down behind his desk. Jodl bowed, then stood at attention. Eisenhower asked Jodl if he understood the terms and was ready to execute them. Jodl said yes. Eisenhower then warned him that he would be held personally accountable if the terms were violated. Jodl bowed again and left.

Eisenhower went out into the war room, gathered the SHAEF officers around him (Kay and Butcher managed to sneak in too), and photographers were called in to record the event for posterity. Eisenhower then made a short newsreel and radio recording. When the newsmen left, Smith said it was time to send a message to the CCS. Everyone had a try at drafting an appropriate document. "I tried one myself," Smith later recalled, "and like all my associates, groped for resounding phrases as fitting accolades to the Great Crusade and indicative of our dedication to the great task just completed."[34]

Eisenhower quietly watched and listened. Each draft was more grandiloquent than the last. The Supreme Commander finally thanked everyone for his efforts, rejected all the proposals, and dictated the message himself. "The mission of this Allied force was fulfilled at 0241 local time, May 7, 1945."[35]

He had managed to grin while the newsreel cameras were on, to hold up the pens in a V-for-Victory sign, to walk without a limp. After signing the last message, he slumped visibly. "I suppose this calls for a bottle of champagne," he sighed. Someone brought one in; it was opened to feeble cheers; it was flat. Utter weariness now descended; everyone went to bed.

It was not at all like the image Eisenhower had held before him for three years. From the time he left Mamie in June 1942, he had sustained himself with the thought of this moment. "When the war ends"—the image of that magic moment had kept him going. When the Germans surrendered, then all would right again. The world would be secure, he could go home, his responsibilities would be over, his duty done. He could sit beside a lazy stream with nothing but a cane pole and a bobber, and Mamie there with him, so that he could tell her about all the funny things that had happened that he had not had time to write about.

By early 1945, he had been forced to modify the fantasy somewhat, as he realized that he would have to remain in Germany for some months at least, as head of the American occupying forces. Still, he clung to the thought that Mamie could be with him immediately after the shooting stopped. Now he had the sinking feeling that even that was not going to be possible.

As to escaping responsibility, decision making, and the burden of command, he had already had to face the fact that such a release was impossible. Worst of all, he already feared that world security was threatened. There had been too many of his own officers who listened with approval to the German whisperings about an anti-Communist alliance; on the other side, the Russian suspicions about Western motives struck Eisenhower as bordering on paranoia (even before he went to bed, Eisenhower received a message that said the Russians would not accept the surrender signed in Reims and insisted on another signing, in Berlin). It made him wonder if it would be possible after all to cooperate with them in rebuilding Europe. Going to bed on that morning of May 7, Eisenhower felt as flat as the champagne.

But Eisenhower's flatness should not preclude a glance at what he had accomplished and what he had to celebrate, had he had the energy to do so. The problem is that, like Smith, one searches in vain for the fitting accolades to acknowledge the accomplishments of Dwight D. Eisenhower in the Second World War—of what he had endured, of what he had contributed to the final victory, of his place in military history.

Fortunately, George C. Marshall, next to Eisenhower himself the man most responsible for Eisenhower's success, spoke for the nation and its allies, as well as the U. S. Army, when he replied to Eisenhower's last wartime message, "You have completed your mission with the greatest victory in the history of warfare," Marshall began. "You have commanded with outstanding success the most powerful military force that has ever been assembled. You have met and successfully disposed of every conceivable difficulty incident to varied national interests and international political problems of unprecedented complications." Eisenhower, Marshall said, had triumphed over inconceivable logistical problems and military obstacles.

"Through all of this, since the day of your arrival in England three years ago, you have been selfless in your actions, always sound and tolerant in your judgments and altogether admirable in the courage and wisdom of your military decisions.

"You have made history, great history for the good of mankind and you have stood for all we hope and admire in an officer of the United States Army. These are my tributes and my personal thanks."[36]

It was the highest possible praise from the best possible source. It had been earned.

Eisenhower earned the praise through a total commitment of his time, energy, and emotion, of course, but even more through his brains, talents, and leadership. He had also been lucky—in his assignments, in his aides and subordinates and superiors, in his opponents, in the weather on D-Day—so many good breaks, in fact, that "Eisenhower luck" became a byword. But much more than luck was involved in his success.

One leadership attribute was his attention to detail, complemented by his intuitive knowledge of which detail to pay attention to. His decisions on the weather on D-Day, for example, were not just pure dumb luck. For a month before June 6, he had made time in his overcrowded schedule to spend fifteen minutes every day with Group Captain Stagg. He would hear Stagg's prediction for the next couple of days, then query him on the basis of the judgment. He wanted to know how good Stagg was, so as to be able to make his own evaluation when he had to make the decision he was born to make.

As a soldier, his chief characteristic was his flexibility. He often said that in preparing for battle, plans were essential, but that once the battle was joined, plans were useless. Nowhere did this characteristic show more clearly or effectively than in his response to the capture of the bridge at Remagen.

He was outstanding at the art of mentally leaping over the front lines to get into the mind-set of the enemy. He alone understood, in September 1944, that the Germans would fight furiously until they had no bullets left, just as he understood, on December 17, that the Germans were launching a counteroffensive in Ardennes, not just a counterattack.

In the Mediterranean, he had been excessively cautious in his generalship, but in the campaign in northwest Europe, he showed boldness and a willingness to take risks. The best example was his decision to go ahead with the D-Day drops of the 82nd and 101st Airborne Divisions in the face of Leigh-Mallory's strongly worded recommendation that they be called off. In view of the contributions of the paratroopers to the success of D-Day, for that decision alone Eisenhower earned his fame.

He made many mistakes, although fewer than he had in the Mediterranean. Some came about because of greater goals—appeasing Montgomery meant the failure to take Caen in mid-June 1944; it meant failure to totally destroy the German Army at Falaise in mid-August; it meant failure to take Antwerp in mid-September. It also cost the Allies dearly in early January 1945, when Monty failed to bag the Germans in the Bulge. Ike's emphasis on the offensive in the late fall of 1944 was the principal cause of the intelligence failure at the Bulge. That failure led to the heaviest losses of the war for the American Army.

To Eisenhower's critics, his biggest mistake was the failure to take Berlin (this author would hotly dispute that judgment). On an even larger scale, he was certainly wrong in 1945 to have such faith (hope) in the future of U.S.-Soviet relations. He should have recognized that the issues that divided the reluctant Allies were too great to be overcome.

But as a strategist, the highest art of command, he was far more often right than wrong. He was right in his selection of Normandy as the invasion site, right in his selection of Bradley rather than Patton as First Army commander, right in his insistence on using the bombers against the French railway system, right to insist on a broad-front approach to Germany, right to see the Bulge as opportunity rather than disaster, right to fight the major battle west of the Rhine. He was right on the big decisions.

He was the most successful general of the greatest war ever fought.

CHAPTER EIGHT

Peace

By the time of the surrender, Eisenhower had become the symbol of the forces that had combined to defeat the Nazis, and of the hopes for a better world. His worldwide popularity was immense. He inspired a confidence that can only be marveled at, rather than accurately measured. In the months following the surrender at Reims, whenever a big job had to be done, his name just naturally came up. Edward R. Murrow told President Truman that Eisenhower was the "only man in the world" who could make the United Nations work. Sidney Hillman, the labor politician, said that Eisenhower was the "only man" who could guide Germany into a democratic future. Alan Brooke told Eisenhower that if there were another war, "we would entrust our last man and our last shilling to your Command."[1] Democratic and Republican politicians alike felt that Eisenhower was the "only man" who could win for them in 1948. Truman himself, in July 1945, told Eisenhower, "General, there is nothing that you may want that I won't try to help you get. That definitely and specifically includes the presidency in 1948."[2]

Eisenhower's personal desire was for a quiet retirement with perhaps a bit of writing and lecturing. But fulfillment of that desire had to wait another sixteen years, because the nation continued to call him to her service, on the grounds that he was the "only man" who could do the job and it was therefore his "duty" to accept. He served in five positions—as head of the American Occupation Zone in Germany, as Chief of Staff, as president of Columbia University, as the Supreme Commander of NATO, and as President of the United States. In each instance, he accepted the responsibility reluctantly, or so at least he told himself, his friends, and the public. There can be no doubt, however, that he enjoyed the challenge, the stimulation, and the satisfaction that his work provided, and that he was, from age fifty-four to age seventy, too active, too involved, too alive, to simply retire. Nor was he immune to the pleasures of power and its uses.

But although Eisenhower's postwar career led to eight years at the pinnacle of world power, it was the case for Eisenhower, as it had been for Washington and Grant before him, that after the war the great moments of his life were behind him. Despite their success in politics, nothing that happened to Washington after Valley Forge and Yorktown, and nothing that happened to Grant after the Wilderness and Appomattox, could surpass those experiences for drama, importance, or personal satisfaction. So too for Eisenhower—nothing could ever surpass D-Day and Reims.

When news of the surrender was flashed around the world, it was, in Churchill's words, "the signal for the greatest outburst of joy in the history of mankind." For Eisenhower, the weeks that followed were full of activity—making arrangements with the Russians, occupation duties, diplomatic difficulties, redeploying the American troops in Europe to the Pacific, entertaining visiting VIPs—but most of his energy went into a hectic, exhausting, satisfying, prolonged celebration.

It began on May 15, when he accepted an invitation to spend a night in London. John, Kay, Jimmy Gault, and Bradley joined him. They took along eighteen bottles of the best champagne in Reims, ate a buffet supper at the Dorchester Hotel, then went to the theater. Kay's mother was a part of the party, and Kay sat beside the general in their box at the theater, which resulted in a famous photograph and added to the gossip about their relationship. It was the first time Eisenhower had seen a show or eaten in a restaurant in three years, indeed his first public appearance since July 1942, and he was astonished to discover how famous and popular he had become. People at the theater cheered, shouted, and called out, "Speech, Speech!" when they saw him. From his box in the balcony he rose and said, "It's nice to be back in a country where I can *almost* speak the language."[3]

The grand centerpiece of the victory celebration came in June, at Guildhall, in the City of London. Churchill insisted that Eisenhower participate in the formal celebration and ignored Eisenhower's request that the ceremonies "be such as to avoid over-glorification of my own part in the victories of this Allied team." Attention centered on Eisenhower. He was told that he would make the principal speech, to a large audience that would include every high-ranking military and civil official in the United Kingdom, in a historic hall filled with British pomp and circumstance at its most extreme and impressive, and that he would receive the Duke of Wellington's sword. He took the assignment with the utmost seriousness, because "this was the first formal address of any length that I had to give on my own." He worked on the speech nightly for three weeks, read it aloud innumerable times to Butcher, Kay, and anyone else who would listen. Butcher suggested that he memorize it, which would give the appearance of spontaneity and allow him to speak without wearing his spectacles. Eisenhower agreed.[4]

The ceremony was held in the morning on June 12. An hour or so before it began, Eisenhower went for a walk in Hyde Park, alone, to collect his thoughts. He was spotted, then surrounded by a mob of well-wishers (it was the last time in his life he ever attempted to go out alone in a city). He had to be rescued by a policeman. From the Dorchester, he and Tedder rode into the City of London in a horse-drawn carriage, past the destruction and rubble around St. Paul's, to bomb-scarred Guildhall. Eisenhower received the sword from the bewigged Lord Mayor of London.

Then Eisenhower began his speech by saying that his sense of appreciation for the high honor being done him was tempered by a sense of sadness, because "humility must always be the portion of any man who receives acclaim earned in blood of his followers and sacrifices of his friends." He spoke of the great Allied team and insisted that he was only a symbol, that the awards and acclaim he was receiving belonged to all the team.

"I come from the very heart of America," he said. He spoke of the differences in age and size between Abilene and London, but then pointed to the kinship between them. "To preserve his freedom of worship, his equality before law, his liberty to speak and act as he sees fit . . . a Londoner will fight. So will a citizen of Abilene. When we consider these things, then the valley of the Thames draws closer to the farms of Kansas." Then, again, he referred to "the great team" that he had led. "No man alone could have brought about [the victory]. Had I possessed the military skill of a Marlborough, the wisdom of Solomon, the understanding of Lincoln, I still would have been helpless without the loyalty, vision, and generosity of thousands upon thousands of British and Americans."[5]

The London newspapers the following day, in what Eisenhower called "an excess of friendly misjudgment," compared the speech to the Gettysburg Address. After he finished, Churchill took him to the balcony to greet a crowd of thirty thousand in the streets below. "Whether you know it or not," Eisenhower responded to the demands for a speech, "I am now a Londoner myself. I have as much right to be down in the crowd yelling as you have." Butcher, the professional public-relations man, was impressed. "[Ike's] words," he said, "came as naturally as if he had rehearsed them for a week."[6]

Eisenhower was the focus of ceremonies in Prague, Paris, and other European capitals, and most of all in the United States. Together with Marshall, he made detailed plans for the return home of his top commanders, so that Bradley, Patton, Hodges, Simpson, and the corps and division commanders would each get their share of the applause of a grateful nation. He himself came home last, because Marshall insisted that anyone who came after Eisenhower would be distinctly anticlimactic.

Eisenhower's triumphant return took place in late June. Huge crowds greeted him and he made numerous speeches. The most important was to a joint session of Congress. Marshall sent him a draft of a speech to read at the Capitol; Eisenhower thanked him for it but said he preferred to speak extemporaneously. The result was a speech full of platitudes and eternal verities, but it was spoken with such sincerity and emotion that it quite overcame the audience. The politicians gave General Eisenhower a standing ovation that was the longest in the history of Congress, and there was not a man in the hall who did not think to himself how wonderful General Eisenhower would look standing at that podium as President Eisenhower.

Later that day, John joined his father for the flight to New York. As they settled into their seats, Eisenhower commented, "Well, now I've got to figure out what I am going to say when I get there." There were an estimated two million people in his audience outside City Hall. His theme was "I'm just a Kansas farmer boy who did his duty," and The New York Times acclaimed his speech as "masterful."[7]

He was in great demand as a speaker. Invitations came in a flood, from the rich, the famous, the heads of worthy organizations and old universities, friends; everyone wanted him to speak. All the causes were good ones; he hated to say no to any of them. But as he told a friend, "One of my greatest horrors is a garrulous general."[8] So far as possible, he held his speechmaking down to a minimum, and except for the Guildhall address he put in a minimum amount of preparation. He usually hit the right note. In Abilene, twenty thousand people (four times the city's population) gathered in City Park to welcome him home. "Through this world it has been my fortune, or misfortune, to wander at considerable distances," Eisenhower said. "Never has this town been outside my heart and memory."[9]

In brief, whether as a writer, or formal speaker, or testifying before congressional committees, or making an impromptu talk to a street crowd, or just riding in an open car, waving his hands like a prizefighter and grinning broadly, and whether in Prague or Paris or London or New York, Eisenhower was a tremendous success. His first words when he stepped off the plane in Washington on June 18 made headlines the next day—"Oh, God, it's swell to be back!" Trailing along behind his triumphant parade in New York, Butcher heard numerous comments—"He waved at me." "Isn't he handsome?" "He's marvelous!" In Washington, Dr. Arthur Burns, an economist at George Washington University, watched Eisenhower drive past in his convertible, caught the friendliness he projected, turned to his wife and said, "This man is absolutely a natural for the Presidency."[10]

Thus did the celebration of the victory add to the already widespread talk about Eisenhower for President. During the war, Eisenhower had responded to such suggestions with a snort or a grunt. When Truman said he would support Eisenhower for the Presidency in 1948, Eisenhower laughed at the idea and replied, "Mr. President, I don't know who will be your opponent for the presidency, but it will not be I."[11] It was an interesting choice of words, as the sentence seemed to identify Eisenhower as a Republican (a subject on which there was intense speculation), and indicated that Eisenhower was shrewd enough to realize that whatever Truman was saying in 1945, Truman himself would be a candidate in 1948.

In August 1945, an old friend from Fort Sam Houston wrote to say he and others in San Antonio were "ready and anxious to organize an 'Eisenhower for President' Club." Eisenhower replied that he was flattered by the suggestion, "But I must tell you, with all the emphasis I can command, that nothing could be so distasteful to me as to engage in political activity of any kind. I trust that no friend of mine will ever attempt to put me in the position where I would even be called upon to deny political ambitions." To Mamie, he wrote, "Many people seem astounded that I'd have no slightest interest in politics. I can't understand *them*."[12]

What he wanted to do was retire. Failing that, he wanted his wife at his side. It was sixteen years before he could achieve the first objective, six months before he realized the second.

Five days after the surrender, Ike wrote his wife to say that he was at work on developing a policy that would make it possible for her to join him in Europe. He wanted her to come as soon as suitable quarters could be found, but warned that it would be difficult and might take time, because "the country is devastated. . . . It is a bleak picture. Why the Germans ever let the thing go as far as they did is completely beyond me!"[13]

On June 4, Eisenhower wrote Marshall. He proposed a policy to bring to Germany wives of enlisted men and officers on occupation duty. He then made his personal case. "I will admit that the last six weeks have been my hardest of the war," he said. "My trouble is that I just plain miss my family." He said he got to see John, then assigned to the 1st Division, about once a month, which was not enough. As to Mamie, he was worried about her health (she had just entered the hospital, suffering from a persistent cold, her weight down to 102 pounds). In a heartfelt plea, he commented, "The strain of the past three years has also been very considerable so far as my wife is concerned, and because of the fact that she has had trouble with her general nervous system for many years I would feel far more comfortable about her if she could be with me."[14]

Three things stand out about the letter. First, the depth of Ike's love and concern for his wife. Second, his concern for what people thought of him. Third, his continued subordination of himself to Marshall. Eisenhower was, after all, Marshall's equal in rank, a five-star general. The other five-star generals—Arnold, MacArthur, and Marshall—had all had their wives at their sides throughout the war. Eisenhower must have known that MacArthur most certainly did not ask Marshall's permission to have Jean join him at his headquarters. Eisenhower did not have to ask Marshall's permission in order to live with his wife; all he had to do was tell her to come on over.

Marshall's response is also extraordinary and caused a subsequent furor. Marshall took the letter to the President for consultation. Truman told him "No," Mamie could not go, as it would be unfair to all the others. Decades later, long after Truman had broken with Eisenhower and at a time when Truman was approaching senility, the former President told reporter Merle Miller, for his book *Plain Speaking*, that Eisenhower had written to Marshall in June 1945 asking permission to divorce Mamie in order to marry Kay. According to Truman's story, he and Marshall agreed that they could never allow such a thing to happen. They told Eisenhower "No," threatened to ruin his career if he did go through with a divorce, and then destroyed the letter.[15]

The story was widely reported in 1973, and widely believed, but completely untrue. Eisenhower did not want to divorce Mamie, he wanted to live with her.

Eisenhower's respect for Marshall and his concern about his own image were so great that, in his response to Marshall's message turning down his request, he apologized for bothering Marshall with a personal problem. Eisenhower said he understood that "from every standpoint of logic and public relations the thing is impossible."[16] He then wrote Mamie to give her the bad news and to tell her, "You cannot be any more tired than I of this long separation, particularly at my age." He said he had talked to John and persuaded him to drop his request for transfer to the Pacific, in order to be around headquarters so that they could be together. "Johnny is really anxious to go to the Pacific," Eisenhower wrote Mamie, "but he realizes I am lonely and need him."[17]

John later wrote that the postsurrender months were "probably the period in my entire life when Dad and I were closest." He was stationed within a half hour's drive. "Dad was a lonely man at that time, let down after the excitement of the war," John recognized, and he tried to help by spending as much time as possible with his father. He went along on trips, including Eisenhower's whirlwind tour of the States in June.[18]

That journey was a disappointment to Mamie, because she had to give up her man to the public. When she met her husband's plane at the Washington airport, she had only the briefest kiss and hug before Ike was hustled off to the Pentagon. For the next eight days, he was constantly making public appearances. Finally, on June 25, Ike, Mamie, John, and Mamie's parents went to White Sulphur Springs for a week of privacy. But as Ike later wrote Charles Harger of Abilene, "In those few days the reaction from the war months and from a rapid series of celebrations was so great that I really didn't get to settle down and relax."[19] When Ike got back to Germany, Mamie wrote about her disappointment over the visit and confessed that she was "back down in the dumps." Ike assured her, "If you'd just once understand how exclusively I love you and long for you then you'd realize how much the week at White Sulphur meant." He said that as a result of the trip, "My hatred of Washington is even greater than it used to be. Which is saying a lot!" and blamed her depression on the city—"I don't see how you could help it [living] in Washington."[20]

What to do about Kay was becoming a problem. She was not a U.S. citizen and therefore could not retain her commission as a WAC or continue working for Eisenhower. In October, she decided to go to the States to take out citizenship papers. When she returned to Germany, Eisenhower asked General Lucius Clay, in Berlin, to give her a job in his office. He told Clay that "I hope you will find a really good job for her and I know that you will remember that she has not only served me with the utmost faithfulness and loyalty but has had more than her share of tragedy to bear in this war. Incidentally, she is about as close-mouthed a person about office business as I ever heard of."[21] To Smith, Eisenhower confessed that he felt bad about Kay, because he knew that "she feels very deserted and alone."[22]

Then, to Kay herself, he dictated a long, businesslike letter that explained why she could no longer work for him. He said he would "not attempt to express the depth of my appreciation for the unexcelled loyalty and faithfulness with which you have worked under my personal direction," and that he was "personally much distressed that an association which has been so valuable to me has to be terminated in this particular fashion." After promising to do anything he could to help her get started on a new career, he concluded, "Finally, I hope that you will drop me a note from time to time—I will always be interested to know how you are getting along." Then he added a handwritten postscript—"Take care of yourself—and retain your optimism."[23]

Kay left the WAC, became a U.S. citizen, and moved to New York. In late 1947 she became engaged, set a date for the wedding, and sent Eisenhower an invitation. He politely declined in a warm but formal reply. Kay soon broke her engagement, however, leading Eisenhower to write in his diary on December 2, 1947, "Heard today . . . that my wartime secretary (rather personal aide and receptionist) is in dire straits." Eisenhower blamed Kay's emotional problems on the death of Colonel Arnold in North Africa in 1943, and commented, "Too bad, she was loyal and efficient and the favorite of everyone in the organization. . . . I trust she pulls herself together, but she is Irish and tragic."[24]

In 1948, Kay published a book about her war experiences, *Eisenhower Was My Boss*. It was a great success and, along with the fees she earned on a lecture tour, made her financially independent. After Eisenhower moved to New York City, in 1948, Kay managed to "accidentally" run into him near his office; he was curt and, by her later account, dismissed her by saying, "Kay, it's impossible. There's nothing I can do."[25]

In 1952, Kay married Reginald Morgan, a New York stockbroker. Then came the publication of *Plain Speaking* (1973), which led Kay to publish a new book of memoirs, *Past Forgetting: My Love Affair with Dwight D. Eisenhower*. In her introduction, Kay said she had been first surprised, then pleased, to discover from Truman's story that Eisenhower had wanted to divorce Mamie to marry her. As Eisenhower was by then dead, and she herself was dying of cancer, she said she had decided to tell the whole truth about their famous affair.

Whether she told the "whole truth" or not, no one can tell. If she did, then General Eisenhower was sexually impotent throughout the war. Kay's book, as a whole, was a vivid and moving account of a wartime romance that was both frustrating and exciting. Nowhere did she claim too much for her own role in his life, but she was always around, a keen and sensitive observer who was, for her part, deeply in love with her boss. Whether Eisenhower loved her in turn or not is less certain, although obviously he had strong feelings about her. In fact, she was the third most important woman in his life, behind only his mother and his wife. But he never thought of marrying Kay, and Kay knew that all along. Mamie, meanwhile, was naturally resentful about Kay, and even Ike, who was so inept in such matters, realized that he could not have both Mamie and Kay. In that circumstance, he unhesitatingly chose Mamie.

No matter how successfully, coldly, even cruelly, he thereafter avoided Kay, the Eisenhower-Summersby romance was too good a story to disappear, and over the years the various rumors and gossip continued to irritate Mamie. When *Plain Speaking* and *Past Forgetting* were published, she was so upset that she authorized John to publish Eisenhower's wartime letters to her, which had previously been sealed. The book that resulted, *Letters to Mamie*, established conclusively that throughout the war years, when Eisenhower was with Kay, his love for Mamie was constant. Throughout the war, his sustaining force was the thought that when it was over he and Mamie could live together again. He loved Mamie for half a century.

But loving Mamie did not necessarily preclude loving Kay. At least, loving her under the special situation in which they lived from the summer of 1942 to the spring of 1945. He was lucky to have her around, and the Allies were lucky she was there. The best advice in attempting to pass any judgment on the Eisenhower-Summersby relationship was that given by Hughes to Tex Lee back in 1943. "Leave Kay and Ike alone. She's helping him win the war."[26]

Eisenhower's occupation headquarters were in the I. G. Farben offices in Frankfurt. His hatred for the Nazis led him to issue strict orders forbidding any fraternization of any kind under any circumstances.

In taking such a tough stance, Eisenhower was expressing accurately the spirit of his operating instructions, which were contained in a document called JCS 1067 (Joint Chiefs of Staff Paper #1067) which had been sent to him on April 26. JCS 1067 was based on the assumption that all Germans were guilty, although some were more guilty than others. It forbade any fraternization between the occupying forces and the Germans. It called for the automatic arrest of large numbers of Germans who had participated in various Nazi organizations. It insisted on denazification, primarily by removing Nazis from public office or positions of importance in public and private enterprises.

It was an impossible policy to enforce, especially the parts about fraternization and the elimination of former Nazis from all positions of responsibility. Eisenhower was slow to realize these obvious truths. Human nature, however, forced him to change his views, first of all with regard to nonfraternization. There was no way in the world to keep GIs whose pockets were bulging with cigarettes and candy away from German girls when most German boys were in P.O.W. camps— where they were suffering terribly because of Eisenhower's insistence that they receive no more food than displaced persons being held in camps. It was Stalin who told his troops that in Germany only the unborn were innocent, but Eisenhower's policies were based on the same principle. The GIs, however, saw little blond, hungry kids, not guilty Nazis, and acted acccordingly.

In June, Eisenhower admitted that it was almost impossible to enforce the nonfraternization rules in the case of small children, and he of course recognized that it was simply silly to forbid soldiers to talk to or give candy bars or chewing gum to German children. Finally, in July, official orders on nonfraternization were amended to include the phrase "except small children." Ultimately the nonfraternization policy became a major embarrassment and was quietly dropped.

Denazification, however, was pursued with sustained vigor, and with the enthusiastic backing of General Eisenhower. His insistence on its application, in fact, was so strong that it led to a breakup of his friendship with Patton.

In Eisenhower's view, if it was a mistake to regard all Germans as guilty, it was certainly correct to regard all Nazis as guilty. In a series of general orders, he directed that no one who had ever been associated with the Nazi party be allowed to hold any position of importance in the American zone. His subordinates in the field complained that the policy was unrealistic. Patton, in command in Bavaria, was the most outspoken. On August 11, he wrote Eisenhower that "a great many inexperienced or inefficient people" were holding positions in local government "as a result of the so-called de-Nazification program." Patton said that "it is no more possible for a man to be a civil servant in Germany and not have paid lip service to Nazism than it is possible for a man to be a postmaster in America and not have paid at least lip service to the Democratic Party, or the Republican Party when it is in power."[27]

Patton continued to use Nazis to run Bavaria. On September 11, Eisenhower wrote Patton a letter that was designed to set him straight on the issue. "Reduced to its fundamentals," Eisenhower told Patton, "the United States entered this war as a foe of Nazism; victory is not complete until we have eliminated from positions of responsibility and in appropriate cases properly punished, every active adherent to the Nazi party." He insisted that "we will not compromise with Nazism in any way ... The discussional stage of this question is long past ... I expect just as loyal service in the execution of this policy ... as I received during the war."[28]

Eisenhower followed up the letter with a personal visit to Patton to emphasize his concern. He said he wanted to extend denazification to cover the whole of German life, not just public positions. But Eisenhower could not convince Patton; as he reported to Marshall, "The fact is that his own convictions are not entirely in sympathy with the 'hard peace' concept and, being Patton, he cannot keep his mouth shut either to his own subordinates or in public."[29]

Patton was trying his best to stifle himself. "I hope you know, Ike, that I'm keeping my mouth shut," he protested. "I'm a clam." But he opened up on September 22, at a press conference. A reporter asked him why reactionaries were still in power in Bavaria. "Reactionaries!" Patton exploded. "Do you want a lot of communists?" After a pause, he said, "I don't know anything about parties. . . . The Nazi thing is just like a Democratic and Republican election fight."[30]

The remark caused a sensation. Eisenhower ordered Patton to report to him in Frankfurt. Patton did so. On the day he arrived, Kay recalled, "General Eisenhower came in looking as though he hadn't slept a wink. I knew at once he had decided to take action against his old friend. He had aged ten years in reaching the decision . . . When General Patton came in, followed by Beetle, the office door closed. But I heard one of the stormiest sessions ever staged in our headquarters. It was the first time I ever heard General Eisenhower really raise his voice."[31]

Eisenhower tried to convince Patton that denazification was essential to the making of a new Germany. Patton tried to convince Eisenhower that the Red Army was the real threat and that the Germans were the real friends. Red-faced, furious, shouting, dealing with the most basic issues, the two old friends reached an impasse. Eisenhower was almost horrified by some of Patton's views on the Russians, and by his loose talk about driving the Red Army back to the Volga. He later told his son that he would have to remove Patton "not for what he's done—just for what he's going to do next." Eisenhower and Patton parted in cold silence. The next day, Eisenhower relieved Patton as commander of the Third Army and put him in a paper command, head of a Theater Board studying lessons from the war. According to one of his biographers, as Patton reflected on the disintegration of his friendship with Eisenhower, he "believed he saw the truth of Henry Adams' phrase that a friend in power is a friend lost."[32]

On October 12 Eisenhower held a press conference in Frankfurt. *The New York Times* reported that he spoke "emphatically, and at times bitterly against the Nazis" and insisted that denazification was being carried out.[33] And it certainly was true that the arrest, trial, and punishment of former Nazis went much further in the American zone than in any of the other three zones. The Americans brought charges against some three million Germans, actually tried two million of them, and punished nearly one million.

All around him, in Frankfurt, in Berlin, in his trips through Germany and Europe, he saw the horrible destruction of war. Germany was pulverized almost beyond belief or repair. "The country is devastated," he told Mamie. "Whole cities are obliterated; and the

German population, to say nothing of millions of former slave laborers, is largely homeless." His inspection trips to German cities, to former concentration camps, to current displaced persons' camps, and his practical and immediate responsibility for handling the problems involved gave him an awareness of the consequences of war that caused him to swear to himself "never again." He told Mamie, "I hope another American shell never has to be fired in Europe," while to a friend he said, "Certainly Germany should not want to see any more high explosives for the next hundred years; I am quite sure that some of the cities will never be re-built." [34]

Worst damaged of all the nations of Europe was Russia. If Eisenhower had thought that nothing could compare to Germany, he learned better in August, when he flew from Berlin to Moscow, at only a few hundred feet of altitude. He did not see a single house standing intact from the Russian-Polish border to Moscow. Not one.

The development of the atomic bomb added to his conviction that war had become too terrible to ever again be a viable option. He hated to hear talk about the "next war" and would not allow his staff or subordinates to indulge in it. This was the major reason he was so furious with Patton, whose irresponsible talk about driving the Red Army beyond the Volga appalled Eisenhower.

Peace, Eisenhower knew, depended above all on Soviet-American relations. As he explained to Henry Wallace in the summer of 1945, in response to a letter from Wallace congratulating him on his success in getting along with the Russians in Germany, "So far as a soldier should have opinions about such things, I am convinced that friendship—which means an honest desire on both sides to strive for mutual understanding between Russia and the United States—is absolutely essential to world tranquillity." [35] When a reporter asked him at a June press conference about a possible "Russo-American war," Eisenhower's face went red with anger. He insisted sharply that there was no possibility of such a war. "The peace lies, when you get down to it, with all the peoples of the world," he explained, and "not just . . . with some political leader . . . If all the peoples are friendly, we are going to have peace. . . . I have found the individual Russian one of the friendliest persons in the world." [36]

It was a theme he would repeat over and over, in speeches, at congressional hearings, in his private letters, in conversation. He was not so naive as to think that friendliness would eliminate the manifold difficulties facing the U.S.-U.S.S.R. relationship, but he was sure that there would be no success without a generally friendly and trusting spirit, while "the alternative to success seemed so terrifying to contemplate" that he insisted on approaching the Russians on the basis of friendship and trust. He hoped that in his contacts and dealings with the Russians in Berlin, where the two nations had to work together, he could establish a "spirit [that would] spread beyond Germany to our own capitals." If that could be done, "we could eventually live together as friends and ultimately work together in world partnership." [37] He also recognized that a major obstacle would be Russian suspicion and distrust of the United States. He made it a personal goal to do everything he could to alleviate that suspicion and distrust.

On June 5, Eisenhower went to Berlin to meet with the Russians and to establish the Allied Control Council. He immediately struck up a warm friendship with Marshal Grigori Zhukov. Despite the language barrier, the two soldiers got on famously. They respected each other and enjoyed talking about professional matters, political philosophy, and indeed a wide range of subjects. They also found they could work together and quickly reached an agreement whereby the United States troops pulled out of the Russian zone, while the Western powers sent their forces into Berlin.

Over the weeks that followed, Eisenhower and Zhukov were often together. They studied each other's campaigns, and their admiration one for the other grew apace. Eisenhower told Montgomery that Zhukov "was in a class by himself . . . His narrative of his campaigns (and he was always at the critical point) coupled with his statement of reasons for each action that he took, including his exploitation of weapons and arms in which he had a superiority, his concern for weather, and his care in providing fully for administration before he delivered his blow, all added up to making him a standout." [38] When Zhukov came to Frankfurt for a visit, Eisenhower hosted an elaborate dinner. In a long and flattering toast to Zhukov ("To no one man do the United Nations owe a greater debt than to Marshal Zhukov"), Eisenhower said that what they both wanted was peace, and they wanted it so badly that "we are going to have peace if we have to fight for it. This war was a holy war," he added; "more than any other in history this war has been an array of the forces of evil against those of righteousness." [39]

Stalin too wanted to meet Eisenhower. He told Harry Hopkins in late May that he hoped Eisenhower could come to Moscow on June 24 for the victory parade. Averell Harriman, the U.S. ambassador to Moscow, urged Eisenhower to accept and said there was "*no* doubt that Stalin was anxious to have him."[40] Eisenhower could not make it for the victory parade, but in August he did fly to Moscow, accompanied by Zhukov, who stayed with him throughout his trip. It was a triumphal march, although the devastation everywhere was depressing. Eisenhower saw most of the sights—the Kremlin, the subway, a collective farm, a tractor factory, etc. He attended a soccer game and delighted the crowd by throwing his arm around Zhukov's shoulder. At a sports parade in Red Square, which lasted for hours and involved tens of thousands of athletes, Eisenhower was invited by Stalin to stand on Lenin's Tomb, a unique honor for a non-Communist and non-Russian.

Another unique honor came when Stalin apologized to him for the actions of the Red Army in April 1945, when it advanced toward Berlin rather than toward Dresden, as Stalin had told Eisenhower it would. As Eisenhower reported to Marshall, "Stalin explained in detail the military reasons for the last-minute change but said that I had the right to charge him with lack of frankness and this he would not want me to believe."[41]

Eisenhower made a strong impression on Stalin. The Russian dictator talked to him at great length, emphasizing how badly the Soviet Union needed American help in recovering from the war. He said that the Russians realized they needed not only American money, but American technicians and scientific assistance. Eisenhower's sympathetic response was much appreciated by Stalin. When Eisenhower left, Stalin told Harriman, "General Eisenhower is a very great man, not only because of his military accomplishments but because of his human, friendly, kind and frank nature. He is *not* a 'grubi' [coarse, brusque] man like most military."[42]

Eisenhower was in his turn impressed by Stalin. He told a *New York Times* correspondent that Stalin was "benign and fatherly," and that he sensed "a genuine atmosphere of hospitality." At a press conference in Moscow, he declared, "I see nothing in the future that would prevent Russia and the United States from being the closest possible friends." But while he was in Moscow, two atomic bombs were dropped on Japan, and suddenly he did see an immediate danger to friendly relations. "Before the atom bomb was used," he told a journalist, "I would have said yes, I was sure we could keep peace with Russia. Now, I don't know. I had hoped the bomb wouldn't figure in this war . . . People are frightened and disturbed all over. Everyone feels insecure again."[43]

• •

On November 11, 1945, Eisenhower flew to Washington. He appeared before the Senate Committee on Military Affairs, then took a train ride with Mamie to Boone, Iowa, to visit her relatives there. Scarcely had they arrived when Mamie was rushed to a hospital suffering from bronchial pneumonia. A few days later Eisenhower, after being assured that she was "on the road to recovery," returned to Washington and to more appearances before congressional committees.

On November 20, Truman accepted Marshall's resignation as Chief of Staff and appointed Eisenhower in his place. Eisenhower, meanwhile, came down with a "speaker's throat," as he called it; in fact he too had bronchial pneumonia. Nevertheless, he forced himself to fly to Chicago to speak before the American Legion on the subject of postwar defense, then returned to Washington and more testifying. On November 22, the doctors put him into the hospital, at White Sulphur Springs. He stayed there for nearly two weeks. He came out on December 3, on which date he took up his duties as Chief of Staff. As he told Swede Hazlett, in a letter dictated while he was in the hospital, "The job I am taking now represents nothing but straight duty."[44]

If being the head of an occupation force in Germany had been a thankless and unwelcome task, being Chief of Staff of the U.S. Army as it demobilized was worse. Eisenhower anticipated, correctly, interminable battles with the other members of the Joint Chiefs of Staff over the issues of universal military training and unification of the armed services, and battles with Congress over the issues of demobilization and the size and strength of the postwar Army. He entered these conflicts not as a supreme commander with a single overriding goal, but as one among equals in power within the JCS, and as a supplicant in his dealings with Congress. On every major front, he was forced to give way or give in; the contrast between the total victory he had just won in Germany and the agonizing struggles and compromises and retreats he would have to endure as Chief of Staff was complete. Small wonder that shortly after taking up his duties he could write his son, John, that the Pentagon "was a sorry place to light after having commanded a theater of war."[45]

Completely new to him was his role as spokesman for the Army. Aside from the Guildhall address, he had never been a public speaker. Now the demands were constant. Every organization in America, it sometimes seemed, wanted him as the principal speaker at its annual meeting, while every congressional committee that had the remotest connection with the War Department wanted the Chief of Staff to testify before it, thus giving the politicians an opportunity to have their picture taken with Eisenhower. In his first year as Chief of Staff, Eisenhower made forty-six major speeches to national organizations, or nearly one per week. He testified before Congress on thirteen occasions. In his second year, 1947, the figures were a little less—thirty and twelve.

The American public loved to hear him speak, and the content and delivery of his speeches could not have done more to add to his luster. The more often he spoke, the more the invitations poured in. He tried to hold his appearances down to a minimum; to one prominent congressman, over the telephone, he said, "Talking Generals are not a very good thing for our country," and begged to be excused. In 1946, he told a friend, "I have always hated talking Generals—I can't understand why there is so much pressure put upon me to appear at every kind of gathering to put some more useless words on the air or over the dinner table." [46] But the requests kept coming, and he could not say no to all of them.

The speeches brought Eisenhower in contact with some of America's richest and most powerful men. Usually the invitations came from the chairman of the board of directors of the various universities or cultural organizations; that chairman (or whatever his title) was typically a wealthy businessman. Like most Americans, these businessmen found Eisenhower's charm and fame irresistible; unlike the average citizen, they were in a position to get to meet and know him. A few had ulterior motives, a desire to manipulate the general for their own purposes, but most were simply hero-worshipers.

The elite of the Eastern Establishment moved in on him almost before he occupied his new office. Thomas J. Watson of IBM, for example, came to the Pentagon in early March 1946 to meet the general and insist that he speak at the Metropolitan Museum of Art in New York. The heads of other great corporations in New York all had their pet project too, and used their position in the organization or university for their initial access to Eisenhower.

He had known almost none of America's business leaders before the war; he had met a few of them during the war; by 1947, he had met or at least corresponded with hundreds of them, including a high percentage of the one hundred richest and most powerful. Many became close personal friends. When Ike and Mamie had last lived in Washington, twenty years earlier, their social life revolved around other obscure Army officers and their wives. From 1946 to

1948, however, their social life included almost no Army personnel; instead they spent their evenings and vacation time with Eisenhower's new, wealthy friends. When they played bridge in the thirties, it was with other majors and their wives; in the late forties, it was with the president of CBS, or the chairman of the board of U.S. Steel, or the president of Standard Oil.

Eisenhower's relationships with wealthy men grew steadily from 1946 onward, to the point that his friends were almost exclusively millionaires. The effect of these relationships on Eisenhower is a matter of some dispute; his critics charge that they gave him a millionaire's view of the world and made him staunchly conservative on fiscal and other issues. According to the charge, Eisenhower was overly impressed by rich men, even a bit in awe of them. The truth was, however, more the other way around—the millionaires were awestruck by the general. For his part, Eisenhower enjoyed being with men who had proved themselves, who thought big, who had handled big problems successfully, who knew how to organize and produce, who exuded self-confidence. He also enjoyed what they could give him.

Not money—he never took money from any of his rich friends. But he would accept the use of a cottage in the north woods, or a fishing camp or hunting lodge in the Deep South, and did so often. In 1946, for example, Cason Callaway, a director of U.S. Steel and one of the largest cotton growers in the world, along with Robert Woodruff, chairman of the Coca-Cola Company, entertained Eisenhower at Callaway's Georgia plantation. The lake was well stocked; the three men caught more than two hundred largemouth bass in an afternoon. The quail hunting was also excellent.

The pattern lasted for the remainder of Eisenhower's life. He went hunting and fishing frequently, and it was always at the top spots in the country, in the finest conditions that money could buy. So too with his passion for golf—he could indulge it on exclusively top-quality courses. Shortly after he became Chief of Staff, Chevy Chase Club made him a member; other exclusive clubs, in New York, Georgia, and elsewhere, did too. On an income of about $15,000 per year, Eisenhower was able to enjoy, on a regular basis, recreation ordinarily reserved only for the very wealthy.

The Eisenhowers' living quarters, too, were the best they had ever had. They occupied Quarters No. One at Fort Myer, in the house Marshall had lived in, and before him, MacArthur. It was a large, sprawling, old brick house, with ample room to absorb all Mamie's furniture and a steady stream of house guests. The grounds were large too, and the Eisenhowers inherited from the Marshalls a chicken flock consisting of three roosters and two dozen Plymouth Rock hens. Eisenhower was delighted to have them—caring for the birds brought out the farmer in him—but soon tragedy struck. In June 1946, Eisenhower began a long letter to Marshall (who was in China), "This is a message of disappointment and disaster. It involves the chickens." First a rooster had died; then two of the hens; eventually half the flock was gone. Eisenhower called in a veterinarian, built a new coop, added vitamins to the feed, and tried other solutions, but to his dismay the chickens kept dying. Marshall took the news with a soldierly fortitude: "Don't worry about those hens," he replied. "Dispose of them if they are a care and a burden." [47]

For the first time in twenty years, Eisenhower had a piece of land he could dig up and plant, which he did with gusto. He went right to the top for his seeds. In 1946 they came from Henry Wallace, who had been a famous plant geneticist before he became Secretary of Agriculture, and in 1947 from W. Atlee Burpee himself. He concentrated on corn, tomatoes, and peas for himself, with petunias for Mamie (Burpee named a new strain of petunia the "Mrs. Dwight D. Eisenhower"). Both years he was so anxious to get started that he planted his garden in mid-March, then had to replant after a late freeze.

He and Mamie were getting along better than ever. They did a great deal of traveling together—they visited every state while he was Chief of Staff—and he loved it, despite his complaints about his brutal schedule, because Mamie went with him. Her doctors had decided that she could be allowed to fly, if the pilot stayed below five thousand feet. They went on a number of overseas journeys, as foreign governments were just as anxious to have Eisenhower as a guest and speaker as were American universities. In 1946 alone, they visited Hawaii, Guam, the Philippines, Japan, China, Korea, Brazil, Panama, Mexico, Germany, Italy, Scotland, and England.

Mamie was putting on weight, was up to 130 pounds. In late 1946, Eisenhower told a friend, "Mamie is in better health than I have ever known her to be. The only difficulty is that she has outgrown all her clothes. This is a tragedy for her." A year later, she still worried about her weight and wardrobe, while her husband was still delighted by her good health. Eisenhower told a friend that "I have been urging her to fulfill a long-held ambition, mainly to buy herself a good fur coat." She agonized over the choice between a dark ranch-bred mink and a lighter wild mink, which cost twice as much. She eventually chose the cheaper coat.[48] Photographs taken while he was Chief of Staff attest to Ike's good spirits and trim and athletic appearance. The tension that so often showed in his eyes, his face, and his body movements during the war was replaced by a relaxed look and carriage.

With President Truman, Eisenhower's relations were correct but formal. They never established an intimacy, nor did they work closely together. Marshall had been Roosevelt's closest adviser on military and strategic matters; Eisenhower's relationship with Truman was entirely different. Truman did not turn to his Chief of Staff for advice, even on the most major decisions of his Presidency, decisions that had crucial military implications, such as the Truman Doctrine, military aid to Greece and Turkey, or the Russian blockade of Berlin.

The absence of any input from Eisenhower on these and other issues was a bit surprising, because Eisenhower and Truman had so much in common. Both men came from sturdy pioneer stock of small farmers and merchants; they had grown up within 150 miles of each other; Truman and Eisenhower's older brother Arthur had been roommates in a Kansas City boardinghouse in 1905; both men were internationalists in outlook despite their midwestern backgrounds.

Eisenhower appreciated Truman's support for genuine unification of the armed forces (Eisenhower himself was such a strong advocate of unification that he proposed a single uniform for the armed services, and a program of sending cadets to Annapolis and midshipmen to West Point for their third year of study). The two men shared the general Army prejudice against the Marine Corps, and, although neither could ever say so publicly, they would have liked to eliminate the Corps (indeed, according to the Marines, that was the chief objective of unification).

But despite all that they had in common, Eisenhower and Truman never became friends; indeed, each man was more than a bit wary of the other. Truman could hardly avoid resenting Eisenhower's standing with the public. When the two men flew to Kansas City on the presidential plane, the *Sacred Cow,* on June 6, 1947, for example, it was Eisenhower—not the President—who attracted the reporters at the airport. And it was Eisenhower who delivered the principal address at the homecoming reunion of the 35th Division, even though the 35th was Truman's old World War I outfit.

•   •

The most difficult military problem facing the United States during Eisenhower's years as Chief of Staff was setting a policy for the atomic bomb. It was an area in which Eisenhower had little influence, partly because Truman, whatever his diffidence toward Eisenhower, was determined to keep the power and responsibility in the White House, and also because Eisenhower was so busy with administrative matters, inspection trips, and speeches that he had little time to think about the implications of the new weapon.

Eisenhower called the bomb "this hellish contrivance,"[49] and favored international control of the weapon, but all attempts to forge a sane nuclear policy ran afoul of the deepening American suspicion of the Soviet Union. When Eisenhower became Chief of Staff the immediate problem with regard to the atomic bomb was that so much was unknown. How great might the explosive power of the weapon become? How long would it take other nations to make a bomb? What kind of delivery systems could be developed? What would the effect of the bomb be on diplomacy? On traditional warfare? In addition to these and many other questions, Eisenhower and the Joint Chiefs were bothered by a widespread public sentiment that held that atomic bombs made armies and navies obsolete, and that possession of an atomic monopoly by the United States constituted a sufficient defense policy by itself.

The ultimate nightmare was that the bomb would be treated as just another weapon, with every nation free to build as many (and as powerful) bombs as it saw fit. But if the United States insisted on attempting to maintain its monopoly, that is exactly what would happen, and in any case monopoly as a policy had little to recommend it, because the general consensus was that within five years the Soviets would have a bomb of their own.

Attitudes toward atomic policy were so closely interwoven with attitudes toward the Soviet Union that the two cannot be discussed separately; thus this is the appropriate place to examine Eisenhower's evolving view of the Russians. When he returned from Germany, he remained committed to a friendly, cooperative approach to the Soviets. In November 1945, he was asked while testifying before a congressional committee to comment on the chances of Russia starting a war. He replied, "Russia has not the slightest thing to gain by a struggle with the United States. There is no one thing, I believe, that guides the policy of Russia more today than to keep friendship with the United States."[50]

Three days after taking up his duties in the Pentagon, he wrote

Mamie Doud, 1914. "The one who first attracted my eye instantly," Ike later recalled of their first meeting, "was a vivacious and attractive girl, smaller than average, saucy in the look about her face and in her whole attitude."

Ike's West Point graduation photograph, 1915. He went to the Academy for a free education, and to play football. He was an average student who got more than his share of demerits and had his share of fun. He took from the Academy an intense devotion to duty.

Lieutenant Eisenhower at Fort Sam Houston, Texas, 1915. Mamie Doud took one look at him and thought to herself, "He's a bruiser," and then, "He's just about the handsomest male I have ever seen." Within weeks, they were going steady. In less than a year, they were married.

In 1919 Ike joined George Patton as an instructor at the Infantry Tank School at Camp Meade, Maryland. Both young officers wrote articles on the future of the tank, emphasizing speed and independent operation. Because this differed from the Army's official line, which called for tanks to support infantry, Ike and Patton were told to cease writing or leave the Army.

The Eisenhowers in San Remo, Italy, August 1929. Ike had spent the previous year in Paris, writing a guidebook to American battlefields in France. He then took a 17-day, 1,800 mile motor trip through Europe.

Aboard the *President Coolidge*, July 1938. Ike had shaved his head because of the heat of the Philippines. Still a lieutenant colonel, after 23 years in the Army and at age 43, he was expecting to be retired in a year. He was, however, about to be discovered by General Marshall as the U.S. Army prepared for World War II.

Ike and Monty observe armored maneuvers at Gillingham, England, March 1, 1944. By this time Ike had led three major invasions —North Africa, Sicily, Italy. Just two months earlier, he had taken command of the Allied Expeditionary Force.

Ike and Churchill at Newbury Race Course, March 23, 1944. The two men had some sharp disagreements during the war, but they retained their mutual respect, admiration, and liking for each other. Churchill doubted Overlord: about this time he told Ike: "I am in this thing with you to the end, and if it fails we will go down together." But after a formal briefing in mid-May, he said, "I am hardening toward this enterprise."

Eisenhower and de Gaulle in Granville, Normandy, outside the Supreme Allied Commander's headquarters, August 21, 1944. De Gaulle was urging on Ike the military benefits of liberating Paris immediately; Ike wanted to bypass the city.

Ike at Le Havre, France, February 22, 1944, watching the arrival of fresh troops. He felt it was important to let the men at least get a look at the general who was sending them into combat; he always looked them straight in the eyes.

Ike with members of the 101st Aiborne Division at Greenham Common Airbase, about 10:30 PM, June 5, 1944. Ike asked, "Is there anyone here from Kansas?" Lieutenant Wallace C. Strobel replied, "I'm from Kansas, sir." Giving the thumbs up, Ike said, "Go get 'em, Kansas!"

The look of victory. Generals Eisenhower, Patton, Bradley, and Hodges, at Hodges's First Army HQ near Remagen, Germany, March 25, 1945. The previous day American troops had broken out of their bridgeheads to begin the final drive through Germany.

Ike and Patton watch a football game, Nürnburg, October 14, 1945. Ike had relieved Patton of his Third Army command because Patton would not enforce the War Department's anti-Nazi policies. Patton wrote in his diary, "Ike is bitten with the presidential bug and is also yellow. He will never be president!"

Ike and his mother, June 23, 1945, on the porch of the home he grew up in. Speaking in the Abilene City Park that day, he said, "Through this world it has been my fortune, or misfortune, to wander at considerable distances. Never has this town been outside my heart and memory." Neither had his mother.

WIDE WORLD PHOTOS

COURTESY OF HOWARD MEAD

The Eisenhower brothers all inherited their mother's big grin. Left to right: Arthur, Milton, Earl, Dwight, and Edgar react to Earl's sitting down on a fishing plug during a fishing vacation at Manitowac, Wisconsin, 1947.

During the vacation, Ike took a stroll to the downtown waterfront, where Boy Scout campers surrounded him. He spent an hour talking to them.

COLUMBIA UNIVERSITY

The President of Columbia University, 1949. He enjoyed the job more than most people thought, and he was better at it than the Columbia faculty was willing to grant.

Ike had the most expressive face. Here a photographer catches his reaction to the news that President Truman had just fired General MacArthur, April 1951.

Just back from France, November 3, 1951, the SACEUR and two of his grandchildren, Susan and David.

STARS AND STRIPES/
EISENHOWER LIBRARY

UNITED STATES ARMY

In June 1952, Ike began his race for the Republican nomination for the presidency. Here he tells Truman's Secretary of State, Dean Acheson, what was wrong with American foreign policy. The President and the Secretary very much resented the General's charges, especially because Ike had been an active agent in carrying out their policies in Europe.

June 1, 1952, Ike meets with Secretary of Defense Robert Lovett, President Truman, and Secretary of the Army Frank Pace. Ike and Truman had gotten on well—indeed, in 1948 Truman offered the Democratic nomination to Ike, saying he would join the ticket as Vice Presidential candidate—but when Ike announced that he was a Republican, the relationship went stone cold.

Colorado, August 1952. Republican nominee Eisenhower gives his running mate some tips on fly casting. He had met Nixon only twice; this was their getting-acquainted session.

With Senator Robert Taft, Chicago, July 1952, immediately after Ike's nomination. The candidate's first impulse was to get Taft on his team. The deep disappointment of Taft's supporters is etched on the faces of the women in the rear.

Ike and Mamie play Scrabble at Camp David, July 1954. During the war, Ike's flirtation with his secretary, Kay Summersby, led to all sorts of rumors, but the truth was that Mamie was the woman he wanted to live with.

Father and son, 1956. John went to Normandy following his graduation on June 6, 1944; his first assignment was to ETO; he was on occupation duty in Germany with his father; after service in Korea, he became Goodpaster's assistant and a liaison officer between the White House and the CIA. He helped his father write his Presidential memoirs.

The President and the Premier at Camp David, September 25, 1959. They agreed on the need to disarm but not on how to achieve the goal. Khrushchev assured Ike, "Your old friend Zhukov is all right. He's down in the Ukraine fishing."

Ike and Nixon on one of the few occasions they played golf together. The President had deep reservations about his Vice President, saying of him once that he just couldn't understand how a man could live his life without friends, and on many occasions complaining that he lacked maturity. But Ike kept Nixon on the ticket in 1956 and supported him in 1960 and 1968.

A meeting of legislative leaders in the Oval Office, March 6, 1959. Left to right: Charles Halleck, Allen Dulles, Everett Dirksen, Christian Herter, Sam Rayburn, Neil McElroy, Ike, Lyndon Johnson, Nixon.

Ike and Secretary of State John Foster Dulles, October 25, 1954. Typically, they are at the airport, aides are scurrying behind them, the plane is about to take off, and Dulles is waiting for Ike's approval of his next speech before departing for who knew where.

A fateful handshake. Ike and McCarthy, Milwaukee, October 1952, on the occasion of Ike's removal of a paragraph praising George Marshall, in deference to McCarthy. Some of Ike's worst problems as President flowed from this handshake; eventually, he broke with McCarthy when the Senator began charging that Communists had infiltrated the U.S. Army.

Ike and Kennedy on their way to Kennedy's inauguration. The oldest President to date had to hand over to the youngest man elected to the office, and he hated doing it. His opinion of Kennedy, already low, went to rock bottom a few months later, after the Bay of Pigs and the erection of the Berlin Wall.

Ike leaves the White House, August 30, 1965. He was very hawkish on Vietnam and consistently urged Johnson to go for victory. Johnson wanted his support but would not take his advice.

VIRGIL PINKLEY

Walter Cronkite interviews Ike for the CBS program, "D-Day Plus Twenty Years." They are sitting in Southwick House, Ike's invasion HQ, in front of the operations map at SHAEF, set for dawn, June 6, 1944.

Ike and California Governor Ronald Reagan enjoy a laugh together at an impromptu press conference at the Eldorado Country Club, March 14, 1967. Ike said he did not believe that Reagan was as much of a right-winger as everyone thought.

Dwight David Eisenhower, 34th President of the United States, October 22, 1953.

a warm letter to Zhukov, inviting him to come to the States for a visit in the spring, and expressing the hope that many other Soviet officials could also pay a visit, because such exchanges would promote understanding and confidence. Zhukov replied that he hoped to come; in the meantime, he sent Eisenhower some New Year's presents, including a large white bearskin rug. In March 1946, Zhukov sent Eisenhower a selection of delicacies from Russia. Eisenhower thanked him, again asked him to come for a visit, and concluded, "I still look upon the hours that I spent in friendly discussion with you as among the most pleasant and profitable that I have ever experienced."[51]

By April, however, Zhukov had left Berlin for Moscow, where he stayed only briefly before going on to a command in Odessa. Beetle Smith, whom Truman had appointed ambassador to Russia, reported to Eisenhower that Zhukov had fallen from favor. It was rumored that one reason for Zhukov's virtual disappearance was his known friendship with Eisenhower. There never would be a Zhukov visit to the United States.

Through 1946, Eisenhower deplored the rapidly developing breakdown of relations, the loose talk in the United States about the "inevitability" of conflict between the two systems. On June 11, Truman called a conference at the White House. The Secretary of State and the JCS discussed the possibility of an imminent Russian offensive in Europe. Such talk made Eisenhower angry, as he felt it had no basis in fact. "I don't believe the Reds want a war," he told Truman. "What can they gain now by armed conflict? They've gained about all they can assimilate."[52]

His conclusions were based on practical considerations, not hunches or a sense of trust in the goodness of Soviet intentions. Eisenhower told Truman, forcefully, that the Russians simply were not strong enough to undertake an offensive. At this meeting, and on a number of similar occasions, he demanded evidence, hard evidence. What was there to indicate that the Russians intended suddenly to sweep across Western Europe? He knew from experience the kind of elaborate logistical support there had to be for such an offensive. Where was the evidence of the necessary buildup of supplies in East Germany?

A month later William C. Bullitt, a former ambassador to Russia, sent Eisenhower a copy of his recent book on world affairs. Bullitt was a convinced Cold Warrior and a leader of the anti-Soviet group in the State Department. His views were simple but alarming: "The

Soviet Union's assault upon the West is at about the stage of Hitler's maneuvering into Czechoslovakia," he asserted. After thus linking Stalin with Hitler, an increasingly popular analogy in Washington, Bullitt flatly declared, "The final aim of Russia is world conquest." Eisenhower thought such notions fantastic. He never for a minute believed any such thing. He told Smith that Bullitt's book was "an excoriation of Russia" and said he could not bring himself to read any more of it.[53] Nor did he read George F. Kennan's famous "Mr. X" article, which also indicated a Russian desire for world conquest.

Montgomery stood with Eisenhower. From his post as Chief of the Imperial General Staff, he wrote Eisenhower in early 1947 that "the Soviet Nation is very, very tired. Devastation in Russia is appalling and the country is in no fit state to go to war." He thought it would be fifteen or twenty years before the Russians would be able to fight another major war, and argued that in the meantime the English-speaking democracies ought to be building friendly relations with the Soviets, rather than hurling threats and insults. Eisenhower told Montgomery that he heartily agreed.[54]

Eisenhower's belief in the vital necessity of peace combined with his faith in international cooperation to make him a strong supporter of the United Nations, far stronger than most of his peers or even his own staff. He expected that the U.N. would establish a genuine peace-keeping force, and that the United States would send a sizable contingent to it. He assigned one of his best officers, General Matthew Ridgway, to the potential peace-keeping force. He was a prudent soldier and was not ready to give up the atomic monopoly until he was assured of an adequate inspection system within the Soviet Union. But he still managed to believe that sooner or later the U.N. would have control of atomic weapons, an outcome he very much favored.

Events, Soviet actions in Eastern Europe, and the climate of opinion around him, however, were steadily eroding Eisenhower's hopes for an active cooperation with the Soviets. In Poland and elsewhere, the Soviets were acting with high-handed brutality, ignoring the promises they had made in the Yalta Agreements to hold free and unfettered elections in Eastern Europe. In Germany, East and West were growing further apart in their policies with each passing week. In the U.N. Security Council, the U.S. and the U.S.S.R. were hurling accusations at each other. And in Greece, where a civil war raged, the Soviets appeared to be adopting new methods, "political pressure and subversive tactics" as Eisenhower called them, in an attempt to bring new territories under their control.[55] Alarmingly, in February 1947 the British, who had been supporting the Greek monarchists, announced that they were broke and would have to pull out of Greece. Truman and the State Department reacted with speed and vigor, Truman announcing on March 12 the doctrine of containment.

Eisenhower talked with Marshall, who was by then Secretary of State and who had just returned from a meeting of the foreign ministers in Moscow. Marshall, whose own hopes for a new, better world based on cooperation between the victors were as great as Eisenhower's, and who was by no means anti-Soviet, confessed that getting along with the Russians was beginning to seem impossible. The great problem, Marshall told Eisenhower, was Germany. European recovery, so obviously necessary on humanitarian grounds as well as to prevent the spread of Communism, was dependent on the recovery of German production, but Russian fears of the Germans were so great that they would not allow a German revival. Eisenhower agreed with this analysis, and with Marshall's more general point that European recovery was crucial to America's self-interest.

"I personally believe," Eisenhower wrote in his diary one month before the Marshall Plan was announced, "that the best thing we could now do would be to post 5 billion to the credit of the secretary of state and tell him to use it to support democratic movements wherever our vital interests indicate. Money should be used to promote possibilities of self-sustaining economies, not merely to prevent immediate starvation."[56]

By mid-1947, then, Eisenhower was moving, reluctantly and slowly, but nevertheless surely, toward a Cold War position. He had decided that the Soviets were in fact aggressive, although certainly not in the way that Hitler had been. Unlike many Cold Warriors, he did not believe that the Soviets were preparing for war. He continued to insist that peace was possible and essential, even if active cooperation with the Russians was not likely in the immediate future. In the parlance of the day, he was "soft" on the Soviets, much softer than Truman, and much less likely to seek a military solution to the problem of coexistence.

In 1947 the most pleasurable experience in his private life was the addition of a daughter-in-law to the Eisenhower family. John, on occupation duty in Vienna, had fallen in love with Barbara Thompson. Barbara was also an Army brat, the daughter of Colonel and Mrs. Percy Thompson. Preparations for the wedding took six months. Ike liked to pretend that while Mamie was all nerves and excitement, he was calm and indifferent, but in fact he was deeply involved, sending John (in Vienna, on occupation duty) long letters about arrangements, making suggestions on what John should do about his career before and after the wedding, manipulating the ceremony itself, purchasing a small automobile as a wedding present. John was his only child, after all, and this wedding was his only chance to play the father of the groom.

The ceremony was held on June 10, 1947, in the chapel at Fort Monroe, Virginia. Within six weeks of the wedding, Ike was beginning to hint to his son that a grandchild would be most welcome.

For the public Eisenhower, 1947 was dominated by politics, and specifically by demands that he become a candidate for President, an experience he found irksome, irritating, and almost impossible to deal with. During the war, he had been able to brush aside various suggestions that he become a candidate. In 1946, it had not been so easy, as the number of people and groups asking him to run, and their seriousness, increased dramatically. Reporters frequently asked him about running; to them his usual answer was that he could not conceive of any circumstances under which he would enter politics.

Late in 1947, Harry Truman called Eisenhower to his office, where—according to Eisenhower—he made a most remarkable offer. If Eisenhower would accept the Democratic nomination, Truman said he would be willing to run as the vice-presidential candidate on the same ticket. At that time, Truman's chance for re-election appeared to be nil. Eisenhower assumed that Truman wanted to use him to pull the Democrats out of an impossible hole. The general wanted nothing to do with the Democratic Party; his answer was a flat "No."

Most of those urging Eisenhower to run assumed that if he did so, he would win in a runaway. Eisenhower did not agree. With no party identification, no political experience, no support or base, no record, and no organization, he doubted that there was any reality to an Eisenhower boom. He either was not fully aware of the depth and extent of his own popularity, or he refused to believe what seemed obvious to others.

That he was sincere in saying that he did not want to follow the examples of Washington and Grant there can be no doubt, but he could not convince others. They assumed that he was being coy. In his diary, he confessed that even his friends would not believe him.

It was a mark of his self-confidence that he never said publicly, or in his private correspondence, that he did not feel qualified for the job. What he did say, emphatically and repeatedly, was that he did not want it. In Vicksburg, Mississippi, on July 4, 1947, at a time when speculation about his political future was intensifying, he replied to a question on the subject, "I say flatly, completely, and with all the force I have—I haven't a political ambition in the world. I want nothing to do with politics." [57] But even his brother Edgar did not believe him. Neither could Swede Hazlett, who urged him to issue an "unequivocal statement on the subject—one that no one can shoot holes in!" [58]

What Hazlett, and many others, wanted was the classic Sherman statement, "If nominated I will not run, if elected I will not serve." Anything short of that they regarded as equivocal. The fact that he would not make such a statement, combined with the well-known fact that he regarded "duty" as a sacred obligation, together with the widespread feeling that it *was* his duty to become the nation's leader, all kept the boom alive.

Eisenhower agonized over his position. He had an intense dislike for partisan politics. The idea of asking people for their support was alien to him, as was the thought of making political deals, fighting for a nomination and election, distributing patronage, and all the rest that goes into party politics. But the nation, from some of its biggest businessmen and most prominent politicians to tens of thousands of former GIs and other ordinary citizens, would not allow him to simply say no. The persistence of the demands that he become a candidate was forcing him to realize that there was no easy way out, and at the same time forcing him to think about what it would be like to be President. He was, after all, within a year of retirement from the Army, with no job prospect in civilian life in hand. He confessed to John that he did sometimes wonder about being the nation's leader. But daydreaming about being President was much different from running for the office, and if being a candidate implied making political promises and deals, Eisenhower wanted no part of it.

A nomination and election by acclamation, on the other hand, would be a different matter. In that event, he told Beetle Smith, he would be forced to regard service in the White House as his duty. He did not expect that to happen, but if it did by some miracle, he would have to serve. But, he insisted, in an October 1947 letter to Cornelius Vanderbilt, Jr. who had urged him to run, "No man since Washington has been elected to political office unless he definitely desired it."

To his brother Milton, he said that "we are not children and we knew that under the political party system of this country it would certainly be nothing less than a miracle" if there ever were a genuine "draft" at a nominating convention.[59]

In January 1948, a group of New Hampshire Republicans entered a slate of delegates pledged to Eisenhower in the March 9 primary. Leonard Finder, publisher of the Manchester *Union-Leader*, endorsed Eisenhower, then in an open letter to Eisenhower said, "No man should deny the will of the people in a matter such as this." Eisenhower wrote on his copy of Finder's letter, "We'll have to answer —but I don't know what to say!"

It took him more than a week to compose an answer to Finder. He brought home various drafts every night, making many changes. On January 22, he made his reply public. He said that because the office of the President "has, since the days of Washington, historically and properly fallen only to aspirants," and as he had made it clear he had no political ambition, he had hoped that the Eisenhower boom would die. It had not. He had not issued a "bald statement" that he would not accept a nomination because "such an expression would smack of effrontery," and because he did not want to be accused of avoiding his duty. But with actual primary elections coming up, he did not want people wasting their votes, so he had decided he needed to clarify his position.

He then did so in a ringing declaration: "It is my conviction that the necessary and wise subordination of the military to civil power will be best sustained, and our people will have greater confidence that it is so sustained, when lifelong professional soldiers, in the absence of some obvious and overriding reasons, abstain from seeking high political office." He went on, "Politics is a profession; a serious, complicated and, in its true sense, a noble one." He concluded, "My decision to remove myself completely from the political scene is definite and positive."[60]

Many people, then and later, assumed that had Eisenhower answered Finder differently, had he agreed to run, he could have had the Republican nomination and the Presidency. The assumption was not tested, but Eisenhower doubted its validity, and he may well have been right. So few states held primaries in 1948 that even had he won them all, he would have gone into the convention with far less than half the delegates pledged to him. Neither Robert Taft nor Thomas Dewey, the leading Republican contenders, were likely to give up without a struggle. Considering how strong a fight Taft made in 1952, it is certainly possible that together with Dewey he could have turned back an Eisenhower nomination in 1948. That is what Eisenhower meant when he told Milton, "We are not children." He realized that his supporters were amateurs. The professional politicians who were so active in his behalf in 1952 were noticeably absent in 1948. Neither the enthusiasm of the amateurs nor Eisenhower's standing in the polls (the Gallup Poll found that he was the public's first choice, regardless of party affiliation) could produce the delegate votes necessary to capture the nomination.

Equally, however, it should be noted that Eisenhower's rejection of a candidacy in 1948 seemed to take him out of the presidential picture permanently. His assumption was that Dewey would get the Republican nomination, then win the election, and succeed himself in 1952. By the time of the 1956 election, Eisenhower would be sixty-six years old, presumably too old to be a candidate. By saying "No" in 1948, then, Eisenhower believed he was saying "No" for good.

Had he chosen to fight for the nomination in 1948, he had an excellent chance of winning it—from either party. It stretches the truth, perhaps, but only slightly, to say that Eisenhower, in 1948, turned down the Presidency of the United States.

One of the remarkable aspects of the Eisenhower boom was that he never indicated, even to his closest friends, his party preference. Democrats as well as Republicans found it easy to assume that a man as smart as Eisenhower *must* be a member of their party. (He was aware that this was a factor in his popularity, and that the moment he took a stand on a controversial issue, he would lose the support of most of those on the opposite side.) The only member of the Eisenhower family who had been involved in the Washington scene was Milton, and he had served successfully under both Democratic and Republican Administrations. General Eisenhower was careful never to say a word on domestic political issues, so no one knew where he stood on them. His commitment to internationalism was well known, of course, but at a time when a bipartisan approach to foreign policy was the norm, that stand indicated nothing about party preference.

As a career soldier, he was obliged to avoid commentary on domestic political issues, and keeping silent on such matters as deficit financing, the welfare state, government regulation of industry and agriculture, or race relations was second nature to him. The views that he did hold, he held strongly, but they were consistently in the middle of the political spectrum. Indeed he had a penchant for expressing emphatically and earnestly his belief in values that were so widely accepted and acknowledged as to be commonplace.

"I believe fanatically in the American form of democracy," he said in a private letter to one of his oldest friends, Swede Hazlett, "a system that recognizes and protects the right of the individual and that ascribes to the individual a dignity accruing to him because of his creation in the image of a supreme being and which rests upon the conviction that only through a system of free enterprise can this type of democracy be preserved."[61] To cynics it sounded like pure corn, and surely, they thought, it must be a put-on. But that was the way Eisenhower talked, in private, with his friends.

When Eisenhower talked or wrote on foreign affairs, he was on firmer ground, and his views were more sophisticated. As noted, he was a proponent of the Marshall Plan before it was announced, and a firm supporter afterward. Senator Taft was not. Taft said American money ought not be poured into a "European T.V.A." in a "vast giveaway program." Along with other Republicans, Taft thought that the Europeans had gone too far in the direction of socialism already, and that they would use Marshall Plan money to nationalize basic industries, including American-owned plants. Eisenhower put his emphasis on the joint nature of the plan, which required the Europeans to get together among themselves for self-help. And he said—in a letter to James Forrestal in January 1949—that "a virtual economic union" between the West European states was a precondition to success. He added that "some kind of *political* accord may have to be achieved among these European countries before they will be willing to make the required economic concessions. . . . A possible practicable approach would be to establish a Combined Chiefs of Staff for the study of common defense problems." He said that "these things are none of my business and my ideas may be completely screwy," but he knew that there were "tremendous political obstacles" to be overcome before a common market could be created, and they had to be faced.[62] Starting with some form of defensive alliance—in practice, he was suggesting what became NATO—seemed to Eisenhower to be in order. Truman, of course, agreed. In this area, Eisenhower was much closer to the President's position than to that of Senator Taft.

So too in his developing views on the Soviet Union. By the fall of 1947, Eisenhower's feelings about the Soviets were running parallel with Truman's and those of other hard-line Cold Warriors. The Russian repression of the freedoms in Eastern Europe that Eisenhower had fought to preserve, perceived Russian aggression in Greece, Turkey, and Iran, Russian intransigence in Germany and the U.N., all a part of the intensifying Cold War, led Eisenhower to abandon his hope for friendly cooperation and instead to see an inevitable conflict between the U.S. and the U.S.S.R.

"Russia is definitely out to communize the world," he wrote in his diary in September 1947. "It promotes starvation, unrest, anarchy, in the certainty that these are the breeding grounds for the growth of their damnable philosophy." He felt that "we face a battle to extinction between the two systems." To win that battle, the U.S. had to oppose Russian expansion, whether it was attempted by direct conquest or through infiltration. Eisenhower wanted to go beyond Truman's policy of containment, however, and "over the long term to win back areas that Russia has already overrun," meaning, of course, the liberation of the East European satellites. In addition, America had to help rebuild Western Europe, through the Marshall Plan, because unless their economies were restored, the peoples of Western Europe would "almost certainly fall prey to communism, and if the progress of this disease is not checked, we will find ourselves an isolated democracy in a world controlled by enemies." In the diary entry, he stated his conclusion as dramatically as he could put it: "To insure the health of American democracy," he wrote, "unity is more necessary now than it was in Overlord."[63]

Although Eisenhower had done a complete turnaround in his attitude toward the Russians, he did not in the process give way to the near hysteria that swept in waves across the country during the early Cold War, or to the view of the Russians as some kind of supermen. When Beetle Smith, U.S. ambassador to the Soviet Union, wrote from Moscow that if America stood firm, "we have little to fear," Eisenhower wholeheartedly agreed. "It is a grievous error," he said, "to forget for one second the might and power of this great republic."[64]

On October 14, 1947, Eisenhower was fifty-seven years old. He would shortly be leaving the Pentagon (Truman had promised him he would not have to serve as Chief of Staff beyond two years). He had rejected politics as a career. As a five-star general, he was technically on active duty for life, and thus drew a salary of $15,000 per year. But he had no savings, owned no property, stocks, or bonds.

What would he do? Where would he live? In his entire adult life, he had never had to answer those basic questions for himself—the Army had always provided the answer.

Offers he had, an embarrassing number. Major corporations

wanted him for president or chairman of the board. They offered some "fantastic sums," Eisenhower told his father-in-law, but "I will under no circumstances take a position where I could be accused of merely 'selling a name' for publicity purposes for a corporation."[65] He therefore thought that the presidency of a small college somewhere would be best. After a few years of that activity, he wanted to go into full retirement. He and Mamie thought they would retire to San Antonio, and spend their summers in northern Wisconsin. He knew of a small cottage on a lake that would be suitable and affordable. Meanwhile, Eisenhower had friends looking for a ranch near San Antonio for him. He eventually found a ranch he wanted, but finally had to turn it down because the price was too high. He confessed that, never having had a mortgage before, he was highly uncomfortable at the thought of committing himself to payments for the next twelve years.

On April 2, 1946, Eisenhower had spoken at the Metropolitan Museum of Art, then stayed at the Waldorf-Astoria as Tom Watson's guest. Watson was a member of a Columbia University trustees' committee searching for a president. Watson asked Eisenhower if he would consider taking the job. Eisenhower's instant reply was that Columbia had asked the wrong Eisenhower—the university should go after Milton, who was an experienced educator. No, Watson said, Columbia wanted the general. Eisenhower said that he would not be available for nearly two years, and that he therefore could not consider the offer at that time.

Thirteen months later, Watson called on Eisenhower. "To my chagrin," Eisenhower wrote Milton, Watson again offered the Columbia position, urging "the importance of the public service I could perform in that spot" and painting "the rosiest possible picture of what I would be offered in the way of conveniences, expenses, remuneration and so on." Eisenhower repeated that Milton was the man Columbia wanted; Watson repeated that Columbia wanted the general and pressed for an answer. Eisenhower resented the pressure and told Milton that if Watson forced him to make a quick answer, it would be "No."[66]

Watson argued that by accepting the position, Eisenhower could remove his name from political speculation, an idea that appealed to Eisenhower mightily. It should be noted here that the popular impression that Watson and the other wealthy Republican trustees at Columbia wanted Eisenhower in order to begin grooming him for the Presidency of the United States is altogether wrong. In November

1947, Watson "exhortated" Eisenhower to "have nothing to do with this political business," and in fact Watson and most of the Columbia trustees were Dewey supporters who expected Dewey to win in 1948 and then serve until 1956.[67]

Eisenhower, who had made so many momentous decisions, found the process of making this one extremely painful. "It was almost the first decision I ever had to make in my life that was directly concerned with myself," he told Smith. In making it, he "had to struggle against every instinct I had."[68]

On June 23. 1947, Eisenhower wrote to Columbia to indicate that if a formal offer were made to him, he would accept. He said that he and Mamie had gone through some definite inner battles and indeed experienced feelings "akin to dismay" at the prospect of living in New York City, but after hours of "anxious and prayerful thought . . . the finger of duty points in the direction of Columbia." He insisted that the trustees must understand, before they acted, the nature and extent of the verbal agreements he had made with Watson. These included no involvement in purely academic matters, no responsibility for fund raising, no excessive entertaining, and no burdensome administrative details.

What on earth would he do? He would, in his words, "devote my energies in providing internal leadership on broad and liberal lines for the University itself and promote basic concepts of education in a democracy." On those vague conditions, Columbia asked Eisenhower to become its president, at a salary of $25,000 per year. He accepted. He would take office after commencement in June 1948.[69]

In the middle of his twenty-seven-month tour of duty as Chief of Staff, Eisenhower had written in his diary, "It has been a most difficult period for me, with far more frustrations than progress." In October 1946, he complained, "My life is one long succession of personnel, budgetary, and planning problems, and I am getting close to the fed up stage."[70]

He was, therefore, glad to be handing the position over to Bradley. The ceremonies took place at noon on February 7, 1948. Just before leaving his office for the last time, Eisenhower dictated a final message. It was addressed "To the American Soldier." In it, he spoke of his nearly four decades of service, of his pride in the Army and its accomplishments, of the satisfaction his career had brought him. He concluded, "I cannot let this day pass without telling the fighting men —those who have left the ranks and you who still wear the uniform

—that my fondest boast shall always be: 'I was their fellow-soldier.' " [71]

Then he walked across the hall to the Secretary of the Army's office, where he administered the oath of office to Bradley. President Truman pinned a third Oak Leaf Cluster to Eisenhower's Distinguished Service Medal. By prior agreement, the Eisenhowers were to stay on at Quarters No. One until they moved to New York City in May. A few days after Bradley's swearing-in, Eisenhower bought a car, a brand-new Chrysler. The dealer brought it out to Fort Myer. After Mamie approved, Eisenhower wrote a check in full payment. Then he took Mamie by the hand, pointed to the sedan, and said,"Darling, there's the entire result of thirty-seven years' work since I caught the train out of Abilene." He was broke. [72]

His prospects, however, were, to say the least, excellent. Aside from his continuing Army salary and the salary he would soon be drawing from Columbia, he had finally managed to set aside some time—February to June 1948—to write his memoirs. Throughout 1946 and 1947, publishers had approached Eisenhower with offers for his memoirs. In December, Douglas Black, president of Doubleday, along with William Robinson of the *New York Herald Tribune* (a man Eisenhower liked immediately; they quickly became close friends), approached the general to argue that he owed it to "history" to write his memoirs. [73] Whenever Eisenhower talked with publishers, they made his head spin with their explanations of options and first serial rights and second serial rights and movie rights and translations and on and on. What Black and Robinson offered was much more appealing to him—a one-shot deal, in which they would pay a flat sum for all rights. Within a few days, Eisenhower discovered that the deal they offered was even more attractive, because Joseph Davies, who was serving informally as Eisenhower's legal representative in the talks, advised Eisenhower that he would pay a capital gains tax on the money, not a personal income tax.

That seemed too good to be true, but Eisenhower checked with the Undersecretary of the Treasury, who gave him an official ruling, which was that Davies was correct. As a nonprofessional writer, Eisenhower was entitled to pay only a capital gains tax *if* he sold the manuscript in its entirety, together with all subsidiary rights. It had often been done before, the Treasury assured Eisenhower. Eisenhower then agreed to write his memoirs. Black and Robinson paid him $635,000; he paid $158,750 in taxes; the nearly half million dollars that he got to keep made him a wealthy man.

After Eisenhower had completed his manuscript and turned it over, he told the publishers he was afraid he was sticking them with a white elephant. They smiled and said that, to the contrary, they were not sure they were treating him fairly. That was indeed the truth. The book that resulted was reprinted and serialized and appeared in many different editions, and was translated into twenty-two foreign languages. It sold by the millions; indeed by some accounts only Dr. Benjamin Spock and the Bible outsold Eisenhower in the twentieth century. On a regular contract, the publishers would have had to pay out far more in royalties to Eisenhower than they did in the one-lump-sum payment, and even after paying personal income taxes on the royalties, Eisenhower would have retained much more than he did get to keep. The real beneficiary of the deal was the publisher, not Eisenhower.

In preparing himself for the task of writing the manuscript, Eisenhower began by rereading Grant's *Memoirs*. It was the best possible choice of a model, and Eisenhower used it well. He gathered together his wartime letters, reports, diary entries, and other documents. He employed three secretaries, and immediately after turning over his job to Bradley, he started writing. Or rather, dictating. His method was to begin at 7 A.M., over breakfast. At lunch, he was often joined by the editors. He would continue dictating until 11 P.M. He worked at this sixteen-hour-a-day pace for most of February and all of March and April. It was a blitz, as he called it, one that few men of his age could have done. Or many younger men, either—the determination, self-discipline, and concentration he had to summon to maintain such a schedule was enormous. He never complained, indeed enjoyed reliving the war, and having all that money waiting for him when he finished—the money that would buy him and Mamie that retirement home someday—was highly motivating.

The book itself, *Crusade in Europe,* published in late 1948, was greeted with almost unanimous critical acclaim, along with praise for its author's modesty, candor, fairness, tact, and general humanity. It was called the best American military reminiscence (with the possible exception of Grant's), and "the work of the best soldier-historian since, perhaps, Caesar and his commentaries."[74] *Crusade in Europe* not only gave Eisenhower financial security; it stood the test of time (it was still selling briskly in the 1980s), and it added immeasurably to his popularity. It was a book worthy of the man and his services to the nation.

CHAPTER NINE

Columbia, NATO, and Politics

ON MAY 2, 1948, immediately after finishing *Crusade*, Eisenhower left Quarters No. One. He took a month's vacation, as William Robinson's guest, at the Augusta National Golf Club. The vacation provided him and Mamie with a needed rest, and introduced him to a group of men who became and remained his closest friends. "The gang," as he called the members of the group, were all millionaires whose great passions were playing golf and bridge, and talking politics. With one exception, they were all Republicans. They were also united by their hero-worship of General Ike.

For his part, Eisenhower was impressed by the gang's business success, appreciated the members' devotion to him, and enjoyed their easy banter, nonstop flow of jokes, and their eagerness to play golf and bridge with him. He sought their advice on politics, economics, and finance, both in general and with regard to his personal fortunes. He accepted from them many gifts, services, free trips, etc. To the end of his life he spent as much time with the gang as he could possibly spare; when they were separated he carried on an extensive correspondence with the members. With them, he could relax as he could with no one else.

Bill Robinson was the leader of the gang. Ten years younger than Eisenhower, Robinson had met the general in connection with *Crusade*. A large, beefy Irishman with a keen political sensitivity, Robinson was on intimate terms with nearly every important East Coast

Republican. Next in importance was Clifford Roberts, a New York investment banker who took charge of Eisenhower's personal investments. Robert Woodruff, chairman of the board of Coca-Cola, one year older than Eisenhower, and W. Alton (Pete) Jones, six months younger and president of Cities Service Company, were other members. The only Democrat in the gang was George Allen, a rotund Mississippian who was a close friend of Truman's and a member of the Democratic National Committee. Ellis (Slats) Slater, four years Eisenhower's junior and president of Frankfort Distilleries, was the last member of the gang. His wife, Priscilla, became Mamie's closest friend.

The gang made Eisenhower a member at Augusta, built him a cottage there, and put in a fish pond, well stocked with bass, for his private use. When Eisenhower moved to New York City, in June of 1948, Robinson made him a member of Blind Brook Country Club in Westchester County. Every member of the gang had his own circle of rich and powerful friends; through the gang, Eisenhower met on a social and private basis innumerable members of the American business, financial, publishing, and legal elite, nearly every one of whom, after a few minutes with the general, became an Eisenhower-for-President booster, putting their time, money, energy, experience, and contacts into the cause.

The object of their adulation, however, still insisted that he had no interest in a political career. Democrats who feared that Truman was a certain loser in 1948 continued to try to draft Eisenhower for the Democratic nomination. At Augusta, Eisenhower told Bill Robinson and the gang that he knew the Democrats "were desperately searching around for someone to save their skins," but that his friends in the Midwest "would be shocked and chagrined at the very idea of my running on a Democratic ticket for anything." When Robinson said that the right-wing Republicans might turn to Mac-Arthur in order to block Dewey's nomination, Eisenhower blurted, "My God, anything would be better than that!" But "anything," he quickly added, did not include an Eisenhower candidacy.[1]

In late June, the Republicans nominated Dewey. The Democrats were meeting in mid-July. Party bosses implored Eisenhower to allow them to put his name before the convention. Again Eisenhower refused. When Senator Claude Pepper of Florida told Eisenhower that he intended to place Eisenhower's name before the convention, with or without the general's permission, Eisenhower wrote Pepper, "No matter under what terms, conditions, or premises a proposal might be couched, I would refuse to accept the nomination."[2] Truman was duly nominated. The furor surrounding Eisenhower subsided.

During the campaign that followed, Eisenhower refused a number of requests that he endorse Dewey, although he told his friends that he was voting for Dewey and expected him to win. He thoroughly enjoyed his freedom from political pressure, for the first time since the end of the war, and —anticipating a Dewey victory, followed by Dewey's re-election in 1952—believed that he had finally put politics completely behind him. He intended to do a good job at Columbia, retire after a few years, then perhaps do a bit of writing on national and international affairs.

That dream was shattered on election night, 1948. John Eisenhower later described November 2, 1948, as the darkest day of his life, because of the way in which Truman's upset of Dewey thrust his father's name back into the forefront of politics.

At Columbia, in June of 1948, the Eisenhowers moved into the president's home on Morningside Drive. They were unhappy with the home, which was too palatial for their tastes; they spent most of their time on the upper two floors, which the trustees had had remodeled for them into a modern apartment. Eisenhower had a new hobby, painting in oils, which he had taken up at the urging of Churchill and after watching Thomas Stephens paint a portrait of Mamie. He did his painting in his penthouse retreat; usually his subjects were portraits. Admitting that "my hands are better suited to an ax handle than a tiny brush," he destroyed two out of every three of his attempts. Nevertheless, the activity gave him great pleasure and he tried to spend a half hour a day or more at it, usually between eleven and midnight.[3]

Time was a problem. The trustees had assured him that no heavy demands would be placed upon him, that he would be free to concentrate on general policy for the university. But after five months on the job, he confided to Bill Robinson that he feared he had made an awful mistake in coming to Columbia. He was appalled at the terrible "demands" on his time; he said he had never realized what a big operation Columbia was, with its "countless numbers" of postgraduate and professional schools. So fully and freely did Eisenhower exercise what he insisted was "the soldier's right to grouse"[4] about his life at Columbia that it has become a standard feature of his biographies to call these the unhappiest and least productive years of his career. And, so the story goes, Columbia suffered as much as the general did. One popular story among the Columbia faculty was to never send the general a memorandum of more than one page, else his lips would get tired.

There was some truth in these judgments. The general and the professors were strange to each other. Grayson Kirk, then a professor of international relations at Columbia, later Eisenhower's successor as president of the university, noted that "he had a tendency born out of his long military experience to want to have all the problems presented to him in very brief form . . . He would shoot from the hip in order to dispose of the problem . . . He felt it was better to make a decision than to postpone it." The professors, on the other hand, much preferred discussion—however protracted—to decision.[5]

Faculty meetings were Eisenhower's special hell. "He thought they could be deadly dull," John Krout, dean of the graduate faculty, reported. "He felt, well, here we spent an hour and a half to two hours, we haven't done a single thing. We've done a lot of talking, didn't amount to much; we haven't advanced one inch so far as doing anything for the university is concerned." At first he tried to attend committee meetings on a regular basis, but as the professors talked and talked in more and more detail about less and less consequential subjects, his eyes would glaze over with total boredom, and he soon gave that up, too.[6]

After almost two years on the job, Eisenhower recorded in his diary, "There is probably no more complicated business in the world than that of picking a new dean within a university."[7] While he was Chief of Staff of the Army, Eisenhower had thought that there could be no bureaucracy in the world that generated so much paper work as the U.S. Army; seven months after coming to Columbia, he wrote, "One of the major surprises . . . is the paper work. . . . I thought I was leaving those mountainous white piles forever." He tried to insist that every project be presented on one typewritten page, the very idea of which reduced the prolific professors to helpless rage or laughter.[8]

Columbia was an outstanding university with a brilliant faculty composed of highly sophisticated specialists who were dedicated to their research. They regarded Eisenhower as hopelessly naïve. When one scholar told Eisenhower that "we have some of America's most exceptional physicists, mathematicians, chemists, and engineers," Eisenhower asked if they were also "exceptional Americans." The scholar, confused, mumbled that Eisenhower did not understand—they were research scholars. "Dammit," Eisenhower shot back, "what good are exceptional physicists . . . exceptional anything, unless they are exceptional Americans." He added that every student who came to Columbia must leave it first a better citizen and only secondarily a better scholar.[9] To the faculty, that attitude was embarrassing—Eisenhower made Columbia sound like a high school civics class. When Eisenhower raised nearly a half million dollars for Teachers College to carry out a Citizenship Education Project, and another huge sum for a Chair of Competitive Enterprise, the embarrassment deepened.

The professors benefited immediately and immensely from Eisenhower's ability to raise money, but snobs that they were, they continued to sneer at him. That they could hold in contempt the intellectual powers of the man who had out-thought Rommel, the man who had organized Overlord, told far more about the professors than it did about Eisenhower. Columbia was lucky to have him, even if the faculty never knew it.

After seven years at the center of world events, accustomed to seeing the latest top-secret intelligence every morning, to making decisions involving millions of men, to dealing on a daily basis with men like Churchill and de Gaulle, Eisenhower felt left out at Columbia. He could only comment upon, not shape, events; his decisions affected only a few thousand people; his contacts were social ones with his millionaire friends, not business meetings with heads of government. The worst part was that he seemed to be working as hard as ever, but had little to show for it.

The Truman Administration was anxious to get Eisenhower involved, in part because it was obviously prudent for the Administration to draw upon the general's reputation and experience, but more to make him a supporter of Administration policy. As a five-star general he was, by law, on active duty for life, and thus available. In 1947 Congress passed the National Defense Act, creating the office of Secretary of Defense and bringing the three services together in a loose federation. In December 1948, Truman asked Eisenhower to come to Washington for "two or three months" to act as a military consultant to the first Secretary of Defense, James Forrestal. Forrestal was involved in the thankless task of trying to bring about some genuine unification among the services.

When Eisenhower arrived in Washington in January 1949, he was appalled. The "Revolt of the Admirals" had broken out; the Navy wanted a much larger share of the Department of Defense's money than had been appropriated, and went after it by ridiculing the Air Force and the Army, meanwhile demanding a larger role for the

Navy. Eisenhower told Swede Hazlett that "our present Navy can scarcely be justified on the basis of the naval strength of any potential enemy." He thought the Navy's proposed supercarrier would just be a supertarget. He objected to the Navy's insistence on a strong Marine Corps. Why, he asked Swede, should the Navy have its own land army of hundreds of thousands of men? [10]

What bothered Eisenhower most was the way in which the Joint Chiefs were going before Congress as individuals to plead their special cases. Eisenhower feared that "some of our seniors are forgetting that they have a commander in chief." [11] Forrestal was having a terrible time trying to get the Chiefs to concentrate their attention on the Russians, instead of one another.

Eisenhower's advice to Forrestal was to establish a "majority rule" principle for the JCS. The Chiefs should be free to argue for their services when the budget was being drawn up, but all their votes should be secret, and once decisions had been reached, they should "carry [them] out faithfully, loyally, enthusiastically." Over the next two years, Eisenhower continued to take the train to Washington once a week; he sent long letters of advice and suggestions on reorganization to Forrestal; he continued to advocate his own program of universal military training; but he was more politely tolerated than listened to, because he always remained an outsider. [12] Truman wanted his prestige, not his advice; Forrestal was, in Eisenhower's words, "nervous, upset, preoccupied, and unhappy." [13] (In May 1949, Forrestal committed suicide.) Meanwhile, the Chiefs continued to bicker, loudly and in public.

In the spring of 1949, Truman asked Eisenhower to serve as the informal chairman of the JCS. The position had no legal basis and, as Eisenhower was in Washington for only a day or two per week, no real clout. He could not possibly keep up with the details of the arguments between the Chiefs, and in that atmosphere, mastery of detail was crucial. He urged Truman to spend more money on defense, but the President insisted on attempting to balance the budget and would not go above $15 billion. Eisenhower had a feeling of déjà vu; "Of course the results [of an inadequate defense policy] will not show up until we get into serious trouble," he predicted in June 1949. "We are repeating our own history of decades, we just don't believe we ever will get into a real jam." [14]

Being a part-time, informal chairman of the JCS gave Eisenhower maximum exposure and minimum influence, which suited the Truman Administration nicely, but left the general depressed. Despite Eisenhower's logic, his reputation, and his charm, the Chiefs continued to bicker among themselves. "The bitter fight still goes on," Eisenhower wrote in his diary. "The whole performance is humiliating—I've seriously considered resigning my commission, so that I could say what I pleased, publicly." [15]

For much of his life, Eisenhower had suffered from occasional stomach cramps. The attacks were isolated and capricious and without apparent cause. On March 21, 1949, while he was in Washington, Eisenhower had an acute attack. His friend and personal physician, General Howard Snyder, suspected some form of enteritis (the ailment was in fact chronic ileitis) and kept Eisenhower in bed for a week on a liquid diet. Truman offered Eisenhower the use of the Little White House that he maintained in Key West. Eisenhower accepted the offer and spent three weeks recuperating in the sun. In April, he moved north to Augusta, where he spent the next month with the gang, playing golf and bridge, fishing, and loafing.

While he was at Key West, Eisenhower had been told by Snyder that he would have to cut down from four packs of cigarettes per day to one. After a few days of limiting his smoking, Eisenhower decided that counting his cigarettes was worse than not smoking at all, and he quit. He never had another cigarette in his life, a fact that amazed the gang, his other friends, the reporters who covered his activities, and the public. Eisenhower was frequently asked how he did it; he replied that it was simple, all he did was put smoking out of his mind. It helped, he would add with a grin, to develop a scornful attitude toward those weaklings who did not have the willpower to break their enslavement to nicotine. He told Cliff Roberts, "I nursed to the utmost . . . my ability to sneer." [16]

Shortly after Eisenhower returned to Columbia, John—currently an instructor in English at West Point—and Barbara had their second child, Barbara Anne. The Eisenhowers' first grandchild, Dwight David Eisenhower II, had been born in 1951. The Eisenhowers were doting grandparents. The general wanted his grandchildren with him for as long and as often as possible; he loved playing with them, teaching them things, buying them presents, giving them lectures. His relationship with his namesake—who was called David, not Dwight—was especially close, and grew even closer as David grew older.

With the coming of grandchildren, Mamie wanted a place of her own more than ever. In thirty-four years of marriage, she had never had one. In the fall of 1950, Eisenhower found one for them, near a farm George Allen had purchased outside Gettysburg, Pennsylvania (Allen later bought up all the land around the Eisenhower farm so that it would be completely protected from encroachment). The farm appealed to the Eisenhowers because of its location, Gettysburg's historic significance, and the worn-out nature of the soil. Eisenhower looked forward to building the soil back up again, restoring it to the condition it was in when the Eisenhowers first came to Pennsylvania from Germany. Mamie looked forward to restoring the old farmhouse; eventually, however, all but the outer walls had to be torn down and a new home built. Mamie designed it for a retirement home, with large, airy rooms and lovely views. Eisenhower began raising cattle in partnership with Allen.

In the late summer of 1949, Eisenhower severed all his ties with the Administration. The issue was the budget. Truman was determined to cut spending on defense to below $15 billion a year; Eisenhower wanted it raised to $16 billion. Defense Secretary Louis A. Johnson asked Eisenhower to help him distribute the allocation (about $13.5 billion) among the three services. Eisenhower did so, but he fought with Johnson at nearly every step of the way, and when the process ended he asked to be relieved of his assignment. He returned to Columbia, "convinced that Washington would never see me again except as an occasional visitor." [17]

But for a man who expected never to return to Washington to live, and for a man who continued to insist that he had no interest in any political career, Eisenhower was acting suspiciously like a man who in fact planned to be the Republican candidate for the Presidency in 1952. He could not avoid thinking about his intentions, because his friends, and a virtual army of citizens, were urging him to enter the race.

Daily, in one form or another, he was asked, "Don't you want to be President?" He emphatically denied it, in his private conversations with his family, the gang, his other intimate friends; he denied it in his private diary; he denied it in his correspondence; he denied it in every public utterance he made on the subject. There is not a single item in the massive collection at the Eisenhower Library prior to late 1951 that even hints that he would seek the job or that he was secretly doing so.

And yet, his actions could not have been better calculated to put him into the White House. His numerous public appearances, his association with the rich and powerful, and the content of his speeches all increased the demand that he become a candidate. No professional politician could have plotted as successful a campaign for the general as the one he directed himself.

To be a successful candidate, he had to appear not to be a candidate. Until after a nomination, he had to avoid partisanship. His speeches had to be forceful without being controversial, seeking the great middle ground of American politics while avoiding any position on current specific disputes. He needed to make himself visible around the country, not as a candidate pleading for votes but as a public servant speaking out on some great issue on which the majority already agreed. He had to put some distance between himself and the Democrats without appearing ungrateful to FDR and Truman for the opportunities they had given him. He had to have access to men of great wealth, and to assure them that his views, especially on taxes and the economy, were safely conservative. He had to keep his image as the Supreme Commander—tough, decisive, highly intelligent, dignified, a man at ease with Churchill and de Gaulle and the other great men of the age—as well as his image as "Ike"—friendly, outgoing, personable, just plain folks, the Kansas farm boy who retained his modesty and was a bit bemused by all the attention that surrounded him, just a simple soldier trying to do his duty.

All this he did, and it led unswervingly to the White House. Yet at every step of the way he protested that he had no ambition to serve as President. He frequently complained that no one, not even the gang, believed his denials, but then how could they, given his actions? None of this recital of his ambivalent behavior is meant to suggest that he sat down, sometime after the night of Truman's re-election, and charted a course for himself that had as its goal the White House. Most of what he did in the period from November 1948 to the end of 1950 he would have done even had Dewey won in 1948 and thus ended all talk about Eisenhower for President. But as he knew better than anyone else, his activities kept his political options open. He did not decide that he wanted to be President and gear his actions to that end, but he carefully made certain that the possibility remained open, indeed that it increased. He did not seek the Presidency, but he so successfully managed his public and private life that, more so than any other candidate in American history, save only George Washington, the Presidency sought him.

He said that he would never willingly seek a vote, and he would never consent to becoming a candidate unless there was an overwhelming demand that convinced him it was his duty to run. Then he created the conditions that convinced him.

• •

Eisenhower's progress toward the White House began the day after Truman's re-election. Ed Bermingham of Alabama, a highly successful investment broker, asked Eisenhower to be the guest of honor at a dinner in Chicago that would have as its audience the leading businessmen, publishers, and bankers in the Midwest. Eisenhower instantly accepted; his remarks at the dinner about the dangers of big government and big labor, high taxes, and creeping socialism were greeted with sustained applause. Shortly after he returned to New York, he was the honored guest of Winthrop Aldrich of the Chase Manhattan Bank at a dinner party at the Racquet & Tennis Club in Manhattan. When Frank Adams, chairman of Standard Oil of New Jersey, asked him to give a little off-the-record talk to his company's top officials on the "broad economic, political and social problems of the day,"[18] Eisenhower accepted the next day. He thus established a pattern that continued, without letup, for the next two years. By the end of that time, there was scarcely a successful businessman, publisher, or financier in the country who had not experienced Eisenhower's firm handshake, seen that big grin, reacted to that bouncy enthusiasm, been impressed by "Ike's" grim determination.

Meanwhile, he tried to avoid the politicians, but they came to him, usually secretly, or through an emissary. The man he least wanted to be seen with in public was Governor Dewey. Thus when Dewey asked for a private meeting in July 1949, Eisenhower agreed, but only if Dewey would come in via the back door and without any publicity.

The governor told Eisenhower that he was "a public possession," that his standing with the citizenry was "likewise public property," and that he had to "carefully guard" his image so that it could be used "in the service of all the people." The governor explained that Eisenhower was the "only" man who could "save this country from going to Hades in the handbasket of paternalism, socialism, dictatorship." Eisenhower replied that he would never "want to enter politics," that he would never seek a vote, that he would of course do his duty, but that "I do not believe that anything can ever convince me that I have a duty to seek political office."[19] That only made plainer to Dewey what he already knew—that his task was to "convince" Eisenhower where his "duty" lay.

Throughout 1949 and on into 1950, Eisenhower repeatedly stated in his diary, "I am not, now or in the future, going willingly into politics," but always there was the "unless." "If I ever do so it will be as the result of a series of circumstances that crush all my arguments, that there appears to me to be such compelling reasons to enter the political field that refusal to do so would always thereafter mean to me that I'd failed to do my duty." He said he could not believe he could be convinced, and added that "if I should ever, in the future, decide affirmatively . . . it will be because I've become oversold by friends."[20] Then he gave his friends every reason to try to so convince him, as he went around the country decrying the state of the nation's defenses, America's position in the world, and the drift to socialism and dictatorship.

In July of 1950 he went to the very heart of right-wing Republicanism, the Bohemian Grove, a retreat in California where millionaires gathered each year to talk, listen to speeches, play, drink, relax, and establish contacts. Herbert Hoover was the reigning figure at the Grove; members called him "The Chief." Eisenhower made the trip on a special train provided for him by the president of the Santa Fe Railroad; in California, he delighted the men at the Grove (including Congressman Richard Nixon, who chatted briefly with Eisenhower at this, their first meeting) by his informality, friendliness, and attacks on the New Deal.

On June 25, 1950, the North Koreans invaded South Korea. Truman reacted immediately; the United Nations adopted an American resolution denouncing the aggression and committing the U.N. to the defense of South Korea, while Truman sent in the U.S. Navy and Air Force, with ground troops to follow.

No one in the Administration thought to invite General Eisenhower to Washington for consultation, but he went anyway, three days after the war began. At the Pentagon he talked with the high command and was disappointed. "I went in expecting to find them all in a dither of effort, engaged in the positive business of getting the troops, supplies, etc., that will be needed to settle the Korean mess," he wrote in his diary. But "they seemed indecisive." Eisenhower assured them that he supported Truman's decision, then emphasized that an "appeal to force cannot, by its nature, be a partial one . . . for God's sake, get ready! . . . We must study every angle to be prepared for whatever may happen, even if it finally came to the use of an A-bomb (which God forbid)."[21]

He returned to Washington a week later, to meet with Pentagon officials, testify before a Senate committee, and have lunch with Truman and George Marshall. Eisenhower and Marshall told Truman that they "earnestly supported" his actions, then advised him to put as much strength, as quickly as possible, into Korea. But although Truman and the Pentagon officials assured Eisenhower that in Korea General MacArthur was getting "all he asked for," Eisenhower felt "there seems no disposition to begin serious mobilizing. . . . [Truman's] military advisers are too complacent." [22]

The mood in Washington in late June and July of 1950 was not at all similar to the mood of urgency and dedication that characterized December 1941. For Eisenhower personally, being an outsider commenting on events without benefit of the latest information, rather than being at the center of the action, as he had been in 1941, was frustrating. But whatever the drawbacks to being an outsider, there were advantages. Eisenhower was in the happy position of being able to give advice without having to make decisions. Thus he could tell Truman to undertake a rapid rearmament program, without having to consider all the President's legal, economic, and political problems. Thus he could argue—as he did, later, when it became an issue—that he had advised the government to do more in Korea, but had been ignored.

By the fall of 1950, Eisenhower clearly needed to get out of Columbia. The nation was at war, the world in crisis, and the old soldier wanted to be in on the action.

His luck held, his opportunity came. In 1949, the United States had joined with the nations of Western Europe in the North Atlantic Treaty Organization (NATO). European rearmament, almost nonexistent before the Korean War began, was now under way. Truman had committed the United States to a massive program of rearmament and indicated that he would send a goodly portion of the forces raised to Europe, to join in a NATO military organization. Leaders on both sides of the Atlantic unanimously agreed that Eisenhower was the "only man" who could take command of the NATO forces. In October 1950, Truman called Eisenhower to a meeting at the White House, where he "requested" the general to accept the appointment. Eisenhower took the position that "I am a soldier and am ready to respond to whatever orders my superiors" may give.[23]

It was an ideal appointment. As NATO commander, with headquarters in Paris, he could avoid making any comments about domestic and partisan issues. His return to Europe would insure front-page coverage around the world. He could speak out, forcefully, on the issue closest to his heart, the Atlantic Alliance. He would be in daily working contact with the heads of government of Western Europe, which would only add to his image as one of the world's leading statesmen. His reputation as the Western world's greatest soldier would be enhanced. The post put Eisenhower at the center of great events. It represented a challenge worthy of his talents. As he explained to his son, John, "I consider this to be the most important military job in the world."[24] He could renew and strengthen his relations with his many British and French friends, and establish new ones with the West German leaders. His only worry, he said, was his wife; Mamie's "heart condition deteriorates a bit year by year and I hate to contemplate" forcing her to move once again. But as for himself, he knew he would be happy when he could feel that "I am doing the best I can in what I definitely believe to be a world crisis."[25]

Best of all, he would be in a position to preserve the victory he had directed in 1945. The specter of the Europe that he had liberated being overrun and enslaved by the Red Army—a prospect that in late 1950 seemed entirely possible—was too painful to contemplate. He told Swede, "I rather look upon this effort as about the last remaining chance for the survival of Western civilization."[26]

But if Truman had provided Eisenhower with a perfect platform, it was still Eisenhower who would have to perform. The job was hardly ceremonial; the challenges were real; there was a definite possibility of failure. The only firm decision that the NATO Council of Ministers had made was that they wanted Eisenhower for the Supreme Command.

But of what? A multinational force? Independent national armies joined together in a loose alliance? How many troops? Where would they come from? Truman had said he intended to send more American divisions to Germany—there were two there already—but Taft and other Old Guard Republicans had challenged the President's right to ship American troops to Europe in peacetime.

And although few dared to say so publicly, all the NATO partners knew that NATO without German troops would never be able to match the Red Army. Eisenhower himself felt that "the safety of Western Europe demands German participation on a vigorous scale," but West Germany was not yet sovereign, was not a member of NATO, and in any case the French, Dutch, Belgians, and others were horrified at the prospect of rearming the Germans only five years after they had been liberated from the Nazis. German rearmament was going to be a hard sell. So too would be general European rearmament.

To the Europeans, NATO meant a guarantee that the United States would not desert them, that they could count on the atomic bomb to deter the Red Army. They could see no reason to add a significant military component to NATO, especially when the price would include German rearmament as well as higher taxes and more sacrifices for their economies, at a time when they were just beginning to emerge from the ashes of World War II. Rearmament would merely provoke the Russians, critics said, without creating sufficient strength to repel them—at least without using atomic bombs, which was already assured by American participation in NATO. To succeed as Supreme Commander, Eisenhower would have to persuade the Europeans that the Germans were their allies, not their enemies; that they could build ground and air forces strong enough to hurl back the Red Army; that a genuine military alliance of the NATO partners was, even though unique in history, nevertheless workable.

He was disturbed by American leadership. Taft and his fellow isolationists in the Republican Party were simply hopeless. Truman was not much better. There was no sense of direction, Eisenhower complained, "and poor HST [is] a fine man who, in the middle of a stormy lake, knows nothing of swimming."[27] In late 1950, as the Chinese armies rolled southward in Korea, as the Europeans continued to resist either German or their own rearmament, and as the Americans continued to bicker among themselves about the size of their commitment to NATO, Eisenhower wrote in his diary, "Something is terribly wrong."[28]

His friends kept telling him that he was the "only man" who could lead America and the Atlantic Alliance out of its morass. He was finding it increasingly difficult to disagree with them. He still insisted that there were many fine men around and that he wanted no part of politics, but hardly anyone believed him. By December, Eisenhower had been convinced that one more Democratic victory would end the two-party system in the United States, but he was unhappy about Taft. His concern was with Taft's policies, not on domestic matters, where the two men thought alike, but in foreign affairs, and most of all with Taft's commitment to NATO (Taft had voted against the treaty).

So, before leaving for Europe, Eisenhower arranged a meeting with Taft. He wanted Taft's support for NATO; if he got it, he was ready to "kill off any further speculation about me as a candidate for the Presidency." Before Taft arrived Eisenhower wrote out a statement he intended to issue that evening, if Taft would agree to the principles of collective security and an all-out American commitment to NATO. Eisenhower's statement read, "Having been called back to military duty, I want to announce that my name may not be used by anyone as candidate for President—and if they do I will repudiate such efforts."

But the talk with Taft was disheartening. The senator objected to Truman's program of sending additional American divisions to Europe, said that the President did not have the right to do so. Eisenhower insisted that the President certainly did have such a right. Then Eisenhower asked Taft if he and his followers would "agree that collective security is necessary for us in Western Europe" and would support NATO as a bipartisan policy.

Taft equivocated. He seemed to Eisenhower to be "playing politics," and appeared to be primarily interested "in cutting the President, or the Presidency, down to size." He moved the discussion from principle to detail, mumbling several times, "I do not know whether I shall vote for four divisions or six divisions or two divisions." Eisenhower said he had no interest in such details, that he wanted support for the concept of NATO, but Taft would not respond. After the senator left, Eisenhower called in two aides and in their presence tore up his drafted statement, which was Sherman-like enough to take him out of the presidential race forever. He decided to retain "an aura of mystery" about his plans.[29]

Eisenhower began his tour as Supreme Allied Commander, Europe (SACEUR), with a January 1951 trip that took him to the eleven European capitals of the NATO countries. He started in Paris, where he made a Europe-wide radio broadcast. He took the opportunity to assert his great love for Europe: "I return with an unshakable faith in Europe—this land of our ancestors—in the underlying courage of its people, in their willingness to live and sacrifice for a secure peace and the continuance and the progress of civilization." He said that he had no "miraculous plans," and that he brought with him no troops or military equipment, but he did bring hope.[30]

And his name, the power of which he knew. At the initial NATO planning session, General Lauris Norstad of the U.S. Air Force recalled, "I've never heard more crying in my life." All the staff officers from the various countries said they did not have this, they did not have that, how weak they were. "And I could see General Eisenhower becoming less and less impressed with this very negative approach, and finally he just banged that podium . . . got red faced . . . and said in a voice that could have been heard two or three floors below that he knew what the weaknesses were . . . 'I know there are shortages, but I myself make up for part of that shortage—what I can do and what I can put into this—and the rest of it has to be made up by you people. Now get at it!' And he banged the podium again and he walked out. Just turned around, didn't say a word, just walked out. And believe me there was a great change in attitude. Right away there was an air of determination—we *will* do it." [31]

One of Eisenhower's goals on the January trip was to get from the Europeans positive commitments to NATO that he could use back in the States to counter Taft and the others who were charging that since the Europeans were unwilling to rearm, the United States should not bear the burden and the cost. In Lisbon, Eisenhower told Prime Minister Salazar that the Europeans would have to develop "the same sense of urgency and desire for unity and common action to preserve peace as existed in the United States," and asked Salazar to give him "concrete evidence to take back to the American people that the European countries were giving their defense effort chief priority." [32] He repeated these demands at every stop, and he could be blunt and direct in doing so.

Eisenhower also used the trip to give pep talks to the Europeans. He was at his most dramatic in Paris, where he told Premier Pleven "that the French do not have enough confidence in their own potentialities; that, after all, they have only been defeated once and that the public officials in a country of such glorious traditions should be constantly exhorting the people to again rise to the height of which the French people are capable." He urged Pleven to "beat the drums to reaffirm the glory of France." The official recorder noted that "the impression Eisenhower made on M. Pleven was very noticeable. M. Pleven said, 'I thank you; you have aroused new confidence in me already.'" When Eisenhower's chief of staff, Alfred Gruenther, told him he had been "superbly eloquent," Eisenhower grunted, "Why is it that when I deliver such a good talk it has to be to an audience of one!" [33]

Part of the pep talk included urging the Europeans to get along with one another. He asked Prime Minister de Gasperi of Italy, for example, if it was not possible "for the Italians to think in friendly terms about Yugoslavia," as he had high hopes of eventually including Yugoslavia in NATO in order to strengthen his southern flank. (His overtures to Marshal Tito, a sort of Darlan Deal in reverse, aroused the fury of Republicans, who were upset enough at the thought of helping Europe's socialist governments. The idea of giving military aid to Communist Yugoslavia made them livid. But Eisenhower in 1951, as in November 1942, would take allies wherever he could find them.) De Gasperi, citing the struggle between Italy and Yugoslavia for control of Trieste, noted that "it was a sad fact that in Europe nations were usually friendly with other nations which were not their neighbors."[34]

Two neighbors who shared a long frontier and deep hatreds were France and West Germany. When talking with the French, Eisenhower avoided the delicate subject of German rearmament, but he did begin to lay a basis for the creation of a German army by making a trip to a U.S. air base in West Germany, where he held a press conference. He opened by saying that when he had last come to Germany, "I bore in my heart a very definite antagonism toward Germany and certainly a hatred for all that the Nazis stood for, and I fought as hard as I knew how to destroy it." But, he added, "for my part, by-gones are by-gones," and he hoped that "some day the great German people are lined up with the rest of the free world, because I believe in the essential freedom-loving quality of the German people." When a German reporter pointed out that many Frenchmen wanted a permanently neutralized Germany, Eisenhower replied that "in this day and time to conceive of actual neutrality . . . is an impossibility." When asked whether he thought a German contribution was essential to the defense of Europe, he hedged a bit, but finally admitted "the more people on my side the happier I will be."[35]

In his extensive private correspondence, with the gang, with other millionaires, with politicians and publishers, Eisenhower concentrated on selling NATO. Most of the incoming letters were pleas that he run for the Presidency; his standard reply was that he had no interest in politics and that in any event the job he held was so important that he had to concentrate his full energy and time on it. Then he would launch into a sales pitch for NATO, usually ending by urging the recipient to spread the word.

The word was that "the future of civilization, as we know it, is at stake." The word was that the true defense of the United States was on the Elbe River. The word was that the American way of life was dependent upon raw materials that could come only from Europe and its colonies, and upon trade and scientific exchanges with Europe and the rest of the free world. The word was that by supporting European rearmament, the United States could buy as much security for itself by spending $1 as it could by spending $4 to build up American forces. The word was that only through collective security could the United States and Europe meet the Soviet threat.[36]

In his correspondence, Eisenhower dealt directly with the two major objections to American support for NATO. The first was that the Europeans, led by the Labour Party in Britain, were going socialist, which caused many of Eisenhower's friends to ask, "Why in hell should we support a bunch of pinkos?" Eisenhower reassured them that Europe was fully committed to a free, democratic way of life, that it was not about to go Communist (unless the United States abandoned it), and that "it would be a terrific mistake to demand conformity in all political and economic details. We would soon fall apart!"[37]

The second objection, far more serious, was that the United States was committing itself to an indefinite defense of Europe, at a tremendous cost that would continually go higher. Eisenhower admitted the force of the objection. "We cannot be a modern Rome guarding the far frontiers with our legions," he said. He recognized that the economic strength of the United States was the greatest asset the free world had, and he agreed that the expenditure of billions of dollars for defense would, in the long run, bankrupt the United States, thus presenting the Soviets with "their greatest victory." But he insisted that a program of support for NATO was a short-run proposition. American aid for NATO was essential now, in 1951, but it could be phased out rather quickly. To Ed Bermingham, he flatly declared, "If in ten years, all American troops stationed in Europe for national defense purposes have not been returned to the United States, then this whole project will have failed."[38]

Within Europe, Eisenhower considered morale to be his biggest problem. Less than six years after the most destructive war in history, Europeans just did not want to think about fighting—or building the forces to fight—another war. Further, the figures on ground strength were so stark and discouraging—NATO had only 12 divisions, the Russians 175—that it seemed impossible to stop the Red Army without using atomic bombs, and if the Americans were going to use atomic bombs anyway, why bother to build European ground strength, especially when it would be so expensive, would slow or halt economic recovery, and would only provoke the Russians?

Eisenhower thought that sufficient conventional strength could be built and that it was both mad and immoral to rely upon the atomic bomb. In his talks with the European leaders, Eisenhower attempted to build their confidence. Inevitably, he had to ask them to dig deeper, spend more, but he did so within the context of recognizing political realities. As his principal aide, Andrew Goodpaster, later explained, "He had a great sense of how the governments of the various countries worked and what the practical constraints were on the political leaders that you couldn't crowd them too far, you couldn't ask too much of them." [39]

Eisenhower therefore emphasized morale, which cost little or nothing to build. "Civilian leaders talk about the state of morale in a given country as if it were a sort of uncontrollable event or phenomenon, like a thunderstorm or a cold winter," he complained in his diary, while "the soldier leader looks on morale as . . . the greatest of all his problems, but also as one about which he can and must do something." Thus he continued to urge, cajole, encourage. He asked the governments to remind each and every citizen daily "of his own conceptions of the dignity of man and of the value he places upon freedom; this must be accompanied by the reminder that freedom is something that must be earned every day that one lives!"

On the seventh anniversary of Overlord, Eisenhower went to Normandy to deliver a Europe-wide radio broadcast that reminded the Europeans of what was at stake. "Never again," he said "must there be a campaign of liberation fought on these shores." [40]

Germany remained Eisenhower's most delicate problem. No matter how successful he was in persuading the other nations of Western Europe to increase their defense spending, his goal of forty divisions was simply unattainable without a German army. Eisenhower had extracted from the French a promise of twenty-four divisions for NATO, but in fact the French had only three divisions in West Germany and six in France, with no immediate prospect of making any further contribution, because ten French divisions were tied down in Indochina in an apparently endless war. Whenever Eisenhower asked the French for more support for NATO, they countered with a request for more American support for their effort in Indochina. "I'd favor heavy reinforcement to get the thing over at once," Eisenhower wrote in his diary, "but I'm convinced that no military victory is possible in that kind of theater." [41] In his view, the French had to give Vietnam, Laos, and Cambodia their independence, then let them fight their own war, while the French Army came home to defend France. But he could not convince any French leader of the wisdom of that course, which meant that the only alternative for NATO was to create a German army, but the French would not allow that either.

"We are either going to solve this German problem," Eisenhower believed, "or the Soviets will solve it in their favor."[42] Or as Chancellor Konrad Adenauer put it, "The Western Allies, especially France, have to . . . answer the question of which danger is the greater: the Russian threat or a German contribution to a European defense community."[43] After going through various contortions, including a proposal that the Germans provide the enlisted men while the French supplied the officers, the French finally offered the "Pleven Plan." The Germans would build an army that would have no unit larger than a division, as part of an integrated NATO force commanded by Eisenhower; the German contribution would be limited to 20 percent of the integrated force.

Eisenhower told Marshall, "The plan offers the only immediate hope that I can see of developing, on a basis acceptable to other European countries, the German strength that is vital to us." In addition, he had a larger goal. "I am certain that there is going to be no real progress towards a greater unification of Europe except through the medium of specific programs of this kind."[44] In other words, rather than waiting for the creation of a United States of Europe to achieve an all-European army, he felt that by forming the army first, the political unification would naturally follow.

He thought the new supernation should include all the European NATO members, plus Greece, Sweden, Spain, and Yugoslavia. A United States of Europe, he argued, would "instantly . . . solve the real and bitter problems of today . . . It is a tragedy for the whole human race that it is not done at once." He brushed aside objections. "I get exceedingly weary of this talk about a step-by-step, gradual cautious approach," he told Harriman. He saw no reason why a "socialist Sweden could [not] live alongside a capitalist Germany" so long as there was a simple bill of rights in the constitution, and the elimination of trade barriers and all economic and political restraint on free movement. He thought the United States could and should go to "any limit" to support such a venture.[45]

In December 1951, he urged Premier Pleven to issue a call to the European members of NATO "to meet in an official constitutional convention to consider ways and means for promoting a closer union." Such a "dramatic and inspiring call to action," he said, would be a great help in getting a European army under way. But although Pleven was the sponsor of the European army idea, and although Eisenhower carefully flattered Pleven, he did not respond.[46] The French, in short, could not yet answer Adenauer's question: Which do you fear most, the Red Army or a new German army?

The British too had to be wooed. They were not so opposed to a German army as were the French, but a united Europe was "anathema to them." Eisenhower went after the British in his typical fashion —public speeches, private meetings with politicians, and an extensive correspondence with his many friends in the British government. On July 3, 1951, he delivered a major address to the English-Speaking Union at Grosvenor House on Park Lane, to an audience of 1,200 British leaders. Foreign Secretary Herbert Morrison introduced him as "the First Citizen of the Atlantic"; Prime Minister Clement Attlee referred to him as "the man who won the war"; the then opposition leader, Winston Churchill, led the standing ovation. The attitude of the audience toward Eisenhower, according to Bill Robinson, who was there, "amounted to worship."

In his speech, Eisenhower issued a ringing call for a United States of Europe. He recognized the difficulties—"this project faces the deadly danger of procrastination, timid measures, slow steps and cautious stages"—then held out the vision of what could be gained: "With unity achieved, Europe could build adequate security and, at the same time, continue the march of human betterment that has characterized Western civilization. Once united, the farms and factories of France and Belgium, the foundries of Germany, the rich farmlands of Holland and Denmark, the skilled labor of Italy, will produce miracles for the common good." The next day Churchill told Eisenhower that he was too deaf to have heard the speech, but having now read it, he wanted to say, "I am sure this is one of the greatest speeches delivered by any American in my lifetime."[47]

At his home outside Paris, Ike had Mamie with him, as well as Moaney as his valet, Sergeant Dry as his driver, and Colonel Craig Cannon as his personal aide. There was a golf course on the property, and a fish pond well stocked with trout, and room for a vegetable garden. Initially the house was too French for Mamie's taste, too grand in its appearance, both inside and out, while the plumbing and electricity were unreliable. But after it was fixed up it became one of her favorite homes.

Ike took great pleasure in his garden and his painting. "We have had sweet corn, two kinds of beans, peas, radishes, tomatoes, turnips and beets . . . in great quantity," he told his son in September, and bragged that "our corn did better than almost any other we have ever planted."[48] His painting abilities had not improved, he told Swede; there was still "no faintest semblance of talent." But he added that because he could no longer indulge himself in "serious and steady reading," he needed "some kind of release" and he found it in paint-ing. "For me the real benefit is the fact that it gives me an excuse to be absolutely alone and interferes not at all with what I am pleased to call my 'contemplative powers.' "[49]

He needed time to contemplate, as the pressure on him to enter politics continued to grow. In the summer of 1951 his friends in the states formed a volunteer organization, Citizens for Eisenhower. Cliff Roberts financed the effort, with help from Ellis Slater, Pete Jones, and the rest of the gang, along with such Republican financiers as John Hay Whitney, L. B. Maytag, and George Whitney, the president of J. P. Morgan and Company. Citizens for Eisenhower then oversaw and encouraged the innumerable Ike Clubs that began springing up around the country. Because the group included no professional politicians, the movement gave the appearance of a spontaneous grass-roots demand.

But as the Ike Clubs boomed, inevitably the professional politi-cians began to get involved, through letters, telegrams, speeches, and visits to Paris. Eisenhower was polite to all of them. Senator Joseph McCarthy sent him a copy of one of his speeches; Eisenhower made a noncommittal, but friendly, reply. Senator Richard Nixon made a special trip to Paris in late May to meet the general and express his support for NATO.

Insofar as the Ike Clubs claimed to be nonpartisan, and insofar as Eisenhower was so much closer to the Democrats than the Taft-dominated Republicans on foreign policy, and insofar as Eisenhower would be an absolutely sure thing as a Democratic candidate, some Democrats still had hopes of capturing the general. In August 1951, Oregon Democrats filed petitions putting him on the Democratic primary ballot. Eisenhower protested that as SACEUR he could not take a partisan position and asked that his name be removed. Tru-man, meanwhile, was remaining as mysterious about his plans as Eisenhower was; it was generally acknowledged that he could have the Democratic nomination if he wanted it, but most observers felt he would not have much chance in the general election (his approval rating in the polls was below 30 percent).

In November, when Eisenhower was in Washington for consul-tation on NATO matters, Truman met him privately in Blair House and there repeated an offer he had made earlier through George Allen—the President would "guarantee" Eisenhower the Democratic nomination and give him his full support. "You can't join a party just to run for office," Eisenhower replied. "What reason have you to think I have ever been a Democrat? You know I have been a Republican all my life and that my family have always been Republicans." Truman pressed the offer; Eisenhower rejoined that his differences with the Democrats over domestic issues, especially labor legislation, were too vast for him to even consider accepting.

Had Eisenhower accepted, given that he had more support from Democratic than Republican voters, he would have won a certain victory, probably bringing a Democratic majority to Congress with him. But he would not consider it. For one thing, the Republican Party had to be saved from itself; for another, there were the general's personal feelings. As he noted in his diary, "I could never imagine feeling any compelling duty in connection with a Democratic movement of any kind."[50]

Taft, meanwhile, was piling up delegates. Equally alarming to Eisenhower's political supporters, the Citizens for Eisenhower group was plagued by problems—internal bickering, fighting for position, poor organization. On September 4, 1951, Senator Henry Cabot Lodge of Massachusetts visited Eisenhower in Paris. He came as a spokesman for numerous East Coast Republicans, and he insisted that it was time to put some professional expertise into the Eisenhower campaign. Getting the nomination would be the hard part, Lodge said. The election was a cinch. Lodge therefore insisted that Eisenhower had to permit the use of his name in the Republican primaries, and to allow professionals to take control of the Citizens for Eisenhower organization. Speed was essential; otherwise Taft soon would have the nomination sewed up. Eisenhower promised to think it over.[51]

In the States, the professionals were trying to infiltrate the Citizens organization. Lucius Clay sent Eisenhower a series of reports on their activities, all done in a simple code. ("Our Friend up the river" was Dewey; "F" was Harold Stassen; "G" was Taft; "A" was Senator James Duff of Pennsylvania; etc.) Clay was disturbed by their infighting—F would not join up if A was a part of the movement; Our Friend did not like A; and so it went. On a more positive note, Clay reported that "I am convinced that the President will not run if you run. He has made this statement to two separate and reliable persons. He will run if G does, and in my opinion would beat G to a frazzle."[52] Eisenhower responded that he would do whatever duty dictated. He then added that he had been assured by Harold Stassen, who had made a strong bid for the Republican nomination in 1948 and was attempting to do so again in 1952, that at the proper moment he, Stassen, would deliver his delegate votes to Eisenhower. Eisenhower also assured Clay that "you need not worry that I shall ever disregard Our Friend," then ended with a heartfelt handwritten postscript: "Wouldn't it be nice if we could just forget all this kind of thing?"[53]

That was obviously impossible. On November 10, Clay met in New York with Dewey, Lodge, and a number of Dewey's high command from 1948, including his campaign manager, New York lawyer Herbert Brownell, and his economic adviser, Gabriel Hauge. The group agreed to name Lodge as Eisenhower's campaign manager. Lodge was free of the onus of being a Dewey man (he had supported Arthur Vandenberg in 1948) and had enthusiasm, drive, and professional know-how. As the meeting broke up, Dewey said, "And don't forget, let's get a hell of a lot of money."[54]

When Eisenhower flew to New York in November, he spent three hours sitting in the airplane at LaGuardia Airport while Mamie went to Morningside Heights to collect a few things. On the plane, Eisenhower held a meeting with the gang. Milton Eisenhower and Clay also were there. Throughout his brief stay in the States, Eisenhower had been harassed by reporters wanting to know his political preference; he had just come from Washington, where he had turned down Truman's offer; he was exhausted, irritable, and unhappy. But he was also moved by Milton's position, which was that if the choice before the voters in 1952 was to be Truman or Taft, then "any personal sacrifice on the part of any honest American citizen is wholly justified." Robinson pointed out that "in no circumstance could you ever avoid the burden of worry over the country's future course, and there would seem to be fewer frustrations for the leader than there would be for the commentator." Eisenhower replied that he would respond to a genuine draft, that he would do nothing to bring it about, that he would not repudiate the efforts of the Citizens for Eisenhower, and that he wished the whole thing were over, because he certainly did not want to be President.[55]

What it came down to was that Eisenhower wanted to be nominated by acclamation, but his friends knew that was impossible. He was expecting too much; he would have to enter the fight for delegates before Taft had them all. Eisenhower refused. He cited his NATO job, the need for him to remain above politics, and—most of all—Army regulations, which forbade a serving officer from seeking political office.

At least, his friends said, allow us to announce that you are a

Republican, because Taft's great advantage in the struggle for delegates was his argument that no one knew what political party the general belonged to. Still Eisenhower refused, but he did agree that Milton could make a statement to the effect that the Eisenhower family had always been Republican.

Growing pressure caused growing resentment. The more he saw of professional politicians, the less he liked them. Shortly after returning to Paris in November, he wrote Robinson, "Every passing day confirms and hardens my dislike of all political activity as a personal participant."[56] Because of that reaction Eisenhower was increasingly ambiguous, increasingly doubtful that he wanted to pay the price of a political career.

He was distressed by reports from Clay of trouble in the organization. Senator Duff was "full of ego and determined to be the 'anointed.'" Duff did not like Lodge; Lodge could not stand Duff; Dewey was doubtful about both Duff and Lodge; no one trusted Stassen; there were difficulties with the finance managers.[57] It all made Eisenhower's head spin.

The pressure mounted. Paul Hoffman, whom Eisenhower admired enormously, wrote him on December 5: "Whether you like it or not, you have to face the fact that you are the one man today who can (1) redeem the Republican party, (2) change the atmosphere of the United States from one impregnated with fear and hate to one in which there will be good will and confidence, and (3) start the world down the road to peace."[58] Clay, Robinson, and dozens of other men Eisenhower respected bombarded him with similar statements. Aldrich sent him a poll taken in Texas that indicated Eisenhower would carry the state by a wide margin.

It was that prospect—that all he had to do was say yes and he could be President, and that as President he could save the country —that kept him from repudiating the efforts in his behalf. That, and his feeling that "the presidency is something that should never be sought, [but] could never be refused."[59]

Then, on December 8, what Eisenhower called a crisis arose. Lodge told him that he simply had to return to the States and make a positive announcement or "the whole effort is hopeless." Eisenhower's response was immediate and negative. To involve himself in pre-convention activity, he said, "would be a dereliction in duty—almost a violation of my oath of office."[60] Therefore, the effort in "which you and your close political associates are now engaged should, logically, be abandoned." He wanted Lodge to announce that since Eisenhower's backers had concluded that his nomination without his active participation was impossible, and since "it is impossible for me in my position as a military commander" to campaign, the Citizens for Eisenhower group was being disbanded. In his diary, he outlined these developments, then wrote "Hurrah."[61] As far as he was concerned, it was over—or so it seemed.

Getting out was hardly going to be that easy. Stassen flew over to see him and argue for the cause. Clay wrote a long letter, in effect accusing Eisenhower of going back on his word, given at the La-Guardia Airport meeting, that "if a group could prove it was your duty, on their advice you would return home."[62]

Cliff Roberts and Bill Robinson flew over to Paris. He told them that his "feeling midway between aversion and reluctance is 100% real," and that he was "more devoted to the success of his [NATO] mission than intrigued by the idea of being President." Then he came down from Olympus, explaining his own political judgment and in the process revealing political calculations of his own.

There were, he said, advantages to his staying at his post and making no political statements. First of all, his success in Europe was the *sine qua non* of a successful bid for the Presidency. He could not claim success until the late February meeting of the NATO Council of Ministers in Lisbon, or until he had issued his Annual Report, in April. Next, he pointed out that "the seeker is never so popular as the sought. People want what they think that they can't get." His nonparticipation in the delegate struggle insured that he had made no deals nor incurred any obligations. If he returned to the States and began to campaign, he would have to take a stand on various emotional issues, which would "alienate more strength than it would develop." Further, he would be subjected to more direct and severe attacks than his opponents would dare risk while he was SACEUR. By avoiding a debate with Taft, he might be able to prevent a split in the party and a bitter personal rivalry.

These were powerful arguments, and they convinced his friends. Robinson's conclusion was that "it would seem that there is more to be gained than lost by staying on the job in Europe."[63]

Robinson carried back to Lodge the arguments Eisenhower had made against his returning home and announcing that he was a Republican. Lodge was unconvinced. The general's position, Lodge agreed, would be a positive factor in winning a general election, but it would not help him win the nomination. Lodge's job was to win delegates, and he could not do so for a man who would not even identify himself as a Republican. Lodge decided to force the issue. On January 6, 1952, he announced that he was entering Eisenhower's name on the Republican ballot in the New Hampshire primary. In response to questions, Lodge told reporters that Eisenhower was indeed a Republican, that he would accept the Republican nomination if it were offered to him, and that the general himself would confirm these statements.

Eisenhower was furious. Lodge's presumption, he told Roberts, "has caused me a bit of bitter resentment."[64] He sent a sharp letter of rebuke to Clay, then issued a coy statement of his own. He did not directly confirm Lodge's claim that he was a Republican, but admitted that he did vote for that party. He did not say he would accept a Republican nomination, but did admit that Lodge and his associates had the right "to place before me next July a duty that would transcend my present responsibility." He did not give his approval to the actions of the Citizens, although he added that all Americans were free "to organize in pursuit of their common convictions." He ended with a promise: "Under no circumstances will I ask for relief from this assignment in order to seek nomination for political office, and I shall not participate in . . . preconvention activities."[65]

But events continued to drive him toward a different course. On January 21, Truman submitted his budget, with its $14 billion deficit, to Congress, which led Eisenhower to dictate an eight-page furious protest in his diary. On February 8, Herbert Hoover joined Taft and sixteen other prominent Republicans in a statement that urged that "American troops should be brought home" from Europe. Which was worse, the danger of bankruptcy or isolation, Eisenhower hardly knew, but he felt he had to stop both trends.

There was also the pressure of being wanted as well as needed. It was the pressure he was apparently waiting to see. His friends and the politicians kept telling him how much the American people yearned for his leadership, and on February 11, he got a dramatic demonstration of how right they were. Jacqueline Cochran, the famous aviator and wife of Floyd Odlum, the financier, flew to Paris with a two-hour film of an Eisenhower rally in Madison Square Garden, held at midnight following a boxing match. It had been carefully stage-managed by Eisenhower's friends and the Citizens. Some fifteen thousand people attended, despite—according to Cochran—a total lack of cooperation from the city officials (all, of course, Democrats). The film showed the crowd chanting in unison, "We want Ike! We want Ike!" while waving "I Like Ike" banners and placards. Eisenhower and Mamie watched in their living room and were profoundly moved.

When the film was over, Eisenhower got Cochran a drink. As they raised their glasses, she blurted out a toast: "To the President." She later recalled, "I was the first person to ever say this to him and he burst into tears . . . Tears were just running out of his eyes, he was so overwhelmed . . . So then he started to talk about his mother, his father and his family, but mostly his mother, and he talked for an hour."

Cochran told him that he would have to declare himself and go back to the States, that "I'm as sure as I'm sitting here and looking at you that Taft will get the nomination if you don't declare yourself." Eisenhower told her to return to New York and tell Clay to come to Europe for a talk, then added, "You can go tell Bill Robinson that I'm going to run."[66]

On March 11, 1952, in the New Hampshire primary, Eisenhower beat Taft and Stassen with 50 percent of the vote to their 38 percent and 7 percent. A week later, in Minnesota, Eisenhower received 108,692 write-in votes while Stassen, his name on the ballot in his home state, got 129,076 (Taft did not run). As Stassen had privately assured Eisenhower of his support at the convention, those delegates could be added to the Eisenhower total. He was on his way.

He was not entirely happy about it. Robert Anderson, a forty-two-year-old Texas lawyer, politician, and financier, who flew to Paris to consult with the candidate about the Federal Reserve Board, found Eisenhower "working himself into physical exhaustion" as he tried to finish his NATO duties and prepare himself for the campaign.[67] Eisenhower was not going to go into a battle expecting to lose. He had earlier told Robinson, "If ever I get into this business, I am going to start swinging from the hips and I am going to keep swinging until completely counted out."[68] He was ready to start swinging, although not ready to begin making statements on the issues. As he explained to George Sloan of Chrysler, "A premature consumption of all the ammunition in a battle is certain to bring defeat—everything must be so calculated that the effort constantly increases in its intensity towards its ultimate maximum, which is the moment of victory."[69] Privately, he sent long letters to his business friends, bemoaning high taxes and government bureaucracy; he counted on them to pass the letters around. He met regularly, if secretly, with prominent Republican politicians. He assured Texans that he was on the side of states' rights in the tidelands oil dispute with the federal government. He assured doctors that he was completely opposed to socialized medicine. He wrote a long, friendly letter to Drew Pearson on the subject of Christianity versus communism. He opened a correspondence with various Republican governors.

He continued to arm himself for battle. He asked experts for background papers on mortgage financing, farm subsidies, public housing, and a myriad of other subjects. He asked John Foster Dulles to give him a statement on the problems of dealing with the Russians. Herb Brownell came over to Paris to assure Eisenhower that Dewey had the New York delegation solidly behind the general, and could deliver other East Coast delegations. The two men discussed the mechanics of a presidential campaign, scheduling, speeches, platforms, organization needs, and such issues as Social Security, race relations, and the budget.

Now he was a full-time candidate, pure and simple. His supporters began to bombard him with advice, telling him what he should say on this or that issue. The advice was often cynical. "It seems necessary to walk around some of the questions presented," he wrote Milton. "I seem to sense a difference between a man's convictions and what he believes to be politically feasible."[70] The politicians wanted Eisenhower to "take a stand." He resisted. "Frankly," he told Clay, "I do not consider either race relations or labor relations to be issues. And I don't believe the problems arising within either of them can be ended by punitive law or a statement made in a press conference."[71]

When he did express his views, he got into trouble. After his pro-Texas views on the tidelands matter became known, Lodge wrote in alarm—Eisenhower's stand would hurt him in the Northeast, and he should retreat from a flat endorsement of the Texas claims. Eisenhower replied, "I am compelled to remark that I believe what I believe." He said the original treaty between Texas and the United States specifically guaranteed the tidelands to the state, which as far as he was concerned settled the matter. He added that he would not "tailor my opinions and convictions to the one single measure of net vote appeal."[72]

With all the conflicting advice, with all that Brownell had told him about the rigors of a presidential campaign, with the attacks on him that the Taft people were already launching, with the wrench that came with packing up and moving again, Eisenhower's mood was glum. "Soon I shall be coming home," he wrote Cliff Roberts on May 19, "and I really dread—for the first time in my life—the prospect of coming back to my own country."[73]

• • •

Why then was he going? Of all the arguments used to induce him to enter the campaign, three were decisive. First was the matter of duty, and the man who had presented that case in a decisive fashion was his brother Milton. Milton had been opposed to his brother's entering politics and thereby endangering his reputation and his place in history, not to mention the personal sacrifices involved. But when Milton told Dwight that if he did not run, the nation would have to choose between Taft or Truman, and that in the case of such a disaster any sacrifice was justified, Dwight had to agree. Second was the matter of a mandate, and the woman who made it clear to him that he had one was Jacqueline Cochran. "Even though we agree with the old proverb, 'The voice of the people is the voice of God,'" Eisenhower had written Clay, "it is not always easy to determine just what that voice is saying."[74] Cochran's dramatic presentation of the Madison Square Garden rally convinced him that the people wanted him.

But the most decisive argument was the one put forward by Bill Robinson, sitting in the airplane at LaGuardia Airport. "In no circumstance could you ever avoid the burden of worry over the country's future course," Robinson had said, "and there would seem to be fewer frustrations for the leader than there would be for the commentator."[75] The truth was that Eisenhower was not ready to retire or abandon his country to others. At sixty-one years of age, he was in excellent health. Indeed, despite his irritability at being pushed and pulled in every direction, most observers thought that he never looked better. As he had done for the past decade, he was working a twelve- to fourteen-hour day, seven days a week. He was intensely involved, totally active.

And, despite his oft-expressed modesty, he was supremely self-confident, certain that of all the candidates for national leadership, he was the best prepared for the job. Although he never said so, even to himself, he knew that he was smarter, more experienced, and had better principles than his competitors, and thus was the right man to lead America through the world crisis. He wanted what was best for his country, and in the end he decided that he was the best and would have to serve.

CHAPTER TEN

Candidate

On June 1, Eisenhower returned to the States. The following day he paid Truman a courtesy call. They got to talking politics. Already the Taft people were circulating stories about Mamie's alleged drinking habits, about Eisenhower's supposedly being Jewish, about Eisenhower's presumed secret and continuing love affair with Kay Summersby, and other slanderous material. Truman expressed his sympathy, then said, "If that's all it is, Ike, then you can just figure you're lucky."[1] Eisenhower then flew off to Kansas City. There he was met by Governor Dan Thornton of Colorado, a big, outgoing man wearing cowboy boots, a ten-gallon hat, and a huge smile. "Howya, pardner!" Thornton boomed as he gave Eisenhower a powerful slap on the back. A reporter noted, "There was a tense moment as the General's eyes blazed and his back stiffened. Then, with great control, he gradually unfroze into a smile and reached out his hand to say, 'Howya, Dan.' "[2]

Politics, American style. In England, Eisenhower ruefully noted, men "stood" for office, but in America they had to "run." He had feared that he was going to hate the whole process; now he was sure he had been right. Still, he had promised Bill Robinson that "if ever I get into this business, I am going to start swinging from the hips," and he told "Gee" Gerow that "having put my hand to the plow I intend to see the job through to the end of the furrow."[3] He was determined to win, even if it meant ignoring base slurs on his personal life, mindless attacks on his public record, and affronts to his dignity. He was also willing to pander to those whose support he needed, even if it meant tailoring his views to meet their desires.

The Republican Party of 1952, after twenty years without power or responsibility, was frustrated, angry, negative. What it did best was to criticize, charge, accuse. When it went after the New Deal in general, Eisenhower was in perfect agreement, although on such specific issues as Social Security he was more inclined to take a moderate position. But on foreign policy, he had a major problem. Senator McCarthy's assault against George Marshall ("part of a conspiracy so immense, an infamy so black, as to dwarf any in the history of man") was perhaps a bit more extreme than most Republicans would indulge in, but only a bit. But it was from the midwestern and western Republicans, men who had voted against the Marshall Plan and NATO, that Eisenhower would have to find the delegate votes to beat Taft. Therefore his initial national appearances would not be national at all, but rather appeals to the right wing of the GOP. And for the Old Guard, of all the infamies committed by the Democrats in their "twenty years of treason," the greatest were Yalta and the loss of China. To them, Yalta was the focal point of their hatred of FDR, China of their hatred of Truman.

Now, the truth was that Eisenhower had been one of FDR's principal agents in carrying out his foreign policy in Europe during the war, and Truman's Chairman of the JCS when China was "lost." Eisenhower was hardly an unwilling agent. No matter how much he dodged, equivocated, denied, or explained his actions, it was inescapable that he had loyally, indeed enthusiastically, helped implement FDR's policy. His refusal to race the Russians to Berlin and his attempts to get along with Zhukov in the second half of 1945 gave the strongest possible support to the Yalta agreements. His close involvements with the Truman Administration in 1948 and 1949 had given at least implied consent to the China policy. These facts were the major obstacle to his winning the nomination. He knew it, and knew he had to leap over it.

Thus in his early speeches, he reassured the Old Guard. He was an enemy of inflation, he said, and of excessive taxation, of centralization of government, of dishonesty and corruption, etc. Most of all, he deplored the secrecy of Yalta and the loss of China. Although he did condemn "the utter futility of any policy of isolation,"[4] his emphasis on Yalta and China was exactly what the uncommitted delegates wanted to hear; it also set the tone for the campaign that followed.

In New York, he held a week of meetings with East Coast delegations. The most important of these was Pennsylvania, because it was split: 20 for Ike, 18 for Taft, and 32 uncommitted. The meeting was a success; Eisenhower joked and bantered with the politicians, answered their questions in his simple, forthright manner, and gave them a flash of Eisenhower anger. When he was asked whether he was prepared to wage an enthusiastic campaign, he snapped that it was a "funny kind of question to put to a man who has spent forty years of his life fighting."[5]

When the New Hampshire delegation came to Morningside Heights, Eisenhower met Governor Sherman Adams for the first time. Few people actually liked Adams—thin, nervous, crisp to the point of rudeness, Adams had a face that looked as if it had been carved from New Hampshire granite, a demeanor as cold as a New Hampshire winter—but Eisenhower saw in him many of the qualities that Bedell Smith possessed, and sensed that he would have the same kind of loyalty and efficiency. Eisenhower therefore agreed to Lodge's suggestion that Adams be designated the floor manager for the Eisenhower forces at the convention.

After a week in New York, the Eisenhowers took the train to Denver, stopping en route to address forty thousand people in Cadillac Square in Detroit. He had a prepared speech, but announced that he was abandoning it to talk from the heart. Then he asserted that he had had no personal responsibility for the diplomatic blunders at Yalta and Potsdam and that the decision not to go into Berlin was a political one beyond his control. Then he defended that decision, and in effect contradicted himself, when he reminded the audience that "none of these brave men of 1952 have yet offered to go out and pick the ten thousand American mothers whose sons would have made the sacrifice to capture a worthless objective." He concluded by leading the crowd in reciting the Pledge of Allegiance.[6]

In Denver, he set up headquarters in the Brown Palace Hotel, where he received delegations from the Midwest and West. On June 26, he gave a national radio-TV address before a Denver Coliseum crowd of eleven thousand. Eisenhower denounced Yalta, blamed the Democrats for the loss of China, and accused Truman of being too soft on corruption at home and on Communism abroad. "If we had been less trusting," Eisenhower said, "if we had been less soft and weak, there would probably have been no war in Korea!" He repeated his commitment to sound fiscal practices: "A bankrupt America is a defenseless America."[7]

The next morning he embarked on a ten-day trip back and forth across the Great Plains, Taft country. He met privately with politicians, and gave series of public addresses, with the emphasis on the positive things he could accomplish. Taken all together, it was an adroit campaign. It was by no means, however, a complete success. Old Guard delegates enjoyed meeting the general; they were impressed by him and by the response his foreign-policy positions brought forth from their constituents; they were satisfied that the general's domestic views were safe. But their hearts belonged to Taft, and if not their hearts, then their pocketbooks did, because Taft controlled the party machinery and had been nurturing for years the party faithful who made up the delegates. On the eve of the convention, the Associated Press calculated that Taft had 530 delegates, Eisenhower 427.

Many of the delegates still chafed under their party's defeat in 1948, and "Mr. Republican" was determined to use his lead to stop Eisenhower by portraying Eisenhower as a front man for the hated Dewey. Taft now brought to the fight his finely honed skills as a practical politician. He was, after all, the son of William Howard Taft, the man who had kept the 1912 GOP nomination from the most popular of all early-twentieth-century Republicans, Theodore Roosevelt.

Like his father in 1912, Taft had the southern delegations in his pocket. Lodge set out to steal them for Eisenhower. Through a complex parliamentary process, Lodge got the convention to vote on a "Fair Play" amendment that almost no one understood, except for the point that counted—a vote for "Fair Play" was a vote for Ike. By a narrow margin, Lodge got the amendment passed. Critical help came from Senator Richard Nixon, who pulled a successful power play on Governor Earl Warren to get the California delegation behind "Fair Play" (and thus kill Warren's chances to become the compromise candidate).

Everything that followed was anticlimactic. Eisenhower swept to the nomination on the first ballot.

After winning the prize, Eisenhower's first impulse was to be conciliatory. He called Taft on the telephone to ask if he could come across the street to meet with the senator. Taft, surprised, agreed. Eisenhower's advisers, the men who had fought it out in the trenches with the Taft forces and were still bitter (some of them had been spat upon), were all against it. They wanted to relish their triumph and told Eisenhower that a trip to Taft would violate precedent. But Eisenhower was now the nominee, the man in command. His staff could not push him around anymore, and he insisted.

He did so because, although he might be bewildered by the actions of the politicians gathered in convention, an area in which even a lifelong expert like Taft could get lost, Eisenhower knew better than any politician how to exert leadership on a national stage. He was determined to lead a team, and to have a team he had to bring the Taft people back into the mainstream of the Republican Party. Not so much for the vote in November, which he had been told, and believed, was a sure thing. He wanted—he had to have—a team in order to govern, beginning in January 1953. He had to have a united Republican Party to achieve his program. He had not sought the Presidency for personal reasons, and he felt no great sense of personal triumph over Taft. Rather his first thought was to get Taft on the team, for without him there would be no team and nothing could be accomplished.

The meeting itself was matter-of-fact. It took Eisenhower a half hour to work his way through the crowd of cheering supporters. When he finally got to Taft's hotel room (passing in the hall Taft workers who were weeping), he told the senator, "This is no time for conversation on matters of any substance; you're tired and so am I. I just want to say that I want to be your friend and hope you will be mine. I hope we can work together."[8] Taft thanked him; they went into the hall for photographs; Eisenhower returned to the Blackstone Hotel.

That was all. But crossing that Chicago street set Eisenhower on a path that he would follow for the next eight years, a path whose destination was an accommodation with the Old Guard, one based on the Old Guard's acceptance of NATO and all that it implied. Through his Presidency, Eisenhower stuck to the path, often complaining along the way about the hopelessness, ignorance, or perfidy of various Republican right-wing senators. He never really made it to his destination, and the right wing never came out of its room to meet him halfway. But he never stopped trying to educate and appease the Old Guard.

Eisenhower's second step on the path was his selection of a running mate. On this decision, his advisers were completely with him, because they too recognized the obvious factors in the situation that dictated who the running mate would be. The criteria, in order of importance, were: a card-carrying member of the Old Guard who nonetheless was acceptable to the moderates, especially the Dewey people; a prominent leader of the anti-Communist cause; an energetic and vigorous campaigner; a relatively young man, to offset

Eisenhower's age; a man from the West, to offset Eisenhower's association with Dewey and New York; a man who had made a contribution to Eisenhower's winning the nomination. The only name on the list to satisfy all the criteria was, as Eisenhower well knew, Richard Nixon. So it was done. Brownell called Nixon and asked him to come over to the Blackstone to meet Eisenhower.

Eisenhower was coldly formal. He told Nixon he wanted his campaign to be a crusade for all that he believed in and the things he thought America stood for. "Will you join me in such a campaign?" Nixon, somewhat bemused by the pretentious lines, answered, "I would be proud and happy to."

"I'm glad you are going to be on the team, Dick," Eisenhower said. "I think that we can win, and I know that we can do the right things for this country."

Then he smacked his forehead with the palm of his hand. "I just remembered," he said. "I haven't resigned from the Army yet!" He dictated a telegram to the Secretary of the Army, resigning his commission. The scene brought tears to Milton and Arthur Eisenhower's eyes.[9]

Eisenhower's third step along the path of accommodation to the Old Guard was his acceptance of the party platform. This was an extreme right-wing document; by asserting that he could and would campaign on it, Eisenhower reached out for party unity.[10] The platform charged that the Democrats "have shielded traitors to the Nation in high places," and sanctimoniously declared, "There are no Communists in the Republican Party." The GOP, it promised, "will appoint only persons of unquestioned loyalty." The foreign-policy section, drafted by John Foster Dulles, who hoped to be Secretary of State, pledged the GOP to "repudiate all commitments contained in secret understandings such as those of Yalta which aid Communist enslavement." It damned Truman's containment policy (of which NATO was the most important part) as "negative, futile and immoral," because containment "abandons countless human beings to a despotism and godless terrorism." Then, in an open appeal not only to the Old Guard, which had been thundering about Yalta since 1945, but also to the normally Democratic ethnic vote, Dulles' platform said that a Republican Administration would look "happily forward to the genuine independence of those captive people" of Eastern Europe, whom the Democrats had "abandoned . . . to fend for themselves against Communist aggression." (The Old Guardsmen were, indeed, a strange set of isolationists. They doubted the wisdom of giving any help to Western Europe, but claimed to be ready to liberate Eastern Europe and Asia.) The platform did contain, at Eisenhower's insistence, an endorsement of NATO, but to balance that pledge it renounced any intention of sacrificing the Far East to preserve Western Europe.[11]

In his acceptance speech, Eisenhower avoided foreign policy. Instead, he spoke positively. "I know something of the solemn responsibility of leading a crusade," he told the convention. "I accept your summons. I will lead this crusade." He would bring an end to the "wastefulness, the arrogance and corruption in high places, the heavy burdens and the anxieties which are the bitter fruit of a party too long in power." He vowed a "program of progressive policies, drawn from our finest Republican traditions." He asked all the delegates to join his team, then concluded that "since this morning I have had helpful and heartwarming talks with Senator Taft, Governor Warren and Governor Stassen. I want them to know, as I want you now to know, that in the hard fight ahead we will work intimately together." Nixon followed with his acceptance speech, in which he praised Taft to an almost embarrassing degree.[12]

Then Eisenhower was off for a ten-day vacation at Aksel Nielsen's ranch at Fraser, Colorado. At 8,700 feet, on the western slope of the Divide, it was a perfect place to be in late July. Eisenhower fished, cooked steaks and trout, and painted. George Allen and other members of the gang were there; Allen insisted on listening to the Democratic convention on the radio. Eisenhower joined him to listen to the acceptance speech of the nominee, Governor Adlai Stevenson of Illinois. Eisenhower was impressed by Stevenson's speaking ability. Allen snorted, "He's too accomplished an orator; he will be easy to beat."[13] Eisenhower was not so sure. With the nomination behind him, and a specific rival to worry about, the candidate and his advisers could suddenly think of all sorts of things that might go wrong. Dewey's supreme confidence, right up to election night in 1948, was always there to haunt them. The Democratic Party was by far the majority party in the country, it controlled federal patronage, it was accustomed to winning against the heaviest of odds. Taft had withdrawn into a shell; his supporters continued to snarl at Eisenhower; the Republican Party was beset by the twin obstacles of overconfidence and internal division. At Fraser, Eisenhower began preparing for his campaign, working almost as hard as he had in preparing Overlord.

The first problem, as with Overlord, was to pick a staff. Lodge, the obvious man to serve as campaign manager and chief of staff, had his own senatorial campaign to run in Massachusetts. Eisenhower had been much impressed by Sherman Adams' performance at the convention and asked Adams to travel with him through the campaign and serve as his chief of staff. Jim Hagerty, Dewey's press secretary, took on that job for Ike.

With these men, Ike then planned his campaign. What worried him most was the Yalta issue. He wanted to denounce Yalta, but he did not want to hold out hope of American military aid to an uprising in Eastern Europe. He did want to hold out the hope of liberation, but he did not want another tragedy like the premature Warsaw uprising of late 1944.

Despite the obvious dangers and risks of a call for liberation, the rewards were too great to ignore. Liberation was what the Old Guard wanted to hear; it helped disassociate Eisenhower from Yalta and FDR; it would bring thousands of voters of Eastern European backgrounds into the GOP camp for the first time. So, when Eisenhower went to New York on August 24 to speak to the American Legion convention, and to set up a new headquarters in the city, he took the theme with him. He told the Legion that the United States should use its "influence and power to help" the satellite nations throw off the "yoke of Russian tyranny." He said that he would inform the Soviet Union that the United States would "never" recognize the "permanence" of the Soviet occupation of Eastern Europe, and that American "aid" to the "enslaved" peoples would not stop until their countries were free.[14]

But Eisenhower was never comfortable with loose talk about war, much less thinly veiled threats to use the atomic bomb. Earlier, in April, when Dulles had said that the United States should develop the will and the means to "retaliate instantly against open aggression by Red armies, so that if it occurred anywhere, we could and would strike back where it hurts, by means of our own choosing," Eisenhower had protested. What if the Communists moved politically, Eisenhower asked, as in Czechoslovakia, to "chip away exposed portions of the free world? . . . Such an eventuality would be just as bad for us if the area had been captured by force. To my mind, this is the case where the theory of 'retaliation' falls down."[15] Dulles, always anxious to please, replied that Eisenhower had put his finger on a weakness in his theory.

Eisenhower agreed with Dulles' position that it would be immoral to abandon the peoples of Eastern Europe, but he insisted that moral means had to be used for moral purposes, and he was upset at Dulles' continuing belligerent tone. He got Dulles on the telephone and told him that from then on he absolutely had to use the words "all peaceful means" whenever he discussed liberation.[16]

Having given the Old Guard what it wanted on liberation, Eisenhower tried to put some distance between himself and McCarthy. At an impromptu press conference in late August, reporters confronted him with a recent Nixon statement that Eisenhower would support McCarthy and other Old Guard senators as members of the Republican team. Eisenhower said he would support McCarthy "as a . . . Republican," but added forcefully, "I am not going to campaign for or give blanket endorsement to any man who does anything that I believe to be un-American in its methods and procedures." Pressed about McCarthy's charges against Marshall, Eisenhower became angry, got up from his desk, began to pace around the room. "There is nothing of disloyalty in General Marshall's soul," he said, stating what most would have thought to be the obvious with great emphasis. He described Marshall as "a man of real selflessness." In an oblique reference to McCarthy (whom he never mentioned by name), Eisenhower said, "I have no patience with anyone who can find in his [Marshall's] record of service for this country anything to criticize."[17]

Eisenhower's advisers told him not to waste his time campaigning in the South, but he insisted on going, and indeed began his formal campaign with an early September swing through Dixie. He traveled on his special train nicknamed the "Look Ahead, Neighbor," accompanied by Mamie, Adams, more than three dozen political advisers and staff members, and the working press.

It was the last whistle-stop barnstormer campaign. All the hoopla of American politics was there. The train would stop; the local Republicans would have the crowd waiting; Eisenhower would appear on the rear platform, accompanied by Mamie; he would deliver a set speech that concentrated on cleaning up the mess in Washington and asking the audience to join him in his "crusade"; the whistle sounded; they were off again. Between stops, Eisenhower conferred with local Republican candidates, all of whom wanted their pictures taken with the general.

He carried out a brutal schedule. So brutal, indeed, that the Democrats never dared make an issue of his age. At sixty-one, he was a much more vigorous, active, energetic campaigner than Stevenson, who was nine years his junior. He traveled more than his opponent, spoke more, held more press conferences, and never displayed the kind of utter exhaustion that Stevenson sometimes did. In private, he exercised the soldier's right to grouse: "Those fools on the National Committee!" he once growled when told of yet another motorcade. "Are they trying to perform the feat of electing a dead man?" But he always bounced back, ready to go full speed again the next morning, after enjoying what speech writer Emmet John Hughes described as "the physical miracle that is a soldier's night's sleep."[18]

As always, the crowds responded to his presence, the power of his personality, his appearance, his confidence and sincerity. No matter how corny his speech—in truth, the more corny it was—he managed to make the most commonplace utterances sound like inspired insights, the most unsophisticated and timeworn expressions of his patriotism and religious beliefs sound like fresh and profound conviction.

Mamie proved to be a great asset. She was uneasy with crowds, did not much like politicians, gave no speeches, granted no interviews, and found the whole experience exhausting. But she was a trouper and she seized this opportunity to make a positive, public contribution to her husband's career. No matter how weary, she roused herself at every stop, stood by her husband's side, smiled and waved at the appropriate moments. She looked smashing; her bangs became an overnight fad. The most famous picture of the campaign came in Salisbury, North Carolina, when a crowd gathered around the train at 5:30 A.M. and began chanting for Eisenhower. The general and his wife woke, groaned, put on their bathrobes, and groped their way to the rear platform, where they waved back at the crowd. Ike had his arm around Mamie's shoulder; they both had big grins spreading across their faces. The photograph, as Jim Hagerty said, was "dynamite."

Nixon, meanwhile, was campaigning vigorously, concentrating on K_1C_2 ((Korea, Communism, and corruption). He called Stevenson a graduate of Dean Acheson's "Cowardly College of Communist Containment," and poked fun at Stevenson's urbane manner and intellectualism. He also took a holier-than-thou attitude toward the corruption that had plagued the Truman Administration in its last years, where gift giving of such items as home freezers and fur coats to public officials had assumed—according to Nixon—alarming and scandalous proportions. Repeatedly, Nixon assured audiences that the Eisenhower "crusade" would clean the crooks and Communists out of Washington.

On September 18, Nixon was hoisted with his own petard. "SE-CRET NIXON FUND!" screamed the headline in the *New York Post*. "SE-CRET RICH MEN'S TRUST FUND KEEPS NIXON IN STYLE FAR BEYOND HIS SALARY." The *Post* story said that Nixon had accepted contributions in the amount of some $18,000 from California millionaires. Nixon helped blow the story up by his own overreaction; he immediately, and instinctively, labeled the story a smear by the Communist elements that were out to get him.

That would not wash with Ike's gang, however; every member urged Ike to dump Nixon. Most of Eisenhower's professional advisers also urged him to get rid of Nixon. The reporters on the Eisenhower train were forty to two in favor of dropping Nixon, and they told Eisenhower that unless he did so, his crusade was doomed.

Eisenhower, the supposed political novice, realized immediately how much was at stake. His first comment to Adams was "Well, if Nixon has to resign, we can't possibly win." [19] He was one of the few to recognize this central fact.

Eisenhower's response was patient, calculated, clearheaded, and in the end he turned apparent disaster into stunning triumph. In the process, however, he lost whatever chance there was of establishing a warm, close, trusting relationship with Nixon.

Eisenhower scarcely knew Nixon. The two men had met fewer than half a dozen times, only once alone, and all their discussions had been formal affairs, primarily about scheduling speeches and other campaign appearances. They had held no philosophical or political discussions of any substance; they had never played cards together, or shared a meal, or a drink. At thirty-nine years of age, Nixon was young enough to be Eisenhower's son. Eisenhower's reputation rested on a lifetime of accomplishments as manager, organizer, commander; Nixon's reputation, aside from his slashing campaign style, rested on a single investigation, that of Alger Hiss. Except for the delivery of the California vote at the convention, Eisenhower owed Nixon nothing.

Eisenhower's virtues included patience and fair-mindedness. "Make no mistakes in a hurry" was one of his favorite maxims, and it would have been patently unfair to simply dump Nixon without hearing his side, just as it would have been foolish to endorse him without knowing the facts. Eisenhower also wanted to let the uproar die down a bit before taking any action, if only to gauge the public response.

Eisenhower held an informal press conference on his train. "I don't care if you fellows are forty to two [against Nixon]," he declared. "I am taking my time on this. Nothing's decided, contrary to your idea that this is a setup for a whitewash of Nixon." Then he added, "Of what avail is it for us to carry on this crusade against this business of what has been going on in Washington if we, ourselves, aren't clean as a hound's tooth?"[20] The following day, the colorful "hound's tooth" phrase made headlines across the country.

At this point Dewey, always the broker, called Nixon to suggest that Nixon go on national TV to explain the fund. Dewey said that the people around Eisenhower, both on the train and in the New York headquarters, constituted a "hanging jury" and that the proposed appearance was the only way to take the decision out of their hands. "At the conclusion of the program," Dewey advised Nixon, "ask people to wire their verdict in to you." If the replies ran no better than 60–40 in Nixon's favor, he should offer his resignation; if they were 90–10, he could stay on. "If you stay on," Dewey concluded, "it isn't blamed on Ike, and if you get off, it isn't blamed on Ike."[21] Dewey, it is important to note, had not cleared this suggestion with Eisenhower, who had no intention of leaving the decision in Nixon's hands.

That evening, Eisenhower called Nixon. He said he had not decided what to do, then paused waiting for a reply. Nixon let the line hang silent. Finally Eisenhower said, "I don't want to be in the position of condemning an innocent man. I think you ought to go on a nationwide television program and tell them everything there is to tell, everything you can remember since the day you entered public life." Nixon asked if, after the program, an announcement could be made, "one way or the other." Eisenhower quibbled. Nixon, furious, said that there came a time to stop dawdling, that once he had made his speech, the general ought to decide.

"There comes a time in matters like this when you've either got to shit or get off the pot," Nixon said. Catching himself, he added apologetically, "The great trouble here is the indecision."

There was another long silence, as Eisenhower caught his breath and regained his composure. Then he said, "We will have to wait three or four days after the television show to see what the effect of the program is."[22] Eisenhower was, in short, going to let Nixon hang until he—Eisenhower—had had an opportunity to judge the speech itself, and its impact.

The conversation was a crucial moment in their relationship. Nixon's people were already outraged at Eisenhower's people for their obvious anti-Nixon attitude, and for their determination to protect the general's reputation, no matter at what expense to Nixon's career. From the time of the fund incident onward, the relationship between the two camps was always characterized by tension, hostility, mistrust. As for the two principals, Nixon could never forget or forgive Eisenhower for not backing him unhesitatingly during this crisis, while Eisenhower would never forget Nixon's unfortunate phrase—no one, not Churchill, not de Gaulle, not FDR, not Marshall, had ever presumed to talk to Eisenhower like that.

So far as the Eisenhower-Nixon relationship was concerned, there was worse to come. The RNC gathered the money; Nixon went on television. Eisenhower, together with Mamie and a couple of dozen members of his team, watched in Cleveland, where he was about to make an appearance. Nixon's speech itself is one of the great classics of American political folklore, so well known that it need not even be summarized here.

There was, however, one part to the speech that affected Eisenhower directly and personally which has not received the attention that has been given to the dog Checkers or Pat Nixon's cloth coat. It had just been revealed that Stevenson too had a fund, which he had not accounted for and which he used to supplement the salaries of some of his personal appointees in Springfield. Further, Nixon knew that Democratic vice-presidential nominee John Sparkman had his wife on his Senate payroll. After Nixon had laid bare his own (modest) financial position, and demonstrated that he had used the fund for legitimate political expenses, he called on Stevenson and Sparkman to make full revelations of their financial history, because, Nixon said, "a man who's to be President and a man who's to be Vice President must have the confidence of all the people."

Eisenhower had a pad of legal paper in one hand, a pencil in the other. When Nixon called for full financial disclosure from Stevenson and Sparkman, Eisenhower jabbed the pencil into the pad so hard that he broke the pencil point and made a hole in the paper. The blood rushed to his face. Nixon had turned the spotlight on Eisenhower, because if three out of the four candidates made their finances public property, Eisenhower would have to do so too.[23]

Eisenhower had spent a lifetime learning how to control his temper. He realized that Nixon had saved himself with his brilliant presentation, that he was now stuck with Nixon. When Nixon concluded, Eisenhower dictated a message to Nixon, praising him for his "magnificent" performance, but still leaving Nixon hanging: "My personal decision is going to be based on personal conclusions." (At the end of his speech, Nixon had asked viewers to write or wire the RNC as to whether or not he should remain on the ticket, a bold attempt to take the decision out of Eisenhower's hands.) Just in case Nixon still did not get the point as to who was in charge, Eisenhower added, "I would most appreciate it if you can fly to see me at once. Tomorrow I will be at Wheeling, West Virginia." He concluded, "Whatever personal affection and admiration I had for you—and they are very great—are undiminished." Not enhanced, just undiminished. Nixon was distraught. "What more can he possibly want from me?" he angrily asked one of his aides. He said he would not go to Wheeling, that he would not humiliate himself any further. Calmer heads in the camp prevailed, and he agreed to go.[24]

Eisenhower, meanwhile, went out to face the Cleveland audience. It had listened to Nixon over the radio, and it roared with enthusiasm: "We want Dick! We want Dick!" Eisenhower had anticipated that reaction, and when the crowd finally quieted down, he declared, "I like courage. Tonight I saw an example of courage. . . . When I get in a fight, I would rather have a courageous and honest man by my side than a whole boxcar full of pussyfooters." [25]

Inwardly, he continued to seethe. Stevenson and Sparkman both said the following week that they would release their tax returns extending over the past decade. Reporters asked Hagerty whether Eisenhower would also make his financial situation public property. Hagerty said he did not know, but turned to Milton, who was with him. Milton said that of course Eisenhower would follow the example of the others. Twenty years later, Hagerty—who was at Eisenhower's side daily through eight years—recalled that he never, ever saw Eisenhower madder than when he was informed of Milton's remark. Eisenhower "blew his stack." He told Hagerty that he would not do it, ever.

Eventually, of course, he had to yield. In early October, Hagerty released Eisenhower's tax returns, which showed earnings over the past ten years of $888,303, including $635,000 for the one-time sale of the rights to *Crusade,* and taxes of $217,082, including $158,750 in capital gains taxes on the book. No one protested or raised any questions, but Eisenhower nevertheless was furious. He hated having to make his private finances public knowledge. It went against every fiber of his being. And he never forgave Nixon for making him do it.

Still, Eisenhower emerged from the crisis as the man unquestionably in command. He had not panicked when others had; he had resisted the pressure from both wings of the Republican Party to either endorse or dump Nixon; he had kept the final decision in his own hands. If anyone, including Nixon, had any doubts on the point of who was the commander in chief, Eisenhower set them straight in his first words to Nixon when they met at the Wheeling airport. By that time, the evening after the speech, it was obvious that Nixon had received an overwhelmingly positive response from the public. As Nixon was helping his wife put on her now famous coat, Eisenhower rushed up the steps to the plane, hand outstretched.

Astonished, Nixon mumbled, "General, you didn't need to come out to the airport."

"Why not?" Eisenhower grinned. "You're my boy!"[26] As far as Eisenhower was concerned, that "my boy" phrase put their relationship in the proper perspective.

In late September, Eisenhower flew to New York for strategy sessions before embarking on a train trip through the Midwest. After Illinois, he was going to Wisconsin, which meant that the question of what to do about McCarthy had to be faced. Eisenhower said to Emmet Hughes, "Listen, couldn't we make this an occasion for me to pay a personal tribute to Marshall—right in McCarthy's back yard?" Hughes, the self-styled liberal in Eisenhower's headquarters, was enthusiastic. He drafted a paragraph that praised Marshall "as a man and as a soldier . . . dedicated with singular selflessness and the profoundest patriotism to the service of America." Charges of disloyalty against Marshall, the paragraph concluded, constituted "a sobering lesson in the way freedom must *not* defend itself."[27]

Someone at headquarters—it was never discovered who—told the Wisconsin Republicans of Eisenhower's intentions. On October 2, while Eisenhower's train was in Peoria, Illinois, for an overnight stop before heading north to Wisconsin, the Wisconsin governor Walter Kohler, the national committeeman Henry Ringling, and the junior senator Joe McCarthy, flew by private plane to Peoria to confront the general. Eisenhower, staying at the Pere Marquette Hotel, was told that they were in town and wanted to see him. He said he would meet with McCarthy, alone. They met for half an hour. McCarthy asked Eisenhower to make his defense of Marshall in another state.

The following day, as the train headed toward Green Bay, Adams showed Kohler the draft of Eisenhower's Milwaukee speech, his major address in Wisconsin. It was pretty much standard Republican anti-Communist rhetoric, well laid on, but it did contain, almost as a gratuitous afterthought, a paragraph defending Marshall. Kohler told Adams he liked the speech but wanted the Marshall paragraph removed, as it was unnecessarily insulting to McCarthy in his home state. He suggested that Eisenhower could defend Marshall somewhere else.

From Green Bay, the train headed south, stopping first in Appleton, McCarthy's home town. McCarthy made the introduction and stood by the general's side as he delivered a twelve-minute address that contained no reference to McCarthy or his methods. As the train moved toward Milwaukee, the argument over the Marshall paragraph continued. Kohler told Adams that he felt it stood out as an "unnecessarily abrupt rebuff to McCarthy" and said that it would cause serious problems for the Republicans in Wisconsin in the election (Wisconsin had gone Democratic in 1948).

Adams then went to the rear of the train to argue Kohler's case with Eisenhower. "Are you suggesting that the reference to George Marshall be dropped from the speech tonight?" Eisenhower asked. Adams responded, "Yes, not because you're not right, but because you're out of context." The general then said, "Well, drop it. I handled the subject pretty thoroughly in Denver and there's no reason to repeat it tonight."

In their various reminiscences, Eisenhower's staff tried to make it all sound just that simple—the general dropped the paragraph because it was out of place—and they expressed surprise at the uproar that followed, which came about, they claimed, because someone had leaked an advance copy of the speech and thus the excision of the paragraph became known. But Eisenhower's aides had been telling reporters all day, "Just wait till we get to Milwaukee, and you will find out what the general thinks of Marshall." Everybody on the train was talking about the stinging rebuke McCarthy was going to get. Further, Eisenhower did not merely remove the paragraph; in deference to the senator he also weakened some paragraphs denouncing McCarthy's methods.[28]

In Milwaukee, Eisenhower made no reference to Marshall. Instead, he said that the Truman Administration had been infiltrated by Communists. The loss of China and the "surrender of whole nations" in Eastern Europe to the Communists was due, he said, to the Reds in Washington. Their penetration of the government, he added, in his most McCarthy-like statement of the campaign, "meant —in its most ugly triumph—treason itself." Lamely, he added that "freedom must defend itself with courage, with care, with force and with fairness," and he called for "respect for the integrity of fellow citizens who enjoy their right to disagree. The right to question a man's judgment carries with it no automatic right to question his honor." [29] As much as the general may have been convinced that he had thereby established a clear distinction between himself and McCarthy, with McCarthy behind him on the stage they sounded like pretty naive quibbles. When Eisenhower finished, McCarthy reached awkwardly over a few rows of chairs to vigorously shake Eisenhower's hand.

The reaction was immediate and intense. *The New York Times* editorialized, "Yesterday could not have been a happy day for General Eisenhower . . . nor was it a happy day for many supporters." [30] *Times* publisher Arthur Hays Sulzberger privately cabled Adams, "Do I need to tell you that I am sick at heart?" Joseph Alsop later reported that Eisenhower's personal staff on the train were soon referring to the Milwaukee visit as "that terrible day." [31] Herblock published a cartoon in *The Washington Post* (which was supporting Eisenhower) showing the leering ape-man McCarthy standing in a pool of filth and holding a sign reading, "ANYTHING TO WIN." About the only public figure who had no public reaction, either then or later, was Marshall himself.

Perhaps the best thing that can be said about the incident is that Eisenhower, having decided to run for the Presidency, was so determined to win that he was willing to do whatever seemed necessary to do so. That he was ashamed of himself, there can be little doubt. He tried to never refer to the Milwaukee speech. When he came to write his memoirs, ten years later, he wanted to ignore it altogether; when his aides insisted that he could not simply pass it over, he wrote, discarded, wrote again, discarded again, and finally printed a version in which he said that if he had realized what the reaction to the deletion was going to be, "I would never have acceded to the staff's arguments, logical as they sounded at the time." He claimed that the reaction constituted a "distortion of the facts, a distortion that even led some to question my loyalty to General Marshall." [32] That was as close as he ever came to making a public apology to Marshall; whether he made a private apology or not is unknown.

The Nixon fund and the never-delivered Marshall paragraph were the two most famous incidents of the campaign, the ones remembered for decades afterward. Other incidents, recalled with fondness, chagrin, or disgust, depending on the point of view, included McCarthy's "slip of the tongue" when he confused the names "Alger" and "Adlai"; Nixon's rampaging assaults on the Democrats, highlighted by his constant association of Stevenson and Hiss; and

Truman's late but enthusiastic entry into the debate, as the President gave back a bit of what the Republicans were dishing out, including some personal attacks on Eisenhower. Taken all together, 1952 is recalled as one of the bitterest campaigns of the twentieth century, and the one that featured the most mudslinging. Few, if any, of the participants could look back on it with pride.

The high point of Eisenhower's campaign came in Detroit, on October 24, when he announced that, immediately after his election, he would "forego the diversions of politics and concentrate on the job of ending the Korean war. . . . That job requires a personal trip to Korea. I shall make that trip. Only in that way could I learn how best to serve the American people in the cause of peace. I shall go to Korea."[33]

It was an electrifying announcement, coming less than two weeks before the election, and it practically guaranteed the result (one Associated Press reporter heard the speech, packed up his typewriter, and left the campaign trail, declaring that it was all over). Eisenhower had always maintained a comfortable lead in the polls; Stevenson had been moving up a bit in October; with Eisenhower's Korean announcement, he re-established and then added to his lead.

Stevenson wisely kept quiet about Eisenhower's pledge, but Truman denounced it as a gimmick of the worst sort, and said that if Eisenhower really wanted to seek peace he should go to Moscow, not Korea. But it was no gimmick; it was so obviously something that the President-elect should do that Stevenson himself, some weeks earlier, had decided that if he won he would make such a trip. But he and his advisers realized that for the governor of Illinois to make such a pledge would most certainly look like a grandstand play, and they could only hope that the idea of such an announcement would not occur to General Eisenhower. But it had always been in Eisenhower's mind to make such a trip, which he equated with his frequent visits to the front lines during the war. In 1952, as in 1942–1945, he wanted to see for himself. The thought of making his intention public first occurred to Emmet Hughes; C. D. Jackson, an aide, brought a draft of the speech to Eisenhower, read it to him, and got the general's immediate endorsement.

The response was enthusiastic. The nation's number-one hero, her greatest soldier and most experienced statesman, was promising to give his personal attention to the nation's number-one problem. It was reassuring, it was exciting, it was exactly what people wanted to hear. He had not, it is important to note, made any promises about what he would do once in Korea. Those who thought a military victory was still possible could imagine that General Ike would find a way to achieve it; those who wanted an earlier end to the war could believe that Eisenhower was the one man who could deliver it. This ambiguity was not only helpful in the quest for votes; more important to Eisenhower, who was going to win anyway, it kept his options open. The truth was that he did not know what he was going to do about Korea; he wanted to reserve judgment until he had seen for himself; in the meantime, his pledge was a dramatic and effective way to use his prestige and reputation to win votes while retaining flexibility.

After a Boston appearance, Eisenhower and Mamie took the train to New York, where they arrived early on election day, November 4. They voted, then went to Morningside Heights and went to bed. Although the professional pollsters, so badly burned in 1948, were hedging, Eisenhower was confident of success. He was right, of course. The early returns that evening showed a massive switch to the Republicans. Across the country, Eisenhower was getting 55 percent of the vote. His decision to campaign in the South was justified, as he carried Texas, Tennessee, Virginia, Florida, and Oklahoma, and barely missed in Louisiana and South Carolina, thereby beginning the historic process of breaking up the Solid South.

Eisenhower got 33,936,234 votes to Stevenson's 27,314,992, or 55.1 percent to 44.4 percent. Eisenhower received 442 electoral votes to Stevenson's 89 (from West Virginia plus eight Deep South states). Eisenhower ran ahead of the Republican ticket everywhere, and was especially pleased that he got 100,000 more votes in Wisconsin than McCarthy received. He managed to bring a Republican Congress with him, although by the slimmest of majorities (eight in the House; a tie in the Senate, which with Vice-President Nixon's vote meant Republican control).

It was a smashing victory. Millions of middle-aged Republicans who voted for Eisenhower had never before cast their ballot for a presidential winner. After five successive victories the Democrats, if not repudiated, were certainly rebuffed. By far the most important reason was Eisenhower's personal popularity; it was, every analyst agreed, much more his triumph than the Republicans'.

As the returns came in, the Eisenhowers watched on TV in their suite at the Commodore Hotel. The gang, plus Milton and a few other close friends and political associates, joined them. Mamie sat on the floor, tears running down her cheeks. When Stevenson conceded, at 1:30 A.M. the Eisenhowers joined the celebration in the ballroom long enough for the President-elect to make a brief speech, then returned to their suite.

Eisenhower threw himself down on a bed, exhausted. Clare Boothe Luce approached him. "Mr. President," she said, "I know how tired you are. But there is one more thing you *have* to do." She told him what it was. Groaning, he went to the phone and put through a call to the last Republican President, Herbert Hoover.[34] Then he and Mamie decided to return to Morningside Heights. When they got into their car, on Park Avenue, they were momentarily astonished to see that Sergeant Dry had been replaced by two complete strangers. They were Secret Service men.

Now he was President-elect. He was in that position because of his proved competence as a general, as a statesman, and as a leader. People had turned to Eisenhower not so much because of what he stood for, although that counted, as because of who he was and what he had accomplished. He was the hero who could be trusted to lead the nation to peace and prosperity. In ten weeks, he would become the most powerful man in the world. (Just how powerful was exemplified by an event that occurred on the last weekend of the campaign. On November 1, at Eniwetok, the United States exploded its first hydrogen device, 150 times more powerful than the atomic bomb dropped on Japan.) He would be directly responsible for dealing with the world's most pressing problems. Despite his penchant for portraying himself as a political novice, few of these problems would be new ones to him. Indeed, it can be argued that no man elected to the Presidency was ever better prepared for the demands of the job than Eisenhower. The man who had organized and commanded Overlord was confident that he could organize and run the United States as it faced the challenges of the Cold War. For all his reluctance as a candidate, he was eager to assume the duties and responsibilities of his new office.

CHAPTER ELEVEN

Getting Started

No MAN CAN EVER be truly ready to take over the office of the President, but Eisenhower was more ready than most. Ironically, this was in part because he was so keenly aware of the limits on the President's power. Having been a prime maker of policy himself, in war and in peace, he realized that "this idea that all wisdom is in the President, that's baloney. I don't believe this government was set up to be operated by anyone acting alone; no one has a monopoly on the truth and on the facts that affect this country."[1]

A major, critical part of presidential leadership, Eisenhower knew, was selecting the right men for the right jobs and working with them. He wanted competent, proven administrators, men who thought big and acted big. Always impressed by successful businessmen who had made it on their own and knew how to run huge organizations, he sought out the high achievers, men he could turn to for advice and with whom he could share both responsibility and praise.

Personal friendship counted for nothing. In selecting his Cabinet and White House staff, Eisenhower did not pick a single old friend. Some of the most prominent selections were of men he had never met; the others were men he had met only during the course of the campaign.

His first selection was for the premier post of Secretary of State. His choice was John Foster Dulles, and he never seriously considered anyone else. The appointment was, indeed, inevitable. In 1919 Dulles had been a part of the American delegation to the Versailles Peace Conference; he was a senior partner in Sullivan and Cromwell, the law firm that represented many of America's greatest corporations in their international dealings; he had written the Japanese Peace Treaty; he had been the Republican spokesman on foreign policy for the past decade. "Foster has been in training for this job all his life," Eisenhower explained to Sherman Adams.

Eisenhower had first met Dulles at SHAPE, in April 1952. He appreciated Dulles' commitment to NATO, foreign aid, and internationalism. Further, Eisenhower was impressed by Dulles' comprehensive knowledge of world affairs. Eisenhower once told Emmet Hughes, "There's only one man I know who has seen *more* of the world and talked with more people and *knows* more than he does— and that's *me*."[2]

In addition, Eisenhower actually liked Dulles. In this he was virtually unique. Nearly everyone else found Dulles impossibly pompous, a prig, and unbearably dull (according to a popular saying, "Dull, duller, Dulles"). Dulles loved to give sermons, to moralize, to monopolize conversations. But Eisenhower appreciated Dulles' penchant for hard work, his mastery of detail, and his willingness to serve.

Eisenhower wanted Lodge to serve as either Assistant to the President (really, Chief of Staff) or Ambassador to the United Nations. Lodge chose the latter post, which Eisenhower elevated to Cabinet rank with seniority just below that of the Secretary of State. Eisenhower then asked Adams to be the Assistant to the President, also according that position Cabinet rank. He had thought of Brownell for the post, but decided he wanted Brownell—one of the top lawyers in New York and Dewey's closest associate—to be his Attorney General. Dewey, still the governor of New York, told Brownell he did not wish to be considered for any position in the Administration.

Dewey's running mate in 1948, Earl Warren, was also a serving governor, in California. Eisenhower called him on the telephone to say that he had been considering Warren for Attorney General, but had decided instead to appoint Brownell. Warren replied that Brownell would make a splendid choice. Eisenhower then said, "I want you to know that I intend to offer you the first vacancy on the Supreme Court." It was something Eisenhower had discussed with Brownell, who—like Eisenhower—was much impressed by Warren's bearing, character, and knowledge. Eisenhower told Warren, "That is my personal commitment to you."[3]

For Secretary of Defense, the man who would head the department that was the world's biggest employer and purchaser, Eisenhower picked Charles E. Wilson, president of General Motors, the world's largest private corporation. As the reputedly highest-paid executive in American business, Wilson presumably would know how to run the vast Pentagon empire. For Secretary of the Treasury, he selected George M. Humphrey, president of the Mark A. Hanna Company of Cleveland, a far-flung conglomerate. Eisenhower had never met either man, but he accepted them on his advisers' recommendation. He found Wilson to be narrow and simplistic, but he liked Humphrey enormously. Indeed, Humphrey was the only man in the Cabinet—save Dulles—with whom Eisenhower established a warm and close personal relationship. They were almost exactly the same age, had the same horror of deficit financing, and shared a love for hunting and fishing. At their first meeting, Eisenhower grinned at the balding Humphrey, stuck out his hand, and said, "Well, George, I see you part your hair the same way I do."[4]

For Secretary of the Interior, Eisenhower picked the outgoing governor of Oregon, Douglas McKay. Before entering politics, McKay had been a successful automobile dealer. Sinclair Weeks, another conservative businessman, from Massachusetts, became Secretary of Commerce. After one of their first meetings, Eisenhower wrote of Weeks in his diary, "[He] seems to be so completely conservative in his views that at times he seems to be illogical. I hope . . . that he will soon become a little bit more aware of the world as it is today."[5] Eisenhower offered Arthur Summerfield, the chairman of the Republican National Committee (RNC), a choice—he could continue in that post or become Postmaster General. Summerfield chose to become Postmaster General. For the sprawling Department of Agriculture, Eisenhower turned to Milton for advice, based on Milton's many years of service in the department. Milton named Ezra Taft Benson, a member of the Council of Twelve of the Mormon Church, agent for farm cooperatives, and a conservative who had supported Taft for the nomination.

Eisenhower told his advisers he wanted one woman in the Cabinet. They selected Mrs. Oveta Culp Hobby, a Texas newspaper publisher and one of the Texas "Democrats for Eisenhower" who had helped make his nomination possible. Eisenhower had known Hobby during the war, when she was the head of the Women's Army Corps.

He told her he planned to ask Congress for the consolidation of health, welfare, and education responsibilities into a single department, and that when it was done he would name her as its head. Meanwhile, he wanted her to serve as head of the Federal Security Agency, and she accepted.

One of the most difficult appointments was that of Secretary of Labor. The Republicans anticipated trouble with organized labor, which was demanding wholesale changes in, if not outright repeal of, the Taft-Hartley Act. Eisenhower wanted a man from the ranks of labor itself; he picked Martin Durkin of Chicago, head of the AFL plumbers' union. Durkin was the only Democrat in the Cabinet, and the only Catholic.

So the Cabinet was selected. *The New Republic* commented, "Ike has picked a cabinet of eight millionaires and one plumber."[6] What was more remarkable about it was the absence of any experienced administrators in government (but then having been out of power since 1933, the Republican Party had none to offer). But without exception, they were all highly successful businessmen, or lawyers, or plumbers, and nearly all self-made men.

In New York, the Eisenhowers continued to live on Morningside Heights, home of the president of Columbia University. Mamie's life was a hectic one of buying clothes for the inaugural and preparing to move once again. She had the consolation that this time, for the first time in thirty-five years, she could count on living in the same house for four straight years. Barbara and the three grandchildren were visiting at Morningside Heights for the holidays, which made Christmas Eve and Day especially nice. Ike gave Mamie a gold bracelet with three heart bangles inscribed "David," "Barbara Anne," and "Susan." On Christmas Day, however, even as Ike was carving the turkey, Mamie fell ill. Dr. Howard Snyder, who had lived with the Eisenhowers for years and was their personal physician, gave her sulfa and confined her to bed. There she stayed for the next few days, meanwhile trying to arrange for the shipment of furniture from New York to Washington. A major problem was remembering which items belonged to her, which to Columbia.

In early January, Mamie learned that John was coming home for the inaugural ceremonies. She asked her husband who had ordered John to leave Korea; he asked Omar Bradley, the Army Chief of Staff; Bradley did not know. John's arrival did for Mamie what the sulfa had not accomplished; her health improved and she was out of bed. After their reunion, John went up to Highland Falls for a few days with his family, then brought his wife and children back to Morningside Heights. During the ten days before the inaugural, Mamie and Barbara shopped, while John attended meetings with his father.

Eisenhower was leading a hectic life, but he was accustomed to it. He had long since learned what it was like to live a life in which virtually all of his time was scheduled, with meetings, interviews, appearances, speeches, working lunches, and trips. Nevertheless, he tried to live by regular habits and insofar as possible did so.

His day began early, around 6 A.M. He got up quietly, so as not to wake Mamie, went to his dressing room, and selected a suit from those Moaney had laid out. Most of his extensive, custom-made wardrobe was given to him by New York clothes manufacturers; he seldom wore a suit more than twice. Over a light breakfast he would read the morning papers. Although it was one of his little conceits to claim that he never read the papers, in fact he pored over them. An extremely fast reader, he could get the essential stories quickly. He usually read the Washington papers, *The New York Times,* and the *Herald Tribune* (by far his favorite).

Eisenhower was in his office by 8 A.M. and worked without a break until 1 P.M. Most of his lunches were working affairs. He would then work at his desk until 6 P.M., sometimes later. There was a wide variety to the type and scope of the problems that came to him for decision. He tried to hear all sides before deciding, to expose himself to every point of view, which required a great deal of reading, listening intently to oral presentations, and asking penetrating questions. It was hard work, in other words, that required him to use his mind constantly and intensively.

After a day in the office, he would relax with a cocktail. He was strict with himself about the use of alcohol; his usual limit was a single highball before dinner. Food, unless he had done the cooking, was of little interest to him. To Mamie's continuing distress, he bolted down whatever was put in front of him. In 1952 he started another practice that Mamie had to resign herself to—eating off a TV tray while watching the evening news. After dinner, if he had no speaking or other engagements, he would study papers, reports, proposals, until about 11 P.M., when he enjoyed an hour of painting before going to bed. His bedside reading still consisted of Wild West stories. In them, there were no complications, no complexities. Decisions were clear-cut, because they were based on easily answered questions of right and wrong. To read such stories, Eisenhower had to suspend all his critical faculties and enter into a fantasy world. By doing so, he could clear his mind for its necessary rest. The stories were, for Eisenhower, the most effective sleeping pills available.

More complete relaxation came from his hobbies—fishing, painting, golf, and bridge. They all allowed him complete escape, because they required complete concentration. Whether trying to decide which fly to use, or which color to put on a painting, or what iron to select for his next shot, or how to bid an unusual hand, he was momentarily free of the burdens of his duties and responsibilities. Ellis Slater, who played a great deal of both golf and bridge with Eisenhower, noted that "I don't believe I've ever known a person with such concentration. When doing anything . . . he has an ability to completely lose himself."[7]

He had always lived in a world of men. The only genuine relationships he had ever formed with women revolved around role images that he felt comfortable with, specifically those of mother, wife, and secretary. No one can look at a photograph of the general with his mother, or of the general and his wife, and doubt that he had a perfect love for Ida and Mamie. But his relationships with them were limited. He never discussed his professional life with either of them, or otherwise shared his concerns.

His relationship with Mamie was happy, uncomplicated, and old-fashioned. Except during World War II, they had always slept together, and planned to do so in the White House. In 1946, at Fort Myer, Mamie had ordered a huge double bed specially built. In 1948 it had been shipped from Washington to New York City. Mamie was going to install it in the White House, saying that she liked to reach over in the middle of the night "and pat Ike on his old bald head anytime I want to."[8]

That bed was her command post. She enjoyed staying in it until noon at least, sometimes all day. From it, she answered her correspondence, ran her household staff, and received visitors. Eisenhower enjoyed pampering her, which added to a general impression that she was lazy, spoiled, and more or less empty-headed. In fact, like her husband, she was hardworking. She was also devoted to him. Although she never engaged in Eisenhower's business, she nevertheless provided him with crucial support, in public as well as in private. When her husband became a world figure, she overcame her natural shyness and became a major asset in his career. She entertained his rich and powerful friends and their wives; she presided over numerous large and formal social affairs; she carefully answered every letter written to her; she made certain that every member of the small army of aides, advisers, and secretaries that existed to do Eisenhower's bidding was remembered with gifts at birthdays and Christmas. She appeared cheerfully, well groomed and beautifully dressed, at the general's side on public occasions. She did, in short, all that Eisenhower wanted a wife to do, and more. If her share in his life was limited, it was nonetheless satisfying, rewarding, and giving.

There was one woman with whom he did share his professional life. She occupied a specific, well-defined role, that of secretary. Her name was Ann Whitman. Ann had joined Eisenhower's team "for a few days" just before the 1952 campaign began; she stayed with him for more than eight years. She was competent at her job, highly intelligent, comfortable to be around. She knew his professional concerns intimately. He could, and often did, comment to her in detail on matters of world importance. He knew she would understand the most cryptic remark; even better, he knew she would be completely on his side, because her devotion to him was unquestioning. He drove her like a slave, dawn to dusk. He made impossible demands on her —have this paper out by so-and-so, he would say—and she met those demands. Ann gave him an outlet for that big gutsy laugh, or for that terrible temper. With her, he could be as angry or as contemptuous toward another man as he wished, without having to fear that the story of his outburst would be all over town the next day.

On November 29, 1952, Eisenhower flew to Korea. He took with him Bradley, Wilson, and Brownell. En route, they were joined at Iwo Jima by Admiral Arthur Radford, Commander in Chief, Pacific. Radford so impressed Eisenhower during the next few days that Eisenhower decided to name him as Bradley's replacement when Bradley's tour as chairman of the JCS ended in August 1953. The decision on Radford was one of the few positive results of the trip.

Indeed, what was most noteworthy about the Korean inspection was what Eisenhower did *not* do. South Korean President Dr. Syngman Rhee was anxious to convince Eisenhower that a renewed invasion of North Korea could work, that it would unify the country, turn back the Communists, and contribute to stability in Asia. But Eisenhower practically ignored Rhee; he met with him only twice, for a total of one hour, and gave Rhee no opportunity to present his plans for an all-out offensive.

Mark Clark, Commander in Chief of the U.N. forces in Korea, also had worked out plans for an offensive designed to drive the Chinese back across the Yalu River and unify Korea. To Clark's admitted surprise and probable astonishment, Eisenhower never gave him an opportunity to present his plan. Instead, for three days, Eisenhower did what he had done so often during World War II; he visited front-line units and talked with the senior commanders and their men. Despite the bitter cold and snow-covered ground, Eisenhower bundled up in a heavy pile jacket, fur-lined hat, and thermo boots to see for himself. He flew a reconnaissance mission over the front. He studied an artillery duel with his binoculars, chatted with the troops, ate outdoor meals from a mess kit, and came to the conclusion that the situation was intolerable.

That was the real result of the trip. Not that Eisenhower had not already made up his mind that the Korean War had to be ended, as quickly as possible on the best terms he could get, but that this instinctive judgment was reinforced by his study of the terrain. He regarded Rhee's and Clark's plans for an all-out assault as bordering on madness. "In view of the strength of the positions the enemy had developed," he wrote, "it was obvious that any frontal attack would present great difficulties."

With the offensive option eliminated, the remaining choices were to negotiate seriously (armistice talks had been under way for nearly two years, but no agreements had been reached because of the POW issue) or to continue the military stalemate, neither accepting a negotiated peace nor seeking victory. The trouble with a negotiated peace was that, aside from having to agree to a forcible repatriation of the Chinese POWs, it would abandon North Korea to Communism, and this by an Administration that had pledged itself to seek liberation for Communist satellites. The trouble with accepting continued stalemate, however, was even worse; as Eisenhower later wrote, "My conclusion as I left Korea was that we could not stand forever on a static front and continue to accept casualties without any visible results. Small attacks on small hills would not end this war." [9]

On January 18 Eisenhower, his wife, son, daughter-in-law, grandchildren, and aides traveled by train to Washington, where the party settled into the Statler Hotel. There his brothers and closest friends met him for a joyous reunion with the family and gang.

On Inauguration Day, January 20, 1953, the Eisenhower family, accompanied by 36 relatives and some 140 members of the incoming

Administration, attended services at the National Presbyterian Church. When they returned to the Statler, Eisenhower said to Mamie, "You always have a kind of special sense of propriety in such matters. Do you think it would be appropriate for me to include a prayer in my Inauguration Address?" Mamie was enthusiastic about the idea, whereupon Eisenhower took ten minutes to write a prayer.[10]

Then it was time to drive to the White House to pick up Harry and Bess Truman. Since the brief meeting in November, Eisenhower had sent only one communication to the President, a telegram of January 15. Eisenhower said in it that he had read in the papers that Truman intended to take the train to Independence, Missouri, immediately after the swearing-in ceremony, and "it occurs to me that it may be much more convenient for you and your family to make the trip in the *Independence* rather than in the Pullman." If Truman wanted the airplane, Eisenhower said he would "be more than glad to express my desire to the Air Force that they make the plane available to you."[11] Truman did not reply (and on January 20, after the ceremonies, he and Bess took the train home).

When the Eisenhower car arrived at the portico of the White House, the President-elect showed his animosity toward the President by refusing an invitation to come inside for a cup of coffee; instead, Eisenhower waited in the car for Truman to appear. They rode together to the Capitol in a frosty atmosphere. According to Truman, Eisenhower broke the silence by remarking, "I did not attend your Inauguration in 1948 out of consideration for you, because if I had been present I would have drawn attention away from you." Truman snapped back, "Ike I didn't ask you to come—or you'd been here." Eisenhower denied that any such exchange took place. He did recall asking Truman who had ordered John back from Korea for the Inauguration. According to Eisenhower, Truman simply replied, "I did." According to Truman, what he said was, "The President of the United States ordered your son to attend your Inauguration. The President thought it was right and proper for your son to witness the swearing-in of his father to the Presidency."[12]

Three days after the ride to the Capitol, Eisenhower sent Truman a letter "to express my appreciation for the very many courtesies you extended to me and mine during the final stages of your Administration . . . I especially want to thank you for your thoughtfulness in ordering my son home from Korea . . . and even more especially for not allowing either him or me to know that you had done so."[13] That was his last communication with Truman, just as January 20 was the last time they were together, except for George Marshall's funeral, until after Eisenhower himself had left the Presidency.

Eisenhower and Truman walked through the Rotunda to the east front of the Capitol, where a platform had been erected for the ceremonies. The crowd was huge—the largest for an inaugural in American history—and festive. The Republicans were there to celebrate with unabashed joy; as movie actor and future Republican senator George Murphy put it, "It is all just so wonderful, it's like walking into bright sunshine after being in darkness for a long time." [14] And indeed, the sun had broken through the clouds—Eisenhower luck, everyone agreed—to turn it into a pleasant, if chilly, day. Eisenhower wore a dark-blue double-breasted overcoat and had a white scarf around his neck. At 12:32 P.M., Chief Justice Fred Vinson administered the oath of office.

As Eisenhower turned to deliver his Inaugural Address, his grim, determined expression gave way to that famous grin, and he shot his hands over his head in the old V-for-Victory sign. After the cheering stopped, he read the prayer he had composed that morning, asking Almighty God to "make full and complete our dedication to the service of the people in this throng, and their fellow citizens everywhere." Not forgetting the Democrats, he added, "May cooperation be permitted and be the mutual aim of those who, under the concepts of our Constitution, hold to differing political faiths; so that all may work for the good of our beloved country and Thy glory. Amen."

Then he began his Inaugural Address. "The world and we have passed the midway point of a century of challenge," he said. The challenges that had to be faced now, he insisted, were those of the dangers of war and aggressive Communism. In a speech devoted exclusively to foreign policy, he promised that his Administration would "neither compromise, nor tire, nor ever cease" to seek an honorable worldwide peace. But people had to realize that "forces of good and evil are massed and armed and opposed as rarely before in history." The urgency of seeking peace in such a climate of hostility was all the greater because "science seems ready to confer upon us, as its final gift, the power to erase human life from this planet." [15]

Taken all together, the speech was hardly what the Old Guard wanted to hear from the first Republican elected to the Presidency since 1928. There was no denunciation of the New Deal, nor of Yalta, no promise to cut taxes or balance the budget. Instead, Eisenhower had summoned the American people to yet another crusade; in so doing, he sounded far more like Truman announcing the containment policy than he did like Taft or indeed any other Republican. Senator Lyndon B. Johnson, the new Democratic minority leader, called it "a very good statement of Democratic programs of the last twenty years." [16]

But for the moment, it hardly mattered. Taft praised the speech, and the Republicans prepared to celebrate. The parade took forever; "Not until nearly seven o'clock," Ike complained, "did the last two elephants go by." [17] Then he and Mamie drove to the White House, and as she took his arm, they walked together into their new home.

That evening, the Eisenhowers attended two inaugural balls (the crowds were so large that one hall could not hold them all). Finally at 1 A.M.—accompanied by John, Barbara, and the grandchildren—the Eisenhowers drove home and went to bed.

The next day, Eisenhower got started on his job. At the end of the day, he took a minute to make an entry in his diary. "My first day at the president's desk," he wrote. "Plenty of worries and difficult problems. But such has been my portion for a long time—the result is that this just seems (today) like a continuation of all I've been doing since July 1941—even before that." [18]

The contrast between Eisenhower's confident attitude and that of his predecessor after *his* first day on the job could not have been greater. On April 13, 1945, Harry Truman had told reporters, "Boys, if you ever pray, pray for me now. . . . When they told me yesterday what had happened, I felt like the moon, the stars, and all the planets had fallen on me." [19]

Eisenhower's preparation for the Presidency was, obviously, much better than Truman's had been. Roosevelt's death had thrown Truman into a whole new world, one completely strange to him. But Eisenhower was simply continuing a life that he had long since grown accustomed to leading. He had not had a private life since June 1942, when he arrived in London. He had had aides at his elbows and advisers behind him for ten years. He was used to being surrounded by reporters whenever he was in a public place, to having his photograph taken, to having his every word quoted. Most important of all, Eisenhower was accustomed to being held in awe, to being the center of attention, to having the power to make the decisions.

Eisenhower had resigned himself to the loss of many ordinary human pleasures, but also learned to accept the privileges that went with his station. Except for an occasional private banquet, he had not eaten in a restaurant in ten years. His schedule seldom allowed him sustained leisure for the serious reading of history he so loved to do. He had learned to take infrequent and short vacations, to expect them to be interrupted, and to take along plenty of work. To leave his mind and his time free, he had others to do the most basic of human chores for him. He did not dress himself—John Moaney, his valet, put on his underwear, socks, shoes, pants, shirt, jacket, and tie. Eisenhower did not drive a car, never had to worry about a parking place. He did not even know how to use a dial telephone. He had never been in a laundromat or a supermarket. He did not keep his own checkbook or manage his own finances. He handled money only when it was time to settle up on the golf course or at the bridge table, where he hated to lose and hated even more having to pay up. His travel arrangements were always made for him.

Eisenhower was also ready for the physical demands of the Presidency. Three weeks before the election of 1952, he had celebrated his sixty-second birthday. Despite his age, Eisenhower was in good health. At 175 pounds, he weighed only a few pounds more than he had when he played football at West Point. He ate and drank in moderation, and in 1949 he had quit tobacco cold turkey. He exercised regularly, either on the golf course or in a swimming pool. His face was usually sun-tanned, his complexion ruddy. His erect military bearing provided convincing evidence of his good muscle tone and strong constitution. Although he was of medium height (five feet ten inches) he somehow seemed taller. Wherever he went, he stood out, not only because of his reputation, but also because of his animation. His immense storehouse of energy and warmth was sensed, felt, communicated to everyone around him. His associates drew on that apparently inexhaustible source of energy; his political opponents were confounded by it.

Among most men, Eisenhower inspired confidence. Those who knew him well, and millions who did not, looked to him instinctively for guidance and leadership. But Harry Truman had his doubts about Eisenhower's trustworthiness, and was certain that Eisenhower would not be able to provide the country with competent leadership. As prepared as Eisenhower was for the life-style the Presidency would force on him, he was not, in Truman's view, at all prepared for the real work facing him in the task ahead. Reflecting on the problems the general-become-President would face, in late 1952 Truman mused, "He'll sit here, and he'll say, 'Do this! Do that!' *And nothing will happen.* Poor Ike—it won't be a bit like the Army. He'll find it very frustrating." [20]

Whether it would be the ho-hum Ike who could handle the problems of running the country with the back of his hand, or the frustrated Ike who would learn that he commanded nothing, was now to be discovered.

CHAPTER TWELVE

The Chance for Peace

AFTER EISENHOWER had been in office for slightly more than a month, Robert Donovan of the *Herald Tribune* asked him at a news conference, "How do you like your new job?" Eisenhower replied that he had never said nor thought that "I would like it. It is not a job that I suppose it is intended one should like."[1]

Eisenhower was being a bit coy. Despite his almost blasé remark in his diary at the end of his first day in the Oval Office, he was finding the job to be fascinating, absorbing, challenging, and fulfilling. He once—only once—admitted that he found the clash of wits with German generals during the war to be "exhilarating." In a different way, so was the Presidency.

The range of problems was much greater; so were the possibilities of using his talents to bring about compromise and to find a *modus vivendi* among warring factions. Most of all, even for the former Supreme Commander, it was a heady experience to feel that he was "at the center of the world." The "excitement" of working daily on a wide variety of difficult problems of the greatest importance, he confessed, was "exhilarating."[2]

One of Eisenhower's major goals was the creation of a United States of Europe. During his year and a half as SACEUR, 1951–1952, he had pushed that concept hard, in public and in private. In his State of the Union message, he called for a "more closely integrated economic and political system in Europe." He sent Dulles and Stassen on a tour of the European NATO capitals, with instructions to pressure the Europeans toward a ratification of the European Defense Community (EDC), which was designed to create an all-European army. Eisenhower's idea was that no political unity could be achieved in Europe without a spur, and that EDC was the best possible spur. A treaty had been signed creating EDC; the French were holding up ratification; Eisenhower wanted to force action.

The Europeans told Dulles that they could not afford to spend any more on defense, and that their idea was that the United States ought to increase its nuclear arsenal in Europe (which currently stood at sixteen bombs of twenty kilotons each). Eisenhower reminded the Europeans that "if, on the other side of the Iron Curtain, a backward civilization with a second-rate production plant can develop the power to frighten us all out of our wits, then we, with our potential power can, through work, intelligence and courage, build any countering force that may be necessary." [3]

Thus patterns were early established. Eisenhower was determined to force the Europeans to spend more on defense, and to achieve political and military unity. Dulles, highly visible and quotable, flew around the world, apparently acting on his own but in fact operating under instructions from Eisenhower. So tightly did Eisenhower control Dulles that Dulles, each evening that he was on a trip, sent a cable reporting on what had transpired that day and what he intended to say the following day. Dulles carried messages; he did not make policy. And, frequently, Dulles had to be saved from his own mistakes, which Eisenhower was more than willing to do, even at his own expense.

NATO was a matter of great concern to Eisenhower, but the war in Korea was of more immediate importance. On February 11, Eisenhower met with the NSC to consider the situation and the options. Bradley gave a briefing in which he discussed recent reports, and a request, from General Clark. The reports concerned a Chinese buildup in the Kaesong sanctuary, a twenty-eight-square-mile area created through the armistice negotiations and which "was now chock-full of troops and material." Clark believed the Chinese were preparing an offensive; he asked permission to attack Kaesong "as soon as he believes that the Communist attack is imminent." Dulles agreed with Clark; he said the time had come to end the arrangements for immunity at Kaesong, which had been designed to facilitate armistice negotiations that were now defunct. Eisenhower asked about the possibilities of using atomic weapons on Kaesong, as "it provides a good target for this type of weapon." He did not like that option, but "we can not go on the way we are indefinitely."

Bradley thought it unwise to consider using atomic weapons. Dulles mentioned the moral problem "and the inhibitions on the use of the A-bomb, and Soviet success to date in setting atomic weapons apart from all other weapons as being in a special category." He said in his opinion "we should try to break down this false distinction." Eisenhower knew that the U.N., and especially Britain and France, would object strongly to using atomic weapons; in that case, he added, "we might well ask them to supply the three or more divisions needed to drive the Communists back."

But, on reflection, he concluded that there should be no discussion "with our allies of military plans or weapons of attack." As to Clark's request to attack Kaesong, Eisenhower said he "doubted the validity" of any advance information Clark might obtain on Chinese intentions. He said that although "I have never been able to understand why the U.N. command had ever abandoned its right of hot pursuit of enemy aircraft to the bases" in Manchuria, he nevertheless would not give Clark the authority to attack Kaesong. He also told Dulles not to broach the subject of ending Kaesong's immunity with the NATO allies.[4]

Instead, Eisenhower wanted to increase the psychological pressure on the Chinese. He intended to let them know, "discreetly," that unless the armistice negotiations resumed and satisfactory progress was made, the United States would "move decisively without inhibition in our use of weapons . . . We would not be limited by any worldwide gentleman's agreement."[5] Unleashing Chiang was a part of the pressure; so was Eisenhower's announcement that he was increasing military assistance to the Army of the Republic of Korea (ROK); so were his frequent statements that the situation in Korea was "intolerable."

But the greatest pressure, by far, was his own reputation. The Chinese were fully aware that in the war against Germany, Eisenhower had used every weapon at his disposal. They knew that he had atomic weapons available in the Far East, that he would not accept a stalemate, and that he was not demanding their unconditional surrender, but only that they agree to an armistice. The substance behind Eisenhower's threat was Eisenhower's reputation, backed by America's atomic arsenal.

• •

On Tuesday, February 17, Eisenhower held his first presidential news conference. He had already announced that he intended to meet with the press on a regular basis, weekly if possible, and that he was considering allowing TV cameras into the Executive Office Building for the conferences. Eight years later, he had met with the press on 193 occasions, and starting in 1955 with the cameras present. He thus subjected himself to the questions of the press far more often than any other President in American history. He did so despite the jeers of his critics, who had great fun with his jumbled syntax, his confessions that he "did not know" about this or that issue, and his often inappropriate or impossibly confusing answers.

Eisenhower was proud of his command of the English language, as he had a right to be. But showing that he could get his verbs and nouns to agree, that he knew better than to end a sentence with a preposition, or that he could turn a phrase, was not part of his purpose in the news conferences. Rather, he used the reporters, and later the TV cameras, to reach out to the nation. One of his basic principles of leadership was that a man cannot lead without communicating with the people. Through the conferences, he could educate and inform, or confuse if that suited his purpose. The conferences helped him stay in control; through his answers, he could command the headlines and the national discussion of issues. The Tuesday-morning meetings allowed him to set the national agenda for that week. By downplaying an issue, he could get it off the front pages; by highlighting an issue, he could make it the prime item of national interest. He could, in short, decide when there was a crisis, and when there was not. He could also obfuscate an issue when he was not yet sure how he would deal with it.

As he had done during the war, and in the period 1945–1952, he cultivated the press corps, especially the senior members. Reporters who covered his vacations would find themselves invited to a feast of fresh-caught trout, cooked by the man who had caught them, the President himself. Sometimes he played golf with reporters. And although he could not, and did not, expect the kind of loyal cooperation he had gotten from the press during the war, when he considered the reporters to be quasi members of his staff, he never allowed his relationship with them to degenerate into one of antagonism. In his opening remarks at his first news conference, he praised the American press corps, saying that in the eleven years he had been a world figure, "I have found nothing but a desire to dig at the truth . . . and be openhanded and forthright about it." And he was aware of, and thanked the reporters for, the sympathetic treatment he had received: "I feel that no individual has been treated more fairly and squarely over the past many years . . . than I have by the press."

There was an obvious major difference between being Supreme Commander and being President. In the first instance, Eisenhower was executing policies made by Roosevelt, and in his press conferences he could concentrate on how he was carrying out his responsibilities. Reporters did not ask him about, much less criticize, his plans and intentions. As President, he was making policy, which meant that his conferences concentrated on what he was going to do, and why. Further, all reporters were on his side as a general, but as President he faced a press corps of which at least half the working members were Democrats. Despite the differences, it was as true of President Eisenhower as it was of General Eisenhower that he established and maintained an excellent rapport with the press.

In this first presidential news conference, Andrew Tully of Scripps-Howard Newspapers wanted to know if he had "discovered any other secret agreements besides the one signed at Yalta?" No, Eisenhower responded, he had not. What about the repudiation of Yalta? Eisenhower had promised to send an appropriate resolution to Congress on that subject; he now explained, "I am merely talking about those parts of agreements that appeared to help the enslavement of peoples, or, you might say, have been twisted by implication to mean that." In so saying, he made a major concession to the Democrats. The Republican position was that Roosevelt had handed over Eastern Europe to Stalin; the Democrats maintained that Roosevelt had entered into the best possible agreement, one which should have guaranteed freedom to the Poles, but that Stalin had violated his pledged word.

May Craig of the Portland *Press Herald* then asked if he was aware that "many members of Congress feel that the agreements were never binding, anyway, because they were not presented to the Senate" for ratification. Of course he was aware, but he confused the issue; "Well, I think there are, in our practice, certain things that are of course binding when the people are acting as proper representatives of the United States—say, in war, as in establishing staffs and that sort of thing. That extends out into some fields that are almost politico-military in nature."

Unsatisfied, Craig pressed on. "Are you aware that many members of Congress also feel that the President had no right to take us into Korea without consulting Congress, also that he had no right to send troops to Europe?" Eisenhower cut her off: "That all took place long before I came to this office. I have a hard time trying to determine my own path and solve my own problems. I am not going back and try to solve those that someone else had." (Two weeks later, Craig pressed again; Eisenhower then told her, sharply, "I have no interest in going back and raking up the ashes of the dead past.")

Eisenhower also used his news conferences to send messages to Congress. When a reporter wanted to know if he intended to sponsor a bill to retain the excess-profits tax, which was due to expire on June 30, he replied, "I would say this—I can't answer that in exact terms —I shall never agree to the elimination of any tax where reduction in revenue goes along with it."[6] Then, giving the reporters a wave and a big grin, he left the room, leaving them to figure out what he had said and what he meant, but with the distinct impression that everything was under control.

Like most Presidents, Eisenhower had difficulty distinguishing between attacks on his policies and attacks on himself. When Ken Crawford of *Newsweek* wrote a critical piece, Eisenhower told an aide, "I don't understand how he could write a piece like that because I've always regarded him as a friend of mine." The aide replied, "Well, he admires you and he is a friend of yours. His trouble is that he hates Republicans." Eisenhower rubbed his chin, grinned, and replied, "He may have something there."[7]

Indeed, in his first months in office, Eisenhower had far greater difficulty with his own party than with the Democrats. On February 7, Eisenhower had noted in his diary, "Republican senators are having a hard time getting through their heads that they now belong to a team that includes rather than opposes the White House."[8] He had in mind the Old Guard, and most especially Senator McCarthy.

A fight between Eisenhower and McCarthy was inevitable. The senator was not about to give over to the Administration the issue that had catapulted him to international prominence, Communism in government. And he was hardly alone. With control of the congressional committees in hand, the Republicans were determined to use their investigative powers to expose the undesirables who, in their view, had taken over the federal bureaucracy. By the time Eisenhower made his diary entry, congressional committees had already launched eleven different investigations of just the State Department. Nearly every Republican wanted to participate; of the 221 Republican representatives, 185 had requested assignment to the House Un-

American Activities Committee (HUAC). But, as had been true since February 1950, McCarthy stood pre-eminent in the anti-Communist crusade.

During the 1952 campaign, aides on Eisenhower's staff had urged him to denounce McCarthy. He refused to do so because, he said, he could not repudiate a fellow Republican. Now, as President, he needed the support of the Republican senators, and according to popular belief (shared by Eisenhower), McCarthy controlled seven or eight votes in the Senate.

McCarthy's opportunity to make trouble came when Eisenhower sent to the Senate his appointees for State Department and foreign posts. With a Republican majority, Eisenhower expected a *pro forma* confirmation. He was therefore astonished and furious when he learned that McCarthy was holding up his first nominee's confirmation. That nominee was Walter B. Smith, for Under Secretary of State. He was a man whom Eisenhower trusted and admired without stint. Smith had conservative views, to say the least—he once told Eisenhower that he thought Nelson Rockefeller was a Communist— and he had served the Truman Administration as head of the CIA, as well as ambassador to Russia. Eisenhower could not conceive of any possible objection to Smith, but his morning *Times* informed him that McCarthy was taking "an interest" in the case, because Smith had defended John Paton Davies, who was on Smith's staff in Moscow. Smith had characterized Davies as "a very loyal and capable officer." Insofar as Davies was one of McCarthy's favorite targets, high up on the senator's famous list of known Communists in the State Department and a prime example of bumbling State Department China hands, Smith's praise for Davies made Smith, in McCarthy's view, a possible fellow traveler.

To make Smith into a suspect was, in Eisenhower's view, preposterous, degrading, embarrassing. It gave Eisenhower an intimate sense of the true meaning of McCarthyism. Eisenhower came to loathe McCarthy, almost as much as he hated Hitler. He was determined to destroy McCarthy, as he had destroyed Hitler, but his campaign against the first was much different from his campaign against the second. The direct assault against Hitler was replaced by an indirect assault against McCarthy, one so indirect as to be scarcely discernible, and one which contributed only indirectly—at best—to McCarthy's downfall. Eisenhower went after Hitler with everything he had; with McCarthy, he kept all his ammunition in reserve. During the war, he had insisted on keeping Hitler at the center of everyone's attention; in his first years as President, he did his best to get people to ignore Joe McCarthy.

Why the difference? Beyond such obvious factors as nationality and party affiliation, Eisenhower cited two basic reasons for his non-approach to McCarthy. The first was personal. "I just won't get into a pissing contest with that skunk,"[9] he said to his friends, many of whom—including Milton—were encouraging him to do just that. But Eisenhower never adversely mentioned McCarthy by name. Not once. He explained his position to Bill Robinson: "No one has been more insistent and vociferous in urging me to challenge McCarthy than have the people who built him up, namely, writers, editors, and publishers." He thought they should have a touch of guilty con-science, protested that McCarthyism existed "a long time before I came to Washington," and complained that as McCarthy grew in headline value, "the headline writers screamed ever more loudly for me to enter the list against him. As you and I well know—and have often agreed—such an attempt would have made the Presidency ri-diculous."[10]

Aside from the dignity of the Presidency, Eisenhower refused to speak against McCarthy because he convinced himself that ignoring McCarthy was the way to defeat McCarthy. He explained his reason-ing in his diary: "Senator McCarthy is, of course, so anxious for the headlines that he is prepared to go to any extremes in order to secure some mention of his name in the public press." Eisenhower, with Smith in mind, knew what he was talking about. Thus his conclusion: "I really believe that nothing will be so effective in combating his particular kind of troublemaking as to ignore him. This he cannot stand."[11]

Eisenhower's second reason for attempting to ignore McCarthy, and indeed to appease him whenever possible, was his need for McCarthy's support in the Senate. Some of his advisers strongly dis-agreed. C. D. Jackson argued that to cooperate with McCarthy would only embolden him further, while costing the President independent and moderate support. But Eisenhower insisted that if anyone should censure McCarthy, it should be the Senate itself, not the President, and that anyway if given enough rope, McCarthy would hang him-self. Jackson retorted that appeasing McCarthy was poor arithmetic (referring to the Senate votes) and worse politics. But Nixon and White House aide Jerry Persons urged Eisenhower in the direction his feelings were already taking him. They said that an attack on McCarthy would only divide the party and publicize the senator even more. "The best way to reduce his influence to the proper proportion," Nixon said, "is to take him on as part of the team."[12]

That was no part of Eisenhower's view. He never saw McCarthy as a possible member of his team. But McCarthyism, broadly considered, was the most divisive issue of the day. Eisenhower wanted to bring the nation together, through cooperation, not tear it further apart by confrontation. Behind McCarthy stood millions of Americans; they were an important part of the electorate that had put him in office; to attack and alienate McCarthy would be to alienate the senator's supporters, driving them farther away from the middle road in American politics.

Further, Eisenhower was more on McCarthy's side than not on the issue of Communism in government. It was McCarthy's methods he disapproved of, not his goals or his analysis. At a February 25 news conference, Eisenhower said he had no doubt at all that "almost one hundred percent of Americans would like to stamp out all traces of Communism in our country," and added that if there had been a known Communist on his faculty at Columbia, he would have had the man fired, or he would resign.[13]

But he was no McCarthyite. The senator's methods, the way in which his charges and investigations set American against American, leaving innocent victims in the wreckage, were themselves evil. Eisenhower knew this, he felt it in his bones, but he was faced with the fact that McCarthy was an enemy of his enemies, and a friend of a good many of his friends. So while McCarthy had to be destroyed, his followers had to be educated and brought into the mainstream, not alienated. The best way to do that, Eisenhower thought, was to destroy McCarthy by ignoring him, or by letting him destroy himself. He believed this so strongly that he even ignored McCarthy when the senator called into question the good name of his old friend Beetle.

Instead, Eisenhower worked behind the scenes, as he would do countless times in the future, for he was not averse to hastening the process of McCarthy's withering away. In this instance, he called Taft and told him to put an immediate stop on this nonsense about Beetle. Taft did as told, it worked, and Eisenhower began to have a better impression of Taft. Smith was confirmed, McCarthy got no headlines out of the case, battle had been avoided.

What McCarthy and his friends really wanted from Eisenhower and Dulles were major policy and structural changes. In policy, the Old Guard wanted a flat repudiation of the Yalta agreements, to be followed by action—the form of which was unspecified—to free the East European satellites.

As a candidate, Eisenhower had felt free to denounce Yalta. As President, his freedom of action was much more limited. When he turned to serious consideration of the effect of a repudiation of the agreements, he realized that such an action would have negative effects on American foreign policy and would needlessly alienate the Democrats. Further, having assumed power, he did not want to waste his assets by scavenger hunting into the past. Yalta had given the Americans their occupation rights in West Berlin and in Vienna; how could such guarantees be continued if they had been granted by an invalid agreement? The British, among others, warned that if the Americans could repudiate their pledged word, so could the Russians. Anthony Eden said bluntly that the U.K. would never participate in a repudiation. And of course the Democrats would resist with all their power any implied or real repudiation of FDR. Any resolution that passed Congress by a slim, partisan majority would have little if any effect. Eisenhower told the Republican leaders that "solidarity is the important thing." He wanted politics to stop at the water's edge.

So, on February 20, when Eisenhower presented to Congress his proposed resolution on Yalta, it did not repudiate the agreements, but instead merely criticized the Soviet Union for violating the "clear intent" of Yalta and thereby "subjugating whole nations." The United States, Eisenhower's resolution declared, rejected "interpretations" of Yalta that "have been perverted to bring about the subjugation of free peoples." It "hoped" that these peoples would "again enjoy the right of self-determination." [14]

The Old Guard denounced Eisenhower for this betrayal of basic Republican principles. Taft, under pressure from Eisenhower to go along, tried to bridge the gap by proposing a reservation to Eisenhower's resolution: "The adoption of this resolution does not constitute any determination by the Congress as to the validity or invalidity of any of the provisions of the said agreements." The Democrats, meanwhile, led by Lyndon B. Johnson of Texas, hailed Eisenhower's original resolution and opposed any change in it.

This put the Old Guard in a dilemma. If it allowed Eisenhower's resolution to pass unamended, it would imply acceptance of Yalta; if it amended the resolution, it would be guilty of partisanship and of splitting with a Republican President. But the Old Guard could not simply drop Yalta. Senator Hickenlooper wanted a clear and strong repudiation, and he had a number of allies on the Senate Foreign Relations Committee, which held hearings on the subject.

Then Stalin, of all people, came to Eisenhower's aid. On March 4, word came from Moscow that the Soviet dictator was near death. Under the circumstances, passing a repudiation resolution would be regarded as particularly callous; further, the imminent change in Soviet leadership made it inopportune to reopen old wounds. Nevertheless, Eisenhower was ready to go ahead with his own resolution. On March 5 he told a news conference that "what I really want to do is to put ourselves on record . . . that we never agreed to the enslavement of peoples that has occurred."

When he was asked to comment on suggestions that the Taft amendment represented "a break between you and Senator Taft," Eisenhower replied, "So far as I know, there is not the slightest sign of a rift or break between Senator Taft and me. And if anyone knows of any, I don't." Four days later, Eisenhower met with Taft and other Republican leaders to discuss the issue. Taft admitted that it was probably better "to forget the whole thing." Eisenhower's "powder-puff resolution" was not worth fighting for, while opposing it or amending it would be too costly. Stalin's death, on March 5, allowed everyone to escape the dilemma by shelving permanently any resolution on Yalta.[15]

The death of the man who had single-handedly led the world's second most powerful nation, and America's principal enemy, was an event of momentous importance. The trouble was that no one in the United States knew what to do about it, how to take advantage of it, or what was going to happen next. Eisenhower, relieved to have escaped the need to denounce FDR in public for Yalta, privately told his Cabinet that American unpreparedness was a "striking example of what has not been done" by the Democrats while they held power. Since 1946, he said, there had been much talk about what would happen when Stalin died, but the net result of seven years' talk "is zero. There is no plan, there is no agreed-upon position." He added that was why he had brought Robert Cutler down from Boston to give some form, direction, and organization to the work of the National Security Council (NSC). SHAEF had always had contingency plans ready in the event of Hitler's death, and he wanted the NSC to be equally prepared in the future.[16]

Eisenhower was equally unhappy with the failure of the NSC, and the JCS, to think through the implications of the defense budget, which had soared more than 300 percent in the past two and a half years. Ike wanted it cut, and ordered Wilson to get at it, which was done.

Except for the Secretary of the Treasury, George M. Humphrey, only a handful of Republicans supported Eisenhower on these cuts, although few went public with the opposition. The Democrats felt no such constraints. After Defense Secretary Charles E. Wilson announced his program of major reductions, Senator Symington launched an attack—one that the Democrats would continue and intensify over the next eight years—charging that Eisenhower's determination to balance the budget through defense cuts was leaving the United States vulnerable to Soviet aggression.

When Eisenhower was asked about Symington's charges, at a March 19 news conference, he used the occasion to educate the American people. "Ladies and gentlemen," he said, "there is no amount of military force that can possibly give you real security, because you wouldn't have that amount unless you felt that there was almost a similar amount that could threaten you somewhere in the world." [17]

At a Cabinet meeting the following day, the President was even blunter. Dulles was opposed to making a balanced budget top priority. He warned Eisenhower that if the United States cut back on defense spending, it would have the effect of saying the crisis was over. The Europeans would then feel that in that case, they too could cut back on military expenditures. This, he gravely warned, "would take the heart out of NATO." Eisenhower immediately disagreed. There could be no security, he told Dulles, without a sound economy, which was dependent upon a balanced budget. Dulles charged that the decision to balance the budget was made in a vacuum.

He then tried to pose a dilemma for Eisenhower: what were they going to do about Korea? Continue the stalemate? If so, they would lose congressional support. Try to win? If so, they needed more money for defense. Eisenhower held his position. "There is a limited kind of striving for a victory," he said, "but we simply cannot have these succeeding deficits."

Dulles tried another approach. The French were coming to Washington to ask for more help in Vietnam. Dulles thought that "we can clean up Indochina by an eighteen-month all-out effort" of military aid to France. It made good sense to Dulles to spend the money now, in order to effect greater savings later. So too in Korea —victory there now, whatever the cost, would mean savings later.

Eisenhower admitted that there was some truth in what Dulles said, but not enough. He pointed out that just getting sufficient force in Korea to drive the Communists back a few miles, so that the front lines would run across the narrow waist of the peninsula, would cost $3 or $4 billion. "How much better off are we at the waist," he wondered, "and how much do we want to pay to get there?" Dulles said driving forward to the waist would improve Korean morale. Eisenhower replied that that was "an imponderable."

Turning to a broader theme, Eisenhower flatly declared that "the defense of this country is not a military matter. The military has a very limited sector." If military spending continued at present levels, "then we've got to call for drastic reductions in other things," such as veterans' benefits, Social Security, farm programs. Eisenhower also warned his Cabinet that "any notion that 'the bomb' is a cheap way to solve things is awfully wrong. It ignores . . . the basic realities for our allies. It is cold comfort for any citizen of Western Europe to be assured that—after his country is overrun and he is pushing up daisies—someone still alive will drop a bomb on the Kremlin." [18]

Shortly after taking office, Eisenhower had a telephone conversation with Omar Bradley about the situation in Korea. Hanging up the phone, he turned to Ann Whitman and said, "I've just learned a lesson." Bradley had called him "Mr. President," after a lifetime of calling him "Ike." Eisenhower told Ann that it was a shock to hear it, and made him realize that as long as he was in the White House he would "be separated from all others, including my oldest and best friends. I would be far more alone now than [during the war]." [19]

To overcome those feelings of loneliness, Eisenhower turned first of all to his wife. They almost always ate their evening meal together, in the West Sitting Hall, usually with Mamie's mother, Mrs. Doud, who lived in the White House with them. Later in the evening, when Ike painted, Mamie would sit with him, reading or answering correspondence. They took their vacations together, whether to Augusta in the winter or Colorado in the summer. In the late winter of 1953, following Mamie's first visit to the presidential retreat in Maryland's Catoctin Mountains, named Shangri-La by FDR, Mamie announced that she would not go back to the rustic, rather shabby place unless it was modernized. But there was no money in the White House budget to do so. A member of the staff suggested to Mamie that since the place was operated by the Navy, the Navy might pay for remodeling. Mamie said, "I think I'll just pass a hint along to the Commander-in-Chief." The work was done; Eisenhower renamed the retreat Camp David after his grandson; therefore, until the Gettysburg farm was remodeled, Ike and Mamie spent numerous weekends together in the mountains.[20]

Ike's son, daughter-in-law, and grandchildren also helped him preserve some modicum of a normal family life. John and Barbara stayed in the White House until after the inaugural: Ike liked having them around, and they liked being there. The morning of January 22, Mamie had discovered Barbara sitting in a big four-poster in the Royal Suite, having her breakfast served to her. Mamie laughed at the sight; Barbara said that she would "never be nearer heaven than right then."[21] In the months and years that followed, Barbara was often back, with her children, which added immeasurably to Ike's pleasure, and to his sense that the White House was a real home, not an institution.

But neither Mamie nor the family could fully satisfy Ike's need for friendship and companions. Mamie seldom woke before 10 A.M., and did not get out of bed before twelve. "I believe that every woman over fifty should stay in bed until noon," she said, quite seriously.[22] She would study the papers, looking for bargains, whether in foods, clothes, or gifts, which she would then order over the telephone. She closely supervised the White House staff and took charge of the social functions, deciding on the menu, flowers, and seating arrangements. "I have only one career, and his name is Ike," she frequently declared, but in fact she was so busy—not to mention his schedule—that they seldom saw each other in daylight. John had his own career to pursue—he returned to Korea and the front lines shortly after the inaugural—and Barbara and the grandchildren lived in New York State. Further, Mamie never played golf, and she refused to play bridge with her husband, for the good reason that he yelled at her every time she misplayed.

Fortunately, he had friends who shared his love of golf and played bridge to his satisfaction. Even better, they were devoted to him. Following his election, his gang got together and agreed that they would always be available to the President whenever he had a free moment for golf and bridge. They were men of large affairs with crowded schedules of their own, but they felt that since they had played a major role in convincing their friend to take on the Presidency, they owed him whatever they could give him—which was primarily their time and their friendship. Over the next eight years, they were always available. Ann could telephone them in the morning, tell them that the boss wanted to play, and they would immediately get on a plane to Washington. Or, on a few occasions, to England or the Continent.

Ike told Slater he was especially delighted at the gang's willingness to come to Washington at a moment's notice, because most of his favorite partners and opponents in Washington were Democrats. He enjoyed playing with Chief Justice Fred Vinson, Senator Symington, and others he had known for years in the capital, but he feared that if he continued to play with them "some Republicans might not understand."[23]

In his memoirs, Ike paid a handsome tribute to his gang. "These were men of discretion," he wrote, "men, who, already successful, made no attempt to profit by our association. It is almost impossible for me to describe how valuable their friendship was to me. Any person enjoys his or her friends; a President needs them, perhaps more intensely at times than anything else."[24]

In the middle of February, Robinson, Roberts, and Slater came down from New York to spend the weekend at the White House. After golf in the afternoon and dinner on Saturday night, the party went to the movie theater in the White House to see *Peter Pan*. Slater asked Ike how the Presidency was going to work out for him financially. "Hell," Ike replied, "this job is no easy touch. Truman says I'll be lucky if I don't use $25,000 a year of my own money." Mamie added that the government only allowed her $3,000 for redecoration, and complained about "the stingy small bath towels."

Later in the afternoon, Robinson accompanied Ike to the study in which he did his painting. As Ike worked on a self-portrait Milton had requested, he talked to Robinson about various political problems. "Ike always likes to be in motion of some kind when he is talking and thinking," Robinson noted. "He seldom sits in the same chair for very long during a discussion and abhors sitting behind a desk in any extended conference. During our two- or three-hour talk he was all over the room and he continued to talk animatedly while he worked on the painting."

When Robert Donovan asked Eisenhower on February 25 how he liked his job, Ike mentioned "the confinement, and all the rest—those things are what you pay." Wanting always to be in motion, he hated having to spend hours, days, or weeks on end in his office, without a break from the routine, and he got away as often as possible. On February 7, Ann noted in her diary that "today the President wanted to play golf, very, very badly. He awoke to a cold and drizzly rain. He peered at the sky frequently during the morning, and finally, after another excursion out to the porch, announced, 'Sometimes I feel so sorry for myself I could cry.' "[25]

Later that month, Eisenhower was delighted when the American Public Golf Association offered to build a putting green on the South Lawn. Ike accepted, and had it placed just outside his office window. He practiced his approach shots and putts on his way to and from the office. He was furious with the squirrels, which were almost tame because Truman liked to feed them, and who buried acorns and walnuts in the green. Ike told Moaney, "The next time you see one of those squirrels go near my putting green, take a gun and shoot it!" The Secret Service talked him out of that idea, substituting traps instead; soon most of the squirrels had been transported to Rock Creek Park.[26]

Ike's favorite place to play golf was not on the White House lawn, nor at the Burning Tree Golf Club outside Washington, but at Augusta National. There he and Mamie could entertain their friends, relax, and play cards. On February 27, he made his first trip there for a weekend; the gang flew down from New York in a Chase National Bank plane; everyone had a great time. Ike played golf with the world's most famous golfer, Bobby Jones; he vowed to return often.

He needed all the relaxation he could get, because among other problems, Joe McCarthy was on another series of rampages. He had charged, for example, that Dr. Ralph Bunche, a Negro American who had won the 1950 Nobel Peace Prize and who was working at the U.N., was a Communist. It was a ridiculous charge that made Ike furious.

McCarthy, in Eisenhower's view, sought headlines, not Communists. A whirlwind tour of Europe that spring by McCarthy's young aides, Roy Cohn and G. David Schine, seemed to the President to prove the point. Cohn and Schine were "investigating" Communist penetration of the Voice of America by examining the holdings of America's overseas libraries. Those libraries had already been pretty thoroughly purged by Dulles' orders, but Cohn and Schine announced that they had found books written by 418 Communists or fellow travelers still being circulated. McCarthy demanded that Dulles trace the book orders and find out who had authorized the purchase of books by such people as Foster Rhea Dulles (the Secretary's cousin, a distinguished historian), John Dewey, and Robert M.

Hutchins. Dulles then banned the works of all Communist authors and "any publication which continuously publishes Communist propaganda." Some books were burned. Dulles also dismissed some 830 employees of the Voice.

The spectacle was more than many columnists could bear. Richard Rovere, Walter Lippmann, Bruce Catton, and others demanded that Eisenhower speak out. He refused. "I deplore and deprecate the table-pounding, name-calling methods that columnists so much love," he explained to one correspondent. "This is not because of any failure to love a good fight; it merely represents my belief that such methods are normally futile." [27] On May 9, Eisenhower's friend Harry Bullis of General Mills warned him "that the senator has unlimited personal ambitions, unmitigated gall, and unbounded selfishness. In the opinion of many of us who are your loyal friends, it is a fallacy to assume that McCarthy will kill himself. It is our belief that McCarthy should be stopped soon."

Still Eisenhower refused. He told Bullis that "this particular individual wants, above all else, publicity. Nothing would probably please him more than to get the publicity that would be generated by public repudiation by the President." That would only "increase his appeal as an after-dinner speaker and so allow him to raise the fees that he charges," which Eisenhower thought was McCarthy's chief motivation. Eisenhower said he realized "it is a sorry mess," and admitted that "at times one feels almost like hanging his head in shame." [28] But shame or no, he would not act.

Even if Eisenhower tried to ignore McCarthy, no one else would. Cohn and Schine were dominating the news, pushing the major issues of statecraft off the front pages, and there was a veritable national uproar over the holdings of America's overseas libraries. In Europe, if possible, the uproar was even greater. Philip Reed of General Electric went to Europe to assess the damage for Eisenhower. Reed reported that "it was surprising how seriously McCarthy and his tactics are taken in Europe" and spoke of the "shattered morale" in America's leading propaganda agency. He advised Eisenhower to "take public issue with McCarthy" in order to correct the European impression of "abject appeasement." [29]

On June 14, at Dartmouth College commencement exercises, Eisenhower did speak out. Talking without notes, he began with a rambling discourse on college life, golf, and patriotism. Then, leaning forward, he admonished the graduates, "Don't join the book burners. Don't think you are going to conceal faults by concealing evidence that they ever existed. Don't be afraid to go in your library and read every book." [30]

The pronouncement caused great excitement among the press, which speculated that Eisenhower was finally, at last, going to go after McCarthy. But it was not to be. The next day, Dulles asked Eisenhower if he wanted recent restrictions on material in the overseas libraries lifted. Eisenhower said no, "it would be undesirable to buy or handle books which were persuasive of Communism." [31] At a news conference on June 17, Merriman Smith asked the President whether the Dartmouth speech was "critical of a school of thought represented by Senator McCarthy." Eisenhower immediately backtracked.

"Now, Merriman," he began gently, "you have been around me long enough to know I never talk personalities." He said he was opposed to the "suppression of ideas," but then added, "if the State Department is burning a book which is an open appeal to everybody in those foreign countries to be a Communist, then I would say that falls outside of the limits I was speaking, and they can do as they please to get rid of them." Did that mean he approved of book burning? Well, no, not exactly. [32]

Eisenhower was equally vague in the privacy of his Cabinet meetings. On June 26 he told Dulles it was all becoming too embarrassing, and he wanted the Secretary to issue yet another statement on book policy (seven had already been sent out). Dulles, harassed himself, charged that Voice employees were burning books "out of fear or hatred for McCarthy," and out of a desire to embarrass the Secretary of State. Eisenhower said that he "could not conceive of fighting the Commies by ducking our heads in the sand," but then, on the other hand, he did not want American libraries distributing Communist propaganda. On still another hand, he said he knew for a fact that the German people "love our libraries," that he was proud to know that a library in Bonn carried a book that "severely criticizes me—on the battle of the Rhine or something." [33] Dulles finally escaped his predicament by issuing yet another directive, which said that books in overseas libraries should be "about the United States, its people and policies." McCarthy, meanwhile, was off after new targets, and Eisenhower had avoided an open break with the senator.

Eisenhower's refusal to go after McCarthy brought widespread criticism, and not just from Democrats. Nor were the criticisms limited to McCarthy; General Ike was a great military commander, people were saying, but President Ike is no political leader.

In Eisenhower's view, the complaints about his refusal to exercise real leadership were misdirected. The critics were watching the periphery, while he concentrated on the main battles. These included taxes, the budget, the war in Korea, the level of defense spending, foreign aid, and the general problem of world peace. On all these momentous issues, Eisenhower insisted, he provided firm, direct, and, most of all, effective leadership. He used all the weapons at his command, including private meetings with congressional leaders, his persuasive powers with the Cabinet, patronage, and his ability to mold public opinion through his news conferences and speeches. He left no doubt where he stood on any of the issues he felt were important, and he got his way—despite intense opposition—on every one of them.

Taxes are a problem for every President, of course, but they were especially irksome for Eisenhower because of Republican insistence that they be cut, at once, regardless of the size of the deficit. To that end, seventy-seven-year-old Congressman Daniel Reed of New York, chairman of the House Ways and Means Committee, had introduced a bill (H.R. 1) to advance from January 1, 1954, to July 1, 1953, a scheduled elimination of the 11 percent increase in personal income taxes adopted because of the Korean War. He also announced his intention to let the Korean War excess-profits tax expire as scheduled on June 30, 1953. These two measures would cost the government some $3 billion in revenue. Eisenhower repeated over and over that he would not allow a tax cut until he had a balanced budget; he wanted to postpone the cut in excise taxes and to extend the 11 percent increase in income taxes.

The battle lines were clearly drawn. "I used every reason, argument, and device," Eisenhower later recalled, "and every kind of personal and indirect contact to bring Chairman Reed to my way of thinking."[34] Nothing worked. Eisenhower made it plain to other Republican congressmen that if they wanted their share of the patronage, they would have to give him their votes on taxes. That brought a few members around. Eisenhower asked Taft to use his influence, which the senator reluctantly did. In July, Eisenhower finally got what he wanted.

Part of his success was due to his promise to bring down federal spending. That was the argument that had moved Taft. The senator was therefore appalled when, at a Legislative Leaders' Meeting on April 30, Eisenhower outlined his budget for the coming fiscal year. Although it made heavy cuts in defense, they were not enough to satisfy Taft; he objected strongly to the continuation of foreign aid at levels only slightly less than those of Truman; he refused to believe that more cuts could not be made and the first Republican budget in twenty years could not come out balanced.

Red-faced, raising his voice, snapping out his words, Taft declared, "I can't express the deepness of my disappointment at the program the Administration presented today." As Eisenhower recounted in his diary, "[Taft] accused the security council of merely adopting the Truman strategy and, by a process of nicking here and chipping there, built up savings which he classed as 'puny.' He predicted that acceptance by the Congress of any such program would insure the decisive defeat of the Republican party in 1954. He said that not only could he not support the program, but that he would have to go on public record as fighting and opposing it." Eisenhower found himself "astonished at the demagogic nature of his tirade, because not once did he mention the security of the United States . . . he simply wanted expenditures reduced, regardless."

Eisenhower broke in. "Let's go back," he said. Looking directly at Taft, he continued; "The essentials of our global strategy are not too difficult to understand." Europe must not fall; we can't take it over; we must make it stronger. "Next, the Middle East. That's half of the oil resources. We can't let it go to Russia." Southeast Asia was another critical point; we had to support the French in Vietnam. Taft's idea about relying exclusively on atomic weapons, based in the United States, brought from Eisenhower a scornful comment: "Reprisal alone gives us no assurance of security." America had to maintain a position of strength, or the Russians "will take these over gradually without fighting." He then gave Taft a detailed explanation of his defense policy.

Finally, a simple conclusion: "I cannot endanger the security of my country," and the meeting ended. Eisenhower commented in his diary that Taft did not have "considered judgment," because "he attempts to discuss weighty, serious, and even critical matters in such an ill-tempered and violent fashion." And, in a telling judgment on the subject of self-control, Eisenhower said of Taft, "I do not see how he can possibly expect . . . to influence people when he has no more control over his temper [than that]." [35]

Aside from the basic question of war or peace, the most important problem any modern President faces is the size of the defense budget. Everything else—taxes, the size of the deficit, the rate of unemployment, the inflation rate, relations with America's allies and with the Soviet Union—is directly related to how much DOD spends. All of Eisenhower's major goals—peace, lower taxes, a balanced budget, no inflation—were dependent upon his cutting the defense budget.

He knew it and was determined to do it. Indeed, an important factor in his decision to enter politics was his unhappiness with Truman's defense policy. As Taft had noted, spending for the military went up and down between 1945 and 1953 at a dizzying pace. On the eve of the Korean War, Truman had reduced defense to $13.5 billion. Eisenhower had opposed such drastic cuts, and often said that he personally believed there never would have been a Korean War if Truman had not demobilized so rapidly as to force the Army to withdraw its divisions from South Korea in 1948. By 1952, Truman was projecting more than $50 billion for defense, and had committed the United States to building up a maximum strength—to a near total-war footing—by 1954, the so-called "year of maximum danger." (By 1954, according to the Pentagon, the Soviet Union would have a hydrogen bomb and possess the means of delivery.)

Eisenhower told Republican leaders that this target date business was "pure rot." He said, "I have always fought the idea of X units by Y date. I am not going to be stampeded by someone coming along with a damn trick formula of 'so much by this date.'" What he wanted, instead, was a steady buildup, based on what the country could afford. When he announced his program, however, all the services objected strenuously. The Air Force, which had been scheduled to get the largest share of the Truman buildup, was especially upset, and not in the least hesitant in going public with its criticisms. Air Force objections got wide publicity. The Air Force argued that it had to have 141 groups by 1954 or it could not meet its responsibilities.

"I'm damn tired of Air Force sales programs," Eisenhower told the Republican leaders. "In 1946 they argued that if we can have seventy groups, we'll guarantee security forever and ever and ever." Now they come up with this "trick figure of 141. They sell it. Then you have to abide by it or you're treasonous." Eisenhower said he had told Defense Secretary Wilson to put his house in order, to force the generals and admirals to keep their mouths shut. "I will not have anyone in Defense who wants to sell the idea of a larger and larger force in being." The main Air Force spokesman on Capitol Hill, Senator Stuart Symington, charged that Eisenhower's program would leave the United States open to a Russian strategic bombing campaign. Eisenhower thought that too was "pure rot."

"We pulverized Germany," he reminded the congressmen, "but their actual rate of production was as big at the end as at the beginning. It's amazing what people can do under pressure. The idea that our economy will be paralyzed is a figment of Stuart Symington's imagination." Eisenhower looked at the problem from the other end —he pointed to the effect on the economy if the United States continued to build toward Truman's target date. What would happen after 1954? Could the country simply shut down the plants that had geared up to produce all those tanks, ships, and planes?

Still the politicians objected to Eisenhower's cuts. Surely the Air Force knew better than anyone else what its needs were. Eisenhower said that was "bunk." He reminded the congressmen that "I've served with those people who know all the answers—they just won't get down and face the dirty facts of life." The politicians were not convinced. How could they, mere civilians, argue with the Pentagon? Eisenhower replied that he knew the Pentagon as well as any man living; he knew how ingrained was the tendency to overstate the case, to ask for more than was really necessary.[36]

These remarks were made in private meetings, but Eisenhower was just as emphatic in public. At an April 23 news conference, Richard Harkness of NBC asked him if the "stretch out" in defense spending meant that he was looking to a ten-year buildup. "Well," Eisenhower responded, "I would object to ten years just as much as I object to two. Anybody who bases his defense on his ability to predict the day and the hour of attack is crazy. If you are going on the defensive, you have got to get a level of preparation you can sustain over the years."[37]

A week later, when the subject came up again, Eisenhower gave a history lecture. The situation in the 1950s, he said, was not at all like the situation in June of 1944 when "I went across the Channel." At that time, he said, "we knew the day. We knew when we wanted our maximum force. We knew the buildup we wanted. We knew exactly what we were up against." None of that was true in 1953.[38]

An integral part of Eisenhower's defense posture was reliance upon allies. That meant specifically that he wanted more funds for Mutual Security Assistance (MSA), so that he could distribute military hardware to the Koreans, to the NATO allies, and to other friends around the world. Eisenhower believed that it was cheaper for the United States to pay the costs of keeping a British or a German force on the Elbe River, or a French force in Vietnam, than it was to keep an American force there. Here he ran into the firm opposition of a majority of Republicans in Congress. They were tired of the Marshall Plan, tired of foreign aid, tired of "giving away" America's money. It was in this area, rather than in Pentagon appropriations, that they saw an opportunity to cut spending. Like Taft, they wanted a "Fortress America" program, although unlike Taft they were unwilling to reduce the size of the fortress.

To Eisenhower, this was just another instance of congressional stupidity. "Consider British bases," he told the Republican leaders. From Britain, the United States could strike the Soviet Union with B-47 bombers instead of having to use B-52s. He reminded them of the "huge difference" in initial costs, in operation, and in maintenance.[39] He managed to get most of what he asked for on MSA, and the Pentagon budget did go down. Together with maintaining the existing level of taxes, these were major triumphs. Eisenhower, more than any other individual, was responsible for winning them.

The most obvious way for Eisenhower to reduce defense spending was to reduce the level of tension in the world. Since 1945 the United States and the Soviet Union had been hurling the most horrendous charges at each other as they built and maintained armed forces designed to fight the battle of Armageddon. Eisenhower's election and Stalin's death provided an opportunity for a fresh start. Stalin's immediate successor, Georgi Malenkov, seized the chance. On March 15, he declared that there was no existing dispute between the two countries that "cannot be decided by peaceful means, on the basis of mutual understanding." The Soviet propaganda machine then went into high gear on a "peace offensive." Eisenhower had to respond. He had a sense of urgency about the need to do so, because he had just read a CIA report on the world reaction to the Soviet moves. "It begins to look to me," he told Dulles, "that if I am to make a speech on this question of peace, I should do it soon." Dulles was opposed—he did not believe a word of what Malenkov was saying—but Eisenhower insisted.[40]

In late March, Eisenhower met with Hughes in the Oval Office. After going over some routine matters, Eisenhower "began talking with the air of a man whose thoughts . . . were fast veering toward a conclusion."

Hughes recalled the scene vividly—Eisenhower's head "martially high," his "strong mouth tight, the jaw set—and the blue eyes agleam and intent." Eisenhower "wheeled abruptly" toward Hughes and went on: *"Here* is what I would like to say. The jet plane that roars over your head costs three-quarters of a million dollars. That is more money than a man . . . is going to make in his lifetime. What world can afford this sort of thing for long? We are in an armaments race. Where will it lead us? At worst, to atomic warfare. At best, to robbing every people and nation on earth of the fruits of their own toil."

Eisenhower said he wanted to see the resources of the world used to provide bread, butter, clothes, homes, hospitals, schools, "all the good and necessary things for decent living," not more guns. To help bring that about, he wanted to make a speech that would not include the standard indictment of the Soviet Union. "The past speaks for itself. I am interested in the future. Both their government and ours now have new men in them. The slate is clean. Now let us begin talking to each other. *And let us say what we've got to say so that every person on earth can understand it."*

Hughes injected a word of caution. He said he had just talked to Dulles about how the United States would react if the Communists accepted an armistice in Korea. Dulles had said he would be sorry, because *"I don't think we can get much out of a Korean settlement until we have shown—before all Asia—our clear superiority by giving the Chinese one hell of a licking."*

Eisenhower's head snapped around. He stared at Hughes. Then he said, "All right, then. If Mr. Dulles and all his sophisticated advisers really mean that they can *not* talk peace seriously, then I am in the wrong pew. For if it's war we should be talking about, I *know* the people to give me advice on that—and they're not in the State Department. Now either we cut out all this fooling around and make a serious bid for peace—or we forget the whole thing." [41]

Eisenhower told Hughes, and C. D. Jackson, to get to work on a speech on peace. He monitored every word of the many drafts, often providing them with imagery and telling phrases. Over the next two weeks, they worked hard at it.

On April 16, 1953, Eisenhower went to the Statler Hotel in Washington to give the American Society of Newspaper Editors the finest speech of his Presidency. He called it "The Chance for Peace." Insofar as it was a response to the Soviet peace offensive, it was propaganda—eloquently put, but still propaganda. Eisenhower welcomed recent Soviet statements on the need for peace and said that he would believe they were sincere when the words were backed with deeds. Specific deeds, including the release of POWs held since 1945, a Soviet signature on an Austrian treaty, the conclusion of "an honorable armistice" in Korea, Indochina, and Malaya, agreement to a free and united Germany, and the "full independence of the East European nations."

In return for such actions by the Russians, Eisenhower said he was prepared to conclude an arms-limitation agreement and to accept international control of atomic energy designed to "insure the prohibition of atomic weapons." All this would be supervised by "a practical system of inspection under the United Nations."

Eisenhower knew that most of his demands for proof were unacceptable to the Russians. Under no circumstances would they pull out of Eastern Europe; the idea of German reunification gave them nightmares; they could not be expected to (or even be able to) call off the guerrilla warriors in Vietnam and Malaya; and their opposition to on-site inspections within the Soviet Union was implacable, and well known.

The specific charges, demands, and proposals in "The Chance for Peace," in other words, were little more than a restatement of some of the oldest Cold War rhetoric. They were not what made the speech great. What did make it great was Eisenhower's warning about the dangers and the cost of continuing the arms race.

"The worst to be feared and the best to be expected can be simply stated," he declared. "The worst is atomic war. The best would be this: a life of perpetual fear and tension; a burden of arms draining the wealth and the labor of all peoples." Then he added up the price: "Every gun that is made, every warship launched, every rocket fired, signifies, in the final sense, a theft from those who hunger and are not fed, those who are cold and are not clothed."

Suddenly Eisenhower began perspiring. As the sweat beaded up on his face, he became so dizzy he feared he would faint. Then he was racked by chills. He reached forward and grabbed the podium with both hands to steady himself. He had had an intestinal attack the previous evening, and that morning Dr. Snyder had given him sedatives, but now the attack was worse than ever. With an effort of will, Eisenhower drew himself together, managed to concentrate on the text, and read on, skipping some passages so as to emphasize the important ones.

"This world in arms is not spending money alone," he continued. "It is spending the sweat of its laborers, the genius of its scientists, the hopes of its children." He picked up his voice, looked out at his audience, and began ticking them off: "The cost of one modern heavy bomber is this: a modern brick school in more than thirty cities. It is two electric power plants, each serving a town of sixty thousand population. It is two fine, fully equipped hospitals." Sweat was pouring from his brow, but he read on: "We pay for a single fighter plane with a half-million bushels of wheat. We pay for a single destroyer with new homes that could have housed more than eight thousand people."

Looking out again, he pronounced his judgment. "This is not a way of life at all, in any true sense. Under the cloud of threatening war, it is humanity hanging from a cross of iron."

Eisenhower's conclusion, pointing to the alternative, was as splendid as his evocation of the costs of the arms race. He said that if the Soviets showed by deeds that they too were ready for peace, the United States would devote "a substantial percentage of the savings achieved by disarmament to a fund for world aid and reconstruction . . . to assist all peoples to know the blessings of productive freedom. The monuments to this new kind of war would be these: roads and schools, hospitals and homes, food and health."[42]

The reception to his speech, in the Western world, was overwhelming. The American press outdid itself in praising him; so did the British and Continental newspapers; messages from American embassies around the world reported the greatest enthusiasm to any statement by an American since George Marshall outlined the European Recovery Program.

There was much in "The Chance for Peace" that was pure propaganda, but the overall tone of the speech was so reasonable and moderate, Eisenhower's sincerity so apparent, as in his willingness to speak the blunt truth about the arms race in such vivid terms, and the reception of the speech was so favorable, that the Soviets had to respond. How, and when, remained to be seen.

CHAPTER THIRTEEN

Peace in Korea
—Coup in Iran—
Atoms for Peace

WHEN EISENHOWER returned to Washington, Korea was at the center of his attention. The Communists said they were ready to begin again the armistice talks with the U.N. team at Panmunjom. Dulles wanted to reject the offer. At an NSC April 8 meeting, he told Eisenhower that "it was now quite possible to secure a much more satisfactory settlement in Korea than a mere armistice at the thirty-eighth parallel, which would leave a divided Korea." Dulles believed that if a military armistice was not followed by a "political settlement," meaning the unification of Korea, the United States would have to break the armistice.

Eisenhower would have none of that. He told Dulles "it will be impossible to call off the armistice and to go to war again in Korea. The American people will never stand for such a move."[1]

In Panmunjom, meanwhile, both sides were negotiating seriously, taking new positions on the complex problem of Chinese and North Korean POWs who did not want to return home. The Indian government was proposing a compromise solution that appealed to both sides. But not to Dulles. He flew to Karachi for talks with Prime Minister Jawaharlal Nehru. This trip has since become famous, because during the talks Dulles supposedly told Nehru that the United States might feel compelled "to use atomic weapons if a truce could not be arranged." In fact, no such direct warning was made, nor was it necessary. The full text of Dulles' report to Eisenhower on his conversation with Nehru read: "Nehru brought up Korean armistice, referring particularly to my statement of preceding day, that if no (repeat no) armistice occurred hostilities might become more intense. He said if this happened it difficult to know what end might be. He urged withdrawal our armistice proposals as inconsistent with the Indian resolutions. He made no (repeat no) alternate proposal. He brought up again my reference to intensified operations, but I made no (repeat no) comment and allowed the topic to drop."[2]

Dulles did not need to make any direct threats, much less depend on Nehru to pass them along to the Chinese. The Communists already knew that Eisenhower had a nuclear option; they knew that his patience was limited; they knew that he was under pressure to widen the war; they knew that the Americans had atomic warheads in Okinawa. On June 4, the Chinese presented a POW proposal that was in substantial accord with the last U.N. offer. Peace was in sight.

Rhee was furious. He had already told Eisenhower that a simple military armistice would mean "a death sentence for Korea without protest." He proposed, instead, a simultaneous withdrawal of both the Chinese and U.N. forces in Korea, a mutual-defense pact between South Korea and the United States, and an increase in military aid. If this program was unacceptable, he begged Eisenhower to allow the Koreans to continue the fighting, for this "is the universal preference of the Korean people to any divisive armistice of peace."[3]

In a long and sympathetic reply, Eisenhower told Rhee that "the moment has now come" for peace. "The enemy has proposed an armistice which involves a clear abandonment of the fruits of aggression." As the cease-fire line would follow the front lines, which were slightly north of the 38th parallel, Rhee would emerge from the conflict with his territory intact, "indeed somewhat enlarged." Eisenhower pledged that the United States "will not renounce its efforts by all peaceful means to effect the unification of Korea," agreed to a mutual-defense pact, and promised substantial reconstruction aid for South Korea. He concluded, "Even the thought of a separation at this critical hour would be a tragedy. We must remain united."[4]

On June 8, the Communists at Panmunjom agreed to the voluntary repatriation of POWs, with the provision that the processing of the prisoners would be observed by representatives of both sides. All that now remained was to establish a cease-fire line. That, and bringing Rhee around.

Rhee was in a strong position. Two-thirds of the battle line was manned by his troops. He could upset any armistice agreement by marching north. Further, his soldiers were the guards at the POW compounds. He had the sympathy of many Americans. And he had the apparent complete support of his own people. When the announcement of the POW agreement was made in Seoul, some 100,000 South Koreans took to the streets in a massive demonstration demanding a march to the north. The South Korean assembly rejected the proposed truce by a vote of 129 to 0.

On June 19, Eisenhower was holding a regular Cabinet meeting. An aide came in with a message. Rhee had released some twenty-five thousand POWs, Chinese and Korean, and they had quickly scattered over the countryside. This was a direct violation of the armistice agreements, and inevitably made the Chinese ask "whether the United States was able to live up to any agreement to which the South Koreans might be a party." Eisenhower turned to his Cabinet, reported on what he had just learned, and commented that "we are coming to the point where it is completely impossible." He said he could not understand the "mental processes of the Oriental. One thing I learned in five years out there is that we don't know to what they will react." Rhee, in Eisenhower's view, was committing his people to national suicide.

Dulles thought Rhee had a legitimate point of view and suggested, "Let's merely hold the line; try to carry on what we've done the last two years," that is, continue the war. Eisenhower objected: "This would be a complete surrender to his blackmail." Wilson said that was the other side of the "Oriental mind—he doesn't consider it blackmail. After all, we dumped him out of the truce talks." Humphrey said that the "only thing for us to do is what we can to keep face." Eisenhower burst into laughter—"Imagine," he said, "Westerners saving face!"

Dulles had the last word. He gravely informed Eisenhower that "this situation is inherent in the type of foreign policy we're trying to pursue." Failure to fight the Communists everywhere, failure to drive them back behind the Yalu, failure to support Chiang in an offensive on the mainland, failure to go for an all-out victory in Vietnam, all coupled with Eisenhower's glittering promises in "The Chance for Peace," made it impossible for the United States to pursue a clear and direct policy of resistance to Communism.[5] The implication of Dulles' remarks was clear—break off the truce talks and go for victory.

Eisenhower would not consider that. Instead, he sent Walter Robertson, an Assistant Secretary of State, to Seoul to try to talk reason to Rhee. Eisenhower also sent a stern warning to Rhee. Reminding the South Korean President that the Koreans had agreed to give the U.N. Command "authority over all land, sea, and air forces of the ROK during the period of the present state of hostilities," Eisenhower said that the release of the prisoners "constitutes a clear violation of this assurance and creates an impossible situation." Eisenhower told Rhee that "unless you are prepared immediately and unequivocally to accept the authority of the U.N. Command to conduct the present hostilities and to bring them to a close, it will be necessary to effect another arrangement."[6] Robertson, acting under Eisenhower's direction, told Rhee what those "other arrangements" would be—a withdrawal of American troops, no more military support for the ROK, no reconstruction funds for South Korea, no mutual-defense pact.

Rhee resisted the pressure, helped by reports from the States that seemed to indicate a near revolt by Republican senators against their own Administration. Ralph Flanders had said that Robertson was putting "us in the position of threatening the Korean government with an attack from the rear while the ROKs were attacking the Communists at the front." Bridges and McCarthy believed that "freedom-loving people" should applaud Rhee's defiance of the armistice. An Old Guard representative introduced a resolution in the House commending Rhee for releasing the prisoners. And on July 5, the acting majority leader, Senator William Knowland (Taft was in the hospital for treatment of a cancer in his hip), blamed Eisenhower for a "breach" with Rhee and announced his support for Korean unification before any armistice agreement was signed.[7]

Despite the clamor, Eisenhower insisted that Robertson be firm with the old man. He was, and ultimately persuaded Rhee that it was futile for South Korea to try to go it alone. On July 8, Rhee finally issued a public statement promising to cooperate.

At 9:30 P.M. on July 26, Eisenhower received word of the truce signing. A half hour later, he made a radio and television address to the American people. The shooting was over, he said, a fact that he greeted with "prayers of thanksgiving." Still, he felt it necessary to remind the American people that "we have won an armistice on a single battleground—not peace in the world. We may not now relax our guard nor cease our quest." There were no victory celebrations, no cheering crowds in Times Square, no sense of triumph. Instead Republicans like William Jenner, McCarthy, and House Speaker Joe Martin complained because the Administration had not sought vic-

tory, while Lyndon Johnson warned that the armistice "merely re-
leases aggressive armies to attack elsewhere."[8]

The armistice was, despite its reception, one of Eisenhower's
greatest achievements. He took pride in it. He had promised to go to
Korea; he had implied that he would bring the war to a close; he had
made the trip; despite intense opposition from his own party, from
his Secretary of State, and from Syngman Rhee, he had ended the
war six months after taking office. Eisenhower was the only American
who could have found and made stick what he called "an acceptable
solution to a problem that almost defied . . . solution."[9] His solution
was acceptable only because he had put his own immense prestige
behind it; he knew that if Truman had agreed to such a settlement,
Republican fury might have led to an impeachment attempt and
certainly would have had a divisive effect on the country.

What stands out is Eisenhower the leader. The Supreme Allied
Commander of 1945, the victor who would accept nothing less than
unconditional surrender, had become the peacemaker of 1953, a
man who would accept a compromise settlement that left him far
short of victory, much less unconditional surrender. There were fundamental differences in the two situations, obviously, but this should
not obscure the truth. The truth was that Eisenhower realized that
unlimited war in the nuclear age was unimaginable, and limited war
unwinnable. This was the most basic of his strategic insights.

One alternative between unimaginable and unwinnable was continued stalemate. That was the policy urged on him by nearly all his
advisers, Republican colleagues, and most Democrats. At this
thought, Eisenhower the man rebelled. The U.S. Army had suffered
nearly one thousand casualties a week in Korea during the time since
Rhee released the prisoners, on the eve of a successful completion of
the truce. The thought of those five thousand dead and wounded
boys made Eisenhower sick. The man who had ordered the Allied
troops back onto the Continent and into the hell of the Bulge could
not bear the thought of American boys dying for a stalemate. He
wanted the killing ended, and he ended it.

Eisenhower liked to make up lists in his diary, lists of men who
had pleased him or disappointed him, of events, of accomplishments.
From the end of July 1953 onward, whenever he listed the achievements he was proudest of, he always began with peace in Korea.

One thing he did not brag about, even in the privacy of his diary,
was the overthrow of Iranian Prime Minister Mohammed Mossad-

egh. Not that he was not pleased with the outcome, or proud of it, but that he just didn't want it discussed, because he felt that the CIA's triumphs should be kept secret.

Mossadegh headed a government that had seized the Anglo-Persian Oil Company (British owned) and then broken diplomatic relations with London. The British had retaliated by setting up a *de facto* blockade of Iranian oil; meanwhile the British, along with American oilmen, told Ike that Mossadegh was a Communist. In the spring of 1953, Foreign Secretary Eden came to Washington, to propose a joint effort between the British Secret Service and the CIA to topple Mossadegh.

Eisenhower was receptive, because of the emphasis he was putting on both the underdeveloped world and the CIA. Eisenhower and Foster Dulles spent many a cocktail hour together, holding wide-ranging discussions. More often than not, their talk came around to the underdeveloped world and the need to keep the poorer nations from going Communist. With NATO in place, an armistice in Korea, the battleground for the Cold War had shifted to the so-called Third World. Latin America, India, Egypt, Iran, Vietnam—these were the places where the free world was being challenged, or so Eisenhower and Dulles believed.

In meeting the challenge, Eisenhower intended to use the CIA in a much more active role than Truman had given it. Under Truman, the Agency had concentrated on its first responsibility, gathering and evaluating intelligence from around the world. Eisenhower believed the Agency could be used more effectively, indeed could become one of America's chief weapons in the Cold War. Partly this was based on his experiences in World War II; he had been impressed by and grateful for the contribution to victory made by the British Secret Service, the French Resistance, and the American OSS. More important was Eisenhower's fundamental belief that nuclear war was unimaginable, limited conventional war unwinnable, and stalemate unacceptable. That left the CIA's covert action capability. Under Eisenhower's leadership and Allen Dulles' direction, the size and scope of the CIA's activities increased dramatically during the 1950s. The beginning came in Iran in 1953.

It was the CIA's first big-time coup. It was planned in the early summer of 1953. It was prepared by Allen and Foster Dulles, Beetle Smith, and Charlie Wilson. The aim of their plot was to depose Mossadegh and bring the Shah back to power; the means were out-and-out bribes for the Iranian Army officers. Code name for the plan was Ajax.

Before going into operation, Ajax had to have the approval of the President. Eisenhower participated in none of the meetings that set up Ajax, he received only oral reports on the plan, and he did not discuss it with his Cabinet or the NSC. Establishing a pattern he would hold to throughout his Presidency, he kept his distance and left no documents behind that could implicate the President in any projected coup. But in the privacy of the Oval Office, over cocktails, he was kept informed by Foster Dulles, and he maintained a tight control over the activities of the CIA.

Ajax was a great success. The Iranian Army arrested Mossadegh, the Shah returned, he cut a new oil deal that gave the American oil giants 40 percent of Iran's oil, Eisenhower announced an $85 million economic aid package for Iran, and everyone was happy—except the Iranian people, and the British oil executives, who lost their monopoly.

Eisenhower had ordered the Mossadegh government overthrown, and it had been done. It seemed to him that the results more than justified the methods. That was an additional side of the man who had insisted on making peace in Korea and trying new approaches to Russia on disarmament. Where he thought it prudent and possible, he was ready to fight the Communists with every weapon at his disposal—just as he had fought the Nazis. There was no squeamishness, no doubts. Do it, he told the CIA, and don't bother me with any details.[10]

The methods used were immoral, if not illegal, and a dangerous precedent had been set. The CIA offered the President a quick fix for his foreign problems. It was there to do his bidding; it freed him from having to persuade Congress, or the parties, or the public. The asset of the CIA greatly extended the President's powers—at the expense of also greatly extending the risks of his getting into deep trouble.

Taft's death from cancer, on July 31, was a blow. The senator had surprised and pleased Eisenhower by his cooperative attitude. Despite Taft's outburst when first informed of the Administration's budget plans, he had persuaded many of the Old Guard congressmen to go along with Eisenhower's proposals on such basic matters as taxes and expenditures. Responding to Eisenhower's heartfelt pleas, he had managed to save much of the MSA appropriation. With Taft's help, Eisenhower could deal with the Old Guard; without it, he anticipated great difficulties. Eisenhower released a statement saying that America had "lost a truly great citizen and I have lost a wise counselor and a valued friend." Along with Mamie, Eisenhower paid a call on Taft's widow in Georgetown. Holding Martha Taft's hand in both of his, Eisenhower said, "I don't know what I'll do without him; I don't know what I'll do without him." [11]

Eisenhower meant what he said, if only because Taft's successor as majority leader in the Senate was William Knowland. Eisenhower's contempt for the California senator was complete. "In his case," Eisenhower wrote of Knowland in his diary, "there seems to be no final answer to the question 'How stupid can you get?' " [12]

What especially bothered Ike about Knowland was the Senator's blind opposition to any foreign involvement (save all-out aid to Nationalist China). Eisenhower wanted to get on with building a United States of Europe. To that end, he wanted Germany rearmed, unified, and brought into NATO and EDC as a full partner.

These had been among Eisenhower's major goals as SACEUR, and he continued to make them the centerpiece of his European policy as President. Through Dulles, and through his private correspondence with European leaders, he pushed the projects. In September, he told French Premier Joseph Laniel that it was "urgent" that the French, in their relations with West Germany, "be guided by a new spirit of friendship and trust." He said he was aware of the difficulties for the French involved in ratifying EDC, as "we are not blind to history." But still he urged Laniel not to miss "this historic opportunity for a Franco-German rapprochement." [13]

Eisenhower's high hopes for EDC involved not only what he felt it could accomplish for Western Europe, but also the promise it held for the United States. A closely knit Western European community, held together by economic and military ties, protected through NATO by the American nuclear umbrella and through EDC by numerous all-European ground divisions, would not only be a source of security for the world but would end the need for MSA funds and allow Eisenhower to cut even further the American military budget. EDC, in short, would simultaneously provide greater security for the West, a smaller defense establishment for the United States, and lower taxes. EDC ratification received a new emphasis on August 12, when the Soviets successfully tested their own hydrogen bomb.

There was another explosion coming on, one that Eisenhower paid little attention to although, like the Russian hydrogen bomb, it was one that he wished would never happen. It was the explosion in race relations in the United States.

Much as Ike wanted to ignore it, however, his Attorney General would not let him do so, and Ike had developed an unbounded admiration for Brownell. In his diary, Eisenhower wrote that Brownell was a man of consummate honesty, incapable of an unethical practice, a lawyer of the first rank, and an outstanding leader. He summed up, "I am devoted to him and am perfectly confident that he would make an outstanding president of the United States." [14] So Eisenhower necessarily had to pay attention when Brownell came to him to discuss the school segregation cases that were coming up before the Supreme Court.

Brownell told Eisenhower that the Court had requested the Attorney General to file a brief and an opinion in the cases. Requests for such *amicus curiae* briefs from the Court, Brownell assured Eisenhower, were not unique, although by no means was it an established practice. Eisenhower was not bothered by the Court's request for a statement of fact on the Fourteenth Amendment as it related to segregation in the schools, but he did object to the Court's further request that the Justice Department also submit its opinion on the subject. This, to Eisenhower, represented an abdication of responsibility. One reason he felt that way was his attitude toward separation of powers. "As I understand it," he told Brownell, "the courts were established by the Constitution to interpret the laws; the responsibility of the Executive Department is to execute them." He suspected the Court was trying to duck out of or avoid the most controversial social problem in America, that "in this instance the Supreme Court has been guided by some motive that is not strictly functional." [15]

Brownell very much wanted to give his own opinion, which was that segregation by race in public schools was unconstitutional. There was the rub. Eisenhower was fearful of the effect of a ruling outlawing segregation. Partly this reflected his own background and attitudes. Eisenhower was six years old when *Plessy* v. *Ferguson* established the doctrine of "separate but equal"; he had lived all his life with it. There were no Negroes in his home town, none at West Point. Eisenhower had spent virtually all his prewar career at Army posts in the South, or in the Canal Zone or the Philippines, where racism was, if possible, even more blatant. During the war, he had commanded a Jim Crow Army. Eisenhower had left the Army before Truman, in 1948, ordered the armed forces desegregated. Eisenhower had many southern friends and he shared most of their prejudices against Negroes. When he went down to Augusta, he listened to the plantation owners tell their jokes about the "darkies"; when he returned to Washington, in the privacy of his family, he would repeat some of those jokes.

During the campaign, Eisenhower had denied that race relations were an issue, a startling statement in view of the Democratic Party split in 1948 over the Fair Employment Practices Commission (FEPC). Indeed, Eisenhower had bid for southern votes by his own refusal to endorse FEPC. But one of his core beliefs about the office he now held was that he was the President of all the people. That included Negro Americans. He had therefore announced, in his State of the Union message, that he would use his full authority to end segregation in the District of Columbia and in the armed forces.

That was done, to Ike's credit, but those changes had little or no effect on the great bulk of Negro Americans. *Plessy* remained the law of the land. The sum total of Eisenhower's program for the 16 million Negro Americans who were outside the federal establishment was to appeal to the southern governors for some sign of voluntary progress. Since every one of those governors had been elected by a virtually all-white electorate, and since every one of them was thoroughly committed to segregation as a way of life, as were the vast majority of their white constituents, the President could not have anticipated rapid or dramatic progress.

Not that he really wanted it. The civil-rights movement presented problems he did not understand, nor wish to study, much less to solve. He wanted to put those problems off, leave them to his successor. This was his great weakness as a political leader. His unwillingness to grapple with long-term problems and his inability to see clearly moral questions were to cost the nation, his party, and his reputation beyond measure.

Inadvertently, however, and unknowingly, he made a powerful contribution, indeed a critical one, to the civil-rights revolution. It happened because of the man he chose to be Chief Justice.

On the morning of September 8 the President was informed that Chief Justice Fred Vinson had died of a heart attack. Eisenhower flew back to Washington for the funeral. He mourned the passing of his old bridge-playing friend, but inevitably his mind turned to the appointment of a successor. Eisenhower had already promised Earl Warren that he would have the first vacancy on the Court, but when he made that promise he did not expect that the vacancy would be that of the Chief Justice himself. Eisenhower therefore felt free to canvass other possibilities, and did so—including John W. Davis of West Virginia, the 1924 Democratic nominee for the Presidency and a lawyer who was arguing the South's side in the segregation cases. Eisenhower also thought of John Foster Dulles, and indeed asked Dulles if he would take the appointment. Dulles said no, he preferred to stay with the State Department.

It was not that Eisenhower wanted to renege on Warren. Eisenhower had talked to Warren about his basic philosophy and was much impressed by the California governor. Brownell later recalled that Eisenhower "saw Warren as a big man; and his respect turned into a real crush." To his brother Edgar, Eisenhower wrote that "from the very beginning of my acquaintanceship with Warren, I had him in mind for an appointment to the high court."[16]

But Eisenhower wanted to think long and hard before making what probably would be the most important appointment of his Presidency. "I'm not going to make any mistakes in a hurry," he told one consultant. To the dean of the Columbia Law School, who had suggested some names, Eisenhower explained his approach. "My principal concern is to do my part in helping restore the Court to the position of prestige that it used to hold, and which in my opinion was badly damaged during the New and Fair Deal days." He said he was seeking "a man of broad experience, professional competence, and with an unimpeachable record and reputation for integrity."[17]

Warren had all those qualifications, and others. Eisenhower could not be accused of paying off a political debt, because Warren had stayed in the race against him until the end at the convention. Warren was middle-of-the-road, so much so that Eisenhower's reactionary brother Edgar denounced him as a left-winger, while Milton reported that he and his friends considered Warren to be dangerously to the right. Eisenhower responded to Milton: "Warren has been very definitely a liberal-conservative; he represents the kind of political, economic, and social thinking that I believe we need on the Supreme Court."[18]

In late September, Eisenhower announced a recess appointment of Warren as Chief Justice (Congress was not in session). Eisenhower made the appointment for all the reasons cited above, but the one that stands out is simplicity itself. Eisenhower personally knew many great lawyers, great judges, great men. He was a shrewd judge of character and talent. He wanted this appointment to be his best. He was convinced that Warren was the best man in the country for the post of Chief Justice.

When Congress gathered again in January 1954, Eisenhower sent Warren's formal nomination to the Senate. There Senator Langer, helped by other Old Guard senators, held up confirmation. Eisenhower scribbled in his diary, "[If the] Republicans as a body should try to repudiate him [Warren], I shall leave the Republican Party and try to organize an intelligent group of independents, however small."[19] Despite his many difficulties with Warren over the next seven years, he remained convinced that he had made the right choice.

On October 8, Eisenhower opened a news conference with a prepared statement. The subject was the recent Soviet test of a hydrogen bomb. The President said the test had not come as a surprise, and added that the Soviets "now possess a stockpile of atomic weapons . . . and the capability of atomic attack on us, and such capability will increase with the passage of time." Turning to the American situation, he said, "We do not intend to disclose the details of our strength in atomic weapons of any sort, but it is large and increasing steadily." He assured the press that the armed forces had sufficient nuclear arsenals to carry out the specific tasks assigned to them. And he warned that "this titanic force must be reduced to the fruitful service of mankind."[20]

Millions agreed with Eisenhower's final sentence. More important, leading American scientists agreed, and indeed had already been calling for disarmament followed by research on peaceful uses of atomic power. Most important, the former scientific head of the Manhattan Project, J. Robert Oppenheimer, agreed. In July of 1953 Oppenheimer had published, in *Foreign Affairs*, an article titled "Atomic Weapons and American Policy." In the article, Oppenheimer warned that an atomic arms race between the superpowers could only have disastrous results, and in any case it made no sense, because when America built its "twenty-thousandth bomb it . . . will not offset their two-thousandth." In a vivid image, Oppenheimer compared the United States and the Soviet Union to "two scorpions in a bottle, each capable of killing the other, but only at the risk of his own life." He insisted that the American people had to be told the truth about the size and power of their atomic arsenal, and called for "candor on the part of the representatives of the people of their country."[21]

Oppenheimer's article sharpened, but did not begin, the debate in the Eisenhower Administration over atomic policy. As this was unquestionably the most momentous problem Eisenhower faced, he treated it with the utmost seriousness. He had made Oppenheimer the head of an advisory group to report to the President on what to do about the arms race; in addition, Oppenheimer had been chairman of the General Advisory Committee of the Atomic Energy Commission (AEC). Eisenhower read and was impressed by Oppenheimer's views; he agreed with the physicist that an atomic arms race was madness; he also believed that if the American people were told, in graphic detail, of the destructive power of the H-bomb, they would support him in any genuine disarmament proposal. The President therefore put C. D. Jackson to work on a speech designed to meet Oppenheimer's call for candor. Jackson called the preparation of the speech "Operation Candor," and worked on it through the spring and summer of 1953. He was an enthusiastic supporter of Oppenheimer's basic idea.

Other top advisers were firmly opposed. Dulles had no faith whatsoever in any disarmament proposal. He believed in dealing with the Russians only from a position of overwhelming strength, and insisted that the various Soviet proposals so far received for disarmament were merely propaganda devices, designed to weaken NATO and to discourage the French from ratifying EDC. Admiral Lewis Strauss, chairman of the AEC, agreed with Dulles.

Strauss was a self-made millionaire (on Wall Street) and had been James Forrestal's assistant during the war (thus his rank of admiral). Truman had first put him on the AEC in 1946; three years later Strauss had engaged in a bitter dispute with Oppenheimer over the hydrogen bomb. Oppenheimer did not want to build one, while Strauss—and Truman—did. In July 1953, Eisenhower appointed Strauss the chairman of the AEC (although he hardly knew the man). After Strauss's swearing-in ceremony, Eisenhower took him aside and told him, "My chief concern and your first assignment is to find some new approach to the disarming of atomic energy."[22] Strauss ignored the President's directive.

Eisenhower was between Oppenheimer and Strauss in his thinking, "encouraging both without offending either." The President said that Jackson's various drafts (which insiders were calling the "Bang! Bang! papers"), with their descriptions of atomic horrors leaving "everybody dead on both sides with no hope anywhere," were too frightening to serve any useful purpose. "We don't want to scare the country to death," Eisenhower told Jackson, because he was afraid it would set off a congressional demand for outlandish and largely ineffective defense spending. On the other hand, ever since he had read his first report on the initial H-bomb test, he had had an impulse to inform the public about the awesome destructive power thereby unleashed. But each time he read another of Jackson's drafts, the fear of an overreaction by Congress to a "Bang! Bang!" presentation overcame his insistence to tell the truth, and he kept instructing Jackson to tone it down. "Can't we find some hope?" he asked Jackson.[23]

Jackson could not. Nor were his advisers much help. They either told him to build bigger bombs as fast as possible (Strauss) or build none at all (Oppenheimer).

Eisenhower mulled it over. He realized that he would have to come up with an idea of his own for a disarmament proposal, one that would not endanger security, that the Russians would not be likely to dismiss out of hand, and that would contain some genuine hope. Finally he hit on it. The United States and the Soviet Union could, he thought, make donations of isotopes from their nuclear stockpiles to a common fund for peaceful purposes, such as developing nuclear generators. In one stroke, the proposal would solve many problems. It would replace despair over atomic energy with hope; it did not require on-site inspection, always a stumbling block in any disarmament proposal; its propaganda advantages were obvious and overwhelming.

Further, it would reassure the American people "that they had not poured their substance into this whole development with the sole purpose of its being used for destruction." Best of all, as Eisenhower wrote in his diary, if the Russians cooperated, "The United States could unquestionably afford to reduce its atomic stockpile by two or three times the amounts that the Russians might contribute . . . and still improve our relative position in the cold war and even in the event of the outbreak of war." Finally, "Underlying all of this, of course, is the clear conviction that as of now the world is racing toward catastrophe."[24]

Even as Eisenhower groped his way toward a genuine, new disarmament proposal, he got hit by a secret report from the Secretary of Defense that indicated the most famous American atomic scientist could not be trusted. Wilson told the President, over the telephone, that he had just received a report on Oppenheimer. It consisted of a letter from William Borden, the former director of the Joint Congressional Committee on Atomic Energy, to the Secretary of Defense. Borden charged that it was "more likely than not that J. Robert Oppenheimer is a Communist spy."[25] Borden had no new evidence to substantiate this charge, which had been around a long time, had been investigated, was widely known, and was widely disbelieved. What disturbed Wilson—and Eisenhower—was not so much what

Borden was saying, but that McCarthy had become aware of the charges. It was imperative that the Administration act before McCarthy made the Oppenheimer charges his case.

The following morning, December 3, Eisenhower convened Strauss, Brownell, Wilson, Cutler, and Allen Dulles in the Oval Office. Eisenhower demanded to know how on earth Strauss could have cleared Oppenheimer for the AEC back in 1947, and why there had been no investigation of him since the Republicans took office. Strauss muttered that they could not have built the atomic bomb without Oppenheimer. Eisenhower then said that while he "wished to make it plain that he was not in any way prejudging the matter," he wanted a "blank wall" placed between Oppenheimer and any further access to top-secret information until such time as a hearing had been completed. He told Brownell to get the entire FBI file on Oppenheimer and study it. He said he had himself examined the Borden charges and thought they provided "no evidence that implies disloyalty on the part of Dr. Oppenheimer." However, Eisenhower added, "this does not mean that he might not be a security risk." Eisenhower said he realized that if Oppenheimer had been feeding information to the Soviets, then cutting him off at this point "would not be a case of merely locking the stable door after the horse is gone; it would be more like trying to find a door for a burned-down stable."[26] He appointed a three-man committee to investigate the charges; Oppenheimer meanwhile was put into a state of suspension. McCarthy was blocked from exploiting the case.

Simultaneously with the Oppenheimer case, Eisenhower had to deal with the segregation cases coming up before the Supreme Court. Unhappy with the idea of the Attorney General expressing his opinion on the unconstitutionality of segregation in the schools, Eisenhower nevertheless accepted Brownell's advice that it had to be done. Indeed, he helped Brownell write his opinion. Still he worried. As always when he got back from Augusta, Eisenhower was full of sympathy for the white southerner's point of view. He asked Brownell what would happen if the southern states abandoned public education, as they were threatening to do, and repeated his fear that the Court would make education a function of the federal government. Brownell assured him that the South "will work it out in ten to twelve years."[27]

On December 2, Brownell told Eisenhower that Justice Warren "told me last night that my brief on the segregation cases was outstanding." Eisenhower made it clear that he wanted no part for himself in the compliment.[28] He had begun the process of refusing to associate himself and his prestige in any way with *Brown* v. *Topeka*.

At 2 P.M. on December 8, Eisenhower gave his "Atoms for Peace" speech to the General Assembly. After opening words of praise for the U.N., Eisenhower launched into the Operation Candor part of his speech. It was much reduced from his original intention. He informed the world that the United States had conducted forty-two test explosions since 1945, that America's atomic bombs were now twenty-five times more powerful than the original bombs used against Japan, "while hydrogen weapons are in the ranges of millions of tons of TNT equivalent." Oppenheimer's and Jackson's thought that the President ought to reveal the size of the American arsenal gave way to this paragraph: "Today, the United States stockpile of atomic weapons, which, of course, increases daily, exceeds by many times the explosive equivalent of the total of all bombs and all shells that came from every plane and every gun in every theater of war in all of the years of World War II." Eisenhower gave one additional illustration: "A single air group can now deliver to any reachable target a destructive cargo exceeding in power all the bombs that fell on Britain in all of World War II." Atomic weapons, he added, had now achieved "virtually conventional status within our armed services."

But the Russians also had the bomb, and were building more. An atomic arms race was under way. To continue it, Eisenhower said, "would be to confirm the hopeless finality of a belief that two atomic colossi are doomed malevolently to eye each other indefinitely across a trembling world." Anything would be better. Eisenhower asserted that he was prepared to meet with the Soviets (and he announced that the four-power talks the Russians had requested would begin promptly) to discuss such problems as an Austrian treaty, Korea, and Germany, as well as disarmament.

In such talks, Eisenhower said, the United States "would seek more than the mere reduction or elimination of atomic materials for military purposes." It was not enough "to take this weapon out of the hands of the soldiers. It must be put into the hands of those who will know how . . . to adapt it to the arts of peace." Then, "this greatest of destructive forces can be developed into a great boon, for the benefit of all mankind."

Eisenhower thereupon made his specific proposal. The U.S., the U.K., and the U.S.S.R. should make joint contributions from their stockpiles of fissionable materials to an International Atomic Energy Agency. That agency would be set up under the aegis of the U.N. He recognized that initial contributions would be small, but "the proposal has the great virtue that it can be undertaken without the irritations and mutual suspicions incident to any attempt to set up a completely acceptable system of worldwide inspection and control."

The proposed agency would draw on the talents of scientists from all over the world, who would study ways to use atomic energy for peaceful activities. "A special purpose would be to provide abundant electrical energy in the power-starved areas of the world. Thus the contributing powers would be dedicating some of their strength to serve the needs rather than the fears of mankind." He outlined other advantages inherent in his proposal: a reduction in the world's atomic stockpile dedicated to destruction; proof that the superpowers were "interested in human aspirations first"; and the opening of "a new channel of peaceful discussion." He closed with a pledge: The United States was ready "to devote its entire heart and mind to find the way by which the miraculous inventiveness of man shall not be dedicated to his death, but consecrated to his life." [29]

Eisenhower had not been interrupted once by applause, and when he finished there was dead silence. Then the thirty-five hundred delegates began to cheer—even the Russians joined in—in an outburst of enthusiasm unprecedented in U.N. history. Outside the Communist countries, world reaction was overwhelmingly positive and even extravagant. Eisenhower appeared to have cut the Gordian knot. He had replaced fear with hope.

But the Russians stalled. They gave no immediate response, nor did they respond during the next year, or the next. Not until 1957 was an International Atomic Energy Agency created. By that time, the arms race had moved on to new levels and such an agency was irrelevant to current problems.

A great opportunity had been lost. Eisenhower's proposal of Atoms for Peace was the most generous and the most serious offer on controlling the arms race ever made by an American President. All previous offers, and all that followed, contained clauses about on-site inspection that the Americans knew in advance were unacceptable to the Russians. But it was the strength of Eisenhower's proposal, the measure of his genius, and the proof of his readiness to try something new to get out of the arms race that Atoms for Peace seemed to have a real chance of acceptance. It was not loaded against the Russians. Eisenhower believed that, to the contrary, the proposal had to be tempting to them. He hoped they would accept it and he thought that they would.

They did not. The Communists allowed their suspicions to override their judgment. They felt, evidently, that a reduction of their stockpile of fissionable matter would only widen the American lead. But Eisenhower had proposed contributions at a level of five American units to one Russian, and that was only a starting figure, open to negation. Still the Russians were not interested. They let the numbers frighten them. The United States might get two or three thousand bombs ahead of them.

Thus did the logic of the nuclear arms race take over. It was a logic unique to itself, with no connection to experience or reality. Everyone agreed that the sole purpose of making atomic weapons was to deter the enemy from aggression. All agreed that to deter you need only be in a position to threaten to destroy one major city. (Eisenhower once told this author, "There is nothing in the world that the Communists want badly enough to risk losing the Kremlin." [30]) Why then build arsenals of thousands of bombs, when a few hundred would be more than enough to make the threat meaningful?

At this point the numbers game took over. Strategists and leaders on both sides were terrified at the thought of the other side getting too far ahead. Eisenhower and the Americans wanted—demanded —a clear American superiority. How they would use that lead—except to insure deterrence, which could be achieved with one hundred bombs anyway—they did not know. For their part, the Russians could not accept such a huge American advantage. They were determined to close the gap, if not catch up. Like the Americans, they did not know what they were going to do with all those bombs. They only knew they wanted them.

So they spurned Eisenhower's proposed Atoms for Peace plan. It was a true tragedy. With only a bit of exaggeration, it can be said that Eisenhower's proposal was the best chance mankind has had in the nuclear age to slow and redirect the arms race. Had the Russians put their own enthusiasm into it, it is possible to project an idyllic scenario: a generation of money, energy, and scientific skill going into peaceful uses for the atom, with both sides content to maintain but not add to their existing arsenals. To Eisenhower, the worst possible outcome, as he looked ahead in 1953, would have been a continuation of the numbers game, only by the 1980s at a level of tens of thousands of bombs, and with peaceful uses of atomic power generally unexploited, or—when in place—highly controversial and expensive. But that is exactly how it turned out.

Part of the blame is Eisenhower's. He played the numbers game in nuclear weapons vigorously, although not so vigorously as all the JCS, nearly all Democrats, and most Republicans wanted him to. Atoms for Peace was his one great bid to get out of what he knew was a losing game. He had pride of authorship in the original idea, which added to his depression when the Russians stalled on the proposal. He thought his idea was worth a try, and the lack of Russian response made him harden his attitude toward the Soviet Union. He had been rebuffed on the major goal of his Presidency. His attempt to explore a new approach to arms control was never even tried. That was the sad result of Atoms for Peace.

CHAPTER FOURTEEN

McCarthy and Vietnam

EISENHOWER, on domestic politics, was neither reactionary nor reformer, but rather in the middle of the road. The result was a series of bland policies that angered the conservatives as well as the liberals but found support from a majority in Congress and the public. On health care, for example, Ike rejected Truman's proposal for national health insurance and the American Medical Association's position that there be no federal involvement in health whatsoever. Eisenhower asked for legislation that would provide federal support for the private health-insurance industry. He was opposed to a high tariff and managed to keep it down. He wanted private development of nuclear power plants, under a licensing system administered by the AEC, and he got it. On Labor Day 1954, at Shippingport, Pennsylvania, ground-breaking ceremonies marked the beginning of the first atomic power plant in America.

Eisenhower's most significant legislative victory was Social Security. He had tried to expand the system in 1953, failed to get action, and repeated his request in 1954. With an election coming in November, Republicans were more amenable to improving rather than destroying the system, and Eisenhower got a bill that increased benefits and put ten million people not previously covered into Social Security. He also got the funds for American participation in the St. Lawrence Seaway and put through a tax-revision bill that did not lower rates but did increase deductions, thereby providing a tax cut of $7.4 billion for 1954. Thanks to reductions in defense expenditures, he was bringing the budget into balance despite the tax cut.

In the spring of 1954, the country went into a mild, post-Korea recession. Eisenhower was determined that the Republican Party shed the label of "party of depression," and repeatedly warned his Cabinet and the Republican leaders that they could not afford to "get tagged like Mr. Hoover did, unjustly, of not doing anything to help in economic bad times."[1] Eisenhower spent an enormous amount of his time studying the state of the economy with his chief economics adviser, Dr. Arthur Burns, and with his associates. He was ready to move decisively in the event unemployment got much above 5 percent (it had been 2.9 percent in 1953, and peaked at 5.5 percent in 1954).

Fortunately for Eisenhower and the Republicans, the recession was short-lived. Whether the early recovery was due to the Administration's policies, or to simple good luck based on the inherent strength of the economy, was unclear. In any event the Republicans had avoided a depression, and thereby laid to rest at least some of the fear, so widely held from 1929 onward, that a Republican Administration meant widespread unemployment and an uncaring government. In the economic field, Eisenhower was approaching or realizing his major goals—a balanced budget, no inflation, tax reduction, a growing GNP, and a low rate of unemployment.

By no means were all the President's relations with Congress happy ones. His attempt to undercut McCarthy by ignoring him had failed. McCarthy continued to dominate the headlines and the White House news conferences. Eisenhower was genuinely perplexed by this situation; insofar as he felt he could explain it, he laid the blame on the news media. He told Bill Robinson, "We have here a figure who owes his entire prominence and influence in today's life to the publicity media of the nation," and he complained that "now these same media are looking around for someone to knock off the creature of their own making."[2] He wanted the press to be a part of his team, working together for the good of the country, just as the press in the war had been on his side.

On a more realistic level, Eisenhower wanted the press to provide, at a minimum, accurate reporting. At the end of January, Ellis Slater came down to spend a weekend in the White House. On Sunday morning, the two men read the papers while eating breakfast. Slater recorded that Eisenhower "remarked that after twelve years in public life, during which he had been in a position to know the real stories back of the news, he had about come to believe it was virtually impossible for a news reporter to get any story exactly right." [3]

A prime example was Secretary of the Army Robert T. Stevens' "surrender" to McCarthy. The incident had its origins in McCarthy's various investigations of Communist infiltration into the Army, which had led him to discover that a dentist, Dr. Irving Peress, who had been drafted, was a "Fifth Amendment Communist." But although Peress had refused to sign a loyalty oath, or to answer McCarthy's questions in a hearing, he had been promoted (the promotion was required by the doctors' draft law) and then given an honorable discharge. McCarthy, furious, called the Camp Kilmer commanding officer, General Ralph Zwicker, to testify. Through most of February, McCarthy's sole question of Zwicker—"Who promoted Peress?"— dominated the national news. Zwicker said he knew nothing about it. McCarthy browbeat Zwicker in the most abusive fashion, telling the general that he did not have "the brains of a five-year-old child" and that he was "not fit to wear" his uniform. Stevens then ordered Zwicker not to testify further. McCarthy thereupon ordered Stevens himself to appear before his committee. On February 24, Stevens had lunch with McCarthy in Everett Dirksen's Senate office. McCarthy promised to stop abusing witnesses in return for Stevens' promise to permit further testimony by Zwicker and to release "the names of everyone involved in the promotion and honorable discharge of Peress." [4]

When Stevens emerged, McCarthy beside him, the reporters and photographers were waiting. McCarthy announced that Stevens had agreed that he and his subordinates would come back to the hearings. He neglected to add that he in turn had promised to act responsibly, and Stevens did not think to point this out to the press.

As the newspapers then broke the story, Eisenhower and his Administration had surrendered. *The New York Times* headlined its story, "Stevens Bows to McCarthy at Administration Behest. Will Yield Data on Peress." Eisenhower, returning from a speaking trip to California, was "very mad and getting fed up." Hagerty noted in his diary, "it's his Army and he doesn't like McCarthy's tactics at all." Eisenhower swore, "This guy McCarthy is going to get into trouble over this. I'm not going to take this one lying down . . . He's ambitious. He wants to be President. He's the last guy in the whole world who'll ever get there, if I have anything to say." [5]

Behind the scenes, Eisenhower was meeting with Dirksen and

Senator Karl Mundt, extracting from them promises to make Joe behave. But his more significant act was a telephone call he placed to Brownell. His subject was the power of a committee of Congress to subpoena. "I suppose the President can refuse to comply," Eisenhower said, "but when it comes down to people down the line appointed to office, I don't know what the answer is. I would like to have a brief memo on precedent, etc.—just what I can do in this regard."[6] Eisenhower thereupon prepared the foundation for what would be his sole significant action against McCarthy, denial of access to executive personnel and records.

On March 3, Eisenhower had a prepared statement for his news conference. He said that the Army had made "serious errors" in the Peress case, that it was correcting its procedures, and that he had complete confidence in Stevens. He then read some homilies about McCarthyism ("In opposing Communism, we are defeating ourselves if we use methods that do not conform to the American sense of justice"), about the Army (it was "completely loyal and dedicated"), and about Congress (which had a responsibility "to see to it that its procedures are proper and fair"). After asserting his own "vigilance against any kind of internal subversion," Eisenhower ended curtly: "and that is my last word on any subject even closely related to that particular matter."[7]

McCarthy answered within the hour. He declared defiantly that "if a stupid, arrogant, or witless man in a position of power appears before our committee and is found aiding the Communist Party, he will be exposed. The fact that he might be a general places him in no special class as far as I am concerned." Then, in a classic McCarthyism, delivered by the master himself, McCarthy said, "apparently the President and I now agree on the necessity of getting rid of Communists." To make sure his followers got the point, he publicly deleted the "now" a half hour later.[8]

Still Eisenhower held back from any direct attack against McCarthy. He continued to urge the Republican senatorial leaders, especially Knowland, Dirksen, and Mundt, to keep the Army-McCarthy hearings (which were about to begin) orderly and fair. He told his Cabinet, in a formal memorandum, that "each superior, including me, must remember the obligations he has to his subordinates. These comprise . . . the protection of those subordinates, through all legal and proper means available, against attacks of a character under which they otherwise might be helpless."[9] Beyond that, he would not go. His belief was that McCarthyism was based on fear, and that the fear would subside, and McCarthy would lose his power and influence as the nation concentrated its interest on matters of substance.

Much of Eisenhower's incoming mail was telling him that McCarthy "has it within his power to destroy our system of government." He scoffed at the notion: "When the proposition is stated as baldly as this, then it becomes instantly ridiculous." He also scoffed at Adlai Stevenson's charge, "that the Republican Party was one-half Eisenhower and one-half McCarthy." When asked at a news conference to comment, Eisenhower replied "At the risk of appearing egotistical, I say 'nonsense.' " [10]

Thus Eisenhower decided, again, that McCarthy was not so great a threat to the nation or to the party as so many feared. But the forces McCarthy represented, and the methods he used, were another matter. "There is a certain reactionary fringe of the Republican Party that hates and despises everything for which I stand," he told Robinson. He thought if the Republican leaders had done their job, McCarthy would have long since been relegated to his proper sphere. Knowland, especially, had let him down; Eisenhower wrote of the majority leader in the Senate, "It is a pity that his wisdom, his judgment, his tact, and his sense of humor lag so far behind his ambition." As to McCarthy's methods, Eisenhower said, "I despise them." [11]

Nevertheless, he thought that his many close friends who were urging him to publicly label McCarthy with derogatory titles were badly mistaken. It would make "the Presidency ridiculous and in the long run make the citizens of our country very unhappy indeed." Instead of speaking out, he would stick to his lifelong principle, so often stated so vehemently: "To avoid public mention of any name unless it can be done with favorable intent and connotation; reserve all criticism for the private conference; speak only good in public." [12]

Sound principle, but there were other principles Eisenhower also held, one of which was loyalty. He was, after all, not only the Commander in Chief but also the former Chief of Staff of an Army that McCarthy was viciously attacking. He was also the Supreme Commander of 1944; under his orders, General Zwicker, a West Pointer, had gone ashore on D-Day as chief of staff for the 2d Division, been wounded, and won a decoration. Since the war, Zwicker had had a distinguished career. Now Eisenhower was standing aside while McCarthy told Zwicker that he was not fit to wear the uniform. One might have thought that such assaults on such targets would have brought Eisenhower charging into the action. He himself had said (of the Republican senatorial leaders), "They do not seem to realize when there arrives that moment at which soft speaking should be abandoned and a fight to the end undertaken. Any man who hopes to exercise leadership must be ready to meet this requirement face to face when it arises; unless he is ready to fight when necessary, people will finally begin to ignore him." [13] But despite McCarthy's extreme provocations, Eisenhower was not ready to abandon soft speaking.

The next storm broke when McCarthy announced that he would hold his seat as a voting member of the committee, despite the fact that he was on trial as much as the Army was (the Army charged that Roy Cohn, counsel to McCarthy's subcommittee, had used his position to exert pressure for special favors for G. David Schine, Cohn's former associate, who had been drafted). At a news-conference briefing, Eisenhower's aides were split on how to respond. Jerry Persons, always the most conservative of the advisers, wanted the President to say that McCarthy's vote was a matter for the Senate to decide. Hagerty, Cutler, and others said that the President was the moral leader of the nation and that if he did not speak out he would "get murdered on this one." Eisenhower stopped their arguing by announcing, "Look, I know exactly what I am going to say. I'm going to say he [McCarthy] can't sit as a judge. I've made up my mind you can't do business with Joe and to hell with any attempt to compromise." [14]

At his news conference, he was not quite so tough. "I am perfectly ready to put myself on record flatly," he said, "that in America, if a man is a party to a dispute, directly or indirectly, he does not sit in judgment on his own case, and I don't believe that any leadership can escape responsibility for carrying on that tradition." [15] No one could disagree with that statement, and so McCarthy was considered "spanked," and he abandoned his demand to have a vote, although he did retain his right to cross-examine witnesses. And, of course, the right to subpoena.

It was this last point that had Eisenhower worried. He did not want McCarthy running rampage, demanding that personnel from the Executive Branch appear before him, and that they produce records. McCarthyism was the result of fear, the President had insisted, but he was reluctant to admit that he also was afraid. He feared that McCarthy would get into the records or haul government officials before him. On March 29, he again asked Brownell to prepare a statement that he could use in the event that he had to order his subordinates not to appear before McCarthy.

What Eisenhower feared specifically was the Oppenheimer case. Eisenhower's withholding of Oppenheimer's top-secret clearance, pending investigation, had been done secretly, but inevitably word was getting out. What bothered Eisenhower most was that McCarthy had just charged that the H-bomb development had been held up for eighteen months "because of Reds in the government." Joe's statement was getting uncomfortably close to Oppenheimer.

"We have to move fast," Hagerty noted, "before McCarthy breaks the Oppenheimer investigation and it then becomes our scandal." Hagerty worried about the public-relations aspects: "It's just a question of time before someone cracks it wide open and everything hits the fan—if this breaks it will be the biggest news we've had down here yet—real hot."[16] Eisenhower worried about something much bigger than public relations; his concern was the morale of the nation's scientists and the state of the nation's defenses.

The seriousness Eisenhower assigned to keeping McCarthy out of the Oppenheimer case was best illustrated by the fact that the President spent most of three full days, April 9 through 11, on the Oppenheimer matter. Strauss gave the President information that made it clear Oppenheimer had indeed tried to delay the H-bomb project. Eisenhower was not particularly concerned about the politics of Oppenheimer's wife, or those of his brother and sister-in-law, or even about Oppenheimer's having lied, under oath, about his associations. Eisenhower respected the man for his accomplishments, thought that such a unique genius should be given maximum leeway for idiosyncrasies, even in politics, and had been impressed by the moral arguments Oppenheimer had made against the H-bomb.

What Eisenhower found inexcusable was that once Truman had made the decision to go ahead with the H-bomb, Oppenheimer did not get on the team. Worse, he tried to slow down the project. Eisenhower wanted him removed from all contact with the AEC, because he did not want to give Oppenheimer the opportunity to spread moral doubts in the minds of the scientists. Oppenheimer's removal from the AEC had to be done carefully, however, because of his unique stature and prestige among his fellow scientists, men on whom the fate of the nuclear arms race rested. Eisenhower also did not want to let McCarthy give the country the impression that all scientists were disloyal. "We've got to handle this so that all our scientists are not made out to be Reds," Eisenhower told Hagerty. "That goddamn McCarthy is just likely to try such a thing."[17]

Adding to the difficulties, as Hagerty noted, was that "McCarthy knows about case and it was Nixon who talked him out of using it earlier because of security reasons." And Hagerty realized, as did

Eisenhower, that McCarthy, "with back to wall, could easily try to get out from under by splashing Oppenheimer."[18]

So Eisenhower decided to back off, or rather to stay backed off, from McCarthy. He would not push the senator, but allowed events to run their course, including ignoring McCarthy's gross insults to Zwicker, hoping that McCarthy would not get so far back against the wall that he opened an Oppenheimer investigation. When Eisenhower was asked at a news conference about McCarthy's charge of an eighteen-month delay in the H-bomb, he denied any knowledge of it at all. "I never heard of any delay on my part, never heard of it." Even in his memoirs, written after the accusation had been made that Oppenheimer had been removed from the AEC because of his opposition to the H-bomb, Eisenhower said, "Certainly I . . . gave no weight to this fact."

Also in his memoirs, Eisenhower said his main concern about the Army-McCarthy hearings was that they be done "with minimum publicity and maximum dispatch."[19] He certainly failed in that goal. But his real aim was to keep McCarthy away from Oppenheimer, and to avoid a debate among scientists about the morality of working for the government on the H-bomb. In this goal he succeeded brilliantly.

The hearings began on April 22 and dragged on for two months. They were on national TV and attracted a huge and fascinated audience. McCarthy got maximum publicity with minimum dispatch— indeed, too much publicity. The senator had put himself into an impossible position. He could only destroy himself before the biggest audience of his career. Eisenhower watched the spectacle on TV as fascinated and appalled as everyone else. "The McCarthy-Army argument, and its reporting, are close to disgusting," he told Swede Hazlett. "It saddens me that I must feel ashamed for the United States Senate."[20] As the spring wore on, he was content to watch McCarthy hang himself, and quite pleased that the subject of the H-bomb never came up in the hearings.

The H-bomb was very much at the center of the President's attention. On March 1, the AEC had detonated a multimegaton nuclear device on Bikini Island. Code named Bravo, the blast was the first in a series called Castle. Eisenhower had given his approval to Castle after being told by Strauss that it was probable that the Russians were ahead in H-bomb technology. The device the AEC had set off in November 1952 had not been small enough to carry in an airplane, while the Russians seemed to have accomplished that goal in their test. American scientists needed to increase their efforts, which was one reason Eisenhower was so concerned about the Oppenheimer case breaking just as the United States prepared to start Castle.

Eisenhower wanted to keep the tests themselves secret too, but it proved impossible to hide them. Among other problems, a Japanese fishing boat had been showered with radiation, the crew fell ill, and the Japanese government and people raised a roar of protest. On March 24, at a news conference, Eisenhower decided he had to respond to persistent questions about radiation, even though he had promised Hagerty he would tell reporters to wait for Strauss' return from the Pacific testing grounds. Eisenhower told the press, "It is quite clear that this time something must have happened that we have never experienced before, and must have surprised and astonished the scientists. Very properly, the United States has to take precautions that never occurred to them before."[21]

The President's admission allowed the reporters to speculate that the H-bomb testing had gotten out of hand, that the blast was uncontrollable. Then on March 30 the AEC, no longer attempting to hide the basic testing, announced that a second H-bomb had been tested that morning. That led to more concerned headlines. Meanwhile, Strauss had returned to Washington, and on March 31 Eisenhower took him to his news conference. Eisenhower had told Strauss to read a prepared statement "setting at ease fears that bombs had gotten out of control," then answer questions about Bravo, and finally try to relieve people's worries.

Strauss told the press that Bravo was never out of control, that the main problem had been a shift in wind that blew the radioactive material over the Japanese fishing boat, that there was no truth to stories about contaminated tuna fish or about radioactive currents moving on Japan, and that overall the fallout danger was being greatly exaggerated. The radioactivity would disappear quickly, but the military gains for the United States would be enduring. He said that the nation should "rejoice" that the tests had been so successful and that "enormous potential has been added to our military posture by what we have learned."

That piqued the reporters' curiosity, and one of them asked how big an H-bomb might be made. Strauss replied, "It can be made to be as large as you wish, as large as the military requirement demands, that is to say, an H-bomb can be made as—large enough to take out a city." Cries of "What?" went up around the room. "How big a city?"

"Any city," Strauss replied. "Any city, New York?" "The metropolitan area, yes."[22]

On the way back to the Oval Office, Eisenhower told Strauss, "Lewis, I wouldn't have answered that one that way." Instead, the President said, Strauss should have told the reporters to "wait for the movie." He was referring to a movie the AEC had made on Bravo. Eisenhower said he wanted the truth told—"Hell, I'd let everyone see the movie," he told Hagerty. "That's the purpose of it, to let everyone in." But then he let Strauss change his mind and decided not to release the movie, for fear of frightening people even further.[23]

The Oppenheimer case, meanwhile, became public knowledge when the committee Eisenhower had charged with investigating Oppenheimer reported, by two to one, that while Oppenheimer was not disloyal, he had "fundamental defects of character" and therefore recommended that his security clearance be taken away. (By a vote of 4 to 1, with Strauss leading the way, the AEC later upheld that decision.) The announcement of the committee recommendation met Hagerty's objective of beating McCarthy to the headlines on Oppenheimer, but it also set off the split that Eisenhower had feared in the American scientific community. The ensuing uproar also met Eisenhower's objective of keeping the development of the H-bomb out of the debate. The ugly charge of anti-Semitism was hurled about, and Oppenheimer's supporters said that Eisenhower had done it only to appease McCarthy. Eisenhower was careful to point out that he was not punishing Oppenheimer in any way, nor finding him guilty of anything, merely separating him from the AEC. He was not even averse to having Oppenheimer work for the government, if the project was safe enough. "Why do we not get Dr. Oppenheimer interested in desalting sea water?" Eisenhower wrote to Strauss.[24] And in a press conference, he was ready to praise Oppenheimer, albeit in a rather muddled way: "I have known Dr. Oppenheimer and, like others, I have certainly admired and respected his very great professional and technical attainments; and this is something that is the kind of thing that must be gone through with what I believe is best not talked about too much until we know whatever answers there may be."[25] And with that, and with the end of the Castle series, and with the Army-McCarthy hearings reaching their height, the public interest in Bravo and its implications faded.

Throughout the period of Castle and the announcement about lifting Oppenheimer's security clearance, Eisenhower complained about the way in which the Army-McCarthy hearings were detracting public attention from the real issues. But he was the chief beneficiary. He wanted Bravo and Oppenheimer kept as quiet as possible, and McCarthy diverted enough attention so that few noticed, in the spring of 1954, that Eisenhower had launched the United States into an H-Bomb race with the Soviets, including a race to build intercontinental missiles. Eisenhower had made momentous decisions about this most critical of issues, and had done so with a minimum of public debate. He had even managed to keep Oppenheimer's dismissal from raising the question of the morality of building the H-bomb.

Eisenhower, depressed by the failure of the Russians to respond to Atoms for Peace, was fully committed to the H-bomb. It had become the centerpiece of his strategy, and of his defense policy. It had allowed him to cut spending while increasing America's nuclear lead. It made possible the "New Look," as Wilson's Pentagon public-relations people called it—fewer conventional forces, more atomic firepower, less cost.

The basic structure of the New Look was an expanded strategic air force and a much-reduced conventional force on land and at sea. It depended upon a huge American lead in nuclear weapons. Critics, led by Army Chief of Staff Matthew Ridgway, charged that it was unbalanced and thereby forced America into an "all or nothing" posture. Ridgway was right, of course, as Dulles made clear in a mid-January speech, when he announced that Eisenhower and the NSC had made a "basic decision" that in the future the United States would confront any possible aggression by "a great capacity to retaliate instantly by means and places of our own choosing." Eisenhower, asked to comment, said that Dulles "was merely stating what, to my mind, is a fundamental truth and really doesn't take much decision; it is just a fundamental truth." [26]

But that only deepened and did not elucidate the mystery. If American policy was to retaliate instantly and massively against Soviet aggression, what happened to the congressional power to declare war? In March, Dulles explained: "If the Russians attacked one of America's allies, there was no need for the President to go to Congress for a declaration of war." Congress was unhappy with that response; so were the reporters. Through the spring, they pressed Eisenhower for clarification.

He explained that "there is a difference between an act of war and declaring war." If he was faced with a Soviet assault against the

United States, "a gigantic Pearl Harbor," he would act instantaneously, but he would also assemble Congress as fast as possible, because "after all, you can't carry on a war without Congress." As to the precise legal and constitutional question, Eisenhower admitted, "I could be mistaken, and I would not argue it." In a sentence that said volumes about the Eisenhower-Dulles relationship, the President added, "I would like to discuss it with Foster Dulles, but having talked to him, I am sure that we are absolutely in agreement as to what we mean about it."

The point was that the reporters wanted to know what he meant by "it." Did it mean that if there was a war in Korea or that Americans decided to support the French in Vietnam, nuclear weapons would be delivered against Moscow or Peiping? "No war ever shows the characteristics that were expected," Eisenhower replied. "It is always different." Avoiding the question of how massive retaliation could work in a small war far outside Russian or Chinese borders, Eisenhower returned to the Pearl Harbor theme, again warning that in the age of nuclear weapons a surprise attack could be horrendous. Under those circumstances, if the President did not act immediately, he "should be worse than impeached, he should be hanged."[27]

The war raging in Vietnam made the subject of massive retaliation more than academic. The French were holding their own, but barely. Paris was weary of war. The cost, in lives and money, had become unendurable. For the Americans, too, the situation was intolerable. A continued stalemate would drain French resources to such an extent that France would never be able to meet its NATO obligations, always a prime consideration with Eisenhower. Further, the French were demanding more American money, and even American planes and troops, and they were simultaneously using EDC, which Eisenhower very much wanted, to blackmail the United States. Without support in Indochina, the French were saying, they could not ratify EDC.

A French defeat in Vietnam would be worse than continued stalemate. There was first of all global strategic balance to consider. There was in addition the political position of the Republican Party to be considered. A major theme of Eisenhower's campaign had been a rejection of containment and an adoption of a policy of liberation. Now the Republicans had been in power for more than a year. They had failed to liberate any Communist slave anywhere. In Korea they had accepted an armistice that left North Korea in Communist hands.

Eisenhower was keenly aware that by far his most popular act had been to achieve peace in Korea, but he was just as aware that Republican orators had been demanding to know, ever since 1949, "Who lost China?" Could he afford to allow Democrats to ask, "Who lost Vietnam?" He told his Cabinet he could not.

The obvious way out of the quandary was a French victory, but the problem was how to achieve it without introducing American planes and troops. Under no circumstances was Eisenhower going to send American troops back onto the Asian mainland less than a year after signing an armistice in Korea. Even had he wanted to do that, the New Look precluded such an effort—the troops simply were not available.

Eisenhower did increase direct American military assistance to the French. How much of the war the Americans were paying for at this time is impossible to say because the figures were hidden in so many different ways, but the general estimate is around 75 percent. The French now wanted twenty-five bombers and four hundred Air Force personnel to service them; Eisenhower gave them ten bombers and two hundred people.

On February 8, at a meeting of Republican leaders, Senator Leverett Saltonstall anxiously raised the question about American servicemen going to Indochina. Was yet another President, this one a Republican, going to take the country into yet another war by the back door? That was Saltonstall's implied question, and Eisenhower took it seriously. He carefully explained his reason for giving U.S. Air Force weapons to the French to be used against the Vietminh, and assured Saltonstall that none of the personnel would be in a combat zone. Eisenhower admitted that he was "frightened about getting ground forces tied up in Indochina," and promised that he would pull all two hundred men out of the area on June 15.[28]

Still, for all Eisenhower's emphasis on reduced numbers and a definite date for withdrawal, he had sent the first American military personnel to Vietnam. Of course, as Eisenhower insisted, it was hardly an irrevocable step. But still, it had been taken. He was worried about what it might lead to. Earlier, in January, he had told the NSC (in the words of the stenographer), "For himself, said the President with great force, he simply could not imagine the United States putting ground forces anywhere in Southeast Asia, except possibly in Malaya, which we have to defend as a bulwark to our offshore island chain. But to do this anywhere else, said the President with vehemence, how bitterly opposed I am to such a course of action. This war in Indochina would absorb our troops by divisions!"[29]

Long before the Gulf of Tonkin Resolution of 1964, Eisenhower was even more emphatic and prophetic about an American ground involvement in Vietnam. When writing his presidential memoirs, in 1963, he declared, "The jungles of Indochina . . . would have swallowed up division after division of United States troops, who, unaccustomed to this kind of warfare, would have sustained heavy casualties. . . . Furthermore, the presence of ever more numbers of white men in uniform probably would have aggravated rather than assuaged Asiatic resentments."[30] (When he published the memoirs, nearly a year later, he deleted that passage, because by then the country was getting involved in Vietnam and he did not want to be critical of the President.) Nevertheless, throughout the long period in 1954 of the French agony at Dien Bien Phu a grim specter dominated his thinking.

In mid-March, the upbeat reports from Vietnam suddenly reversed. Allen Dulles said the French now felt they had only a 50-50 chance at Dien Bien Phu. Furthermore, French Premier René Pleven told Ambassador to France Douglas Dillon that "there was no longer the prospect of a satisfactory military solution."[31]

On March 23 French Army Chief of Staff Paul Ely came to Washington to discuss increasing the flow of American material. Eisenhower and Dulles had a series of meetings with Ely. He wanted additional American aircraft, while Eisenhower pressed him on the status of granting independence. Finally, Eisenhower agreed to furnish the French with some C-119 Flying Boxcars that could drop napalm, "which would burn out a considerable area and help to reveal enemy artillery positions." But Eisenhower would not commit the United States to any military policy of direct intervention until he "got a lot of answers" from Paris on outstanding issues, primarily EDC and Indochinese independence.[32]

Then Eisenhower set about building the support he would need to withstand the strident demands for intervention that he knew would come when Dien Bien Phu fell. He did so by putting conditions on American involvement. They were deliberately created to be impossible of fulfillment, and there were a number of them. First, a full and clear grant of independence by the French. Second, British participation in any venture. Third, at least some of the nations of Southeast Asia had to be involved. Fourth, Congress had to give full and clear prior approval. Fifth, he would want the French to turn the war over to the Americans, but keep their troops in combat. Sixth, the French had to prove that they were not just asking the Americans to cover a fighting withdrawal.

Eisenhower's conditions, impossible as they were, seemed to him to be based on principles that could not be broken. As Dulles told Ely point-blank, the United States could "not afford to send its flag and its own military establishment and thus to engage the prestige of the United States," unless it expected to win. Eisenhower expressed for himself another basic principle, when in an unpublished portion of his memoirs he wrote that "the strongest reason of all for the United States [to stay out] is the fact that among all the powerful nations of the world the United States is the only one with a tradition of anti-colonialism. . . . The standing of the United States as the most powerful of the anti-colonial powers is an asset of incalculable value to the Free World . . . The moral position of the United States was more to be guarded than the Tonkin Delta, indeed than all of Indochina." [33]

So Eisenhower refused to go very far in meeting Ely's demands. The French general went to Radford, who was much more forthcoming. Together they approved joint U.S.-French plans, made in Saigon, for Operation Vulture, an air strike against the Vietminh around Dien Bien Phu. Ely's hope, and Radford's, was that as the end drew near at Dien Bien Phu, Eisenhower could not resist the pressure to intervene. Indeed, some of Eisenhower's aides thought that the French were deliberately losing at Dien Bien Phu in order to force an American intervention.

On the morning of April 5, Dulles called Eisenhower to inform him that the French had told Ambassador Dillon that their impression was that Operation Vulture had been agreed to, and hinted that they expected two or three atomic bombs to be used against the Vietminh. Eisenhower told Dulles to tell the French, through Dillon, that they must have misunderstood Radford. Eisenhower said that "such a move is impossible," that without congressional support an air strike would be "completely unconstitutional and indefensible." He told Dulles to "take a look to see if anything else can be done," then again warned, "We cannot engage in active war." [34]

So Eisenhower had rejected intervention. But he had not decided to leave Southeast Asia to its own devices. He very definitely wanted to form a regional grouping that could draw a line and thus institute a policy of containment. As Truman had done in Europe in the late forties, Eisenhower would seal off the Communists in Southeast Asia. To achieve that goal, he first of all had to convince Congress, the American people, and the potential allies that Indochina was worth the effort. After all, if the Americans were not ready to fight beside the French, why should they, or anyone else, be prepared to fight for whatever was left of a non-Communist Indochina?

At his April 7 news conference, Eisenhower made his most important—and his most famous—declaration on Indochina. Robert Richards of Copley Press asked him to comment on the strategic importance of Indochina to the free world. Eisenhower replied that first of all, "You have the specific value of a locality in its production of materials that the world needs." Second, "You have the possibility that many human beings pass under a dictatorship that is inimical to the free world." Finally, "You have the broader considerations that might follow what you would call the 'falling domino' principle. You have a row of dominoes set up, you knock over the first one, and what will happen to the last one is the certainty that it will go over very quickly. So you could have a beginning of a disintegration that would have the most profound influences." He thought that the "sequence of events," if the United States abandoned Southeast Asia altogether, would be the loss of all of Indochina, then Burma, then Thailand, then Malaya, then Indonesia. "Now you begin to talk about areas that not only multiply the disadvantages that you would suffer through loss of materials, sources of materials, but now you are talking really about millions and millions of people." Even worse, the loss of Southeast Asia would be followed by the probable loss of Japan, Formosa, and the Philippines, which would then threaten Australia and New Zealand.[35]

By April 23, the situation at Dien Bien Phu had become desperate. Dulles sent a series of alarming cables to Eisenhower. "France is almost visibly collapsing under our eyes," the Secretary declared. He deplored the worldwide publicity being given to Dien Bien Phu, because "it seems to me that Dien Bien Phu has become a symbol out of all proportion to its military importance." Dulles insisted that there was "no military or logical reason why loss of Dien Bien Phu should lead to collapse of French will, in relation both to Indochina and EDC." In another cable, Dulles said the French insisted there were only two alternatives; Operation Vulture or a request for cease-fire. (There was great confusion about Vulture; Radford, Ely, and Nixon all believed it involved three atomic bombs, while Dulles thought it would be a "massive B-29 bombing" by U.S. planes using conventional bombs.)[36]

Eisenhower wrote a long, thoughtful letter to Al Gruenther, Supreme Allied Commander, Europe (SACEUR), whom he depended upon as his most reliable link to the French leadership. After repeating once again that unilateral American intervention was out of the question ("it would lay us open to the charge of imperialism and colonialism or—at the very least—of objectionable paternalism"), Eisenhower complained that "ever since 1945 France has been unable to decide whether she most fears Russia or Germany. As a consequence, her policies in Europe have been nothing but confusion; starts and stops; advances and retreats!" Eisenhower said of Dien Bien Phu, "This spectacle has been saddening indeed. It seems incredible that a nation which had only the help of a tiny British Army when it turned back the German flood in 1914 and withstood the gigantic 1916 attacks at Verdun could now be reduced to the point that she cannot produce a few hundred technicians to keep planes flying properly in Indochina." Eisenhower thought the French problem was one of leadership and spirit. "The only hope is to produce a new and inspirational leader—and I do *not* mean one that is 6 feet 5 and who considers himself to be, by some miraculous biological and transmigrative process, the offspring of Clemenceau and Jeanne d'Arc."

Then Eisenhower turned serious, ticking off points he wanted Gruenther to make to the French. The loss of Dien Bien Phu did not mean the loss of the war. Eisenhower wanted the French Army to remain in Vietnam and promised that "additional ground forces should come from Asiatic and European troops already in the region" (that is, there would be no American troops but America would pay the bills). The French should grant independence. The ultimate goal, Eisenhower told the SACEUR to pass on to the French, was to create a "concert of nations" in Southeast Asia on the NATO model.[37]

This was Eisenhower's first direct mention of the idea of a Southeast Asia Treaty Organization (SEATO), and it was significant that he made it to the SACEUR. He thought first of NATO. His own vehement anti-Communism certainly played the major role in his Vietnam policy, tempered of course by his realism, but his anxieties about the French were also important considerations. He felt the French had to be dealt with like children. He had to support Pleven, now reportedly his only hope for getting EDC ratified by the French. And if EDC failed, German rearmament would be even more difficult to achieve. And without German rearmament, NATO would continue to be a hollow shell. In some part, then, SEATO came about because of the needs of NATO.

On May 1, Cutler brought the President a draft of an NSC paper that was exploring the possibilities of using atomic bombs in Vietnam.

Eisenhower told Cutler, "I certainly do not think that the atom bomb can be used by the United States unilaterally." He went on, "You boys must be crazy. We can't use those awful things against Asians for the second time in less than ten years. My God."[38]

On May 7, Dien Bien Phu surrendered. Eisenhower tried to keep up the pretense that the French had lost only a battle, not the war. He told the NSC of his "firm belief that two, and only two, developments would really save the situation in French Indochina." First, Paris had to grant independence; second, the French needed to appoint a better general to take charge of the campaign. The French could still win, but time was running out. Cutler then joined Nixon and Stassen in again urging a unilateral American intervention. Eisenhower ignored them.[39]

So Eisenhower's policy was set: to accept partition, although only after obstructing and delaying the process as long as possible, and then to create SEATO. He had managed to avoid involvement in the war, but he was determined to make as firm a commitment to the non-Communist remainder of Southeast Asia as America had made to the NATO countries.

Of all Eisenhower's reasons for staying out of Vietnam, the one that meant most to him was the potential effect of intervention on the American people. The Korean War had been divisive enough; Eisenhower shuddered to think of the consequences of getting into a war to fight for a French colony less than a year after the armistice in Korea. That was the reason for his stress on prior congressional approval; if he could get it, he would be leading a united nation. But he doubted that he could get it, precisely because the nation was badly divided.

Eisenhower's decision to stay out of Vietnam did not have the dramatic quality to it that his 1944 D-Day decision had, because it was made over a longer period of time. Nevertheless, it was as decisive, in its way, because in both cases what happened next depended solely upon his word. At any time in the last weeks of Dien Bien Phu he could have ordered an air strike, either atomic or conventional. Many of his senior advisers wanted him to do just that, including his chairman of the JCS, his Vice-President, his head of the NSC planning staff, his MSA adviser, and (sometimes) his Secretary of State. Eisenhower said no, decisively. He had looked at the military options, with his professional eye, and pronounced them unsatisfactory. On June 5, 1944, they had been satisfactory, and he said go; in April 1954, they were unsatisfactory, and he said don't go.

From that moment on, Eisenhower supporters could claim, "He got us out of Korea and he kept us out of Vietnam."

In his memoirs, Eisenhower complained that the day Dien Bien Phu fell, the banner headlines covered not that event but rather McCarthy's demand for a test of Eisenhower's right to use executive privilege to bar secret data to congressional investigators. Ten years later, Eisenhower said, it was plain to see that the action in Vietnam was far more important than McCarthy, who "ceased to command public attention shortly after that day in history."[40] What Eisenhower could not know was that almost exactly *twenty* years later the precedent of executive privilege he created would be used by Nixon in his response to Watergate. In May 1974 it would not have been quite so self-evident that the headline writers had put the wrong story on top back in 1954.

Eisenhower took McCarthy's demand far more seriously than he implied in his memoirs. In March, he had asked the Attorney General if the President could order federal personnel not to appear before McCarthy on the grounds that they were being abused. The reply was that there was no such precedent. On May 3 and 5, Eisenhower asked for further briefs on his power to withhold confidential information from Congress.

What bothered Eisenhower was how far down he could extend the blank wall. On May 11, Wilson called him to report that the McCarthy committee had demanded the names of all Army personnel who had any connection with the Peress case. Wilson said that Ridgway "violently objected" to this, and asked Eisenhower what to do. Eisenhower said that in this case the Army had better give in to avoid the appearance of a "cover-up."[41]

Two days later, McCarthy was threatening to subpoena White House personnel. Eisenhower began to feel the pressure. In a conference with Adams and Hagerty, Eisenhower said it might be necessary to send one man from the White House, probably Adams, before the committee. He should give his name, and title, and then refuse to answer all questions under presidential order.

The following day, May 14, Eisenhower told Hagerty that he was not even going to send Adams. "Congress has absolutely no right to ask them to testify in any way, shape, or form about the advice that they were giving to me at any time on any subject." Eisenhower was angrier than he had ever been with McCarthy, because McCarthy had now pushed him to the point where he had to act. His response to McCarthy's demands had become the central issue. With Adams, Lodge, and the others before his committee, McCarthy could have a field day. It made Eisenhower shudder to think what McCarthy might bring up. Worst of all would be Oppenheimer.

What was at stake, as Eisenhower saw it, was the modern Presidency. Previous Presidents had been exceedingly reluctant to withhold information or witnesses from Congress, and Brownell was never able to find any convincing precedent for a doctrine of executive privilege. What Eisenhower felt so keenly was the *need* for such a doctrine for a President in the nuclear age. The reason there were no precedents was precisely because the situation was unprecedented. There were so many things Eisenhower felt he had to keep secret, like Oppenheimer, the H-bomb tests, the CIA's covert activities, and a host of others, that he was willing to vastly expand the powers of the Presidency to do it. He told Hagerty, "If they want to make a test of this principle, I'll fight them tooth and nail and up and down the country. It is a matter of principle with me and I will never permit it." [42]

On May 17, at a leaders' meeting, Eisenhower said that "any man who testifies as to the advice he gave me won't be working for me that night. I will not allow people around me to be subpoenaed and you might just as well know it now." Knowland protested that it would be a terrible thing if Eisenhower challenged Congress' right to subpoena. Eisenhower repeated that "my people are not going to be subpoenaed." [43]

That afternoon, Eisenhower released a letter to Wilson, directing Wilson to withhold information from the committee. The President put his case in sweeping terms: "It is essential to efficient and effective administration that employees of the Executive Branch be in a position to be completely candid in advising with each other on official matters." Therefore "it is not in the public interest that *any* of their conversations or communications, or *any* documents or reproductions, concerning such advice be disclosed." [44] This was the most absolute assertion of presidential right to withhold information from Congress ever uttered to that day in American history. Earlier Presidents had held that their conversations in Cabinet meetings were privileged and confidential, but none had ever dared extend this privilege to *everybody* in the Executive Branch. Congress was upset, Republicans and Democrats alike.

McCarthy was livid. His real source of power was the power to subpoena, and he knew at once that his whole career was at stake. He therefore made a public appeal to federal employees to disregard Eisenhower's orders and report directly to him on "graft, corruption, Communism, and treason." Eisenhower took up the challenge. When Hagerty discussed McCarthy's appeal with Eisenhower, the red-faced President damned "the complete arrogance of McCarthy." Pacing around the room, speaking in rapid-fire order, Eisenhower said, "This amounts to nothing but a wholesale subversion of public service . . . McCarthy is deliberately trying to subvert the people we have in government. I think this is the most disloyal act we have ever had by anyone in the government of the United States."

Eisenhower told Hagerty to make sure the subject came up at his next press conference, so that he would have the opportunity to tell the reporters "that in my opinion this is the most arrogant invitation to subversion and disloyalty that I have ever heard of. I won't stand for it for one minute."[45] But between the time of that discussion and the press conference, Eisenhower spent another afternoon on the Oppenheimer case. He was beginning to think that the case was even worse than he had feared, that Oppenheimer really was a Communist, and really had significantly held back H-bomb development. But whatever the facts, Eisenhower remained determined to avoid a public debate on Oppenheimer, with its probable demoralizing effect on the atomic scientists. So he did not want to push McCarthy too far against the wall. He did not deliver the rough treatment that he had promised to give McCarthy at the press conference; instead he refused to answer any questions on the subject. He simply held to his order on executive privilege.

The Army-McCarthy hearings droned on to their doleful conclusion. On June 18, the day after they ended, Eisenhower called Army counsel Joseph Welch to the Oval Office, where he congratulated Welch on his prosecution of the Army's case. Welch said that the only good thing to come out of the hearings was that they had given the nation an opportunity to see McCarthy in action. Eisenhower agreed.

And that indeed was the effective end of McCarthy. He still retained considerable strength in the polls, he still had his committee chairmanship, but he no longer had the power to frighten. The Army-McCarthy hearings had degenerated to ridiculous points of trivia, primarily because Eisenhower denied to the committee access to people and records that could have provided McCarthy with sensational disclosures. But with nothing substantial to go after, McCarthy was reduced to ranting and raving (and increasingly heavy drinking), which cost him his credibility. It was not the things Eisenhower did behind the scenes but rather his most public act, the assertion of the right of executive privilege, that was his major contribution to McCarthy's downfall. At the time, few noticed and fewer commented on Eisenhower's boldness in establishing executive privilege, which quickly came to be regarded as traditional.

In the spring of 1954, the Supreme Court was scheduled to make its pronouncement in the school segregation cases. Brownell told Eisenhower that he thought the Court wanted to delay making a ruling as long as possible. Eisenhower laughingly replied that he hoped they would defer it until the next Administration took over. More seriously, the President said, "I don't know where I stand, but I think I stand that the best interests of the United States demand an answer in keeping with past decisions."[46] He invited Warren to the White House for a stag dinner, along with Brownell, John W. Davis, who was counsel for the segregationists, and a number of other lawyers. Eisenhower had Davis sit near Warren, who in turn was on the President's right hand. During dinner, Eisenhower—according to Warren—"went to considerable lengths to tell me what a great man Mr. Davis was." And as the guests were filing out of the dining room, Eisenhower took Warren by the arm and said of the southerners, "These are not bad people. All they are concerned about is to see that their sweet little girls are not required to sit in school alongside some big overgrown Negroes."[47]

If Eisenhower intended to influence Warren, he failed. On May 17, the Court handed down its decision in the case of *Brown* v. *Topeka*. It declared segregation by race in public schools to be unconstitutional. Eisenhower was "considerably concerned," Hagerty recorded in his diary the next day. The President thought that the southerners might "virtually cancel out their public education system," putting in its place all-white "private" schools to which state money would be diverted. "The President expressed the fear that such a plan if it were followed through would not only handicap Negro children but would work to the detriment of the so-called 'poor whites' in the South."[48]

Although Eisenhower personally wished that the Court had upheld *Plessy* v. *Ferguson,* and said so on a number of occasions (but only in private), he was impressed by the 9 to 0 vote and he certainly was going to meet his responsibilities and enforce the laws. But he would not comment on it in public. At a May 19 press conference, he was asked if he had any advice to give to the South as to how to react. "Not in the slightest," Eisenhower replied."The Supreme Court has spoken and I am sworn to uphold the constitutional processes in this country; and I will obey." [49]

That refusal to give the South any advice was a strange thing for a man who had fought hard to become the nation's leader to say. It was an abdication of responsibility. What hurt even more was Eisenhower's refusal to give *Brown* v. *Topeka* a public endorsement. As with McCarthy, Eisenhower insisted time and again that he had neither need nor right to comment. Even as violence flared across the South, as the implementation of desegregation began, Eisenhower refused to ever say that he thought segregation was morally wrong. That allowed the bitter-end segregationists to claim that Eisenhower was secretly on their side, which they said justified their tactics. Warren, and many others, thought that one word from Eisenhower would have made possible a smoother, easier, and quicker transition period.

But Eisenhower never said the word. He insisted that it was not his role to comment on Court decisions, just as firmly as he insisted that the Court's ruling had a "binding effect" on everyone. He told Hazlett, "I hold to the basic purpose. There must be respect for the Constitution—which means the Supreme Court's interpretation of the Constitution—or we shall have chaos. This I believe with all of my heart—and shall always act accordingly." [50] That was a long way from President Andrew Jackson's famous dictum, "John Marshall has made his decision; now let him enforce it." But it was also a long way from saying that *Brown* was morally right. He missed a historic opportunity to provide moral leadership. In fact, until Little Rock in 1957 he provided almost no leadership at all on the most fundamental social problem of his time.

The most serious foreign problem Eisenhower had to face in the summer of 1954, and the one of the largest long-term significance, was Vietnam. The Geneva Conference was under way, with Beetle Smith there as the American representative. With Dien Bien Phu gone, the Communists at Geneva were stalling on the talks while the Vietminh regrouped after their victory and prepared to attack the French throughout the delta region of Vietnam. Which upset Eisenhower most—French defeatism or British refusal to cooperate—would be impossible to say. Australia and New Zealand had told Dulles they were willing to join a regional alliance. On May 5, Eisenhower told a news conference that "we will never give up," and gave a strong pitch for SEATO. [51]

Meanwhile a major war scare ensued. The French convinced

themselves that the Chinese were on the verge of intervening. If that happened, the French wanted a guarantee of a massive and immediate American intervention.

Dulles was breathing fire. He thought Chinese intervention in Vietnam would be the "equivalent of a declaration of war against the United States." He advised the President to get a resolution through Congress at once, authorizing him to respond to a possible Chinese intervention as he saw fit. Eisenhower told Dulles (as recorded in notes taken by Cutler), "If he was to go to the Congress for authority he would not ask any halfway measures. If the situation warranted it, there should be declared a state of war with China; and possibly there should be a strike at Russia." That took Dulles' breath away. The President's next point eliminated the idea of a unilateral intervention by the United States. Eisenhower said, "He would never have the United States go into Indochina alone." Returning to his first point, Eisenhower said: "If the U.S. took action against Communist China, . . . said there should be no halfway measures or frittering around. The Navy and Air Force should go in with full power, using new weapons, and strike at air bases and ports in mainland China."[52]

Then Eisenhower called in the JCS. He told the Chiefs that an atomic assault against China would inevitably bring Russia into the war; therefore if the United States were to launch a preventive attack, it had to be against both Russia and China simultaneously. Looking directly at Radford, Eisenhower asked, suppose it were possible to destroy Russia. "I want you to carry this question home with you. Gain such a victory, and what do you do with it? Here would be a great area from Elbe to Vladivostok . . . torn up and destroyed, without government, without its communications, just an area of starvation and disaster. I ask you what would the civilized world do about it? I repeat there is no victory except through our imaginations."[53]

With all the loose talk going on in Washington about atomic strikes, reporters inevitably heard about the JCS and NSC recommendations. At a news conference, Eisenhower was asked to comment on preventive war. He replied, "I don't believe there is such a thing; and, frankly, I wouldn't even listen to anyone seriously that came in and talked about such a thing." Was his answer based on military or moral considerations? "It seems to me that when, by definition, a term is just ridiculous in itself, there is no use in going any further," Eisenhower replied.[54]

Syngman Rhee flew to Washington to tell Eisenhower that the moment had come to strike hard at the Communists. "Let me tell you that if war comes," Eisenhower replied to Rhee, "it will be horrible. Atomic war will destroy civilization. War today is unthinkable with the weapons which we have at our command. If the Kremlin and Washington ever lock up in a war, the results are too horrible to contemplate. I can't even imagine them."[55]

Fortunately, the war scare in Indochina went away as quickly as it came on. The Chinese did not intervene. They did not have to, as the Vietminh were driving forward on their own, and the Laniel government in Paris was tottering.

On June 12, the Laniel government fell by a narrow margin, 306–293. On June 18 Pierre Mendès-France took office as Premier on the strength of a pledge that he would secure a peace in Indochina by July 20. Privately, he told Smith—who had flown from Geneva to Paris—that he might be meeting with Chou En-lai. Smith strongly advised him not to. Smith suspected a French sell-out. Neither he, Dulles, nor Eisenhower wanted to be a part of the surrender arrangements at Geneva. Smith therefore returned to the United States, and the American delegation at Geneva was reduced to an "observer" status.

Meanwhile, Churchill and Eden came to Washington; one of the things they discussed with Eisenhower was the French and EDC. Laniel had been a strong supporter of EDC, but Mendès-France was shaky. The final vote on ratification was imminent. Without EDC, there was no program for German rearmament. To influence both the French and the British on the EDC vote, Eisenhower had Knowland steer through the Senate a resolution, adopted unanimously, authorizing the President to take any steps necessary to "restore sovereignty to Germany and to enable her to contribute to the maintenance of peace and security." In other words, if France and Britain did not get behind EDC, the Americans would help the Germans rearm themselves, outside an all-European army, but inside NATO as a full partner.

On July 21, the Geneva agreements were signed. They established a cease-fire, partitioned Vietnam, called for nationwide elections within two years, forbade the introduction of new military equipment from foreign nations into either part of Vietnam, provided for free movement of people between the two parts of Vietnam, and established a three-nation supervisory commission (Poland, India, and Canada). This was an outcome to which Eisenhower had long since resigned himself. It was acceptable to him because it sealed off the Communist breakthrough and because SEATO was now well on track to establish a new defensive line in Southeast Asia. Ho Chi Minh was the big loser.

Nevertheless, Eisenhower and the Republicans were embarrassed by the loss of northern Vietnam to the Communists, so Eisenhower had Smith issue a declaration that said that United States took note of the agreements, would not use force to upset them, but would not sign them. When Eisenhower informed a news conference on July 21 of the refusal to sign, he emphasized that "the United States has not itself been a party to or bound by the decisions taken." He added that he was immediately dispatching ambassadors to Laos and Cambodia, and that he was "actively pursuing discussions . . . with view to the rapid organization of a collective defense in Southeast Asia." [56]

What Eisenhower had done was face the realities. The French were not going to continue to fight; if the war went on, Ho Chi Minh would win everything in Indochina. At the critical juncture, the United States had neither the air nor troop strength to prevent a Vietminh victory, short of a unilateral atomic strike. But although there was extreme pressure to do just that, from a majority of Eisenhower's military and civilian advisers, he set political and military obstacles that he knew could not be overcome. Of these, the most important were British cooperation, congressional approval, and a JCS facing of the fact that an atomic strike had to be directed against Russia as well as China, and could hardly be limited to Vietnam. As he had done in the crisis of late April over Dien Bien Phu, Eisenhower in July 1954 again kept America out of Vietnam.

Then he put America into Vietnam. Dulles spent most of August flying around the world, signing up allies for SEATO. By September 8, the process was completed. France, Britain, Australia, New Zealand, Thailand, the Philippines, Pakistan, and the United States together pledged themselves to defend Southeast Asia. The treaty extended the protection of SEATO to Laos, Cambodia, and South Vietnam. Less than one month later, Eisenhower pledged full American support to the Prime Minister of South Vietnam, Ngo Dinh Diem.

The debacle in Indochina badly strained the NATO alliance. As Gruenther had warned, many Frenchmen put the blame on the United States. They had an opportunity to vent their anger on August 30, when the French Assembly voted on EDC. Dulles had been active in Paris, putting every kind of pressure he could on the French.

Eisenhower, at a news conference, added to the pressure by announcing that if the French failed to ratify EDC, the United States would move alone to "secure a better relationship with Germany." He wanted the French to know that one way or another there was going to be a German rearmament.[57] Nevertheless, the Assembly voted to reject EDC, 319 to 264, with 43 abstentions.

Eisenhower had suffered a major setback. Since December 1950, he had labored to create EDC and the all-European army that would go with it, not only in order to get German rearmament under way but also to provide a spur for a United States of Europe. He was disappointed and perplexed. He asked Hagerty, "Are the French deliberately saying they are going to tie up with Russia?" He recalled a meeting he had with the French Cabinet when he was SACEUR, when he had lost his patience and said to the members, "I obviously have a hell of a lot more fear of what happens to France than you do." Eisenhower said that some of the Frenchmen present "broke down and cried," but now look, they were rejecting their own proposal, EDC.[58]

As in Vietnam, Eisenhower had his backup position ready. Immediately upon hearing the result of the vote, he told Smith—who was Acting Secretary of State while Dulles was in Paris—to arrange a meeting of the NATO countries, "with a view of including Germany as an equal partner therein."[59] Thus the chief result of the French vote was to restore German sovereignty, bring Germany into NATO, and create an independent German Army.

Taken together, the loss of North Vietnam and of EDC were serious defeats for Eisenhower. But he had lost only a couple of battles, not the war against Communism. As he so often reminded his Cabinet, "Long faces don't win wars." He insisted on remaining optimistic as much as he insisted on being realistic.

A full generation later, after South Vietnam had fallen to the Communists but the remainder of the dominoes had not, Ike's prophecy looked as ill-considered as his notion that all Communists everywhere were but puppets on Moscow's string. EDC, meanwhile, had long since been forgotten completely, but Ike's idea of a United States of Europe remained very much alive. There was no European army, but there was a Western European economy and a European Parliament. Eisenhower's optimism on that point had proven to be well founded.

CHAPTER FIFTEEN

ChiNats and ChiComs

IN LATE AUGUST 1954, Eisenhower went to Denver for the start of his vacation. On September 3, he got word from Washington that there was yet another Far East crisis, this one about halfway between Korea and Vietnam. The Chinese had begun shelling two tiny islands, Quemoy and Matsu.

These islands were less than two miles off the Chinese coast. Unlike Formosa and the nearby Pescadores, which had been held by the Japanese for some fifty years, Quemoy and Matsu had always been a part of China. When Chiang fled to Formosa in 1949, he retained his hold on the islands, garrisoned them heavily, and used them to observe the mainland, to stage raids against the mainland, and to disrupt Chinese coastal shipping. Eventually, Chiang hoped to use them as stepping stones for his invasion of the mainland.

The U.S. Seventh Fleet had orders, originated by Truman and continued by Eisenhower, to prevent a Chinese assault against Formosa. Whether Quemoy and Matsu were included in the defensive area was unclear. There were technical and political problems; the U.S. Navy could not get its ships between the islands and the mainland for lack of depth of water, and intervention threatened to put the United States squarely into the Chinese civil war at a time when none of America's allies, except Chiang, was willing to risk World War III over two tiny offshore islands. Nevertheless Chiang insisted that the fall of Quemoy and Matsu would only be a preliminary to the invasion of Formosa itself, and Eisenhower was told that National-ist Chinese morale would fall precipitously if no attempt was made to defend them. The JCS informed Eisenhower that although the islands were not militarily necessary to the defense of Formosa, Chiang could not hold them without American assistance.

On September 12, Dulles and the JCS flew to Denver for a con-ference on what Dulles called "this horrible business." The Chinese were shelling the islands on a regular basis but had not yet invaded. Radford, backed by the Air Force and Navy chiefs, recommended not only putting American forces on the islands, but also that the United States join Chiang in carrying out bombing raids against the mainland. This was the third time in less than six months that Rad-ford had recommended aggressive action, to include atomic weapons, against China. Eisenhower again rejected the advice. As before, the President said that "if we attack China, we're not going to impose limits on our military actions, as in Korea." And, the President added, "If we get into a general war, the logical enemy will be Russia, not China, and we'll have to strike there." [1]

By late October, the Chinese appeared to be ready to launch their invasion. Despite Eisenhower's dressing down in September, Radford and the JCS still assumed that when China attacked, the United States would strike hard at the Chinese mainland. Eisenhower told them to make no such assumption. He said he was distressed at their lack of understanding of the constitutional responsibilities of the President. The United States had no treaty with Chiang Kai-shek; the President could not plunge America into a war with China (and possibly Russia) without congressional approval, and especially not over the fate of such insignificant places as Quemoy and Matsu. He told the JCS that if the Chinese attacked Formosa, the Seventh Fleet should act defensively; simultaneously, he would call an immediate session of Congress. There would be no retaliation against the Chinese mainland, no invoking the doctrine of massive retaliation, "pending congressional consideration of the matter." [2]

Through November, the threat intensified as the Chinese bombed other small islands held by Chiang's forces and continued their buildup opposite Quemoy and Matsu. Then, on November 23, the Chinese announced the verdict of a trial of thirteen American fliers who had been shot down over China during the Korean War. They received prison terms ranging from four years to life for espi-onage. In as much as all but two of the fliers had been in uniform, and in as much as the Korean armistice agreements specified that all

POWs would be returned, there was a predictable roar of protest in the United States. Senator Knowland spoke for millions of Americans when he demanded a total blockade of the Chinese coast.

Eisenhower had to respond somehow. Early in December, he signed a mutual-defense treaty with the Nationalist Chinese. It declared that an armed attack on either party would be regarded as an act of war against the other. Chiang agreed not to attack the mainland unilaterally. Eisenhower insisted on restricting the treaty to Formosa and the Pescadores, deliberately leaving out Quemoy and Matsu.

The major concern of most politicians in America in the second half of 1954 was not Germany, nor Vietnam, nor China, but getting re-elected. Eisenhower was also concerned about the elections, if only because of the thin margins the Republicans held in both houses of Congress. He wanted his party to retain control of Congress, and despite his constant reiteration of his nonpartisanship, he exhorted his Cabinet members to do all they could to elect Republicans.

Despite Eisenhower's efforts, the Republicans lost seventeen seats in the House and two in the Senate, which gave the Democrats control of both chambers of Congress. Most observers felt that only Eisenhower's last-minute intervention had prevented an even bigger Democratic victory, and Eisenhower pointed out that Republican losses in the off-year election were much less than was customary for the party in power.

One cause of the losses was the Secretary of Defense. Wilson had shot off his mouth during the campaign about unemployed auto workers in Detroit. "I've always liked bird dogs better than kennel-fed dogs myself," Wilson announced. "You know, one who'll get out and hunt for food rather than sit on his fanny and yell."[3] It was an absurd comparison—bird dogs live in kennels and they do not hunt, kill, and eat the quail, but only point them out to the hunter—and the unnecessary insult of equating the unemployed with lazy dogs set off a storm that cost the Republicans votes. Eisenhower was also unhappy with Wilson because of the Secretary's inability to control the Chiefs. In preparing his budget for the next fiscal year, Eisenhower had again made substantial cuts in the Army and Navy. The Army would drop from 1.4 million to 1 million, with a budget reduction from $12.9 billion to $8.8 billion; the Navy from 920,000 to 870,000, and from $11.2 to $9.7 billion. The Air Force got a slight increase, from $15.6 to $16.4 billion. All the Chiefs were unwilling to accept these figures. Ridgway was the most outspoken—he said he could not be responsible for the security of American troops in Europe, Korea, and elsewhere with so small an army—but the Navy and Air Force Chiefs also went before Congress to denounce the Eisenhower budget and demand more money.

In December, Eisenhower summoned Wilson and the Chiefs to the Oval Office. General Andrew Goodpaster, Ike's staff secretary, took notes. Eisenhower gave a brief outline of his military budget, acknowledged that each service could find shortcomings in it, insisted that he had to look at the whole picture, including the state of the economy, and then ordered each of the chiefs to get on the team.

Thus did Eisenhower set the nation's post-Korea, post–Dien Bien Phu defense policy. The New Look put the emphasis on massive retaliation, on more bang for a buck, on cutting costs everywhere except for the Strategic Air Force and its ability to wage atomic war. The New Look meant big savings, and much grumbling. At times it seemed that except for Humphrey, Eisenhower was the only man in Washington who supported it. From 1955 onward, the Democrats would concentrate their criticisms of Eisenhower on his defense policy, charging that the President—and Humphrey—were allowing their Neanderthal fiscal views to endanger the security of the nation. Despite Eisenhower's direct order, the JCS continued to supply his critics with countless facts and figures to prove that more money had to be spent on conventional forces.

So strongly, and so often, did the Chiefs—all of them—object to the New Look that Eisenhower was nearly driven to distraction. "Let us not forget that the armed services are to defend a 'way of life,' not merely land, property, or lives," Eisenhower wrote Swede Hazlett. "So what I need to make the Chiefs realize is that they are men of sufficient stature, training, and intelligence to think of this balance— the balance between minimum requirements in the costly implements of war and the health of our economy."

A major problem was that although each Chief agreed that the sums allocated to the other services were entirely adequate, the amounts provided for his own service were entirely inadequate. Eisenhower told Hazlett that he could run a blue pencil through the Pentagon requests for more money because he knew the Pentagon game so well, "but some day there is going to be a man sitting in my present chair who has not been raised in the military services and who will have little understanding of where slashes in their estimates can be made with little or no damage." Eisenhower then expressed his great fear: "If that should happen while we still have the state of tension that now exists in the world, I shudder to think of what could happen in this country."[4]

The more general complaint about Eisenhower's New Look was linked to widespread dissatisfaction with the way he was waging the Cold War. Critics—including not only the opposition party but also the Old Guard, the JCS, the NSC, and often the Secretary of State— wanted a more vigorous prosecution of the conflict, as evidenced by the number of times in 1954 they urged the President to launch an atomic strike against China. But Eisenhower would have no part of nuclear war, unless the Russians actually marched across the Elbe River, and he wanted no more Koreas.

He was, however, more than willing to wage an aggressive covert offensive, implemented by the CIA, against the Communists. The CIA was carrying on assorted covert operations around the world. Because it was his chief instrument for waging the Cold War, and because it was so controversial, Eisenhower kept a close watch on the CIA. In late October, he spent an afternoon with General Jimmie Doolittle and the other members of the committee he had created to investigate the Agency. At the end of the meeting, Doolittle handed Eisenhower the committee's report. Its conclusion was chilling: "It is now clear that we are facing an implacable enemy whose avowed objective is world domination . . . There are no rules in such a game. Hitherto acceptable norms of human conduct do not apply. . . . We must . . . learn to subvert, sabotage, and destroy our enemies by more clever, more sophisticated, and more effective methods than those used against us."[5] That was a concise summary of Eisenhower's own views, and described accurately the methods he had already used in Iran, Guatemala, and North Vietnam.

The CIA's other main function was the less glamorous one of collecting and interpreting intelligence. Like everyone else of his generation, Eisenhower had been deeply scared by the intelligence failure at Pearl Harbor; by the fifties, the advantage of surprise to an attacker who had atomic weapons was incalculably greater than it had been in the early forties. Eisenhower wanted information from within the Soviet Union; he especially wanted an early warning on any mobilization of planes or troops. But the CIA had been unable to place any spy networks inside Russia.

Early in 1954, Eisenhower set up a Surprise Attack Panel to advise him on what to do. The chairman was Dr. James R. Killian, president of MIT. A key member was Edwin H. Land, inventor of the Polaroid camera and winner of a Nobel Prize (1952). Land re-

ported that new cameras were available that made high-level precision photography possible. The trick was to get the cameras over
Russia. The Air Force had made several attempts, using redesigned
bombers and unmanned balloons, but the results were disappointing.

Meanwhile, Clarence ("Kelly") Johnson, the top designer at
Lockheed, had proposed a high-altitude single-engine reconnaissance aircraft that was really more a kite with an enormous wingspan,
a single jet engine, and an ability to fly long distances above seventy
thousand feet. Lockheed called the plane the U-2. Allen Dulles liked
it; Killian liked it; Land liked it. On November 24, they went to see
Eisenhower to ask authorization to build thirty U-2s at a cost of $35
million. The CIA and the Defense Department would split the bill.
Foster Dulles, who was also present, indicated "that difficulties might
arise out of these flights, but we can live through them." Allen Dulles
put Richard Bissell in charge. At the conclusion of the meeting,
Goodpaster noted, "The President directed those present to go ahead
and get the equipment, but before initiating operations to come in
for one last look at the plans."[6]

Immediately after the U-2 meeting, Eisenhower, his family, and
his gang went to Augusta for Thanksgiving. Accompanying them was
Field Marshal Montgomery, who had—Ike complained—"invited
himself." At Thanksgiving dinner, the two old soldiers regaled the
party with war stories. They got to talking about Gettysburg. Ike gave
a lecture on his favorite battle. When he got to Pickett's charge, he
said that Lee's reply to Pickett's suggestion that he attack the enemy
—"Do it if you can"—was a most unusual one. As a commanding
general himself, Ike said, he would never give a subordinate so much
leeway. Montgomery said he had good reason to know that was true.

Later, Monty got started on all the things he did not know about
America. He said he had never heard of Princeton, only Harvard
and Yale. On the liner crossing the Atlantic, he recounted, he was
introduced at the captain's table to a man named Spencer Tracy.
Monty had to ask Mr. Tracy what business he was in. After dinner,
the men settled down to play bridge, all except Monty, who did not
play cards and therefore had Mamie teach him to play Scrabble.

The following morning, Monty asked Ike about what it was like
to be the President. "No man on earth knows what this job is all
about," Ike replied. "It's pound, pound, pound. Not only is your
intellectual capacity taxed to the utmost, but your physical stamina."[7]

The Eisenhowers returned to Augusta for Christmas and New

Year's. On this occasion there was an unusual tension in the air because Eisenhower had to wait out the French vote on German rearmament. He worried that he would have to return to Washington if the vote went badly. There was, therefore, great relief all around when on December 30 word arrived that the French Assembly had ratified the agreement.

Thus did Eisenhower's second year in office end on a happy and successful note. French acceptance of his program for Germany had led to a stronger NATO, one of Eisenhower's proudest achievements. There were many other victories to toast that New Year's Eve. McCarthy had been censured. SEATO was functioning. The budget was almost in balance. Defense spending was sharply down. Eisenhower's popularity, according to the polls, was remarkably high—he had a 60 percent or higher approval rating. There had been setbacks, of course. The ones Eisenhower felt most strongly were the loss of North Vietnam, the failure to bring the Old Guard into the mainstream of moderate politics, and the election losses that turned control of the Congress over to the Democrats. There were also ongoing issues, fraught with danger, such as Quemoy and Matsu, the stability of South Vietnam, and of course all the domestic problems. But as Eisenhower looked back on 1953 and 1954, the deep sense of personal satisfaction he felt about his record was based upon, far and above all other considerations, his success in making and keeping peace.

Eisenhower had told Hagerty that his "one purpose" was "the job of keeping this world at peace."[8] At times it appeared that he was the only man who could do it. In mid-1953, most of his military, foreign-policy, and domestic political advisers were opposed to accepting an armistice in place in Korea. But Eisenhower insisted on peace. Five times in 1954, virtually the entire NSC, JCS, and State Department recommended that he intervene in Asia, even using atomic bombs against China. First, in April, as the Dien Bien Phu situation grew critical. Second, in May, on the eve of the fall of Dien Bien Phu. Third, in late June, when the French said the Chinese were about to enter the Indochina conflict. Fourth, in September, when the Chinese began shelling Quemoy and Matsu. Fifth, in November, when the Chinese announced the prison terms for the American fliers.

Five times in one year the experts advised the President to launch an atomic strike against China. Five times he said no. He did so most dramatically in a news conference in late November, when he was asked about the possibilities of a preventive strike against the Chinese. Eisenhower took ten minutes to reply, in off-the-cuff remarks that were delivered with visible emotion. After giving a lengthy analysis, Eisenhower leaned forward and said he wanted "to talk a little bit personally." He admitted that "a President experiences exactly the same resentments, the same anger, the same kind of sense of frustration almost, when things like this occur to other Americans, and his impulse is to lash out." He said he knew that would be the "easy course" as well. The nation would be "united automatically." It would close ranks behind the leader. The job would become a simple one—win the war. "There is a real fervor developed throughout the nation that you can feel everywhere you go. There is practically an exhilaration about the affair." Eisenhower confessed that he was not immune to those feelings: "In the intellectual and spiritual contest of matching wits and getting along to see if you can win, there comes about something . . . an atmosphere is created . . . an attitude is created to which I am not totally unfamiliar."

Five times in one year the experts had advised him to enjoy that experience once again. But Eisenhower had other memories too. He reminded the reporters of his own favorite line from Robert E. Lee: "It is well that war is so terrible; if it were not so, we would grow too fond of it." He said he had personally experienced "the job of writing letters of condolence by the hundreds, by the thousands, to bereaved mothers and wives. That is a very sobering experience." So he pleaded with the reporters, and through them to the people, to think things through before rushing off to act. Try to imagine the results, he said. "Don't go to war in response to emotions of anger and resentment; do it prayerfully."[9]

Five times in 1954 Eisenhower prayed over the question of war or peace. Each time, he made the decision to stay at peace.

On New Year's Day, 1955, Chiang Kai-shek predicted "war at any time" over Quemoy and Matsu. On the other side of the Formosa Straits, Chou En-lai said that a Chinese invasion of Formosa was "imminent."[10] Thus did the two Chinese rivals intensify the Formosa Straits crisis, which soon became one of the most serious of Eisenhower's eight years in office. Indeed the United States in early 1955 came closer to using atomic weapons than at any other time in the Eisenhower Administration.

On January 10, the ChiCom Air Force raided the Tachen Islands, two hundred miles from Formosa but held by ChiNat troops.

(For the sake of simplicity, this account will use the terminology of the Eisenhower Administration in distinguishing the two sides— ChiComs were the Chinese Communists, while the ChiNats were the Chinese Nationalists.) Eisenhower decided that "the time had come to draw the line." [11] This decision immediately raised the problem of *where* to draw the line, a problem that was never fully resolved and that deepened the crisis. Certainly the Americans were going to fight to defend Formosa—Eisenhower had made treaty arrangements in December of 1954 that required the United States to do so—and the Pescadores were included in the area to be defended.

But what of Quemoy and Matsu? They were so close to the Chinese mainland, so unquestionably a part of China, so far from Formosa (and in any case so small that they could not be used as a platform for the invasion of Formosa) that almost no one, except Chiang, thought they were worth defending. The Tachens added to the problem: Were they also vital to the defense of Formosa?

Eisenhower decided to let the Tachens go, while deliberately remaining vague about Quemoy and Matsu. He managed to maintain the vagueness throughout a series of war scares during the crisis. It was the cornerstone of his policy, and he held to it despite the manifold problems it created for him with his European allies, his own military and JCS, Chiang, Congress, and the American public.

On January 19, Eisenhower met with Dulles to discuss a resolution Eisenhower wanted Congress to pass, giving him authority to commit American armed forces to the defense of Formosa and the Pescadores. Dulles agreed there was a need for such a resolution, but he wanted to include Quemoy and Matsu, which Eisenhower would not permit. Instead, Eisenhower said the wording he wanted would allow the President to react in defense of Formosa and the Pescadores and "such other territories as may be determined." [12]

The resolution Eisenhower wanted was something new in American history. Never before had Congress given the President a blank check to act as he saw fit in a foreign crisis. Fully aware of the unprecedented nature of his request, Eisenhower talked with all the congressional leaders before submitting it. He explained his thinking and his wishes to Joe Martin, the minority leader, and Sam Rayburn, the Speaker of the House; they assured him that the House would "approve his action and without any criticism whatsoever." [13]

On January 24, Eisenhower sent his message to Congress, asking for a resolution that would "clearly and publicly establish the authority of the President as Commander in Chief to employ the armed forces of this nation promptly and effectively for the purposes indicated if in his judgment it became necessary." The "purposes indicated" included not only the defense of Formosa and the Pescadores, as required by treaty, but also the defense of "closely related localities," which meant—or did it?—Quemoy and Matsu.[14] The President did not, would not, say.

The House responded as Martin and Rayburn said it would; within the hour of receiving the message, it gave the President unlimited authority to act as he saw fit, by a vote of 410 to 3.

On January 28, by a vote of 83 to 3, the Senate passed the resolution. For the first time in American history, the Congress had authorized the President in advance to engage in a war at a time and under circumstances of his own choosing.

He was also free to use whatever weapons he saw fit. Dulles urged him to drop a couple of atomic bombs on the Chinese mainland airfields. Eisenhower replied that he did not want any talk about atomic bombs. Nor would he consider sending American troops to Formosa. But he did want to do something.

What the President needed was more precise information on the situation in Quemoy and Matsu. He was dissatisfied with the intelligence he was getting from the CIA. He therefore decided to send his closest and most trusted adviser, Goodpaster, to the Pacific. Pulling Goodpaster aside after the NSC meeting, Eisenhower told him to find out "how fast ChiCom attacks in various forms might develop," and how long the ChiNats could hold out on their own if they had American logistical support.[15] Goodpaster went, investigated, and returned to report that the ChiNats were rapidly improving their defense on Quemoy and Matsu, rushing in troops, and would be capable of defending themselves against a ChiCom attack, unless the ChiComs threw their air force into the battle. In that case, "U.S. support would be required, and would probably have to include special weapons."[16]

The use of "special weapons" had, by the time Goodpaster returned, become a matter of public debate. On March 12, Dulles said in a speech that the United States had "new and powerful weapons of precision which can utterly destroy military targets without endangering unrelated civilian centers." Three days later, he was even more specific, saying that the United States was prepared to use tactical atomic weapons in case of war in the Formosa Straits. This was a clear and unambiguous threat, much clearer than those Dulles and Eisenhower had made against the ChiComs two years earlier with regard to Korea. Dulles cleared his statement with the President before making it.[17] Inevitably, it set off an uproar within the U.S. and throughout the world.

At Eisenhower's March 16 news conference, Charles von Fremd of CBS asked him to comment on Dulles' assertion that in the event of war in the Far East, "we would probably make use of some tactical small atomic weapons." Eisenhower was unusually direct in his answer: "Yes, of course they would be used." He explained, "In any combat where these things can be used on strictly military targets and for strictly military purposes, I see no reason why they shouldn't be used just exactly as you would use a bullet or anything else." But would not the United States itself be destroyed in a nuclear war? Eisenhower replied, "Nobody in war or anywhere else ever made a good decision if he was frightened to death. You have to look facts in the face, but you have to have the stamina to do it without just going hysterical."[18]

Democrats found it difficult to avoid hysteria when the President started comparing atomic weapons to bullets. Lyndon Johnson warned against undertaking "an irresponsible adventure for which we have not calculated the risks," and Adlai Stevenson expressed "the gravest misgivings about risking a third world war in defense of these little islands."

On the other side, Radford could barely suppress his excitement; the chairman of the JCS said that "there is a distinct possibility that war can break out at any time." And Senator Wiley pronounced his judgment: "Either we can defend the United States in the Formosa Straits—now, or we can defend it later in San Francisco Bay." General James Van Fleet wanted to send American troops to Quemoy and Matsu; if the Chinese continued shelling the islands, Eisenhower could "shoot back with atomic weapons and annihilate the Red effort." Knowland added his perspective—there should be no "appeasement," no matter what the risks. Dulles, in a speech on March 20, managed to raise the tension even higher by referring to the ChiComs in terms usually reserved for use against nations at war. The Secretary said the Chinese were "an acute and imminent threat . . . dizzy with success," more dangerous than the Russians. He compared their "aggressive fanaticism" with Hitler's.[19]

Three days later, Eisenhower was walking with Hagerty from the White House to the Executive Office Building for a press conference. Hagerty said he had just received a frantic plea. "Mr. President, some of the people in the State Department say that the Formosa Strait situation is so delicate that no matter what question you get on it, you shouldn't say anything at all." Eisenhower laughed and replied, "Don't worry, Jim, if that question comes up, I'll just confuse them." [20]

He did. Joseph C. Harsch asked him about using atomic weapons in the Formosa Straits, and he responded with a long, rambling reply that was incomprehensible. Years later Eisenhower still got a chuckle out of thinking about the difficulties Chinese and Russian intelligence analysts must have had in trying to put his remarks into their language and then explain to their bosses what the American President meant. Eventually, Harsch interjected, "Sir, I am a little stupid about this thing," and asked for further clarification. Eisenhower explained that he could not be precise. "The only thing I know about war are two things: the most changeable factor in war is human nature in its day-by-day manifestation; but the only unchanging factor in war is human nature. And the next thing is that every war is going to astonish you in the way it occurred, and in the way it is carried out. So that for a man to predict, particularly if he had the responsibility for making the decision, to predict what he is going to use, how he is going to do it, would I think exhibit his ignorance of war; that is what I believe. So I think you just have to wait, and that is the kind of prayerful decision that may some day face a President." [21]

But in fact, by mid-April the crisis was over. On April 23, Chou spoke at Bandung about Chinese friendship for the American people and said that the ChiComs "do not want to have a war with the United States." He offered to negotiate. Eisenhower responded positively, saying he was ready to talk "if there seemed to be an opportunity for us to further the easing of tensions." Chou continued his conciliatory line, saying that the ChiComs "are willing to strive for the liberation of Formosa by peaceful means as far as this is possible." The shelling of Quemoy and Matsu eased off; by mid-May, it ceased entirely. On August 1, talks between American and Chinese representatives began. [22]

Throughout the crisis, Eisenhower had been beset by conflicting advice. As he recounted it in his memoirs, "The administration heard the counsel of Attlee (liquidate Chiang), Eden (neutralize Quemoy and Matsu), [Democratic Senators] (abandon Quemoy and Matsu), Lewis Douglas (avoid entry into a civil war, on legal principle), Radford (fight for the Tachens, bomb the mainland), Knowland (blockade the Chinese coast), and Rhee (join him and Chiang in a holy war of liberation)." [23] But the only counsel Eisenhower really took was his own. As a result, he emerged from the crisis with all his objectives secured. Chiang still held the islands, and the American commitment to defend Formosa was stronger than ever. These results satisfied all but the most extreme members of the China Lobby and the Old Guard.

Eisenhower had gotten a blank check from Congress that gave him total freedom of action. As a result, he had managed to so confuse the ChiComs as to whether or not the United States would use atomic bombs against them in the defense of Quemoy and Matsu that they decided not to attack. True, his comparison of an atomic bomb to bullets scared the wits out of people around the world, but through his actions and press-conference ambiguities Eisenhower had managed to convince the Europeans, and others, that he was neither hysterical nor cold-blooded. He never had to use the bomb; he did not plunge the world into war; he kept the peace without losing any territory or prestige.

Eisenhower's handling of the Quemoy-Matsu crisis was a *tour de force,* one of the great triumphs of his long career. The key to his success was his deliberate ambiguity and deception. As Robert Divine writes, "The beauty of Eisenhower's policy is that to this day no one can be sure whether or not he would have responded militarily to an invasion of the offshore islands, and whether he would have used nuclear weapons." [24] The full truth is that Eisenhower himself did not know. In retrospect, what stands out about Eisenhower's crisis management is that at every stage he kept his options open. Flexibility was one of his chief characteristics as Supreme Commander in World War II; as President, he insisted on retaining that flexibility. He never knew himself just how he would respond to an invasion of Quemoy and Matsu, because he insisted on waiting to see the precise nature of the attack before deciding how to react. What he did know was that when the moment of decision came, he would have the maximum number of options to choose from.

The Formosa experience made Eisenhower yearn, more than ever, for a genuine peace. To attain that goal, he would have to deal with the Russians. The last time the leader of the United States sat down with the leader of the Soviet Union had been in 1945, at Yalta and Potsdam. Because of the outcome of those conferences, the Old Guard was dead set against another summit. Eisenhower, too, had objections to a summit. For one thing, it was not clear who was in command in the Kremlin. For another, Eisenhower thought the major outstanding problems—two Germanies, two Koreas, two Vietnams, two Chinas, and arms control—were intractable.

Still, he wanted to reach out. His urge was reinforced by changes in the Soviet leadership. Nikolai Malenkov was gone. Bulganin had become chairman of the Council of Ministers; Nikita Khrushchev was First Secretary of the Communist Party; Marshal Zhukov had become Minister of Defense. Together they formed a troika. In May 1955, they reached out to Eisenhower when they announced that the Soviet Union was ready to sign the Austrian peace treaty, which would restore Austria's independence and make Austria neutral, on the Swiss model. This was the "deed" Eisenhower had been demanding as proof of the Soviets' sincere intentions. On June 13, a month after the Austrian Treaty was signed, the Foreign Ministers announced that there would be a summit in Geneva beginning on July 18.

Anticipation of the first Summit Conference since Yalta and Potsdam, coupled with the end of the Formosa Straits crisis and the general peace that prevailed around the world, added to a feeling of near-euphoria millions of Americans enjoyed in 1955. Everything was going beautifully for the Eisenhower Administration. For the first time in their lives, Eisenhower took pride in declaring, Americans born after 1929 were experiencing peace, progress, and prosperity simultaneously. The short-lived post-Korean War recession was over, thanks in some part to Eisenhower's extension of Social Security benefits, his stepped-up expenditures during the recession, and his ability to convince Congress to extend unemployment compensation to some four million workers not previously covered. In addition, Eisenhower got Congress to raise the minimum wage from seventy-five cents per hour to one dollar per hour.

In mid-1955, George Meany, head of the AFL-CIO, told his associates: "American labor has never had it so good."[25] By early 1955 a boom was on, but without inflation—consumer prices went up only 1 percent. The result was a buying spree. The auto industry benefited most dramatically. In 1955, Detroit sold 7.92 million cars, which was up more than 2 million over 1954 and remained the record for one-year sales until 1965. The percentage of families owning automobiles jumped from 60 percent in 1952 to 70 percent in 1955 (and reached 77 percent by 1960). When some five thousand wives of the National Association of Automobile Dealers came to the White House, Mamie —who met them—told her husband "that is one crowd that is prospering! I never saw so many furs and diamonds."[26]

The American people for their part had never seen so many cars; the problem was that the road system was woefully inadequate. Except in New York, Chicago, and Los Angeles, the major urban areas had few or no high-speed expressways. Except for the Pennsylvania Turnpike and a few other toll roads in the East, the country had no four-lane highways connecting the cities.

Ever since a cross-country trip by Army convoy in 1919, Eisenhower had been concerned about America's highways. Like almost every other American who fought in Germany in 1945, he had been impressed by Hitler's system of *Autobahnen*. There had been many stops and starts by Congress over the past two decades in an attempt to upgrade and modernize the American road system, but almost no real action, primarily because of federal-state disputes over who would pay for the construction, a problem compounded by the trucking industry, the American Automobile Association, and the many other parts of the "highway lobby," which was composed of so many different interest groups that it could never present a unified position to Congress.

Eisenhower wanted the highways built. To him, it was an ideal program for the federal government to undertake. First, the need was clear and inescapable. Second, a unified system could only be erected by the federal government. Third, it was a public-works program on a massive scale, indeed the largest public-works program in history, which meant that the government could put millions of men to work without subjecting itself to the criticism that this was "make-work" of the WPA or PWA variety. By tailoring expenditures for highways to the state of the economy, Eisenhower could use the program to flatten out the peaks and valleys in unemployment.

Eisenhower was often called by his critics a "Whig President," with the implication that he was a "do-nothing" leader. But by advocating a highway program on a gigantic scale, Eisenhower was putting himself and his Administration within the best and strongest tradition of nineteenth-century American Whigs. John Quincy Adams, Henry Clay, and the other great Whigs had all been advocates of internal improvements paid for by the federal government. Eisenhower's highway program brought that tradition up to date.

In July 1954, Eisenhower had made his first move. At that time, he was trying to "build up" a possible successor for 1956; as a part of that effort, he sent Nixon to speak at a Governors' Conference and gave him a major policy speech to make. Nixon staggered the audience with the scope of the Administration's proposal. Eisenhower's grand plan advocated a comprehensive program, including roads for farm-to-market travel and rapid intercity and interregional travel. He suggested spending $5 billion per year for the next ten years, in addition to the $700 million already being spent annually. Nixon's speech had an "electrifying effect" on the governors, and on the public. In September 1954, Eisenhower put Lucius Clay at the head of a blue-ribbon private citizens' committee to study methods of financing. By the summer of 1955, a road-building bill was working its way through Congress.[27]

CHAPTER SIXTEEN

The Geneva Summit
and a Heart Attack

THE FIFTIES were a decade in which Americans, including their President, lived on the high edge of tension. Every decade of the nuclear age has been full of tension, obviously, but the fifties felt it most. America's leaders had had Pearl Harbor burned into their souls, and Americans of the fifties, already superconscious of the danger of surprise attack, were the first to have to live with long-range bombers, and to know that ICBMs were being built, and Polaris submarines. Most frightening of all, the weapons these delivery systems carried were H-bombs, big enough, in Strauss' words, "to take out a city. Any city."

Eisenhower wanted to lessen, if he could not eliminate, the financial cost and the fear that were the price of the Pearl Harbor mentality. But he could not bring himself to respond to Russian, or any other, calls for nuclear disarmament. To him, security for America required building more bombs, because that was the only area in which America had a lead on the Soviet military machine. But building more bombs only increased the cost and raised the tension.

Eisenhower searched for a way out of his dilemma. In 1955 he came up with an idea. It was one of his boldest. He decided to propose that the Soviets and the Americans open their airspace to each other, and provide each other with airfields from which to operate continuous reconnaissance missions. That simple step might solve the dilemma. Eisenhower maintained that the United States could never launch a first strike, both because of American morality and because of the open nature of American society, which precluded secret mobilization. Thus the United States had nothing to lose and much to gain by opening its airspace to the Russians. If American pilots had the same rights over the Soviet Union, it would be impossible for the Russians to launch an undetected nuclear Pearl Harbor, or to otherwise secretly increase their military might.

Eisenhower had used air reconnaissance extensively during the war, and was well aware of advances in cameras and photo interpretation techniques that had taken place since 1945. He had already tried various ways of flying over the Soviet Union, without success but without abandoning the project. Lockheed's U-2 was coming along nicely, he was told, and would soon—perhaps within a year— be operational. Then would come satellites, which Eisenhower was told were only two or three years away. They too would be able to carry cameras and beam pictures back to earth. Technology was going to open the skies to spy cameras in any case; whether the Russians agreed or not, the United States was soon going to be taking high-altitude photographs of the Soviet Union. By offering unlimited inspection, Eisenhower was trying to use inevitable technological advances to reduce, rather than raise, tensions.

Two weeks were taken up with preparations for the Geneva Summit. There were many practical arrangements that had to be made for the American delegation. Ike was delighted that Mamie had agreed to fly over with him, only her second flight across the Atlantic; adding to his pleasure was the fact that John, who had just completed the course at the Command and General Staff School and who thus had a one-month furlough, would also be along.

Eisenhower flew to Geneva full of curiosity about the new Russian leaders. He had met Foreign Minister V. M. Molotov in Moscow in the summer of 1945, and he had always felt a special tie with Zhukov, who had fallen into such disfavor with Stalin that Eisenhower had at one time thought him dead. He was anxious to see Zhukov again, find out what had happened, explore the possibility of re-establishing the working partnership the two of them had created in Germany after the war, and find out if Zhukov, as Defense Minister, had become a real leader in the post-Stalin government, or was only window dressing.

Eisenhower had not met either Bulganin, chairman of the Council of Ministers, or Khrushchev, First Secretary of the Communist Party. He had seen CIA studies on them, as well as estimates of who was really in charge, but none of it was conclusive. Eisenhower could hardly believe that four strong-willed Russian Communists were genuinely sharing power, so he set as one of his objectives at Geneva discovering who the real boss was. To that end, he set John to work. Eisenhower recalled that John had been a big hit with Zhukov during the 1945 trip to Moscow, and asked John to stick by Marshal Zhukov's side throughout the conference. Zhukov just might, Eisenhower said, drop something around John that he might otherwise withhold.

Eisenhower's natural curiosity was reinforced by his practical need to know. If Zhukov, for example, was really in charge of defense policy, Eisenhower felt certain he could get a positive response to his inspection proposal. During the opening rounds of cocktail parties, Eisenhower devoted himself exclusively to the Russians, much to the dismay of Eden and Dulles.

At one party, Eisenhower, John, and Zhukov were together in the garden and Zhukov remarked that his daughter was getting married that day but that he had passed up the ceremony to see his "old friend." Eisenhower turned to an aide and had some presents brought out, including a portable radio. Zhukov, visibly embarrassed, said softly that "there are things [in Russia] that are not as they seem." To both Eisenhowers, Zhukov seemed only a shell of himself, a broken man, almost pathetic. Father and son recalled the "cocky little rooster" they had known at the end of the war; now Zhukov spoke "in a low monotone . . . as if he was repeating a lesson that had been drilled into him. . . . He was devoid of animation, and he never smiled or joked, as he used to do." The President noted a feeling of "sadness" and thereafter dismissed Zhukov from his mind. Whoever was in charge, it certainly was not Zhukov.[1]

At dinner that evening, Eisenhower sat with Khrushchev, Bulganin, and Molotov. He appealed to their reason. "It is essential," Eisenhower declared in a loud voice, "that we find some way of controlling the threat of the thermonuclear bomb. You know we both have enough weapons to wipe out the entire northern hemisphere from fall-out alone. No spot would escape the fall-out from an exchange of nuclear stockpiles." The Russians nodded their vigorous agreement.[2]

Eisenhower did a masterful job of stage-managing his inspection proposal. On July 18, in his opening statement, he took an extremely tough line, one that indeed seemed intransigent and certainly was not a part of the "spirit of Geneva" he had been promoting. Eisenhower said the first issue the conference should discuss was "the problem of unifying Germany and forming an all-German government based on free elections. Beyond that, we insist a united Germany is entitled as its choice, to exercise its inherent right of collective self-defense." In other words, the reunified Germany would be a full partner in NATO. Next, Eisenhower wanted to discuss East Europe and the failure to implement the Yalta promises. Then there was "the problem of international Communism." Stirring up revolutions around the world was something the United States "cannot ignore." Eisenhower knew that the chances of getting a Soviet response on any of these demands were zero.

Over the next two days, the discussions were generally acrimonious and never profitable. The Russians concentrated on denouncing Eisenhower's position on Germany. Then, on July 21, at the Palais des Nations, speaking from some note cards, Eisenhower said, "I have been searching my heart and mind for something that I could say here that could convince everyone of the great sincerity of the United States in approaching this problem of disarmament." Turning to look directly at the Soviet delegation, he said he wanted to speak principally to them. He thereupon proposed "to give to each other a complete blueprint of our military establishments, from beginning to end, from one end of our countries to the other." Next, "to provide within our countries facilities for aerial photography to the other country." The Americans would make airfields and other facilities available to the Russians, and allow them to fly wherever they wished. The Russians would provide identical facilities for the United States.

When Eisenhower finished, there was a tremendous clap of thunder, and all the lights went out. When he recovered from his surprise, Eisenhower laughed and said, "Well, I expected to make a hit but not that much of one." More than twenty years later Vernon Walters, Eisenhower's translator, said that "to this day, I am told, the Russians are still trying to figure out how we did it."[3]

The French and British expressed their hearty approval of the idea. Bulganin spoke last. The proposal, he said, seemed to have real merit. The Soviet delegation would give it complete and sympathetic study at once. But when the session ended, Khrushchev walked beside Eisenhower on the way to cocktails. Although he was smiling, he said, "I don't agree with the chairman." Eisenhower could hear "no smile in his voice." Eisenhower realized immediately that Khrushchev was the man in charge. "From that moment," he recalled, "I wasted no more time probing Mr. Bulganin." Instead, he stayed after

Khrushchev, arguing the merits of what was being called Open Skies. Khrushchev said the idea was nothing more than a bald espionage plot against the Soviet Union.[4]

Why Khrushchev reacted so adversely is a puzzle. Eisenhower made the offer sincerely, and he emphasized that it would be "only a beginning." The President could not see what the Russians had to lose. Overflights, the Russians surely knew, were inevitable within two or three years anyway. How Open Skies would have worked out, no one knows, although the difficulties were surely huge; imagine, for example, the problems involved in having a Soviet air base in the middle of the Great Plains, or in New England, not to mention those of the exchange of military blueprints. But no one knows because Open Skies never was tried. Khrushchev had killed it within minutes of its birth.

Disappointed though he was by Khrushchev's quick rejection, which Eisenhower correctly decided was authoritative, Eisenhower nevertheless continued to build the spirit of Geneva. The next day, July 22, he made his presentation on the need for more trade between the U.S.S.R. and the United States, as well as a "free and friendly exchange of ideas and of people." And his parting words, at the last session of July 23, were: "In this final hour of our assembly, it is my judgment that the prospects of a lasting peace with justice, well-being, and broader freedom, are brighter. The dangers of the overwhelming tragedy of modern war are less." He was specific about what he had learned and accomplished: "I came to Geneva because I believe mankind longs for freedom from war and rumors of war. I came here because of my lasting faith in the decent instincts and good sense of the people who populate this world of ours. I shall return home tonight with these convictions unshaken . . ."[5]

That final statement, coupled with Eisenhower's proposals, was what made Geneva a dramatic moment in the Cold War. For the five years before Geneva, there were war scares on an almost monthly basis, with major wars going on in Korea and Indochina. For the five years after Geneva, war scares were relatively rare, except at Suez in 1956, and no major wars were fought. The leaders of the two sides had met and agreed among themselves that they were indeed two scorpions in a bottle. Bulganin's parting words to Eisenhower were "Things are going to be better; they are going to come out right."[6]

As Dulles had warned would be the case, nothing had been settled at Geneva. But as Eisenhower had determined would be the case, Geneva produced an intangible but real spirit that was felt and appreciated around the world. The year following Geneva was the calmest of the first two decades of the Cold War.

In late August, Ike and Mamie flew to Denver for their summer vacation. The fishing was the best Eisenhower could remember. He enjoyed cooking the trout for his gang and the press corps. The weather for golf at Cherry Hills, Eisenhower's favorite course, was perfect. Lowry Air Force Base in Denver provided him with a complete communications hookup, and an office where he could work a couple of hours a day.

Eisenhower used his vacation to do some thinking and talking about the 1956 presidential election. His friends told him that they would feel he was letting them down if he retired. He resented their pressure, and insisted that he had given them no reason to think he would run again so he could not be guilty of letting them down. He told Milton that he wanted to "retain as long as possible a position of flexibility," but barring some unforeseen crisis, he would not run again.[7]

He had his health to think about. He was not at all sure he could or should take the mental pounding for another four years. He had another worry. Churchill had not been at Geneva. Eisenhower had found it strange to be at an international meeting without him, but he also knew from his own dealings with Churchill before the old man finally retired that Churchill had held on to power far too long. What worried Eisenhower was, as he told Swede, "Normally the last person to recognize that a man's mental faculties are fading is the victim himself." Eisenhower said, "I have seen many a man 'hang on too long' under the definite impression that he had a great duty to perform and that no one else could adequately fill his particular position." Eisenhower feared that this might happen to him, because "the more important and demanding the position, the greater the danger in this regard."[8]

Ike spent September 19 to 23 at Aksel Nielsen's ranch at Fraser, Colorado. On the morning of the twenty-third, he was up at 5 A.M. to cook breakfast for George Allen, Nielsen, and two guests. He skipped the wheat cakes and made only bacon and eggs. At 6:45 they left Fraser and drove to Denver. Eisenhower went to his office at Lowry; Ann Whitman later wrote in her diary that "I have never seen him look or act better." He was in a good mood, went through his work cheerfully, read a letter from Milton and handed it to Whitman, saying, "See what a wonderful brother I have."[9]

About 11 A.M. he and Allen drove out to Cherry Hills and began to play. Twice Ike had to return to the clubhouse for phone calls from Dulles, only to be told that there was difficulty on the lines. He had a hamburger with slices of Bermuda onion for lunch and returned to the course. Again he was called to the clubhouse to talk to Dulles, there to be told that it was a mistake. He was scoring badly, his stomach was upset, his temper flaring. Giving up on golf, he and Allen drove to Mamie's mother's home, where they were spending the evening. Ike and Allen shot some billiards before dinner, declining a cocktail. At 10 P.M., Eisenhower went to bed.

About 1:30 A.M. Ike woke with a severe chest pain. "It hurt like hell," he later confessed, but he did not want to alarm Mamie. Nevertheless his stirring about woke her. She asked if he wanted anything. Thinking of his indigestion the previous afternoon, Ike asked for some milk of magnesia. From the tone of his voice, she knew there was something seriously wrong. Mamie called Dr. Snyder, who arrived at the bedside about 2 A.M. Noting that the patient was suffering with pain in the chest area, Snyder broke a pearl of amyl nitrite and gave it to Ike to sniff while he prepared a hypodermic of one grain of papaverine and immediately thereafter one-fourth grain of morphine sulphate. He then told Mamie to get back into bed with her husband and keep him warm. Forty-five minutes later, Snyder gave Eisenhower another one-fourth grain of morphine to control the symptoms.[10]

Ike slept until noon. When he woke, he was still groggy, had not shaken off the effects of the morphine, did not know what had happened to him. But his first thoughts were of his responsibilities. He told Snyder to tell Whitman to call Brownell "for an opinion as to how he could delegate authority." Snyder insisted on taking an electrocardiogram first; it located the site of the lesion in the anterior wall of the heart. Eisenhower had suffered a coronary thrombosis. Snyder decided to transfer him to a hospital immediately. As the stairs were too narrow for a stretcher, and as Snyder thought it better for both physical and morale factors for the President to walk, Ike walked, heavily supported, to the car for the drive to Fitzsimons Army Hospital in Denver. Before leaving his bedroom, and once again in the car with Snyder, Ike asked about his wallet, about which he was terribly concerned. He asked Mamie several times about it. She assured him she had brought it along.[11]

In the hospital, Ike was put into an oxygen tent. Snyder continued his medication, discontinuing morphine after the second day. John flew down from Fort Belvoir. Arriving at Fitzsimons, he conferred with Mamie, who was being tough, strong, and confident. Then he went to see his father. "You know," Ike said after their greeting, "these are things that always happen to other people; you never think of them happening to you." Then he asked John to hand him his wallet. He explained that he had won a bet from George Allen and wanted to give the money to Barbara. John withdrew to let his father rest; Hagerty told him in the corridor that the heart attack was moderate, "not severe but not slight either." [12]

By the end of the second day, Ike was resting comfortably, feeling well, beginning to talk about getting back to work. Mamie was living on the eighth floor of the hospital with him, doing her best to cope with the shock and find some therapy for herself (she lost ten pounds during the first two weeks) to keep her busy. She decided to answer, by hand, each of the thousands of letters and cards that were coming in from all over the country. John confessed, "I thought she was out of her mind," but he later saw the wisdom of her finding something for herself to do. And she actually completed the task. [13]

The President's heart attack inevitably put a great strain on the relations among the members of the Administration. In the first couple of weeks of Eisenhower's recuperation, no one knew whether or not he would be able to resume his place as President at any time, much less in the near future. There was a general and widespread assumption that whatever else it meant, the heart attack precluded a second term. Thus any jockeying for power in September 1955 was over not just the next year but the next five years.

Nixon was in the most difficult position. Almost anything he did would be wrong. If he shrank from seizing power, he would look uncertain and unprepared; if he attempted to seize power, he would look ruthless and uncaring. But he managed to find a narrow middle ground, helped in no small part by Eisenhower's early insistence that Cabinet and NSC meetings go forward as scheduled, with Nixon in the chair. On September 29, Nixon met with the NSC, the next day with the Cabinet. He issued a press release which emphasized that "the subjects on the agenda for these meetings were of a normal routine nature." He also called in photographers to observe the harmony among Eisenhower's "family" and to record how the teamwork was so effective that the government was functioning "as usual." [14]

Despite the appearance of unity in the Administration, an intense behind-the-scenes struggle for power was going on. Dulles, not Nixon, was the leading figure at the meetings, and Dulles insisted on sending Sherman Adams to Denver to be at the President's side to handle all liaison activities. Nixon questioned this arrangement, indicating that he thought Adams ought to stay in Washington while he, Nixon, went to Denver. But Dulles prevailed. Dulles also stressed that there would be no further delegation of powers by the President.

The best reporters in Washington could hardly miss the real story. James Reston had already reported, on September 26, that the Eisenhower Republicans were anxious to keep control in the hands of Sherman Adams and away from Nixon, because they were not going to hand over the party to Nixon, and with it the 1956 nomination. Dulles, Humphrey, Adams, Hagerty, and the others felt that Nixon would allow the right wing to dominate the party, and that he would lose to Stevenson (a Gallup Poll in October showed Nixon losing to Stevenson while Warren came out ahead in a race with Stevenson). Richard Rovere observed, in *The New Yorker,* that Adams "regards himself as the President's appointed caretaker and is doing everything he can to cut Mr. Nixon down to size." Nixon, meanwhile, received a telegram from Styles Bridges, which advised, "You are the constitutional second-in-command and you ought to assume the leadership. Don't let the White House clique take command."[15]

As the power struggle progressed, Eisenhower was having a smooth convalescence. His color, his appetite, his energy, and his general demeanor all improved rapidly. He rather enjoyed his enforced rest. His doctors decided to keep newspapers from him, but after the first few days allowed Whitman and Hagerty to bring him news and answer questions.

The timing of the heart attack was fortunate in the extreme; if it had come at any time during the series of war scares of 1954 and 1955, when Eisenhower's firm hand was crucial to keeping the peace, there is no way of knowing what might have happened. But the world scene was quiet in the fall of 1955, thanks in large part to the spirit of Geneva, and during the crisis over the President's illness the Russians stayed discreetly silent and in the background. Had it come later, when the 1956 campaign was already under way, Eisenhower would not have had time to recuperate or think through his options, and Nixon would have had the nomination by default. Eisenhower was also lucky in that the attack came when Congress was not in session, so there were no bills for him to sign or veto. If there ever was a time when the United States in the Cold War could get by without a functioning President for a few weeks, it was the fall of 1955.

• •

Eisenhower wanted to see some of his own gang. He asked especially for Slater. On November 3, Slater flew to Denver. When he arrived at Fitzsimons the following day, he found Ike in Mamie's room helping her balance her checkbook. Ike wanted to talk about his retirement. They conversed at length about Angus cattle, about Eisenhower's plans for the Gettysburg farm. Ike said he wanted to plow as much money as he could into the farm now, while he was in a high tax bracket. He was concerned about improving the soil at Gettysburg.

On October 25, Eisenhower went for his first walk since entering the hospital. On November 11, he and Mamie flew to Washington, where a crowd of five thousand greeted him at the airport. Eisenhower walked to the microphone and said a few words, then drove up to Gettysburg.

Gettysburg was the ideal place for his recovery. The house was large and comfortable. The major feature was a glassed-in porch, where the Eisenhowers spent most of their time. It had large sliding glass doors that opened onto a terrace; beyond the terrace there was a putting green, farther out a pasture. The doctors said Ike could practice his putting so long as he did not overdo it. The Slaters came for a visit; Mamie took them for a tour of the house. Slater noted that it was beautifully done, "but what makes it really charming is Mamie's enthusiasm over the whole place and her own pride and delight in having created her first home of their own."

Ike had Slater join him in a golf cart for a tour of the farm. When they got to the pasture where the Angus cattle were grazing, Ike grinned impishly, pulled out a cattle horn, blew it, and laughed delightedly when—to Slater's surprise—the cattle came running.

Like millions of other Americans, Slater was intensely curious about Eisenhower's political plans. He assumed that Mamie wanted no part of a second term, especially so since her home was now complete, and after her husband's heart attack. Mamie never said that directly to him, however. Slater himself, like the rest of the gang, wanted Eisenhower to retire and thought he deserved it. But Slater also noted that "he's been too active to sit at home on the farm and wait for people to come to him." [16]

Mamie was one of the first to sense this truth. Dr. Snyder had told her, while Ike was still in Fitzsimons, that her husband's life expectancy might be improved if he ran for a second term rather than withdraw to a life of inactivity. She knew Snyder was right, that inactivity would be fatal for Ike. John was with her when Snyder gave her his view; as the three of them talked, Mamie volunteered another reason for a second term. "I just can't believe that Ike's work is finished," she declared.[17]

Neither could he. In mid-December, Eisenhower had a series of talks with Hagerty about politics and 1956. Eisenhower said that he was concerned about the welfare of the country, particularly in the foreign field. Hagerty recorded in his diary, "He was appalled by the lack of qualified candidates on the Democratic side and particularly pointed to Stevenson, Harriman, and Kefauver as men who did not have the competency to run the Office of President." Harriman, currently the governor of New York, was in Eisenhower's view "a complete nincompoop. He's nothing but a Park Avenue Truman."[18]

During his conversations with Hagerty, Eisenhower threw out ideas. At one meeting Adams was also present. "You know, boys," Eisenhower said, "Tom Dewey has matured over the last few years and he might not be a bad presidential candidate. He certainly has the ability and if I'm not going to be in the picture, he also represents my way of thinking." The remark left Adams and Hagerty speechless. The following day, Eisenhower brought up Dewey's name again. This time Hagerty said that if Eisenhower tried to foist Dewey off on the Republican Party once more, the right wing would revolt and nominate Knowland. "I guess you're right," Eisenhower sighed, dismissing Dewey from his mind.[19]

Eisenhower asked about Nixon's chances. Hagerty, who from early October on had insisted that Eisenhower would have to run again, said he thought "Nixon is a very excellent vice-presidential candidate," but not ready for the top spot. On December 14, Hagerty showed Eisenhower a David Lawrence column in the *Herald Tribune*. Lawrence speculated that if the doctors told Eisenhower he was physically capable of continuing in office, Eisenhower would say, "I had no desire to come to public office in the first place . . . But if the people want me to serve, I shall obey their wish and serve if elected." Eisenhower read it through, laughed, and exclaimed, "Well, I'll be goddamned." Turning to Hagerty, Eisenhower said, "Jim . . . that's almost exactly the words that are forming in my own mind should I make up my mind to run again."[20]

By Christmas 1955, Eisenhower felt fully recovered. He found that he could conduct Cabinet and NSC meetings without undue difficulty, meet with his advisers on a regular basis in the Oval Office, and perform his other duties, all without fatigue or weariness. He was ready to resume a full daily work schedule and was convinced that his recovery from his heart attack would be complete. But that did not mean he would necessarily run again. He was still keeping his options open, although he remained distressed by the failure to locate anyone in the Republican Party who could successfully replace him. John, Barbara, and the grandchildren came to the White House for the holidays; on Christmas Day, as the family was driving to church, Ike turned to John and said, "I told the boys four years ago that they ought to get someone who'd want to run again for a second term."[21]

The day after Christmas, Eisenhower called Nixon into his office for a private chat. A number of Eisenhower's aides, led by Adams, had been urging him, if he decided to run again, to dump Nixon. They provided Eisenhower with the results of current polls, which indicated that Nixon would cost Eisenhower three or four points in a race with Stevenson. Eisenhower cited the figures to Nixon, then said that in his opinion Nixon could strengthen himself for 1960 by accepting a Cabinet post, where he could get some experience in administration. Eisenhower offered Nixon any post he wanted, except that of Secretary of State or Attorney General, but urged him to replace Charlie Wilson at Defense.

Nixon smelled the very obvious rat. He knew—and he at least suspected that Eisenhower knew—that the press would interpret such a move as a demotion, so serious a demotion as to probably ruin Nixon's chance to ever be President. Nixon told Eisenhower that putting someone else on the ticket in 1956 would "upset the many Republicans who still considered me [your] principal link with party orthodoxy." Nixon then asked Eisenhower, directly, whether the President believed that the Republicans would be better off with someone else as the vice-presidential candidate.[22]

Eisenhower did not answer. He would not order Nixon off the ticket. Still, he wished Nixon would leave voluntarily, and suggested again that Nixon could pick up some badly needed experience as Secretary of Defense. The conversation ended on that inconclusive note.

At the beginning of the new year, Ike flew to Key West for a week in the sun. Slater, Bill Robinson, George Allen, and Al Gruenther joined him there. Ike's friends agreed that there had been a "great change . . . in his apparent health, his enthusiasm, and completely relaxed attitude . . ." They played bridge almost nonstop, with "a great deal of banter and kidding and laughing." When Ike reneged, he was the butt of the jokes for the remainder of the evening. Slater said he feared they were overdoing the bridge, that they were taxing Eisenhower's strength. Allen replied that he had "never seen the President in such good spirits," and told Slater that their bridge games were as nothing compared to the poker games he used to play with Truman in the White House; Truman's games sometimes began early in the morning and would "go on and on until late at night," often with "dire results" for Truman.

Inevitably in an election year, much of the talk around the bridge table was political. The burning question was, of course, whether or not Ike would run again. The members of the gang agreed among themselves that he would. Allen had it straight from Mamie—who was in Gettysburg—that she wanted him to stay in office. Slater too thought Ike would stand for re-election, because he had done such a good job of organizing his office that "things seem to move with clocklike precision." [23]

But a number of factors made the decision in 1956 more difficult for Eisenhower than 1952 had been. He was sixty-five years old, had suffered a heart attack, had persistent stomach problems, was not sleeping well, and claimed that he resented the idea that one man was indispensable. He also claimed he had grown immune to the argument that he had a "duty" to serve. Surely neither the nation nor the Republican Party had any right to ask more of him.

As with every recovering heart-attack patient, death was very much on his mind. "As I embark on the last of life's adventures," he wrote by hand on a sheet of White House stationery in early February, "my final thoughts will be for those I've loved, family, friends and country." [24] Under the circumstances, would it be fair and right for him to run again? What if he died or were incapacitated between the convention and the election, or after the election? Such questions added not only to his personal anxiety but also to his concern about what would happen to his party and his country. His choice of a running mate in 1956 would be far more critical than it had been in 1952, not so much in terms of voter appeal, but in the possibility that the running mate might have to become the candidate, or succeed Eisenhower upon his death. That was why Eisenhower had tried to persuade (and continued to try to persuade) Nixon to take a Cabinet post.

Eisenhower's feelings about Nixon were ambiguous. In their three years together, they had not developed an intimate relationship. Eisenhower appreciated Nixon for his obvious qualities—he was extremely hardworking, highly intelligent, loyal, devoted to Eisenhower and the Republican Party, an effective campaigner who could take the low road, allowing Eisenhower to stay on the high road. On January 25, in a press-conference briefing, Eisenhower told Hagerty that "it would be difficult to find a better Vice-President." As compared to Knowland and most other prominent Republicans, Eisenhower much preferred Nixon, who had, in the President's view, learned a great deal since 1952. But, Eisenhower added, "people think of him [Nixon] as an immature boy." Eisenhower did not say that he agreed with that judgment, but did indicate that he thought Nixon should leave the Vice-Presidency, where he might become "atrophied," to assume a post in the Cabinet.[25]

In a conversation with Dulles, Eisenhower was more direct. He said "he was not sure" it was a good idea for Nixon to stay on the ticket. Using the approach that he had fixed in his mind as the best way to ease Nixon out, he claimed that another term as Vice-President would ruin Nixon politically (a judgment neither Nixon nor anyone else accepted, not only because a "dump Nixon" move would be sure to damage his career, but for the more obvious, if crass, reason that as Vice-President, Nixon had only a recent heart-attack victim between himself and the White House). Eisenhower nevertheless seriously told Dulles that Nixon ought to become Secretary of Commerce. Dulles doubted that Nixon would take it, and suggested that Nixon succeed him as Secretary of State. Eisenhower laughed and said Dulles was not going to get out of his job that easily, then added that "he doubted in any event that Nixon had the qualifications to be Secretary of State."[26]

In a January 25 press conference, Eisenhower was asked if, in the event he decided to seek re-election, he wanted Nixon for a running mate. Eisenhower replied that "my admiration, respect, and deep affection for Mr. Nixon . . . are well known." Then he said, in a statement that was the direct opposite of the truth, that "I have never talked to him under any circumstances as to what his future is to be or what he wants it to be, and until I confer with him I wouldn't have anything to say."[27] That fell far short of an endorsement and left Nixon in agony, but it allowed Eisenhower to keep his options open.

Eisenhower's sense of himself as the nation's steward, meanwhile, which had come on him so strongly after the heart attack, had grown in the months of recuperation. It was at this time that Eisenhower put his greatest efforts into such programs as the Soil Bank and the Interstate Highway System. As another example, he made more diary entries in January 1956 than in any other month of his Presidency, or indeed during the war. Most of the entries were concerned with long-range problems. One was about a report he had read on the damage that could be anticipated in the United States in the event of an all-out nuclear war. There were a number of scenarios, but even at best, the country would suffer 65 percent casualties. To Eisenhower, this was "appalling." Even if the United States were "victorious," "it would literally be a business of digging ourselves out of ashes, starting again." [28]

Nuclear war had to be avoided at all costs. But so did surrender. Eisenhower looked around him and could see no one whom he could trust to take his place. He could not trust Nixon or Knowland to act deliberately in a crisis; he could not trust Warren to act soon enough. That was one reason why he never told Nixon—as FDR had told two of his Vice-Presidents, Garner and Wallace—that the time had come for them to part. There was no one else around he liked or trusted any more than he did Nixon, except Warren, but Warren could not be asked to leave the Court to be a Vice-President.

So Eisenhower was stymied, both by the actual situation and by his own perception of himself and his contemporaries. In finding shortcomings in every possible successor, Eisenhower was coming to see himself as indispensable. He never said so directly, in fact denied it vehemently every time his supporters told him he was the "only man" who could keep the peace. He never wrote it in his diary. But nevertheless, he had come to think of himself as indispensable.

His associates reinforced the belief. At every opportunity, they told him it was so. Nixon did so, of course, at some length. So did Hagerty and all the aides. So did the Secretary of State, who met with the President over cocktails two days before Eisenhower announced his decision. In his memo on the conversation, Dulles wrote, "I expressed my feeling that the state of the world was such as to require the President to serve." Dulles believed that America's standing in the world had never been higher, that Eisenhower was the most trusted leader around the world and the greatest force for peace. Eisenhower wrote in his diary, "I suspect that Foster's estimate concerning my own position is substantially correct." [29]

Eisenhower's mind was made up. He would run again if the doctors gave him a go-ahead. On February 12, he went to Walter Reed for a series of tests; two days later the doctors declared, "Medically the chances are that the President should be able to carry on an active life satisfactorily for another five to ten years." [30] After the tests,

Eisenhower went down to Humphrey's plantation in Georgia for some quail shooting. On February 25 he returned to Washington. Four days later he announced his decision at a press conference. He would be a candidate for re-election.

Eisenhower's announcement was tantamount to his nomination. Thus he immediately had to face the question every nominee faces: Who would be his running mate? Eisenhower refused to answer, "in spite of my tremendous admiration for Mr. Nixon." The President said "it is traditional . . . to wait and see who the Republican Convention nominates" before announcing the vice-presidential candidate. That was too coy to satisfy the reporters. Charles von Fremd of CBS asked for clarification: "Would you like to have Nixon?" Eisenhower replied, "I will say nothing more about it. I have said that my admiration and my respect for Vice-President Nixon is unbounded. He has been for me a loyal and dedicated associate, and a successful one. I am very fond of him, but I am going to say no more about it."[31]

What to do about Nixon? Ike continued to urge Nixon to pick a Cabinet post for himself (but not State or Justice), to insist on something that seemed ridiculous to every other observer, that Nixon would thereby strengthen himself for 1960. In Eisenhower's press conferences that spring of 1956, Nixon was the number-one topic. The more Eisenhower tried to praise him, it somehow seemed, the more tongue-tied he got; the more he tried to endorse Nixon's leadership qualities, the more doubtful he sounded. Thus on March 7, in response to a question as to whether he would "dump Nixon" or not, he began indignantly: "If anyone ever has the effontery to come in and urge me to dump somebody that I respect as I do Vice-President Nixon, there will be more commotion around my office than you have noticed yet." Then he said he "had not presumed to tell the Vice-President what he should do with his own future." He added that he had told Nixon that "I believe he should be one of the comers in the Republican Party. He is young, vigorous, healthy, and certainly deeply informed on the processes of our government. And so far as I know, he is deeply dedicated to the same principles of government that I am."

Well, then, if Nixon wanted to stay on the ticket, would Eisenhower be content? Eisenhower snapped back, "I am not going to be pushed into corners here . . . I do say this: I have no criticism of Vice-President Nixon to make, either as a man, an associate, or as my running mate on the ticket."[32] What Eisenhower did not tell the press, but did say to Nixon, was that Nixon would be better off running one of the big departments, but "if you calculate that I won't last five years, of course that is different." It was cruel, really, of Eisenhower to put it bluntly—what on earth could Nixon answer? The Vice-President contented himself with mumbling that "anything the President wanted him to do, he would do." [33]

Two weeks later, at a press-conference briefing, Eisenhower told Hagerty, "The idea of trying to promote a fight between me and Dick Nixon is like trying to promote a fight between me and my brother. I am happy to have him in government." That sounded like an endorsement, but Eisenhower immediately added, "That still doesn't make him Vice-President. He has serious problems. He has his own way to make." Eisenhower said he did not know what Nixon was going to do, "but there is nothing to be gained politically by ditching him." Ambiguous as always about Nixon, Eisenhower then said he did not want to give Nixon the inside track to the nomination in 1960. "I want a bevy of young fellows to be available four years from now." [34]

Despite the lack of intimacy between the two men, despite Eisenhower's frequently expressed private doubts about Nixon's ability either to run the government or to win votes, despite Hagerty's warning to Eisenhower that "not one person was for Nixon for Vice-President for a second term," Eisenhower would not act decisively to get rid of Nixon. Despite Eisenhower's undoubted admiration for many of Nixon's talents, despite Eisenhower's frequently expressed public satisfaction with Nixon's actions as Vice-President, despite Nixon's popularity with the Old Guard, which was insisting that he stay on the ticket, Eisenhower refused to endorse Nixon. Instead, he remained indecisive.

Ever since the *Brown* decision was announced, and even before, Eisenhower had gone to great lengths to divorce himself from the problem of race relations, and especially integration of the schools. Integration, he said over and over, was the responsibility of the courts. The judges should exercise the leadership. There was no executive responsibility. He would not involve himself or his Administration.

In early January, in his State of the Union address, Eisenhower called for a bipartisan commission to investigate the racial situation and make recommendations for appropriate legislation. He hoped that such a commission would act as a buffer to keep the race issue out of partisan politics and reduce tension. Brownell, meanwhile, was eager to sponsor a new civil-rights bill (none had been passed since Reconstruction, eighty-five years earlier). Eisenhower told Brownell to get to work on it.

On January 25, at a news conference, Eisenhower was asked how he felt about race relations. He began his answer by asserting "these things aren't simple." He reiterated, "My devotion to the decisions of the Supreme Court, particularly when they are unanimous, I hope is complete." He said, "I believe in the equality of opportunity for every citizen of the United States," but immediately repeated, "It isn't quite as simple as that." Eisenhower emphasized that "we want the schools now," and reminded the reporters that the Supreme Court itself had said that desegregation should be "implemented gradually." The President said he had to recognize "the deep ruts of prejudice and emotionalism that have been built up over the years in this problem." He wanted moderation on the race issue.[35]

Moderation was hard to find. To the black community, words like "moderate" and "gradual" had come to mean "never," which was exactly what the majority of the white South wanted—never. Racial violence, always endemic in the South, increased, almost always by the whites against the blacks.

But Eisenhower and his aides felt that the black community was guilty of pushing too hard, too fast, and of ingratitude. In February 1956, Eisenhower expressed his disappointment at the results of a study of black voting in the 1954 congressional elections. Eisenhower felt that after all he and the Republicans had done for Negroes—the desegregation of military base facilities and of Washington, D.C.— the percentage of Negroes voting Republican should have gone up. But it had not.

The South's counterattack against *Brown* by 1956 was being launched with vigor and imagination. In February, four southern state legislatures passed interposition resolutions that claimed the Supreme Court decision in *Brown* had no force or effect in their states. Eisenhower was asked at a February 29 news conference about his reaction to the doctrine of interposition. Eisenhower ducked: "Now, this is what I say: there are adequate legal means of determining all of these factors." He would leave interposition to the courts. He expected that "we are going to make progress," but emphasized that "the Supreme Court itself said it does not expect revolutionary action suddenly executed. We will make progress, and I am not going to attempt to tell them how it is going to be done."[36]

On March 1, Eisenhower showed again his capacity for caution on the race issue. A federal judge ordered the University of Alabama to enroll Autherine Lucy; university officials then expelled her on the astonishing grounds that in her suit against the university, she had lied when she said that her race was the reason she had earlier been denied admittance. This seemed a clear-cut case of defiance of federal court orders, something Eisenhower had sworn many times he was pledged to and determined to enforce. But he remained aloof, strengthening the view in the South that the Eisenhower Administration would never intervene to enforce integration.

In early March, the South's counterattack escalated from the state to the federal level, as 101 southern members of the House and Senate signed a "manifesto" in which they committed themselves to try to overturn the *Brown* decision. On March 14, Eisenhower was asked to comment. He managed to see the thing from the South's point of view. "Let us remember this one thing," he said, "and it is very important: the people who have this deep emotional reaction on the other side were not acting over these past three generations in defiance of law. They were acting in compliance with the law as interpreted by the Supreme Court [in the *Plessy* case]." *Brown* had "completely reversed" *Plessy,* Eisenhower pointed out, "and it is going to take time for them to adjust their thinking and their progress to that."

How much time? "I am not even going to talk about that; I don't know anything about the length of time it will take." Eisenhower criticized "extremists" on both sides, and offered this advice: "If ever there was a time when we must be patient without being complacent, when we must be understanding of other people's deep emotions as well as our own, this is it."

As to the manifesto, Eisenhower was quick to point out that the signers "say they are going to use every legal means," that they did not intend to act outside the law, that "no one in any responsible position anywhere has talked nullification," which Eisenhower admitted would put the country in "a very bad spot" if it happened.[37]

Eisenhower hoped that would be the end of his involvement, but when 101 congressmen formally declare they intend to change a Supreme Court decision, the President cannot escape that easily. At his next news conference, Eisenhower was asked how he, the Chief Executive, felt about defiance of Supreme Court orders. Eisenhower asserted that no one had used the words "defy the Supreme Court" and again spoke of the difficulty southerners had readjusting from *Plessy* to *Brown.* Then he said, "These people [white southerners] have, of course, their free choice as to what they want to do." He could hardly have meant it the way it sounded, but he was getting irritated by the whole issue and wanted to be done with it. His conclusion was less than resounding: "As far as I am concerned, I am for moderation, but I am for progress; that is exactly what I am for it in this."[38]

Martin Luther King, Jr., was leading a bus boycott in Montgomery, Alabama, protesting segregated seating on the city buses. Black citizens were shot, their homes and churches were bombed, but the city police were arresting the boycotters. Eisenhower told his Cabinet that he was "much impressed with the moderation of the Negroes in Alabama," and that he thought the South had made "two big mistakes," one in not admitting Miss Lucy and the other in opposing the reasonable demands of the Montgomery black community. But when Robert Spivack asked Eisenhower to comment publicly, at a press conference, on King's Montgomery crusade, Eisenhower backed away. "Well, you are asking me, I think, to be more of a lawyer than I certainly am. But, as I understand it, there is a state law about boycotts, and it is under that kind of thing that these people are being brought to trial." He could see no reason for federal involvement.[39]

A common white southern assertion at this time was that integration was a Communist plot. Eisenhower was hardly so naive as to believe that, but he did fear that the Communists would take advantage of the racial unrest. On March 9, J. Edgar Hoover presented to Eisenhower and his Cabinet a twenty-four-page briefing on the explosive situation in the South. Hoover damned the extremists on both sides, the NAACP and the White Citizens Councils. He said blacks were so terrified that they would refuse to testify as to the violence they had seen or suffered, or even talk to FBI agents. But Hoover emphasized that his greater concern was with the efforts of the Communists to infiltrate the civil-rights movement and use it to add to social unrest. For his part, Eisenhower feared that the Communists were trying to "drive a wedge between the Administration and its friends in the South in that election year . . ."

After Hoover made his presentation, Brownell outlined the civil-rights bill he was proposing. It called for a bipartisan commission, created by Congress, with the power to subpoena and to investigate alleged civil-rights violations; for a new Assistant Attorney General in charge of civil rights in the Justice Department; for new laws enforcing voting rights; and for strengthening existing civil-rights statutes to protect privileges and immunities of citizens. Eisenhower was enthusiastic about the proposals and told Brownell to go ahead with them. But Humphrey objected to Brownell's bill, which he charged went too far and too rapidly toward desegregation. Humphrey insisted that progress had to be evolutionary. He also gave a warning. "We've talked about the Deep South," he said, "but your worst problems can come in Detroit, Chicago, et al. All they need to run wild is a little expectation of backing." Wilson agreed that there were real dangers in Detroit. He pontificated: "A social evolution takes time. You can't speed it up."

"I'm at sea on all this," Eisenhower confessed. "I want to put something forward that I can show as an advance." But he was fearful. "Not enough people know how deep this emotion is in the South. Unless you've lived there you can't know . . . We could have another civil war on our hands." More probably, pressure from the North might lead the South to abandon public education altogether. The whites would then have their own church-related schools, Eisenhower said, while the blacks would have no education at all. He used the word "dilemma." "I must enforce the law," but he did not know how to do it. "They come in and say I should force the university to accept Miss Lucy," he complained. He could not do it, because education was a local matter. His hands were tied.[40]

Eisenhower's moderate, middle-of-the-road stance with regard to race relations was, of course, consistent with his general approach to all his problems. He often asserted that a person who stood at either extreme on a political or social question was always wrong. And in his memoirs, he made the best possible case he could for his position of refusing to act even while violence flared all across the South. He said he was committed to the cause of civil rights, but "I did not agree with those who believed that legislation alone could institute instant morality, [or] who believed that coercion could cure all civil rights problems . . ."[41]

Whenever Eisenhower stated his position on extremists always being wrong, he would add, "except on a moral issue." He did not see the desegregation crisis as a moral issue, but rather as one of practical politics, in which every point of view (meaning that of the white southerners) had to be considered and responded to. His critics charged that he was guilty of moral equivocation; his supporters replied that he was carefully and safely guiding the country through dangerous times.

What he had not done was provide leadership, either moral or political. What he wanted—for the problem to go away—he could not have. Around this time, Goodpaster warned him that problems that were put off could grow into unmanageable problems. But the President would not attack this one. He was trapped by his own prejudices, a prisoner of his own limited view.

The Democrats nevertheless were hard pressed to find an issue to use against Eisenhower in the presidential campaign. In February, Senator Symington of Missouri tried an issue that did not quite catch on in 1956, but which came to be a major one in 1960. It was the missile gap.

The American ballistic-missile program got started shortly after World War II, but in the cost-cutting days of the Truman Administration only a few millions of dollars had been appropriated for it (less than $7 million for ICBMs, for example). Nor did Eisenhower put any emphasis on it during his first year in office. But in 1954, following the Castle series of tests in the Pacific, the AEC reported to Eisenhower that nuclear weapons could be so drastically reduced in size that a missile could be designed and built powerful enough to carry the bombs. (Previous atomic warheads weighed nine thousand pounds.) Eisenhower then ordered research and development on missiles speeded up; in 1955 he put a half billion dollars into it, and asked for $1.2 billion in 1956. One reason for doubling the budget in 1956 was another recommendation from the scientists, that the U.S. develop an IRBM with a range of fifteen hundred miles.

Eisenhower agreed, but he also divided the programs and then split them again. The Air Force had two separate projects for ICBMs, Atlas and Titan; the Army (Jupiter) and the Navy (Thor) had IRBM responsibility. Within the Administration, there was some grumbling about this division of responsibility, and Eisenhower worried about the inherent waste involved because of duplication, but the President nevertheless decided that competition and the full use of all existing resources would speed development. In addition, in connection with the International Geophysical Year (which would begin in July 1957), in 1955 Eisenhower had created yet another program, Project Vanguard, designed to put an earth satellite in orbit.

With all the money involved, at a time when Eisenhower was continuing to reduce appropriations for conventional forces, the President told his Cabinet that he expected "to be called on to justify this money." But to his surprise, "I find out that newcomers are saying why aren't you doing more."[42] The newcomer he had in mind was Senator Symington, who at the beginning of February 1956 charged that the United States lagged seriously behind the Soviet Union in the production and development of guided missiles. At a press conference on February 8, Eisenhower was asked to comment.

"Now, I just want to ask you one thing," Eisenhower said to the reporters, "and if there is anyone here that has got the answer to this one, you will relieve me mightily by communicating it to me here or in private: Can you picture a war that would be waged with atomic missiles . . . ? It would just be complete, indiscriminate devastation, not [war] in any recognizable sense, because war is a contest, and you finally get to a point [with missiles] where you are talking merely about race suicide, and nothing else." [43]

Under those circumstances, he was damned if he was going to speed up spending on ICBMs.

CHAPTER SEVENTEEN

The 1956 Campaign

IT WAS a curious fact, but true—the man who had made the D-Day decision, and countless others since, the man who had insisted upon keeping control of events in his own hands, in 1956 was unable to decide who his own running mate should be and left the decision in other people's hands.

Had he wanted Nixon, all he needed to do was say one word at any time in the first half of 1956 and that would have been that. Had he wanted to dump Nixon, all he needed to do was say one word and he would have been rid of the Vice-President. But instead of saying the word on this momentous subject, fraught with significance for the post-Eisenhower Presidency, Eisenhower remained silent, thereby turning the decision over to others. His indecision can only be seen as an indication of his ambiguous and complex attitude toward Nixon.

The adjectives Eisenhower used to describe Nixon in his private diary are generally cold and indifferent; Nixon was "quick," or "loyal," or "dependable." Eisenhower told Arthur Larson that Nixon "isn't the sort of person you turn to when you want a new idea, but he has an uncanny ability to draw upon others' ideas and bring out their essence in a cool-headed way."[1]

Eisenhower's most persistent complaints about Nixon were that he was too political and too immature. As to the first charge, it was as much Eisenhower's fault as Nixon's. Although obviously Nixon enjoyed blasting the Democrats, and although Eisenhower frequently told him to tone it down, it was nevertheless the case that Eisenhower used Nixon in both presidential campaigns, as well as in the off-year congressional elections, for the hard-hitting partisan speeches, which allowed the President to stay above the battle.

As to the second charge, Eisenhower's comments to Larson were typical of those he made to many others. When Nixon was forty-five years old, in 1958, Eisenhower told Larson, "You know, Dick has matured." Six years later, in 1964, Eisenhower repeated, "You know, Dick has matured." Three years after that, in 1967, Eisenhower reminded Larson, "You know, Dick has really matured." But in the spring of 1956, when Eisenhower had to make the crucial decision about Nixon's career, he told Emmet Hughes, "Well, the fact is, of course, I've watched Dick a long time, and he just hasn't grown. So I just haven't honestly been able to believe that he is presidential timber."[2]

That leaves another problem. In 1956, Eisenhower was a sixty-five-year-old heart-attack victim. There was a good chance he would not live through a second term. Eisenhower loved his country and wanted the best for it. If he thought Nixon was not the best, much less unqualified to be President, Eisenhower was the one man in America who could push Nixon out of the Vice-Presidency, in order to get a man whom he trusted to serve as his potential successor. But he either could not find such a man, or, having found him, could not persuade him to take on the job of ousting Nixon.

On April 9 Eisenhower met with Nixon. The President, to Nixon's consternation, continued to urge him to take a Cabinet post, perhaps HEW or Commerce, in order to build his administrative experience. But, Eisenhower added, "I still insist you must make your decision as to what you want to do. If the answer is yes, I will be happy to have you on the ticket." He urged Nixon to take his time.[3]

On April 25, at a press conference, Eisenhower was asked if Nixon had yet charted his own course and reported back to the President. "Well," Eisenhower replied, "he hasn't reported back in the terms in which I used the expression . . . no." The following morning, Nixon asked for an appointment with the President. That afternoon, in the Oval Office, Nixon told Eisenhower, "I would be honored to continue as Vice-President under you." Eisenhower said he was pleased with Nixon's decision. The President got Hagerty on the telephone. "Dick has just told me that he'll stay on the ticket," Eisenhower said. "Why don't you take him out right now and let him tell the reporters himself. And," he added, "you can tell them that I'm delighted by the news."[4]

Republican preconvention activity was quiet and dignified. In 1952, Eisenhower and the Republicans had won a campaign in which they took the offensive, leveling various accusations against the Democrats. This time, Eisenhower intended to run on the defensive, pointing to his record of accomplishments instead of to the shortcomings of the opposition. Given the record levels of employment, the general prosperity, and the achievement of peace in the world, pointing to the record was obviously a wise and prudent decision. In addition, Eisenhower had many specific pieces of legislation he could point to with pride; his own favorite was the National System of Interstate and Defense Highways, which he signed into law on June 29, 1956.

There were, however, three outstanding problems the Republicans had to face in the weeks before the convention. First was civil rights. Second was the Middle East, where the situation threatened to escalate to a war that would damage Eisenhower's reputation as a peacemaker. Third was the festering sore in Eastern Europe, recently made worse by Khrushchev's secret speech denouncing Stalin and hinting at a liberalization of the Soviet control of the area.

On civil rights, Eisenhower's chief initiative in the summer of 1956 was Brownell's civil-rights bill. Republican leaders were cautious about the bill; although they loved putting the Democrats on the defensive by forcing the southern senators to take a stand, they worried about losing their best chance to crack the Solid South. They therefore advised Eisenhower to go slow, and told him Brownell's bill was too stringent. Eisenhower told the leaders that Brownell had been under terrific pressure "from radicals on his staff" to write an even tougher bill, and that the one Brownell had produced could hardly be "more moderate or less provocative." He complained that the southerners, who were already denouncing the bill, had not even bothered to read it. But then he turned his attention to the other side, saying that "these civil-rights people" never consider that although the President could "send in the military" he could not "make them operate the school." He then repeated a little story he had heard from Bobby Jones down at Augusta; one of the field hands was supposed to have said, "If someone doesn't shut up around here, particularly these Negroes from the North, they're going to get a lot of us niggers killed!"[5]

Brownell sent his civil-rights bill to Congress. After prolonged infighting, in July the House passed the two mildest provisions of the bill, one creating a bipartisan commission to investigate racial difficulties, the other establishing a civil-rights division in the Justice Department. Voting rights and federal responsibility for enforcing civil rights were dropped from the compromise package. Nevertheless, the bill died in the Senate Judiciary Committee, where the chairman was Senator James Eastland of Mississippi.

A major feature of the 1952 Republican platform had been the call for "liberation" of the East European satellites. Nothing that Eisenhower or his associates had done since had brought liberation any closer; indeed, as noted, Dulles thought that Eisenhower's going to the Geneva Summit had signaled an American acquiescence in Soviet domination of Eastern Europe. But in the spring of 1956, as a result of action by the Russians, not the Americans, the prospects for liberation suddenly seemed bright again.

In his famous secret speech to the Twentieth Party Congress, Khrushchev denounced Stalin for his crimes against the Russian people, and seemed to promise that in the future there would be a relaxation of Communist controls both inside Russia and in the satellite countries. The CIA obtained a copy of the speech; with Eisenhower's permission, Allen Dulles gave it to *The New York Times*. On June 5, the paper printed the speech in its entirety. Publication caused great excitement throughout Eastern Europe. Perhaps, just perhaps, the long-awaited breakup of the Soviet empire was at hand. Republicans wanted another strong plank on liberation. Eisenhower insisted that they proceed cautiously. He told Jerry Persons "that this particular plank should make it clear that we advocate liberation by all peaceful means, but not to give any indication that we advocate going to the point of war to accomplish this liberation."[6]

In the Mideast, Eisenhower had other problems. Insofar as possible, he wanted to stay out—he refused to sell arms to either Israel or the Arabs—but he also wanted to keep the Russians out. Further, he wanted good relations with the Egyptians, and had promised their leader, Gamal Abdel Nasser, American financial and technical support for the Aswan Dam. But when Nasser recognized the government of Red China and purchased arms from the Czechs, the Eisenhower Administration withdrew its support. Nasser reacted quickly and boldly: on July 26 he nationalized the Suez Canal and took control of its operations. He said he would use the revenue to pay for the dam. "The fat," as Eisenhower wrote in his memoirs, "was now really in the fire."[7]

Prime Minister Anthony Eden was ready for action. On July 27, he sent a cable to Eisenhower, arguing that the West could not allow Nasser to seize Suez and get away with it. They must act at once, together, or American and British influence throughout the Middle East would be "irretrievably undermined." He said that the interests of all maritime nations were at stake, because the Egyptians did not have the technical competence to run the canal. Eden said he was preparing military plans and said the West must be ready, as a last resort, to "bring Nasser to his senses" by force.

Eisenhower was drawn in different directions by his various desires and needs. He said that the U.S. "must let the British know how gravely we view this matter, what an error we think their decision is, and how this course of action would antagonize the American people . . ." As to the British claims that Egypt had committed a crime, Eisenhower could only say that "the power of eminent domain within its own territory could scarcely be doubted," and that "Nasser was within his rights." As to the British claim that the Egyptians could not run the canal, Eisenhower scoffed at it. The Panama Canal, he said, was a much more complex operation; he had no doubt the Egyptians could run it. But he also said that "thinking of our situation in Panama, we must not let Nasser get away with this action."[8]

On August 21 Eisenhower flew off to California to attend the Republican National Convention. It was San Francisco in August, and it could hardly have been better. Everyone had on "I Like Ike" buttons, or "Ike and Dick." Peace and prosperity were the theme. Ike had Mamie, John, Barbara, Milton, and Edgar with him. All the members of his gang came out.

On August 22, the convention nominated Eisenhower by acclamation, and Nixon as vice-presidential candidate. Ike made an appropriate acceptance speech, then went off for a few days' vacation on the Monterey Peninsula. The gang was along and they played golf and bridge for four days. On the plane ride back to Washington, Ike had his friends join him. They played nonstop bridge for eight and one-half hours. Ike returned to the White House sun-tanned, buoyant, eager to go to work on his problems.

Politics had provided an interlude in the Suez crisis, but only a brief one. As soon as Eisenhower returned to Washington, the Middle East—not the upcoming campaign—was his central concern, to which he wanted to give his undivided attention.

But of course he could not. The issue of elementary schools, for example, was pressing in on him, because simultaneously with the Suez crisis and the campaign, the 1956–1957 school year began across the nation. At all levels, college, secondary, and elementary, it was the largest opening in the history of the Republic. The classroom and teacher shortage was acute. Eisenhower often said that education was as important, or even more important, than defense, yet the sole significant contact his government had with these millions of children, who everyone agreed were the nation's greatest asset, was a school-lunch program. The two great needs of the education system, teachers and classrooms, were not addressed in any way by the federal government. The baby-boom children were being shortchanged in their education.

By no means was it entirely Eisenhower's fault, but at least some of the responsibility for this situation was his. Although he had no proposal to help the teacher crisis, beyond urging the states to raise salaries, he did propose a federal program of loans and grants to the states for school construction. He put conditions on his program, however, that made it—as he had certainly been told that it would— unacceptable to Congress. His principal condition was that the money go to the poor states; rich states like California or New York could solve their own problems. In practice, that meant most of the money appropriated for schools would go to the Deep South. There it would be used to strengthen a segregated school system existing in open defiance of the Supreme Court. Eisenhower refused to widen his proposal to send money to all the states, which would have insured passage. Instead, he did nothing. He hoped the states would solve the problem, or that it might otherwise somehow go away.

It did not, could not, has not. As schools opened, mob violence broke out in Clinton, Tennessee, and in Mansfield, Texas, as school officials attempted to carry out court-ordered desegregation. On September 5, Eisenhower was asked at a press conference whether he thought "there is anything that can be said or done on the national level to help local communities meet this problem without violence." Eisenhower thought not. It was a local problem. "And let us remember this," he said, "under the law the federal government cannot . . . move into a state until the state is not able to handle the matter."[9] But he could not get off that easily, because the desegregation crisis was getting closer to the basic point every year. That point was the question, Would the federal government use force to insure court-ordered desegregation? If it would, then integration would prevail, and the South (and the nation) thereby change forever. If it would not, segregation would continue.

Everyone involved in the crisis knew those basic facts. Everyone knew that the ultimate test had to come. Eisenhower admitted to Whitman, "Eventually a district court is going to cite someone for contempt, and then we are going to be up against it," that is, forced to act.[10] As in Suez, Eisenhower wanted to delay as long as possible, to allow people to cool down.

But others wanted the test now. Governor Allan Shivers of Texas, who had supported Eisenhower in 1952, sent Texas Rangers to defy a court order, reassigned the Negro pupils, and then said, "I defy the federal government. Tell the federal courts if they want to come after anyone, to come after me and cite me in this matter." Edward Morgan of ABC asked the President, "Would you consider that an incident in which the federal government had a responsibility, and, if not, can you give us an idea of what the formula is that would have to be followed for the government to intervene?"

Eisenhower was clear in answering one part of the question, while managing to ignore the other. If a federal court cited someone for contempt, Eisenhower said, of course U.S. marshals would serve the warrants and take the man to jail or force him to pay a fine. But as to using marshals, or any other form of federal force, to put the Negro children back into the school to which the court had assigned them, Eisenhower said not a word. Instead, he deplored violence, then expressed the hope that the states would meet their responsibilities, both to maintain law and order and to enforce the court orders on desegregation.

Eisenhower was asked if he had any advice for young people in the border states who would be attending desegregated schools that fall. Eisenhower's thoughts immediately turned to the white children, not to the Negro students. He expressed his sympathy for their situation, said he recognized that "it is difficult through law and through force to change a man's heart." The South, he said, was "full of people of good will, but they are not the ones we now hear." Eisenhower then condemned "the people . . . so filled with prejudice that they even resort to violence; and the same way on the other side of the thing, the people who want to have the whole matter settled today." (Eisenhower's comparison of civil-rights activists to southern mobs infuriated the NAACP.) Eisenhower also said, "We must all . . .

help to bring about a change in spirit so that extremists on both sides do not defeat what we know is a reasonable, logical conclusion to this whole affair, which is recognition of the equality of men."

That statement led to the next question: Did Eisenhower endorse the *Brown* decision, or merely accept it, as the Republican platform did? Eisenhower replied, "I think it makes no difference whether or not I endorse it. The Constitution is as the Supreme Court interprets it; and I must conform to that and do my very best to see that it is carried out in this country." [11]

It was an attitude he carried with him through the campaign. He refused to discuss the *Brown* decision or the topic of desegregation, except to point with pride to his ending of Jim Crow in Washington, D.C., and at Army and Navy posts. Since desegregation was not a subject the Democrats could afford to raise, Eisenhower managed to successfully avoid the issue for another year. At what cost to the nation's children, and especially those who were black and lived in the South, no one can say.

Before the convention, Eisenhower had warned the Republicans that if they nominated him, he would not undertake a strenuous or wide-ranging campaign. Instead, he intended to limit himself to four or five major speeches on national TV. One reason was his health; another was that unlike 1952, he had a record to run on; a third was that, as President, he simply did not have the time to devote to campaigning that he had had when he was only a candidate. One month after the nomination, on September 19, he made his first address. He gave a sober review of the world situation, stressing his Administration's success in maintaining peace. He dismissed Stevenson's call for a nuclear test ban as a "theatrical gesture." [12]

Eisenhower's private view of the opposition was scathing. He told Gruenther, "Stevenson and Kefauver, as a combination, are the sorriest and weakest pair that ever aspired to the highest office in the land." Eisenhower never had any doubts that he and Nixon would prevail, so he felt comfortable in letting Nixon do the vast majority of the campaigning. But, as in 1952, professional Republicans could imagine all sorts of things going wrong. "I notice that as election day approaches," Eisenhower wrote Gruenther, "everybody gets the jitters. You meet a man and he is practically hysterical with the confidence of overwhelming victory, and sometimes you see that same man that evening and his face is a foot long with fright." [13]

Pressed by the RNC to do more talking, Eisenhower convinced

himself that it was necessary. He explained to Swede that he not only wanted to win, but to win by a substantial margin. Without a mandate, he said, he would "not want to be elected at all." He gave two reasons. First, his work in "reforming and revamping the Republican Party" was far from complete, and his influence over the party would depend, in large measure, on the size of his victory. Second, he expected the Democrats to retain the House and Senate. Working with the Democrats, although it often came easier to Eisenhower than working with the Republicans, would also depend on his margin of victory. He therefore decided to "do a bit of traveling in the campaign," and made campaign speeches in half a dozen cities. He went partly for the fun of it—he always enjoyed traveling—and partly "to prove to the American people that I am a rather healthy individual." [14]

Insofar as there was an issue that got him going, it was Stevenson's call for a test ban. Insofar as there was a reason for his increasing contempt for Stevenson, it was the inept and confused way in which Stevenson raised and used the issue. Stevenson's campaign was indeed a mishmash; he wanted to end the draft, end testing, but greatly accelerate spending on missiles. Eisenhower thought that testing was far too complex and dangerous a subject to be discussed in a political campaign, and he would have preferred to leave it alone. Stevenson's advisers also told him that he was foolish to attempt to attack Eisenhower on any question concerning national defense. Stevenson nevertheless insisted on making an end to testing a central theme in his campaign, but he got nowhere with it.

Through September, the British and French continued to put the pressure on Nasser, as Eisenhower continued to urge them to go slowly. Meanwhile, the U-2 spy plane had become operational. Flights over the Middle East revealed an Israeli mobilization and the presence in Israel of some sixty French Mystère jets. Eisenhower was incensed, because under the terms of the 1950 Tripartite Declaration, the United States, the United Kingdom, and France were committed to maintaining a *status quo* in arms and borders in the Middle East. France had earlier asked for, and received, American permission to sell Mystères to Israel, but only twenty-four, not sixty. Thus Eisenhower now knew that the French were arming the Israelis in contravention of the 1950 agreement, and lying to the Americans about it.

Eisenhower did not suspect an Israeli attack on Egypt; his attention was riveted on Jordan. He told Dulles to "make it very clear to the Israelis that they must stop these attacks against the borders of Jordan." If they continued, the Arabs would turn to the Russians for arms, and "the ultimate effect would be to Sovietize the whole region, including Israel."

Eisenhower told Dulles he thought "Ben-Gurion's obviously aggressive attitude" was due to his belief that the political campaign in America would hamstring the Eisenhower Administration. Eisenhower told Dulles to set the Israelis straight: "Ben-Gurion should not make any grave mistake based upon his belief that winning a domestic election is as important to us as preserving and protecting the peace." Dulles should also tell Ben-Gurion that in the long term, aggression by Israel "cannot fail to bring catastrophe and such friends as he would have left in the world, no matter how powerful, could not do anything about it." [15]

Over the next two weeks, there was a virtual blackout on communication between the United States on the one side and the French and the British on the other. Simultaneously, American interceptors picked up heavy radio traffic between Britain and France. American code breakers were unsuccessful in unraveling the content of the messages; they could only report that the sheer volume of traffic was ominous. Eisenhower's own expectation was that the Israelis would attack Jordan, supplied by the French with covert British sanction, and that the British and the French would then take advantage of the confusion to occupy the canal. He was, in other words, badly misinformed, and had reached the wrong conclusions. He was about to be as completely surprised as he had been on December 7, 1941, by Pearl Harbor, or on December 16, 1944, by the Ardennes counteroffensive. The difference was that this time it was his friends who were fooling him.

How could it have happened? The United States maintained a huge, complex, and generally efficient intelligence system, of which the CIA was only one part. There were American reporters in London, Paris, and Tel Aviv, all filing daily dispatches about activities in the capitals. The State Department had flourishing embassies in all three capitals, plus a secret line of communication to send word on developments. The U-2s were overflying the eastern Mediterranean and sending back photographs that revealed major military moves. The CIA had spies at various levels scattered through the area. Most of all, Eisenhower had close personal friends in Eden's Cabinet and in the British military, as well as in the French government and military. But there is no evidence he made any attempt to get in touch, secretly, with his friends (Macmillan, for example, or Mountbatten, both of whom opposed Eden's adventurism) in order to find out what was going on. As a result, he was surprised.

Part of the reason was, obviously, preoccupation with the campaign, precisely the point the British, the French, and the Israelis relied upon as they did their plotting together. The more important reason for the American intelligence failure was the nature of the act itself. To Eisenhower in 1956, it made no sense—indeed was self-destructive—for the British and the French to attempt to seize and hold the canal, or for the Israelis to act aggressively when they were surrounded by a sea of Arabs, and it especially made no sense to him for Britain and France to attempt to act independently of the United States, much less against the expressed policy of the Eisenhower Administration.

So Eisenhower was badly surprised. He hated to be surprised, but experience had taught him—as he said so many times—that he had to expect to be surprised. The proper response was to remain cool, gather all the information he could, consider the options, and use them to take control of events. That was what he had done in December 1944, in one of his greatest moments as Supreme Commander. It was what he intended to do, and did, in October–November 1956, in one of his greatest moments as President.

While Britain, France, and Israel were completing the preparations for their bizarre plot, great events were occurring in Eastern Europe. Disturbances and riots in Poland, sparked by publication of Khrushchev's secret speech to the Twentieth Party Congress, swept the Soviet-dominated government out of power and brought in Wladyslaw Gomulka, a man earlier dismissed by the Soviets as a Titoist. Gomulka announced that "there is more than one road to Socialism," and warned that the Polish people would "defend themselves with all means; they will not be pushed off the road of democratization." On October 22, the Poles' successful defiance of the Soviets set off demonstrations throughout Hungary, where the demand was that Imre Nagy, who had been deposed by the Soviets in 1955, be returned to power.

Although these were spontaneous events, and quite unpredictable, they nevertheless had long been expected by the Eisenhower Administration, where it was an article of faith that sooner or later the satellites would rise up against Russia. But although the United States had anticipated a revolt, and had indeed encouraged it, both through Voice of America and Radio Free Europe broadcasts and through CIA-created underground resistance cells within Eastern Europe, when the revolt actually came, the government had no plans prepared. There was a good reason for this shortcoming—there was nothing the United States could do anyway. As always in grand strategy, geography dictated the options. Hungary was surrounded by Communist states, plus neutral Austria, and had a common border with the Soviet Union. It had no ports. There was almost no trade going on between the United States and the Russians. There was no pressure, in short, save for the amorphous one of world public opinion, that Eisenhower could bring to bear on the Soviets in Hungary. He knew it, had known it all along, which made all the four years of Republican talk about "liberation" so essentially hypocritical.

On October 23, the Hungarian government installed Nagy as Premier; he promised "democratization and improved living standards." But the riots went on, and the Soviets sent troops to Budapest to restore order. The following day, Hungarian freedom fighters began hurling homemade Molotov cocktails at Russian tanks in Budapest. Eisenhower issued a statement deploring the intervention, but he turned down frantic requests from the CIA that it be allowed to fly over Budapest and air-drop arms and supplies. Liberation was a sham. Eisenhower had always known it. The Hungarians had yet to learn it.

On October 26, Eisenhower presided over a meeting of the NSC. Allen Dulles reported on the entry of Soviet troops into Hungary, the desertion of large numbers of Hungarian Army troops, and the fighting in Budapest. Eisenhower said he wanted to proceed cautiously, that he did not want to give the Soviets any reason to think that the United States might support the Hungarian freedom fighters. Pointing to the dangers involved, he wondered if the Soviets "might not . . . be tempted to resort to extreme measures" to maintain their hold over the satellites, "even to start a world war."

Foster Dulles then reported on the developments in the Middle East, where Egypt had joined with Jordan and Syria in the Pact of Amman, which provided for military cooperation among them, and an Egyptian commander to take charge of their armed forces in the event of war with Israel. Ben-Gurion said the pact put Israel in "direct and immediate danger," and Dulles said he expected an Israeli attack on Jordan momentarily.[16]

On October 28, Eisenhower learned that Israel had ordered a general mobilization of its reserves. In addition, there was heavy radio traffic between Israel and France. Eisenhower decided to evacuate American dependents from the Middle East. He also sent a stern warning to Ben-Gurion "to do nothing which would endanger the peace." U-2 flights revealed heavy military concentrations by the British and the French on Cyprus. Most disturbing was the increase in the number of troop transports and air forces. It appeared that they had concerted a plan to take advantage of the imminent Israeli attack on Jordan to occupy the canal. Whitman, monitoring a call to Dulles, recorded, "President said he just cannot believe Britain would be dragged into this." Dulles said he had just talked to the French ambassador and the chargé. "They profess to know nothing about this at all . . . But, he [Dulles] said, their ignorance is almost a sign of a guilty conscience, in his opinion." [17]

Eisenhower and Mamie left the White House for a political trip to Miami, Jacksonville, and Richmond. About midafternoon, while his plane, the *Columbine*, was en route between Florida and Virginia, the Israelis attacked on a broad front with everything they had. But their target was Egypt, not Jordan. And the Israelis were sweeping the Egyptians before them. Eisenhower got some of the news in Richmond. He went ahead with his speech, then flew up to Washington, arriving at 7 P.M. He met with the Dulles brothers, Hoover, Wilson, Radford, and Goodpaster. Radford thought that it would take the Israeli forces three days to overrun Sinai and get to Suez, which would be the end to the whole affair. Foster Dulles disagreed. "It is far more serious than that," he said. The canal was likely to be closed, the oil pipelines through the Middle East broken. Then the British and the French would intervene. "They appear to be ready for it," Dulles said, "and may even have concerted their action with the Israelis." [18]

Finally, the Americans had caught on. Britain, France, and Israel had entered into a cabal, aimed against Egypt, not Jordan. The details of their plot had yet to be revealed, but that they had plotted together there could be no doubt. Dulles speculated that they must have convinced themselves that in the end the United States would have to give its grudging approval, and support.

The moment for decision had come. Eisenhower's strategy of delay had to give way to action. His British friends, men who had fought beside him in the war, men he admired and loved without stint, had convinced themselves that they had reached a critical moment in their history, and at such a moment they expected the United States to stand beside them. They could not believe their great friend

Ike would desert them. The French counted on Eisenhower's unbreakable commitment to NATO to force him to tilt toward them. The Israelis thought that the election, and the importance of the Jewish vote in it, would force Eisenhower to at least stay neutral, if not support them. But good as their reasoning appeared to them to be, the conspirators were as badly wrong about Eisenhower as he had been about their plans.

Eisenhower's immediate decision, from which he never retreated one inch, was that the cabal could not be allowed to succeed. The plot reeked of nineteenth-century colonialism of the worst sort; it reeked of bad planning; it reeked of bad faith and perfidy. It also violated the 1950 Tripartite Declaration. Under the circumstances, Eisenhower said (as summarized by Goodpaster): "We cannot be bound by our traditional alliances, but must instead face the question how to make good on our pledge [in the Tripartite Declaration]." As a first step, he wanted to take a cease-fire resolution to the U.N. in the morning. "The President said, in this matter, he does not care in the slightest whether he is re-elected or not . . . He added that he did not really think the American people would throw him out in the midst of a situation like this, but if they did, so be it." He wanted to tell the British, immediately, that the U.S. would side with Egypt, even though "we recognize that much is on their side in the dispute," because "nothing justified double-crossing us." [19]

Eisenhower announced that he intended to support the Tripartite Declaration, one part of which pledged the United States to support the victim of an aggression in the Middle East. The only honorable course, he said, was to carry out that pledge. He issued a White House statement to that effect.

Eisenhower began the next day, October 30, by reading a message Goodpaster handed him from Ben-Gurion, saying that Israel had to strike to save itself and rejecting any thought of a cease-fire in Sinai, much less a retreat. Arthur Flemming came in to warn that Western Europe would soon be in critical need of more oil. "The President said he was inclined to think that those who began this operation should be left to work out their own oil problems—to boil in their own oil, so to speak." [20]

At 10 A.M., Eisenhower went into a meeting with Dulles, Hoover, Sherman Adams, and Goodpaster. There was a wire-service report that British and French landings in the Suez were "imminent." Eisenhower said "that in his judgment the French and British do not have an adequate cause for war . . . He wondered if the hand of Churchill might not be behind this—inasmuch as this action is in the mid-Victorian style." He also wondered what they proposed to do to meet their oil needs. Dulles said they probably figured "we would have no choice but to take extraordinary means to get oil to them." Eisenhower said that "he did not see much value in an unworthy and unreliable ally and that the necessity to support them might not be as great as they believed." But that was just agitated talk; he knew Dulles was correct in saying that "the U.S. could not sit by and let them go under economically." [21]

At midday, Eisenhower exchanged a series of messages with Eden, arguing about whether the Tripartite Declaration was still valid or not. In New York, the Security Council was considering the U.S. resolution asking all members of the U.N. to refrain from using force in the Middle East. When the vote came that afternoon, Britain and France vetoed it. They also used the veto to defeat a Soviet resolution calling on Israel to pull back to the starting line.

At 2:17 P.M., still October 30, Dulles called to tell the President that Britain and France "gave a twelve-hour ultimatum to Egypt that is about as crude and brutal as anything he has ever seen." Dulles saw no point to studying it, because "of course by tomorrow they will be in." But Eisenhower wanted Dulles to read the ultimatum to him, as he had just received a copy and had not had time to read it. The ultimatum revealed, for the first time, the scope of the plot.

Britain and France told Egypt and Israel that unless both sides withdrew ten miles from the canal and permitted Anglo-French occupation of the key points along it, Britain and France would take the canal by force to keep the two sides apart. The Israelis, of course, agreed. If the plot worked, Israel would get to keep Sinai, the British and French would have the canal, Nasser would be toppled. To Eisenhower, such pipe dreams bordered on madness. He sent urgent cables to Eden and Mollet, at 3:30 P.M., pleading with them to withdraw the ultimatum. [22]

At dawn, October 31, the news included the results of a vote of confidence on Eden in Commons; he had survived, 270 to 218. Israeli forces were still driving westward across Sinai. But Allen Dulles, who gave the morning briefing, had some good news. The Russians had announced they would withdraw their troops from Hungary, had apologized for past behavior toward the satellites, and had pledged "noninterference in one another's internal affairs." Eisenhower feared it was too good to be true. Allen Dulles said, "This utterance is one of the most significant to come out of the Soviet Union since the end of World War II." Eisenhower replied, "Yes, if it is honest." [23]

At 9:47 A.M., Senator Knowland telephoned from California to ask if Eisenhower intended to call a special session of Congress. Eisenhower said he did not. Knowland expressed his shock at British actions. Eisenhower said what amazed him was that Eden was going ahead with the thing on the basis of a 270 to 218 vote. "I could not dream of committing this nation on such a vote." Eisenhower went on to say, "I am about to lose my British citizenship. I have done my best. I think it is the biggest error of our time, outside of losing China."[24]

In New York, meanwhile, Lodge had told the General Assembly that the United States intended to introduce a resolution calling upon Israel and Egypt to cease fire, on Israel to withdraw to its original borders, and on all U.N. members to refrain from the use of force, and to participate in an embargo against Israel until it withdrew.

At 11:45 A.M., Lodge phoned Eisenhower to tell him that "never has there been such a tremendous acclaim for the President's policy. Absolutely spectacular." The small nations of the world could hardly believe that the United States would support a Third World country, Egypt, in a struggle with colonial powers that were America's two staunchest allies, or that the United States would support Arabs against Israeli aggression. But it was true, and the small nations were full of admiration and delight.[25]

The introduction of the American resolution to the U.N. was, indeed, one of the great moments in U.N. history. Eisenhower's insistence on the primacy of the U.N., of treaty obligations, and of the rights of all nations gave the United States a standing in world opinion it had never before achieved.

Despite this overwhelming demonstration of world public opinion (even the small nations of Europe were privately telling Lodge what a great thing this was), despite the narrow vote in the House of Commons, despite Eisenhower's warnings, despite a thoroughly botched preparation for an invasion (the British and French forces were in disarray even before they went into action), Eden gave the order to strike. By midday, October 31, Eisenhower learned that British planes were bombing Cairo, Port Said, and other targets. Nasser had resisted, ineffectively, but he had managed to block the canal by sinking a 320-foot ship, previously loaded with cement and rocks; in the next few days, he sent thirty-two ships to the floor of the canal, blaming all the sinkings on the British.

Eisenhower spent most of the afternoon with Hughes, preparing for a national TV broadcast at 7 P.M. Hughes noted that the "press was edgy with expectancy, since no moment since Korea has seemed so charged with war peril. Even technicians around cameras were hushed and anxious." [26]

Eisenhower began with Poland and Hungary. He said the U.S. was ready to give economic help to new and independent governments in Eastern Europe without demanding any particular form of society, and reassured the Soviets by saying the United States wanted to be friends with these new governments but did not regard them as potential allies. Turning to the Middle East, Eisenhower said the United States wished to be friends with both Arabs and Jews. He pointed out that he had not been consulted in any way about the assault on Egypt. Britain, France, and Israel had the right to make such decisions, just as the U.S. had the right to dissent. American policy was to support the U.N. in seeking peace, and to support the rule of law.

At 9 A.M. on November 1, Eisenhower presided over an NSC meeting. Allen Dulles began with an intelligence briefing. Egypt had broken diplomatic ties with Britain and France, and Nasser had pulled most of the Egyptian Army out of Sinai to fight the British and the French in defense of the canal. In Hungary, the new Premier, Imre Nagy, told the Russians that Hungary was withdrawing from the Warsaw Pact (created in 1955 as the Soviet answer to NATO), declaring its neutrality, and appealing to the U.N. for help. The developments in Hungary, Dulles said, "are a miracle. They have disproved that a popular revolt can't occur in the face of modern weapons. Eighty percent of the Hungarian Army has defected. Except in Budapest, even the Soviet troops have shown no stomach for shooting down Hungarians." Eisenhower thanked Dulles for his presentation, then said that "he did not wish the council to take up the situation in the Soviet satellites." Instead, he wanted to concentrate on the Middle East.

Foster Dulles took the floor. His pessimism was as deep as his brother's optimism was high. The Secretary of State declared that "recent events are close to marking the death knell for Great Britain and France." Like Eisenhower, Dulles was furious with the French, British, and Israelis for plotting behind his back. Adding to the fury was the lost opportunity to exploit Soviet difficulties in Eastern Europe. "It is nothing less than tragic," Dulles said, "that at this very time, when we are on the point of winning an immense and long-hoped-for victory over Soviet colonialism in Eastern Europe," Western colonialism in Egypt was the center of the world's attention. It was maddening that the British and the French were forcing the U.S.

to choose between them and Egypt. Dulles concluded, "Yet this decision must be made in a mere matter of hours—before five o'clock this afternoon." At that hour, Dulles was scheduled to address the U.N. General Assembly, at which time he had intended to formally introduce the American cease-fire resolution. Eisenhower ordered Dulles to issue a statement about sanctions against Israel, and to go ahead that afternoon in New York with the original American cease-fire resolution.[27]

Dulles did as he was told. As darkness fell on November 1, the General Assembly began its debate on the American cease-fire resolution. That evening, Eisenhower made his last campaign speech, in Philadelphia. Referring to the Middle East, he declared, "We cannot subscribe to one law for the weak, another law for the strong; one law for those opposing us, another for those allied with us. There can be only one law—or there shall be no peace."[28] Eisenhower then canceled the rallies he had been scheduled to attend in the last week of the campaign.

The next day, November 2, Eisenhower dictated a letter to Gruenther, beginning, "Life gets more difficult by the minute." He confessed that "sleep has been a little slower to come than usual. I seem to go to bed later and wake up earlier—which bores me." But the news that morning was good—the U.N. General Assembly had adopted the U.S. cease-fire resolution by a vote of 64 to 5 (Britain, France, Australia, New Zealand, and Israel opposing). Lester Pearson of Canada then proposed a U.N. police force to interject itself between the warring parties to insure the effectiveness the cease-fire. By this time, Israeli forces had taken virtually all of Sinai and the Gaza Strip. The Egyptian Air Force had been destroyed; the Israelis had five thousand Egyptian prisoners and large quantities of Soviet-made arms. British and French planes continued to bomb Egypt, and their troops had not yet landed.

Eisenhower was appalled by both British tactics and British strategy. "If one has to fight," he told Gruenther, "then that is that. But I don't see the point in getting into a fight to which there can be no satisfactory end, and in which the whole world believes you are playing the part of the bully and you do not even have the firm backing of your entire people." Eisenhower said he had talked to an old British friend who was "truly bitter" about Eden's gunboat diplomacy, and who had declared, "This is nothing except Eden trying to be bigger than he is." Eisenhower said he "did not dismiss it that lightly. I believe that Eden and his associates have become convinced that this is the last straw and Britain simply had to react in the manner of the Victorian period."[29]

The news over the weekend was quite disheartening. On Saturday, Dulles had entered Walter Reed for an emergency cancer operation, which took place that day. For the immediate future, Herbert Hoover, Jr., would be the acting Secretary. In the Middle East, the Syrians blew up oil pipelines running through their country from Iraq to the Mediterranean. In Britain, Eden rejected the U.N. call for a cease-fire, unless Egypt and Israel accepted French-British possession of Suez until a U.N. force could arrive. On Sunday morning, at 3:13 A.M., the Security Council met to consider an American resolution calling upon the Russians to withdraw from Hungary. The Soviet Union vetoed the resolution. That morning the Red Army launched a major assault on Hungary, following an ultimatum that Hungary rejected. Some 200,000 troops accompanied by 4,000 tanks moved on Budapest. Nagy fled to the Yugoslav Embassy, and a new Hungarian government, under Janow Kadar, took office. The Hungarian freedom fighters resisted. Eisenhower sent a message to Bulganin, reminding him of the Soviet declaration of "nonintervention" made only four days earlier, praising him for that statement, and urging him to put it into action.[30]

Meanwhile, U-2 flights revealed that the British-French armada from Cyprus was finally approaching the Egyptian coast. Eisenhower again asked Eden to turn back. Eden replied that "if we draw back now everything will go up in flames in the Middle East . . . We cannot have a military vacuum while a U.N. force is being constituted."[31]

The Hungarians, meanwhile, wanted help. They thought they had been promised it by Radio Free Europe, and by Dulles' many references over the years to liberation. Eisenhower, however, had no intention of challenging the Russians so close to their borders. American intervention, of any type, would have appeared to the Russians as an attempt to break up the Warsaw Pact, and they would fight before they would allow that to happen. Eisenhower again refused the CIA permission to air-drop arms and supplies to the Hungarians, and he would not consider sending U.S. troops to Hungary, which he characterized as being "as inaccessible to us as Tibet."[32] Eisenhower knew that there were limits to his power, and Hungary was outside those limits.

On Monday morning, November 5, the day before the election, all hell broke loose. British and French paratroopers landed around

Port Said on the Suez Canal. Amphibious landings soon followed. Bulganin sent messages to Eden, Mollet, and Ben-Gurion, telling them that the Soviet Union was ready to use force to crush the aggressors and restore the peace. There was a thinly veiled threat to use nuclear missiles against London and Paris if the Franco-British force was not withdrawn from Suez. Bulganin also wrote Eisenhower, proposing that the U.S. and the Soviet Union join forces, march into Egypt, and put an end to the fighting. "If this war is not stopped, it is fraught with danger and can grow into a Third World War," Bulganin warned.[33]

At 5 P.M., Eisenhower summoned Hoover, Adams, and Hughes to discuss a reply to Bulganin's preposterous proposal that the United States and the Soviet Union join hands against Britain and France. To Hughes, Eisenhower seemed "poised and relaxed," although fatigued. The discussion was somber. The conferees agreed on the word "unthinkable" in dismissing Bulganin's suggestion. They worried about the Russians, whom they recognized were torn by hope and fear—hope that the Suez crisis would lead to a breakup of NATO, and fear that Hungary would lead to a breakup of the Warsaw Pact.

Eisenhower described their position: "Those boys are both furious and scared. Just as with Hitler, that makes for the most dangerous possible state of mind. And we better be damn sure that every intelligence point and every outpost of our armed forces is absolutely right on their toes." Under the circumstances, Eisenhower said, "we have to be positive and clear in our every word, every step. And if those fellows start something, we may have to hit 'em—and, if necessary, with *everything* in the bucket." Eisenhower directed Hoover to issue a statement that would include clear warnings—if the Russians tried to put troops into the Middle East, the U.S. would resist with force.[34]

November 6 was election day. At 8:37 A.M., Eisenhower met with Allen Dulles, Hoover, and Goodpaster for the latest intelligence briefing. Dulles reported that the Soviets had told the Egyptians they intended to "do something" in the Middle East. He thought it possible that they would send air forces into Syria. Eisenhower told Dulles to send U-2 flights over Syria and Israel, "avoiding, however, any flights into Russia." If the Soviets attacked the British and the French, Eisenhower said, "we would be in war, and we would be justified in taking military action even if Congress were not in session." If reconnaissance "discloses Soviet air forces on Syrian bases," Eisenhower said, he thought "that there would be reason for the British and French to destroy them." Goodpaster's memo on the conference concluded on a chilling note: "The President asked if our forces in the Mediterranean are equipped with atomic antisubmarine weapons."[35]

At 9 A.M. Eisenhower and Mamie drove to Gettysburg to vote, then took a helicopter back to Washington, arriving around noon. Goodpaster met him at the airport to report that the U-2 flights had discovered no Soviet planes on Syrian airfields, or any moving into Egypt. World War III was not about to begin. In the White House Cabinet Room, Eisenhower met with Radford. The question was, Should the U.S. mobilize? Eisenhower wanted mobilization put into effect by degrees, "in order to avoid creating a stir." As a start, he wanted Radford to recall military personnel on leave, an action that could not be concealed and that would give the Russians pause.[36]

At 12:55 P.M., Eisenhower put through another call to Eden, who had just announced British willingness to accept a cease-fire. (The war had already cost the British nearly $500 million; further, the British and the French now claimed control of the canal.) Eisenhower said, "I can't tell you how pleased we are." Eisenhower added that the U.N. peace-keeping force was "getting Canadian troops—lots of troops." Eden wanted American troops. Would they be a part of the U.N. force? Eisenhower said he wanted none of the great nations in it. "I am afraid the Red boy is going to demand the lion's share. I would rather make it no troops from the big five." Eden reluctantly agreed. "If I survive here tonight [he faced a vote of confidence]," Eden concluded, "I will call you tomorrow." Then he asked how the election was going for Eisenhower. "We have given our whole thought to Hungary and the Middle East," Eisenhower responded. "I don't give a damn how the election goes. I guess it will be all right."[37]

Eisenhower spent the afternoon resting, to prepare for the excitement of the long night ahead. He canceled his plans to go to Augusta the next day, because of the Suez situation, a decision that he hated to make. "He's as disappointed as a kid who had counted out all the days to Christmas," Whitman reported.[38] At 10 P.M. he left the White House for the Republican headquarters. As predicted, the early returns showed that he was winning by a landslide, but that the Democrats were going to retain control of Congress.

In the excitement of the contest, Eisenhower shed his supposed indifference to the outcome. He told Hughes, "There's Michigan and Minnesota still to see. You remember that story of Nelson—dying, he looked around and asked, 'Are there any of them still left?' I guess

that's me. When I get in a battle, I just want to win the whole thing
. . . six or seven states we can't help. But I don't want to lose any
more. Don't want any of them 'left'—like Nelson. That's the way I
feel." [39]

Eisenhower got the mandate he wanted from the American people, who voted 35,581,003 for him, 25,738,765 for Stevenson. That
10,000,000-vote margin was almost double the margin of 1952. Stevenson carried only seven southern states.

Eden too survived his vote of confidence. At 8:53 A.M. on November 7, he called Eisenhower to ask for an immediate—that day
or the next—summit conference in Washington between himself,
Eisenhower, and Mollet. Eisenhower feared that Eden was trying to
back out of British acceptance of a cease-fire and a U.N. force taking
control in Suez, but Eden said that what he wanted to discuss was
what happened next. Well, Eisenhower replied, "If we are going to
talk about the future and about the Bear—okay." [40]

Eisenhower next met with Adams and Goodpaster. They both
told him the proposed conference was a terrible idea. Goodpaster
emphasized that such a meeting would give the appearance "that we
were now concerting action in the Middle East independently of the
U.N. action." Hoover joined them. He agreed with Goodpaster and
said he had just talked to Dulles, who also opposed the meeting.
Hoover also said he had a report from Allen Dulles stating that the
Soviets had offered Egypt 250,000 volunteers and that preparations
for their departure were under way. Eisenhower asked Goodpaster
to check on that report. While he did so, Eisenhower called Eden to
inform him that the meeting would have to be postponed. Goodpaster returned to report that there was nothing solid in the intelligence
data, but certainly the Soviets did not have 250,000 troops on the
move. [41]

That morning, Ben-Gurion issued a statement saying Israel rejected the U.N. order to withdraw Israeli forces from Sinai and Gaza
and to permit U.N. forces to enter. Eisenhower sent him a strong
protest. Then the President received a message from Bulganin: "I
feel urged to state that the problem of withdrawal of Soviet troops
from Hungary . . . comes completely and entirely under the competence of the Hungarian and Soviet governments." [42] The fighting in
Budapest, meanwhile, had passed its peak. Hungarian refugees were
fleeing to Austria at the rate of three to four thousand a day; there
were forty thousand dead freedom fighters.

As had happened so many times before, and would again, the

United States found itself unable to influence in any significant way events in Eastern Europe. The Russians violated their pledge of safe-conduct to Nagy, seized him, held a secret trial, and executed him. All that Eisenhower could do was announce that the U.S. was ready to accept 21,000 of the 150,000 Hungarian refugees, and that he would ask for emergency legislation to let more Hungarians enter the United States.

In Egypt, meanwhile, by the end of November, the U.N. force was moving into place, and the British and the French were almost out. Eisenhower lifted the embargo on oil sales to Britain, and the United States soon was shipping 200,000 barrels a day. The Americans loaned money to the British to tide them over. By Christmastime the French and the British troops were gone and the Egyptians had started to clear the canal.

At a meeting with Republican leaders on New Year's Eve, Eisenhower was asked about British and French attitudes toward the United States "Underneath," the President replied, "the governments are thankful we did what we did. But publicly, we have to be the whipping boy." Anyway, "The whole darn thing is straightening out very rapidly." A recent NATO meeting had gone "very well." The alliance had survived the crisis.[43]

After all the nuclear saber rattling that had gone on, relations with the Russians were still tense. Three days after the election, Eisenhower had proposed to Hoover that the United States take advantage of the worldwide fright, a fright that Bulganin presumably shared, to make some progress on disarmament. Eisenhower was willing to make a dramatic offer, such as pulling NATO forces behind the Rhine and withdrawing American ground troops in Germany. Hoover doubted that Dulles would agree. Eisenhower said he just wanted the Secretary to have the thought, because "as long as we are before the world, just calling each other names, being horrified all the time by their brutality, then we get nowhere."[44] But nothing came of the President's idea.

One reason was Soviet reaction to continued U-2 overflights. During the crisis, Eisenhower had to know what military moves the Soviets were making, and after the election he authorized additional flights. The Soviets protested, privately but strongly. On November 15, Eisenhower met with Hoover, Radford, and Allen Dulles to discuss the flights. Eisenhower thought that they were beginning to "cost more than we gain in form of solid information." Hoover pointed out that "if we lost a plane at this stage, it would be almost catastrophic." Eisenhower agreed, and added "Everyone in the world says that in the last six weeks, the U.S. has gained a place it hasn't held since World War II." The country had to "preserve a place that is correct and moral." Still, he worried about those Russians and what they might do with the Red Army, so he approved flights over Eastern Europe, "but not the deep one." The pilot should "stay as close to the border as possible."[45]

The Russians continued to protest. One month later, on December 18, Eisenhower talked to Foster Dulles about the overflights of Eastern Europe. Eisenhower said he was "going to order complete stoppage of the entire business." As to the Russian protests, Dulles said, "I think we will have to admit this was done and say we are sorry. We cannot deny it." Eisenhower said he would call Charlie Wilson "and have him stop it." Dulles reminded the President that "our relations with Russia are pretty tense at the moment." Eisenhower agreed that this was no time to be provocative.[46]

The problem of the Hungarian refugees remained. On November 26, Eisenhower gave a warm and heartfelt greeting to the first arrivals, who came to the White House to see the President. He expressed his shock and horror at Russian actions and assured the Hungarians that they were most welcome in the U.S.

On the day after Christmas, Eisenhower held an 11 A.M. meeting with Nixon, who had just returned from a trip to Vienna to get an overview on the refugee situation. Nixon remarked on the high caliber of the refugees. They were mostly young, well educated, leadership types who had to flee because they had participated in the rebellion. Eisenhower recalled a remark that Zhukov had made to him in the summer of 1945: "If you get rid of the leaders of a country, you can do anything you want to." But the only thing the Americans could do for poor Hungary was accept refugees—yet the law prevented that. Nixon said there were still seventy thousand in Vienna. Eisenhower remarked that the Hungarians were productive people, and that it would be "a tremendous thing" if some of the Middle East countries would take in refugees. The Latin Americans also ought to try to take some—God knew they could "use the skills the Hungarians have." Meanwhile, he wanted the State Department to continue to process applications, even if the quota had been used up, because if the processing stopped, "the pick of the refugees will go to other countries."[47]

The best of Hungary's young people but not freedom for Hungary—that was what the United States got for four years of agitation about liberation.

CHAPTER EIGHTEEN

Little Rock
and Sputnik

"New forces and new nations stir and strive across the earth," Eisenhower declared in his Second Inaugural Address. "From the deserts of North Africa to the islands of the South Pacific one-third of all mankind has entered upon an historic struggle for a new freedom: freedom from grinding poverty." Across this world, he said, "the winds of change" were blowing. The Communists were trying to get those winds blowing their way, in order to exploit the Third World. The great battleground of the Cold War had shifted away from Europe and Korea and Formosa, where the situation was relatively stable, to Africa, the Middle East, and the Indian subcontinent, where the situation was in active ferment. Suez was only the most spectacular event in the process of the breaking up of European colonialism. New nations were emerging, or struggling to emerge, from the wreckage. Most had not been prepared by their rulers for independence. Many had raw materials unavailable elsewhere, particularly oil and minerals that were crucial to the Western industrial system. All of the new nations appeared to be more or less in danger of falling to the Communists.

Suez made Eisenhower almost painfully aware of the importance of the Third World to the United States, which was why he made it not only the theme of his second inaugural but of much of his second term. "No people can live to itself alone," he told the American public. If living conditions were not improved in the Third World, it would go Communist. "Not even America's prosperity could long survive if other nations did not also prosper."[1] Even before the inaugural, Eisenhower had set his Administration to work on a searching review of the U.S. foreign-aid program. When the reports came in, two months later, they concluded—as Eisenhower already had—that economic assistance to the Third World would lead to economic development, which would lead to political stability and the evolution of democratic societies.

Convincing the American people was the trick. Over the next four years, Eisenhower would try every form of persuasion at his command to demonstrate to his countrymen the importance of the Third World to the United States. It was one of the most frustrating experiences of his life. He could not convince the people; he could not convince the Republican Party; he could not even convince his own Secretary of the Treasury. Humphrey opposed independence for Third World colonies, on the grounds that with European managers they would get richer, faster. He opposed loans to independent Third World countries on the grounds that they would never be paid back and would unbalance the American budget. Citing his own experiences in the Philippines, Eisenhower explained the obvious to Humphrey, that through national independence people obtained "fierce pride and personal satisfaction."

Eisenhower wanted Humphrey to understand "that the spirit of nationalism, coupled with a deep hunger for some betterment in physical conditions and living standards, creates a critical situation in the underdeveloped areas of the world." He pointed out that "Communism is not going to be whipped merely by pious words, but it can be whipped by . . . a readiness on the part of ourselves . . . to face up to the critical phase through which the world is passing and do our duty like men."[2]

Eisenhower's exhortation to Humphrey to be a man did not succeed. The President himself, agreed with one part of Humphrey's position. On July 2, at a leaders' meeting, the Republicans told Eisenhower that Senator John F. Kennedy was going to make a long speech on Algeria, and propose a resolution in support of Algerian independence. They wanted to know how to reply. Eisenhower, citing Humphrey, admitted that "the people of Algeria still lacked sufficient education and training to run their own government in the most efficient way." Eisenhower was also concerned about the effects on relations wth France if the Senate supported Algerian independence.

But strong as those arguments were, the President continued, they had to give way to even stronger ones. "The United States could not possibly maintain that freedom—independence—liberty—were necessary to us but not to others." Therefore, the Republicans could not argue against the Algerian cause. "Perhaps," the President concluded, "Republicans might best just chide Mr. Kennedy a bit for pretending to have all the answers."[3]

Eisenhower put his time, prestige, energy, and persuasive powers into the effort to get his foreign-aid package through Congress. He met interminably with the Republican leaders, with the Democratic leaders, with groups and associations interested in the subject. He made speeches. He devoted nearly every one of his stag dinners to convincing his guests to become missionaries for foreign aid. But he could not get the money. Time and again, Congress cut his requests. It left Eisenhower furious.

To Swede, he wrote, "I am repeatedly astonished, even astounded, by the apparent ignorance of members of Congress in the general subject of our foreign affairs." He realized that congressional penny-pinching "reflects abysmal ignorance" among the general public as well. Each congressman, he said, "thinks of himself as intensely patriotic; but it does not take the average member long to conclude that his first duty to his country is to get himself re-elected," a conviction that led to a "capacity for rationalization that is almost unbelievable."

"Again and again," he said, he had patiently explained to congressmen that foreign aid represented America's "best investment."[4] It helped keep down the cost of the American military establishment and provided consuming power in recipient nations. Most of the foreign-aid money was spent in the United States to provide goods and services for the Third World countries. It was a program that, to the President, was so obviously good for America that he could not understand how anyone could be opposed. But opposed Congress was, and his virtual one-man attempt to push through an adequate foreign-aid program failed.

Fortunately for Ike, as he battled with Congress over his budget, foreign aid, and other problems, he was able to get away most weekends to Gettysburg. There he could relax, check on his cattle, oversee the planting of his vegetable garden, play golf and bridge with the gang, and take pleasure in Mamie's happiness as she put the finishing touches on the place. Ike enjoyed everything about the farm, even the drive from Washington to Pennsylvania.

Invitations to spend a weekend with the First Family at the farm were rare and precious. Ordinarily, only Eisenhower's closest personal friends received one. Field Marshal Montgomery solved that problem by inviting himself. He arrived in June. Ike took Monty on a tour of his favorite battlefield. As the two old generals scrambled over the rocks on Little Round Top, or studied the lay of the land from Cemetery Ridge, Ike explained the action to Monty, reporters trailing behind recording every word.

"As you know," Eisenhower later told a friend, "Monty can never resist a newspaper reporter nor a camera." Finally, Ike said, "I got a bit tired of Monty raising his voice, knowing well that he was doing it for the benefit of eavesdroppers." So Ike walked over to the car, while Monty kept talking. Monty called over the heads of the crowd, "Both Lee and Meade should have been sacked." He added something about incompetence, then called out, "Don't you agree, Ike?"

Eisenhower merely replied, "Listen, Monty, I live here. I have nothing to say about the matter. You have to make your own comments." [5]

Nevertheless, the story got page-one space on Sunday, the reports claiming that Ike had agreed with the field marshal that Lee and Meade should have been sacked. At his Tuesday press conference, Ike was asked about it. He would not comment directly, but he did point out that he had the portraits of four men on his Oval Office wall—Franklin, Washington, Lincoln, and Lee—and insisted on his great admiration for Lee.

Monty gave Ike a set of the galley proofs of his memoirs, indicating passages that discussed Ike. The President read the marked sections, then told Whitman that Monty "is pretty clever . . . He says I am so loving and kind that I let him have his own way and he really planned the war." When he read that "Ike reached his greatest heights as President of the United States," Eisenhower grunted and said, "He doesn't want to say I was responsible for winning the war." [6]

Eisenhower could hardly have expected praise from Monty, but he did receive that year some high praise from an unexpected source. Henry Wallace, the Progressive Party candidate for President in 1948 and a leading critic of American policy in the Cold War, sent Eisenhower a copy of the talk he had given in which he said he found certain similarities in the characters of Presidents Washington and Eisenhower. Eisenhower was quite sincerely flattered. He wrote Wallace, "My sense of pride is all the greater because I've never been able to agree with those who so glibly deprecate his [Washington's] intellectual qualities." Subconsciously describing himself as well as Washington, Eisenhower went on: "I think that too many jump at such conclusions merely because they tend to confuse facility of expression with wisdom; a love of the limelight with depth of perception." Speaking directly of himself, Eisenhower concluded, "I've often felt the deep wish that The Good Lord had endowed me with his [Washington's] clarity of vision in big things, his strength of purpose, and his genuine greatness of mind and spirit."[7]

On every possible occasion, Eisenhower told the press, the politicians, and the public that the only way to reduce the budget, stop inflation, and cut taxes was through disarmament. So long as the arms race went on, the United States would be putting $40 billion or so, nearly 60 percent of the total budget, into what Humphrey had called the "dump heap." Even at those levels, however, the JCS were unhappy and demanding more; indeed they had originally requested $50 billion for 1958. In December of 1956, while the budget was being written, Eisenhower told Dulles he was going to "crack down on defense people," and complained that "I am getting desperate with the inability of the men there to understand what can be spent on military weapons and what must be spent to wage the peace."[8]

With no disarmament treaty in sight, Eisenhower concentrated on making savings where he could. Personnel was a major item; he ordered the armed forces, especially the Army, to make even further cuts in their manpower. Wilson and the JCS protested. Eisenhower told his Cabinet, "I think I know more about this subject than anyone else. What would we do with a large Army if we had it? Where would we put it?" Eisenhower told Wilson to reduce, and where to do it. The President wanted to streamline the forces in Germany, saving thirty-five thousand men there; he ordered a reduction of forty thousand in Japan and another twenty-five thousand elsewhere.[9]

As difficult as Congress had been for Eisenhower to deal with on such issues as the budget, it was worse when the subject was civil rights. In his State of the Union address on January 10, Eisenhower had again submitted Brownell's civil-rights bill. It was a multifaceted bill, but Eisenhower put his own emphasis on the right to vote. He was "shocked" to discover that out of 900,000 Negroes in Mississippi, only 7,000 were allowed to vote. He investigated and found that the registrars were asking Negroes attempting to register such questions as "How many bubbles are there in a bar of soap?" In Louisiana, the registrars had closed their doors in the face of five thousand Negroes lined up to register; a local grand jury found "no case" against the state officials.[10]

Through the late winter and early spring, the House debated the civil-rights bill. Eisenhower gave it public and private support. He pushed the bill in his meetings with Republican leaders. He met with Arthur Hays Sulzberger of *The New York Times* to urge him to support the bill. (Sulzberger "shamefacedly admitted, for private use only, that even he would not want his granddaughter to go to school with Negro boys.")[11] On June 18, the House passed the bill, which then went to the Senate. Lyndon Johnson warned Eisenhower over the phone that "the Senate is going to fight on the civil-rights issue—tempers are flaring already and will be worse." Eisenhower protested that what he was asking for was the mildest civil-rights bill possible—he stressed that he himself had lived in the South and had no lack of sympathy for the southern position. He said he was a little struck back on his heels when he found this terrific uproar.[12]

But uproar there was. On July 2, Senator Russell of Georgia described the bill as "a cunning device," designed not to guarantee the right to vote, but to use the power of the Justice Department and "the whole might of the federal government including the armed forces if necessary, to force a commingling of white and Negro children."

At a news conference the following day, James Reston asked Eisenhower to comment. The President was mild and hesitant in his reply. Certainly his own desire was only to protect and extend the right to vote, "simple matters that were more or less brought about by the Supreme Court decision, and were a very moderate move." Now, he said, he discovered that "highly respected men" were making statements to the effect that "this is a very extreme law, leading to disorder." Eisenhower confessed that he found such a reaction "rather incomprehensible, but I am always ready to listen to anyone's presentation to me of his views on such a thing."

Reston asked if Eisenhower was willing to rewrite the bill, so that it dealt only with the right to vote. Eisenhower said he did not want to answer, because "I was reading part of that bill this morning, and there were certain phrases I didn't completely understand. So, before I make any more remarks on that, I would want to talk to the Attorney General and see exactly what they do mean."[13]

It was a stunning confession of ignorance. Eisenhower had been pushing the bill for two years, had managed to get it through the House and considered by the Senate, and yet now said he did not know what was in it. Eisenhower's admission was an open invitation to the southern senators to modify, amend, emasculate his bill, and they proceeded to do just that. They offered an amendment that would assure a jury trial to anyone cited for contempt of court in a civil-rights case. Insofar as the jury lists were made up from the voting lists, which were virtually all white, the amendment would have the practical effect of nullifying the bill, since it was unlikely, indeed almost unthinkable, that a southern white jury would convict another white man of violating the rights of a Negro. But the right of an accused to a trial by a jury of his peers was so deeply ingrained in the American tradition, and so sacred, that the amendment attracted support from such northern liberals as Joseph O'Mahoney of Wyoming and Frank Church of Idaho. Eisenhower appealed to Republicans to resist the amendment, and Knowland said on the Senate floor that a vote for jury trial "will be a vote to kill for this session . . . an effective voting-rights bill." Lyndon Johnson replied, "The people will never accept a concept that a man can be publicly branded as a criminal without a jury trial." [14]

On July 10, in the Oval Office, Eisenhower had an hour-long meeting with Russell. Ann Whitman wrote in her diary that Russell, "while emotional about the matter, had conducted himself very well." Then Whitman, always loyal to Eisenhower and nearly always unquestioningly on his side, noted that the President "is not at all unsympathetic to the position people like Senator Russell take." Eisenhower was "far more ready than am I, for instance, to entertain their views." Whitman chided him for supporting segregationists. "I have lived in the South, remember," the President reminded his secretary. She hoped, and believed, that "he is adamant on the fact that the right to vote must be protected." Then, speaking for millions of Americans, Negro and white, Republican and Democrat, North and South, liberal and conservative, Whitman declared, "It seems so ridiculous to me, when it has been in the Constitution for so many years and here at last we get around to believing it might be possible for some of our citizens to really have that right." [15]

On July 22, as the Senate debate continued, Eisenhower wrote Swede, who had lived in North Carolina for two decades. "I think that no other single event has so disturbed the domestic scene in many years," the President said, "as did the Supreme Court's decision of 1954 in the school segregation case." In his view, "Laws are rarely effective unless they represent the will of the majority." Further, "when emotions are deeply stirred," progress must be gradual and take into account "human feelings." Otherwise, "we will have a . . . disaster." The South had lived for three score years under *Plessy* as a law-abiding area; it was therefore "impossible to expect complete and instant reversal of conduct by mere decision of the Supreme Court."

In the next paragraph, Eisenhower gave Swede the most eloquent and concise statement on the role of the Supreme Court in American life that he ever delivered. "I hold to the basic purpose," he began. "There must be respect for the Constitution—which means the Supreme Court's interpretation of the Constitution—or we shall have chaos. We cannot possibly imagine a successful form of government in which every individual citizen would have the right to interpret the Constitution according to his own convictions, beliefs, and prejudices. Chaos would develop. This I believe with all my heart—and shall always act accordingly."[16]

That was a private letter to a private citizen. The day he wrote it, the President received a letter (already made public) from Governor Jimmy Byrnes of South Carolina, supporting the sacred right of trial by jury. In response, Eisenhower said that "as I read your letter, it seems to me that what you are really objecting to is the giving of authority to the Attorney General to institute civil actions." Eisenhower told Byrnes that the right to vote was what was really sacred. Although "the last thing I desire is to persecute anyone," Eisenhower told Byrnes that "the right to vote is more important to our way of life" than anything else.[17]

Taken altogether, the President's various statements on civil rights, whether made in private, or in meetings, or in letters to southern governors, or in news conferences, confused more than they clarified. As southern politicians chose to hear what he was saying, the President had a firm commitment to the Constitution, but it was more ritualistic than active. What came through to them was Eisenhower's sympathy for the white South, and his extreme reluctance to use force to insure compliance with *Brown*. The President's moderation, the southerners felt, gave them license to defy the Court, and to emasculate the civil-rights bill.

At a July 17 news conference, Eisenhower as much as said so directly. Merriman Smith asked the first question. Was the President aware that under laws dating back to Reconstruction, he had the power and authority to use military force to put through integration? Yes, Eisenhower said, he was aware that he had such power. But, he added, "I can't imagine any set of circumstances that would ever induce me to send federal troops into any area to enforce the orders of a federal court, because I believe that [the] common sense of America will never require it." Few paid any attention to his qualification, because after further questioning he said, "I would never believe that it would be a wise thing to do in this country."[18]

For Eisenhower, the whole experience was one of the most agonizing of his life. He wanted to uphold the Supreme Court, but he did not want to offend his many southern friends. He wanted to enforce the law, but he did not want to use force to do so. He did not want to antagonize anyone, but "anyone" always seemed to turn out to be white southern segregationists. He had waged two successful campaigns to become the nation's leader, but he did not want to lead on the issue of civil rights. The upshot of his conflicting emotions and statements was confusion, which allowed the segregationists to convince themselves that the President would never act.

In his letter to Swede, Eisenhower had concluded, "Possibly I am something like a ship which, buffeted and pounded by wind and wave, is still afloat and manages in spite of frequent tacks and turnings to stay generally along its plotted course and continue to make some, even if slow and painful, headway." But to many observers, it appeared that the ship of state was in fact caught in a storm without a rudder, without power, without a captain; that it was, if the truth be told, drifting aimlessly in unknown and uncharted waters.

In August and September 1957, the efforts by southern segregationists to resist *Brown* and its implications reached a peak. The climax began on August 2, in the wee hours, after an exhausting session of Senate debate over Eisenhower's civil-rights bill, when the Senate voted, 51 to 42, to adopt the jury trial amendment to the bill.

Eisenhower, told of the vote when he woke, was furious. At a 9 A.M. Cabinet meeting, he opened by saying the vote was "one of the most serious political defeats of the past four years, primarily because it was such a denial of a basic principle of the United States," the right to vote. Eisenhower said he could not find much forgiveness in his soul for those Republicans who had voted with the South (twelve had done so, including Barry Goldwater of Arizona). In a statement issued later that morning, the President declared that the jury-trial amendment would make it impossible for the Justice Department to obtain convictions of southern registrars who refused to enroll Negroes. He spoke of how "bitterly disappointing" the result of the Senate vote had been to the millions of "fellow Americans [who] will continue . . . to be disenfranchised."[19]

Despite the President's relatively strong words, the Senate proceeded, on August 7, to pass the emasculated civil-rights bill, 72 to 18. It then went to a Senate-House Conference (the House had earlier passed the bill Eisenhower wanted), where the differences would be worked out.

He was unsure of what he should do if the House agreed to the crippling jury-trial amendment. He was getting conflicting advice. The White House mail mainly urged him not to sign a "phony" bill. Prominent Negro leaders joined the chorus. Ralph Bunche wrote, "It would be better to have no bill than one as emasculated as that which has come out of the Senate." Jackie Robinson, the baseball player, wired to state his opposition. "Have waited this long for bill with meaning," Robinson said, "can wait a little longer." Robinson was one of the newest civil-rights leaders; one of the oldest leaders, the grand old man of the movement, A. Philip Randolph, joined him in opposition. "It is worse than no bill at all," Randolph declared. But the NAACP concluded that half a loaf was better than no bread at all, and therefore wanted Eisenhower to sign it. So did Martin Luther King, Jr.[20]

The bill that came out of the conference satisfied no one. It gave the judge the right to decide whether a defendant should receive a jury trial; it created a Civil Rights Commission with a two-year life; it set up a Civil Rights Division in Justice; and it empowered the Attorney General to seek an injunction when an individual was deprived of the right to vote. But the penalties for violation were so relatively light, and the obstacles in the way of the Attorney General so relatively heavy, that the final bill was a long way away from providing the guarantees of basic civil rights that Eisenhower had insisted were the birthright of all Americans. Some civil-rights leaders blamed the southern senators for this outcome, but others said it was Eisenhower's responsibility, because of his failure to speak forcefully and clearly on the issue.

The battered and bruised bill was hardly Eisenhower's exclusive fault, but the bill's confused and hesitant approach to the problem of civil rights did symbolize the President's own confusion and hesitancy. He still could not make up his mind whether to sign it or not. By the time he did decide, on September 9, to sign, events in Little Rock had overshadowed the bill, and its enactment into law passed virtually unnoticed. Nor can it be said that its enforcement ever attracted much attention, or much action. Essentially, Eisenhower passed on to his successors the problem of guaranteeing constitutional rights to Negro citizens.

• •

On September 4, weary from his battles with Congress, Eisenhower and Mamie flew to Newport, Rhode Island, to spend their summer vacation at the naval base there. Upon their arrival in Newport, Eisenhower said a few words at a reception by the mayor and other local dignitaries. "I assure you no vacation has ever started more auspiciously," he said.[21]

Actually, no vacation had ever begun more inauspiciously, because the previous day the governor of Arkansas, Orval Faubus, had presented Eisenhower with exactly the problem he had most wished to avoid, outright defiance of a court order by a governor. Faubus had called out the Arkansas National Guard, placed it around Central High School in Little Rock, and ordered the troops to prevent the entry into the school of about a dozen Negro pupils.

After various legal maneuverings, a federal judge on September 20 enjoined Faubus and the Arkansas Guard from interfering with the process of integration at Central High. Faubus read a statement questioning the federal court's authority. That afternoon, Eisenhower called Brownell, who told him of Faubus' action, then said that the governor might withdraw the Guard, turning over the streets around Central High to a racist mob, or he might follow a path of "straight defiance." In either case, Brownell said, the President was going to have to make some difficult decisions, including the possible use of the U.S. Army to enforce the court orders.

Eisenhower said he was "loath to use troops." He feared that the "movement might spread—violence would come." He had no doubt whatever about his authority to call out the troops, but said again that he hated to do it. Then Eisenhower expressed his deepest and most persistent fear. He asked Brownell, "Suppose the children are taken to school and then Governor Faubus closes the school? Can he do that legally?" Brownell said he would look it up. Eisenhower feared that the federal government would be helpless in the event the South abolished its public school system, and that the precedent thereby set for defiance of constitutional authority could have devastating results, for Negroes, for poor white southerners, and for the nation.[22]

Monday morning, September 23, a howling racist mob gathered around Central High, screaming protests against integration. Variously estimated at from five hundred to "several thousand" strong, the mob rushed two Negro reporters. As the mob knocked down and beat up the newsmen, nine Negro pupils slipped into the school by a side door. The mob, learning of this development, grew even more enraged. It rushed the police barricades and fought to get into the school, vowing to "lynch the niggers." On orders from the mayor of Little Rock, the police then removed the Negro students. Integration at Central High had lasted three hours.

In his four and one-half years as President, Eisenhower had gotten through many a crisis simply by denying that a crisis existed. His favorite approach was to conduct business as usual, stick as close to a routine as possible, speak and act with moderation, and wait for the inevitable cooling down of passions. Moderation and deliberation, however, were hard to find in Little Rock that morning. There the mob, now swollen in size to many thousands, again took control of the streets. The mayor, Woodrow Wilson Mann, sent Eisenhower a frantic telegram: "The immediate need for federal troops is urgent . . . Situation is out of control and police cannot disperse the mob . . ."[23]

Eisenhower realized immediately that his entire policy had broken down. By allowing events to run their course, by attempting to negotiate with Faubus, by failing to ever speak out forcefully on integration, or to provide real leadership on the moral issue, he found himself in precisely the situation he had most wanted to avoid. His options had run out. Mayor Mann's telegram gave him no choice but to use force.

He did have a choice as to what type of force he would use. At 12:08 P.M., he called Brownell to say that he finally agreed, force would have to be used. He said he wanted to use the U.S. Army. He accepted Brownell's suggestion that he simultaneously call the Arkansas National Guard into federal service and use it side by side with the regulars.[24] At 12:15 he called General Taylor and gave the order. He wanted Taylor to move quickly in order to demonstrate how rapidly the Army could respond. Within a few hours, Taylor had five hundred paratroopers of the 101st Airborne Division in Little Rock; another five hundred were there by nightfall.

Throughout the South, white segregationists were outraged by the "invasion." Marching protestors carried banners that played on the words of the Army's recruiting slogan: "Join the Army and See the High Schools!" Lyndon Johnson proclaimed: "There should be no troops from either side patrolling our school campuses." Senator Eastland said that "the President's move was an attempt to destroy the social order of the South." Senator Olin Johnston boldly proclaimed, "If I were a governor and he came in, I'd give him a fight such as he's never been in before."[25]

The following morning, the 101st Airborne dispersed the mob, with only minor incidents (one man was pricked by a bayonet), while nine Negro students entered Central High and, under Army guard, sat through a full day of classes. Central High was integrated. That was the result the segregationists had vowed to prevent, and that Eisenhower's orders had made possible. Faubus had forced Eisenhower to face one ultimate question: Could the southern governors use the state's armed forces to prevent integration? But because Faubus had been forced to pose the question within the context of outright defiance of the orders of the federal court, he gave Eisenhower no choice but to act. He could not have done otherwise and still been President. Eisenhower had to be pushed to the wall before he would act, but at the critical moment, he lived up to his oath of office. In the process, he convinced most white southerners that they could not use force to prevent integration.

Slowly, the crisis faded. Faubus continued to shout defiance, but by October 14 the situation was stable enough for Eisenhower to withdraw half the Army troops and to defederalize 80 percent of the Guardsmen. The next week, Brownell carried out his long-standing intention of resigning, to return to private practice, an act that helped cool passions, as many southerners saw Brownell as the villain in the piece. By October 23, Negro students entered Central High without military protection. In November, the last of the 101st left. The Guard remained, under federal control, until the end of the school year, in June 1958. In September of that year, Faubus did what Eisenhower had so feared—he closed Central High altogether (it was reopened on an integrated basis in the fall of 1959).

Little Rock had been, for Eisenhower, "troublesome beyond imagination."[26] By the time the crisis ended, however, it had become little more than an irritant, because by then it had been eclipsed by another crisis in American education, this one brought on by the Russians.

Eisenhower had endured many a discouraging autumn. In 1942, he was stuck in the mud of Tunisia, in 1943 in the mud of Italy, in 1944 along the West Wall. In 1954, he lost control of Congress in the fall elections. In late September 1955, he had suffered his first heart attack. In October 1956, it was Suez, and in September 1957, Little Rock. That should have been enough for any man, but still the dreary list grew. On October 4, 1957, the Soviet Union fired into orbit the world's first man-made satellite, named Sputnik ("traveling companion"). This impressive achievement came as "a distinct surprise" to

Eisenhower and his Administration. But as Eisenhower confessed in his memoirs, "Most surprising of all . . . was the intensity of the public concern."[27]

He had no excuse for being surprised by the near-hysterical reaction of the American press, politicians, and public to Sputnik. He himself had said repeatedly, when discussing the American missile program, that the ICBMs were far more important in terms of psychological factors than as military weapons. He had predicted that the achievement of operational ICBMs by the Russians would throw the American people into a fright bordering on panic, because the idea that the enemy could send nuclear warheads across the oceans to obliterate American cities was certain to create uncontrollable anxieties. But predicting and experiencing were two distinct things, and Eisenhower was indeed almost overwhelmed by the intensity of the American response to Sputnik.

Eisenhower had anticipated the fear that Sputnik engendered; what really surprised him was the way in which Sputnik swept away certain basic American assumptions and caused a crisis in self-confidence. For a dozen years, since the victory in the war, Americans had taken for granted that theirs was not only the richest and freest and most powerful nation in the world, but also the best educated and most technologically advanced.

Most commentators, then and later, linked this remarkable self-satisfaction to President Eisenhower. "Trust Ike" was the watchword. He was so comforting, so grandfatherly, so calm, so sure of himself, so skillful in managing the economy, so experienced in insuring America's defenses, so expert in his control of the intelligence community, so knowledgeable about the world's affairs, so nonpartisan and objective in his above-the-battle posture, so insistent on holding to the middle of the road, that he inspired a trust that was as broad and deep as that of any President since George Washington. Even southern Democrats could not bring themselves to dislike Ike, and the Democratic Party as a whole never hated Eisenhower as the Republicans hated FDR and Truman, or as the Democrats later hated Nixon. Thus Eisenhower is praised—or blamed—for the complacency and consensus of the fifties.

Actually, Eisenhower was given far too much credit—or blame—for the character of the fifties. In large part, it was plain good luck. The economic boom would have taken place even if Taft or Stevenson had won in 1952. America's preponderant position in military and financial power was a legacy Eisenhower inherited. Eisenhower had been a participant in the process of changing the isolationist America of 1939 into the world colossus of 1952, but not the maker of that policy. His task as President was one of managing America's rise to globalism, not bringing it about. As Eisenhower himself was always first to point out, it was plain silly to give all the credit, or blame, to one man.

Similarly, the complacency had always been fragile, as was demonstrated when one Russian satellite, weighing less than two hundred pounds and carrying no scientific or military equipment, broke it down. Democrats cashed in on the shame, shock, and anger Americans felt, as they blamed the Republicans for various "gaps"—in education, in missiles, in satellites, in economic growth, in bombers, in science, and in prestige. Almost all Americans wanted to be "number one" in everything, which helped explain the overreaction to Sputnik and gave the Democrats the rallying cry that would carry them to victory in the 1958 and 1960 elections—Let's get the country moving again. "If we do have to stress party differences," Eisenhower had told the Democratic leaders at the beginning of 1957, "let us do it on relatively small matters." But after Little Rock and Sputnik, the differences were over big matters, civil rights and national defense, as complacency and consensus disappeared.

Eisenhower's first response to Sputnik was to call a meeting to review American missile development and find out how the Russians had won the race to space. The backbiting and blame fixing had already begun, the day after Sputnik, when two Army officers said that the Army had a rocket, Redstone, that could have placed a satellite in orbit many months ago, but the Eisenhower Administration had given the satellite program to the Navy (Project Vanguard), and the Navy had failed.

Sputnik not only set the services to bickering among themselves; it had a remarkable effect on the White House press corps, usually so friendly to Eisenhower. On October 9, five days after Sputnik, Eisenhower held a news conference that was one of the most hostile of his career. Merriman Smith, ordinarily a great admirer of Eisenhower, set the tone in his opening question. Reading from a note card, Smith began, "Russia has launched an earth satellite. They also claim to have had a successful firing of an intercontinental ballistic missile, none of which this country has done." Raising his eyes, Smith looked directly at the President. "I ask you, sir, what are we going to do about it?"

Eisenhower began by denying that there was a link between a satellite and the ICBM. He gave a brief history of American involvement in a satellite program. He denied that there ever was a race to get into space first. He promised to have an American satellite in orbit before the end of 1958. As to the Russian ICBM, Eisenhower said that Sputnik had certainly proved that "they can hurl an object a considerable distance." It did not prove that the ICBMs could hit a target. American missile research was going forward full speed, and the United States had a lead in the ICBM race.

Eisenhower was asked if the B-52 was "outmoded," as Khrushchev claimed. Absolutely not, the President replied. Robert Clark wanted to know how the Russians had gotten ahead in launching an earth satellite. Eisenhower replied that "from 1945, when the Russians captured all of the German scientists in Peenemunde . . . they have centered their attention on the ballistic missile." Eisenhower then downplayed the Russian achievement, although he admitted that they had gained a "great psychological advantage."

May Craig wanted to know if the Russians could use satellites as space platforms from which to launch rockets. "Not at this time, no," Eisenhower replied. "There is no . . ." he went on, but paused, smiled, and commented, "Suddenly all America seems to become scientist, and I am hearing many, many ideas."

Hazel Markel of NBC then asked the question all of America was asking. "Mr. President," Markel said, "in light of the great faith which the American people have in your military knowledge and leadership, are you saying at this time that with the Russian satellite whirling about the world, you are not more concerned nor overly concerned about our nation's security?" Eisenhower spoke to the whole nation in his reply, in an attempt to calm a jittery public. "As far as the satellite itself is concerned," he said, "that does not raise my apprehensions, not one iota. I see nothing at this moment, at this stage of development, that is significant in that development as far as security is concerned."[28]

Later that day, Eisenhower met with Lyndon Johnson. Senator Symington was beginning an investigation into the American missile program, with the obvious purpose of putting the blame for the loss of the space race on the Republicans. Eisenhower hoped to keep the whole subject out of partisan politics. He told Johnson that Symington and his friends should be aware "that the Democrats could be blamed." Truman had spent literally nothing on missile research before 1950, and only a pittance after that. Eisenhower promised that the Republicans "would not be first to throw the stone." Johnson said he had been urged to call a special session of Congress; Eisenhower said "he saw no need of it now." After Johnson left, Eisenhower told Whitman that he had "said all the right things. I think today he is being honest."[29]

Having faced the Chiefs, the press corps, and the politicians, Eisenhower met next with the scientists. On October 15, he called fourteen of the leading scientists in America to the Oval Office. It was his first meeting with so broad-gauged and representative a group. Strauss had always managed to control the access of scientists to the President, and brought him only such men as Drs. Lawrence and Teller. (Teller, incidentally, had called Sputnik a greater defeat for the United States than Pearl Harbor, which was exactly the kind of talk Eisenhower deplored.)

The meeting was a long one. Eisenhower began by asking "whether the group really thought that American science is being outdistanced, and asked for an expression of the state of mind of the members." Dr. Isidor Rabi, a Columbia physicist whom Eisenhower knew and admired, spoke first. He said that he, and all the group, wanted federal support for scientific research and training, not because America had fallen behind, but because the Soviets "have picked up tremendous momentum, and unless we take vigorous action they could pass us swiftly just as in a period of twenty to thirty years we caught up with Europe and left Western Europe far behind." Then Dr. Land, who had developed the camera equipment for the U-2, "spoke with great eloquence." He said that science "needs the President acutely." The Russians were in a pioneering stage and frame of mind. They were teaching Russian students basic sciences and beginning to reap the rewards. "Curiously, in the United States we are not now great builders for the future but are rather stressing production in great quantities of things we have already achieved," Land said, while the Russians looked to the future. Land wanted the President to "inspire the country—setting out our youth particularly on a whole variety of scientific adventures." He complained that "at the present time scientists feel themselves isolated and alone."

Eisenhower disagreed with Land's analysis. He said that the Russians had "followed the practice of picking out the best minds and ruthlessly spurning the rest." Nor did he think that he alone could give a new spirit to scientific training and research in America. He did agree that "perhaps now is a good time to try such a thing. People are alarmed and thinking about science, and perhaps this alarm could be turned to a constructive result." Rabi pointed out that Eisenhower lacked a scientific adviser. Eisenhower admitted that such an individual could be "most helpful."[30] Soon thereafter he appointed Dr. James Killian, the president of MIT, to the post, making the widely popular Killian the head of the President's Science Advisory Committee (PSAC).

Shortly thereafter, Eisenhower met with Nathan Twining to discuss ways and means of cutting down costs in the nuclear development field. The President wondered why the AEC and JCS wanted so many bombs. He asked, "What is going to be done with this tremendous number of enormous weapons?" With an existing arsenal of thousands of weapons, Eisenhower said, "we are certainly providing for elaborate reserves, and making very pessimistic estimates as to what can get to the target." He thought the B-52 had "great penetrating power." Twining confirmed that assumption, but then said that "the Air Force will not be happy until they get one [hydrogen bomb] for every aircraft plus a sizable reserve."[31]

Costs were very much on Eisenhower's mind. Sputnik had stimulated almost unmanageable demands for more spending, on space and missile research, for conventional forces, for federal aid to colleges and universities, for fallout shelters, and a myriad of other projects. But the economy was slipping; 1957 was a recession year, federal income was down as a result, and the balanced budget of the previous two years was about to become a deficit budget. At a November 1 meeting, the Cabinet bombarded Eisenhower with proposals. "Look," the President finally exploded, "I'd like to know what's on the other side of the moon, but I won't pay to find out this year!"[32]

National sentiment was otherwise. Eisenhower was getting advice from individuals, groups, organizations, all centering around the theme that "security is more important than balanced budgets." Ike said he knew he could get whatever he asked for from Congress in the way of defense spending in the next session, but the suggested expenditures were "unjustifiable." He admonished one committee that "we must remember that we are defending a way of life, not merely property, wealth, and even our homes . . . Should we have to resort to anything resembling a garrison state, then all that we are striving to defend . . . could disappear."[33] Eisenhower refused to bend to the pressure, refused to initiate a fallout shelter program, refused to expand conventional and nuclear forces, refused to panic.

It was one of his finest hours. If in September 1957, at Little Rock, he had failed to exercise leadership and consequently suffered through one of the low moments of his Presidency, then in October and November 1957, in his response to Sputnik and the uproar it created, he reached one of the highest points.

It is doubtful if any other man could have done what Eisenhower did. The demands for shelters, for more bombers, for more bombs, for more research and development of missiles and satellites, was nearly irresistible. Only Ike could have gotten away with saying no. His unique prestige among his countrymen made his unassailable on the question of national defense. The Ford Foundation, the Rockefeller brothers, the JCS, Congress, indeed almost all of what would be called in the sixties "the Establishment," clamored for more defense spending.

But Eisenhower said no, and kept saying no to the end of his term. He thereby saved his country untold billions of dollars and no one knows how many war scares. Eisenhower's calm, common-sense, deliberate response to Sputnik may have been his finest gift to the nation, if only because he was the only man who could have given it.

CHAPTER NINETEEN

1958—

A Most Difficult Year

ON NOVEMBER 25, after his lunch, Eisenhower went to his office, sat at his desk, began to sign some correspondence, and suddenly felt dizzy. Shaking off the feeling, he reached for another paper. He had difficulty picking it up, and when he did he discovered that the words seemed to run off the top of the page. Frustrated, bewildered, angry, he dropped his pen. Finding himself unable to pick it up, he got up from the chair, suffered another wave of dizziness, and had to grasp the back of the chair for stability.

He collapsed back into the chair and rang for Ann Whitman. When she came in, he tried to tell her what had happened, only to discover that he could not talk intelligibly. Words came out, but not the ones he wanted to say. Nor were they in any order that made sense.

Whitman was stunned to find the President in the Oval Office talking gibberish. She called for Andy Goodpaster. He came in from his adjacent office, assessed the situation, and took charge. Grasping Eisenhower's arm, he helped him out of the chair and led him toward the door, saying, "Mr. President, I think we should get you to bed." Eisenhower had no difficulty walking with Goodpaster's support, nor did he feel any pain. When they got to his bedroom, Goodpaster helped him undress and lie down. Dr. Snyder was there in a matter of minutes. His patient was comfortable, and turned over to take a nap.[1]

Snyder called in two neurologists, while Goodpaster called John Eisenhower, and Whitman told Mamie what had happened. The initial medical diagnosis was a minor stroke. Snyder speculated that the President may have had a spasm in one of the small capillaries of his brain. Sherman Adams joined the group in the living room. He said he had called Nixon both to alert him and to ask the Vice-President to replace the President at a state dinner that evening.

To their collective horror, the door opened and there stood the President, in bathrobe and slippers, a big grin on his face, expecting to be congratulated on his quick recovery. As he sat down, Mamie gasped, "What are you doing up, Ike?" Softly and slowly, he replied, "Why shouldn't I be up? I have a dinner to go to." Snyder, Mamie, John, and Adams all protested simultaneously that he would do no such thing. "There's nothing the matter with me!" he said. "I am perfectly all right." Mamie explained to him that Nixon would take over at the dinner, and warned that if he went, she would not.

Again Eisenhower began to insist that he would go, and to discuss the activities scheduled for the rest of the week that he did not intend to miss. But his words were still jumbled and mispronounced. He was aware that he was making no sense, and his anger swelled up in him. Mamie turned to Adams in dismay. "We can't let him go down there in this condition," she said. They finally convinced him to go back to bed. As he left the room, he mumbled, "If I cannot attend to my duties, I am simply going to give up this job. Now that is all there is to it."[2]

He slept comfortably, with John and Snyder sharing a night watch at his bedside. In the morning, the doctors found his pulse normal. He continued, however, to have difficulty with words. Pointing toward a watercolor on the wall, he tried to say its name, but could not. The harder he tried, the more frustrated he became. He thrashed about on the big double bed, beating the bedclothes with his fists. John, Snyder, and Mamie shouted any word that came to mind, until Mamie finally remembered the title. *"The Smugglers,"* she blurted out. Eisenhower shook his finger at her, demanding a repeat. But even after hearing it a second time, he could not say it. He sank back into the bed, exhausted. Later that day, he did some painting of his own. Adams and Nixon came to see him. Nixon said that the state dinner had gone well, and that he was planning to substitute for the President at a NATO conference, scheduled for mid-December.

The following day, November 27, a Wednesday, Eisenhower worked in his room on various papers; on Thanksgiving, he and Mamie attended church services, then drove to Gettysburg for the weekend.[3] His speech seemed completely recovered, to everyone but himself. Always very clear and precise in his pronunciation of words, it bothered him thereafter, until the end of his life, that occasionally he would reverse syllables in a long word. In private conversations or public speeches, few if any listeners ever noticed.

But the President was, in the winter of 1957–1958, noticeably more irritable and short-tempered, and complained about his job more than he ever had. The Presidency had begun to take its toll. From the time of Suez onward, as Eisenhower had told Swede, his life had been a succession of crises. They did not bother him so much as did the swelling criticism of his Administration. Although few Democrats were ready to go after General Ike personally, many columnists were, especially on such specific issues as the Middle East crisis, Hungary, Little Rock, and, most of all, Sputnik. Critics were questioning his leadership abilities, and pointing to the inept attempt to put through a civil-rights bill with some meaning and the recession as examples of his failures. The charge that hurt the most was that he had "lost" the space race and had neglected the nation's defenses. Implicit in all the criticism was the idea that he was too old, too tired, too sick, to run the country.

Especially frustrating was the problem of a test ban. The American position, that the United States would cease testing nuclear weapons only when the Soviets simultaneously accepted a ban on further weapons production, had been consistently turned down by the Russians. Instead, Bulganin proposed, on December 10, 1957, a two- or three-year moratorium on nuclear tests. When Eisenhower went to the NATO meetings a week later, he discussed the test ban with the British and the French. They were unalterably opposed; Britain had tests scheduled, and the French were striving to perfect their own atomic bomb. The Western nations decided to stall by proposing disarmament talks on the Foreign Ministers' level. The British and the French also agreed to accept American IRBMs on their soil when the missiles were operational.

Not until January 12, 1958, did the President respond to Bulganin's call for a summit meeting and his offer of a moratorium. Eisenhower said he was willing to meet with Bulganin (and Khrushchev, who was the real power in Russia), but only after meetings at the Foreign Ministers' level. He could not agree to a moratorium that was not linked to a cutoff in nuclear weapons' production. Bulganin rejected the proposal.

Then, on March 27, Bulganin resigned, making Khrushchev the

Russian dictator in name as well as in fact. On March 31, Khrushchev announced that Russia was unilaterally halting all further tests of nuclear weapons. The overwhelmingly positive worldwide response made Eisenhower and his advisers furious, because they felt it was so transparently insincere. The Russians had only just concluded their most extensive series of tests ever, and they knew that an American series (code name Hardtack) was just about to begin. Especially infuriating was the Russian statement that if the United States and the United Kingdom did not stop their tests, "the Soviet Union will, understandably, act freely in the question of testing atomic and hydrogen weapons."[4] It would be some months before the Soviets could prepare for a new series of tests in any case; Khrushchev's shrewd maneuver gave him a built-in excuse to resume testing without disruption in the Russian nuclear program, and to put the blame on Hardtack.

On April 2, at a news conference, Eisenhower responded to Khrushchev's move by dismissing it as "just a side issue." He said, "I think it is a gimmick, and I don't think it is to be taken seriously, and I believe anyone that studies this matter thoroughly will see that." The editors of *The Nation* commented, "If all this is a 'gimmick,' one can only wish to God that our statesmen could concoct such gimmicks once in a while."[5]

In April, a new group entered the debate. In the wake of the post-Sputnik demands that the President have a full-time scientific adviser, Eisenhower had created the President's Science Advisory Committee (PSAC) and put Dr. James R. Killian, president of MIT, at its head. Killian and his people, especially physicists Hans Bethe and Isidor Rabi, undertook a thorough review of American policy. They concluded that an inspection system could be created that, although not absolutely foolproof, could detect any nuclear blast down to as low as two kilotons. Dulles then telephoned Eisenhower to recommend that the President write Khrushchev, accepting an earlier Soviet offer to undertake technical talks on a possible test-ban inspection system. Eisenhower said that was fine, then added, "Our position is that we want to look on testing as a symptom rather than a disease."[6]

On April 26, Dulles met with Gruenther, Robert Lovett (Truman's Secretary of Defense), Bedell Smith, and John J. McCloy. It was a carefully selected group—Eisenhower had great admiration for each member of it, and would be impressed by a recommendation from such men. Dulles gave them a full briefing, then got their assent to advise Eisenhower to take the initiative in seeking a test-ban agreement. With their backing, Dulles wrote a draft of a letter from Eisenhower to Khrushchev, repeating his earlier proposal for technical talks on an inspection system, and saying, "Studies of this kind are the necessary preliminaries to putting political decisions into effect."[7]

In other words, Dulles wanted to take a decisive step and divorce production of future weapons from a nuclear test ban. That marked a fundamental change in the American disarmament position. To Strauss' consternation, and Dulles' delight, Eisenhower accepted the recommendation and on April 28 sent the letter to Khrushchev. Three days later, Eisenhower told Dulles he had made the historic shift in position because "unless we took some positive action we were in the future going to be in a position of 'moral isolation' as far as [the] rest of the world is concerned."[8]

For the first time in the nuclear age, the superpowers were engaged in serious disarmament talks that offered some prospect of success. Ironically, the man most responsible for convincing Eisenhower to accept the inherent risk in agreeing to such talks, John Foster Dulles, was the man who got most of the blame for the long delay.

By 1958, Dulles had softened considerably on the question of spending for national defense. During Eisenhower's first term, the Secretary of State had been the leading proponent in the Cabinet for more funds for the Department of Defense (DOD). He had insisted that America had to maintain a clear lead over the Russians in order to have an effective foreign policy. But in the greatest crises of his career, Suez and Hungary in late 1956, Dulles had learned that American military strength was irrelevant in Eastern Europe, where he had hoped for so much, and equally irrelevant in the Middle East, where American economic pressure, not military force, had compelled the French, British, and Israelis to withdraw. After those experiences, and with George Humphrey out of the Cabinet, Dulles became the leading proponent of less spending by DOD.

Not that Eisenhower had lost his concern over defense spending. In the wake of the post-Sputnik hysteria, the President had stood firm against emergency appropriations and crash programs. When on January 28 the Republican leaders told him that the demand for more B-52s was "irresistible," he complained that "we do things in defense that are just so damn costly," and pointed out that he could not conceive of any Russian attack that was so successful "that there wouldn't be enough bombers escaping to go do their job. If six hundred won't do it," Eisenhower continued, "certainly seven hundred won't."[9]

At an April 25 NSC meeting, Eisenhower continued to complain about the exorbitant cost of defense. He said that every time there was a test firing of a Titan missile, "we are shooting away $15 million." At that price, "he hoped there would be no misses and no near-misses!" After the DOD people gave a spirited defense of their program, and justified its costs, Eisenhower commented that "we are now beginning to think of aircraft as becoming obsolescent, and so it is also with first-generation ballistic missiles." He thought it a mistake to "go ahead full steam on production," and predicted that the B-52s would remain usable long after the early missiles were obsolete. To attempt to mass-produce both more bombers and new missiles "will create unheard-of inflation in the United States."

Dulles then entered the discussion. To everyone's surprise, he thought even the President was going too far in defense spending. Dulles raised fundamental points about the arms race. He reminded Eisenhower that the President had often quoted to the NSC George Washington's words on "the desirability that the United States possess a respectable military posture." In his view, Dulles said, "The United States should not attempt to be the greatest military power in the world, although most discussions in the NSC seemed to suggest that we should have the most and best of everything." He wondered if "there was no group in the government which ever thought of the right kind of ceiling on our military capabilities?" Dulles suggested that a "respectable military posture," not overwhelming superiority, was the proper goal. "In the field of military capabilities," Dulles said, "enough is enough. If we didn't realize this fact, the time would come when all our national production would be centered on our military establishment." He wanted the Russians to "respect" the American military, not be frightened to death by it.

Eisenhower was startled. Since Taft's death, he almost never had to defend his Administration from charges that it was spending too much on defense; it was usually the other way around. And he had not anticipated that Dulles, of all people, would advocate spending less, not more. He therefore replied to Dulles' basic critique that saving money was, of course, "one of the great preoccupations of the JCS." Dulles interrupted to say "that he was not at all sure that this was so." He recognized that it was the business of the JCS "to recommend military capabilities which would provide the utmost national security. He did not blame them for this. It was right and it was their job." But there was another side to the problem, and he complained that it never came out in NSC discussions.[10]

Allen Dulles and the CIA provided some support for the Secretary of State's position. The CIA was, at this time, a source of discomfort to the President. The Russians were protesting vigorously against continuing U-2 flights. On March 7, Eisenhower told Goodpaster that he should inform the CIA that the President had ordered the flights "discontinued, effective at once."[11] A week later, Cutler brought in the CIA's latest "Estimate of the World Situation," pronouncing it "a very superior piece of work." Eisenhower did not agree. He told Cutler that it "could have been written by a high-school student."[12]

But in June, the CIA brought in its latest estimates on Soviet bomber and missile production, and although the report admitted that the Agency had previously grossly exaggerated the scope of the Soviet effort, Eisenhower was pleased with the new conclusions, as the report indicated there was not so much to worry about after all. For example, in August of 1956 the CIA had estimated that by mid-1958 the Russians would have 470 Bison and Bear bombers and 100 ICBMs. But in June of 1958, the estimate was that the Soviets actually had 135 bombers and no operational ICBMs. Eisenhower commented that "the Soviets have done much better than have we in this matter. They stopped their Bison and Bear production, but we have kept on going, on the basis of incorrect estimates and at a tremendous expense in a mistaken effort to be 100 percent secure." Secretary Dulles heartily concurred.[13]

With such strong backing from the CIA and the State Department, Eisenhower was able to hold off the political demands for more military spending. At a Republican leaders' meeting on June 24, he declared flatly that he did not want any nuclear carriers, because "they would be useless in a big war" and were not needed in a little one. As for more missiles and B-52s, the President said he "just didn't know how many times you could kill the same man!" Senator Leverett Saltonstall said the country needed more Army reserves, more National Guard, and more Marines. "The President wanted to know why." He said he had "great admiration" for the Marines, but pointed out that "he had made the two largest amphibious landings in history and there hadn't been a Marine in them. To hear people talk about the Marines, you couldn't understand how those two great landings were ever accomplished!"[14]

● ●

No matter how often the President assured the country that America was well ahead in nuclear delivery systems, few people would believe him until the nation had put a satellite into orbit. In December 1957, amid extensive publicity, the United States had tried with a Vanguard rocket, but it had caught fire, fallen back to earth two seconds after takeoff, and was totally destroyed. Such an embarrassment might prove as costly to the budget as to American pride. Knowland, on January 7, warned Eisenhower that if the United States did not get a satellite into orbit soon, the demands on the budget were going to go "hog-wild." [15]

Nelson Rockefeller, running for governor of New York, was one of those who thought there was no limit to the amounts of money available for every conceivable project including flying to the moon. On January 16, he told the President that if the United States used nuclear explosions for propulsion, it could launch a satellite that could reach the moon and return, and predicted that it would be "the most notable accomplishment of our time." Eisenhower was dubious.[16] On February 4, he told Republican leaders that "in the present situation, he would rather have a good Redstone [IRBM] than be able to hit the moon, for we didn't have any enemies on the moon!" [17] But the idea of flying to the moon was too exciting to pass up. On February 25, at a meeting in the Oval Office, Killian and Deputy Defense Secretary Donald Quarles proposed a nuclear aircraft, and expenditures of $1.5 billion over the next few years in order to send a nuclear-powered rocket to the moon.

Eisenhower was not convinced. He regarded such talk as Buck Rogers fantasy, unrelated to reality. On March 6, he announced that he was rejecting any proposal to build atomic-powered airplanes, holding that such a prestige effort was a waste of scarce resources and talent. Scientists were critical. Eisenhower ignored them.

On January 31, the United States had put its first satellite into orbit, but it was almost as much of an embarrassment as Vanguard, because the satellite, named Explorer I, weighed only thirty-one pounds. In March, the Navy finally got a Vanguard rocket to work, but the satellite it put into orbit weighed only three pounds. The embarrassment deepened in May when the Russians put Sputnik II into space—it weighed three thousand pounds.

Eisenhower's basic approach to missiles and satellites had been to let each service develop its own program and hope that one of them would score a breakthrough. The result had been failure. The generals and admirals squabbled with one another, made slighting remarks about their fellow services' efforts, and ignored the Secretary of Defense. In January 1958, Eisenhower proposed a reorganization of the Pentagon, to give more power to the Secretary and to keep the service Chiefs away from congressional committees (where they always said that the Eisenhower Administration was not giving them enough funds to carry out their missions). But Congress was extremely reluctant to give up its power to appropriate separately for the services, and some of Eisenhower's critics charged that he was trying to create a Prussian General Staff. Others pointed out that Eisenhower was asking for centralization at the top, but ignoring the real problem, which was waste and duplication in the space program; they wanted him to put all space activities into one super agency, outside the Department of Defense.

Eisenhower was opposed to the creation of a separate Department of Space. He feared it would put its priority on satellites, while he wanted to keep the priority on missiles. He regretted not putting all space activities into the office of the Secretary of Defense in the first instance, and he wanted nothing to do with any moon shots, or other prestige operations, because he did not want to "put talent etc. into crash programs outside the Defense establishment." [18]

But the President could not hold his ground in opposition to nearly every Democrat, most Republicans, and a majority of columnists and scientists. On April 2, he retreated. He asked Congress to establish a National Aeronautics and Space Administration (NASA). The bill gave NASA control of all space activities "except those that the President determined were primarily associated with national defense." At a press conference two weeks later, James Reston said he had "often wondered why" it had taken the President five years to get around to establishing NASA.

"I think the answer to that is I have had plenty of troubles over the five years," Eisenhower snapped back. He then became completely incomprehensible. Even after the editors of his transcripts had smoothed out his reply, it read: ". . . it did not seem that that was a big factor that we should advance in an argument that, to my mind, has become very, very important." [19] But jumbled syntax or not, and Eisenhower's misgivings notwithstanding, the United States had a civilian space agency.

Sherman Adams, meanwhile, was in deep trouble. No one, except Eisenhower himself, had ever liked him very much. Adams' abruptness and absence of emotion were principal reasons for his vast unpopularity. The man just seemed to have no human feelings at all. Once Eisenhower had painted a portrait of Adams, taken from a color photo. The President worked on it many hours. When he presented it, Adams' only remark was "Mr. President, thank you, but I think you flattered me." He then turned on his heel and walked out. [20]

Foolish stories, wildly exaggerated, about Adams' supposed immense influence with the President were a standard feature of Washington gossip and newspaper columns. The truth was that Adams had almost no influence on the President's policies—he was the gatekeeper, the schedule maker, the man who smoothed things over, but never was he involved in making decisions. Nevertheless, every man who had had a request turned down by the White House blamed Adams; every man whom Eisenhower did not want to see in the Oval Office blamed Adams for his failure to gain admission; every man who objected to a specific Eisenhower decision blamed Adams. Old Guard Republicans hated the man, whom they blamed for Eisenhower's refusal to adopt their pet projects. The Democrats hated him because he was a Republican, and because in January 1958 he had delivered a blistering attack on the Democratic Party, blaming it for Pearl Harbor and the loss of the space race.

The Democrats controlled Congress, and thus the committees and investigations. Like the Republicans from 1953 to 1955, they wanted to use that power to expose their political enemies. In early June 1958, a subcommittee of the House Interstate and Foreign Commerce Committee charged that Adams had allowed a New England industrialist named Bernard Goldfine to pay some of his hotel bills in Boston, and that in return Adams had engaged in influence peddling for Goldfine, who was having tax and regulatory problems with the SEC.

On June 17, Adams made his appearance before the committee. He admitted to a lack of prudence in his dealings with Goldfine, but insisted that the only thing he had done for the man was to place one phone call to the SEC, asking it to expedite its hearings in Goldfine's case. The following day, Eisenhower opened a news conference with a prepared statement. He issued a ringing defense of Adams. No one, the President said, could doubt Adams' "personal integrity and honesty." As for himself, Eisenhower said, "I personally like Governor Adams. I admire his abilities. I respect him because of his personal and official integrity. I need him." [21] But the Democrats, smelling blood, were not deterred. The investigation continued, more Goldfine gifts were uncovered, and the Old Guard Republicans, seeing their opportunity, began demanding Adams' resignation (Barry Goldwater and Bill Knowland were the first to do so).

On June 23, Eisenhower expressed his feelings about the uproar to Paul Hoffman. "Nothing that has occurred has had a more depressive effect on my normal buoyancy and optimism than has the virulent, sustained, demagogic attacks made upon Adams," he said. Eisenhower admitted that Adams had been "less than alert" in his dealing with Goldfine, but "the fact remains that he is not only honest, effective, and dedicated, but in most cases, his attackers know this to be true." At the least, Eisenhower said, he would have hoped the Republicans would not add to the clamor. "I grow to despise political expediency more every day." [22]

Nevertheless, Eisenhower could not completely ignore what was becoming an almost unanimous Republican demand that Adams resign. In July, the President sent Nixon to talk to Adams about the situation, emphasizing that he felt such deep loyalty to Adams "that he did not want to even discuss the possibility of a resignation." But he did want Nixon to point out to Adams what a liability he had become. [23] In his talk later that morning with Adams, Nixon put the stress on the upcoming congressional elections. He warned Adams that if the Republicans did badly (which was widely anticipated), they would inevitably, if unfairly, blame Adams. But Adams refused to resign. He told Nixon that only Eisenhower could decide what the proper course of action should be. Meanwhile the investigation went on. Goldfine appeared before the committee and made an awful impression. The Republican Party was distraught, Eisenhower hardly less so.

In January of 1958, Nasser had announced that Egypt and Syria were uniting into a new nation, the United Arab Republic (UAR). The UAR then began propaganda broadcasts over the radio to appeal to pan-Arab sentiment in Jordan, Iraq, Saudi Arabia, and Lebanon. In response, the feudal monarchies of Jordan and Iraq formed their own federation, the Arab Union.

By that time, too, a situation had developed that Eisenhower had said he never wanted to see take place—there was an active arms race in the Middle East, with the United States supplying Saudi Arabia, Iraq, Jordan, and (to a slight extent) Lebanon with military equipment, while the Russians supplied Syria and Egypt, and the French sold arms to Israel. As the Middle East became an armed camp,

Eisenhower's worries increased. Although for public relations purposes he said his concern was with internal Communism in the Arab
countries, he had no evidence to support such a charge, and solid
evidence against it, beginning with the fact that the Communist Party
was outlawed in Egypt.

What Eisenhower really feared was radical Arab nationalism.
Nasser was almost openly appealing to the Arab people of the feudal
states of Jordan, Iraq, and Saudi Arabia to revolt against their mon-
archs and join the UAR. If he succeeded, and continued to rely on
the Soviets for arms and money, Khrushchev might possibly get a
stranglehold on the Western world's basic energy source, and Israel
could be crushed. Under those circumstances, Eisenhower could only
conclude that America's vital interests were at stake. He therefore
began searching for a way to demonstrate, unequivocally, America's
readiness and capability for action, and its determination to use force
to prevent the domination of the area by anti-Western pan-Arab
nationalism.

On July 14, pro-Nasser forces in Iraq pulled off a coup in Bagh-
dad, overthrowing the Hashemite monarchy and assassinating the
royal family. Although there was no direct evidence linking Nasser
to the coup, Radio Cairo was urging regicide throughout the feudal
Arab states. Hussein was the target of plots in Jordan; Saud was
worried and demanding that the United States send troops to the
Middle East, else he would be forced "go along" with the UAR. In
Lebanon, Allen Dulles reported, President Chamoun had requested
British and American intervention. The entire Middle East seemed
on the verge of falling into the hands of anti-Western pan-Arabs
controlled by Nasser.

This was a major crisis. To deal with it, Eisenhower called the
Dulles brothers, Nixon, Anderson, Quarles, Twining, Cutler, and
Goodpaster into the Oval Office. Cutler recalled that the President
"sat sprawled back in the chair behind his desk in a comfortable
position, the most relaxed man in the room. . . ." Cutler had the
feeling that Eisenhower "knew exactly what he meant to do." [24]

He did indeed; as Eisenhower put it in his memoirs, "This was
one meeting in which my mind was practically made up . . . even
before we met. The time was rapidly approaching, I believed, when
we had to move into the Middle East, and specifically into Lebanon,
to stop the trend toward chaos." [25]

Eisenhower turned to Twining to discuss the readiness of the
Sixth Fleet and the Marines in the eastern Mediterranean. Secretary

Dulles asked, almost plaintively, "Would you wish to hear my political appreciation?" Obviously embarrassed, Eisenhower replied: "Go ahead, Foster, . . . please." Dulles said the Russians would be content with making noise, but he warned that "if the United States went into Lebanon we could expect a very bad reaction from most Arab countries." He feared for the pipelines and the canal. But he assured Eisenhower that from a legal viewpoint, an American landing in Lebanon was far different from that of the British-French attack on Suez, because Chamoun had invited American troops into his country. He also warned, however, that few people would make the distinction.

Eisenhower knew all that already. Cutler noticed that the President, "calm, easy, and objective . . . was dealing with something which he thoroughly understood. His unruffled confidence was apparent to all." He told Dulles to have Lodge request an emergency meeting of the Security Council for the following morning; he told Jerry Persons to assemble the legislative leaders that afternoon; he told Twining to start the Sixth Fleet and the Marines toward Lebanon. [26]

Intervention proved to be a difficult proposition to sell to Congress. The legislative leaders were not at all enthusiastic. Some argued that intervention would undo America's good reputation; Sam Rayburn feared that America was getting into a civil war; Senator Fulbright doubted seriously that this crisis was Communist-inspired. Only three men supported action. But Eisenhower had not called the congressmen together to elicit support, or for consultation—he had called them in to inform them of what he intended to do. At the conclusion of the meeting, he met with the Dulles brothers, Twining, Quarles, Hagerty, and Goodpaster to "fix firmly upon specific action steps." Eisenhower told Twining to send the Marines ashore at 3 P.M. Lebanon time, which was 9 A.M., July 15, Washington time. No one, not even Chamoun, should be given advance notice, because the President did not want to give the rebels in Lebanon an opportunity to prepare resistance. Eisenhower instructed Foster Dulles to have Lodge tell the Security Council that the United States sought only to stabilize the situation until the U.N. could act. [27]

Eisenhower then called Macmillan. The Prime Minister had also received Chamoun's call for help, as well as one from Hussein of Jordan—"the two little chaps," Macmillan called them. Eisenhower informed Macmillan that American Marines were on their way to Lebanon. Macmillan laughed and said, "You are doing a Suez on me." Eisenhower laughed at his end. Macmillan wanted to act jointly; Eisenhower insisted on a unilateral American intervention in Lebanon, and asked Macmillan to be prepared to move into Jordan with British paratroopers. The President did not want to give the impression that the two countries were acting in collusion (although obviously they were), so he promised full logistical support for the British in Jordan, but refused to include American armed forces in that movement. He also assured Macmillan that he would not abandon his ally.[28]

Thus did Eisenhower unleash the American military for the only time in his Presidency. A quarter of a century later, his motives still seemed unclear. Lebanon was under no real threat; Chamoun had already announced that he would not seek a second term; evidence of any Russian, or Egyptian, involvement in Lebanon or in the coup in Iraq was lacking; there were no vital American interests in Lebanon itself. Eisenhower's decision to intervene, in addition, contrasted sharply with his response to the various crises in the Far East from 1953 through 1955. Then he had been cautious and prudent, far more so than his professional and political advisers. Now he was much more eager to intervene than were the politicians or the State Department people; indeed he had been eager to go into Lebanon for more than a year, and was just waiting for a proper excuse. Why was he so much more aggressive in the Middle East than in the Far East?

For one reason, because the chances of a clash between the superpowers were so much less in Lebanon, and the potential for indigenous resistance was far less in Lebanon than in Indochina or on the Chinese coast. Further, by 1958 one of the Democratic charges against Eisenhower had become his defense policy, with its emphasis on big planes and big bombs. Maxwell Taylor, as Army Chief of Staff, had joined the Democrats in this criticism, which had become widespread, and claimed that for America it was all or nothing—the country had no capability of making a flexible response appropriate to the occasion. By intervening in Lebanon, Eisenhower proved that was not true. Within two weeks, he had the equivalent of a full division in the country, equipped with Honest John rocket batteries that had atomic weapons, with another two divisions alerted on a few hours' flight from Germany. Lebanon, in short, was a show of force—and a most impressive one.

Against whom was it directed? Not the Soviets, who already knew, roughly, what American capability was. Not the Lebanese, virtually unarmed. The real target was Nasser. As Eisenhower later summed it up, he wanted to bring about a change in Nasser's attitude. Nasser, according to the President, "seemed to believe that the United States government was scarcely able, by reason of the nation's democratic system, to use our recognized strength to protect our vital interest." Eisenhower wanted to impress Nasser, and to show him that he could not count on the Soviets, in order to give him "food for thought." Eisenhower was also anxious to demonstrate to King Saud that the United States could be counted on to support its friends. (The President had told the legislative leaders that Saud had made it clear that "if we do not come in we are finished in the Middle East.") Most of all, Eisenhower's gunboat diplomacy in the Middle East was based on his perception of the importance of the area to the United States and its allies. In his judgment, the Middle East was more vital to the interests of the United States than the Far East. [29]

The Marines landed without incident, to find a country going about its business. Having made the commitment, Eisenhower downplayed its significance. In a special message to Congress, in Cabot Lodge's announcement to the Security Council, and in his own nationwide radio and television address that evening of July 15, Eisenhower expressed the hope that the U.N. could quickly come into Lebanon and "permit the early withdrawal of United States forces." He used the words "stationed in" Lebanon rather than "invading." American forces would secure the airfield and the capital, but would otherwise not operate in Lebanon.

Two days later, on July 17, the British sent twenty-two hundred paratroopers to Jordan to bolster King Hussein's shaky regime. Macmillan still wanted direct American participation; Eisenhower again refused. By early August the United States began to withdraw from Lebanon. The Russians, as Eisenhower had predicted, limited their response to diplomatic maneuvers (Krushchev was calling frantically for a summit meeting to deal with Lebanon, while denouncing American aggression). In less than four months, the crisis was over; by October 25, the last American troops were withdrawn. Eisenhower had accomplished his basic objectives without risking general war (Nasser had flown to Moscow in July, only to find that the Soviets had no interest in challenging the United States in the Middle East). The whole affair, Eisenhower noted in his memoirs, brought about "a definite change in Nasser's attitude toward the United States." [30]

Despite the impressive demonstration of American strength in Lebanon, the Democrats continued to charge that Ike was neglecting the nation's defenses. Senator Symington took the lead. In public, he said that the President had left the country vulnerable to a Soviet attack. Ike called him into the Oval Office for a meeting and carefully explained to him that the CIA had been overestimating Soviet development and capability; in fact, America had a significant lead in all categories of strategic weapons. In a grand understatement recorded by Goodpaster, "the President said he thought it would be out of character for him to be indifferent to valid assessments of Soviet strength." Symington was not convinced. [31]

Ike was even having trouble with his own administration. Neither John McCone, Strauss' successor as head of the AEC, nor Quarles, nor Neil McElroy were convinced that Eisenhower's desire for a test ban was good for the country. They wanted more tests. In late July, they proposed to the President a new series designed to test the ABM. The AEC and DOD proposed conducting the tests from Eglin Airfield, on the Florida Gulf Coast, firing out into the Gulf. Secretary Dulles was appalled; he said it would do great damage to relations with both Cuba and Mexico. (No one at the meeting raised the question of what the American residents of the Gulf Coast might think.) On the basis of Dulles' advice, Eisenhower ordered the series canceled.

In Geneva, meanwhile, the technical experts from Russia and the United States continued their deliberations in an attempt to agree on an inspection system that would justify a test ban. On August 4, Killian reported that they were making progress. Eisenhower told Killian that "if full technical agreement is reached, the weight of argument for doing so [ceasing the tests] would be very great." Both Twining and McCone strongly protested, but Eisenhower insisted.

On August 21, the Geneva experts adopted their final report. It concluded that "it was technically feasible" to create "a workable and effective control system to detect violations of an agreement on the worldwide suspension of nuclear weapons' tests." There was some disagreement among the experts on the number of control posts needed, and on the ability to detect small underground blasts, but that could not obscure the fact that for the first time in the nuclear age, Soviets and Americans had reached an agreement on atomic matters. Eisenhower told the State Department to begin test-ban negotiations with the Soviet Union. On August 22, Eisenhower issued a public statement, offering to enter into test-ban negotiations with the Russians on October 31. [32]

Five days later, before Khrushchev had replied to Eisenhower's proposal, McCone met with Eisenhower to ask for "one more test." He said he needed a decision "immediately." Eisenhower "expressed some irritation, saying that he had announced the tests' suspension and now 'they' wanted to have another big test." But McCone persisted, and finally got a weary President to agree; Eisenhower said "he supposed that AEC might as well go ahead." Part of the reason was undoubtedly the roar of protest that had greeted his announcement, from such people as Teller, Strauss, Hanson Baldwin, and Henry Kissinger. Another factor may have been Macmillan's actions; on August 22, the day of the announcement, the British began their latest series of tests with an explosion at Christmas Island.[33]

On August 29, Khrushchev indicated his willingness to enter into negotiations at the end of October; that same day, the AEC began a new series, officially named Hardtack II but called Operation Deadline by the press. Hardtack II set off nineteen separate explosions, most of them in the low-kiloton range, and including one of a nuclear bazooka shell designed to be fired by two men at a range of less than two miles. The Soviets also participated in this orgy of last-minute testing, starting their own series on September 30 and setting off fourteen weapons, most in the megaton range, and in the process releasing vast quantities of radioactive material. In 1958, the year that saw the first respite in testing since 1945, the three nuclear powers set off more bombs than in any other year (the Soviets set off more in October 1958, alone, than they had in all of 1957). The final total was eighty-one blasts. Radioactivity levels were at their peak. But at least there was, for the first time, some genuine hope that it all might soon end.

Hopelessness, meanwhile, was the dominant mood in the Republican Party as the off-year elections came closer. Eisenhower's veto of a farm bill was one reason, and the relatively lackluster candidates the party was offering another. Little Rock and Sputnik added to Republican woes. The Democrats, anxious to increase their lead in Congress and thus lay a base for the 1960 presidential election, were conducting a vigorous campaign, one in which they were able to reverse the roles of the 1952 campaign—they were on the offensive, while the Republicans were thrown back on the defensive. Under the circumstances, a Democratic sweep seemed certain.

Almost every Republican wanted a scapegoat. Most put the blame on Sherman Adams. In early September the demands for his resignation became irresistible. Still, Eisenhower hated to let Adams go. Both as general and as President, Eisenhower found it extremely difficult to fire a man who had served him well and loyally, no matter how great a handicap the man had become. So it was with Adams.

Eisenhower, greatly depressed, finally said, "My mind is pretty well cleared up as to what would be the better thing to do. The difficulty is to find a good way to do it." He asked Meade Alcorn, chairman of the RNC, to get together with Nixon and talk to Adams. Alcorn said he would.[34]

They did, without results. Adams told them, "I will have to talk to the boss myself." Eisenhower agreed to a meeting, then commented to Whitman, "How dreadful it is that cheap politicians can so pillory an honorable man."[35] At the meeting, on September 17, Adams indicated that he was willing to hand in his resignation, but that he wanted to wait a month or so to get the personnel situation straightened out. Eisenhower told him, "If anything is done and we make any critical decision, as I have always said, you will have to take the initiative yourself." But after the meeting, the President changed his mind and called Adams on the telephone to tell him that he could not drag the thing out for a full month. Then he added that he wanted to protect Adams "from anything that looks cold and indifferent."[36]

Five days later, on September 22, Adams announced his resignation. Eisenhower accepted it with the "deepest regret." The boil had been lanced, but whether the surgery would cure the desperately ill Republican Party remained to be seen.

Shortly thereafter, Ellis Slater and the rest of the gang spent a weekend at the White House with the First Family. Just before Saturday's dinner, nine-year-old David came in to present his grandfather with a bill for the work he had done on the farm the past two weeks. David had put the bill in an envelope addressed to "President Dwight Eisenhower"; it tabulated his days and hours—twenty-four hours' total at thirty cents per hour, with fifty cents for a previous loan deducted from the bill, which Eisenhower then paid. At the President's suggestion, David marked the bill paid in full and signed it.

Eisenhower cooked Sunday breakfast—cantaloupe from his farm, stacks of wheat cakes, and big link sausages—all served on trays on stands while the guests sat in easy chairs. They talked for three hours, mainly about farming and cattle and fertilizer and fields. Eisenhower said he was desperately looking forward to January 20,

1961, when he could retire and "just sleep and rest and be himself." Mamie commented that she had a lot of work to do before they left the White House, and said "it wasn't going to be fun getting ready to vacate that place." The morning, Slater wrote in his diary, was "refreshing and diverting" for the President.

Toward the end of the breakfast session, however, Eisenhower got to talking about what a terrible year he had had; he called 1958 "the worst of his life." He then commented that years ending in eight always seemed to be bad ones for him. In 1918, he said, he had missed World War I. In 1928, he had been in Paris, writing a guidebook—pleasant enough, but it had given him a feeling of treading water in his career. In 1938, his last year in the Philippines, he had gone through some bitter battles with MacArthur and feared he would never get away from the islands or the man. In 1948, he had retired from the Army and gone to Columbia, where he found much frustration and little satisfaction. In 1958, he had suffered a stroke, found himself in frequent disagreement with his chief foreign-policy adviser and with Congress, lost Sherman Adams and Lewis Strauss, endured a series of international crises and an economic recession, and had to anticipate major Republican defeats in the next election. Small wonder he was looking forward to retirement.[37]

But he was naturally an optimist. In a letter full of grousing to George Humphrey, he concluded, "Actually, of course, the sun is shining . . . the United States is still populated by relatively happy people, and by and large our grandchildren do not seem too much worried." He thought everything would work out all right.[38]

Even with the departure of Sherman Adams, Eisenhower and the Republican Party were gloomy on the eve of the off-year elections. The Democrats were hitting them hard in the campaign, most of all on the charge that "six years of leaderless vacillation have led us to the . . . brink of having to fight a nuclear war inadequately prepared and alone.[39] The charge that Eisenhower had allowed a "missile gap" to develop, which Stevenson had used without much success in 1956, and which Symington had been using since, began paying off for the Democrats in the 1958 elections.

Eisenhower tried to keep the issue out of politics. His first effort was to attempt to convince the Democratic critics that they were wrong; to do so, he had Allen Dulles give them a briefing. But he would not allow Dulles to reveal any hard information about the U-2 program, so Dulles, unable to cite his sources, was unconvincing. In his press conferences, meanwhile, Eisenhower always managed to say a word or two about how adequate America's defenses were, and to pooh-pooh any missile gap, but he did so in such a vague manner, without citing statistics or sources, that he too was unconvincing.

Another favorite Democratic charge was that the Republican Party was hopelessly split between the Old Guard and the moderate Eisenhower Republicans. Eisenhower tried to turn that one on its head. On October 20, in a major campaign speech in Los Angeles, the President declared that the Democratic Party "is not one—but two—political parties with the same name. They unite only once every two years—to wage political campaigns." One wing consisted of southern conservatives, the other of "political radicals," the wild spenders. A Democratic victory would mean innumerable new social programs, more money for defense, and a tax cut, all of which would lead to uncontrollable inflation and an unstoppable growth of the federal government.[40]

On November 4, 1958, the Republican Party, despite Eisenhower's warnings and efforts, suffered its worst defeat since the advent of the Depression. In the new Congress, Democrats would outnumber Republicans by nearly two to one in both houses. The Democrats had thirty-five governors, the Republicans only fourteen. Rockefeller's victory in New York had been balanced by Knowland's defeat in California, where he had run for governor. It was, all together, a humiliating defeat for the Republican party, which had been decisively rejected by the people even though its leader was a highly popular President. It left Eisenhower with the dubious distinction of being the first President to face three successive Congresses controlled by the opposition party.

Since 1954 and the CIA-supported overthrow of the Arbenz government in Guatemala, the United States had more or less ignored Latin America, as Eisenhower and Dulles concentrated on Europe, the Middle East, and Asia. The Administration, and especially its expert on Latin America, Milton Eisenhower, had called for more economic assistance to the area, but obtaining funds from Congress was difficult at best, and little was accomplished. As always, Latin radicals blamed Uncle Sam for the widespread poverty and discontent; as always, the United States ignored the agitation so long as it did not threaten to actually overthrow a pro-American government.

It was in Cuba, one of the most prosperous of the Spanish-speaking countries, that the policy fell apart. There Fidel Castro was leading a revolt against the corrupt and reactionary dictator, Fulgencio Batista. Batista had an odious record; Castro was young, romantic, dynamic.

On New Year's Day of 1959, Batista fled Cuba as Fidel entered Havana in triumph. The United States joined other American countries in recognizing the new regime. Castro appointed Cuban liberals to the top posts in his new government, a cause for hope in Washington, but in mid-January he made the Communist Party legal in Cuba, and by the end of the month his first Premier had resigned in protest over the executions of Batista supporters and the increasingly anti-American quality of Castro's speeches. On February 13, Castro himself became Premier, and in the ensuing weeks the executions and the attacks on the United States mounted.

The classic American response to radicalism in Latin America was to send in the Marines, an option that Eisenhower would not even consider, because of Castro's popularity not only in Cuba but throughout Latin America and even within the United States, and because of the probable effect of such action on world public opinion. In any event, the CIA gave him an alternative to the Marines.

Under Allen Dulles' direction, and with Eisenhower's encouragement, the CIA had been conducting covert operations around the world. None were as successful or spectacular as Iran in 1953 and Guatemala in 1954, and some—for example, Hungary in 1956—had been disastrous failures. Nevertheless, covert operations remained one of Eisenhower's chief weapons in the Cold War. The trick now was to find a way to use the CIA capabilities to get rid of Fidel.

On October 31, 1958, in Geneva, the Conference on the Discontinuance of Nuclear Weapons Tests commenced. One week earlier Gordon Gray met with the President to discuss the line the American negotiating team should follow. Gray was taking his post as National Security Adviser seriously. He was more forward than Cutler had been in raising subjects with Eisenhower, more bellicose and more active. He had even less trust in the Russians than Foster Dulles had, and he warned Eisenhower to be extra cautious in the test-ban talks. Eisenhower, however, thought it was necessary to take some risks. Although he insisted he would never jeopardize the real security interests of the United States, Eisenhower said that because of the numbers of such weapons and the improving means of delivery, "he would wish in any negotiation to err somewhat on the liberal side." To continue testing and the arms race, he said, "frightened him."[41]

Despite the President's attitude, the talks got off to a bad start. On the first day, they deadlocked. The issue was the agenda. The Russians wanted to begin by discussing a comprehensive test ban, while the Americans insisted on starting with discussions of an inspection system. These were becoming classic positions that left little room for negotiating anything. But at least there was a voluntary moratorium on testing. Although the Russians had cheated and conducted two tests in the first week of the Geneva talks, Eisenhower had promised if they would stop testing, so would he, and after November 3 the Russians did no more testing. Thus, as *Time* magazine pointed out, Eisenhower had done what he had always claimed he would not do, "stopped [American] tests primarily on good faith, without any provision of inspection." [42]

Having gotten from Eisenhower the unsupervised test ban they had wanted, the Russians finally agreed at Geneva to put the inspection system first on the agenda. The negotiators accepted an 180-post inspection system, but then deadlocked again when the Russians insisted on a veto in the seven-nation control commission. Eisenhower, eager to find a way out of the impasse, was therefore receptive to a mid-November proposal from Senator Albert Gore, a member of the American delegation in Geneva. Gore had concluded that there was no hope for a comprehensive test-ban agreement because of the inspection problem. He urged Eisenhower to announce a three-year unilateral ban on atmospheric tests, the type that spread radioactivity around the world. Gore told Eisenhower that the Russians have been "whaling us over the head" on fallout, but if the United States limited itself to underground tests, "the Soviets would have to do the same or be put on the defensive propaganda-wise." [43]

Eisenhower was perplexed. He wanted a test ban badly; he wanted more than just a ban, in fact, he wanted some real disarmament. But he felt he could not trust the Russians. On December 9, he explained to the visiting Queen Frederika of Greece that "we cannot be naive and put the whole safety of the free world in their [the Soviets'] hands." If America pulled out of NATO and surrendered its lead in nuclear weaponry, "then we have no recourse except to try to accept the communist doctrine and live with it." Eisenhower said "he would not want to live, nor would he want his children or grandchildren to live, in a world where we were slaves of a Moscow Power," because at that point "you would pay too big a price to be alive." [44]

On January 12, Dr. George Kistiakowsky, a Ukrainian-born chemist who was a member of the PSAC, warned the President that in his opinion that Russians had an operational ICBM force. Eisenhower remarked that it might possibly be so, but he still doubted that they had the numbers or the accuracy to do much damage with them. "He then asked the question, if the Soviets should fire these weapons at us, where this action would leave them. They would still be exposed to destruction. In his mind there is the question whether this is a feasible means of making war; he granted that it is a feasible way of destroying much of the nation's strength, but the resulting retaliation would be such that it does not make sense for war." [45]

Back in 1956 most of the scientists who later joined the PSAC had been opposed to further testing, Killian most of all. In the spring of 1958, Killian and the others had concluded, again, that a test ban would benefit the United States, and that a relatively small number (180) of inspection sites would discover all but the lowest-yield underground tests. It was on that basis that Eisenhower had agreed to the Geneva talks and the unilateral suspension of testing.

But once the scientists became formal advisers to the President, a number of them—led by Killian and Kistiakowsky—began to have doubts about the wisdom of a ban. In late December, the PSAC informed the President that it had decided it could not detect underground blasts as large as twenty kilotons, and that therefore thousands of inspection sites would be required to police a comprehensive test ban. Eisenhower was understandably furious with the scientists, because he knew that the demand for a quantum leap in the number of inspection sites would give the Russians an opportunity to charge that they had been double-crossed, and because he hated being given the wrong information, and even worse having acted on it.

But he felt he had to stick by his scientists, so on January 5, 1959, the American delegation at Geneva revealed the results of its latest findings and demanded more inspection sites. The Russians refused to even discuss the data, and the talks deadlocked again. Eisenhower instructed Killian to set up a new committee to find ways of making adequate inspection without so many sites.

On January 16, McCone came to the President with a request that the AEC be allowed to build a new reactor, in order to produce more bombs, as required by the DOD. Eisenhower exploded that there were no "requirements" until he had approved them, and stated that he could see no point to building bombs at a faster rate than the current pace of nearly two per day. He said the Defense people were getting "themselves into an incredible position—of having enough to destroy every conceivable target all over the world, plus a threefold reserve." He said "the patterns of target destruction are fantastic." Eisenhower had seen a graph on America's projected atomic weapons figures by 1968, which called for numbers of bombs that he could only regard as "astronomical." "Some of these days," he continued, "we are going to realize how ridiculous we have been and at that time we will try to retrench."

Eisenhower concluded by saying that "we are taking council of our fears," and by suggesting "that we indoctrinate ourselves that there is such a thing as common sense."[46]

Common sense, however, was hard to find. On February 18, Eisenhower met with Gordon Gray. During the course of a wide-ranging conversation, Eisenhower returned to the subject of numbers of weapons, and to earlier JCS claims that by hitting seventy targets inside Russia, the Soviets would be effectively destroyed. The new plans contemplated targets in the thousands, involving tremendous numbers of weapons of megaton size. The JCS were planning on using thousands of weapons averaging 3.5 megatons in an all-out war; Eisenhower "wondered what would be the cumulative effect of ground bursts of such a magnitude of megatonage on the Northern Hemisphere . . . He expressed his concern that there just might be nothing left of the Northern Hemisphere." The United States already had a stockpile of "five thousand or seven thousand weapons or whatnot." Eisenhower wondered why more were needed.[47]

(Getting accurate figures on the American nuclear arsenal was the most difficult research task in this study. The figures were always given to the President in oral form, by the head of the AEC. As far as the author can tell, Eisenhower inherited an arsenal of about fifteen hundred weapons ranging from the low-kiloton yield to bombs of many megatons. If there were six thousand or so weapons by 1959, the AEC had built about forty-five hundred weapons during the first six years of the Eisenhower Administration, or more than two per day.)

The American ability to hit the Russians was already awesome. In late November of 1958, the President undertook a review of the DOD budget request for fiscal 1960. The JCS had asked for $50 billion; DOD had brought that figure down to $43.8 billion; Eisenhower wanted it reduced to $40 billion. In a discussion with McElroy, Twining, Quarles, Gray, Goodpaster, and others, Eisenhower examined the current retaliatory capacity. In addition to SAC (which still carried the most and biggest bombs and was virtually invulnerable), there were the various IRBM and ICBM projects going forward, including the implanting of IRBMs in Europe, and six Polaris submarines were under construction. After looking it all over, Eisenhower asked rhetorically, "How many times do we have to destroy Russia?" Still the JCS and DOD wanted more of everything, including a second nuclear-powered aircraft carrier. Eisenhower objected. He said he did not "visualize a battle for the surface of the sea," and that existing conventional carriers provided sufficient mobility to meet the purposes of any small war, or of an intervention as in Lebanon. The DOD and JCS people kept coming back to the nuclear carrier, however, until the President snapped that "Our defense depends on our fiscal system." He insisted that the carrier be put on hold, and that other cuts in defense be made, bringing the total down to $40 billion, because "unless the [federal] budget is balanced sooner or later, procurement of defense systems will avail nothing."[48]

Eisenhower's campaign for fiscal integrity, coupled with his use of the veto, worked. When the Democrats proposed spending $450 million per year for four years for urban renewal, Eisenhower objected strongly enough, and got enough support from southern congressmen, to defeat the bill. When Congress finally did pass a housing bill, with lowered expenditures, Eisenhower vetoed it. The Senate failed to override the veto, because of southern votes. That pattern held throughout the year, and to his delight Eisenhower ended up fiscal 1960 with a surplus of a billion dollars.

CHAPTER TWENTY

A Revival

FOLLOWING the disappointments and frustrations of 1958, Eisenhower rallied, took command, and led his people with all the instincts of the good steward. Soon columnists were talking about a "new" Eisenhower, a man who asserted himself more powerfully than he had ever done before.

The "new" Eisenhower was noticeably friendlier toward the Soviets, more willing to see issues from their point of view, more willing to take some risks to achieve a first step toward a test ban, more willing to consider a summit meeting, than he had ever been before. Some observers attributed this development to the absence of Foster Dulles, but that was only partly true at best. A number of factors had come together by February 1959, when Dulles took his leave of absence, that were pushing Eisenhower toward a summit and some form of accommodation with the Soviets.

First of all, after November 4, 1958, he had his last election behind him. The next one belonged to Nixon. This put Nixon in the awkward position of having to be simultaneously a loyal member of the Administration, a supplicant, and his own man. It put Eisenhower in the worrisome position of realizing that in two years he would have to hand over the Presidency to Nixon—or, worse, to the Democrats. Were the opposition to take charge, Eisenhower anticipated an orgy of spending on defense and on social programs with a tax cut—a prospect he regarded with horror.

Nor could he regard a Nixon succession with optimism. After six years of standoffish relationship, Eisenhower remained ambiguous about Nixon. He did not doubt the man's loyalty, or honesty, or even ability, but he did worry about Nixon's ambition. On June 11, Whitman recorded in her diary that Eisenhower had breakfast with Nixon. The Vice-President asked the President if he would take some of Nixon's friends—all rich men, potential contributors—for a weekend on a Navy yacht and play some golf with them at Quantico. Eisenhower, who prided himself on not mixing politics and his social life (although of course he did), flatly refused. Later, the President told Whitman, "It is terrible when people get politically ambitious."[1]

Another problem in their relationship was that Nixon wanted to do more, be more visible, shoulder more responsibilities, but Eisenhower would not let him. What really made a close relationship impossible, however, was the nature of their concerns. Nixon's position forced him to concentrate all his attention and energies on the 1960 election; Eisenhower's position forced him to concentrate all his attention and energies on what he could accomplish in his last two years. The irony was that Nixon had to make his decisions on a short-term basis of the election, while Eisenhower's short time remaining led him to make his decisions on the basis of long-term considerations. Nixon's goal was votes. Eisenhower's goals were peace, a test ban, disarmament, reconciliation.

On November 10, 1958, Khrushchev had announced his intention of signing at an early date a peace treaty with East Germany. According to Khrushchev, that action would have the effect of terminating Allied rights in West Berlin. According to Eisenhower, it would do nothing of the sort, as the Allied right to be in Berlin rested on the wartime agreements at Yalta and had nothing to do with the East Germans, whose regime the Allies did not recognize.

Khrushchev set a deadline, May 27, 1959. If the Allies did not agree to negotiations for the withdrawal of their troops from Berlin by that date, he would sign the treaty with the East Germans and then the Allies would have to shoot their way through to West Berlin, as they had no treaty with East Germany.

Eisenhower was sure Khrushchev was bluffing, that he would back down if the Allies remained firm. Khrushchev wanted a summit to discuss Berlin. Eisenhower did not. To stall, Ike insisted that there be a meeting of the Foreign Ministers, and that some progress be made on various divisive issues, before the summit.

But while Ike downplayed the event, the country as a whole grossly exaggerated the dangers that threatened. The Democrats, led by Senators Symington and Kennedy, joined the JCS to demand greatly increased spending on new weapons and an expansion of the armed forces. By no means was the pressure to increase military spending limited to Symington or the JCS. There was a general impression around the country, one that was assiduously spread by the huge Pentagon propaganda machine, the arms industry, the Democrats, and columnists, that Eisenhower was underreacting to the Berlin crisis.

The national mood, at least as it was being expressed in the halls of Congress and in the media, was impatient. People wanted to get moving again, to take the offensive in the Cold War, to stop reacting and start acting. Many were eager to shoot the way through to Berlin and teach the Soviets a lesson.

Eisenhower, however, thought much of this aggressiveness was artificially created, by the same forces that created an artificial demand for more missiles, bombers, and other weapons. "I'm getting awfully sick of the lobbies by the munitions," he told the Republican leaders. After looking at the advertisements Boeing and Douglas had published, Eisenhower said, "You begin to see this thing isn't wholly the defense of the country, but only more money for some who are already fat cats." Eisenhower also thought, "This seems to be a hysteria that is largely political." [2]

But whether artificially created or not, the popular impression that more had to be done ran very deep. As Eisenhower had feared would happen, people had become afraid, and in their fright their instinctive response was to strengthen their military. Although they trusted Ike, they were confused by his policies. He talked about being firm in Berlin, but simultaneously announced a cut of fifty thousand men from the armed services.

As Khrushchev's May 27 deadline approached, a war-scare fever began to sweep the country, one reminiscent of those over the Far East in 1954 and 1955, only even more serious because this one pitted the United States directly against the Soviet Union, and the arsenals had quadrupled or more since 1954.

More than any other individual, the man who held the Berlin crisis in check was Dwight Eisenhower. His was an absolutely bravo performance, a combination of master diplomat, statesman, and politician at his best. He gave Khrushchev the room to retreat, he mollified his allies, he kept the JCS and the other hawks in check, he kept the risks at a minimum level, he satisfied the public that his response was appropriate, and he kept the Democrats from throwing billions of dollars to the DOD. His most basic strategy was to simply deny that there was a crisis. His most basic tool was patience, as he carefully explained, over and over, fundamental truths about the nuclear age.

Along the way, he seemed to be almost alone. Dulles was in the hospital, his deputy Christian Herter was feeling his way into his responsibilities, McElroy was on the side of the JCS, and Eisenhower was generally on his own. Even the White House press corps, normally so friendly, turned on him, asking hostile and even insulting questions. May Craig was the worst. She opened by instructing the President on the Constitution, then asked, "Where technically do you get the right to thwart the will of Congress, for instance in cutting the Army and the Marine Corps . . . or for not spending the money which they give you for missiles, submarine missiles, or whatever they be?" Other reporters also expressed their concern about the reduction in the size of the Army.

"What would you do with more ground forces in Europe?" Eisenhower replied rhetorically. "Does anyone here have an idea? Would you start a ground war?" Speaking with great emphasis and deep emotion, he proclaimed: "We are certainly not going to fight a ground war in Europe. What good would it do to send a few more thousands or even a few divisions of troops to Europe?" Chalmers Roberts wanted to know if Eisenhower thought the American public was "sufficiently aware of the possibility of war in this situation?" Indeed, Eisenhower replied, he thought it was *too* aware. "What I decry is: let's not make everything such an hysterical sort of a proposition that we go a little bit off half-cocked."

Then it was back to those fifty thousand troops—what if Congress forced him to take them? "Where will I put them?" Eisenhower asked in his turn. "Well, just some place where it's nice to keep them out of the way, because I don't know what else to do with them."

Edward Folliard asked Eisenhower to comment on the widespread assumption that the Administration "puts a balanced budget ahead of national security." Suppose, Folliard said, there were more money in the budget—would Eisenhower then spend more on the military? Eisenhower replied, "I would say that I would not spend [such] money on the armed forces of the United States . . ."

Eisenhower's responses left the reporters frustrated. Peter Lisagor asked the last question, and he spoke for the others when he expressed his puzzlement. Lisagor quoted the President's previous remark about "nuclear war doesn't free anyone," noted that he had ruled out the possibility of a ground war in Central Europe, and wondered if there was "an in-between response that we could make." The question gave Eisenhower an opportunity to use the news conference not only to calm the American people, but to send a message to the Soviets. "I didn't say that nuclear war is a complete impossibility," he replied to Lisagor's question. "I said it couldn't as I see it free anything. Destruction is not a good police force. You don't throw hand grenades around streets to police the streets so that people won't be molested by thugs." But you just might use them if the Soviets blockaded Berlin.[3]

One of Eisenhower's major tasks was to calm people down. In March, on three separate occasions—to the JCS, to the Republican leaders, and to the Democratic leaders—he made the same point. As recorded by John Eisenhower at the JCS meeting, "The President then stressed the necessity to avoid overreacting. In so doing we give the Soviets ammunition. The President stressed the view that Khrushchev desires only to upset the United States. He expressed once again his view that we must address this problem in terms, not of six months, but of forty years." The Soviets would always attempt to keep America off balance, Eisenhower said. First, Berlin. Then Iraq. Next Iran. Wherever they could stir up trouble, they would, and "they would like us to go frantic every time they stir up difficulties in these areas."[4]

The reason, as Eisenhower explained to the Republican and Democratic leaders, was that—as he claimed anyone who had ever read Lenin knew—"the Communist objective is to make us spend ourselves into bankruptcy." It was wrong to dramatize Berlin, he declared. "This is a continuous crisis . . . that the United States has to live with certainly as long as we are going to be here." He dismissed liberation of Eastern Europe as an illusion, then explained what America's most realistic hope was: "The President went into our long-term policy of holding the line until the Soviets manage to educate their people. By doing so, they will sow the seeds of destruction of Communism as a virulent power. This will take a long time to settle."[5]

It was one of the oddities of the Cold War that each side expected the other to collapse as a result of its internal contradictions. Eisenhower believed deeply that in the end freedom would prevail, but he also recognized—indeed counted on—Khrushchev's equally firm belief that Communism would win. Thus he told his Cabinet on March 13, "There is good reason to believe that the Russians do not want war," because they felt they were winning already. This gave Eisenhower an opportunity to follow a policy of both conciliation and firmness.

The firmness came first. From the beginning, Eisenhower stressed that the United States was not going to abandon the people of West Berlin. He was ready to face the possible consequences of that stand. As he told the Cabinet, "The United States has to stand firm even should the situation come down to the last and ultimate decision, although neither I nor the State Department believe it will ever be allowed to go to that terrible climax. You should not think of this as the beginning of the end, but don't think it is possible to end tension by walking away from it."[6] In innumerable ways, the President conveyed that message to Khrushchev.

Then came the conciliation. It came hard, because at times even Eisenhower's patience ran out and he allowed himself to fantasize a bit about how he might stick it to those impossible Russians. He had no thought of bombing them into the Stone Age, but he did call Herter to ask for a "little study" of what the effects would be of breaking diplomatic relations with the Russians. Eisenhower enjoyed the thought immensely. "Throw out all the Russians in this country," he exclaimed. "Stop all trade . . . who would be hurt? There may be some other things. If we broke relations we could throw the Russians out of the U.N. and deny them visas." Herter interrupted the President's fantasy before he got too carried away by reminding him that "we have a freedom of access agreement in the U.N."[7]

Conciliation, not confrontation, was what Eisenhower wanted anyway, whatever his dreams. He let Khrushchev know that although he was standing firm, he was willing to negotiate Berlin's status. He made new concessions on a test ban, and tried in other ways to reach out to Khrushchev. But his most important act was the declaration of willingness to negotiate, and the hints that he would be willing to attend a summit. The act of negotiation would, in itself, be an agreement to Khrushchev's position that the situation in Berlin was abnormal. But then of course it was—Eisenhower was only admitting the truth—and Eisenhower was ready to discuss a free-city status, so long as the discussions also included reunification of Germany.

The President's proposed solution for this greatest of the outstanding problems left over from World War II, the division of Germany, was to hold nationwide free elections. The Soviets insisted on reunification through merger at the top. Adenauer's position was that reunification was his principal goal, and that no recognition of any sort of the East German regime was possible, but most observers, on both sides of the Iron Curtain, disbelieved him. Khrushchev once told Eisenhower categorically "that Adenauer's support of unification was nothing but a show." Herter told Eisenhower exactly the same thing. On April 4, over the telephone, Herter reported that Bonn was opposed to talking about free elections at any Foreign Ministers' or summit meeting, although Adenauer was not saying so publicly. "Herter said it was obvious that what Adenauer and the Christian Democrats were scared of was that in a reunified free election the opposition Socialist Party in West Germany would form a coalition with certain East German parties and throw the Christian Democrats out of office." Eisenhower's reply, at least for those who believe in democracy, was perfect: "The President said if they get a true free unification, then they have to take their chances on politics."[8]

Conciliation included not only declaring a willingness to talk about Germany, but also some concessions on a test ban. Accordingly, on April 13, the day the Geneva negotiations resumed, Eisenhower wrote Khrushchev, announcing that the United States no longer insisted on a comprehensive test ban, but would be willing to move "in phases, beginning with a prohibition of nuclear weapons' tests in the atmosphere." This would require only a simplified control system.[9] Khrushchev, although he denounced a partial test ban as "misleading," nevertheless indicated a willingness to talk, and the negotiations went on.

On a daily basis, Eisenhower was calling Dulles in the hospital to keep him informed of the test-ban progress, a cause to which Dulles had committed himself so strongly. In one of their last conversations, Eisenhower expressed his desire to halt the "terrific" arms race by at least stopping tests in the atmosphere. "In the long run," Eisenhower concluded, "there is nothing but war—if we give up all hope of a peaceful solution."[10]

On May 24, the end came for John Foster Dulles. Eisenhower's sense of loss and grief was personal and painful. Dulles had served him faithfully and tirelessly for six years. He had frequently disagreed with the President, especially in the early years over policy in the Far East, but he had always acceded to the President's judgment and carried out Eisenhower's policies with skill and enthusiasm. They were never personal friends in any social sense; Dulles did not play bridge or golf, or spend weekends with Eisenhower at Gettysburg or Augusta. But they had deep personal respect for each other, and

they enjoyed working together, because they shared common assumptions about the nature of the Soviet threat and on the need to
stand firm to meet it. In Eisenhower's judgment, Dulles was one of
the greatest of Secretaries of State. That he could not convince others
of that judgment was not for lack of trying.

Dulles' death brought the Foreign Ministers to Washington for
the funeral, which ironically was held on May 27—the original "deadline" date Khrushchev had set for Berlin. Before the funeral, Eisenhower asked the Foreign Ministers to the White House for lunch.
The President explained to a protesting State Department aide that
"what he had in mind was simply to ask them in and tell them that it
is, in his judgment, ridiculous that the world is divided into segments
facing each other in unending hostility. He felt that decent men
should be able to find some way to make progress toward a better
state of things." [11]

Almost unnoticed in the publicity and hoopla surrounding the
Foreign Ministers' meeting was the fundamental outcome of the Berlin crisis of 1959—that Eisenhower had gotten through it without
increasing the defense budget, without war, and without backing
down. The situation in Berlin was unchanged.

With only a year and a half to go in office, Ike's mind turned
increasingly to retirement and death. He told Slater he could not
decide how he wanted to arrange his retirement—whether to take
the President's pension of $25,000 per year, with $50,000 in allowances, or go back to the Army as a five-star general, which would
entitle him free of charge to the services of Colonel Schulz and Sergeants Dry and Moaney. He said he had gotten so accustomed to
having those three around, "it will be hard to get along without
them."

Together with the gang, Ike and Mamie talked about their eventual burial spot. They considered Arlington, West Point, and Abilene.
Ike liked the idea of Abilene, where a private foundation had already
raised the money to build an Eisenhower Museum and was arranging
financing for an Eisenhower Library. The gang urged him to choose
Gettysburg, on the grounds that it was closer to the major population
centers and was already a major tourist site. [12]

In June 1959, Ike had one of the greatest pleasures any grandfather can have—the grandchildren came to live with him. Not at the
White House, but the next best thing, as Barbara and the children
moved in at Gettysburg, while John took a room on the third floor of

the White House. John went up to Gettysburg on weekends, his parents joining him whenever they could.

Eisenhower was beginning to lose a bit of enthusiasm and stamina. In April, he told Slater, "You know, one way I realize I'm not as young as I once was, is that I'm perfectly willing to have a big conference at ten in the morning—I even look forward to it—but the same situation faced at four in the afternoon finds me unhappy about the prospect." [13]

His mind stayed young. In late June, dictating a letter to Whitman, he used the sentence, "I doubt whether a man of my age changes his habits of thinking and of speech." Then he told her to cross out that sentence, and explained that "he had conscientiously tried to change his habits of speech. That since a child he had always thought faster than he could talk, which accounted for the fact that his tongue would 'run away with him' and he might not finish sentences, etc. Since his 'difficulty' of the last couple of years, he said he tried very hard to think before he would speak—to outsiders." [14]

With the Foreign Ministers' meeting stalled and in recess, and with the test-ban talks, also based in Geneva, and also stalled and in recess, if Eisenhower wanted to use the last year and a half of his term to advance the cause of peace, he was going to have to talk directly to Khrushchev. That was exactly what Khrushchev wanted; indeed he had dropped any number of hints that he would like to visit the United States and then invite Eisenhower to Moscow.

Eisenhower was intrigued by the idea. American domestic politics were at a virtual standstill, as the politicians were gearing up for the 1960 election and the only significant issue between Eisenhower and Congress was the budget. Further, technology was making travel so much easier, faster, and more comfortable. In 1959, *Air Force One* replaced the *Columbine* as the President's airplane. The new craft dwarfed the old one, had a much greater range and more room inside, and could fly around the world if the President desired. Travel, just for its own sake, had always been one of Eisenhower's chief delights. There were many places he wanted to see—most especially India—and he had been compiling a mental list of the sites he intended to visit after retirement. But how much nicer to visit them while he was still President, and could use *Air Force One,* and—best of all—could use his prestige and position to further the cause of peace, to which he had committed himself and his Administration.

On July 10, Eisenhower told Herter, Dillon, and Goodpaster that if there was some progress at the Geneva Foreign Ministers' meeting (due to resume in three days), he would ask Khrushchev to visit the United States after he had made an appearance before the U.N. Then in October, he said, he would visit Moscow, afterward flying on to India.

Eisenhower explained that he thought talking to Khrushchev might do some good. He added that a talk with Khrushchev "would be useful for one thing. If Khrushchev were to threaten war or use of force, he would immediately call his bluff and ask him to agree on a day to start." [15]

By July 22, Khrushchev had responded; he would be delighted to come, for a ten-day visit, and there was much he wanted to see. The announcement brought howls of protest from various Cold Warriors. William Buckley, for example, wanted to fill the Hudson River with red dye so that when Khrushchev entered New York Harbor, it would be on a figurative "river of blood." Reporters too were hostile. At an August 12 news conference, held in Gettysburg, Eisenhower was asked what it was in the United States that he wanted Khrushchev to see. Whitman called Eisenhower's reply a "love song to America."

"I would like for him, among other things, to see this," Eisenhower responded. "The evidence that the fine, small or modest homes that Americans live in are not the exception as he seemed to think the sample we sent over to Moscow was." He wanted Khrushchev to see Levittown, a town "universally and exclusively inhabited by its workmen . . . I would like to see him have to fly along in my chopper and just make a circuit of the District, to see the uncountable homes that have been built all around, modest but decent, fine, comfortable homes." Further, "I would like to see him go in the little town where I was born and pick up the evidence . . . and let them tell him the story of how hard I worked until I was twenty-one. I can show him the evidence that I did, and I would like him to see it." Most of all, Eisenhower emphasized, "I want him to see a happy people. I want him to see a free people, doing exactly as they choose, within the limits that they must not transgress the rights of others." [16]

Eisenhower did not tell the reporters, but he did say privately, that he had something else he wanted Khrushchev to see—his opportunity. As Goodpaster recorded it, "The President thought he personally might make an appeal to Khrushchev in terms of his place in history, point out that if he wants to gain such a place through making a change to improve the international climate, the President is confident that something can be worked out." Eisenhower intended to stress that while he had only eighteen months to go, Khrushchev would be in command for many years to come. He felt he had to make such an appeal, he said, if only "to satisfy his own conscience."[17]

De Gaulle and Adenauer were predictably and understandably worried, Macmillan only slightly less so. The thought of Eisenhower and Khrushchev making deals together alarmed them. In order to reassure them, and to try out *Air Force One* and to indulge in some nostalgia, Eisenhower decided to visit the three Western capitals before Khrushchev's September 15 arrival in America.

At 3:20 A.M., August 26, Ike climbed aboard *Air Force One* for the first time. Mamie had gotten up to come see him off (she had been tempted to go along, but there was too much flying involved for her taste), and he showed her the accommodations, which dazzled him but bored her. The flight itself, his first ever in a jet, Ike found an "exhilarating experience." As the big jet went into its "silent, effortless acceleration and its rapid rate of climb," whatever doubts Ike had about the wisdom of spending most of the remainder of his term on world travels vanished. He was hooked.[18]

In Bonn, Adenauer promised that Germany would do more rearming. Eisenhower said he hoped so, and added that he looked forward to the day that the German contingent in NATO was sufficiently large the Americans could reduce their ground forces in Europe. Adenauer, much alarmed, asked Eisenhower to not even mention the possibility.

In London, Eisenhower talked with Macmillan. Their only disagreement was over the test-ban negotiations. Macmillan was willing to accept something short of a verifiable inspection system in order to get a comprehensive test ban, while Eisenhower favored a ban on atmospheric testing only.

In Paris, in his talks with de Gaulle, Eisenhower said he just could not support the French in Algeria. De Gaulle tried to revive the idea of a tripartite worldwide arrangement, to no avail. Eisenhower tried to revive the idea of the European Defense Community, or all-European army. The President reminded de Gaulle that in early 1952, he "swore, prayed, almost wept for the EDC. It was initialed, but after the French Parliament was through with it, there was nothing left." Would de Gaulle like to examine it again?

"Non," replied de Gaulle, as he loftily declared that "an Army can have no morale unless it is defending its own country." Eisenhower blanched, then reminded de Gaulle that "in the Second World

War, when a lot of us were fighting on foreign soil, it seemed we had good morale." [19]

The war was much on his mind. Nothing new had come out of the discussions; nevertheless the trip gave Eisenhower a great boost, because it brought back so many good memories and because of the evidence it provided of Eisenhower's extraordinary popularity in Western Europe. On the twenty-mile drive from the airport to the American Embassy in Bonn, the roads were jammed with cheering crowds; it was a moving experience for Eisenhower, to be cheered by the people he had only so recently conquered. Eisenhower told Adenauer it was "astonishing"; the Chancellor agreed.

In Paris, the people quite outdid themselves. From the airport to the city, the crowds were huge. De Gaulle and Eisenhower rode in a convertible, waving to the wildly enthusiastic throngs. "How many?" Eisenhower asked de Gaulle. "At least a million," de Gaulle told him. "I did not expect half as many," said Eisenhower, deeply moved.

London was the best, although Eisenhower had feared the worst. He had been warned to expect a cool reception, as the British had by no means forgiven him for Suez. In addition, Macmillan had given the trip minimum publicity, as the talks were informal and because Eisenhower had given tentative agreement to making another, formal visit at Christmastime.

But as the motorcade drove from the airport to the city, through a gathering dusk, the people of Britain turned out to honor the man who had such a special place in their hearts. They turned out by the thousands, by the tens of thousands, by the hundreds of thousands. As the crowds grew denser, Macmillan kept repeating, "I never would have believed it, I never would have believed it." As they got to Grosvenor Square, Eisenhower's wartime headquarters, Macmillan told him, "The state visit in December is off. Anything after this would be anticlimax." [20]

Eisenhower hosted a dinner for his wartime comrades. He paid a visit to the royal family. He spent a weekend at Chequers (ah, the memories). He took a few days' vacation at Culzean Castle, given to him for his lifetime by the people of Scotland. The gang flew over to play bridge.

London provided the appropriate setting for the climax of the trip. Eisenhower appeared with Macmillan on television, talking extemporaneously. Eisenhower, discussing the need for greater cultural exchange, showed again that the British always brought out the best in him. Turning to Macmillan, he said with great earnestness, "I like to believe that people, in the long run, are going to do more to promote peace than our governments. Indeed, I think that people want peace so much that one of these days governments had better get out of the way and let them have it."[21]

That was the spirit of his trip, the spirit in which he had, however grudgingly, agreed to a Khrushchev visit, the spirit in which he intended to work in the time remaining to him.

On September 7, Eisenhower returned to the States. A week later, Khrushchev arrived for two days of talks, formal dinners, and a helicopter ride over Washington. Khrushchev gave Eisenhower a gift, a model of a projectile called Lunik II, which had just made a trip to the moon. Eisenhower thought it a bit on the blatant side, but then thought to himself "quite possibly the man [is] completely sincere." In his opening statement at the talks, Khrushchev made the most basic point, one that everyone said they recognized but that no one was willing to act on as a basis of policy. We do not want war, said Khrushchev, and we believe that you know that. Eisenhower said he did, that there was no future in mutual suicide. After that, they really had nothing more to discuss, as on all the outstanding issues—the status of Berlin, of Formosa, Soviet (and American) meddling in the Middle East, disarmament—each man had taken a position from which he would not back down.[22]

Primarily, Eisenhower wanted to appeal to Khrushchev's sense of history, in order to get some progress somewhere, most likely on testing. As he told the Republican leaders, he wanted to make "one great personal effort, before leaving office, to soften up the Soviet leader even a little bit. Except for the Austrian peace treaty, we haven't made a chip in the granite in seven years."[23] He did get a chance to make the point to Khrushchev privately; Khrushchev took it graciously, but said that there would have to be movement toward compromise by both sides. The following morning, he took off for a tour of the country. Eisenhower assigned Cabot Lodge to accompany him. Khrushchev's tour was a media event of the first magnitude. He made great copy and the world press was there to take down his rages, his delights, his off-the-cuff comments, his threats, his blandishments, and to satisfy his desire for headlines.

A highlight came on September 18, when Khrushchev spoke to the U.N. He was proud of his speech—back in Washington, he had tapped his pocket and told Eisenhower, "Here is my speech and no one is going to see it." Thus Eisenhower was completely unprepared for Khrushchev's bombshell, which was nothing less than a call for a total abolition of all weapons, nuclear and conventional, over the next four years, without any provision for inspection or supervision. If the West was not ready for so radical a cure, he was willing to pursue the stalled test-ban issue, which he said was "acute and eminently ripe for solution."[24]

On September 25, Khrushchev returned to Washington. He and Eisenhower took a helicopter to Camp David for two days of talks. Now it was Khrushchev's turn to try to impress Eisenhower. He grew quite expansive in discussing the military and security posture of the Soviet Union (all through the trip, he had been kidding Lodge about how easily the KGB broke the most secret American communications, and hinted that the KGB had a mole highly placed in the CIA). He said the Russians were building more powerful nuclear submarines than the Americans. Khrushchev claimed that the U.S.S.R. had all the bombs it wanted and would soon have all the missiles it needed; he bragged that the number was a "lot." He said he had decided that small tactical atomic weapons were too expensive. So was atomic power for civilian purposes; Khrushchev said the Russians had stopped work on their nuclear power plants and were relying instead on gas, oil, and coal. But, as Eisenhower later told Twining, "Khrushchev gave great emphasis to the tremendous costs of defense, returning to this subject time after time. He repeatedly emphasized the importance of disarmament."[25]

They had a long talk about World War II. Khrushchev assured Eisenhower, "Your old friend Zhukov is all right. Don't worry about him. He's down in the Ukraine fishing—and like all generals he is probably writing his memoirs." Then Khrushchev began talking about the subject Eisenhower had hoped he would, American homes and automobiles, and Eisenhower was more disappointed than ever, because Khrushchev said he was not impressed. In fact, he was shocked at all the waste. Those vast numbers of cars, he said, represented only a waste of time, money, and effort. Well, said Eisenhower, he must have found the road system impressive. No, replied Khrushchev, because in his country there was little need for such roads because the Soviet people lived close together, did not care for automobiles, and seldom moved. The American people, he observed, "do not seem to like the place where they live and always want to be on the move going someplace else." And all those houses, Khrushchev continued, cost more to build, more to heat, more for upkeep and surrounding grounds than the multiple family housing in the Soviet Union.[26]

The only positive note to emerge was Khrushchev's willingness to remove any hint of a deadline or an ultimatum from the Berlin question. On that basis, the two leaders made a tentative agreement to meet at the summit, in Paris, in May. After the summit, Eisenhower and his wife, son, daughter-in-law, and grandchildren would pay a visit to Russia.

Throughout 1960, as throughout his two terms, Eisenhower devoted much of his time, effort, and prestige to holding down spending. He had some success, more than any of his successors. In the recession year of 1958 the government had run a $12 billion deficit, but in 1959, revenues were up by nearly $10 billion, and as the economy recovered, spending for antirecession measures was curtailed. In fiscal 1959, Eisenhower cut federal spending by almost $4 billion. The result was a $1 billion surplus, and a projected $4 billion surplus in 1960.

As always, defense was the most difficult place to hold down spending. The generals and the admirals were determined to stick to the cutting edge of the technological revolution, while they simultaneously wanted the largest nuclear arsenal, the best delivery system, the world's most powerful Navy and conventional Air Force, and a large, mobile standing Army. They, and their many supporters, could be most eloquent in stating their position.

At a June 23 meeting with the top officials in DOD and PSAC, for example, Eisenhower was told that there was unanimous agreement on the pressing need to go forward with the project for a nuclear-powered aircraft. But Eisenhower could not be bamboozled. He asked some probing questions, which revealed that the major reason his military advisers wanted to do it was because they thought it was possible to do it. "The President commented that the next thing he knows someone would be proposing to take the liner *Queen Elizabeth* and put wings a mile wide on it and install enough power plant to make it fly. Dr. York begged him not to let the idea get around, or someone would want to try." [27]

It was not that the President was opposed to new ideas, or that he was incapable of changing his mind. Two years earlier, at the time of Sputnik, he had insisted that the bomber was still much the best delivery system; since then, advances in rocketry had been such as to convince him otherwise. What bothered him most, however, was that the Air Force insisted on having both, indeed wanted to fund a new bomber, the B-70, while increasing ICBM construction. Eisenhower said he was "very skeptical" about the need for any new bombers. "If the missiles are effective, there will be no need for these bombers." He said he wished the Air Force officers would make up their minds, and added (he must have had a grin on his face), "I am beginning to think that the Air Force is not concerned over true economy in defense."

McElroy said that DOD wanted to put money into the B-70 because it represented the state of the art, and would provide spinoff benefits in civilian air transport. Eisenhower said sharply that he could not see us putting military money into a project to develop a civilian transport. He is "allergic" to such an idea. But all the PSAC members jumped in to urge funding for the B-70. And Twining said the Air Force planned to send the B-70 over Russia "to search out and knock out mobile ICBMs on railroads." Eisenhower snorted. "If they think that," he said, "they are crazy!" He explained, "We are not going to be searching out mobile bases for ICBMs, we are going to be hitting the big industrial and control complexes." [28]

When Eisenhower met with the JCS, they too pressed him for the B-70. The Air Force Chief of Staff, General Thomas D. White, argued that all the Air Force wanted was research and development money, and reminded Eisenhower of the "premium we gain from having different systems for attack." Eisenhower replied that in "ten years the missile capacity of both countries will be such as to be able to destroy each other many times over." He thought that "we are going overboard in different ways to do the same thing." White replied that "this is the last aircraft under development in the world" and almost begged Eisenhower to leave it in the program. But Eisenhower "reviewed past examples of weapons that had outlived their era and said he thought we were talking about bows and arrows at a time of gunpowder when we spoke of bombers in the missile age." He refused to support the B-70. [29]

Another military expense Eisenhower wanted to reduce was in the American contribution to NATO. In mid-November, he told the people in DOD that he wanted to pull back some air and ground units from Europe. Eisenhower said that the United States had six divisions in Europe, "which we never intended to keep there permanently." The only reason he could see to maintaining them was that "the NATO allies are almost psychopathic whenever anyone suggests removing them." He also wondered why the United States should maintain the Sixth Fleet in the Mediterranean, which was a British and French responsibility and where the U.S. Navy would only be bottled up in time of war. Eisenhower said this was an area in which he had always been in sharp disagreement with Dulles, who "had practically a phobia against raising the question of reduction of these forces." Eisenhower's response was that by pulling out Americans, the United States could force the Europeans to do more in their own defense.[30]

CHAPTER TWENTY-ONE

1960—High Hopes and Unhappy Realities

FOR EISENHOWER, 1960 turned out to be a bad year, the worst of his Presidency. He made a series of mistakes, particularly in his dealings with Khrushchev and Castro, mistakes brought on by his own fetish for secrecy and his misplaced trust in the CIA. He had hoped to leave office in an atmosphere of budding trust between the superpowers, with the Communist threat turned back in Latin America, Berlin secure, and disarmament under way. These were, however, inherently contradictory aims, which was one overriding reason for the lack of success. On the one hand, Eisenhower was trying to inspire Khrushchev, and the American people, with his vision of peaceful coexistence; on the other hand, he was willing to do almost anything to get rid of Castro. His readiness to take major risks in pursuit of disarmament was counterbalanced by his unwillingness to risk working toward a new relationship with Castro and Cuba specifically or Latin American radicalism generally.

Forces beyond Eisenhower's control were a factor in the failures of 1960. While he tried to concentrate on peace, his fellow politicians concentrated on the presidential election. It was characteristic of such elections, in the era of the Cold War, for each party to try to outdo the other in promising to get tough with the Communists (Eisenhower himself had used that theme against the Democrats in 1952). Getting tough meant, primarily, spending more money on arms; to Eisenhower's disgust, both candidates promised to do just that. The press was far more ready to see dangers in peaceful coexistence than it was to envision hope. Powerful men, in such bureaucracies as the CIA, the AEC, the JCS, and the DOD, and their suppliers in the defense industry, were firmly opposed to any outbreak of peace, and together they helped to sabotage Eisenhower's vision. Despite Eisenhower's efforts, the Cold War by the end of 1960 was more dangerous, more tension-packed, than it had been at the beginning of the year.

By January of 1960, Eisenhower and his advisers were determined to do something about Cuba. Castro's verbal abuse against the United States was reaching new levels, as was his confiscation of American-owned property. There were, however, many problems in dealing with Castro. He was politically astute and adroit. His anti-American diatribes were based on a Latin, not a Communist, critique of Uncle Sam, and he had managed to convince millions of Latins that any attempt by Washington to link him with the Communists was simply the old Yankee trick of accusing all Latin American reformers of being Communists. He was widely popular among the Latin masses, and retained a certain popularity even among liberals in the United States, who were arguing that the United States ought to try cooperation instead of confrontation with the new Cuban government. Privately, the rulers of Latin America were telling Eisenhower that they hoped the United States could get rid of Castro, one way or another, but neither individually nor collectively, through the Organization of American States (OAS), would they speak out against Castro.

The OAS had long since committed itself (in the Caracas Declaration of 1954) to opposition to Communist intrusion in the New World. The problem was proving that Castro was a Communist. The Administration could not prove to the OAS that Castro was Communist because it could not prove it to itself. The ambassador to Cuba told Eisenhower that he personally did not think Cuba was a Communist dictatorship, and he expected that Castro's foreign policy would be to seek neutrality in the Cold War. Secretary of State Herter reported in March 1960 that "our own latest National Intelligence Estimate [prepared by the CIA] does not find Cuba to be under Communist control or domination . . ."

Herter added that because of an uncertainty about the direction in which Castro was moving, the anti-Castro refugees in Florida were unable to unite in their opposition. Some wanted to bring back Batista, others only wanted to be rid of Fidel, none were willing to cooperate to create a government-in-exile. Herter warned against any action to drive Castro from Cuba until responsible Cuban opposition leadership was ready to take over, because otherwise Cuba might end up with someone worse than Castro.[1]

At a January 25 meeting, a frustrated and angry President said that "Castro begins to look like a madman." He indicated that if the OAS would not help remove him, then the United States should go it alone, for example, by imposing a blockade on Cuba. "If the Cuban people are hungry," Eisenhower declared, "they will throw Castro out." Calmer heads prevailed, pointing out that the United States should not punish the whole Cuban people for the acts of one madman. Eisenhower admitted that that was true.[2]

Eisenhower turned to the CIA for help in solving the Cuban problem. In February, the President called Allen Dulles to the Oval Office to discuss Castro. Dulles brought along some U-2 photographs of a Cuban sugar refinery, along with CIA plans to put it out of action by sabotage. Eisenhower scoffed at this puny effort, noting that such damage could easily be repaired and telling Dulles that the CIA had to come up with something better. He told Dulles to go back to his people and return when they had a "program" worked out.[3]

The CIA then began a series of assassination attempts against Castro. There were some harebrained schemes, including using the Mafia to gun Castro down, poisoning Castro's cigars or his coffee, and rigging an exotic seashell with an explosive device to be placed in Castro's favorite skin-diving area. None worked.

Whether Eisenhower knew about these attempted assassinations or not, or whether he ordered them or not, cannot be said. There is no documentary evidence that this author has seen that would directly link Eisenhower with the attempts. He could have given such orders verbally and privately to Dulles, but if he did he acted out of character. Further, Eisenhower himself indicated to the CIA that he did not want Castro removed until a government-in-exile had been formed, because he feared that the probable successor to Castro in the event of a premature assassination would be Raul Castro or Che Guevara, either of whom would be worse than Fidel.

The record is clear on what Eisenhower did approve. On March 17, he met with Dulles and Richard Bissell, the CIA agent Dulles had put in charge of preparing a "program" for Cuba. Eisenhower gave the go-ahead to the program Bissell presented to him. It had four parts: (1) creation of a "responsible and unified" Cuban government-in-exile; (2) "a powerful propaganda offensive"; (3) "a covert intelligence and action organization in Cuba" that would be "responsive" to the government-in-exile; and (4) "a paramilitary force outside of Cuba for future guerrilla action." Eisenhower indicated that he liked all four parts, but put his emphasis on Bissell's first step, finding a Cuban leader living in exile who would form a government that the United States could recognize and that could direct the activities of the covert and paramilitary forces.[4]

In early 1960, Eisenhower's thoughts were primarily on his retirement, and on the upcoming summit conference, where he had high hopes on getting started on some genuine disarmament. Nearly every other politician in America, however, had his thoughts on the upcoming presidential election. Eisenhower stayed aloof from the Democratic struggle for the nomination, although in private he expressed his anger and disgust at Kennedy's constant harping on a "missile gap" and other exaggerated remarks. At a Republican meeting on April 26, for example, Styles Bridges informed the President that Kennedy had said the day before that seventeen million Americans went to bed hungry every night. Eisenhower snorted, then commented, "They must all be dieting!!!"[5]

Similarly, Eisenhower remained aloof from the Republicans' pre-convention activities. Early in 1960, Rockefeller was still a candidate, which gave a bit of drama to the Republicans but no satisfaction to Eisenhower, who had long ago decided that Rockefeller did not have either the brains or the character to be President. He did write Rockefeller a long letter of advice, of which the principal point was to stick to the middle of the road, but he so deplored Rockefeller's deficit financing in New York State, and Rockefeller's calls for more defense spending, that he could never support the man for the Presidency. That left him with Nixon, the only viable Republican candidate, but he was not happy with Nixon either. Still, he had no one else to support, and as between Nixon and any of the Democratic candidates, he much preferred Nixon.

He would not, however, give Nixon his support until the Republicans, meeting in convention, actually nominated him. After Rockefeller withdrew from the race, Marvin Arrowsmith asked Eisenhower at a press conference if he would not now endorse Nixon. Eisenhower refused to do so, maintaining "that there are a number of Republicans, eminent men, big men, that could fulfill the requirements of the position . . ." Then he added lamely that Nixon "is not unaware of my sentiments" toward him. Later in the same conference, William

Knighton asked if the President did not think that the country ought to have the benefit of his advice as to which Republicans he regarded as qualified. Well, Eisenhower replied, "There's a number of them." Then, from Nixon's point of view, he made things worse by saying, "I am not dissatisfied with the individual that looks like he will get it," but still he would not endorse Nixon by name.[6]

Nevertheless, he was not completely resigned to Nixon's nomination. He tried to persuade Robert Anderson to become a candidate; when that failed, he asked Oveta Culp Hobby to get the Texas Republicans to organize behind Anderson as a "favorite son." If that was not possible, he suggested that she might become a candidate herself. He also tried to get Al Gruenther to run.[7] Nothing worked, as no one was ready to take on Nixon, because his strength with the party organization was too great.

One of Eisenhower's major objections to Rockefeller was that the New York governor was sounding like an echo of Kennedy in his positions on defense spending. That Rockefeller would adopt the Democratic position on defense (spend more, now, on every conceivable weapon) irritated Eisenhower no end. So did the partisan use of the issue by the Democrats. "I don't take it very kindly," Eisenhower told a January 13 press conference, "the implied accusation that I am dealing with the whole matter of defense on a partisan basis." Hauling out his heaviest artillery, he pointed out that with regard to national defense, "I've spent my life in this, and I know more about it than almost anybody."[8] In short, he wanted the people to "trust Ike" and turn away from the Democratic critics.

At his private meetings with Republican leaders, Eisenhower was blunt and direct in castigating the Democratic candidates. "By getting into this numbers racket," he said of Kennedy, Symington, and the others, "and by scaring people, they are getting away with murder." The President wondered "how much deterrent could possibly be wanted by the critics. Did they just want to build more and more Atlases for storage in warehouses? It was unconscionable."[9]

The Air Force was the darling of congressional Democrats, and the Air Force's pet project was the B-70 bomber. Eisenhower did not like the project at all. In February, he received a long memorandum on the B-70 from Kistiakowsky that concluded, "Putting it crudely, it is not clear what the B-70 can do that ballistic missiles can't—and cheaper and sooner at that." The President decided to cancel the B-70. General White, Air Force Chief of Staff, testified before Congress that the B-70 was "vital" to the nation's defense. A furious

Eisenhower called Secretary Gates on the telephone. According to Whitman's notes, "The President said that ever since the days of the Fair Deal and the New Deal, discipline had been lost in the high-ranking officers of the services. Nothing does he deplore more. Everyone seems to think he has a compulsion to tell in public his personal views." Once a decision was made by the Commander in Chief, he insisted, every officer in the armed services was duty-bound to support it. To the Republican leaders, Eisenhower complained that "all these fellows in the Pentagon think they have some responsibility I can't see." He continued, "I hate to use the word, but this business is damn near treason."[10]

Eisenhower was fighting virtually a one-man battle on holding down the costs of defense. The JCS would not support him; neither would his new Secretary of Defense, Tom Gates; nor would McCone, the head of the AEC; nor would the Republican leaders, who tried to convince him that the JCS were not out of line in expressing their own views. Further, not a single member of the White House press corps was on his side; the questions he received at his press conferences were uniformly hostile. Why wasn't the United States doing more? When would we catch up with the Russians? Did not the President fear a Soviet first strike? Was not the President's insistence on fiscal soundness imperiling the nation's security?

With a great effort of will, Eisenhower calmly and patiently answered all the questions. He insisted that there was no missile gap, that American prestige was not at stake in the space race, that there was no need to be afraid. He cited history to prove his point: "Only three or four years ago," he said, "there was a great outcry about the alleged bomber gap." Congress appropriated nearly a billion dollars more than Eisenhower had asked for to build new American bombers. "Subsequent intelligence investigation," however, "showed that that estimate was wrong and that, far from stepping up their production of bombers, the Soviets were diminishing it or even eliminating that production."[11]

Eisenhower also tried logic. On February 3, the journalist Merriman Smith wanted to know, "Do you feel any sense of urgency in catching up with the Russians?" Eisenhower replied, "I am always a little bit amazed about this business of catching up. What you want is enough, a thing that is adequate. A deterrent has no added power, once it has become completely adequate, for compelling the respect for your deterrent." But, Rowland Evans protested, the Air Force was insisting that unless the B-52s were put on a full air alert, "our deterrent of heavy bombers cannot be properly safeguarded." Eisenhower's reply was short and scathing: "Too many of these generals have all sorts of ideas."

But neither historical truth nor logic was Eisenhower's best weapon. It was his personal prestige that counted most. When Charles Shutt asked him to comment on Democratic charges that he was "complacent in advising the people of the danger we face in world affairs," and that Eisenhower was allowing his commitment to fiscal soundness to "stand in the way of developing some weapons we may need," Eisenhower stiffened, reddened, glared at Shutt, then replied: "If anybody—anybody—believes that I have deliberately misled the American people, I'd like to tell him to his face what I think about him. This is a charge that I think is despicable; I have never made it against anyone in the world." Then he insisted, "I don't believe we should pay one cent for defense more than we have to," and concluded with a personal assurance: "Our defense is not only strong, it is awesome, and it is respected elsewhere." [12]

But wherever he turned, Eisenhower was confronted with the charge that he, the man most responsible for it, had neglected the nation's security. In March 1960, he attended the annual Gridiron dinner in Washington. Senator Symington was the principal speaker, and his theme was the need for more and better weapons. When he finished, Eisenhower took the mike. The President described the day he moved into the Oval Office, and how the JCS started coming in even before he had hung his pictures on the wall or had the carpet put down. The Chiefs insisted that they had to have more of this and more of that. After he had gotten rid of them, Eisenhower related, he paced the bare floor, looked out the window, and said to himself, "My God, how did I get into this?" Then he went into what one observer called a "magnificent explanation of the responsibilities of the Presidency and how they far exceed the importance of weapons . . . He went into the responsibilities to the whole nation and to the family and the whole man. He talked about the spiritual things as well as material things. He built an awesome and inspiring and yet heartwarming image of the broad scope and high responsibilities that are a President's. And then he said goodnight." [13]

Eisenhower's basic position was that there was no missile gap. The proposition could not be proved, however, without revealing the U-2 flights and showing the photographic evidence demonstrating that the Russians were not building ICBMs on a crash basis. But Eisenhower was extremely sensitive about the flights, and about the resulting Russian protests, and he insisted that the U-2 be kept top secret (within the White House, only he, Gordon Gray, Goodpaster, and John Eisenhower knew about the project). He "exploded," therefore, when *The New York Times* ran a story, based on a leak from unnamed sources, hinting at American knowledge of Russian missile developments at Tura Tam in Central Asia. Kistiakowsky noted that "the President is exceedingly angry and has talked at length about lack of loyalty to the U.S. of these people. In his estimation Joseph Alsop is about the lowest form of animal life on earth . . ."[14]

By early 1960, Eisenhower had made a test-ban treaty, to be followed by some actual disarmament, the major goal of his Presidency, indeed of his entire career. It would be the capstone to his half century of public service, his greatest memorial, his final and most lasting gift to his country. To that end, he wanted to make an offer to the Russians that he felt had a good chance of being accepted by Khrushchev at the summit. On February 11, he announced at his press conference that he was willing to accept a test-ban treaty that would end all tests in the atmosphere, in the oceans, and in outer space, as well as underground tests "which can be monitored."[15]

On March 19, the Russians did indeed respond positively to Eisenhower's proposal. The Soviets would agree to all of it, provided that the United States agreed to a moratorium on low-kiloton tests underground. By so doing, the Russians were making considerable concessions—accepting a supervised test ban for all atmospheric, underwater, and large underground tests, which meant opening their borders to American inspection teams. All they asked in return was a voluntary cessation of small underground tests based solely on good faith.

On March 29, Eisenhower issued a statement outlining his acceptance. At a press conference the following day, he said "that we should try to stop the spreading of this, what you might say, the size of the [nuclear] club. There are already four nations into it [France in February had exploded its first bomb], and it's an expensive business. And it could be finally more dangerous than ever . . ." Eisenhower also insisted that "all the signs are that the Soviets do want a degree of disarmament, and they want to stop testing. That looks to me to be more or less proved."[16]

At another press conference, a month later, after Eisenhower had announced that he, de Gaulle, and Macmillan agreed that disarmament, not Berlin or Germany, should be the number-one topic at the Paris summit, Laurence Burd wanted to know if disarmament would not mean economic depression for the United States. Eisenhower explained why it would not: "We are now scratching around to get money for such things as school construction . . . road building. There are all sorts of things to be done in this country . . . I see no reason why the sums which now are going into these sterile, negative mechanisms that we call war munitions shouldn't go into something positive." [17]

Eisenhower was prepared to go to Paris to seek a genuine accord. Never in the Cold War did one seem closer. A President of the United States was on the verge of trusting the Russians in the most critical and dangerous field, nuclear testing. He had de Gaulle and Macmillan with him, and Khrushchev seemed by every indication to be sincere in his own desire for disarmament. There were, however, powerful men determined to stop the progress.

First, the politicians. The Democrats, controlling the Joint Congressional Committee on Atomic Energy, held hearings on the proposal. Dr. Teller, and many others, testified that the Russians would cheat, that the proposed inspection systems were woefully inadequate, that the whole thing was a disaster for American security interests. John McCone, purportedly the prime mover behind the hearings, told Kistiakowsky that the proposed ban was "a national peril" that might force him "to resign his job." Arthur Krock believed that the Democrats were holding the much-publicized hearings in order to cast doubts in advance on any treaty Eisenhower managed to obtain, so as to deprive the Republicans of the peace issue in the November election. Eisenhower himself thought "that goddamned joint committee will certainly do anything in its power to embarrass me." [18]

Second, the military. The Pentagon wanted no part of a ban, wanted to resume testing, and wanted a major buildup in ICBMs. At an April 1 NSC meeting, Eisenhower "sharply questioned" the Defense people about the rate of proposed buildup. The reply was that they were seeking a production capacity of four hundred missiles per year. Eisenhower, according to Kistiakowsky, "remarked in obvious disgust, 'Why don't we go completely crazy and plan on a force of 10,000?' " [19]

Third, the scientists. Teller and the AEC scientists, and their friends, were determined to continue testing. Their device was through "peaceful" explosions. They appealed to Eisenhower's great desire to use nuclear energy for the good of mankind to make all sorts of proposals. Teller told an April 26 Cabinet meeting that he wanted to dig a tunnel through Mexico and another parallel to the Panama Canal; he wanted to blast a harbor in northern Alaska, with a short channel and a turnaround basin; he wanted to deposit heat in underground caverns by setting off a bomb, then draw on the energy later; he saw splendid opportunities for strip mining through atomic blasts. Given the opportunity, he said, he could squeeze oil out of the sands. All these glittering prospects could become reality only if he were allowed to test. When Defense Secretary Gates asked him how much these experiments would add to weapons developments, Teller assured him a great deal would be learned. He also added that the proposed moratorium "can be evaded with complete safety by us . . . it can easily be evaded." [20]

Fourth, the intelligence community. The CIA and other intelligence gatherers were strongly opposed to any unsupervised ban, and were especially insistent that U-2 flights over the Soviet Union be continued and even expanded. They were concerned about "gaps" in the coverage. In a meeting with the Board of Consultants on Foreign Intelligence Activities, on February 2, General Doolittle urged Eisenhower to use the overflights to the maximum degree possible. Eisenhower, according to Goodpaster's notes, "pointed out that such a decision is one of the most soul-searching questions to come before a President." He added that at Camp David, Khrushchev had outlined for him Soviet missile capability, and "every bit of information I have seen [from the overflights] corroborates what Khrushchev told me."

Goodpaster's notes continue: "The President said that he had one tremendous asset in a summit meeting, as regards effect in the free world. That is his reputation for honesty. If one of these aircraft [the U-2s] were lost when we are engaged in apparently sincere deliberations, it could be put on display in Moscow and ruin the President's effectiveness." [21]

Despite this basic recognition, Eisenhower approved additional flights, but only at the rate of one per month. One reason was the standard assumption by the intelligence community that even if the Soviets ever shot down a U-2, they never would admit it, because they would then also have to admit that the flights had been going on for years and they had been unable to do anything about them. The logic was questionable, but the eagerness to get more photographs was real enough. In late March, Richard Bissell explained to Eisenhower why the CIA thought the Russians might be building new missile sites, while John Eisenhower and Goodpaster traced out for him on a huge map of Russia the proposed flight route.

Eisenhower set aside his personal objections and authorized one flight. It went on April 9. The Russians tracked the U-2 with their radar and made a number of attempts to knock it down with their surface-to-air missiles (SAMs), but the flight was a success. The photographs revealed no new missile construction. In early April, Bissell asked for another flight. Eisenhower authorized him to fly any day in the next two weeks. Every day for the next fourteen days, however, Russia was covered by clouds. The U-2 needed near-perfect weather to get its photographs.

When the weather did not improve, Bissell applied for an extension. Eisenhower told Goodpaster to call Bissell and tell him the flight was authorized for one more week. Goodpaster made it formal with a memorandum for the record: "After checking with the President, I informed Mr. Bissell that one additional operation may be undertaken, provided it is carried out prior to May 1. No operation is to be carried out after May 1." Eisenhower had insisted on that date because he did not want to be provocative on the eve of the summit meeting.[22]

On May 1, the weather cleared. That morning, in Adana, Turkey, Francis Gary Powers, a young pilot employed by the CIA, took off for Bodo, Norway, his flight route taking him directly over the Soviet Union.

Meanwhile, Eisenhower prepared for the summit. In March and April, he met with de Gaulle and Adenauer in the White House, getting their agreement to make disarmament the main topic in Paris. He indicated that he intended to follow the test-ban treaty with a new variation on Open Skies, an offer for continuous aerial inspection, divorced from any disarmament aspects, and operating in selected regions, for example, Siberia and Alaska. Eisenhower's hopes were high. His own desire to make a breakthrough in the arms race, as his final act as a world leader, was greater than ever. His Secretary of State, Herter, was distinctly milder toward the Soviets than Foster Dulles had ever been. Eisenhower had a science adviser who assured him that a test ban would strengthen not only America's moral position but its strategic situation as well. The JCS were no longer his contemporaries, as Bradley and Radford had been in the early years, but relatively junior officers from World War II, men who could not impress him. Macmillan wanted a test ban; de Gaulle wanted peace; Khrushchev wanted an agreement; Eisenhower was ready to take some risks and make some concessions. The atmosphere, on the eve of the summit, could not have been better.

• •

On the afternoon of May 1, two weeks before Eisenhower was scheduled to fly to Paris, Goodpaster called him on the telephone: "One of our reconnaissance planes," he said, "on a scheduled flight from its base in Adana, Turkey, is overdue and possibly lost."

The information was disturbing but not alarming. If the plane had crashed, or been shot down, there was no possibility of the pilot, Francis Powers, escaping alive. Further, the CIA had assured the President "that if a plane were to go down it would be destroyed either in the air or on impact, so that proof of espionage would be lacking. Self-destroying mechanisms were built in." The CIA had not told Eisenhower that the "self-destruct mechanism" had to be activated by the pilot, or that it was only a two-and-one-half-pound charge, hardly sufficient to "destroy" a craft as big as the U-2, or that the hundreds of feet of tightly rolled film would survive a crash and/or fire, thus by itself providing the Soviets with all the evidence they would need. Eisenhower assumed that Powers was dead, his U-2 burned to cinders. He thanked Goodpaster for the information and went on to other business.[23]

The next morning, May 2, Goodpaster came into the Oval Office. "Mr. President," he said, "I have received word from the CIA that the U-2 reconnaissance plane I mentioned yesterday is still missing. The pilot reported an engine flameout at a position about thirteen hundred miles inside Russia and has not been heard from since. With the amount of fuel he had on board, there is not a chance of his still being aloft."[24] If Powers was not aloft, he was dead, and his craft destroyed. Eisenhower therefore decided to do nothing, leaving the next move to Khrushchev, who it was assumed (or hoped) would also do nothing. Having shot down a U-2, the Russians had made their point. If Khrushchev was sincere about the summit, he would either downplay the event or ignore it altogether, contenting himself with a private remark or two to Eisenhower in Paris.

On May 5, Khrushchev made a speech to the Supreme Soviet in which he claimed that the Soviet Union had shot down an American spy plane that had intruded Soviet airspace. Khrushchev angrily denounced the United States for its "aggressive provocation" in sending a "bandit flight" over his country. In the course of a long harangue, Khrushchev said the Americans had picked May Day hoping to catch the Soviets with their guard down, but to no avail. Khrushchev provided his own interpretation of the provocative flight: "Aggressive imperialist forces in the United States in recent times have been taking the most active measures to undermine the summit or at least to hinder any agreement that might be reached." He did not blame Eisenhower, however; instead, he suggested that the militarists were acting without the President's knowledge.[25]

The President decided to make no rejoinder, nor any explanation. He could have refuted the charges immediately. He might have issued a statement taking full responsibility, pointing out that no U-2 flight ever left the ground without his personal approval, insisting that because of the closed nature of the Soviet Union and because of fears of a nuclear Pearl Harbor, the overflights were necessary to the security of his country. In the process, he could have reminded the world that, as everyone knew, the KGB was far more active in spying on the West than the CIA was in spying on Russia. He might have given a brief outline of the history of the U-2, then made the most fundamental point of all—that the evidence gathered by the overflights provided convincing proof that there was no missile gap, despite Khrushchev's boasting about Soviet rockets, and that as a result of the photographs, the United States had been able to keep some kind of control on its own defense spending.

But he did none of these things, because he had a fetish about keeping the U-2 a secret. The odd thing about this fetish was that the U-2 was no secret to the Soviets, and had not been since the very first flight, back in 1956. Indeed, all the governments involved—British, French, Turkish, Norwegian, Formosan, and others—knew about the U-2. The people who did not know were the Americans and their elected representatives.

Another option available to Eisenhower would have been to state that since the Soviets had turned down Open Skies, he had decided to unilaterally put it into effect anyway, and then invite Khrushchev to fly all he wanted to across the United States. To do that, however, Eisenhower would have had to make public the U-2 flights. Although it is difficult to see, a quarter of a century later, when Russian and American spy satellites are constantly in orbit around the world, what damage could have resulted, Eisenhower decided to make a desperate effort to keep the overflights a secret, or at least to deny their existence. Instead of confessing, he launched a cover-up.

He did so because he thought a cover-up would work. Acting on the assumption that Powers was dead and his plane in ruins, Eisenhower believed that Khrushchev could prove nothing. The irony— or perhaps the tragedy, considering what was at stake at the summit —was that Eisenhower himself had pointed out that his greatest single asset was his "reputation for honesty," and that if a U-2 were lost "when we are engaged in apparently sincere deliberations, it could be put on display in Moscow and ruin the President's effectiveness." But he clung to the hope that Khrushchev, without any physical evidence, would be unconvincing.

On the afternoon of May 5, after returning to Washington, Eisenhower approved a statement that was then issued by the National Aeronautics and Space Administration. It began, "One of N.A.S.A.'s U-2 research airplanes, in use since 1956 in a continuing program to study meteorological conditions found at high altitude, has been missing since May 1, when its pilot reported he was having oxygen difficulties over the Lake Van, Turkey, area." Presumably, the U-2 had strayed off course, perhaps crossing the border into Russia. The unstated assumption was that Powers' weather plane was the one the Russians had shot down.[26]

The following day, Khrushchev released a photograph of a wrecked airplane, describing it as the U-2 Powers had flown. It was not, however, a U-2, but another airplane. The Premier was setting a trap. He wanted Eisenhower to continue to believe that Powers was dead, the U-2 destroyed, so that the United States would stick to its "weather research" story, as it did.

Then, on May 7, Khrushchev sprang his great surprise. He jubilantly reported to a "wildly cheering" Supreme Soviet that "we have parts of the plane and we also have the pilot, who is quite alive and kicking. The pilot is in Moscow and so are the parts of the plane." Khrushchev made his account into a story of high drama and low skulduggery, interspersed with bitingly sarcastic remarks about Eisenhower's cover story. Cries of "Shame, Shame!" rose from the deputies as Khrushchev heaped scorn on the CIA, mixed with cries of "Bandits, Bandits!"[27]

Upon receiving the news of Powers' capture by the Russians, news that he found "unbelievable," Eisenhower knew that since Khrushchev had both the plane and the pilot (and the film), there was little point in denying any further the real purpose of the overflights. He was not ready, however, to tell the American people, and the world, that he personally was involved in the distasteful business of spying. Dulles, Herter, and other top officials were frantically trying to find ways to protect the President. On Herter's recommendation, Eisenhower then authorized the State Department to issue a statement denying that Powers had any authorization to fly over the Soviet Union.[28]

That statement was so ill conceived and so poorly timed that it made a bad situation much worse. As James Reston reported in *The New York Times,* "The United States admitted tonight that one of this country's planes equipped for intelligence purposes had 'probably' flown over Soviet territory.

"An official statement stressed, however, that 'there was no authorization for any such flight' from authorities in Washington.

"As to who might have authorized the flight, officials refused to comment. If this particular flight of the U-2 was not authorized here, it could only be assumed that someone in the chain of command in the Middle East or Europe had given the order." [29]

The attempt to cover up continued that afternoon, when Goodpaster called Herter to say that Eisenhower wanted a statement from the State Department that would indicate that the U-2 flights were carried out under "a very broad directive from the President given at the earliest point of his Administration to protect us from surprise attack." But, Goodpaster added, "The President wants no specific tie to him of this particular event." [30]

The resulting statements added to a national sense of humiliation, shame, and confusion. Reston reported, "This was a sad and perplexed capital tonight, caught in a swirl of charges of clumsy administration, bad judgment and bad faith.

"It was depressed and humiliated by the United States having been caught spying over the Soviet Union and trying to cover up its activities in a series of misleading official announcements." [31]

Eisenhower personally remained calm. He told Whitman, "I would like to resign," and he seemed to her to be depressed in the morning, "but by afternoon had bounced back with his characteristic ability to accept the bad news, not dwell on it, and so go ahead." [32] That afternoon, Eisenhower gave a briefing to the congressional leaders. He explained the U-2, gave a bit of its history, praised the overflights for the information they had gathered, admitted that he had fallen into Khrushchev's trap, and concluded, "We will now just have to endure the storm." [33]

Over the next two days, humiliation gave way to fright as the headlines became increasingly alarmist. "Khrushchev Warns of Rocket Attack on Bases Used by U.S. Spying Planes," the *Times* announced on May 10. The following morning, the headline read, "U.S. Vows to Defend Allies if Russians Attack Bases." Khrushchev, at an impromptu news conference in Moscow, announced that he was putting Powers on trial and added, "You understand that if such aggressive actions continue this might lead to war." Eisenhower held his own news conference, where he read a prepared statement. In firm, measured tones, without a hint of regret or apology, Eisenhower said Khrushchev's antics over the "flight of an unarmed nonmilitary plane can only reflect a fetish of secrecy." Because of the nature of the Soviet system, spying "is a distasteful but vital necessity." When asked whether his trip to Russia had been canceled, he replied, "I expect to go." When asked if the outlook for the summit had changed, he replied, "Not decisively at all, no."[34]

But of course it had. No one in Washington could have supposed for a minute that Khrushchev would not exploit the fact that he had caught the Americans red-handed, and that they had lied about it. Some of Eisenhower's advisers urged him to take the way out Khrushchev had offered—deny that he knew anything about the flights and punish someone, presumably Allen Dulles, for them. Such action, the advisers argued, might still save the summit. Eisenhower rejected the advice, first of all because it was not true, secondly because it would be manifestly unfair to Dulles, thirdly because if he did such a thing, Khrushchev could refuse to deal with him at the summit on the grounds that Eisenhower obviously could not control his own Administration.

With only a few days to go before the summit, Khrushchev continued to make belligerent statements, but also continued to express his doubts that Eisenhower personally knew about the flights; at one point, he even said that the KGB often carried on activities that he did not know about. Sorting out Khrushchev's motives is a hopeless task. He seemed determined to destroy the summit before it got started—but he was the one who had been most insistent about a summit meeting. He must have known he could never get Eisenhower to say that such a major operation as a U-2 flight could take place without his knowledge, just as he must have realized that Eisenhower would not make a personal apology—yet he insisted on both. His histrionics, wild charges, and pretended outrage sat ill with a man who had satellites flying over the United States daily—indeed Russian newspapers had even published photographs of the United States taken by cameras aboard such satellites.

The crisis brought the Western allies closer together. Eisenhower, Macmillan, and de Gaulle had first come together in Algeria in 1943, seventeen years earlier. Their common foe then had been the Nazi dictatorship. Now their common foe was a Communist dictatorship. Their determination to oppose totalitarianism and their resolution to maintain democracy and the Western alliance were as great as ever. They knew each other intimately, these three who had been through so much together.

"I don't know about anybody else," Eisenhower said at their first meeting in Paris, "but I myself am getting older." De Gaulle smiled. "You don't look it," he replied.

"I hope," said Eisenhower, "that no one is under the illusion that I'm going to crawl on my knees to Khrushchev." De Gaulle smiled again. "No one is under that illusion," he said. De Gaulle mentioned Khrushchev's threat to attack U-2 bases in Turkey, Japan, and elsewhere. "Rockets," Eisenhower replied without smiling, "can travel in two directions." Macmillan nodded his agreement and pledged his full support.

"With us it is easy," de Gaulle said to Eisenhower, because "you and I are tied together by history."[35] In the crisis, NATO had held firm, which for Eisenhower was a heartwarming experience that justified all the effort and hope he had put into the Western alliance since December 1950. It was unfortunate that strengthening NATO required deepening the split between East and West, but then it was Khrushchev, not Eisenhower or Macmillan or de Gaulle, who made the decision to ruin the summit conference.

On May 14, Eisenhower and his party had flown to Paris. The next afternoon, he met with Herter, Ambassador to the Soviet Union Chip Bohlen, and Goodpaster. They informed him that Khrushchev, already in Paris, had told de Gaulle that he was prepared to go ahead with the summit, but that the Russian leader had given de Gaulle a six-page statement asserting that if Eisenhower did not condemn such actions as the U-2 flight, renounce such acts in the future, and punish those responsible, the Soviets would not take part in the summit. Eisenhower wanted to know why Khrushchev had not made such specific demands five days earlier—it would have saved him a trip to Paris. Bohlen remarked that the content of the statement, coupled with the fact that it was in written form, indicated that Khrushchev had already decided to break up the conference.

At the initial meeting, de Gaulle, the host, had hardly finished calling the meeting to order when Khrushchev was on his feet, red-faced, demanding the right to speak. De Gaulle looked quizzically at Eisenhower, who nodded his agreement, then indicated that Khrushchev had the floor. Khrushchev launched into a tirade against Eisenhower and the United States. Soon he was shouting. De Gaulle interrupted, turned to the Soviet interpreter, and said, "The acoustics in this room are excellent. We can all hear the chairman. There is no need for him to raise his voice." The interpreter blanched, turned to Khrushchev, and began to translate. De Gaulle cut him off and motioned to his own interpreter, who unflatteringly translated into Russian. Khrushchev cast a furious glance at de Gaulle, then continued to read in a lower voice.

He soon lashed himself into an even greater frenzy. He pointed overhead and shouted, "I have been overflown!" De Gaulle interrupted again. He said that he too had been overflown.

"By your American allies?" asked Khrushchev, incredulous. "No," de Gaulle replied, "by you. Yesterday that satellite you launched just before you left Moscow to impress us overflew the sky of France eighteen times without my permission. How do I know you do not have cameras aboard which are taking pictures of my country?" Eisenhower caught de Gaulle's eye and gave him a big grin.

Khrushchev raised both hands above his head and said, "As God is my witness, my hands are clean. You don't think I would do a thing like that?"

After Khrushchev finished his diatribe, which concluded with a statement that Eisenhower would no longer be welcome in the Soviet Union, Eisenhower spoke. He said that Khrushchev hardly needed to go to such lengths to withdraw his invitation, that he had come to Paris hoping to engage in serious discussion, and that it was his wish that the conference could now proceed to matters of substance. Khrushchev and the Russian delegation stalked out of the room. As Eisenhower rose to follow them, de Gaulle caught him by the elbow and drew him aside. De Gaulle said to the President, "I do not know what Khrushchev is going to do nor what is going to happen, but whatever he does, or whatever happens, I want you to know that I am with you to the end."[36]

The summit was over before it started, all the hopes for détente and disarmament gone with it. Eisenhower, with only eight months to serve, would not have another chance to force progress toward genuine peace. He returned home, where he had to endure making a series of reports to various groups, including the public. He issued a formal statement, made a radio and television report, met with the congressional leaders and his Cabinet, and with the NSC. At the latter meeting, Herter said something about the need to "regain our leadership." Kistiakowsky recorded, "This made the President angry. He lost his temper and said we did not lose the leadership and therefore we didn't have to regain it, and he would appreciate it if that expression were never used again, especially before congressional committees." [37]

On May 23, Herter reported to him that the CIA and the Defense Department wanted to continue the U-2 flights. Eisenhower replied that "he had no thought whatsoever of permitting more of these . . . that they may as well realize that these flights cannot be resumed in the next eight months." [38] By August 1960, the United States had reconnaissance satellites in operation, although the U-2 continues to this day to provide photographic reconnaissance of outstanding quality. Powers was eventually exchanged for a Soviet spy, Colonel Rudolf Abel (what happened to Powers' U-2 remains a mystery).

In late May, Eisenhower had a private talk with Kistiakowsky. The President said that the scientists had failed him. Kistiakowsky protested that the scientists had consistently warned that eventually a U-2 was going to get shot down. "It was the management of the project that failed. The President flared up, evidently thinking I accused him, and used some strong uncomplimentary language." After Kistiakowsky explained that he meant the bureaucrats, not the President, were responsible, Eisenhower cooled off. He "began to talk with much feeling about how he had concentrated his efforts that last few years on ending the cold war, how he felt that he was making big progress, and how the stupid U-2 mess had ruined all his efforts. He ended very sadly that he saw nothing worthwhile left for him to do now until the end of his presidency." [39]

Eisenhower's depression was deep, genuine, and appropriate. Of all the events in Eisenhower's long lifetime, this one stands out. If only Eisenhower had not given permission for that last flight. If only Khrushchev had not made such a big deal out of such a small thing. If only the two leaders could have trusted their own instincts just once, rather than their technicians and generals. Eisenhower was on the verge of agreeing to an unsupervised test ban; Khrushchev was on the verge of agreeing to inspection teams within the Soviet Union. No one knows where the momentum thus generated might have taken the Cold War and the nuclear arms race. But both the old men allowed their fears to override their hopes, and the summit was gone, and with it the best chance to slow the arms race of the sixties and seventies and eighties.

•   •

Eisenhower returned to Washington and more problems. Cuba, for one. Although neither Eisenhower nor his advisers could even now decide if Castro was a Communist or not, they nevertheless wanted to be rid of him and the danger he represented. In Eisenhower's view, the worst possibility was Castro allowing Khrushchev to use Cuba as a base for Soviet strategic forces. He did not, however, think that was likely to happen. At a June 29 meeting with Gordon Gray, Eisenhower "observed that he did not believe that Khrushchev would enter into a mutual-security treaty with Castro," and added that Chip Bohlen shared that opinion. Khrushchev must know, Eisenhower said, that the United States "could not tolerate" a military alliance between Cuba and Russia.[40]

On July 6, Eisenhower signed legislation authorizing a major reduction in the Cuban sugar quota, and eliminating it altogether for 1961. As he admitted, "This action amounts to economic sanctions against Cuba."[41]

Along with his diplomatic and economic moves against Castro, Eisenhower considered a full range of military or paramilitary options. At a July 7 NSC meeting, Gates briefed him on possible moves, ranging from evacuating American citizens from Cuba to a full-scale invasion and occupation. Treasury Secretary Anderson "gave a fairly bloodthirsty long speech about the need to declare a national emergency . . . [and] argued that what is happening in Cuba represents an aggressive action by the U.S.S.R."[42]

Eisenhower was not ready to sound the bugles and direct a charge up San Juan Hill. As he explained to Republican leaders— who, like Nixon, were desperate for some definitive action against Castro before the November elections—"If we were to try to accomplish our aims by force, we would see all of [the Latin countries] tending to fall away and some would be Communist within two years. . . . If the United States does not conduct itself in precisely the right way vis-à-vis Cuba, we could lose all of South America."[43]

Nixon wanted public action but Eisenhower continued to refuse. The President was, however, ready to move covertly against Castro. On August 18, he met with Gates, Dulles, and Bissell to discuss implementation of the four-point plan he had approved in March. Bissell reported that point two, a powerful propaganda offensive, was under way; point three, the creation of a resistance organization within Cuba, had been a miserable failure, primarily because of Castro's police-state control. Bissell was making progress on point four, the creation of a paramilitary force from among Cuban exiles. He had moved the original training camp, outside Miami, to the Panama Canal Zone, then to Guatemala, where the CIA had excellent ties with President Miguel Ydígoras Fuentes.

Bissell wanted to expand the training program. Eisenhower agreed. The CIA had shown him photographs of Czech arms in Cuba, which helped convince him. He approved a $13 million budget for Bissell, and authorized the use of DOD personnel and equipment in the operation, although he insisted that "no United States military personnel were to be used in a combat status." Later, he also approved the mounting of a U.S. Navy patrol off the coast of Guatemala, supposedly to block a Cuban invasion, actually to keep the Guatemalan training base a secret.

After giving his approval to Bissell's expanded plans, Eisenhower asked about the original point one—"Where's our government-in-exile?" Bissell and Allen Dulles explained that it was difficult to get the Cubans to work together, because some were pro-Batista, most were anti-Batista, all were hot-tempered and hardheaded, few were willing to compromise. Thus no genuine leader had emerged. Eisenhower, impatient, remarked, "Boys, if you don't intend to go through with this, let's stop talking about it." He would not approve any action, he insisted, without a popular, genuine government-in-exile.[44]

Eisenhower made a halfhearted effort to keep the Geneva disarmament talks going even after Paris, but on June 27 those meetings came to an end when the Soviet delegation walked out. Their collapse, although hardly unexpected, was a blow to Eisenhower, who had in 1953 set disarmament as one of his major goals, but who by 1960 had to recognize that the arms race was out of control. By 1960, the American nuclear arsenal had grown to proportions that by 1953 and 1954 standards Eisenhower had called "fantastic," "crazy," and "unconscionable." Just how big it was becoming, Eisenhower was reminded on August 15, when McCone informed him that the United States was now producing, each year, more bombs than the estimated total requirement had been back in the mid-fifties. Partly this was a result of Eisenhower's own inability to stand up to the AEC and the DOD over the years and say no to the expansion, but as he said, "being only one person, he had not felt he could oppose the combined opinion of all his associates."[45]

America had gone far beyond what it needed for deterrence, at least in Eisenhower's view, without getting anywhere close to a first-strike capability. After paying the cost in money and tension for the arsenal, which now contained more than six thousand weapons of all sizes, the United States was less secure than it had been in 1953. Eisenhower hated that result, but could not do anything about it.

In his last half year in office, Eisenhower's conversations about disarmament proposals were exclusively concerned with propaganda advantage, or the effect of this or that proposal on the election, never with seeking a compromise that could lead to a breakthrough in the talks. Indeed, he agreed, albeit reluctantly and for the first time, to an increase in DOD appropriations, primarily because the Democrats were making such an issue out of national security. In so doing (the amount was one-half a billion dollars), Eisenhower admitted that the additional arms were not necessary for military purposes, but perhaps they "would carry sufficient credibility to create the psychological effect desired."[46]

Despite his increasingly belligerent attitude toward the Russians, the President refused to be swept away on the national-security issue. The NSC, DOD, AEC, and Henry Luce all urged him to institute a nationwide civil-defense program. Nelson Rockefeller joined the chorus. Eisenhower responded that such a program would cost the federal government more than $10 billion and that in any case, building fallout shelters was a responsibility that "rests upon the locality and the private citizen." Eisenhower would not put any federal money into shelters.[47]

Eisenhower also resisted entreaties that he spend more on the space race. Nixon, Republican leaders, and the Defense Establishment were all urging him to go all out on Project Mercury, designed to put a man in orbit around the earth, and on a man-on-the-moon project. Eisenhower called the latter "a multibillion-dollar project of no immediate value . . . He said he felt the project is useless at this moment and he would not think it really worth the money . . . The President said he likes to see us go ahead on useful things but he is not much of a man on spectaculars. He realizes that some stunts, such as the Lindbergh trip across the Atlantic, have some virtue, [but] he emphasized that he would not be willing to spend tax money to send a man around the moon . . . He said there is such a thing as common sense, even in research."[48]

For Eisenhower, the 1960 presidential election campaign was dominated by three thoughts. First, his intense concern about the future of his country, a concern that expressed itself in a partisan manner, as he convinced himself that victory by the Democrats would mean disaster for the country. Second, his feeling that the election was a vote of confidence and approval of his policies over the past seven and a half years. He knew this was silly, even irrational, that if he himself were the candidate there could be no question of the outcome, but he could not escape the feeling. Nor could he escape a third feeling, one of ambiguity about Nixon.

Since the time of the Checkers speech in the 1952 campaign, Nixon had served Eisenhower loyally and effectively, especially at the time of Eisenhower's 1955 heart attack. For Eisenhower, the problem was that he never seemed to grow, never seemed to consider a problem from any point of view other than the partisan political considerations, never seemed quite ready to take over. In 1956, Eisenhower had agreed to run for a second term primarily because he could not think of anyone qualified to succeed him. Repeatedly, in the summer of 1960, he told friends that his greatest failure was the failure to develop more Republican "comers." He regretted that Nixon did not have more competition for the nomination. But—and there was always a "but" in the Eisenhower-Nixon relationship—he thought Nixon a far better man than his only serious competitor, Nelson Rockefeller. And as between Nixon and any of the Democratic hopefuls, Eisenhower never hesitated. Although Eisenhower could not believe that Nixon was even yet ready, Nixon was so superior to any alternative that Eisenhower gave him his backing.

The nature of the campaign put an additional strain on the already difficult Eisenhower-Nixon relationship. It was inevitable that Nixon would stress his experience in government, and in the process claim for himself a leading role in the decision-making process of the Administration. But this was precisely the area in which Eisenhower was most sensitive. The Nixon claim reinforced the standard Democratic criticism of Eisenhower, that he reigned rather than ruled, that he did not make the decisions himself. Eisenhower could not escape thinking of the election as a referendum on his Presidency, and he could not and would not allow it to be said that he delegated his decision-making powers. Nixon, of course, could hardly see the election as a referendum on Eisenhower; it was Nixon versus Kennedy, and he needed all the support from Eisenhower that he could get. He did not want Eisenhower to campaign on the basis of the record of his Administration, but to cite Nixon's great contributions and describe Nixon as "indispensable," "statesmanlike," "judicious," and so forth. But Eisenhower nevertheless spent the campaign defending his own record.

A second major problem revolved around differences in perceptions. When he was a candidate, Eisenhower had instinctively gone into the middle of the road, with the explicit goal of winning the independent vote. He had won the 1952 nomination despite the intense opposition of the Old Guard; he was not a professional politician; he did not draw his strength or his power from the Republican Party; he simply was not a party man. Nixon, by contrast, was the quintessential party man. He drew his strength and his power from the Republican Party. Thus Nixon was more partisan in his approach, especially during the 1960 campaign, than Eisenhower would have wished.

Nixon's felt need to unite the Republican Party, added to his perception of what the voters wanted to hear on the issue of national defense, led to the deepest wound of all. Nixon deserted Eisenhower on defense. Rationally, Eisenhower knew it had to be done, that the clamor for more defense spending had become irresistible. He also knew that Nixon had to be his own man, had to establish himself as something more than "Ike's boy," had to show that the Republican Party was not a standpat party. But emotionally, it felt to Eisenhower like cold rejection of everything he had stood for and fought for over the past seven and a half years.

The result of all these structural difficulties, and of Eisenhower's ambiguity toward Nixon, was that Eisenhower's contribution to Nixon's campaign was worse than unhelpful—it actually cost Nixon votes, and probably the election.

Defense spending was a central issue in the campaign. The Democratic candidates were stumping the country with it, charging that Eisenhower had allowed a "missile gap" and a "rocket gap" to occur, and that as a result America was in retreat around the globe. Nelson Rockefeller joined the chorus. On June 8, he called for a $3.5 billion increase (about 9 percent) in the defense budget. "I suspect that Nelson has been listening too closely to half-baked advisers," Eisenhower commented at a Republican leaders' meeting.[49]

That evening, Rockefeller telephoned Eisenhower. He wanted to know Eisenhower's thinking on whether or not he, Rockefeller, should once again become an avowed candidate. Eisenhower took the occasion to first of all give Rockefeller a short lecture on defense spending. Whitman recorded that "the President said he did not believe it was right to alarm people unnecessarily—he thought a fair question was whether we were doing these things fast enough." As to

Rockefeller re-entering the race, "The President said he was afraid he would be called 'off again, on again, gone again, Finnegan.' . . . he thought Nelson's chances were very remote." Eisenhower told Rockefeller that anyone who wanted a Republican nomination in the next four or five years "would have to get some kind of blessing from the President. He said therefore he hoped that the reasoned and positive approach he had advocated would be adopted by Nelson (instead of jumping on everybody)."[50]

The following day, Rockefeller announced that although his previous withdrawal from the race still stood, he would accept a draft. That same day, June 11, Eisenhower spoke with Mrs. Hobby. She had called him to deplore Rockefeller's defense-spending statement, but she also remarked that "the other one [Nixon] is not easy." Eisenhower assured her that "Dick is growing in stature daily." Hobby complained that Nixon's partisanship was driving away independents and Texas Democrats who had voted for Eisenhower. She asked the President to urge Nixon to be constructive and nonpartisan in his approach. Eisenhower did as requested, dictating a letter to Nixon repeating Hobby's advice and noting, "personally, I concur."[51]

The Democrats, meanwhile, met in Los Angeles and nominated Senator Kennedy as their candidate. He chose Lyndon Johnson as his running mate. Eisenhower was appalled, even though he had predicted the outcome. He was vacationing at Newport at the time. Bill Robinson was with him. Robinson had breakfast with Eisenhower the morning Kennedy was to announce his choice. Eisenhower asked him who he thought it would be. Symington, Robinson replied, then asked Eisenhower who he thought it would be. "He said, without hesitation, Lyndon Johnson." Robinson remonstrated: "How could Lyndon Johnson—having said all the things he did about Kennedy, having said over and over again he wouldn't be a vice-presidential candidate—even consider it?"

Eisenhower replied, according to Robinson's diary, "Of course, that's very sound thinking and fairly good deduction, unless you know Johnson. He is not a big man. He is a small man. He hadn't got the depth of mind nor the breadth of vision to carry great responsibility. Any floor leader of a Senate majority party looks good, no matter how incompetent he may be. Johnson is superficial and opportunistic."[52]

Eisenhower disliked Kennedy even more. He told Ellis Slater, who was a friend of Joe Kennedy's, that he feared if the Kennedys ever got in "we will never get them out—that there will be a machine bigger than Tammany Hall ever was . . . "[53] Eisenhower told one of his big-business friends, "I will do almost anything to avoid turning my chair and the country over to Kennedy." And he gave Kistia-kowsky "a long discourse on how incompetent Kennedy is compared to Nixon, that even the more thoughtful Democrats are horrified by his selection, and that Johnson is the most tricky and unreliable politician in Congress."[54] In 1956, Eisenhower had pronounced the Stevenson-Kefauver ticket "the sorriest" in the history of the Democratic Party. In 1960, he decided that Kennedy-Johnson was even worse.

But in 1956, he could confront Stevenson-Kefauver directly; in 1960, he had to confront Kennedy-Johnson through Nixon. He could and did, however, see to it that Nixon made the confrontation on a platform acceptable to him. The convention was to open on July 25. The week before, Eisenhower talked twice daily at least with Nixon on the telephone; the President told Bill Robinson that he was "quite content with the Nixon position." Then, on July 22, Nixon unexpectedly flew to New York for a meeting with Rockefeller. They hammered out a joint statement, one that reporters immediately called appeasement on Nixon's part, because on most issues (civil rights, housing, schools, and jobs) the statement reflected Rockefeller's more liberal views. But what really upset Eisenhower was the statement on defense: "The United States can afford and must provide the increased expenditures to implement fully this necessary program for strengthening our defense posture. There must be no price ceiling on American security."

Eisenhower confessed that he found the statement, which echoed Kennedy's charges, "somewhat astonishing," especially as it came from two men "who had long been in Administration councils and who had never voiced any doubt—at least in my presence—of the adequacy of America's defenses." Gabe Hauge called Robinson "in somewhat of a panic." He told Robinson that the statement "really involved a repudiation of the President's position on defense." Worse, Rockefeller was insisting on putting the pledge to increase defense spending into the platform. Robinson talked to Eisenhower, who commented that "it would be difficult for Nixon to run on the Administration record if the platform contained a repudiation of it." Eisenhower said he would still be President for six more months and he intended to stick to his policies. "Any position by Nixon or the platform in repudiation of these policies would bring discord and disunity in the Republican Party efforts."[55]

The following day, Eisenhower telephoned Nixon, who claimed

that Rockefeller had put out the statement unilaterally. "What I'm trying to do," he said, "is to find some ground on which Nelson can be with us and not against us." Eisenhower told Nixon that he would find it "difficult . . . to be enthusiastic about a platform which did not reflect a respect for the record of the Republican Administration . . . "[56] Nixon then instructed his lieutenants to eliminate the offensive passage, substituting for it a compromise: "The United States can and must provide whatever is necessary to insure its own security . . . and to provide any necessary increased expenditures to meet new situations. . . . To provide more would be wasteful. To provide less would be catastrophic." That was acceptable to Eisenhower.

On July 26, Eisenhower addressed the convention. He spoke not of Nixon's qualifications to take over the Oval Office, but rather about the accomplishments of his own Administration. Nixon won the nomination easily, then selected Henry Cabot Lodge, Jr., as his running mate. Eisenhower was disappointed—up to the end he had hoped it would be Al Gruenther or Bob Anderson, and he doubted that Lodge would be an effective campaigner—but he accepted Nixon's decision.[57]

Immediately after the Republican Convention, Eisenhower tried to convince Kennedy to tone down his criticism of defense policy. He instructed Allen Dulles to give a briefing to both Kennedy and Johnson. Eisenhower wanted Dulles to put his emphasis on how strong the American defense posture was. But in the briefing, Dulles only wanted to talk about developments in Berlin, Cuba, Iran, the Middle East, Formosa, NATO, and the Congo. The Democratic senators were only interested in developments that might arise during the campaign. Kennedy did ask Dulles directly, "How do we stand in the missile race?" Dulles recorded, in a memorandum for the President on the briefing, that "I replied that the Defense Department was the competent authority on this question . . . "[58] That was hardly a satisfactory answer, and Kennedy felt free to continue to speak of a "missile gap."

Kennedy's campaign made Eisenhower more determined than ever to stop him. He met with Nixon and they agreed that the President would save his effort until the last days of the campaign, when he would barnstorm for Nixon. Behind the scenes, however, Eisenhower began the process of persuading his millionaire friends to put some of their money and energy into the election. On August 8, for example, he called Pete Jones. Jones was one of his gang, as well as head of Cities Service Oil Company. Eisenhower told Jones to use his influence to see to it that "industry do something to talk a little optimistically, not pessimistically, these next three months." He wanted Jones to get active in fund raising. "The President also said that the government was accelerating some of its spending; that certain companies might do the same." [59]

Besides stimulating the economy and raising campaign funds, Eisenhower could most help Nixon through his press conferences. He tried to do so, but the results were bad. No matter what he was asked about Nixon, it seemed, or what he intended to say, his answers could always be read two or more ways, and never constituted that clear-cut, total endorsement that Nixon so desperately needed. The total effect was almost devastating.

On August 10, a reporter asked if Eisenhower was going to give Nixon "a greater voice . . . than you have in the past, in view of his responsibility as the candidate." Eisenhower replied that he alone could make the decisions. He would continue, as always, to consult with Nixon, but if a decision had to be made, *"I'm* going to decide it according to *my* judgment." Did he think that Nixon had gone too far in trying to appease Rockefeller? "Well," Eisenhower replied, "I don't think he *feels* that he was appeasing." Peter Lisagor asked if Eisenhower had any objections to Nixon holding his own press conference, so that he could speak for himself on the defense issue. Eisenhower said he had no objections: "As a matter of fact I am quite sure that while, with the exception of minute detail, he would be saying exactly the same thing I would be, I have no objection to his going and making any kind of public talk . . . "

Sarah McClendon wanted to know if Eisenhower's recent request for larger military appropriations "is a change that you took in light of the world situation or were you influenced to do this by Mr. Nixon or Mr. Rockefeller." Eisenhower snapped back, "I wasn't influenced by anybody except my own military and State Department advisers and my own judgment." Charles Bartlett asked if there were any differences between Nixon and the President on the question of nuclear testing. "Well," Eisenhower responded, "I can't recall what he has ever said specifically about nuclear underground testing." [60]

Nixon's major claim in his confrontation with Kennedy was that he was experienced in making the tough decisions. But at one half-hour press conference, Eisenhower had denied that Nixon, or anyone else, really participated in the decision making. He specifically denied that Nixon had been consulted on increasing the military budget. And he admitted that he could not even remember what Nixon's advice might have been on the testing issue.

Two weeks later, at the next press conference, things got worse. Sarah McClendon asked Eisenhower to "tell us of some of the big decisions that Mr. Nixon has participated in . . . " Eisenhower replied, "I don't see why people can't understand this: No one can make a decision except me . . . I have all sorts of advisers, and one of the principal ones is Mr. Nixon . . . Now, if you talk about other people sharing a decision, how can they? No one can because then who is going to be responsible?"

Later in the same conference, Charles Mohr of *Time* brought the subject up again, justifying it on the grounds that Nixon "almost wants to claim that he has had a great deal of practice at being President." Could not the President give an example of how Nixon fit into the decision-making process? Eisenhower said that Nixon attended the meetings and gave his opinion. "And he has never hesitated . . . to express his opinion, and when he has been asked for it, expressed his opinion in terms of recommendations as to decision. But no one [at the meetings] . . . has the decisive power. There is no voting . . . Mr. Nixon has taken a full part in every principal discussion."

By this point, Eisenhower was obviously becoming irritated at answering the same simple question over and over. But Mohr persisted. "We understand that the power of decision is entirely yours, Mr. President," he said. "I just wondered if you could give us an example of a major idea of his that you had adopted in that role, as the decider and final—".

Eisenhower cut him off. "If you give me a week," he said, "I might think of one. I don't remember." And with that, the conference ended. [61]

Eisenhower realized immediately how terrible that remark sounded. When he returned to the Oval Office, he called Nixon to apologize and express his regret. The Democrats, of course, and the press, made the most of it. Shortly thereafter, Nixon made a plaintive appeal to Eisenhower "to be tied into the President's action in Cuba in some way." [62] (Nixon was urging decisive action against Castro and wanted Eisenhower to give him the credit for it.) Eisenhower refused, saying, "This would be very difficult to do in any acceptable way." To Whitman, Eisenhower complained that Nixon had made a big mistake in 1956, when Eisenhower offered him the job of Secretary of Defense. Had Nixon taken that post, Eisenhower argued, he could have gained all the decision-making experience he wanted, and "he would be in a lot better position today in his bid for the Presidency."[63]

On August 30, Eisenhower went to see Nixon in the hospital—the Vice-President was in Walter Reed Army Hospital with an infected knee. When he returned from the visit, Eisenhower told Whitman that "there was some lack of warmth." Whitman's diary continues: "He mentioned again, as he has several times, the fact that the Vice-President has very few personal friends." Eisenhower confessed that he could not understand how a man could live without friends. Whitman wrote that the difference between Eisenhower and Nixon "is obvious. The President is a man of integrity and sincere in his every action . . . He radiates this, everybody knows it, everybody trusts and loves him. But the Vice-President sometimes seems like a man who is acting like a nice man rather than being one."[64]

The highlight of the campaign was the Nixon-Kennedy debates. Eisenhower advised Nixon against agreeing to debate, on the grounds that Nixon was much better known than Kennedy and therefore should not give Kennedy so much free exposure. Nixon rejected the advice, on the grounds that debate was one of his strongest points. Eisenhower then advised him "to talk on the positive side . . . and not try to be too slick." Nixon replied that "he was going to be gentlemanly, let Kennedy be the aggressor." After the first debate, Nixon phoned Eisenhower. Nixon must have been crushed when Eisenhower explained "that he had not been able to hear the debate . . ." And he must have been hurt as Eisenhower nevertheless proceeded to advise him to "once in a while . . . not appear to be quite so glib, to ponder and appear to think about something before answering a question."[65]

In late October, Eisenhower finally began active campaigning for Nixon. What he talked about, however, was not Nixon's superb preparation for the Presidency, but the record of his own Administration. He told a Philadelphia audience, for example, that in the past eight years personal income was up by 48 percent, individual savings were up by 37 percent, school construction up by 46 percent, college enrollments up by 75 percent, that 9 million new homes had been built, the most ever in one decade, that the GNP was up by 45 percent, that inflation had been controlled, that the Interstate Highway System had become a reality, as had the St. Lawrence Seaway, that in short the past eight years had been wonderful. Few disagreed, although Nixon might have said that the point was that the election was about who was going to lead America forward into the 1960s, not back into the fifties.

Nevertheless, the Eisenhower speeches were eliciting a response. Eisenhower decided he wanted to do more campaigning and indicated that he wished to have an expanded schedule of speeches. Nixon was all for it. But on October 30, eight days before the election, Mamie called Pat Nixon to say that she was distraught at the thought of her man taking on additional burdens, and told Mrs. Nixon she feared that Eisenhower "was not up to the strain campaigning might put on his heart." She had tried to dissuade him, but could not, and therefore "begged" Pat Nixon to have her husband convince Eisenhower to change his mind, without letting Ike know she had intervened. The following morning, Dr. Snyder added his opinion, telling Nixon to "either talk him out of it or just don't let him do it—for the sake of his health."

In his memoirs, Nixon related that "I had rarely seen Eisenhower more animated than he was when I arrived at the White House that afternoon." He showed Nixon an expanded itinerary. Nixon began giving reasons why the President should not take on the extra burden. According to Nixon, "He was hurt and then he was angry." But Nixon insisted and Eisenhower "finally acquiesced. His pride prevented him from saying anything, but I knew that he was puzzled and frustrated by my conduct."[66]

If Nixon was not ready to risk Eisenhower's health in his cause, he was ready to call into question Senator Kennedy's physical condition. On November 4, Whitman noted that an "air of desperation" had taken over the Nixon camp. She cited as an example a statement Nixon wanted the White House to release. Rumors were flying around the country to the effect that Kennedy had Addison's disease. The proposed statement referred to Eisenhower's position in 1956, when he had made public the results of a complete physical examination, and called on the 1960 candidates to do the same. Nixon indicated that after the President signed and issued the statement, he would immediately make his own physical records public.

Jim Hagerty was furious. He called it a "cheap, lousy, stinking political trick." Eisenhower felt the same way. When an aide tried to explain to the President about the rumors of Addison's disease, Eisenhower cut him off and said, "I am not making myself a party to anything that has to do with the health of the candidates." The idea died.[67]

Hagerty's and Ike's attitude is difficult to understand. Nixon was right to point out that Ike had set a precedent in 1956, and Kennedy had already made an issue of Johnson's health (Johnson had had a heart attack; in the preconvention maneuvering, Kennedy had questioned his ability to give full-time service). In the seventies and eighties, the candidates' health became a standard subject for discussion and consideration.

On November 4, the Nixon people called Whitman with another proposal. Nixon wanted to say in a speech that night that if elected, he would send Eisenhower on a good-will tour to the Communist-bloc countries. Eisenhower was "astonished, did not like the idea of 'auctioning off the Presidency' in this manner, spoke of the difficulty of his traveling once he is not President, and felt it was a last-ditch, hysterical action." He told Hagerty to call Nixon's people and tell them no.

Two days later, Nixon's secretary, Rosemary Woods, called Whitman to ask her to make sure the President listened to Nixon's taped speech at 9 P.M. that night. Eisenhower did, and was again astonished as he heard Nixon make the promise to send Eisenhower on a tour. Eisenhower was so angry he told Hagerty to call Nixon and force him to retract the promise. Hagerty got the President calmed down. Then, Whitman reported, "The President dictated . . . a congratulatory telegram on the speech . . . to send to Nixon." Speaking for everyone who has attempted to plumb the depths of the Eisenhower-Nixon relationship, as well as for that larger group that tries to make sense of American politics, Whitman confessed, "I do not understand." [68]

November 8 was election day. Eisenhower joined John and Barbara to watch the returns. The early reports were discouraging, as Kennedy was sweeping the East. At 11 P.M., Eisenhower went to bed, thinking the worst. When he woke the next morning, Nixon had closed the gap in the popular vote, which stood almost dead equal, but still looked to be hopeless in the electoral vote. Shortly after noon, Nixon called from his California headquarters. He thought he would take California, Illinois, and Minnesota, but it would not be enough. Nixon pointed out that he had run some 7 percent ahead of the Republican Party, and that he lost because of the "weakness of the Republican Party." Eisenhower urged Nixon to take a good rest. He then made a remark that summarized nicely his perspective on the campaign and election: "We can be proud of these last eight years." Nixon replied, "You did a grand job." [69]

Nixon later told Eisenhower that he had never heard the President sound so depressed. Eisenhower agreed that it was so. What he did not tell Nixon, but did tell Whitman, was the reason. It was not so much Nixon's defeat as it was his own sense of rejection. All morning, Whitman recorded, "The President kept saying this was a 'repudiation' of everything he had done for eight years."[70]

CHAPTER TWENTY-TWO

Transition

and

Assessment

THE LAST ten weeks of the Eisenhower Administration were a period of marking time. Because Eisenhower's role was that of caretaker, he undertook no new initiatives. Instead, he worked to keep the options open, so that on such issues as nuclear testing, balance-of-payments problems, Indochina, Berlin, and Cuba, the incoming President could make his own decisions. One place where Eisenhower did try to tie Kennedy's hands, however, was the budget. Starting with his vacation at Augusta, he labored over the budget. He told Slater, "You know, I'm going to insist on a balanced budget no matter what Kennedy says he wants. And if he feels otherwise he'll have to declare himself. There just won't be enough money to pay for the already committed things and his new ideas too." [1]

While working on that final budget, Eisenhower was told that such-and-such a program could not be cut. Goodpaster noted, "The President commented that if he were a dictator he thought he could cut the budget before him 20 percent without damage to the country —by knocking out many sacred cows and completely useless but well-established activities." [2] At another budget meeting, this one with Gates and the Defense people, Eisenhower bemoaned the emphasis Kennedy and his advisers were putting on Maxwell Taylor's idea of "flexible response."

Eisenhower's concern was the same in 1961 as it had been in 1953—keeping the economy sound. Goodpaster recorded that Eisenhower said, "We have constantly got to ask ourselves whether we are cutting out everything that can be cut out. For example, he is clear in his mind that the only way we are going to win in the present struggle is by our deterrent. There may be some use in having a few mobile elements but he cannot see any 'little wars.' More and more the matter is a question of big war and the deterrent."[3]

Eisenhower knew, however, that his views had already been examined and rejected by the Kennedy team, which certainly did intend to spend more than it took in, to cut taxes, and to dramatically increase defense spending, both in nuclear arms and delivery systems and in conventional arms, so as to create a "flexible response" capacity.

Despite Eisenhower's unhappiness with Kennedy's policies, he had no personal rancor toward his successor, as he had had toward Truman. It helped that Kennedy had carefully, and wisely, refrained from any direct attacks on Eisenhower personally during the campaign. It also helped that when Kennedy came to the White House on December 6, at Eisenhower's invitation, for a briefing from the President, he arrived sitting alone in the back seat of his limousine. Eisenhower and his staff had feared he would show up with a group of assistants preparing to celebrate their victory. The President was also pleased by Kennedy's manner. At the meeting in the Oval Office, Kennedy listened carefully and intelligently as Eisenhower explained the way the White House functioned.

Eisenhower stressed to Kennedy the seriousness of the balance-of-payments problem. "I pray that he understands it," Eisenhower wrote in his diary. He was pleased that Kennedy's attitude "was that of a serious, earnest seeker for information." Eisenhower told him that because of the gold outflow, and because of his own conviction that America was carrying far more than its share of the free-world defenses, he intended to let the NATO community know that the United States planned to redeploy some troops out of Europe, unless the Europeans pitched in to stop the outflow of gold. Eisenhower assured Kennedy that he would make the announcement of his intention in such a way as to leave Kennedy a free hand in reversing the policy (which Kennedy did a week after taking office). Kennedy then asked about Eisenhower's personal views regarding Macmillan, de Gaulle, and Adenauer. Eisenhower replied that Kennedy ought to go out of his way to meet them and talk with them individually and as a group; if he did, "he would be impressed by their ability and their integrity."

Toward the end of the meeting, Kennedy asked Eisenhower whether he would be prepared to serve the country "in such areas and in such manner as may seem appropriate." Eisenhower replied that of course, "the answer was obvious," but he added that he hoped it would be in the area of serious conferences and consultations on subjects that Eisenhower knew something about, "rather than errands which might necessitate frequent and lengthy travel." Kennedy understood.

Finally, Kennedy asked if he could hold Goodpaster for two months or more into the new Administration. Eisenhower was opposed. He said Goodpaster wanted to return to active duty with troops, that a spot was being held for him, and that he wished Kennedy would appoint someone right now who could sit at Goodpaster's side for the final month. But Kennedy replied that "he would be handicapped" without Goodpaster. Eisenhower reminded Kennedy that he would soon be the Commander in Chief and he could then order Goodpaster to do any duty he wished. Kennedy indicated that he would hold the active-duty spot open for Goodpaster.[4] The meeting ended on that pleasant note of agreement. It had been much smoother than the preinaugural meeting Eisenhower had had with Truman back in 1952.

One of the subjects Kennedy had wanted to discuss was Cuba. Eisenhower responded with a brief summary of a meeting he had held a week earlier. At that meeting, the Administration had considered the options with regard to the CIA's program for Cuba. Gray kept the notes. He recorded: "The President said he wished to ask two questions: (1) Are we being sufficiently imaginative and bold, subject to not letting our hand appear; and (2) are we doing the things we are doing, effectively." Without waiting for a response, Eisenhower "adverted to the impending transfer of government responsibilities and said that we would not want to be in the position of turning over the government in the midst of a developing emergency."

Dulles reported that there were some 184 different groups among the refugees, each demanding to become the recognized government-in-exile. "The President asked how might we proceed to bring them all together and Mr. Dulles responded that this was impossible." Eisenhower remarked that the CIA should not "be financing those we cannot get to work in harness."

Douglas Dillon, Under Secretary of State, spoke up for his department, saying that "the State concern was the operation was no longer secret but is known all over Latin America and has been discussed in U.N. circles." Eisenhower responded "that even if the operation were known, the main thing was not to let the U.S. hand show. As long as we pursued that course he was not too concerned." He added that he did not share the State Department concern about "shooting from the hip as he thinks that we should be prepared to take more chances and be more aggressive."[5]

In late December, Dulles and Bissell reported to Eisenhower on their progress. The brigade was up to six hundred men, which stretched the capacity of the training camp in Guatemala. The refugees were highly trained and motivated. Eisenhower asked about political progress: Did the Cubans have a recognized and popular leader yet? No, Bissell replied, not yet. Eisenhower said that he would not approve of any military plans for the utilization of the paramilitary force until there was a genuine government-in-exile. He hoped he would be able to recognize one before he left office.

Castro, however, moved before Eisenhower could do so. On January 2, 1961, Castro ordered most of the State Department personnel in the embassy in Havana to leave the country within twenty-four hours, charging that they were a den of spies. The next day, Eisenhower met with his top advisers. He announced that "the U.S. should not tolerate being kicked around," and indicated that he was inclined to bring every member of the embassy home and withdraw diplomatic recognition of the Cuban government. Herter mentioned the various problems that such a course of action would create. Treasury Secretary Anderson said that rather than break relations, he favored vigorous action, now, "to get rid of Castro." He wanted the CIA to get going. Dulles remarked that Bissell's paramilitary force would not be ready to move until early March. The problem of finding a legitimate government-in-exile remained acute, meanwhile, and there was another difficulty—finding an excuse for an American-sponsored intervention in Cuba.

Herter suggested that "we should stage an 'attack' on Guantanamo," copying the technique Hitler had used in 1939 on the German-Polish border before he invaded Poland. Bissell warned that whatever was decided, it had to be done soon, because he did not think he could hold his paramilitary force in Guatemala together beyond March 1. He explained that the CIA agents who were supervising the training "think morale will suffer dangerously if action is not taken by early March."

Eisenhower said that it was his opinion that "we had only two reasonable alternative courses of action: (1) Supporting Cubans to go in March or (2) to abandon the operation." He strongly favored the first course. "When we turn over responsibility on the twentieth," he declared, "our successors should continue to improve and intensify the training and undertake planning when the Cubans are themselves properly organized." Meanwhile, he wanted Bissell to increase the size of the force of refugees. "We should permit the Cubans to expand the forces already planned and then find ways to give arms to broader groups."

As to the immediate future, he had decided to withdraw recognition from the Cuban government that day, even though no government-in-exile had emerged. Eisenhower said he was ready to "recognize in a great hurry the leader whenever we do find him." Goodpaster warned that a relatively large military force was being created by the CIA that was not responsible to nor connected with any government, and that the operation was building a momentum of its own which would be difficult to stop. Eisenhower replied that the CIA was only creating an asset, not committing the United States to an invasion of Cuba or anything like that. Whether the refugees would be used or not depended entirely on political developments. There was no need to worry.[6]

For themselves, the Eisenhowers had many chores to do, but they were such old hands at moving that this would be a relatively easy move, physically if not emotionally, because everything was already set up at Gettysburg. Slater spent the first weekend in January at the White House. As he was walking down the hall on Sunday morning, Mamie called him into her bedroom. She was still in bed, but told him she had been up since 5:30 A.M. trying to balance her checkbook. She had already packed the paintings and knickknacks in their bedroom; looking around, she commented to Slater, "Don't things look bare."[7]

Probably no family has ever moved out of the White House gladly, but there were compensations to becoming private citizens. The day after Christmas, 1960, Eisenhower wrote to the members of his gang, and a few other close friends, an identical letter. "During my entire life," he began, "until I came back from World War II as something of a VIP, I was known by my contemporaries as 'Ike.' " He continued, "I now demand, as my right, that you, starting January 21, 1961, address me by that nickname. No longer do I propose to be excluded from the privileges that other friends enjoy."[8]

But of course no former President is simply a private citizen. Already Ike was being bombarded with requests that he speak to this club or that charity, to this organization or that university. Honoraria of $1,000 and more were being offered. One such request came from Edgar out in Tacoma, who was rather pleased with himself at being able to extend to his brother a fee of $1,000 for a twenty-minute speech at the University of Puget Sound. Ike replied that Edgar's letter "shows how little you know your younger brother. I have made it a practice for years never to accept an honorarium for any talk; this policy I adopted right after World War II."[9]

He had no financial worries in any case. Pete Jones and other friends had done a good job of investing his *Crusade* money for him; Gettysburg was paid for; he had his full pension; there was plenty of money. Besides, he still had a high income potential, even without speaker's fees. Given Ike's continuing popularity, given the turbulent years he had just presided over, and given the great success of *Crusade,* every publisher in the country wanted to produce his White House memoirs. Ike decided to stay with Doubleday, primarily because of friendship with the president, Doug Black. He did not sign a contract, but did make an informal arrangement with Black, trusting that Black would treat him fairly, even generously. There was no package deal involved, as there had been with *Crusade;* this time, Ike would receive royalties and pay taxes on a regular basis.

One additional reason Ike made his arrangement with Black was that Black said he could arrange first serial publications in *The Saturday Evening Post.* Ike had been addicted to that magazine when he was a boy—he claimed he read every issue—and he got a great kick out of the idea of appearing in it.[10]

In January, by special act of Congress, Eisenhower regained the five-star rank he had resigned in 1952. Sam Rayburn and Lyndon Johnson took the lead in getting the legislation into law. As a former President, Eisenhower was entitled to a $25,000 per year pension, plus $50,000 for office expenses, which was much more than he would receive as a five-star general. The special act gave him the best of both worlds—he got his rank back, and Congress stipulated that he should receive the full presidential pension and allowance. Further, he got to retain the services of Sergeants Dry and Moaney and Colonel Schulz, as aides, their costs to be deducted from the $50,000 allowance.

On December 14, Whitman typed up a note and sent it into the Oval Office. "Norman Cousins called," she told the President. "His suggestion: that you give a 'farewell' address to the country . . . reviewing your Administration, telling of your hopes for the future. A great, sweeping document."[11] Eisenhower liked the idea. He also liked the work of a young political scientist from Johns Hopkins University, Malcolm Moos, who had joined the staff in late 1958 as a speech writer. Eisenhower talked to Moos, set him to work on a speech, and over the following weeks consulted closely with him to make the text exactly right.

On January 17, 1961, at 8:30 P.M., Eisenhower went on national radio and television to deliver his Farewell Address. His theme was the Cold War. He spoke of war and peace, of police states and of freedom. "We face a hostile ideology," he declared, "global in scope, atheistic in character, ruthless in purpose, and insidious in method." The danger it posed was of "indefinite duration." There would be many crises, and correspondingly many calls to find a "miraculous solution" by spending ever-increasing sums on research and development of new weapons. Eisenhower warned that every such proposal "must be weighed in the light of . . . the need to maintain balance . . . between cost and hoped-for advantage."

The irony of the Cold War was that to maintain the peace and retain its freedom, the United States had to build a huge military establishment, but the cost of building it threatened to create a garrison state in which there would be no freedom. "Our military organization today bears little relation to that known by any of my predecessors . . . " Eisenhower said. In addition, until after World War II, the United States had "no armaments industry." In earlier days, "American makers of plowshares could . . . make swords as well." But because of the Cold War and the technological revolution, "we have been compelled to create a permanent armaments industry of vast proportions."

Then, in ringing phrases, Eisenhower spoke the sentences that would be the most quoted and remembered of his Farewell Address, indeed of his entire Presidency. The sentences summed up his deepest feelings, gave voice to his greatest fears. They were the words of a soldier-prophet, a general who had given his life to the defense of freedom and the achievement of peace. "This conjunction of an immense military establishment and a large arms industry is new in the American experience," he said. "The total influence—economic, political, even spiritual—is felt in every city, every statehouse, every office of the federal government." Then, the direct warning: "In the councils of government, we must guard against the acquisition of unwarranted influence, whether sought or unsought, by the military-industrial complex. The potential for the disastrous rise of misplaced power exists and will persist." The military-industrial complex should never be allowed to "endanger our liberties or democratic processes. We should take nothing for granted."

Eisenhower next spoke of another great change that had occurred in America in his lifetime, and the dangers that change brought. The solitary inventor, working on his own, had been replaced "by task forces of scientists in laboratories and testing fields." Further, in the old days, universities were "the fountainhead of free ideas and scientific discovery." But today, "partly because of the huge costs involved, a government contract becomes virtually a substitute for intellectual curiosity." Therefore, Eisenhower issued a second warning, not so well remembered later as was the military-industrial complex phrase, but equally prophetic. "The prospect of domination of the nation's scholars by federal employment, project allocations, and the power of money is ever present," he said, "and is gravely to be regarded."

Another warning: "We—you and I, and our government—must avoid . . . plundering, for our own ease and convenience, the precious resources of tomorrow. We cannot mortgage the material assets of our grandchildren without risking the loss also of their political and spiritual heritage. We want democracy to survive for all generations to come . . . "

An apology: "Disarmament . . . is a continuing imperative . . . Because this need is so sharp and apparent I confess that I lay down my official responsibilities in this field with a definite sense of disappointment. As one who has witnessed the horror and the lingering sadness of war—as one who knows that another war could utterly destroy this civilization which has been so slowly and painfully built over thousands of years—I wish I could say tonight that a lasting peace is in sight." But the most that he could say was that "war has been avoided." He concluded by praying that "all peoples will come to live together in a peace guaranteed by the binding force of mutual respect and love." [12]

The speech got a highly favorable reception, which put Eisenhower in a good mood the next morning, when he held his 193rd, and last, press conference as President. He thought the transition was going "splendidly," he praised Congress for its cooperation (sic!), he wished Kennedy "Godspeed in his work," he said his greatest disappointment was the failure to achieve peace, he explained his retirement status, and he answered a question about what specific steps he would recommend in dealing with the military-industrial complex. Eisenhower said every citizen should keep well informed, because "it is only a citizenry, an alert and informed citizenry which can keep these abuses from coming about." He added that the potential abuses of power and influence by the arms makers could come about "unwittingly, but just by the very nature of the thing." Every magazine you picked up had an advertisement of a Titan missile or an Atlas or what have you, which represented "almost an insidious penetration of our own minds that the only thing this country is engaged in is weaponry and missiles. And, I'll tell you we just can't afford to do that."

Robert Spivack asked if, over the years, Eisenhower felt the reporters had been fair to him. Eisenhower grinned and shot back, "Well, when you come down to it, I don't see what a reporter could do much to a President, do you?"

William Knighton wanted the President's opinion on the two-term amendment. "A funny thing," Eisenhower replied, grinning again, "ever since this election the Republicans have been asking me this." After the laughter died down, he said he had come to believe that the two-term amendment "was probably a pretty good thing."[13]

The following day, January 19, Eisenhower invited Kennedy to the White House for a final briefing. Eisenhower told Kennedy about the man with the satchel, a satchel that contained the communications equipment that connected the President with SAC and the missile forces. He was, Eisenhower said, "an unobtrusive man who would shadow the President for all of his days in office." To give Kennedy an example of the services available to him, Eisenhower pressed a button and said, "Send a chopper." In six minutes, a helicopter settled down on the lawn outside the Oval Office.

Kennedy wanted Eisenhower's judgment "as to the United States supporting the guerrilla operations in Cuba, even if this support involves the United States publicly." Eisenhower replied "yes," it should be done, because "we cannot let the present government there go on." He told Kennedy that the members of the OAS, who in public consistently spoke against any action designed to eliminate Castro, in private were urging the Administration to "do something." Eisenhower discussed Bissell's operation in Guatemala. He said that this would be a good time to miss "no opportunity to keep our mouths shut." (*The New York Times,* a few days earlier, had carried a story describing the organization and training of the Cuban refugees.)

Then Eisenhower outlined his attempts to "find a man who was both anti-Batista and anti-Castro" to head a government-in-exile. It was "very tough," he said, to find a man of standing that satisfied all the refugees. Eisenhower said that Kennedy's "first job would be to find who that man could be." Then, when the paramilitary force of refugees went into Cuba, "it would have the appearance of a more legitimate operation." No specific plans for an invasion had yet been made, Eisenhower added, and that should be done as soon as a government-in-exile was formed.

Kennedy asked about America's limited-war capability. Eisenhower assured him that the armed services were more than strong enough to cope with any situation, then urged Kennedy to hold down the costs of defense, and to strive for a balanced budget (afterward, Eisenhower commented that "I must say that the President-elect did not seem to be impressed"). Eisenhower returned to the subject of Cuba, telling Kennedy that it was his "responsibility to do whatever is necessary." Clark Clifford, who took notes for Kennedy, saw no "reluctance or hesitation" on Eisenhower's part. Indeed, five days later Clifford sent a memorandum to President Kennedy reminding him that Eisenhower had said "it was the policy of this government" to help the Cubans "to the utmost" and that this effort should be "continued and accelerated." [14]

Inevitably, Inauguration Day came. Inevitably, Eisenhower was leaving the Presidency with some reluctance. A few days before January 20, Henry Wriston came to the Oval Office to deliver the report of the Commission on National Goals, which Eisenhower had appointed a year earlier. With the New Frontier about to take over, the report was already a dead letter, of no interest to anyone. But it had to be received, and photographs taken. While that was going on, Eisenhower heard the clatter of hammers across Pennsylvania Avenue, where a reviewing stand was being constructed for the inaugural. "Look, Henry," Eisenhower said, "it's like being in the death cell and watching them put up the scaffold." [15]

The morning of January 20, John Eisenhower remembered an "eerie" atmosphere in the White House. It had snowed heavily the night before, forcing many of the staff to spend the night in the basement. Secretary Gates assured Eisenhower that he would have every soldier in the Army shoveling snow to make sure the inaugural went ahead without a hitch. Eisenhower spent most of the morning leaning on his empty safe, reminiscing with Ann Whitman. The servants lined up, and Eisenhower and Mamie went down the line, saying goodbye to each of them. Many had tears streaming down their faces. The Kennedys, the Johnsons, and "a small entourage" of Democrats arrived for a short visit and a cup of coffee.[16]

At noon, before Chief Justice Earl Warren, the oldest man ever to serve as President to that date gave way to the youngest man elected to the office. After the ceremonies, when all the attention was centered on the Kennedys, the Eisenhowers sneaked away through a side exit. In so doing, Eisenhower later wrote, they made "a fantastic discovery. We were free—as only private citizens in a democratic nation can be free." They drove to the F Street Club, where Lewis Strauss was the host for a luncheon for the Cabinet and Eisenhower's close friends. Then it was off for Gettysburg, along the route they knew so well, and home to the farm.

By special, unprecedented action on Kennedy's part, Ike was retaining the services of his personal Secret Service bodyguard, Special Agent Richard Flohr, for two weeks. Otherwise, he was as free as he felt. When they got to the farm, Ike hopped out the car door to open the gate. For twenty years, he had had almost every physical need taken care of by others. He never wore his shoes while they were being shined, he had not been in a laundromat, or a barbershop, or a clothing store, or indeed—as President—in a retail store of any kind.

There were all sorts of things Ike did not know how to do. Paying tolls at the automatic lanes on the turnpikes, for example. He had forgotten how to type, and had never learned how to mix frozen orange juice or adjust a television picture. He had no idea in the world about how to make practical travel arrangements, how to buy tickets or even where to buy them. He had told Slater, on January 7, that after a few days in Gettysburg following the inaugural, he wanted to go quail shooting down in Georgia at George Humphrey's place. But, he said, "I can't drive all that way and I'm just wondering how I'll get there." Slater assured him that he could "snitch a ride" on Pete Jones' airplane.

Ike did not even know how to place a telephone call. For the past twenty years, whenever he wanted to make a call, he told a secretary to put it through for him. The last time he had placed a call himself, in late 1941, he did so by telling the operator the number he wanted. So, the evening of January 20, he picked up the phone to call his son, tried to give the number, heard only a buzzing at the other end, shouted for the operator, clicked the receiver button a dozen times, tried dialing it like a safe, shouted again, and slammed the phone down.

Frustrated, red-faced, he bellowed for Agent Flohr. "Come show me how you work this goddamned thing." Flohr did. "Oh! So that's how you do it!" exclaimed a delighted Ike, fascinated by the way the ring clicked around the dial. He rather thought he might enjoy this business of learning to cope with the modern world.[17]

He would especially enjoy it because, even if he had to place his own phone calls, or get out and open a gate, or wonder how to get from one place to another on his own, he would do so as a private citizen. After a full one-half century in its service, the nation had finally allowed Dwight Eisenhower to retire. He was free.

Any attempt to assess Eisenhower's eight years as President inevitably reveals more about the person doing the assessing than it does about Eisenhower. Assessment requires passing a judgment on the decisions Eisenhower made on the issues of his time, and every issue was political and controversial. Further, all the major and most of the minor issues of the 1950s continued to divide the nation's political parties and people in the decades that followed. To declare, therefore, that Eisenhower was right or wrong on this or that issue tends to be little more than a declaration of the current politics and prejudices of the author.

Thus William Ewald, in *Eisenhower the President*, concludes "that many terrible things that could have happened, didn't. Dwight Eisenhower's presidency gave America eight good years—I believe the best in memory."[18] There were no wars, no riots, no inflation—just peace and prosperity. Most white middle-class and middle-aged Republicans would heartily agree with Ewald. But a black American could point out that among the things that did not happen were progress in civil rights or school desegregation. People concerned about the Cold War and the nuclear arms race could point out that no progress was made in reducing tensions or achieving disarmament. People concerned about the Communist menace could point out that no Communist regimes were eliminated, and that in fact Communism expanded into Vietnam and Cuba. On these and every issue, in short, there are at least two legitimate points of view. What did not happen brought joy to one man, gloom to another.

To repeat, then: To say that Eisenhower was right about this or wrong about that is to do little more than announce one's own political position. A more fruitful approach is to examine his years in the White House in his own terms, to make an assessment on the basis of how well he did in achieving the tasks and goals he set for himself at the time he took office.

By that standard, there were many disappointments, domestic and foreign. Eisenhower had wanted to achieve unity within the Republican Party, on the basis of bringing the Old Guard into the modern world and the mainstream of American politics. In addition, he wanted to develop within the Republican Party some young, dynamic, trustworthy, and popular leaders. He never achieved either goal, as evidenced by the 1964 Republican Convention, where the Old Guard took control of the party, nominating a candidate and writing a platform that would have delighted Warren Harding, or even William McKinley. Franklin Roosevelt did a much better job of curbing the left wing of the Democratic Party than Eisenhower did of curbing the right wing of the Republican Party.

Eisenhower wanted to see Senator McCarthy eliminated from national public life, and he wanted it done without making America's record and image on civil-liberties issues worse than it already was. But because Eisenhower would not denounce McCarthy by name, or otherwise stand up to the senator from Wisconsin, McCarthy was able to do much damage to civil liberties, the Republican Party, numerous individuals, the U.S. Army, and the Executive Branch before he finally destroyed himself. Eisenhower's only significant contribution to McCarthy's downfall was the purely negative act of denying him access to executive records and personnel. Eisenhower's cautious, hesitant approach—or nonapproach—to the McCarthy issue did the President's reputation no good, and much harm.

Eisenhower had wanted, in January of 1953, to provide a moral leadership that would both draw on and illuminate America's spiritual superiority to the Soviet Union, indeed to all the world. But on one of the great moral issues of the day, the struggle to eliminate racial segregation from American life, he failed to speak out, to indicate personal approval of *Brown* v. *Topeka*. This did incalculable harm to the civil-rights crusade and to America's image.

In civil rights, as in civil liberties, Eisenhower was not a reluctant leader—he was no leader at all. He just wished the problems would go away. With regard to civil liberties, the excesses of McCarthy and his supporters were so gross that the problem did tend to solve itself. With regard to civil rights, an area in which the depth of commitment by the American people was considerably less than the commitment to civil liberties, Eisenhower's refusal to lead was almost criminal. Who can say what might have been accomplished in dealing with this most permanent of problems had President Eisenhower joined Chief Justice Warren in enthusiastically supporting racial equality and justice? But he did not; and by putting the problem off, by leaving it to his successors, he just made it worse.

In foreign affairs, Eisenhower's greatest failure, in his own judgment, which he expressed on innumerable occasions, was the failure to achieve peace. When he left office, the tensions and dangers and costs of the Cold War were higher than they had ever been. In large part, this was no fault of his. He had tried to reach out to the Russians, with Atoms for Peace, Open Skies, and other proposals, only to be rebuffed by Khrushchev. But his own deeply rooted anti-Communism was certainly a contributing factor to the failure. Eisenhower refused to trust the Russians to even the slightest degree. He continued and expanded the economic, political, diplomatic, and covert-operations pressure on the Kremlin for his entire two terms. This was good policy for winning votes, and may even have been good for achieving limited victories in the Cold War, but it was damaging to the cause of world peace.

Allied with the failure to achieve peace was the failure to set a limit on the arms race (never mind actual disarmament, another of his goals). Better than any other world leader, Eisenhower spoke of the cost of the arms race, and its dangers, and its madness. But he could not even slow it down, much less stop it. The great tragedy here is opportunity lost. Eisenhower not only recognized better than anyone else the futility of an arms race; he was in a better position than anyone else to end it. His prestige, especially as a military man, was so overwhelming that he could have made a test ban with the Russians merely on his own assurance that the agreement was good for the United States. But until his last months in office, he accepted the risk of an expanding arms race over the risk of trusting the Russians.

When finally he was ready to make an attempt to control the arms race by accepting an unsupervised comprehensive test ban, the U-2 incident intervened. Fittingly, the flight that Powers made was one Eisenhower instinctively wanted to call off, but one that his technologists insisted was necessary. In this case, as in the case of building more nuclear weapons, holding more tests, or building more rockets, he allowed the advice of his technical people to override his own common sense. That this could happen to Eisenhower illustrates vividly the tyranny of technology in the nuclear/missile age.

In Central and Eastern Europe, Eisenhower had hoped to take the offensive against Communism. But his unrealistic and ineffective belligerency, combined with his party's irresponsible advocacy of uprisings and liberation within a police state, produced the tragedy of Hungary in 1956, which will stand forever as a blot on Eisenhower's record. In his Administration, "roll back" never got started, as "stand pat" became the watchword. But the free world was not even able to stand pat, as Eisenhower accepted an armistice in Korea that left the Communists in control in the north, another in Vietnam that did the same, and the presence of Castro in Cuba.

These failures, taken together, make at first glance a damning indictment. According to Eisenhower's critics, they came about because of the greatest shortcoming of all, the failure to exert leadership. In contrast to FDR and Truman, Eisenhower seemed to be no leader at all, but only a chairman of the board, or even a figurehead, a Whig President in a time that demanded dramatic exercise and executive power.

The most basic, telling, and realistic criticism of the Eisenhower Presidency is not what he did, but what he did not do. His two terms were the time of the great postponement. This was obviously true of race relations and progress toward the desegregation of American life; it was equally true of such urban problems as the growth of slums, pollution, the loss of the tax base, a decent education for all, care for the elderly, the helpless, the unemployed. Goodpaster had warned the President that sometimes putting off problems meant they would be unmanageable when you finally got around to dealing with them. Ike's reputation would be higher today had he listened more closely to the warning, and American life today would be different. One reason for the excesses of Lyndon Johnson's Great Society in the mid-sixties was the magnitude of the problems Johnson tried to deal with; it is possible that the problems would not have been so big had Ike faced up to them.

Ike liked to describe himself as a conservative on fiscal matters, a liberal on human issues. In fact, his policies are most understandable by reference to his birth—he was the last President to be born in the nineteenth century. At heart, he was always a nineteenth-century conservative, deeply suspicious of government and especially of the central government. He thought of deficit spending as almost sinful and immoral, except in wartime; he felt the same way about government programs designed to help people with their economic, health, or social problems.

In many areas, he never outgrew his Abilene, turn-of-the-century upbringing.

In foreign affairs, too, the Eisenhower era was a time of the great postponement. This was most obviously the case in South and Central America (not that his successors have done much better), and especially in Cuba, where he neither accepted Castro nor tried to destroy him. He put off the problems of postcolonial Africa. In the Middle East, he was essentially negative, saying "No" to the British, the French, and Israel without saying "Yes" to Egypt or the Arabs. Perhaps his greatest foreign failure was in Southeast Asia where he also practiced a policy of postponement. His middle-of-the-road tactics left the Communists in control of North Vietnam without creating a South Vietnam strong enough to stand on its own.

Yet it can be argued that Southeast Asia was the scene of one of his great triumphs in foreign affairs, because it was there that he showed the wisdom and the courage to keep his country out of an unwinnable war.

How effective, if not dramatic, Eisenhower's leadership techniques were can be seen in a brief assessment of his accomplishments as President, an assessment once again based on his own goals and aspirations. First and foremost, he presided over eight years of prosperity, marred only by two minor recessions. By later standards, it was a decade of nearly full employment and no inflation.

Indeed by almost every standard—GNP, personal income and savings, home buying, auto purchases, capital investment, highway construction, and so forth—it was the best decade of the century. Surely Eisenhower's fiscal policies, his refusal to cut taxes or increase defense spending, his insistence on a balanced budget, played some role in creating this happy situation.

Under Eisenhower, the nation enjoyed domestic peace and tranquillity—at least as measured against the sixties. One of Eisenhower's major goals in 1953 was to lower the excesses of political rhetoric and partisanship. He managed to achieve that goal, in a negative way, by not dismantling the New Deal, as the Old Guard wanted to do. Under Eisenhower, the number of people covered by Social Security doubled as benefits went up. The New Deal's regulatory commissions stayed in place. Expenditures for public works were actually greater under Eisenhower than they had been under FDR or Truman. Nor were Eisenhower's public works of the boondoggle variety—the St. Lawrence Seaway and the Interstate Highway System made an enormous contribution to the economy. Eisenhower, in effect, put a Republican stamp of approval on twenty years of Democratic legislation, by itself a major step toward bringing the two parties closer together.

Eisenhower's positive contribution to domestic peace and tranquillity was to avoid partisanship himself. His close alliance with the southern Democrats, his refusal to ever denounce the Democratic Party as a whole (he attacked only the "spender" wing), his insistence on a bipartisan foreign policy, his careful cultivation of the Democratic leaders in Congress, all helped tone down the level of partisan excess. When Eisenhower came into the White House, his party was accusing the other party of "twenty years of treason." The Democrats in turn were charging that the Republicans were the party of Depression. When Eisenhower left office, such ridiculous charges were seldom heard.

In 1953, Eisenhower had also set as a major goal the restoration of dignity to the office of the President. He felt strongly that Truman had demeaned the office. Whether Truman was guilty of so doing depends on one's perception, of course, but few would argue the claim that Eisenhower—in his bearing, his actions, his private and social life, and his official duties as head of state—maintained his dignity. He looked, acted, and sounded like a President.

He was a good steward. He did not sell off the public lands, or open the National Wilderness Areas or National Parks to commercial or mineral exploitation. He retained and expanded TVA. He stopped nuclear testing in the atmosphere, the first world statesman to do so, because of the dangers of radiation to the people who had chosen him as their leader.

In the field of civil rights, he felt he had done as well as could be done. His greatest contribution (albeit one that he had grown increasingly unhappy about) was the appointment of Earl Warren as Chief Justice. In addition, he had completed the desegregation of the armed forces, and of the city of Washington, D.C., as well as all federal property. He had sponsored and signed the first civil-rights legislation since Reconstruction. When he had to, he acted decisively, as in Little Rock in 1957. These were all positive, if limited, gains. Eisenhower's boast was that they were made without riots, and without driving the white South to acts of total desperation. Progress in desegregation, especially in the schools, was painfully slow during the Eisenhower years, but he was convinced that anything faster would have produced a much greater and more violent white southern resistance.

In 1952, when he accepted the Republican nomination for the Presidency, Eisenhower called on the party to join him in a "crusade." Its purpose was to clear the crooks and the Commies out of Washington. Once that task had been accomplished, Eisenhower's critics found it difficult to discover what his crusade was aiming at. There was no stirring call to arms, no great moral cause, no idealistic pursuit of some overriding national goal. Eisenhower, seemingly, was quite content to preside over a fat, happy, satisfied nation that devoted itself to enjoying life, and especially the material benefits available in the greatest industrial power in the world. There was truth in the charge.

Eisenhower's rebuttal also contained an elementary truth. The Declaration of Independence states that one of man's inalienable rights is the pursuit of happiness. Eisenhower tried, with much success, to create a climate in the 1950s in which American citizens could fully exercise that right.

His greatest successes came in foreign policy, and the related area of national defense spending. By making peace in Korea, and avoiding war thereafter for the next seven and one-half years, and by holding down, almost single-handedly, the pace of the arms race, he achieved his major accomplishments. No one knows how much money he saved the United States, as he rebuffed Symington and the Pentagon and the JCS and the AEC and the military-industrial complex. And no one knows how many lives he saved by ending the war in Korea and refusing to enter any others, despite a half-dozen and more virtually unanimous recommendations that he go to war.

He made peace, and he kept the peace. Whether any other man could have led the country through that decade without going to war cannot be known. What we do know is that Eisenhower did it. Eisenhower boasted that "the United States never lost a soldier or a foot of ground in my administration. We kept the peace. People asked how it happened—by God, it didn't just happen, I'll tell you that." [19]

Beyond keeping the peace, Eisenhower could claim that at the end of his eight years, the NATO alliance, that bedrock of American foreign policy, was stronger than ever. Relations with the Arab states, considering the American moral commitment to Israel, were as good as could be expected. Except for Cuba, the Latin American republics remained friendly to the United States. In the Far East, relations with America's partners, South Korea, Japan, and Formosa, were excellent (they were still nonexistent with the Chinese). South Vietnam seemed well on the road to becoming a viable nation.

What Eisenhower had done best was managing crises. The crisis with Syngman Rhee in early 1953, and the simultaneous crisis with the Chinese Communists over the POW issue and the armistice; the crisis over Dien Bien Phu in 1954, and over Quemoy and Matsu in 1955; the Hungarian and Suez crises of 1956; the Sputnik and Little Rock crises of 1957; the Formosa Resolution crisis of 1958; the Berlin crisis of 1959; the U-2 crisis of 1960—Eisenhower managed each one without overreacting, without going to war, without increasing defense spending, without frightening people half out of their wits. He downplayed each one, insisted that a solution could be found, and then found one. It was a magnificent performance.

CHAPTER TWENTY-THREE

Elder Statesman

THROUGH THE war years, through the time of his service in Washington as Chief of Staff, in New York at Columbia, in Paris with SHAPE, and through the eight years of his Presidency, Ike had fantasized about his retirement. He thought that perhaps he would write an occasional article on some national issue, play a lot of golf and bridge, but mainly concentrate on taking it easy. After a half century of service to the nation, he was, he insisted, bone tired, and had to have some rest. No more meetings, no more speeches, no more conferences, no more decisions to make. George Washington at Mount Vernon was his model.

Ike's Mount Vernon was his farm at Gettysburg. Both he and Mamie loved the farm and the area. The climate, except in winter, was temperate. The location was ideal. They lived in a rural setting, but close enough to Washington and New York for occasional trips to those cities, and convenient for their friends to come to them for weekend visits. The farm was on the edge of the battlefield, which enhanced the sense of being a part of the continuity of American history. Because of its location, there were tourists to put up with—every visitor to the battlefield, it seemed, wanted to see the Eisenhower farm too, and most of them hoped to catch a glimpse and take a picture of the former President walking on his land. Ike enjoyed this visible proof that he had not been forgotten. When he went into town, people would take his picture, or ask for an autograph, or assure him that they had voted for him. He complained about it, but immediately added, "Suppose people didn't like us. That would be terrible, wouldn't it?" [1]

The home had a colonial appearance on the outside, but all the modern conveniences inside. The glass-enclosed sun porch was perfect for reading or painting. The furnishings were elegant, the pick of the hundreds of gifts Eisenhower had received over the years from heads of state and American millionaires. Mamie had a priceless collection of Boehm porcelain birds in one room, of which she was very proud but about which Ike would only comment, "God, wouldn't you hate to have to dust them." Through the presidential years, Ike had hardly seen Mamie during daylight; at Gettysburg, he made up for it by spending long hours with her on the sun porch, overlooking the green fields, reading, watching television, or painting.

When the gang or other guests came for a visit, Ike did the cooking, because the only thing Mamie knew how to make, aside from broiling a steak or baking a potato, was fudge. "I was never permitted in the kitchen when I was a young girl," she explained. Otherwise, she was a devoted wife, who appreciated Ike's protective attitude toward her. "For any marriage to be successful," she told one reporter, "you must work at it. Young women today want to prove something but all they have to prove is that they can be a good wife, housekeeper, and mother. There should be only one head of the family—the man." "As for spats," she told the same reporter, "if a quarrel develops, one should leave the room. It takes two to quarrel."

John, Barbara, and the grandchildren lived on a farm in a small home of their own about a mile away. Eisenhower was extremely proud of his only son. Mamie and Barbara were very close and happy in their relationship; the Eisenhowers related to Barbara as a daughter, rather than a daughter-in-law. But it was David, Barbara Anne, Susan, and Mary Jean who gave them their greatest joy. "I just love having them around," Mamie declared. "The girls try on my clothes and watch TV with me. We do a lot of talking and laughing." Inevitably, David was his grandfather's favorite. "When he was smaller we spent more time together," Eisenhower told one reporter. "Today, he likes baseball, football, and soccer, like other boys his age, but these are things I can no longer do with him. I do go fishing, skeet shooting, and play golf with him. And often we just sit around and talk seriously." He was aware of the potential for problems arising from the close proximity of the two families. "Grandparents should be helpful," he admonished a reporter (and himself and Mamie), "but not busybodies. They should help out with their grandchildren's education if they can, but under no circumstances should they get in the way and become prime ministers for them. That's the one way to ruin your children's marriage."[2]

There were many trips, beginning immediately after January 20, 1961. In February of that year, the Eisenhowers took a train to Palm Desert, California, where they stayed on the ranch of Floyd Odlum and his wife, Jacqueline Cochran, the famous aviator who had played a key role in persuading Ike in 1952 to run for the Presidency. Ike intended to just play some golf and bridge and generally relax, but he discovered that he could not put national affairs out of his mind. Riding his electric cart around the golf course at Eldorado, he turned on the radio and listened to an account of Colonel John Glenn's around-the-world astronaut flight. Slater felt that Eisenhower was "a little disappointed that the trip hadn't been made during his administration." He also confessed that he was terribly unhappy about the "careless spending" of the Kennedy Administration, and its "complete lack of interest in the soundness of the dollar and the disregard of what inflation will do to the savers." He was also concerned about Kennedy's "build up of the military, the space scientists and armament industries." Eisenhower warned that "this combination can be so powerful and the military machine so big it just has to be used."[3]

As the quotations indicate, after all those years at the center of power, making the decisions, Eisenhower was finding it difficult to relegate himself to an observer's role. His major concern, however, was less with shaping the future, more with justifying the past, and specifically his own Administration. But writing his presidential memoirs proved to be a much more difficult task than writing *Crusade* had been. *Crusade* had been the story of an unqualified success with a definitive and happy ending, but the White House memoirs covered issues that were still ongoing, the outcome of which no one knew— Cuba, Laos, Vietnam, disarmament, nuclear testing, and so forth. The cast of characters in *Crusade* was relatively limited; in the presidential memoirs, it was endless. Eisenhower found something good to say about almost everyone who appeared in *Crusade,* even Montgomery, and found little cause for the slightest disparagement of his associates, which was not at all the case in his White House memoirs, but he hated to be critical. *Crusade* covered three and a half tightly compressed years, as compared to the eight years in the White House.

Further, in *Crusade* he could tell the story of making a decision, then show how it worked in action, but the situation for the presidential memoirs was more a case of describing a decision made, followed by inaction. That is, he decided not to expand the war in Korea, not to enter the war in Vietnam at the time of Dien Bien Phu, not to accelerate the arms race, not to attack McCarthy directly, or support *Brown* v. *Topeka,* or dismantle the New Deal, or lower taxes, or support the British and the French at Suez, or intervene in Hungary. The two-volume White House memoirs, in short, necessarily had to be negative and inconclusive, while *Crusade* had been positive and conclusive.

Despite their shortcomings, *Mandate for Change* and *Waging Peace* (together titled *The White House Years*) represented a major effort, and they made a major contribution. Neither as salty nor as personal as Truman's memoirs, they nevertheless did cover all the major and most of the minor issues of the Eisenhower Administration. There were few if any errors of fact, a remarkable achievement in a manuscript of nearly three thousand pages, and a tribute to the thoroughness and accuracy of the research effort. The memoirs did achieve what Eisenhower most wanted them to achieve—he got to explain his side of the story and present his motivation in making this or that decision. They therefore immediately became, as they remain, one of the starting points for any serious study of the politics of the 1950s.

Following the publication of the White House memoirs, editors at Doubleday persuaded Eisenhower to write a more informal autobiography, covering those parts of his life not touched upon in *Crusade* or *The White House Years.* In preparing the book, Eisenhower reverted to his old practice of dictating personally. He thoroughly enjoyed going back in his mind to his boyhood days in Abilene, his years as a cadet at West Point, and his experiences as a young officer. He paid handsome tributes to Fox Conner, Douglas MacArthur, George Marshall, to his parents and his brothers, his high school teachers, and his fellow junior officers. He told some funny stories, and some sad ones, and some revealing ones. He called the book *At Ease: Stories I Tell to Friends,* and it received a much warmer reception, and enjoyed far higher sales and more translations, than *The White House Years.*

April was planting time, and in 1961 by the beginning of the month the Eisenhowers were back at Gettysburg, preparing for the new season. On the seventeenth, Bissell's paramilitary force of Cuban refugees, now grown to some two thousand strong, landed at the Bay of Pigs in Cuba. Deprived of air cover or reinforcements, operating with inadequate communications equipment, the men were quickly killed or captured by Castro's armed forces. It was a debacle.

Kennedy called Eisenhower. Could Eisenhower come to Camp David for consultation? Of course, Eisenhower replied, and on April 22 he flew by helicopter from Gettysburg to Camp David. Kennedy met him when he landed, and the two men went to the terrace at Aspen Cottage to talk. Kennedy described the planning, objectives, and anticipated results of the landing, confessed that it had been a total failure, and said the causes of the failure were gaps in intelligence plus some errors in ship loading, timing, and tactics.

The two men began strolling around the grounds, heads bent, deep in conversation. Eisenhower had the impression that Kennedy "looked upon the Presidency as not only a very personal thing, but as an institution that one man could handle with an assistant here and another there. He had no idea of the complexity of the job." Eisenhower asked Kennedy, "Mr. President, before you approved this plan did you have everybody in front of you debating the thing so you got pros and cons yourself and then made your decision, or did you see these people one at a time?" Kennedy confessed that he had not had a full meeting of the NSC to discuss and criticize the plans. He seemed to Eisenhower to be "very frank but also very subdued and more than a little bewildered." He said to Eisenhower, ruefully, "No one knows how tough this job is until after he has been in it a few months." Eisenhower looked at Kennedy, then said softly, "Mr. President, if you will forgive me, I think I mentioned that to you three months ago." Kennedy replied, "I certainly have learned a lot since."

Eisenhower asked Kennedy why on earth he had not provided air cover for the invasion. Kennedy replied that "we thought that if it was learned that we were really doing this rather than these rebels themselves, the Soviets would be very apt to cause trouble in Berlin." Eisenhower gave him another long look, then said, "Mr. President, that is exactly the opposite of what would really happen. The Soviets follow their own plans, and if they see us show any weakness then is when they press us the hardest. The second they see us show strength and do something on our own, then is when they are very cagey. The failure of the Bay of Pigs will embolden the Soviets to do something that they would not otherwise do."

"Well," Kennedy responded, "my advice was that we must try to keep our hands from showing in the affair." Eisenhower, astounded, snapped back, "Mr. President, how could you expect the world to believe that we had nothing to do with it? Where did these people get the ships to go from Central America to Cuba? Where did they get the weapons? Where did they get all the communications and all the other things that they would need? How could you possibly have kept from the world any knowledge that the United States had been assisting the invasion? I believe there is only one thing to do when you go into this kind of thing. It must be a success."

Kennedy seized on the last sentence. "Well," he said, "I assure you that hereafter, if we get in anything like this, it is going to be a success." Eisenhower, pleased, replied, "Well, I am glad to hear that." The former President then told Kennedy, "I will support anything that has as its objective the prevention of Communist entry and solidification of bases in the Western Hemisphere," but also gave him warning: "I believe the American people will never approve direct military intervention, by their own forces, except under provocations against us so clear and so serious that everybody will understand the need for the move."[4]

Eisenhower's unhappiness with Kennedy was increased by one of Kennedy's responses to the Bay of Pigs. Kennedy challenged the Russians to a race to the moon. Eisenhower thought that a terrible mistake, and said so, although only in private. Nevertheless his criticisms got through to the NASA astronauts, and one of them, Major Frank Borman, wrote Eisenhower about it in June of 1965.

Eisenhower sent Borman a long, careful reply. "What I have criticized about the current space program," he said, "is the concept under which it was drastically revised and expanded just after the Bay of Pigs fiasco." Eisenhower gave it as his judgment that the challenge to the Russians to race to the moon was "unwise." American prestige should not have been put on the line in that fashion, because "it immediately took one single project or experiment out of a thoughtfully planned and continuing program involving communication, meteorology, reconnaissance, and future military and scientific benefits and gave the highest priority—unfortunate in my opinion—to a race, in other words, a stunt." As a result, Eisenhower said, "costs went up drastically," while the benefits of the space program were lost.[5]

On October 14, 1963, Ike celebrated his seventy-third birthday. He had been in and out of Walter Reed a half-dozen times since he left the White House, but never stayed more than a few days, as all the ailments were minor ones. His general physical condition, for a man his age who had suffered a major heart attack, a stroke, and undergone major surgery for ileitis, was excellent. He was playing golf regularly, walking about his farm, puttering in his garden, keeping active.

Shortly after Ike moved permanently to Gettysburg, John wrote that he was "shocked and worried at the Old Man's demeanor." To John, his father's movements were slower, his tone less sharp, "and he had time even during the work day to stop and indulge in what would formerly be considered casual conversation. I feared for his health." But, John soon realized, he was wrong—it was simply that his father was relaxed, more so than he had ever been. Ellis Slater thought that Ike "has seldom looked better—[he] seems quite relaxed." He got tired sooner and more often than in the past, but he still had that remarkable ability to bounce back after a good night's sleep. His mind was as sharp as ever, as was his interest in and concern about public affairs.[6]

His friends were passing from the scene. In March 1962, Pete Jones died. After the funeral, the Eisenhowers flew to Baja California, with what remained of the gang, for some fishing, shooting, and bridge. Ike got up at 5 A.M. each morning in order to be in the ravines when the white-wing doves started flying shortly after sunrise. One day he shot a dozen, the next sixteen, and on the following morning he killed thirty birds, tops in the group. After the shoot, he went marlin fishing, where he was again successful, then spent the afternoons swimming in the pool and the evenings playing bridge.

Ike and his gang were well looked after; in addition to Moaney, there was a Mexican manager, a cook, three maids, four workers to handle luggage and other chores, three planes and pilots, two boats with crews, and a platoon from the Mexican Army to arrange for the jeeps to drive to the ravines for the shooting. The pilots flew over the Gulf of California, at Ike's request, so that he could observe the whales nursing their calves. Ike stayed in Baja for two weeks; when he was not otherwise occupied, he wrote articles for *Reader's Digest* and *The Saturday Evening Post* on the futility of summit meetings and the importance of fiscal responsibility. Taken all together, it was exactly the way he had envisioned his retirement. And, it might be said, exactly the kind of a retirement most Americans thought he deserved and ought to have.

Certainly Eisenhower's rich friends thought so. Beginning in the winter of 1961–1962, the Eisenhowers took a train each year to Palm Desert, where a home was provided for them by one friend, while

Jackie Cochran and Floyd Odlum provided the general with an office and made their ranch available to him for entertaining his friends (at their expense). Another friend provided him with a car.

The office was appallingly busy. In his retirement, Ike received an average of seventy-five hundred letters a month; he claimed to answer two-thirds of the mail. It proved to be too much for Ann Whitman. He insisted on dictating to her alone—during the White House years, she was the only human being he ever dictated to. Whitman was accustomed to handling the load, but when her boss was the President, she had twelve typists she could call on. At Palm Desert, and in Gettysburg, she had only two, and unlike the secretaries in the White House, they refused to work more than eight hours a day, five days a week, which meant Whitman had to carry an enormous typing load. Cochran commented that "Ann didn't even take time to eat. I never saw anybody put in the hours that she did in my life." Ike hardly noticed. He was so accustomed to people knocking themselves out for him that he took it for granted.

There was another problem. During the White House years, Mamie seldom saw Whitman, but at Palm Desert and Gettysburg, they were often together. The two women shared a single obsession, Dwight Eisenhower. He took both of them for granted, but they were competitors for his attention, or so it seemed to Mamie, who resented the way in which her husband relied on Whitman. "There was," Cochran remembered, "a lot of dissension between Ann and Mamie."[7] At the end of that first winter in Palm Desert, Whitman joined Rockefeller in New York, which made the general distinctly unhappy. Thereafter, he had little contact with the woman who had given so much of her life to serving him, a woman who had been indispensable when he was President.

By the fall of 1963, conditions in South Vietnam, which had seemed so stable when Eisenhower left office, had deteriorated badly. A major insurgency was under way. Kennedy had committed nearly sixteen thousand American troops to the country, but political intrigue in Saigon continued and intensified. There was a military coup; one result was the assassination of Diem, the man who had generated such enthusiasm in Eisenhower back in 1954 and in the following years. There was speculation that the CIA was involved in the assassination. Eisenhower commented on the subject in a letter to Nixon. "I rather suspect the Diem affair will be shrouded in mystery for a long time to come," he began. "No matter how much the Administration may have differed with him, I cannot believe any American would have approved the cold-blooded killing of a man who had, after all, shown great courage when he undertook the task some years ago of defeating Communists' attempts to take over his country."[8]

Within the month, there was another assassination, equally mysterious and far more shocking. On November 22, 1963, Eisenhower was in New York for a luncheon at the U.N. when he received the news of Kennedy's death.

The following day, November 23, Eisenhower went to Washington to view Kennedy's casket and to pay his respects to the widow. Then, at the request of the new President, he crossed the street and went to the Executive Office Building for a conference with Lyndon Johnson.

As Richard Nixon once noted, Dwight Eisenhower "was not the kind of man who appreciated undue familiarity." He would give chilling looks to anyone who tugged at his arm or tried to slap him on the back. Lyndon Johnson was the kind of man who could not resist pulling, tugging, slapping, or punching the people he was talking to. Jerry Persons remembered the time, in 1959, when Eisenhower had an appointment with Johnson. "I want you to stand between Lyndon and me," Eisenhower told Persons. "My bursitis is kicking up, and I don't want him to grab me by the arm."[9]

But grab Johnson did, figuratively if not literally. At their meeting the day after Kennedy's assassination, Johnson indicated to Eisenhower that he intended to call on him regularly for advice and support. As a beginning, he asked for a memorandum containing specific suggestions. Eisenhower responded that night with a dictated message. He suggested that Johnson call a joint session of Congress to make a speech of not more than ten minutes. "Point out first that you have come to this office unexpectedly and you accept the decision of the Almighty," Eisenhower advised, then promise that "no revolution in purpose or policy is intended or will occur." Further, promise a balanced budget.[10]

During his first years as President, Johnson concentrated on domestic affairs. In that area, his policies and programs were far too liberal for Eisenhower. Knowing this, Johnson did not ask Eisenhower's advice or opinions, although he did send birthday and anniversary presents, Christmas greetings, and the like, always writing in a humble and subservient manner. His attempts to ingratiate himself included innumerable invitations to come to the White House for lunch or for dinner parties, sending Mamie flowers on any excuse, and promoting Goodpaster to three-star rank (not that Goodpaster did not deserve it, but Johnson was careful to let Eisenhower know that he had done it as a favor). In February 1964, Johnson went hundreds of miles out of his way to pay his respects at Palm Desert.

Johnson started a practice of writing or calling Eisenhower on the telephone before every significant act, both to report on what he intended to do and to seek Eisenhower's support and to ask his advice. Although Johnson's letters to Eisenhower were so full of overblown praise and gratitude as to be obsequious and phony, Johnson was quite sincere in his requests for Eisenhower's counsel, to which he gave great weight. Johnson had, after all, come to the White House almost completely innocent of any experience in foreign affairs. All through the fifties he had deferred to Eisenhower's judgment on virtually every foreign-policy crisis. Like almost everyone else in politics, he regarded General Eisenhower as the nation's greatest and wisest soldier. He was obviously aware of how valuable Eisenhower's public support of his Vietnam policy could be to him, and he was not above using Eisenhower for his own purposes in this regard, but the record makes it absolutely clear that as Johnson made his crucial decisions on the conduct of the war in Vietnam, he both sought and was influenced by Ike's advice—except on the basic question of the wisdom of fighting in Vietnam.

It is equally true that Ike's advice was consistently hawkish, and that the main thrust of Eisenhower's criticism of Johnson on Vietnam —insofar as he was critical rather than supportive—was that Johnson was not doing enough. That had also been true of Ike's criticism of Kennedy's foreign policy; in both instances, Ike was far more belligerent, more ready to take extreme action, as an outsider than he had been when he was the man on the spot.

In 1964, Johnson began Operation Rolling Thunder, the bombing of North Vietnam. He also began sending in American combat units, as opposed to advisers. On March 12, 1965, Ike wrote him to pledge his full support and to assure him that he was doing the right thing. Johnson replied that "you are in my thoughts always and it is so valuable to me to have your thoughts, interest, and friendship." [11]

Beginning in April of 1965, Johnson sent Goodpaster to Palm Desert or Gettysburg on a biweekly basis to give Ike a detailed briefing on what was happening, and to seek his advice. These meetings usually lasted two to three hours. At the first such meeting, Ike told Goodpaster that "he strongly recommended getting rid of restrictions and delaying procedures. These result in many cases from attempts to control matters in too much detail from Washington. Such practices normally result from inexperience on the part of governmental officials." Ike urged Goodpaster to tell Johnson to "untie Westmoreland's hands." The President should give General William Westmoreland, who had recently become the commander in Vietnam, whatever he requested, then leave him to fight the war. He thought this was "absolutely essential." [12]

At a June 16 briefing in Gettysburg, Goodpaster said that the President wanted Ike's views on the proper use and size of reinforcements being sent to Vietnam. The JCS wanted to send only one brigade of the air mobile division, and use it to defend coastal base areas. Westmoreland wanted the entire division, and he wanted to use it to operate offensively within South Vietnam. Ike "considered the matter at some length." He then commented that "we have now appealed to force in South Vietnam, and therefore we have got to win. For this purpose, simply holding on or sitting passively in static areas will not suffice. He added that there is no use building bases if they are not put to full use. The only reason for creating them is to make it possible to take the offensive and clear the area." He therefore concluded that "General Westmoreland's recommendation should be supported," and added that "he was strongly impressed by General Westmoreland." [13]

On July 2, 1965, Eisenhower called Johnson on the telephone. Senators Robert Kennedy and Mike Mansfield were becoming increasingly critical of the escalation. Eisenhower urged Johnson to ignore them. "When you once appeal to force in an international situation involving military help for a nation," he said, "you have to go all out! This is war, and as long as the enemy are putting men down there, my advice is do what you have to do!" He advised Johnson to tell the Russians that if they did "not bring about some understanding we will have to go all out."

At this point Johnson asked Eisenhower, in a plaintive voice, "Do you really think we can beat the Viet Cong?" It was his first confession of uncertainty, at least to Eisenhower. Ike was cautious in his reply. He said it was hard to tell, that it depended on how far the North Vietnamese and Chinese were willing to go, and what Johnson was willing to do. As far as Ike was concerned, "We are not going to be run out of a free country that we helped to establish." Johnson, still gloomy, said that if he escalated further, "we will lose the British and Canadians and will be alone in the world." Ike snapped back, "We would still have the Australians and the Koreans—and our own convictions."

Then, as secretary Rusty Brown recorded the conversation, "President Johnson said he wanted General Eisenhower to think about this as he wanted the best advice possible and General Eisenhower is the best Chief of Staff he has." Eisenhower's advice was to go for victory.[14]

Through August of 1965, Eisenhower remained extremely hawkish. On the third, he told Goodpaster, "We should not base our action on minimum needs, but should swamp the enemy with overwhelming force." He wanted to "mine the harbors without delay, telling the world to keep shipping out of Haiphong and making clear that there is to be no sanctuary." He complained that "there seems to him to be too much of a brake on everything we do." Goodpaster said the JCS were worried about getting overextended in Vietnam, which might tempt the Russians to attack in Europe. "General Eisenhower said he was not concerned over this point. If we were to become involved in war in Europe, he would not be for sending large forces into the area, but would be for using every bomb we have."[15]

On August 20, after Goodpaster reported on a "search and destroy" mission in Chulai, Eisenhower said that that was "the way to do it. It was highly professional, overwhelming and quick." He told Goodpaster to tell Johnson "that there is no question about his support for what the President is doing. He supports it strongly."[16]

By October 1965, Johnson's major ground reinforcements were beginning to move into Vietnam. Ike was enthusiastic. He told Goodpaster, "We must now be sure to put in enough to win. He would err on the side of putting in too much rather than too little. He thought that overwhelming strength on our side would discourage the enemy, as well as keep down casualties." Ike did warn that sending conscripted troops to Vietnam would cause a major public-relations problem, and he thought Johnson should try to avoid it by sending only regulars or volunteers. Goodpaster responded that there just were not enough of either category.[17]

In January 1966, Johnson wanted Ike's advice on a suggestion that some of the "old heads," retired general officers from World War II, be consulted about operations in Vietnam. Eisenhower was opposed. "He stated that there is no better man than Westmoreland. The thing to do is give him the means and let him alone to the maximum possible extent." Two weeks later, Johnson asked, through Goodpaster, what Ike thought about the idea of adopting an "enclave" strategy, i.e., digging in around the bases and cities while abandoning offensive operations in the hinterland. "General Eisenhower indicated he would have nothing to do with such proposals. They would put us in a situation where hope of a successful outcome would be lost. They in fact could only result in complete failure on our side."[18]

Ike's impatience over Johnson's gradual application of pressure on the Communists, and his concern over the way in which the Johnson Administration centralized the decision-making power, not allowing Westmoreland the free hand Eisenhower thought he had to have, were growing daily.

Further, Eisenhower was beginning to worry that as the war dragged on, popular support for it would wane. On September 19, Goodpaster recorded that "General Eisenhower said he had been seeing various statements implying that 'small wars,' or hostilities such as those in Vietnam, could go on almost indefinitely. Some comments in fact suggest that such a condition must be regarded as normal, and that our society must be geared to support this as well as other ongoing problems." Ike would not accept such a view. "He felt this is not something that can go on and on, but is something that should rather be brought to an end as soon as possible. He commented that our people inevitably get tired of supporting involvements of this kind which go on for a long time, with no end in sight."[19]

But although he predicted and anticipated antiwar protests, as they increased in volume so did Eisenhower's anger. "Frankly," he wrote Nixon in October 1966, "it seems that the Vietnam War is creating more whimperings and whinings from some frustrated partisans than it's inspiring a unification of all America in the solution of a national problem." And he complained about "the selfish and cowardly whimperings of some of these 'students' who—uninformed and brash though they are—arrogate to themselves the right to criticize, irresponsibly, our highest officials, and to condemn America's deepest commitments to her international friends."[20]

No matter how strident the antiwar protests, however, Eisenhower could not believe that America would cut and run. In February 1967, he wrote George Humphrey (who had told him that his fear was that Johnson would negotiate an agreement and "bring the boys home," thereby winning re-election), "America has invested a lot of lives in Vietnam. I cannot believe the nation will be satisfied with any agreement that our people would recognize as 'phony,' or which the Communists would soon, and with impunity, violate."[21]

Ike wanted victory, not negotiations. And he wanted it soon. In

April 1967, he told Goodpaster to tell Johnson that "a course of 'gradualism' . . . is bound to be ineffective." To make his point, he used one of his favorite examples: If a general sent a battalion to take a hill, he might get the hill, but would suffer heavy casualties in the process, whereas if he sent a division, the casualties would be minimal.[22]

In July, Eisenhower's frustrations were such that he told reporters how opposed he was to a "war of gradualism," and urged Congress to declare war against North Vietnam. That war, he said, "should be given first priority. Other goals, however attractive, should take second place." In October, he said the country should "take any action to win." Asked if he would draw the line at the use of nuclear weapons, he replied, "I would not automatically preclude anything. When you appeal to force to carry out the policies of America abroad there is no court above you."[23]

On November 28, 1967, Eisenhower and Bradley made a television broadcast from Gettysburg over NBC. Together with Truman, the two old generals had joined a short-lived group called the Citizens Committee for Peace with Freedom in Vietnam. Bradley defined the object of the committee as to help the American people understand the war, because "when they understand it, they will be for it, we think." Eisenhower argued that a military victory was possible if certain changes in strategy and tactics were made. "This respecting of boundary lines on the map," he said; "I think you can overdo it." He suggested a foray into North Vietnam "either from the sea or from the hills . . . I would be for what we call 'hot pursuit' " into Cambodia or Laos. He ended with a curt dismissal of the " 'kooks' and 'hippies' and all the rest that are talking about surrendering."[24]

But it was not just kooks and hippies who wanted out, as Eisenhower well knew. He told Goodpaster privately that "many of the people who see him—neither 'hawks' nor 'doves'—are talking in terms of discouragement about the course of the war in Vietnam. They say that nothing seems to be going well and that, perhaps, it would be better to get out of it than to continue." Goodpaster responded with a pep talk—things were going well, he insisted, and there was an end in sight. Ike was encouraged. "He said he is optimistic that we can win this war."[25]

Another presidential election was coming up. The agony of Vietnam was obviously going to be a major issue. In October 1967, Eisenhower spoke in general terms about the kind of candidates he wanted to see nominated. "I don't regard myself as a missionary, and I don't

want to convert anybody," he said. "But if any Republican or Democrat suggests that we pull out of Vietnam and turn our backs on the
more than thirteen thousand Americans who died in the cause of
freedom there, they will have me to contend with. That's one of the
few things that would start me off on a series of stump speeches
across the nation."[26]

In early 1968, Eisenhower wrote an article on the war for *Reader's
Digest.* "The current raucous confrontation," he wrote of the antiwar
movement, "goes far beyond honorable dissent . . . it is rebellion, and
it verges on treason. . . . I will not personally support any peace-at-
any-price candidate who advocates capitulation and the abandonment of South Vietnam."[27]

Simultaneously, the Communists launched their Tet offensive.
They suffered extraordinarily heavy casualties, but the reaction in
the United States verged on panic. No one had anticipated the offensive, or so it appeared, nor had anyone suspected that the Viet Cong
were so numerous and well coordinated. It all reminded Eisenhower
of the reaction to the Battle of the Bulge. He recalled that in December 1944, when he asked for reinforcements to follow up the victory
in the Ardennes, the Allied governments had provided the men he
needed to finish the job. But in 1968, rather than send Westmoreland
the reinforcements he wanted to follow up his victory, the Johnson
Administration put a ceiling on manpower commitments to Vietnam.
In New Hampshire, meanwhile, Senator Eugene McCarthy, running
on an antiwar platform, did surprisingly well in the Democratic primary against Johnson, and Senator Robert Kennedy entered the race
against the President.

Johnson had promised Eisenhower that he would persevere, but
he went on national television to announce that he was halting the
bombing of most of North Vietnam, and that he was personally withdrawing from the presidential race. Eisenhower was filled with anger,
his remarks about Johnson's cutting and running unprintable. Goodpaster went on to a new assignment, and Eisenhower's connection
with the Johnson Administration came to an end.

Vietnam was the main, but not the only, cause of unhappiness
for Eisenhower in the mid-sixties. Longhairs, hippies, rock music,
extensive drug use by teen-agers, and riots in the ghettos were, to
Eisenhower, deplorable. He wrote a British friend in 1965, "Lack of
respect for law, laxness in dress, appearance, and thinking, in conduct and in manner, as well as student and other riots with civil

disobedience all spring from a common source; a lack of concern for the ancient virtues of decency, respect for law and elders, and old-fashioned patriotism."[28]

Like most older Americans, Eisenhower was appalled by many of the trends of the 1960s. Why could not the youth of the sixties be more like the youth of his day? Why were not draft dodgers an object of scorn, as they had been during World War II? Why could not the kids get their kicks out of the fox-trot and beer and cigarettes rather than rock and roll, marijuana, and LSD? Why was not Norman Rockwell, rather than Andy Warhol, the most popular artist of the day? Eisenhower expressed his concern over the decline in "our concept of beauty and decency and morality," over the use by Hollywood and book and magazine publishers of "vulgarity, sensuality, indeed downright filth, to sell their wares," over the sort of painting "that looks like a broken-down tin lizzie loaded with paint has been driven over it."[29]

A major reason for the decline in morality and good taste, he felt, was the decline in the quality of the nation's leadership. That at least could be set right in the 1968 presidential election. He could not escape a sense of personal responsibility for the Republican debacle in 1964, because of his failure to denounce Barry Goldwater or endorse a candidate of his own choosing, and he was determined not to make the same mistake again.

His candidate was Nixon, and in 1968, unlike 1960, he had no hesitancy about him. It was not so much that Nixon had gone up in his estimation—although he had—as it was a case of having no choice. The other contenders, Nelson Rockefeller, George Romney, and Barry Goldwater, were all for various reasons unacceptable, and in comparison to any Democratic candidate, Nixon was in Eisenhower's view light-years ahead.

As early as 1966, Eisenhower made his opinion public. In November of that year, just prior to the congressional elections, Johnson had issued a blast against Nixon, who was speaking around the country for Republican candidates. Johnson called Nixon a "chronic campaigner" who "never did really recognize and realize what was going on." As proof, Johnson cited a remark made in response to a journalist's request in a 1960 press conference for an example of a major idea of Nixon's adopted by Eisenhower. Ike had answered: "If you give me a week I might think of one." Eisenhower called Nixon from Gettysburg and said, "Dick, I could kick myself every time some jackass brings up that goddamn 'give me a week' business. Johnson has gone too far . . . I just wanted you to know that I'm issuing a statement down here." [30]

In the statement, which was widely reported, Eisenhower said he had "always had the highest personal and official regard" for Nixon, who was "one of the best-informed, most capable, and most industrious Vice-Presidents in the history of the United States and in that position contributed greatly to the sound functioning of our government. He was constantly informed of the major problems of the United States during my Administration. Any suggestion to the contrary or any inference that I at anytime held Dick Nixon in anything less than the highest regard and esteem is erroneous." [31] (It must be pointed out that somehow, whenever he talked about Nixon, Eisenhower could not get it to come out right. Thus in this case, in the key sentence, he did not say Nixon was "consulted" about the "major problems"; instead, the verb he used was "informed.")

On March 14, 1967, Eisenhower held an impromptu press conference at the Eldorado Country Club. The governor of California, Ronald Reagan, was with him. Reporters were clamoring for Eisenhower's attention. From one side, a reporter asked his opinion of Reagan; another newsman, on his other side, simultaneously asked his opinion of Nixon. Eisenhower turned to the man who had asked about Nixon and remarked that "he is one of the ablest men I know and a man I admire deeply and for whom I have great affection." Most of the other reporters, however, had heard only the question about Reagan, and assumed that Eisenhower was talking about the governor. Headlines the next day proclaimed that Eisenhower had said, "Governor Reagan is one of the men I admire most in the world." Walter Cronkite reported it that way on the evening television news. Eisenhower called to straighten him out; Cronkite, according to Eisenhower, "was chagrined to admit that his information came from a newspaper and he hoped sometime to change it." Eisenhower, however, was stuck; he could hardly issue a clarification saying that "Reagan is *not* one of the men I admire most in the world." In any case, he *did* admire Reagan; he told Arthur Larson he did not believe Reagan to be as much of a right-winger as he was portrayed to be. Still Nixon was his man. [32]

He made that clear to Republican politicians in private meetings and in his correspondence with them. His standard line (in this case to Fred Seaton of Nebraska) was, "I cannot think of anyone better prepared than Dick Nixon is to undertake the responsibilities of the Presidency." [33]

That was a bit short of an unqualified endorsement. Eisenhower did not say that Nixon was well prepared," or "completely capable," or anything like that, only that he was "better prepared" than anyone else. In March, when the gang came to Palm Desert for the annual visit with the Eisenhowers, the members got to talking politics. Slater recorded that "many of us are still resentful that Nixon did not run a better campaign in 1960 and all had one or more instances to report where things would have been better had he taken advice. The President (meaning Eisenhower) still doesn't understand why Nixon and Lodge didn't call on him for help and why they didn't take the position of wanting to continue the Eisenhower philosophy of how the country should be run." Still, considering the competition, Eisenhower and his friends concluded that "Nixon would probably make the best president." [34]

After President Eisenhower recovered from his September 1955 heart attack, the doctors had told him that there was no medical reason for him not to run for a second term, and they predicted that he could lead an active life for a period of as long as ten years. In November 1965, when he and Mamie were at Augusta for a week, he remarked one night that the ten years were up. The next day, in Mamie's cabin, he suffered a second heart attack. He was rushed to a nearby Army hospital, and two weeks later was transferred to Walter Reed. Recovery was slow, but for a seventy-five-year-old man who had been struck by two major heart attacks, surprisingly good. Soon the doctors were allowing him to play golf again, although they restricted him to a cart and to a par-three course.

Still, his heart was failing, and he knew it. He was a man who had spent his lifetime facing facts. The end was approaching, and he began to prepare for it. He dispersed his herd of Angus cattle and otherwise put his affairs in order. He had already decided he wanted to be buried in Abilene, where he had had a small Meditation Chapel built, just across the street from his childhood home and just west of the Eisenhower Library and Museum. It was a small, simple, dignified chapel constructed with native sandstone, quite in keeping with the quiet little town on the Plains. In 1967 he had Icky's body moved there from Fairmont Cemetery in Denver and placed at the foot of the area reserved for his body and Mamie's.

That winter, on his way to Palm Desert, Eisenhower stopped off in Abilene to visit the chapel. When he arrived in California, he was still upset and depressed, not at the thought of his own death, but by the tiny plaque on the floor over Icky's body, the physical reminder of what he and Mamie had lost in 1921 when four-year-old Icky died. He soon recovered his natural good spirits, helped by his friends, some good cards at bridge, and the opportunity to play golf in the lovely desert climate. Rather than grouse at being restricted to a par-three course, he made jokes about it, telling an old Abilene friend that "I suppose in another year I will be having to play the ladies' tees even on that course."[35] That winter he scored a hole in one, about which he bragged incessantly.

His thoughts were turning back toward his youth. Visitors noted that he was much more inclined to reminisce about his days as a cadet, or his childhood in Abilene, or his experiences as a junior officer, than he was about SHAEF or the White House. In April 1968, he heard that a proposed governmental reorganization plan included transferring all of the affairs of the American Battle Monuments Commission to the Veterans Administration. He immediately wrote President Johnson: "From my viewpoint, both as a junior officer who once served with the Battle Monuments Commission and as one who has followed its affairs over these many years, I hope that you will decline to approve this particular move."

His reason went beyond nostalgia. The commission was in charge of what surely must be some of the most beautiful cemeteries in the world. No American can visit them, especially the one at Omaha Beach, without feeling a surge of pride, so magnificently are they maintained. Eisenhower explained to Johnson that the cemeteries were closed to future burials, and that they were monuments rather than mere cemeteries. "Nearly all of them are in foreign countries and every one of them is precious to the families and relatives of those who died during those two world conflicts. The American Battle Monuments Commission has always maintained the highest possible standards in the care of these cemeteries." Johnson granted the request.[36]

Eisenhower wrote that letter from the hospital at March Air Force Base, because in April of 1968 he had suffered his third major heart attack. A month later, he had recovered enough strength to be moved to Ward Eight at Walter Reed. Despite his invalid status, he had not lost his flair for giving commands. He ordered the commanding officer at March to give the nurses accompanying him on the flight east a few days' leave in Washington before returning to their duties.

At Walter Reed, Eisenhower had the finest care the Army and modern medicine could provide. Mamie moved into a tiny room next to his suite. Dominated by a high hospital bed, it was cramped and uncomfortable, but it was where she wanted to be. (She would not consider living at Gettysburg alone; she once commented, "Whenever Ike went away, the house sagged. When he came home, the house was alive again.") For a woman who loved to surround herself with knickknacks and family photographs, it was surprisingly bare. She passed the time by sewing facecloths together and stuffing them with foam to make pillows for her friends.

By July, Eisenhower had recovered enough strength to take an active interest in the presidential campaign. He remained committed to Nixon, a commitment that was solidified by the courtship then going on between his grandson, David, and Nixon's daughter Julie. He decided to make a preconvention endorsement of Nixon. On July 15, when Nixon stopped in for a short visit, Eisenhower informed him of his decision.

Two days later, Eisenhower released his statement. He said he supported Nixon for the nomination "because of my admiration of his personal qualities: his intellect, acuity, decisiveness, warmth, and above all, his integrity." He sent Nixon a copy of the press release, with a handwritten note across the top: "Dear Dick—This was something I truly enjoyed doing—DE." [37]

The convention opened in Miami on August 5. That evening, Eisenhower put on a business suit, and television cameras were brought into Walter Reed. He gave a speech to the delegates, who stopped their usual frenetic activity for a few minutes and listened in respectful silence as he gave them some words of encouragement. The next morning, Eisenhower suffered yet another heart attack.

This attack took a new form. It did not cause additional muscle damage, but it did upset the rhythm of the heart, causing it to periodically go out of control and fibrillate. Instead of beating, it merely vibrated, pumping no blood. Whenever a fibrillation began, the doctors were able to restore rhythmic beating through electrical impulses. Everyone feared that this was the end. John and Barbara moved into the guesthouse at Walter Reed while their children stayed with friends around Washington. John began the detailed planning for the funeral. But, after a week, the fibrillations stopped, and soon Eisenhower was out of danger. He was even able to receive visitors again.

On Eisenhower's seventy-eighth birthday, the Army Band gathered outside his room to play a serenade for him. Eisenhower was wheeled to his bedroom window, where he acknowledged the tribute with a smile and a wave of a small five-star flag. His extreme weakness was obvious, and brought tears to everyone's eyes.

He was, however, calm and cheerful. He told John that his mind was eased because a law had been passed that provided widows of former Presidents lifetime Secret Service coverage. "This last August," he said, "when it looked like I might cash in my chips, my only worry was about Mamie. This puts my mind at rest on that count at least."

Nixon's victory in November was not by the margin Eisenhower had hoped for, but he was delighted that at least Nixon had won. In December, as Nixon began naming his Cabinet, he asked Eisenhower if he would receive each appointee. Eisenhower agreed, indeed told Nixon, "I am quite anxious to meet the ones I do not know." He also sent Nixon some advice on replacing Earl Warren, who had resigned, asking Nixon to destroy the memo after he read it (Nixon did not; it is now in the Eisenhower Library). Eisenhower suggested Herb Brownell, or elevating Potter Stewart up to Chief Justice and appointing William Rogers to the vacancy on the Court.[38]

As the end approached, his thoughts were increasingly with his family. For Thanksgiving, 1968, Mamie arranged for each member of the family to share the turkey feast with him. "With the precision of an Army drill instructor," Julie Nixon recalled, "Mamie arranged for members of each family [the Nixons as well as the Eisenhowers] to share a course of the meal with Ike in his bedroom." Susan Eisenhower and Tricia Nixon had juice with him, David and Julie shared the fruit cup, and so on, until Barbara Eisenhower and Pat Nixon joined him for the pumpkin pie. Julie was depressed by his appearance: "He was so thin and wasted under the Army-issue sheet. The blueness of his eyes was startling in his dead-white face."[39]

In December, Eisenhower watched on closed-circuit television the wedding of David Eisenhower and Julie Nixon. David's haircut by the standards of his contemporaries in the late sixties was extremely short and made him something of an object of ridicule, but his grandfather thought it much too long. Eisenhower offered his grandson $100 if he would get it cut before the wedding. David had it trimmed, but not short enough to satisfy his grandfather, who did not pay up.

Christmas and New Year's passed without any celebration by the

Eisenhowers, because Mamie had come down with a severe respiratory ailment, which confined her to bed for more than a month. By February, Eisenhower was taking a terrific beating. The doctors informed him that he would have to undergo a major abdominal operation. Complications had arisen from his ileitis operation of twelve years earlier; scar tissue had wrapped itself around his intestine, causing a blockage. The doctors were worried that his heart could not survive the ordeal, but it did. John visited him shortly after the operation.

"It's an eerie feeling," Eisenhower told his son, "to have them hit you with one thing and then another." "Well," John replied, "now that you've had that intestinal blockage taken out, you ought to start feeling better. Maybe now you can gain some weight."

"God, I hope so," Eisenhower sighed.[40]

On Monday, March 24, 1969, Eisenhower suffered a severe setback. His heart was failing. The doctors began giving him oxygen through tubes stuffed into his nose. He was aware that he was dying, and he wanted the end to come soon. He asked Billy Graham to come by; together they talked about spiritual matters.

He still had the old impulse to give something to those who served him. John had just published a book on the Battle of the Bulge entitled *The Bitter Woods,* which had made the best-seller list. Eisenhower ordered a dozen copies and had John autograph them, so that he could give them to the doctors and nurses who had taken care of him. He gave John last-minute instructions: "Be good to Mamie."

The evening of March 27, the electrocardiogram machine above his bed, which monitored his heartbeat, showed a slight improvement. When John came in to say good night, he told his father that the pattern of the cardiogram was a bit better. Eisenhower winced— he wanted his final release. John, in his turn, winced at the sight of his father; he wrote later that it "made me resolve to avoid ever being placed in a hospital where my life would be artificially prolonged."

All his life, Eisenhower had been a man of the most extraordinary energy. He had carried a burden of high command and decision making that was heavier, and lasted longer, than any other leader of the free world. Not even Roosevelt, not even Churchill, not even de Gaulle, had met the demands that Eisenhower had. For twenty years, on a daily basis, he had had to render judgments, make decisions, give orders at the highest level. The process had often left him exhausted. He had always bounced back after that miracle that is a soldier's night's sleep.

But he was tired now, more tired than he had ever been. No amount of sleep would help him bounce back. The ultimate weariness had descended.

He was a man born to command. On his deathbed, he was still in charge. On Friday morning, March 28, John, David, Mamie, the doctors, and a nurse gathered in his bedroom. Eisenhower looked at them. He barked out a command: "Lower the shades!" The light was hurting his eyes. The venetian blinds were pulled; the room became nearly dark.

"Pull me up," Eisenhower told John and one of the doctors. They propped up the pillows behind him and, one on each arm, raised him until they thought he was high enough. Eisenhower looked from side to side. "Two big men," he growled. "Higher." They pulled him higher.

Mamie grasped his hand. David and John stood stiffly at each corner of his bed. The electrocardiogram was fluttering.

Eisenhower looked at John. He said softly, "I want to go; God take me."[41] He was ready to go home, back to Abilene, back to the heart of America, from whence he came. His great heart stopped beating.

Epilogue

His place in history was fixed as night fell on the Normandy beaches on June 6, 1944. Hundreds of thousands, indeed millions, of men and women contributed to Overlord, and 200,000 soldiers, sailors, and airmen participated directly on D-Day itself, but the operation will forever be linked to one man, Dwight Eisenhower, and rightly so. From inception to completion, it bore his personal stamp. He was the central figure in the preparation, the planning, the training, the deception, and the organization of the greatest air and sea armada in history. At the decisive moment, he was the commanding general who, standing alone, weighed all the factors, considered all the alternatives, listened to the conflicting views of his senior subordinates, and then made the decision—and made the right one.

As a politician and statesman, his place in history is a more relative matter. He has to be judged against other Presidents, which means that no judgment can be really fair, because he did not have the opportunities, nor face the dangers, that other Presidents did. (As a general, of course, he had opportunities that others did not.) We cannot know how great a leader he might have been, because he ruled in a time that required him, at least in his own view, to adopt a moderate course, to stay in the middle of the road, to avoid calling on his fellow citizens for some great national effort.

He did not face the challenges that Washington did, or Lincoln, or Franklin Roosevelt. How he would have responded to a Civil War, or to a Depression, or to a world war, we cannot know. What we do know is that he guided his country safely and securely through a dangerous decade.

Shortly after Eisenhower left office, a national poll of academic American historians placed him nearly at the bottom of the list of Presidents. By the early 1980s a new poll placed him ninth. His reputation is almost certain to continue to rise, to the point that he will soon be ranked with Wilson and the Roosevelts as one of the four truly great Presidents of the twentieth century.

One of the measures of greatness in a President is the change he brings about that is permanent and that affects every citizen's life forever after. With Theodore Roosevelt, it was conservation; with Woodrow Wilson, it was the Federal Reserve System; with Franklin Roosevelt, it was Social Security; with Eisenhower, it was the Interstate Highway program. Each man did much more, of course, but these are the innovations that were unique to them and that will always be associated with their names.

In attempting to assess the Eisenhower Presidency, certain comparisons must be made. Since Andrew Jackson's day, only five men have served eight consecutive years or more in the White House—Grant, Wilson, Franklin Roosevelt, Eisenhower, and Ronald Reagan. Of these five, only two—Grant and Eisenhower—were world figures before they became President. Of the five, only three—Eisenhower, Roosevelt, and Reagan—were more popular when they left office than when they entered.

Eisenhower is unique in another way. In contrast to his Democratic predecessors and successors, Eisenhower kept the peace; in contrast to his Republican successors, Eisenhower both balanced the budget and stopped inflation.

Eisenhower gave the nation eight years of peace and prosperity. No other President in the twentieth century could make that claim. No wonder that millions of Americans felt the country was damned lucky to have him.

Whether or not one agrees with his decisions, such as the importance of a balanced budget or to go slow on race relations reform or to accept a stalemate in Korea and make peace, there is no doubt that he was an inspiring and effective leader, indeed a model of leadership.

Leadership did not come naturally to him. During the war, he wrote his son at West Point, "The one quality that can be developed by studious reflection and practice is the leadership of men." The elements of leadership, as practiced by Dwight Eisenhower, were varied, deliberate, and learned. Richard Nixon called him "devious." Fred Greenstein, in his brilliant work *The Hidden-Hand Presidency*, called him a man whose "personal makeup was permeated by contrasts." Others have seen him as skillful and complex.

Yet he exuded simplicity. He deliberately projected an image of the folksy farm boy from Kansas. But in fact he was capable of a detached, informed, and exhaustive examination of problems and personalities, based on wide and sophisticated knowledge and deep study. He also projected a posture of being above politics, but he studied and understood and acted on political problems and considerations more rigorously than most lifelong politicians ever could.

His magnetic appeal to millions of his fellow citizens seemed to come about as a natural and effortless result of his sunny disposition. But he worked at his apparent artlessness. That big grin and bouncy step often masked depression, doubt, or utter weariness, for he believed it was the critical duty of a leader to always exude optimism.

For forty years, he chain-smoked cigarettes, up to eighty a day. At age fifty-eight, he quit cold turkey, and never again touched tobacco. Clearly he was a man of tremendous willpower. He used that willpower to conquer his own most negative characteristic, an awful temper.

Anger that is contrived, that is put on for show and a purpose, an actor's anger, can be an effective tool of leadership. It was one Dwight Eisenhower often used. But genuine anger, deep blind anger, is the enemy of leadership. Ike often felt it—with Monty, with McCarthy, with others—but he did not act on it. One way he controlled his anger was to do his best to follow his own rule, "Never question another man's motives. His wisdom, yes, but not his motives." He also tried to always assume the best about others, until shown otherwise.

He could do so consistently, even in a world full of high-powered men whose motives were often self-serving or base, because of his most outstanding personal characteristic. He was a man full of love, for life and for people.

No one ever caught this better than Richard Nixon, who observed on the day Eisenhower died that "everybody liked Ike" and that the reason was that "Ike loved everybody." Nixon went on to confess that he could scarcely believe such a thing was possible, because in his experience most politicians were men with "strong hatreds."[1] Lord knows that Nixon was a man full of such feelings.

But as for Eisenhower, the only man he ever really hated was Adolf Hitler.

As a political leader, Eisenhower rejected extremes. Deeply conservative in his own beliefs, he nevertheless instinctively sought the middle ground on every political problem. A favorite saying was that the extremes to the right and to the left on any political dispute are always wrong. Whether or not that principle is defendable as a philosophical position is debatable; that it works for the leader of a democracy is obvious.

But no matter how much of his effectiveness as a leader came from conscious study, reflection, and acting, no matter how correct he was in insisting that leadership is the one human quality that can be learned, it is clear that at least in his case his personality was a major contributing factor to his success.

There was, first of all, his intensity and concentration. He would naturally and effortlessly fix those clear blue eyes on a listener or a speaker, and he would draw the man in as the magnet attracts the bits of metal. He *looked* like an honest man with nothing to hide because he *was* an honest man. People trusted him because he was trustworthy.

Then there was the depth of his concern, the way he cared about people and events. Henry Kissinger gives a vivid example of this point. In early 1969, Nixon brought Kissinger to Walter Reed to meet Ike. Kissinger confesses that he brought with him to the meeting a typical academic's near-contempt for Eisenhower the President. In two of his books, he had deplored the vacuum of leadership in the 1950s. He quickly learned that Ike, although literally on his deathbed, knew rather more about leadership and about the realities of Washington politics than he had ever imagined when he was teaching political science up at Harvard.

Kissinger, more out of politeness than genuine curiosity, asked Ike's advice on how to coordinate national foreign policy making. Specifically he asked Ike's opinion of Lyndon Johnson's experiment with a State Department–dominated interdepartmental group. Eisenhower told him that the Defense Department would not "accept State Department domination of the national security process. It would either attempt end-runs or counterattack by leaking." Over the next five years, Kissinger learned how right Ike was.

Kissinger and Nixon returned to the hospital on February 2, 1969, to ask Eisenhower's opinion on the wisdom of the U.S. forcing Israeli concessions in the interest of peace in the Middle East. Ike was opposed; he thought the U.S. should stay out of the area. He also warned Nixon and Kissinger to be wary of leaks from National Security Council meetings. They thanked him and went off to an NSC meeting.

The next morning, Kissinger wrote in his memoirs, "I had not been in my office many minutes before an irate Eisenhower was on the phone. He had just read a *New York Times* story reporting that the NSC meeting had determined that the United States would not pursue a more active policy in the Middle East. With a vigor that belied my memory of his frailty—and a graphic vocabulary at variance with his sunny smile—he berated me for letting down the President by not restricting the number of participants."[2]

Beyond his concern, Eisenhower's self-confidence contributed greatly to his leadership ability. That self-confidence was based on his knowledge that he was smarter than other men, that he knew more, studied more, understood more, and thought things through more objectively. When he gave an order, he believed in it.

Because he believed in his decisions, he was enthusiastic about them. He liked to say that leadership was more than making good decisions—equally important was getting people to *want* to carry them out. As a football coach, as a general, as President, a large part of his success resulted from his ability to create a sense of team and get people to pull together for a common objective.

People liked to be around him. There were many reasons. First and most obviously, because he was who he was. Beyond that, there was that big gutsy laugh, that infectious lop-sided grin, that bouncy step. There was the genuine interest in and concern about others. There was that limitless curiosity, about people, places, and things. There was the pure enjoyment he got out of living.

People liked Ike because Ike liked life. People admired Ike, and worked for him, because he did great and good things for mankind. He was the general who truly hated war, but who hated the Nazis more. He was the President who made a peace and kept the peace and thus provided the conditions that made it possible for the American people to exercise their right to pursue happiness.

NOTES

FOREWORD

1. DE to Swede Hazlett, 12/8/54, EL.

CHAPTER ONE

1. Kornitzer, *Great American Heritage*, 26.
2. Interview Milton S. Eisenhower.
3. Kornitzer, *Great American Heritage*, 26.
4. Interview DE.
5. Interview Milton S. Eisenhower.
6. Davis, *Soldier of Democracy*, 67–68.
7. DE, *At Ease*, 35.
8. Interview Milton S. Eisenhower
9. DE to Pelagius Williams, 10/30/47, EL.
10. DE, *At Ease*, 51–52.
11. *Ibid.*, 94–96.
12. *Ibid.*, 96–97; Kornitzer, *Great American Heritage*, 43–44; Davis, *Soldier of Democracy*, 79–80.
13. Kornitzer, *Great American Heritage*, 44; DE, *At Ease*, 97.
14. DE, *At Ease*, 18.
15. *Ibid.*, 19–20.
16. *The Howitzer*, 1915.
17. DE, *At Ease*, 17.
18. Neal, *The Eisenhowers*, 30.

19. DE, *At Ease*, 8.
20. *Ibid.*, 12.
21. *Ibid.*, 13–14.
22. *The Howitzer*, 1913.
23. Undated letters to Ruby Norman, EL.
24. Lyon, *Eisenhower*, 45; DE, *At Ease*, 16.
25. DE, *At Ease*, 16.
26. *Ibid.*, 113.
27. Neal, *The Eisenhowers*, 35; Hatch, *Red Carpet for Mamie*, 69–70.
28. Hatch, *Red Carpet for Mamie*, 73.
29. DE, *At Ease*, 123; Hatch, *Red Carpet for Mamie*, 97–98.
30. Neal, *The Eisenhowers*, 38.
31. Lt. Ed Thayer to his mother, 1/11/18, EL.
32. DE, *At Ease*, 137.
33. *Ibid.*
34. Davis, *Soldier of Democracy*, 177–78.
35. Miller, *Eisenhower*, 20.
36. Norman Randolph to DE, 6/20/45, EL.
37. Miller, *Eisenhower*, 173.
38. Davis, *Soldier of Democracy*, 180.

CHAPTER TWO

1. DE, *At Ease*, 169; Blumenson, *Patton Papers*, Vol. I.

2. Interview DE.
3. DE, *At Ease*, 181.
4. Neal, *The Eisenhowers*, 64–65.
5. Brandon, *Mamie Doud Eisenhower*, 126–32.
6. Neal, *The Eisenhowers*, 67.
7. DE, *At Ease*, 195; Davis, *Soldier of Democracy*, 197; McCann, *Man from Abilene*, 80.
8. DE, *At Ease*, 187; Brandon, *Mamie Doud Eisenhower*, 154; Conner's efficiency reports on DE are in EL.
9. John Eisenhower, *Strictly Personal*, 9–10; Brandon, *Mamie Doud Eisenhower*, 141.
10. DE, *At Ease*, 202–03.
11. John Eisenhower, *Strictly Personal*, 2.
12. Mrs. Doud to DE, 6/16/26, EL.
13. Patton to DE, 7/9/26, EL.
14. Interview Milton S. Eisenhower; Lyon, *Eisenhower*, 64.
15. Pershing to DE, 8/15/27, EL.
16. MacArthur's efficiency reports on DE are in EL.
17. James, *Years of MacArthur*, I, 564.
18. DE, *At Ease*, 214; Lyon, *Eisenhower*, 69.
19. DE Diary, 9/26/36 and 11/15/36. The diary is in EL.
20. DE, *At Ease*, 213.
21. Interview Merriman Smith.
22. DE, *At Ease*, 220–21.
23. MacArthur to DE, 9/30/35, EL.
24. DE to Milton S. Eisenhower, 1/3/39, EL.
25. DE Diary, 5/29/36.
26. *Ibid.*, 2/15/36.
27. Lyon, *Eisenhower*, 78.
28. DE Diary, 7/1/36.
29. James, *Years of MacArthur*, I, 505–06.
30. DE, *At Ease*, 225–26; Lyon, *Eisenhower*, 79.

31. Lyon, *Eisenhower*, 78.
32. MacArthur to DE, undated, EL; Quezon to DE, 3/10/37, EL.
33. DE to Milton S. Eisenhower, 9/3/39, EL.
34. Patton to DE, 10/1/40, EL.
35. DE to Gerow, 10/11/39, EL.
36. DE, *At Ease*, 231.
37. *Ibid.*, 240–41.
38. DE to Bradley, 7/1/40, EL.
39. DE to Gerow, 8/23/40, EL; DE, *At Ease*, 237.
40. DE, *At Ease*, 383–84.
41. DE to Hughes, 11/26/40, EL.
42. DE to Patton, 9/17/40, EL; Patton to DE, 10/1/40, EL.
43. Davis, *Soldier of Democracy*, 263.
44. *Ibid.*, 266–68.
45. *New York Times*, 9/17/40.
46. Davis, *Soldier of Democracy*, 272.
47. DE to Gerow, 10/25/41, EL.
48. DE to Nielsen, 10/31/40, EL.
49. Davis, *Soldier of Democracy*, 276.
50. Ambrose, *Supreme Commander*, 3.

CHAPTER THREE

1. Interview DE; Pogue, *Ordeal and Hope*, 237–39; DE, *Crusade*, 14–22; "Steps to be Taken" is reprinted in *Eisenhower Papers* (hereinafter cited as EP). The documents in the *Eisenhower Papers* are printed in chronological order; they will be cited by date only.
2. Interview DE; Pogue, *Ordeal and Hope*, 95–98.
3. DE Diary, 10/5/42; DE, *At Ease*, 248.
4. McKeogh and Lockridge, *Sergeant Mickey and General Ike*, 21.
5. DE Diary, 2/22/42.

6. *Ibid.,* 1/24 and 1/27/42.
7. *Ibid.,* 3/11 and 3/12/42.
8. Interview DE; DE, *At Ease,* 248–49.
9. DE Diary, 3/21/42.
10. *Ibid.,* 3/30/42; DE, *At Ease,* 250.
11. DE Diary, 2/23/42:
12. *Ibid.,* 1/6/53.
13. *Ibid.,* 1/30/42.
14. *Ibid.,* 1/17/42.
15. *Ibid.,* 1/17, 22, 27/42.
16. *Ibid.,* 4/20/42.
17. DE, *Crusade,* 50.
18. DE Diary, 5/27/42.
19. Bryant, *Turn of the Tide,* 285.
20. Pogue, *Ordeal and Hope,* 338–40; Lyon, *Eisenhower,* 123–24.
21. DE, *Crusade,* 50; Ambrose, *Supreme Commander,* 47.
22. DE to Akin, 6/19/42, EL.
23. Davis, *Soldier of Democracy,* 317, 322.
24. Butcher Diary, 6/26/42, EL.
25. DE, *At Ease,* 281–82.
26. DE Diary, 7/5/42.
27. Ambrose, *Supreme Commander,* 97.
28. DE memo, 7/19/42, EL.
29. Butcher Diary, 7/23/42, EL.
30. Ismay, *Memoirs,* 258.
31. *Ibid.,* 263.
32. Interview DE.
33. Interviews Frederick Morgan and Ian Jacob.
34. Interview Forrest Pogue.
35. Interview DE.
36. DE to Gailey, 9/19/42, EL.
37. DE, *Letters to Mamie,* 28.
38. *Ibid.,* 35.
39. *Ibid.*
40. *Ibid.,* 26, 41, 48, 50, 51.
41. *Ibid.,* 26–50.
42. DE Diary, 11/9/42.
43. Butcher Diary, 11/9/42, EL.
44. DE to John Eisenhower, 6/3/43, EL.
45. DE's draft introduction to *Crusade* is in EL.

CHAPTER FOUR

1. DE to Smith, 11/13/42, *EP.*
2. DE to John Eisenhower, 4/8/43, *EP.*
3. Macmillan, *Blast of War,* 174.
4. DE to William Lee, 10/29/42, *EP.*
5. DE, *Letters to Mamie,* 66.
6. Butcher Diary, 12/7/42.
7. Ambrose, *Supreme Commander,* 131.
8. DE to CCS, 11/14/42, EP; DE to Churchill, 11/14/42, *EP.*
9. Viorst, *Hostile Allies,* 122–23.
10. DE to Smith, 11/12/42, *EP.*
11. Patton to DE, 7/9/26, EL.
12. Butcher Diary, 12/9/42.
13. DE, *Crusade,* 126.
14. DE Diary, 12/10/42.
15. Butcher Diary, 12/9/42.
16. DE, *Letters to Mamie,* 63–68.
17. *Ibid.,* 74.
18. Lyon, *Eisenhower,* 174.
19. DE to CCS, 12/24/42, *EP.*
20. Ian Jacob Diary, 1/13/43, EL.
21. Bryant, *Turn of the Tide,* 452–55.
22. Tedder, *With Prejudice,* 400.
23. See *EP,* #811, note 2.
24. DE to Marshall, 2/8/43, *EP.*
25. DE, *Letters to Mamie,* 95–96.
26. DE to Fredendall, 2/4/43, *EP;* DE, *Crusade,* 141.
27. DE to Truscott, 2/16/43, *EP.*
28. DE to Marshall, 2/15/43, *EP.*
29. Blumenson, *Kasserine Pass,* 282–83; DE, *Crusade,* 145–46.
30. DE to Marshall, 2/15/43, *EP.*
31. DE to Patton, 3/6/43, *EP.*
32. DE to Gerow, 2/24/43, *EP.*
33. DE to Bradley, 4/16/43, *EP.*
34. Butcher Diary, 4/25/43.
35. DE, *Letters to Mamie,* 99.
36. DE to Arthur Eisenhower, 5/18/43, *EP;* DE to John Eisenhower, 5/22/43, *EP.*
37. DE to Marshall, 5/13/43, *EP.*

38. DE Diary, 6/11/43.
39. DE to Marshall, 4/19/43, *EP*.
40. Butcher Diary, 5/30/43.
41. Bryant, *Turn of the Tide*, 522.
42. Butcher Diary, 5/30/43.
43. DE, *Crusade*, 168.
44. Brandon, *Mamie Doud Eisenhower*, 218.
45. DE, *Letters to Mamie*, 128, 137.
46. *Ibid.*, 136.
47. Irving, *War Between the Generals*, 46–47.
48. *Ibid.*, 65.
49. DE, *Letters to Mamie*, 132.
50. DE to Marshall, 6/11/43, *EP*.
51. Butcher Diary, 7/8/43.
52. DE to Marshall, 7/9/43, *EP;* Garland and Smyth, *Sicily*, 108–09.
53. DE, *Letters to Mamie*, 134–35.
54. Butcher diary, 7/10/43.
55. Ambrose, *Supreme Commander*, 228–29.
56. DE to Patton, 8/17/43, *EP*.
57. Ambrose, *Supreme Commander*, 230–31.
58. *Ibid.*
59. Patton to DE, 8/29/43, *EP*.
60. DE to Marshall, 8/27,28/43, *EP*.
61. Butcher Diary, 8/15/43.
62. DE, *Letters to Mamie*, 146–47.
63. DE to Marshall, 9/6/43, *EP*.
64. DE to Badoglio, 9/10/43, *EP*.
65. DE to CCS, 9/9/43, *EP*.
66. DE to CCS, 9/13/43, *EP;* DE to Wedemeyer, 9/13/43, *EP*.
67. Butcher Diary, 9/13/43.
68. *Ibid.*
69. DE Diary, 9/14/43.
70. DE to Marshall, 9/25/43, *EP*.
71. DE, *Crusade*, 188; Clark, *Calculated Risk*, 199; DE Diary, 9/14/43.
72. Marshall to DE, 9/23/43, *EP*.
73. Butcher Diary, 9/25/43; DE to Marshall, 9/25/43, *EP*.
74. Summersby, *Eisenhower Was My Boss*, 114; DE to Spaatz, 12/24/43, *EP*.
75. DE, *Letters to Mamie*, 150.
76. *Ibid.*, 154–58.
77. DE, *Crusade*, 197; DE Diary, 12/6/43.
78. Butcher Diary, 11/21/43.
79. FDR to Stalin, 12/5/43, EL.
80. Cunningham to DE, 10/21/43, *EP*.
81. Bryant, *Triumph in the West*, 74.
82. DE to Nielsen, 12/6/43, *EP*.
83. Montgomery, *Memoirs*, 484.
84. DE, *Crusade*, 206–07.
85. Butcher Diary, 12/8/43.
86. DE to Marshall, 12/17/43, *EP*.
87. DE to Patton, 11/24/43, *EP*.
88. Marshall to DE, 12/29/43, *EP*.
89. Ambrose, *Supreme Commander*, 318.

CHAPTER FIVE

1. Morgan, *Past Forgetting*, 199.
2. Butcher Diary, 12/31/43; de Gaulle, *Unity*, 216–17.
3. Pogue, *Supreme Command*, 140; DE, *Crusade*, 218.
4. Hatch, *Red Carpet for Mamie*, 192.
5. DE, *Letters to Mamie*, 164–65.
6. DE to Haislip, 1/24/44, *EP*.
7. DE, *Crusade*, 220.
8. DE to Sommerville, 4/4/44, *EP*.
9. DE to CCS, 1/23/44, *EP*.
10. Ambrose, *Supreme Commander*, 349–62.
11. Interview DE.
12. Morgan, *Past Forgetting*, 194.
13. DE, *Letters to Mamie*, 179.
14. Irving, *War Between the Generals*, 81.
15. Tedder, *With Prejudice*, 510–12; Pogue, *Supreme Command*, 124; Harrison, *Cross-Channel Attack*, 219–20.

16. Butcher Diary, 5/12/44.
17. DE, *Letters to Mamie*, 172–75.
18. Interview Thor Smith.
19. Notes to DE to Marshall, 4/29/44, *EP*.
20. *Ibid.*
21. DE to Patton, 4/29/44, *EP*.
22. Butcher Diary, 5/1/44.
23. *Ibid.*
24. Bradley, *Soldier's Story*, 239.
25. *Ibid.*, 241–42; Bryant, *Triumph in the West*, 189–91; de Guingand, *Operation Victory*, 317.
26. Interview DE.
27. DE, *At Ease*, 275.
28. Leigh-Mallory to DE, 5/29/44, *EP*.
29. DE to Leigh-Mallory, 6/1/44, *EP*.
30. DE Diary, 6/3/44.
31. DE, *Letters to Mamie*, 185.
32. DE, *Crusade*, 249.
33. Interviews DE, Kenneth Strong, Walter B. Smith, Arthur Tedder; Butcher Diary, 6/5–7/44.
34. The undated note is in EL.
35. Interview DE; Butcher Diary, 6/7/44.
36. Morgan, *Past Forgetting*, 216; Butcher Diary, 6/7/44.
37. DE to Marshall, 6/6/44, *EP*.
38. Ambrose, *Supreme Commander*, 424.
39. DE, *Letters to Mamie*, 189–190.
40. Morgan, *Past Forgetting*, 221–22.
41. Neal, *The Eisenhowers*, 184.
42. DE, *Letters to Mamie*, 190.
43. *Ibid.*, 190–92.
44. Interview John Eisenhower; John Eisenhower, *Strictly Personal*, 63.
45. Montgomery, *Memoirs*, 43.
46. Weigley, *Eisenhower's Lieutenants*, 210.
47. Interview Kenneth McLean; Montgomery, *Memoirs*, 43.
48. DE to Bradley, 7/1/44, *EP*.
49. DE, *At Ease*, 288–89.
50. DE Diary, 7/5/44.
51. Tedder, *With Prejudice*, 557.
52. Irving, *War Between the Generals*, 232.
53. Butcher Diary, 7/21/44.
54. DE to Montgomery, 7/21/44, *EP*.
55. Bradley, *Soldier's Story*, 343.
56. DE to Bradley, 7/24/44, *EP*.
57. Wilmot, *Struggle for Europe*, 362.
58. *Ibid.*; Bryant, *Triumph in the West*, 181–82.
59. Butcher Diary, 7/25/44.
60. Bradley, *Soldier's Story*, 349; DE, *Crusade*, 272.
61. Tedder, *With Prejudice*, 575; DE to Marshall, 8/9/44, *EP*.
62. Butcher Diary, 8/8/44.
63. Bradley, *Soldier's Story*, 377; Wilmot, *Struggle for Europe*, 424–25.
64. Butcher Diary, 8/14/44.
65. DE, *Letters to Mamie*, 204, 210.
66. Butcher Diary, 8/15/44
67. DE to Marshall, 8/17/44, *EP*.
68. SHAEF Office Diary, 8/29/44, EL.
69. DE, *Crusade*, 279.
70. DE, *Letters to Mamie*, 203.
71. Ambrose, *Supreme Commander*, 510.
72. Butcher Diary, 8/20/44.
73. Montgomery, *Memoirs*, 240.
74. *Ibid.*, 241; DE to Montgomery, 8/24/44, *EP*.
75. Irving, *War Between the Generals*, 250–51.
76. DE to commanders, 8/29/44, *EP*.
77. Pogue, *Supreme Command*, 259.
78. De Guingand, *Operation Victory*, 329–30.
79. Bryant, *Triumph in the West*, 213.

CHAPTER SIX

1. Davis, *Soldier of Democracy*, 507; Irving, *War Between the Generals*, 256.
2. Patton, *War As I Knew It*, 120; Wilmot, *Struggle for Europe*, 469.
3. Weigley, *Eisenhower's Lieutenants*, 266.
4. DE to Montgomery, 9/5/44, *EP*.
5. Montgomery, *Memoirs*, 242–46.
6. Morgan, *Past Forgetting*, 239–40; DE, *Letters to Mamie*, 210–11.
7. Interview DE; Wilmot, *Struggle for Europe*, 488–89.
8. Tedder, *With Prejudice*, 590–91; SHAEF Office Diary, 9/11/44, EL.
9. Tedder, *With Prejudice*, 590–91.
10. SHAEF office diary, 9/11/44, EL.
11. Ambrose, *Supreme Commander*, 518.
12. DE, *Letters to Mamie*, 210–12.
13. DE to Montgomery, 10/9/44, *EP*.
14. EP, No. 2032, note 1.
15. DE to Montgomery, 10/10/44, *EP*.
16. Interview Sir Frederick Morgan.
17. Interview DE.
18. DE to Montgomery, 10/13/44, *EP*.
19. *EP*, No. 2038, note 1; Pogue, *Supreme Command*, 298.
20. Bryant, *Triumph in the West*, 219.
21. DE to Marshall, 11/11/44, *EP*.
22. DE, *Letters to Mamie*, 222.
23. *Ibid.*, 219–22, 224, 228.
24. *Ibid.*, 213–14.
25. *Ibid.*, 219, 220.
26. DE Diary, 12/23/44; Weigley, *Eisenhower's Lieutenants*, 457–58; Bradley, *Soldier's Story*, 464–65;

Pogue, *Supreme Command*, 372–74.
27. DE to Somervell, 12/17/44, *EP*.
28. DE to Bradley, 12/18/44, *EP*.
29. Bradley, *Soldier's Story*, 470; DE, *Crusade*, 350.
30. DE to CCS, 12/19/44, *EP*; Pogue, *Supreme Command*, 376–77.
31. Bradley, *Soldier's Story*, 476; interview with Sir Kenneth Strong; Weigley, *Eisenhower's Lieutenants*, 503.
32. Interview Sir Kenneth Strong; SHAEF office diary, 12/20/44, EL.
33. Bryant, *Triumph in the West*, 272.
34. *Ibid.*, 273.
35. DE to Lee and Bradley, 12/19/44, *EP*.
36. Bradley, *Soldier's Story*, 475–76.
37. *EP*, No. 2194.
38. Bryant, *Triumph in the West*, 278.
39. SHAEF office diary, 12/26/44, EL.
40. *Ibid.*
41. *Ibid.*, 12/27/44.
42. DE to Montgomery, 12/29/44, EP; DE, *Crusade*, 360–61; Montgomery, *Memoirs*, 284.
43. Interviews DE and Sir Arthur Tedder.
44. DE to Bradley and Montgomery, 12/31/44, *EP*.
45. DE to Montgomery, 12/31/44, *EP*.
46. Interview Freddie de Guingand.
47. De Guingand, *Operation Victory*, 348; Montgomery, *Memoirs*, 286.
48. Montgomery, *Memoirs*, 289.
49. Pogue, *Supreme Command*, 387–88; Bradley, *Soldier's Story*, 484.
50. Irving, *War Between the Generals*, 362.

Chapter Seven

1. Ryan, *Last Battle*, 241.
2. Ambrose, *Supreme Command*, 612.
3. John Eisenhower, *Strictly Personal*, 80; Eisenhower press conference notes, 12/2/54, EL.
4. DE, *Letters to Mamie*, 233–41.
5. *Ibid.*, 233; Morgan, *Past Forgetting*, 244–45; John Eisenhower, *Strictly Personal*, 80.
6. Butcher Diary, 3/27/45, EL.
7. DE to Marshall, 3/26/45, *EP*.
8. Bradley, *Soldier's Story*, 510–12; DE, *Crusade*, 378–80; Butcher Diary, 3/8/45, EL.
9. DE to CCS, 3/8/45, *EP*.
10. DE, *Letters to Mamie*, 243–44.
11. Irving, *War Between the Generals*, 392–93.
12. *Ibid.*, 403.
13. Morgan, *Past Forgetting*, 244–45.
14. DE, *Letters to Mamie*, 246–49.
15. DE to CCS, 3/21/45, *EP;* Churchill, *Triumph and Tragedy*, 442–43.
16. Wilmot, *Struggle for Europe*, 690; Ambrose, *Supreme Commander*, 629–30.
17. Butcher Diary, 3/27/45, EL.
18. Bradley, *Soldier's Story*, 535.
19. Ryan, *Last Battle*, 241.
20. Bryant, *Triumph in the West*, 336–41.
21. DE to Marshall, 3/30/45, *EP*.
22. Pogue, *Supreme Command*, 442; Churchill, *Triumph and Tragedy*, 463–65.
23. DE to Churchill, 4/1/45, *EP*.
24. Bryant, *Triumph in the West*, 339; Ambrose, *Supreme Commander*, 639.
25. Note 1, DE to Montgomery, 4/8/45, *EP*.
26. Ambrose, *Eisenhower and Berlin*, 64–65.
27. DE to CCS, 4/7/45, *EP*.
28. Weigley, *Eisenhower's Lieutenants*, 698.
29. DE to Marshall, 4/15/45, *EP*.
30. DE to Marshall, 4/27/45, *EP*.
31. Ambrose, *Supreme Commander*, 661.
32. DE, *Letters to Mamie*, 250.
33. Pogue, *Supreme Command*, 486–87.
34. Interviews DE, Sir Kenneth Strong; Butcher Diary, 5/7/45, EL; Smith, *Eisenhower's Six Great Decisions*, 229.
35. DE to CCS, 5/7/45, *EP*.
36. Marshall to DE, 5/8/45, *EP*.

Chapter Eight

1. DE to Butcher, 9/27/45, and DE to Marshall, 10/13/45, *EP*.
2. DE, *Crusade*, 444.
3. DE, *Letters to Mamie*, 254; Morgan, *Past Forgetting*, 250–53.
4. Butcher Diary, 6/2 and 6/13/45, EL.
5. DE, *At Ease*, 298–300; Morgan, *Past Forgetting*, 257.
6. Butcher Diary, 6/13/45, EL.
7. *Ibid.*, 6/21/45; *New York Times*, 6/20/45.
8. DE to Lewis Douglas, 9/11/45, *EP*.
9. Neal, *The Eisenhowers*, 224.
10. Lyon, *Eisenhower*, 27.
11. DE, *Crusade*, 444.
12. DE to Neill Bailey, 8/1/45, EP; DE, *Letters to Mamie*, 256.
13. DE, *Letters to Mamie*, 253–54.
14. DE to Marshall, 6/4/45, *EP*.
15. Merle Miller, *Plain Speaking*, 339–40.
16. DE to Marshall, 6/9/45, *EP*.
17. DE, *Letters to Mamie*, 259.
18. John Eisenhower, *Strictly Personal*, 113–14.

19. DE to Harger, 10/31/45, *EP*.
20. DE, *Letters to Mamie,* 270.
21. DE to Clay, 11/22/45, *EP*.
22. DE to Smith, 12/4/45, *EP*.
23. DE to Kay Summersby, 11/22/45, *EP*.
24. DE Diary, 12/2/47.
25. Morgan, *Past Forgetting,* 277.
26. Butcher Diary, 10/25/45, EL.
27. Patton to DE, 8/11/45, *EP*.
28. DE to Patton, 9/11/45, *EP*.
29. DE to Marshall, 9/29/45, *EP*.
30. DE, *At Ease,* 307; Lyon, *Eisenhower,* 361.
31. Summersby, *Eisenhower Was My Boss,* 278.
32. DE to Patton, 9/29/45, *EP;* John Eisenhower, *Strictly Personal,* 114; Farago, *Patton,* 818.
33. *New York Times,* 10/13/45.
34. DE, *Letters to Mamie,* 253.
35. DE to Wallace, 8/28/45, *EP*.
36. Butcher Diary, 6/15/45, EL.
37. DE, *Crusade,* 458–59; Lyon, *Eisenhower,* 25–26.
38. DE to Montgomery, 2/20/47, *EP*.
39. Butcher Diary, 6/10/45, EL.
40. Note 1, DE to Marshall, 6/15/45, *EP*.
41. DE to Marshall, 8/16/45, *EP*.
42. Note 1, DE to Harrison, 8/22/45, *EP;* note 1, DE to Marshall, 8/29/45, *EP*.
43. Lyon, *Eisenhower,* 356.
44. DE to Hazlett, 11/27/45, *EP*.
45. DE to John Eisenhower, 12/15/45, *EP*.
46. DE to P. A. Hodgson, 10/30/46, *EP*.
47. DE to Marshall, 6/15/46, *EP*.
48. DE to Hodgson, 10/23 and 10/30/46, *EP*.
49. DE to Hazlett, 7/1/46, *EP*.
50. Lyon, *Eisenhower,* 365.
51. DE to Zhukov, 3/13/46, *EP*.
52. Notes, DE memo to JCS, 6/7/46, *EP*.
53. DE to Smith, 7/29/46, *EP;* Ambrose, *Rise to Globalism,* 123.
54. DE to Montgomery, 2/20/47, *EP*.
55. DE to Patterson and Forrestal, 3/13/47, *EP*.
56. DE Diary, 5/15/47.
57. DE to Carley, 7/10/47, note 3, *EP*.
58. DE to Hazlett, 10/29/47, note 3, *EP*.
59. DE to Milton Eisenhower, 10/16/47, *EP*.
60. DE to Finder, 1/22/48, *EP*.
61. DE to Hazlett, 7/19/47, *EP*.
62. DE to Forrestal, 1/31/48, *EP*.
63. DE Diary, 9/16/47.
64. DE to Smith, 10/29/47, *EP*.
65. DE to Doud, 1/31/47, *EP*.
66. DE to Milton Eisenhower, 5/29/47, *EP*.
67. Note 1, DE to Watson and Milton Eisenhower, 6/14/47, *EP*.
68. DE to Watson, 11/17/47, and to Smith, 7/3/47, *EP*.
69. DE to Parkinson, 6/23/47, *EP*.
70. DE Diary, 11/12 and 12/15/47; DE to Hodgson, 10/30/47, *EP*.
71. The document is in EL, dated 2/7/48.
72. McCann, *Man from Abilene,* 154–55.
73. DE to Simon, 7/31/46, note 1, *EP*.
74. See introduction to 1977 Da Capo Press edition of *Crusade*.

Chapter Nine

1. Robinson memo 4/1/48, and Robinson to Leo Perpen, 6/12/48, EL.
2. DE memo to Harron, 7/5/48, EL; Lyon, *Eisenhower,* 386–87; DE to Lindley, 6/19/48, EL.
3. DE, *At Ease,* 339–41; DE to Hazlett, 8/12/48, EL.

4. DE to Hazlett, 2/24/50, EL.
5. Kirk interview, EL.
6. John Krout interview, EL.
7. DE Diary, 11/14/50.
8. Neal, *The Eisenhowers*, 251.
9. *Ibid.*, 249–50.
10. DE to Hazlett, 1/27/49, EL; DE Diary, 1/8/49
11. DE Diary, 1/8/49.
12. *Ibid.*, 1/7/49; DE to Eberstadt, 9/20/48, and to Forrestal, 11/24/48, EL.
13. DE Diary, 3/19/49.
14. *Ibid.*, 6/4/49.
15. *Ibid.*, 10/14/49.
16. Interview DE; DE, *At Ease*, 554–55; DE to Roberts, 5/3/51, EL.
17. DE, *At Ease*, 358–60.
18. Adams to DE, 6/21/49, and DE to Adams, 6/23/49, EL.
19. DE Diary, 7/7/49.
20. *Ibid.*, 9/27/49.
21. *Ibid.*, 6/30/50.
22. *Ibid.*, 7/6/50.
23. *Ibid.*, 10/28/50.
24. *Ibid.*, 7/6/50.
25. *Ibid.*, 10/28/50.
26. DE to Hazlett, 11/1/50, EL.
27. DE Diary, 11/6/50.
28. *Ibid.*, 12/5/50.
29. DE, *At Ease*, 371–72; DE, *Mandate*, 14; DE to Marshall, 12/12/50, EL.
30. DE, *At Ease*, 366.
31. Interview Lauris Norstadt, EL.
32. Memcon, 1/17/51, EL.
33. Memcon, 1/24/51, EL.
34. Memcon, 1/11/51, EL.
35. Press conference notes, 1/20/51, EL.
36. DE to Lodge, 4/4/52; DE to Woodruff, 8/27/51; and DE to McConnell, 6/29/51, EL.
37. DE to Lovett, 9/25/51, EL.
38. DE to Bermingham, 2/28/51, EL.
39. Interview Andrew Goodpaster.
40. DE Diary, 10/10/51; DE to Lovett, 9/25/51, EL.
41. DE Diary, 3/17/51.
42. DE to Paley, 3/29/52, EL.
43. Quoted in *History JCS,* Vol. IV, 195.
44. DE to Marshall, 8/3/51, EL.
45. DE Diary, 6/11/51; DE to Harriman, 6/30/51, EL.
46. DE to Pleven, 12/24/51, EL.
47. Robinson notes on Eisenhower speech, EL; *New York Times*, 7/4/51; Churchill to DE, 7/5/51, EL.
48. DE to John Eisenhower, 9/27/51, EL.
49. DE to Hazlett, 9/4/51, EL.
50. Krock, *In the Nation*, 194–95; Krock, *Memoirs*, 267–69; DE Diary, 9/25/51.
51. DE, *Mandate*, 18.
52. Clay to DE, 9/29/51, EL.
53. DE to Clay, 10/3/51, EL.
54. Smith, *Dewey*, 579.
55. DE to Duff, 11/13/51; DE to Leithead, 11/18/51; DE to Robinson, 11/8/51; DE to Milton Eisenhower, 11/20/51, all in EL.
56. DE to Robinson, 11/24/51, EL.
57. Clay to DE, 12/7/51, EL.
58. Hoffman to DE, 12/5/51, EL.
59. DE Diary, 10/29/51.
60. DE to Roberts, 12/8/51; DE to Burnham, 12/11/51, EL.
61. DE to Lodge, 12/12/51, EL; DE Diary, 12/11/51.
62. Clay to DE, 12/21/51, EL.
63. Robinson memo, 12/29/51, EL.
64. DE to Roberts, 1/11/52, EL.
65. *New York Times*, 1/8/52.
66. Jacqueline Cochran interview, EL.
67. Parmet, *Eisenhower*, 54–55.
68. DE to Robinson, 11/24/51, EL.
69. DE to Sloan, 2/21/52, EL.
70. DE to Milton Eisenhower, 4/4/52, EL.

71. DE to Clay, 5/20/52, EL.
72. DE to Lodge, 5/20/52, EL.
73. DE to Roberts, 5/19/52, EL.
74. DE to Clay, 2/20/52, EL.
75. Interview Milton Eisenhower.

CHAPTER TEN

1. Lyon, *Eisenhower*, 439.
2. Parmet, *Eisenhower*, 57.
3. DE to Gerow, 6/28/52, EL.
4. *New York Times*, 6/5/52.
5. *Ibid.*, 6/14/52.
6. *Ibid.*, 6/15/52.
7. *Ibid.*, 6/27/52.
8. DE, *Mandate*, 45.
9. Nixon, *Memoirs*, 87; Milton Eisenhower, *The President Is Calling*, 249–50.
10. Parmet, *Eisenhower*, 97–98.
11. *New York Times*, 7/11–13/52.
12. *Ibid.*
13. DE, *Mandate*, 49–50.
14. *New York Times*, 8/25/52.
15. DE to Dulles, 4/15/52, EL.
16. Interview DE.
17. Reeves, *McCarthy*, 436–37.
18. Hughes, *Ordeal*, 22–25.
19. Interview Sherman Adams, Columbia University.
20. Nixon, *Memoirs*, 96; *New York Times*, 9/23/52.
21. Nixon, *Memoirs*, 97.
22. *Ibid.*, 97–98.
23. Ewald, *Eisenhower*, 55.
24. Nixon, *Memoirs*, 105–06; DE to Nixon, 9/25/52, EL.
25. DE, *Mandate*, 69.
26. Nixon, *Memoirs*, 106.
27. Hughes, *Ordeal*, 41–42.
28. Ewald, *Eisenhower*, 62–63; interview Sherman Adams, Columbia University.
29. *New York Times*, 10/4/52; Reeves, *McCarthy*, 440.
30. *New York Times*, 10/4/52.
31. Reeves, *McCarthy*, 440.
32. DE, *Mandate*, 318.
33. *New York Times*, 10/25/52.
34. Interview DE; Hughes, *Ordeal*, 46.

CHAPTER ELEVEN

1. Richardson, *Presidency of Eisenhower*, 25.
2. Hughes, *Ordeal*, 251.
3. Warren, *Memoirs*, 260.
4. Lyon, *Eisenhower*, 466–67; Geelhoed, *Charles E. Wilson*, 19.
5. DE Diary, 2/7/53.
6. *New Republic*, 12/15/52.
7. Slater, *The Ike I Knew*, 39.
8. West, *Upstairs at the White House*, 130.
9. DE, *Mandate*, 95.
10. Robinson memo, 1/5/55, EL.
11. DE Diary, 2/13/53.
12. DE, *Mandate*, 101; Truman, *Mr. Citizen*, 15.
13. DE to Truman, 1/23/53, EL.
14. Murphy to DE, 12/30/52, EL.
15. PP (53), 1–8.
16. Parmet, *Eisenhower*, 166.
17. DE, *Mandate*, 102.
18. DE Diary, 1/21/53.
19. Truman, *Year of Decisions*, 19.
20. Neustadt, *Presidential Power*, 9.

CHAPTER TWELVE

1. PP (53), 67.
2. DE, *Mandate*, 267.
3. DE to Draper, 3/16/53, EL.
4. NSC notes, 2/11/53, EL.
5. DE, *Mandate*, 181.
6. PP (53), 42–55.
7. Crawford interview, EL.
8. DE Diary, 2/7/53.
9. Interview Milton Eisenhower.
10. DE to Robinson, 3/12/54, EL.
11. DE Diary, 4/1/53.
12. Griffith, *Politics of Fear*, 200.

13. PP (53), 63.
14. *Ibid.*, 56–57.
15. *Ibid.*, 81–83; Minnich, LLM, 3/9/53, EL.
16. Minnich, Cabinet, 3/6/53, EL.
17. PP (53), 116–17.
18. Minnich, Cabinet, 3/20/53, EL.
19. DE, *Mandate*, 113.
20. West, *Upstairs at the White House*, 155.
21. Slater, *The Ike I Knew*, 32.
22. West, *Upstairs at the White House*, 175.
23. Slater, *The Ike I Knew*, 33.
24. DE, *Mandate*, 271–72.
25. Whitman Diary, 2/7/53, EL.
26. West, *Upstairs at the White House*, 157–58.
27. DE to Phillips, 6/5/53, EL.
28. Bullis to DE, 5/9/53, and DE to Bullis, 5/18/53, EL.
29. Bischof, "Before the Break," 144.
30. PP (53), 413–15.
31. Dulles memo, 6/15/53, EL.
32. PP (53), 427–37.
33. Minnich, Cabinet, 6/26/53, EL.
34. DE Diary, 5/1/53.
35. *Ibid.*
36. Minnich, LLM, 5/12 and 5/19/53, EL.
37. PP (53), 209–10.
38. *Ibid.*, 337.
39. Minnich, Cabinet, 5/22/53, EL.
40. *Ibid.*
41. Hughes, *Ordeal*, 103–05.
42. PP (53), 179–88.

CHAPTER THIRTEEN

1. NSC notes, 4/8/53, EL.
2. Dulles to DE, 5/22/53, EL.
3. DE, *Mandate*, 183.
4. DE to Rhee, 6/6/53, EL.
5. Minnich, Cabinet, 6/19/53, EL.
6. DE to Rhee, 6/18/53, EL.

7. Parmet, *Eisenhower*, 314.
8. PP (53), 520–22; *New York Times*, 7/28/53.
9. DE, *Mandate*, 190.
10. Roosevelt, *Countercoup;* Cook, *Declassified Eisenhower;* interview Goodpaster.
11. Parmet, *Eisenhower*, 315.
12. DE Diary, 1/10/55.
13. DE to Laniel, 9/21/53, EL.
14. DE Diary, 5/14/53.
15. *Ibid.*
16. Interview Brownell, Columbia University; DE to Edgar Eisenhower, 10/1/53, EL.
17. DE to Dean Smith, 9/14/53, EL.
18. DE to Milton Eisenhower, 10/9/53.
19. Ewald, *Eisenhower*, 81.
20. PP (53), 645–46.
21. Oppenheimer, "American Weapons and American Policy," *Foreign Affairs*, July 1953.
22. Divine, *Blowing on the Wind*, 11.
23. Lear, "Ike and the Peaceful Atom," 11–12.
24. DE Diary, 10/10/53.
25. *Ibid.*, 12/2/53.
26. *Ibid.*, 12/3/53.
27. Ewald, *Eisenhower*, 82–83; DE-Brownell telephone call, 11/16/53, EL.
28. DE-Brownell telephone call, 12/2/53, EL.
29. PP (53), 813–22.
30. *Ibid.*
31. DE to Smith, 3/15/54, EL.
32. E-Dulles telephone calls, 3/24 and 3/25/54, EL.
33. Ewald, *Eisenhower*, 119–20.
34. DE-Dulles telephone call, 4/5/53, EL.
35. PP (54), 382–83.
36. Dulles to DE, 4/22–25/54, EL.
37. DE to Gruenther, 4/26/54, EL.
38. Interview DE.
39. NSC notes, 5/6/54, EL.
40. DE, *Mandate*, 357.

41. DE-Wilson telephone call, 5/11/54, EL.
42. Hagerty Diary, 5/14/54, EL.
43. Minnich, LLM, 5/17/54, EL.
44. PP (54), 483–84.
45. Hagerty Diary, 5/13/54.
46. *Ibid.*, 1/15/54.
47. Warren, *Memoirs*, 291.
48. Hagerty Diary, 5/18/54, EL.
49. PP (54), 491.
50. DE to Hazlett, 7/22/57, EL.
51. PP (54), 450.
52. NSC notes, 6/2/54, EL.
53. Hagerty Diary, 6/19/54, EL.
54. PP (54), 698–701.
55. American-Korean talks, 7/27/54, EL.
56. PP (54), 642.
57. *Ibid.*, 661.
58. Hagerty Diary, 9/2/54, EL.
59. DE, *Mandate*, 404.

Chapter Fourteen

1. DE, *Mandate*, 303.
2. DE to Robinson, 3/23/54, EL.
3. Slater, *The Ike I Knew*, 69.
4. Greenstein, *Hidden Hand Presidency*, 184–85.
5. Hagerty diary, 2/25/54, EL.
6. DE-Brownell telephone call, 3/2/54, EL.
7. PP (54), 288–91.
8. Greenstein, *Hidden Hand Presidency*, 191–92.
9. DE memo, 3/5/54, EL.
10. DE to Robinson, 3/12/54, EL; PP (54), 300.
11. DE to Robinson, 3/12/54, EL.
12. DE to Helms, 3/12/54, EL.
13. DE Diary, 1/18/54, EL.
14. Hagerty Diary, 3/24/54, EL.
15. PP (54), 339.
16. Hagerty Diary, 4/7 and 4/9/54, EL.
17. *Ibid.*, 4/10/54.
18. *Ibid.*, 4/9/54.
19. PP (54), 382; DE, *Mandate*, 312.
20. DE to Hazlett, 4/27/54, EL.
21. PP (54), 346.
22. Divine, *Blowing on the Wind*, 13.
23. Hagerty Diary, 3/31/54, EL.
24. DE to Strauss, 6/14/54, EL.
25. PP (54), 435.
26. *Ibid.*, 58.
27. *Ibid.*, 324–25.
28. Minnich, LLM, 2/8/54, EL.
29. NSC notes, 1/8/54, EL.
30. PP (54), 382–83.

Chapter Fifteen

1. DE, *Mandate*, 461–64.
2. Memcon, 10/30/54, EL.
3. *New York Times*, 10/30/54.
4. DE to Hazlett, 8/20/56, EL.
5. Ambrose, *Ike's Spies*, 188.
6. Goodpaster memo, 11/24/54, EL.
7. Slater, *The Ike I Knew*, 82–83; Whitman Diary, 11/24/54, EL.
8. Hagerty Diary, 10/24/54, EL.
9. PP (54), 1074–77.
10. *New York Times*, 1/2/55.
11. DE, *Mandate*, 466.
12. *Ibid.*, 467; Divine, *Eisenhower and the Cold War*, 57.
13. DE-Rayburn/Martin telephone call, 1/20/55, EL.
14. PP (55), 207–11.
15. Goodpaster memo, 3/15/55, EL.
16. *Ibid.*, 3/15/55.
17. Divine, *Eisenhower and the Cold War*, 62; Hagerty Diary, 3/16/55, EL.
18. PP (55), 332–33.
19. Ambrose, *Rise to Globalism*, 239.
20. Hagerty Diary, 3/19/55, EL.
21. PP (55), 358.
22. Divine, *Eisenhower and the Cold War*, 64; DE, *Mandate*, 482–83.
23. DE, *Mandate*, 483.
24. Divine, *Eisenhower and the Cold War*, 65–66.

25. DE, *Mandate*, 491.
26. DE-Milton Eisenhower telephone call, 1/31/56, EL.
27. Davies, *Age of Asphalt*, 17–22; Rose, *Interstate*, 69–84.

CHAPTER SIXTEEN

1. DE, *Mandate*, 525; John Eisenhower, *Strictly Personal*, 175–76.
2. John Eisenhower, *Strictly Personal*, 176.
3. PP (55), 707–16; interview Vernon Walters.
4. DE, *Mandate*, 521.
5. PP (55), 718, 722–23.
6. See DE to Bulganin, 7/27/55, EL.
7. DE to Milton Eisenhower, 9/12/55, EL.
8. DE to Hazlett, 8/15/55, EL.
9. Whitman Diary, 9/23/55, EL.
10. Snyder to Robinson, 10/5/55, EL.
11. *Ibid.;* Whitman Diary, 9/29/55, EL.
12. John Eisenhower, *Strictly Personal*, 181.
13. *Ibid.*, 182.
14. *New York Times*, 9/30/55.
15. Parmet, *Eisenhower*, 417.
16. Slater, *The Ike I Knew*, 110–15.
17. John Eisenhower, *Strictly Personal*, 183–84.
18. Hagerty Diary, 12/10 and 12/12/55, EL.
19. *Ibid.*, 12/11 and 12/13/55, EL.
20. *Ibid.*, 12/14/55.
21. John Eisenhower, *Strictly Personal*, 184.
22. Nixon, *Memoirs*, 167–68; Parmet, *Eisenhower*, 424.
23. Slater, *The Ike I Knew*, 121–24.
24. DE Diary, 2/7/56.
25. Hagerty Diary, 1/25/56, EL.
26. Dulles memo, 1/25/56, EL.

27. PP (56), 182.
28. DE Diary, 1/23/56.
29. Dulles memo, 2/29/56, EL; DE Diary, 1/10/56.
30. *New York Times*, 2/15/56.
31. PP (56), 266–67.
32. *Ibid.*, 287, 295.
33. Whitman Diary, 2/9/56, EL.
34. *Ibid.*, 3/13/56.
35. PP (56), 186–87.
36. *Ibid.*, 269–70.
37. *Ibid.*, 304–05.
38. *Ibid.*, 335–40.
39. *Ibid.*, 335.
40. Minnich, Cabinet, 3/9/56, EL.
41. DE, *Waging Peace*, 149.
42. Minnich, Cabinet, 2/14/56, EL.
43. PP (56), 235–36.

CHAPTER SEVENTEEN

1. Larson, *Eisenhower*, 10.
2. *Ibid.;* Hughes, *Ordeal*, 173.
3. Nixon, *Memoirs*, 170–71; Whitman Diary, 4/9/56, EL.
4. Nixon, *Memoirs*, 172–73.
5. Minnich, LLM, 4/17/56, EL.
6. Persons Memo, 8/1/56, EL.
7. DE, *Waging Peace*, 34.
8. Memcon, 7/31/56, EL.
9. PP (56), 735.
10. Whitman Diary, 11/14/56, EL.
11. PP (56), 736–37, 758–59.
12. Divine, *Blowing on the Wind*, 88.
13. DE to Gruenther, 11/2/56, EL.
14. DE to Hazlett, 11/2/56, EL.
15. DE memo, 10/15/56, EL.
16. NSC notes, 10/26/56, EL.
17. Whitman Diary, 10/28–30/56, EL.
18. DE, *Waging Peace*, 71–73.
19. Memcon, 10/29/56, EL.
20. *Ibid.*, 10/30/56, EL.
21. *Ibid.*
22. DE-Dulles telephone call, 10/30/56, EL.

23. DE, *Waging Peace*, 78–79.
24. DE-Knowland telephone call, 10/31/56, EL.
25. DE-Lodge telephone call, 10/31/56, EL.
26. Hughes, *Ordeal*, 219–21.
27. NSC notes, 11/1/56, EL.
28. *New York Times*, 11/2/56.
29. DE to Gruenther, 11/2/56, EL.
30. DE, *Waging Peace*, 86–88.
31. *Ibid.*
32. *Ibid.*, 89, 95.
33. *Ibid.*, 89.
34. Hughes, *Ordeal*, 222–23.
35. Memcon, 11/6/56, EL.
36. DE, *Waging Peace*, 91.
37. DE-Eden telephone call, 11/6/54, EL.
38. Whitman Diary, 11/6/56, EL.
39. Hughes, *Ordeal*, 228.
40. DE-Eden telephone call, 11/7/56, EL.
41. Memcon, 11/7/56, EL.
42. DE, *Waging Peace*, 94–95.
43. Minnich, LLM, 12/31/56, EL.
44. DE-Hoover telephone call, 11/9/56, EL.
45. Memcon, 11/15/56, EL.
46. DE-Dulles telephone call, 12/18/56, EL.
47. Whitman Diary, 12/26/56, EL.

Chapter Eighteen

1. PP (57), 60–65.
2. DE to Humphrey, 3/27/57, EL.
3. Minnich, LLM, 7/2/57, EL.
4. DE to Hazlett, 7/22/57, EL.
5. DE to Gerow, 11/15/57, EL.
6. Whitman Diary, 7/15/57, EL.
7. DE to Wallace, 2/22/57, EL.
8. DE-Dulles telephone call, 12/18/56, EL.
9. Minnich, LLM, 3/29/55, EL; Memcon, 6/28/57, EL.
10. Minnich, LLM, 7/30/57, EL.
11. Whitman Diary, 1/3/57, EL.
12. DE-Johnson telephone call, 6/15/57, EL.
13. PP (57), 520–21.
14. DE, *Waging Peace*, 157–58.
15. Whitman Diary, 7/10/57, EL.
16. DE to Hazlett, 7/22/57, EL.
17. DE to Byrnes, 7/22/57, EL.
18. PP (57), 546–47, 555.
19. Minnich, Cabinet, 8/2/57, EL; PP (57), 587.
20. DE, *Waging Peace*, 160; Minnich, LLM, 8/13/57, EL.
21. Whitman Diary, 9/3/57, EL.
22. DE-Brownell telephone call, 9/20/57, EL.
23. DE, *Waging Peace*, 170.
24. DE-Brownell telephone call, 9/23/57, EL.
25. *New York Times*, 9/25–27/57.
26. DE to Reid, 9/28/57, EL.
27. DE, *Waging Peace*, 205–06.
28. PP (57), 719–30.
29. Whitman Diary, 11/6/57, EL.
30. Memcon, 10/15/57, EL.
31. Memcon, 10/31/57, EL.
32. Minnich, Cabinet, 11/1/57, EL.
33. Memcon, 11/4/57, EL.

Chapter Nineteen

1. DE, *Waging Peace*, 227–28; John Eisenhower, *Strictly Personal*, 195–96.
2. John Eisenhower, *Strictly Personal*, 196; Adams, *Firsthand Report*, 196–97.
3. Adams, *Firsthand Report*, 197–98; John Eisenhower, *Strictly Personal*, 196–97.
4. Divine, *Blowing on the Wind*, 200.
5. *Ibid.*, 262; PP (58), 262.
6. Divine, *Blowing on the Wind*, 106–07.
7. Memcon, 4/17/58, EL.
8. Divine, Blowing on the Wind, 210–12.

9. Minnich, LLM, 1/28/58, EL.
10. NSC notes, 4/25/58, EL.
11. Memcon, 3/7/58, EL.
12. *Ibid.*, 3/16/58.
13. NSC notes, 6/3/58, EL.
14. Minnich, LLM, 6/24/58, EL.
15. DE-Knowland telephone call, 1/7/58, EL.
16. DE-Rockefeller telephone call, 1/16/58, EL.
17. Minnich, LLM, 2/4/58, EL.
18. Memcon, 2/6/58, EL.
19. PP (1958), 311.
20. Interview DE.
21. PP (58), 479.
22. DE to Hoffman, 6/23/58, EL.
23. Interview DE.
24. Cutler, *No Time for Rest*, 363–64.
25. DE, *Waging Peace*, 270.
26. Memcon, 7/15/58, EL; Cutler, *No Time for Rest*, 363–64.
27. Minnich, LLM, 7/14/58, EL; Memcon, 7/14/58, EL.
28. DE, *Waging Peace*, 273; DE-Macmillan telephone call, 7/15/58, EL.
29. DE, *Waging Peace*, 290–91.
30. *Ibid.*
31. Memcon, 8/30/58, EL.
32. Divine, *Blowing on the Wind*, 228–33; Memcon, 8/27/58, EL.
33. Divine, *Blowing on the Wind*, 229–34.
34. DE-Alcorn telephone call, 9/4/58, EL.
35. Whitman Diary, 9/16/58, EL.
36. *Ibid.*, 9/17/58.
37. Slater, *The Ike I Knew*, 179–80.
38. DE to Humphrey, 7/22/58, EL.
39. DE, *Waging Peace*, 377.
40. *Ibid.*, 380–81.
41. Memcon, 10/25/58, EL.
42. *Time*, 11/10/58.
43. Memcon, 11/18/58, EL.
44. *Ibid.*, 12/9/58.
45. *Ibid.*, 1/12/59.
46. *Ibid.*, 2/12/59.
47. *Ibid.*, 2/18/59, EL.
48. *Ibid.*, 11/12/58.

Chapter Twenty

1. Whitman Diary, 6/11/59, EL.
2. Minnich, LLM, 6/2/59. EL.
3. PP (59), 226–28.
4. Memcon, 3/9/59, EL.
5. Minnich, LLM, 3/10/59, EL.
6. Minnich, Cabinet, 3/13/59, EL.
7. DE-Herter telephone call, 3/5/59, EL.
8. *Ibid.*, 4/4/59.
9. DE to Khrushchev, 4/13/59, EL.
10. DE-Dulles telephone call, 4/7/59, EL.
11. Memcon, 5/28/59, EL.
12. Slater, *The Ike I Knew*, 197–99.
13. *Ibid.*, 193.
14. Whitman Diary, 6/27/59, EL.
15. Memcon, 7/10/59, EL.
16. PP (59), 576–82.
17. Memcon, 8/25/59, EL.
18. DE, *Waging Peace*, 415.
19. Memcon, 11/24/59, EL.
20. DE, *Waging Peace*, 419; Lyon, *Eisenhower*, 798.
21. PP (59), 625.
22. DE, *Waging Peace*, 435.
23. *Ibid.*, 432.
24. *New York Times*, 9/20/59.
25. Memcon, 9/28/59, EL.
26. DE, *Waging Peace*, 442–44, 446–47.
27. Memcon, 6/24/59, EL.
28. *Ibid.*, 11/16/59.
29. *Ibid.*, 11/18/59.
30. *Ibid.*, 11/16/59.

Chapter Twenty-One

1. Herter to DE, 3/17/60, EL.
2. Memcon, 1/25/60, EL.
3. Ambrose, *Ike's Spies*, 309.
4. *Ibid.*, 310.

5. Minnich, LLM, 4/26/60, EL.
6. PP (60), 144, 147.
7. DE to Hobby, 5/9/60, EL.
8. PP (60), 26.
9. Minnich, LLM, 2/9/60, EL.
10. DE-Gates telephone call, 1/12/60, and Minnich, LLM, 2/9/60, EL.
11. PP (60), 126.
12. *Ibid.*, 145, 198–99.
13. White to Stephenson, 3/18/60, EL.
14. Kistiakowsky, *Scientist at the White House*, 250–52.
15. PP (60), 166.
16. *Ibid.*, 323–29.
17. *Ibid.*, 362–63.
18. Kistiakowsky, *Scientist at the White House*, 290–91; Divine, *Blowing on the Wind*, 310.
19. Kistiakowsky, *Scientist at the White House*, 293.
20. Minnich, Cabinet, 4/26/60, EL.
21. Memcon, 2/2/60, EL.
22. Goodpaster memo, 4/25/60, EL.
23. Ambrose, *Ike's Spies*, 283–84.
24. DE, *Waging Peace*, 543.
25. *New York Times*, 5/6/60.
26. *Ibid.*
27. *Ibid.*, 5/8/60.
28. DE-Herter and DE-Dulles telephone calls, 5/7/60, EL.
29. *New York Times*, 5/9/60.
30. Goodpaster-Herter telephone call, 5/9/60, EL.
31. *New York Times*, 5/9/60.
32. Whitman Diary, 5/9/60, EL.
33. DE, *Waging Peace*, 552.
34. PP (60), 403–07.
35. DE, *Waging Peace*, 558–59; Lyon, *Eisenhower*, 811–14.
36. DE, *Waging Peace*, 555–56; Walters, *Silent Missions*, 343–47; Memcon, 5/16/60, EL.
37. Kistiakowsky, *Scientist at the White House*, 335–36.
38. Memcon, 5/23/60, EL.
39. Kistiakowsky, *Scientist at the White House*, 375.
40. Memcon, 12/5/60, EL.
41. DE to Dillon, 12/15/60, EL.
42. Memcon, 11/29/60, EL.
43. DE, *Waging Peace*, 613–14.
44. Memcon, 8/18/60, EL.
45. *Ibid.*, 8/15/60, EL.
46. *Ibid.*, 8/15/60.
47. DE to Luce, 7/6/60, EL.
48. Memcon, 10/13/60, EL.
49. Minnich, LLM 6/10/60, EL.
50. Whitman Diary, 6/10/60, EL.
51. DE-Hobby telephone call, 6/11/60, EL.
52. Robinson Diary, 7/18–25/60, EL.
53. Slater, *The Ike I Knew*, 229.
54. DE-Fairless telephone call, 8/19/60, EL; Kistiakowsky, *Scientist at the White House*, 402.
55. Robinson Diary, 7/18–26/60, EL; DE, *Waging Peace*, 595.
56. DE-Nixon telephone call, 7/24/60, EL.
57. DE, *Waging Peace*, 596–97.
58. Memcon, 8/3/60, EL.
59. DE-Jones telephone call, 8/8/60, EL.
60. PP (60), 622–27.
61. *Ibid.*, 651, 653, 657–58.
62. Memcon, 10/18/60, EL.
63. Whitman Diary, 10/4/60, EL.
64. *Ibid.*, 8/30/60.
65. *Ibid.*, 10/14/60; DE-Nixon telephone call, 9/25/60, EL.
66. Nixon, *Memoirs*, 222.
67. Whitman Diary, 11/4/60, EL.
68. *Ibid.*, 11/8–9/60.
69. *Ibid.*
70. *Ibid.*

Chapter Twenty-Two

1. Slater, *The Ike I Knew*, 231.
2. Memcon, 12/30/60, EL.
3. *Ibid.*, 12/5/60.

4. DE Diary, 12/6/60.

5. Memcon, 11/29/60, EL.

6. *Ibid.*, 1/31/61; interview Goodpaster.

7. Slater, *The Ike I Knew*, 239.

8. DE to various friends, 12/26/60, EL.

9. DE to Edgar Eisenhower, 1/7/61, EL.

10. DE to C. D. Jackson, 12/31/60, EL.

11. Whitman to DE, 12/14/60, EL.

12. PP (60), 1035–40.

13. *Ibid.*, 1040–45.

14. Wyden, *Bay of Pigs*, 88; DE Diary, 1/19/61; Person memo, 1/19/61, EL.

15. Lyon, *Eisenhower*, 825.

16. John Eisenhower, *Strictly Personal*, 287.

17. DE, *Waging Peace*, 618.

18. Ewald, *Eisenhower the President*, 324.

19. Lyon, Eisenhower, 851.

Chapter Twenty-Three

1. Interview Milton Eisenhower.

2. Ewald, *Eisenhower*, 6–10; *Parade* magazine, 6/26/66.

3. Slater, *The Ike I Knew*, 243.

4. Interview DE.

5. DE to Borman, 6/18/65, EL.

6. John Eisenhower, *Strictly Personal*, 293.

7. Interview Cochran, EL.

8. DE to Nixon, 11/11/63, EL.

9. Nixon, *Memoirs*, 377–78.

10. DE, Notes for the President, 11/23/63, EL.

11. Johnson to DE, 3/16/65, EL.

12. Goodpaster memo, 4/9/65, EL.

13. *Ibid.*, 6/16/65.

14. DE-Johnson telephone call, 7/2/65, EL.

15. Goodpaster memo, 8/3/65, EL.

16. *Ibid.*, 8/20/65.

17. *Ibid.*, 10/11/65.

18. *Ibid.*, 1/25/66.

19. *Ibid.*, 9/19/66.

20. DE to Nixon, 10/7/66, EL.

21. DE to Humphrey, 2/14/67, EL.

22. Goodpaster memo, 4/7/67, EL.

23. *New York Times,* 10/4/67.

24. CBS News Special, 11/28/67.

25. Goodpaster memo, 10/18 and 11/9/67, EL.

26. Lyon, *Eisenhower*, 847–48.

27. *Reader's Digest*, April 1968.

28. DE to Ormerod, 10/25/65, EL.

29. Lyon, *Eisenhower*, 836.

30. Nixon, *Memoirs*, 275–76.

31. *New York Times*, 11/6/66.

32. DE memo for record, 3/14/67, EL; Larson, *Eisenhower*, 191–92.

33. DE to Seaton, 1/31/67, EL.

34. Slater, *The Ike I Knew*, 269.

35. DE to Robert Pat, 2/14/68, EL.

36. DE to Johnson, 4/3/68, EL.

37. *New York Times*, 7/16/68; DE to Nixon, 7/16/68, EL.

38. DE to Nixon, 10/24 and 12/13/68, EL.

39. Julie Eisenhower, *Special People*, 193.

40. John Eisenhower, *Strictly Personal*, 328–37.

41. *Ibid.*

Epilogue

1. Price, *With Nixon*, 61.

2. Kissinger, *White House Years*, 7–10.

BIBLIOGRAPHY

The vast majority of citations are to Eisenhower's own writings, and come from two basic sources. The first is The Papers of Dwight David Eisenhower, *published in nine volumes to date, covering the period December 1941 to February 1948. Quotations taken from these volumes are cited by date, as they appear chronologically in the Papers, which are identified as* EP. *The second source is the Eisenhower Papers at the Eisenhower Library in Abilene, Kansas. There is a bewildering array of boxes, files, and collections within the Eisenhower Papers, but the overwhelming majority used for this work come from one file, identified by the staff of the library as the "1652" file (because it covers the period 1916-1952). Citations to quotations from that file are listed as* EL *(for Eisenhower Library).*

INTERVIEWS BY THE AUTHOR

Omar Bradley
Sir Francis de Guingand
David Donald
Dwight D. Eisenhower
John S. D. Eisenhower
Milton S. Eisenhower
Andrew Goodpaster

Sir Ian Jacob
Sir Frederick Morgan
Forrest Pogue
Thor Smith
Sir Kenneth Strong
Sir Arthur Tedder

INTERVIEWS BY THE STAFF OF THE EISENHOWER LIBRARY

Sherman Adams
Jacqueline Cochran
Kenneth Crawford
John Eisenhower
Milton Eisenhower
Eli Ginzburg
Andrew Goodpaster

Gordon Gray
Helen King
Grayson Kirk
John Krout
Malcolm Moos
Merriman Smith

Interviews by the Columbia Oral History Project (COHP)

Sherman Adams
Winthrop Aldrich
Richard Bissell
Herbert Brownell
Dwight D. Eisenhower
John Eisenhower
Milton S. Eisenhower
Andrew Goodpaster

Loy Henderson
Howard Hunt
Walter Kohler
Lyman Lemnitzer
Ellis Slater
Stuyvesant Wainwright
William Westmoreland

Interview by the Dulles Oral History Project, Princeton

Dwight D. Eisenhower

Published Works

Adams, Sherman. *Firsthand Report: The Story of the Eisenhower Administration.* New York: Harper & Bros., 1961.

Ambrose, Stephen E. *Ike's Spies: Eisenhower and the Espionage Establishment.* Garden City, N.Y.: Doubleday & Co., 1981.

————. *Rise to Globalism: American Foreign Policy Since 1938.* New York: Penguin, 1972.

————. *The Supreme Commander: The War Years of General Dwight D. Eisenhower.* Garden City, N.Y.: Doubleday & Co., 1970.

Bischof, Guenter. "Before the Break: The Eisenhower-McCarthy Relationship." Master's thesis, University of New Orleans, 1981.

Blumenson, Martin. *Breakout and Pursuit.* Washington: U.S. Department of the Army, 1961.

————. *Kasserine Pass.* Boston: Houghton Mifflin Co., 1967.

Bradley, Omar. *A Soldier's Story.* New York: Henry Holt and Co. , 1951.

Brandon, Dorothy. *Mamie Doud Eisenhower.* New York: Charles Scribner's Sons, 1954.

Bryant, Sir Arthur. *Triumph in the West.* London: Collins, 1959.

————. *The Turn of the Tide.* New York: Doubleday & Co., 1957.

Churchill, Winston S. *The Second World War* (especially *The Hinge of Fate, Closing the Ring,* and *Triumph and Tragedy*). Boston: Houghton Mifflin Co., 1948–1953.

Clark, Mark Wayne. *Calculated Risk.* New York: Harper & Bros., 1950.

Cook, Blanche. *The Declassified Eisenhower.* Garden City, N.Y.: Doubleday & Co., 1981.

Davis, Kenneth S. *Soldier of Democracy: A Biography of Dwight Eisenhower.* Garden City, N.Y.: Doubleday, Doran & Co., 1945.

de Gaulle, Charles. *The War Memoirs of Charles de Gaulle,* Vol. II, *Unity.* New York: Simon and Schuster, 1959.

de Guingand, Sir Francis. *Operation Victory*. New York: Charles Scribner's Sons, 1947.

Divine, Robert A. *Blowing on the Wind: The Nuclear Test Ban Debate, 1954–1960*. New York: Oxford University Press, 1978.

———. *Eisenhower and the Cold War*. New York: Oxford University Press, 1981.

Eisenhower, Dwight D. *At Ease: Stories I Tell to Friends*. Garden City, N.Y.: Doubleday & Co., 1967.

———. *Crusade in Europe,* Garden City, N.Y.: Doubleday & Co., 1948.

———. *Letters to Mamie*, ed. John S. D. Eisenhower. Garden City, N.Y.: Doubleday & Co., 1978.

———. *Mandate for Change*. Garden City, N.Y.: Doubleday & Co., 1963.

———. *The Papers of Dwight David Eisenhower* (Vols. I through V edited by Alfred D. Chandler, Jr., *et al.;* Vols. VI through IX edited by Louis Galambos, *et al.*). Baltimore: Johns Hopkins University Press, 1970, 1978.

———. *Waging Peace*. Garden City, N.Y.: Doubleday & Co., 1974.

Eisenhower, John S. D. *Strictly Personal*. Garden City, N.Y.: Doubleday & Co., 1974.

Eisenhower, Milton S. *The President Is Calling*. Garden City, N.Y.: Doubleday & Co., 1974.

Ewald, William Bragg, Jr. *Eisenhower the President; Crucial Days: 1951–1960*. Englewood Cliffs, N.J.: Prentice-Hall, 1981.

Farago, Ladislas. *Patton: Ordeal and Triumph*. New York: Astor-Honor Inc., 1964.

Garland, Albert N., and Howard McGaw Smyth. *Sicily and the Surrender of Italy*. Washington: U.S. Department of the Army, 1965.

Geelhoed, E. Bruce. *Charles E. Wilson and Controversy at the Pentagon, 1953 to 1957*. Detroit: Wayne State University Press, 1979.

Greenstein, Fred I. *The Hidden-Hand Presidency: Eisenhower as Leader*. New York: Basic Books, 1982.

Griffith, Robert. *The Politics of Fear: Joseph R. McCarthy and the Senate*. Published for the Organization of American Historians by the University Press of Kentucky, Lexington, 1970.

Harrison, Gordon A. *Cross-Channel Attack*. Washington: U.S. Department of the Army, 1951.

Hatch, Alden. *Red Carpet for Mamie*. New York: Henry Holt and Co., 1954.

History of the Joint Chiefs of Staff, 4 vols. Washington: Government Printing Office, 1982.

Hughes, Emmet John. *The Ordeal of Power: A Political Memoir of the Eisenhower Years*. New York: Atheneum, 1963.

Irving, David. *The War Between the Generals*. New York: Congdon & Lattès, 1981.

Ismay, Hastings L. *The Memoirs of General Lord Ismay*. New York: Viking Press, 1960.

James, D. Clayton. *The Years of MacArthur*, Vol. I, 1880–1941. Boston: Houghton Mifflin, 1970.

Kornitzer, Bela. *The Great American Heritage: The Story of the Five Eisenhower Brothers.* New York: Farrar, Straus and Cudahy, 1955.

Krock, Arthur. *In the Nation: 1932–1966.* New York: McGraw-Hill, 1966.

———. *Memoirs: Sixty Years on the Firing Line.* New York: Funk & Wagnalls, 1968.

Larson, Arthur. *Eisenhower: The President Nobody Knew.* New York: Charles Scribner's Sons, 1968.

Lear, John. "Ike and the Peaceful Atom." *The Reporter,* January 12, 1956.

Lyon, Peter. *Eisenhower: Portrait of the Hero.* Boston: Little, Brown and Co., 1974.

Macmillan, Harold. *The Blast of War: 1939–1945.* New York: Harper & Row, 1968.

McCann, Kevin. *Man from Abilene.* Garden City, N.Y.: Doubleday & Co., 1952.

McKeogh, Michael, and Richard Lockridge. *Sergeant Mickey and General Ike.* New York: G.P. Putnam's Sons, 1946.

Miller, Merle. *Plain Speaking: An Oral Biography of Harry S. Truman.* New York: Berkley Publishing Corp., 1973.

Montgomery, Bernard Law. *Memoirs.* Cleveland: World Publishing Co., 1958.

Morgan, Kay Summersby. *Past Forgetting: My Love Affair with Dwight D. Eisenhower.* New York: Simon & Schuster, 1976.

Neal, Steve. *The Eisenhowers: Reluctant Dynasty.* Garden City, N.Y.: Doubleday and Co., 1978.

Nixon, Richard. *Memoirs.* New York: Grosset & Dunlap, 1978.

Parmet, Herbert S. *Eisenhower and the American Crusades.* New York: Macmillan Co., 1972.

Patton, George S., Jr. *War As I Knew It.* Boston: Houghton Mifflin Co., 1947.

Pogue, Forrest C. *George C. Marshall: Ordeal and Hope, 1939–1942.* New York: Viking Press, 1966.

———. *The Supreme Command.* Washington: U.S. Department of the Army, 1954.

Reeves, Thomas C. *The Life and Times of Joe McCarthy.* New York: Stein and Day, 1982.

Ryan, Cornelius. *The Last Battle.* New York: Simon and Schuster, 1966.

Smith, Richard Norton. *Thomas E. Dewey and His Times.* New York: Simon and Schuster, 1982.

Smith, Walter B. *Eisenhower's Six Great Decisions.* New York: Longmans, Green and Co., 1956.

Summersby, Kay. *Eisenhower Was My Boss.* New York: Prentice-Hall, 1948.

Tedder, Sir Arthur. *With Prejudice.* London: Cassell, 1966.

Viorst, Milton. *Hostile Allies: FDR and Charles de Gaulle.* New York: Macmillan Co., 1965.

Weigley, Russell. *Eisenhower's Lieutenants: The Campaign of France and Germany.* Bloomington, Ind.: Indiana University Press, 1981.

Wilmot, Chester. *Struggle for Europe.* New York: Harper, 1952.

INDEX

About the Author

STEPHEN E. AMBROSE wrote more than twenty-five works of history, including *D-Day, Citizen Soldiers, Nothing Like It in the World, Band of Brothers,* and *To America* as well as multi-volume biographies of Presidents Eisenhower and Nixon. He was founder of the Eisenhower Center, president of the National D-Day Museum in New Orleans, and recipient of a National Humanities Award in 1999 as well as the Distinguished Civilian Service Medal from the Department of Defense in 2000. He died in October 2002.

The Stephen E.
Available

 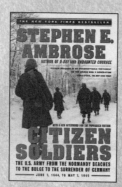 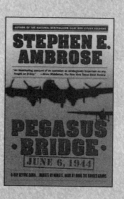 

D-DAY JUNE 6, 1944
The Climactic Battle of World War II

"Historians and public alike should be profoundly grateful to Ambrose...for assembling this comprehensive and permanent record that will be forever a resource for remembering Normandy."

—*Chicago Tribune*

0-684-80137-X

CITIZEN SOLDIERS
The U.S. Army from the Normandy Beaches to the Bulge to the Surrender of Germany: June 7, 1944 to May 7, 1945

"History boldly told and elegantly written...Gripping."

—*The Wall Street Journal*

0-684-84801-5

PEGASUS BRIDGE
June 6, 1944

"The best war story this reviewer has ever read."

—*The Denver Post*

0-671-67156-1

BAND OF BROTHERS
E Company, 506th Regiment, 101st Airborne from Normandy to Hitler's Eagle's Nest

"First-class....Addicts of military history will relish its finely detailed account....Stephen Ambrose's thorough research and clear organization have produced a highly readable account of the heroic service of his 'band of brothers' he so unstintingly admires."

—*San Francisco Chronicle*

0-7432-1645-8
0-7432-1638-5 (Classic Edition)

THE VICTORS
Eisenhower and His Boys: The Men of World War II

"An absolutely wonderful book... a compelling narrative of a time when the average American youth exhibited heroism and grace to save the world."

—*Wisconsin State Journal*

0-684-85629-8

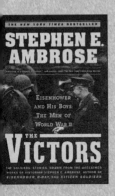
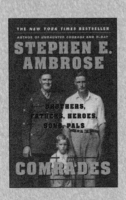